Fourth Edition

Canadian Families Today
New Perspectives

Edited by
Patrizia Albanese

OXFORD
UNIVERSITY PRESS

OXFORD
UNIVERSITY PRESS

Oxford University Press is a department of the University of Oxford.
It furthers the University's objective of excellence in research, scholarship,
and education by publishing worldwide. Oxford is a registered trade mark of
Oxford University Press in the UK and in certain other countries.

Published in Canada by
Oxford University Press
8 Sampson Mews, Suite 204,
Don Mills, Ontario M3C 0H5 Canada
www.oupcanada.com

First Edition published in 2007
Second edition published in 2010
Third edition published in 2014

Library and Archives Canada Cataloguing in Publication
Canadian families today : new perspectives / edited by Patrizia Albanese.
—Fourth edition.

Third edition edited by David Cheal and Patrizia Albanese.
Includes bibliographical references.
ISBN 978-0-19-902576-3 (softcover)

1. Families—Canada—Textbooks. 2. Family policy—Canada—Textbooks.
3. Families—Economic aspects—Canada—Textbooks. 4. Textbooks. I. Albanese,
Patrizia, editor

HQ560.C3586 2018   306.850971   C2017-905536-4

Cover images: Circles vector: © creativika/123RF. Photos (clockwise from top left): © warrengoldswain/
123RF, © Jan Mikat/123RF, © sjenner13/123RF, © Cathy Yeulet/123RF, © Scott Griessel/123RF,
© raywoo/123RF, © Cathy Yeulet/123RF, © Ramzi Hachicho/123RF, © Maria Sbytova/123RF.
Cover design:Sherill Chapman
Interior design: Sherill Chapman

Printed and bound in Canada

6 7 8 - 23 22 21

Contents

Contributors   *v*

Preface   *ix*

I ● Conceptualizing Families, Past and Present   1

1   Introduction to Diversity in Canada's Families: Variation in Forms, Definitions, and Theories   2
Patrizia Albanese

2   Canada's Families: Historical and Contemporary Variations   25
Cynthia Comacchio

3   Same-sex Marriage in Canada   51
Doreen M. Fumia

II ● The Life Course   71

4   Intimacy, Commitment, and Family Formation   73
Melanie Heath

5   Parenting Young Children: Decisions and Realities   95
Amber Gazso

6   Separation and Divorce: Fragmentation and Renewal of Families   115
Craig McKie

7   Families in Middle and Later Life: Patterns and Dynamics of Living Longer, Aging Together   139
Karen M. Kobayashi and Anne Martin-Matthews

III ● Family Issues   161

8   Marriage and Death Rituals   163
Deborah K. van den Hoonaard

9   Paid and Unpaid Work: Connecting Households, Workplaces, State Polices, and Communities   183
Andrea Doucet

10 Family Poverty in Canada: Correlates, Coping Strategies, and Consequences   201
Don Kerr and Joseph H. Michalski

11 The Settlement of Refugee Families in Canada: Pre-migration and Post-migration Trajectories and Location in Canadian Society   225
Amal Madibbo and James S. Frideres

12 Indigenous Families   245
Vanessa Watts

13 Lack of Support: Canadian Families and Disability   267
Michelle Owen

IV ● Problems, Policies, and Predictions   291

14 Violence in Families   293
Catherine Holtmann

15 Investing in Families and Children: Family Policies in Canada   313
Catherine Krull and Mushira Mohsin Khan

16 The Past of the Future and the Future of the Family   341
Margrit Eichler

References   363
Index   411

Contributors

Patrizia Albanese is Professor of Sociology, Chair of the Ryerson University Research Ethics Board, Chair of the Local Organizing Committee for the 2018 International Sociological Association World Congress of Sociology in Toronto, and a past president of the Canadian Sociological Association. She is a book series co-editor with Lorne Tepperman (Oxford University Press); co-editor of *Sociology: A Canadian Perspective* (Oxford, 2016); and co-author of *Making Sense: A Student's Guide to Research and Writing—Social Sciences* (Oxford, 2017), *Growing Up in Armyville* (with D. Harrison; Wilfrid Laurier University Press, 2016), and *Caring for Children: Social Movements and Public Policy in Canada* (with R. Langford and S. Prentice, UBC Press, 2017). She is the author of *Child Poverty in Canada* (Oxford, 2010), *Children in Canada Today* (Oxford, 2016), and *Mothers of the Nation* (UofT Press, 2006). She has been working on a number of research projects that share a focus on understanding family policies in Canada.

Cynthia Comacchio, Professor, Department of History, Wilfrid Laurier University, has a PhD in Canadian history from the University of Guelph. Her research focuses on Canadian social and cultural history, especially the history of childhood, youth, and family. She has published three books on those subjects, most recently *The Dominion of Youth: Adolescence and the Making of Modern Canada, 1920–1950* (Wilfrid Laurier University Press, 2006), which received the Canadian History of Education Association's Founders Award for best English-language monograph. She is currently collaborating with Neil Sutherland on *Ring Around the Maple: A Sociocultural History of Children and Childhood in Canada, 19th and 20th Centuries*, for WLU Press.

Andrea Doucet is the Canada Research Chair in Gender, Work, and Care and Professor of Sociology and Women's & Gender Studies at Brock University. She has published widely on themes of gender and care work, fatherhood, masculinities, parental leave policies, embodiment, reflexivity, and feminist approaches to methodologies and epistemologies. Her book *Do Men Mother?* (UofT Press, 2006) was awarded the John Porter Tradition of Excellence Book Award from the Canadian Sociology Association. She is also co-author of *Gender Relations: Intersectionality and Beyond* (with J. Siltanen, Oxford, 2008). She is currently completing two long-standing book projects—one on breadwinning mothers and caregiving fathers and a second book on reflexive and relational knowing (with N. Mauthner).

Margrit Eichler is Professor Emerita of the University of Toronto/Ontario Institute for Studies in Education. She has published widely in the areas of family policy, biases in research that derive from social hierarchies (e.g. sexism, racism, ableism), women's studies, and sustainability and social justice. She is a member of the Royal Society of Canada and the European Academy of Sciences.

James S. Frideres is Professor Emeritus at the University of Calgary. He was the director of the International Indigenous Studies program and held the Chair of Ethnic Studies. His recent publications include *International Perspectives: Integration and Inclusion* with

J. Biles (McGill Queens) (which is on the *Hill Times* List of top 100 books for 2012) and the ninth edition of *Aboriginal People in Canada* with R. Gadacz (Pearson, 2012).

Doreen M. Fumia is Associate Professor of Sociology and the Jack Layton Chair at Ryerson University. Her work examines lesbians and aging, identities, anti-poverty activism, and neighbourhood belonging in Toronto. She has published in the areas of lesbian motherhood, non-traditional families, informal learning, and same-sex marriage debates.

Amber Gazso is Associate Professor of Sociology at York University. She completed her PhD in Sociology at the University of Alberta in 2006. Her current research interests include citizenship, family and gender relations, poverty, research methods, and social policy and the welfare state. Her recent journal publications focus on low-income mothers on social assistance. She is currently working on two major research projects funded by SSHRC. In one project she is exploring how diverse families make ends meet by piecing together networks of social support that include both government programs (e.g., social assistance) and community supports, and informal relations within families and with friends and neighbours. Another comparative project explores the relationship between health and income inequality among Canadians and Americans in mid-life.

Melanie Heath is Assistant Professor of Sociology at McMaster University. She is the author of *One Marriage Under God: The Campaign to Promote Marriage in America* (NYU Press, 2012). She has published articles in *Gender & Society* and *Qualitative Sociology*. Her current project on "Harm or Right? Polygamy's Contested Terrain Within and Across Borders" is funded by a five-year SSHRC Insight Grant.

Catherine Holtmann is Associate Professor of Sociology at the University of New Brunswick and Director of the Muriel McQueen Fergusson Centre for Family Violence Research. Her research focuses on gender and religion, domestic violence, immigrant women, and social action. She is the lead investigator for the SSHRC-funded AfterGrad NB project team, which explores barriers to post-secondary education for high school graduates.

Don Kerr is Professor of Sociology at King's University College at Western University. His areas of interest are population studies and Canadian demography. His research has focused on social demography, population estimates and projections, environmental demography, the Indigenous population, and family demography.

Mushira Mohsin Khan is a PhD candidate in the Department of Sociology and a Student Affiliate with the Institute on Aging and Lifelong Health at the University of Victoria. Her research focuses on transnational ties and intergenerational relationships within mid- to later-life diasporic South Asian families, ethnicity and immigration, aging, and health and social care. Her work has been published in a collection on health care equity for ethnic minority older adults (SFU, 2015), the Population Change and Lifecourse Strategic Knowledge Cluster Discussion Paper Series (2015), and in *Current Sociology* (2016), and the *International Journal of Migration, Health, and Social Care* (forthcoming). She is the recipient of the SSHRC–Joseph-Armand Bombardier Canadian Doctoral Scholarship (2015–18).

Karen M. Kobayashi is Associate Professor in the Department of Sociology and the Centre on Aging at the University of Victoria. Her research interests include the economic and health dimensions of ethnic inequality in Canada, intergenerational relationships and social support in mid-to-later life families, and the socio-cultural dimensions of dementia and personhood. Her current research programs focus on the relationship between social isolation and health care utilization among older adults, access to health and social care among older visible minority immigrants, living-apart-together (LAT) relationships in adulthood, and an evaluation of quality of care in residential long-term care facilities. Recent work has been published in the *Journal of Aging Studies, Ethnicity and Health, Canadian Review of Sociology,* and the *Journal of Aging and Health.*

Catherine Krull is Dean of the Faculty of Social Sciences and Professor in the Department of Sociology at the University of Victoria. Prior to her arrival at UVic, she was a professor at Queen's University. She has served as editor of *Cuban Studies* as well as editor-in-chief of the *Canadian Journal of Latin American and Caribbean Studies.* Book publications include *Cuba in Global Context: International Relations, Internationalism and Transnationalism* (2014); *Rereading Women and the Cuban Revolution* (with J. Stubbs, 2011); *A Measure of a Revolution: Cuba, 1959–2009* (with S. Castro, 2010) and *New World Coming: The 1960s and the Shaping of Global Consciousness* (with Dubinsky et al., 2009). She has held research fellowships at the Institute for Advanced Studies (University of London), the Institute of Latin American Studies (University of Florida), the Institute of Latin American Studies (David Rockefeller Center, Harvard University), the Department of Sociology (Boston University), and the Centre for International Studies (London School of Economics). Currently, she is working on two monographs, one on the Cuban Diaspora in Canada and Europe (with J. Stubbs, University of London), and *Entangled US/Cuban Terrains: Memories of Guantanamo* (with A. McKercher, McMaster University).

Amal Madibbo is Associate Professor of Sociology at the University of Calgary. Her research focuses on immigration, ethnic relations, globalization, and international development. She has special interest in race and anti-racism, Black francophone immigration to Canada, and race and ethnicity in sub-Saharan Africa.

Anne Martin-Matthews is Professor of Sociology at the University of British Columbia. Her current research focuses on two areas of inquiry in the sociology of aging. The first examines the provision of health and social care to elderly people, examined from the perspectives of agency providers, home care workers, elderly clients, and family carers. Her second area is on widowhood in later life. She is working on CIHR-funded research on home care in Canada.

Craig McKie is a retired professor of Sociology. He taught at the University of Western Ontario for several years, spent more than a decade working for Statistics Canada in

Ottawa, latterly as editor-in-chief of *Canadian Social Trends*, and most recently, from 1990 until retirement, he taught in the Department of Sociology at Carleton University.

Joseph H. Michalski is Associate Professor and Chair of the Department of Sociology, King's University College at Western University. His current theoretical work and research focus is on the geometry of social space in relation to behaviours as diverse as intimate partner violence, welfare, and knowledge production.

Michelle Owen is Associate Professor of Sociology and the Disability Studies Advisory Committee Chair at the University of Winnipeg. She is the director of the Global College Institute for Health and Human Potential and was given the 2011 Marsha Hanen Award for Excellence in Creating Community Awareness. She is working on two disability-related research projects: on how Canadian academics with multiple sclerosis negotiate the workplace, and the experience of intimate partner violence in the lives of women with disabilities.

Deborah K. van den Hoonaard is Professor of Gerontology and Canada Research Chair in Qualitative Research and Analysis at St Thomas University in Fredericton, New Brunswick. She is the author of *Qualitative Research in Action: A Canadian Primer* (OUP, 2015), *By Himself: The Older Man's Experience of Widowhood* (UTP, 2010), *The Widowed Self: The Older Woman's Journey Through Widowhood* (WLU Press, 2001), and co-author (with W.C. van den Hoonaard) of *Essentials of Thinking Ethically in Qualitative Research* (Left Coast Press, 2013).

Vanessa Watts is Academic Director, Indigenous Studies at McMaster University. She is Mohawk and Anishinaabe and is of the Bear Clan. She is currently in the process of completing her PhD in Sociology at Queen's University. Her undergraduate degree is from Trent University in Native Studies and her Master's Degree was in the Indigenous Governance Program at the University of Victoria.

Preface

The fourth edition of *Canadian Families Today* is an introduction to the sociology of family life that draws on a wide range of materials. In 16 chapters, 20 experts in the field cover a wide range of topics that introduce you to families in a Canadian context. Several important updates for this edition reflect the real-word changes experienced by Canadian families, and the way that focuses of study within the sociology of family life have adapted and shifted in turn. Chapters throughout the text have been updated wherever possible with the latest Statistics Canada data—the results of the 2016 Census. Several new authors have been added, including Vanessa Watts, who authors an entirely new chapter on Indigenous families, reviewing the topic in a broad way through the lens of assimilationist state objectives towards the absorption of Indigenous families in Canada.

The book is organized into four parts, reflecting its main themes. Part 1 contains the introductory chapter by Patrizia Albanese, which discusses the diversity of family forms existing in Canada today, reviews different definitions of the family, and considers how the changing definition of this concept has had policy implications for access to programs and privileges or status within society. In Chapter 2, Cynthia Comacchio reviews the major changes and continuities in the history of Canadian families over the past two centuries. In Chapter 3, Doreen Fumia discusses same-sex marriage in Canada and changes in marriage law in the form of Bill C-38—the Civil Marriages Act. She explores how concepts of "normal" and "abnormal" sexuality continue to demarcate relationships and thus persist in relegating many Canadians to a position as "other."

Part 2 provides information about various stages and events in the life course. In Chapter 4, Melanie Heath focuses on how people form relationships. Heath discusses technological innovations that have been affecting dating and sexual relationships in recent years. Amber Gazso, in Chapter 5, focuses on becoming and being a parent of young children. She outlines some of the activities of parenting, with emphasis on how everyday practices of parenting are textured by ideological discourses in our society.

In Chapter 6, Craig McKie focuses on how families fragment through separation or divorce, but often reformulate within the context of a new union. McKie discusses post-separation hardships, but also concludes that these must be weighed against the real risks of physical and emotional trauma in relationships that are full of conflict, risks that are greatly diminished by separation.

Middle age and "old age," two other stages of the life course, are considered in Chapter 7. Karen Kobayashi and Anne Martin-Matthews focus on the transitions that mark middle age (e.g., the "empty nest," caregiving) that are triggered by life events in families including adult children leaving home or care for aging parents. Chapter 7 also highlights the central role that families play in the lives of older adults.

Part 3 of *Canadian Families Today* focuses on some of the many challenges, decisions, and strategies that families face in light of the shifting social, economic, and political contexts. In Chapter 8 Deborah K. van den Hoonaard focuses special attention on the rituals associated with marriage and death. She considers how rituals have evolved over time, and notes that individuals now exercise greater scope in their choices about how to conduct rituals. In Chapter 9, Andrea Doucet describes patterns of paid and unpaid work in families by looking at the relationship between gender and paid work. Doucet also examines the relationship between state policies and paid and unpaid work.

Don Kerr and Joseph H. Michalski, in Chapter 10, focus on recent poverty trends affecting families today, while also considering some of the broader structural shifts in the Canadian economy and in government policies. They examine the high rates of poverty among female-headed lone-parent families and among recent immigrants, and discuss the coping strategies that these families use to survive. In Chapter 11, Amal Madibbo and James Frideres discuss the pre- and post-migration experiences of refugee families. Among other things, they explore the social and economic position of visible minority refugee families in Canadian society and its impact on family structure and family experiences. Michelle Watts, in Chapter 12, presents past and recent trends in family life among Indigenous people in Canada. She traces the impact of devastating colonial policies on family life and the resilience that has come to characterize many Indigenous families. In Chapter 13, Michelle Owen writes about the impact that disability has on families. She begins by discussing the problem of defining disability, and then aims to show that disabled Canadians and their families, like racialized families discussed in Chapter 11, continue to be marginalized in our society.

Finally, Part 4 of the book looks at issues that, if not unique to families, are often central and those with which many contemporary families must grapple: violence, shifts in public policy, and questions regarding the future. Chapter 14, by Catherine Holtmann, analyzes how power differences in the family can lead to mental, physical, or sexual abuse. At the same time, she argues that the powerlessness and dependency cycles in families that make children, women, and aged persons vulnerable can be broken. Catherine Krull and Mushira Mohsin Khan, in Chapter 15, discuss government policies affecting families in Canada, which they believe have a great impact on family life. The authors point out that Canada lacks a comprehensive national family policy, unlike some other countries around the world. In the concluding chapter, Margrit Eichler discusses the extensive history of predictions for and about the future of the family, pointing out that in the past there have been a number of spectacular misprognoses about the future of families. She concludes with predictions of her own.

Acknowledgments

Statistics Canada information is used with the permission of Statistics Canada. Users are forbidden to copy the data and disseminate them, in original or modified form, for commercial purposes, without permission from Statistics Canada. Information on the availability of the wide range of data from Statistics Canada can be obtained from www .statcan.gc.ca.

Patrizia Albanese
January, 2017

PART I

Conceptualizing Families, Past and Present

The first three chapters of this book provide an introduction to the study of family life in Canada. They present some of the changes in the study of families, with a special focus on Canada, while presenting an overview of historical diversity in family life. Multiple perspectives on understanding families are presented, and the complexity of family life is stressed.

In Chapter 1, Patrizia Albanese discusses the diversity of family forms existing in Canada today, reviews different definitions of the family, and considers how the changing definition of this concept has had policy implications for access to programs and privileges or status within society. Albanese also introduces some of the different theories of family life and discusses the influence that theoretical assumptions have on ways of seeing the world. She examines recent changes in family life in Canada and concludes the chapter by noting that today, as in the past, Canadian families take on a number of diverse forms. The changing definition of family simply reflects a reality that change has been, and continues to be, a normal part of family life.

In Chapter 2, Cynthia Comacchio reviews the major changes and continuities in the history of Canadian families over the past two centuries. She discusses how in the past, as is the case today, "the family" as a social construct is an idealization that reinforces hierarchies of class, "race," gender, and age. Throughout the chapter, she underscores the fact that, despite prevailing ideas about what properly constitutes "the family" at various points in time, Canadian families are and have been in constant flux. Comacchio makes it clear that the importance of families to both individuals and to society is a constant, both in ideal and in practice; at the same time, the form and experience of actual families have always been diverse.

Chapter 3, by Doreen M. Fumia, examines same-sex marriage in Canada. She walks us through changes in marriage law in Canada in the form of Bill C-38—the Civil Marriages Act—which shifted the definitions about which couples could legally marry. She argues that while social acceptance of this change is ongoing, social stigmas remain. She goes on to present two arguments: one that advocates for the inclusion of same-sex couples into the institution of marriage, as an avenue towards equal rights and full citizenship participation. The other argument insists that the institution of marriage is still exclusionary and calls for its total dismantling. Through this debate, she challenges readers to decide for themselves who marriage is for.

Introduction to Diversity in Canada's Families

Variations in Forms, Definitions, and Theories

PATRIZIA ALBANESE

LEARNING OBJECTIVES

- To gain an overview of some changing Canadian demographic trends

- To discover that Canadian families have taken, and continue to take, diverse forms

- To see that definitions of *family* have changed over time, and continue to evolve

- To recognize the implications of defining *family* in certain ways—restricting who has access to programs, policies, and privileges and who does not

- To learn about some of the theories that guide our understanding of families

- To understand that theoretical orientations guide what we study and how we study it

---

Introduction

On August 23, 2016, about 200 Indigenous people gathered in Toronto to protest the Sixties Scoop, a period in the 1960s and 1970s during which Indigenous children were removed from their families as part of the work of "child protection services" and placed "in care" with non-Indigenous families. The demonstration by surviving family members took place outside of a courthouse in Toronto where a judge was hearing a class action lawsuit against the federal government over the practice. Among the 200 were Thomas Norton and his sister Karen Rae, who he had just met for the first time. They explained that Karen had been taken from their parents' home on the Sagueen First Nation before Thomas was born. Decades later, as adults, this family was reunited. Thomas Norton shared with the media that he "had no idea what she was doing in her life and she had no idea what I was doing." He added, "you need to build the relationship and gather strength from that as a family" (CBC News 2016: online).

This case reminds us of the meaning, vulnerability, tenacity, and importance of family ties that many in Canada experience, and that some of us, at times, take for granted. It hints at just how diverse in form and experience Canadian families are, and at some of the government policies and practices that shape and constrain who and what a family has been allowed to include or involve. Above all, it reminds us of how powerful and deeply rooted our family ties are to our sense of self and our sense of belonging.

We begin this chapter with an overview of some recent trends in family life as they are captured by broad-sweeping national statistics. We will see that Statistics Canada data capture a considerable amount of change and diversity in family forms, though we must keep in mind that the data may actually mask variations, fluctuations, and "oddities" that encompass everyday life for the millions of people who make up families in Canada today.

Following a review of recent trends in family forms, we assess various definitions of family, to determine which ones, if any, reflect the diversity that we see and experience around us. Following that, we review theories used to help us understand and explain what is happening to, with, and in family life. We see, through the trends, definitions, and theories covered in this chapter, that change and diversity are the norm when it comes to understanding families. We will—throughout this chapter and the rest of the book—see that Statistics Canada data, while they offer evidence of change to family structures over time, fail to accurately depict the full breadth of complex, lived experiences of Canadians.

Changing Trends in the Diversity of Family Forms

In 2016 there were 9,519,945 families in Canada, up from 9,389,700 only five years before (Statistics Canada 2012a; Statistics Canada 2017a). According to Canadian Census data, today, there are proportionally fewer households than in the past composed of a "mother, father and children"; with more people living alone, as couples without children, or as multi-generational families. The 2016 Census revealed that married couples remained the dominant family form, but as in past Census years, this number is declining over time in relation to other family forms. For example, since the 2006 Census, the number of common-law couples has risen, as has the number of lone-parent families and individuals living alone (Statistics Canada 2017b). The growth in the number of individuals living alone—28.2 percent of households in Canada—was especially striking (Statistics Canada 2017b).

In 2016, there were 72,880 same-sex couples in Canada, representing 0.9 per cent of all couples. One-third, or 33.4 per cent of these same-sex couples were married, with the rest living common-law. About 12 percent of all same-sex couples that were counted had children living with them at the time of the 2016 Census, (Statistics Canada 2017c). Those numbers reflect a long journey—after decades of political mobilizing and many legal battles, same-sex families in Canada have gone from a time when homosexuality was illegal, to being invisible, to fully recognized marriages and families for the first time in the 2006 Canadian census (see Chapter 3).[1] Increasingly, we also have come to acknowledge the existence, reality, and complexity of trans families and families with **transgender** members of all ages (see Box 1.1). Clearly, as a result of social change, including changes in the way we define and count families, Canadian families today come in a plurality of forms, with no one family portrait capturing the incredibly rich diversity.

For more on legal changes to same-sex marriage in Canada, see "Passing Bill C-38: The Civil Marriage Act" in Chapter 3, pp. 58–9.

Daily Life for a 12-year-old Transgender Girl

Alexis Knox was assigned male at birth, but at 12 years old, identifies as a transgender girl. She came out to her parents, Amanda and Mark Knox, and her two brothers, in 2014, starting with an email to her father.

Alexis told CBC journalist, Hallie Cotnam, on the *Ottawa Morning* show:

"I was pretty scared. I didn't know what to say, or what to do."

"With email, you can type out and erase, and you can type it out in a new way. You can just kind of get it all out in the perfect way. I just didn't know what else to do. I knew I didn't want to live my life that way."

Her father, Mark Knox, said that when he received the email he was shocked, but not surprised, recalling:

"She says, 'More than anything, I feel like a girl. I want to be a girl.'"

"After I got over the initial reaction to it, it was a special day. We gained a daughter."

Since the email, the family has made some adjustments. Alexis is on puberty blocking medication and is being home-schooled while she adjusts to her new life.

Alexis described the year since coming out to her family as "definitely more challenging," but she notes that it is better than it used to be:

"I'm happier. I'm not just sitting in my room playing Minecraft eight hours a day, every day."

The family's next challenge has been to prepare for the reactions of others as people outside their close circle begin to see and understand the transition Alexis has been going through. As part of this, in a post on her blog, Amanda Knox introduced her readers to her daughter Alexis.

Alexis wants to be more public and to advocate for herself.

Source: CBC News. "Family of transgender girl, 12, opens up about first year." Apr 14, 2015. CBC Licensing.

Questions for Critical Thought

Imagine that a beloved member of your family is transgender. What kinds of challenges do you expect they would encounter? What could you do to support your loved one through some of the challenges?

With time, official measures like the Canadian Census have evolved to capture more of the diversity that makes up everyday life. Blended families, often called "stepfamilies," are those consisting of parents and their children from this and any previous relationships, and are increasingly common. It's only recently, since the 2011 Census, that they have been officially counted. But even before official counting, we have known that following divorces and other break-ups, many second and subsequent unions take place, in the form of remarriages and common-law unions. Not surprising then, to capture changing reality, for the first time in 2011 the Census was changed to include and count stepfamilies. The 2016 Census found that among the 5.8 million children under the age of 14, 69.7 per cent were living with both of their biological or adoptive parents, and no step-siblings or half-siblings; while 30 per cent were living in a lone-parent family, in a stepfamily; or in a family without their parents but with grandparents, with other relatives or as foster children (Statistics Canada, 2017 d). This is increased from the 12.6 per cent of all families in Canada that were stepfamilies in 2011 (Statistics Canada 2012a). In 2016, 62.8 per cent of children in stepfamilies were living with one of their biological or adoptive parents and a step-parent. Just over half of these children had no half-siblings or step-siblings (were in a simple stepfamily). Just under half were in complex stepfamilies where they lived with at least one half-sibling or step-sibling (Statistics Canada 2017d). In 2016, 62.8 per cent of children in stepfamilies were living with one of their biological or adoptive parents and a step-parent. Just over half of these children had no half-siblings or step-siblings (were in a simple stepfamily). Just under half were in complex stepfamilies where they lived with at least one half-sibling or step-sibling (Statistics Canada 2017d). The other 37.2 per cent of children in stepfamilies (3.6 per cent of all children aged 0 to 14) had both of their biological or adoptive parents present. Children in this situation had at least one brother or sister with whom they had only one parent in common: a half-sibling.

Many step-parents face a number of unique challenges and experiences. At the same time, they have much in common with some other families today.

Other types of families we recognize today include transnational families, which have been around a long time, certainly, but have been invisible to most. Recent years have seen an increase in interest, research, and information on **transnational, multi-local families** (Beiser et al. 2014; Bernhard et al. 2006; Burholt 2004; Dhar 2011; Waters 2001). Interest in transnational families has been sparked by the growing awareness of some of the challenges faced by immigrant families, refugee claimants, foreign domestic

Table 1.1 Distribution (Number and Percentage) and Percentage Change of Census Families by Family Structure, Canada, 2001–2011

Census family	2001	2006	2011	Percentage change
Total census families	8,371,020	8,896,840	9,389,700	5.5
Couple families	7,059,830 (84.3%)	7,482,775 (84.1%)	7,861,860 (83.7%)	5.1
Married	5,901,420 (70.5%)	6,105,910 (68.6%)	6,293,950 (67.0%)	3.1
Common-law	1,158,410 (13.8%)	1,376,865 (15.5%)	1,567,910 (16.7%)	13.9
Lone-parent families	1,311,190 (15.7%)	1,414,060 (15.9%)	1,527,840 (16.3%)	8.0
Female parents	1,065,360 (12.7%)	1,132,290 (12.7%)	1,200,295 (12.8%)	6.0
Male parents	245,825 (2.9%)	281,775 (3.2%)	327,545 (3.5%)	16.2

Source: Statistics Canada, 2017 and 2012a, p. 5 (Table 1), available at (www12.statcan.gc.ca/census-recensement/2011/as-sa/98-312-x/98-312-x2011001-eng.pdf).

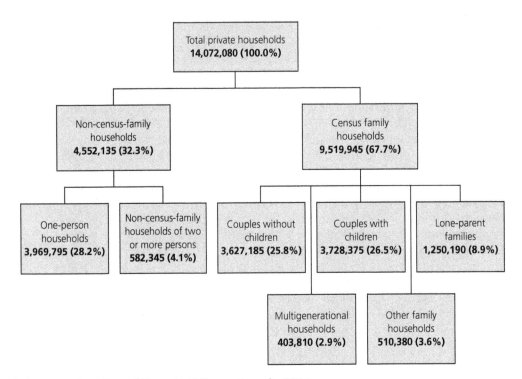

Figure 1.1   Overview of Household Types, Canada, 2016
Source: Statistics Canada, Census of Population, 2016.

workers from the Caribbean and Philippines, migrant workers, visa students, and individuals and families with "less-than-full" legal status.

For more on the challenges refugee families face, see "Family Issues" in Chapter 11, pp. 231–3.

Thousands of people living in Canada currently find themselves temporarily separated from their children and spouses as part of a strategy to secure a better economic future and opportunities for their family. Some have been called **satellite families** or *satellite children*, a term first used in the 1980s to describe Chinese children whose parents immigrated to North America, usually from Hong Kong or Taiwan, but returned to their country of origin leaving children, and sometimes spouses, in Canada (Newendorp 2008; Tsang et al. 2003). Researchers studying transnational families have been documenting the changes and challenges that arise from parent–child separations (for more on parenting, see Chapter 5), long-distance relationships, extended family networks providing child care, and the often emotionally charged reunifications that follow from multi-local family arrangements (Beiser et al. 2014; Bernhard et al. 2006a; Burholt 2004; Dhar 2011; Tsang et al. 2003; Waters 2001).

In 2011, just over 7.2 million people living in Canada (22.0 per cent of the population) were first generation, born in one of over 200 countries around the globe (Dobson, Maheux, and Chui 2013). Nearly half of them arrived in Canada after 1985. In 2014 alone, 260,404 people arrived as permanent residents (CIC 2015).

Most newcomers, like other Canadians, lived in nuclear families; however, family sizes tended to be larger for immigrant families (Bélanger 2006). Partners in recent-immigrant households were more likely to be legally married, rather than living common-law. Recent-immigrant families were also less likely to be headed by single-parents compared to other Canadian families, and were more likely than others to live in overcrowded housing (CIC 2007).

Newcomers today are much more likely than earlier immigrants or those who are Canadian-born to live in families with incomes below the median family income in Canada (income that falls in the middle of the income range or spectrum in a society).

Recent reports reveal that racialized immigrants make up 54 per cent of all immigrants in Canada. However, they make up 71 per cent of all immigrants living in poverty (National Council of Welfare 2013). Furthermore, 90 per cent of racialized persons living in poverty are first-generation immigrants (National Council of Welfare 2013). The factors behind these rates include an over-representation of racialized groups in low-paying jobs, labour market failure to recognize international work experience/ credentials, and "racial" discrimination in employment (Campaign 2000 2007). In contrast, children of immigrants who came to Canada before 1981 and had below-average earnings in the first generation were found to have surpassed their parents in the second generation, and were more educated and earned more on average than Canadians of similar age whose parents were born in Canada (Statistics Canada 2005). A great many factors have changed the social and economic landscape affecting immigrant families more recently, as they have affected all Canadian families (see Duffy, Corman, and Pupo 2015). For example, because of economic shifts, many younger Canadians today find themselves increasingly unable to leave their parental homes and establish independent households.

For more on family poverty, see "Economic Well-being Among Indigenous and Racialized Communities" in Chapter 10, p. 214.

In 1981, about 28 per cent of Canadians between the ages of 20 to 29 lived with their parents. By 2011, this increased to 41 per cent (Beaujot 2004; Milan 2016). In 2011, four in 10 young people either remained in or returned to live in their parental home (Milan 2016). Because of changing economic circumstances and difficulty finding stable, long-term, decent-paying work, coupled with an increasing demand for post-secondary education and large debt loads, researchers have seen the postponement of home-leaving or delayed **child launch**. Linked with this trend is an increase in the number of "boomerang children" or "velcro kids" (Beaupré, Turcotte, and Milan 2006; Milan 2016; Mitchell 1998a; Mitchell 1998b; Tyyskä 2001)—young adults who leave their parental homes for work or school, only to return due to large debt loads, shifting employment prospects, or changing marital status (for more on unions and breakups, see Chapter 4 and Chapter 6).

For more on work and families, see "The Rise of Non-standard Employment" in Chapter 9, pp. 185–6.

While many young people today don't expect to live with their parents or in-laws into their thirties and forties (though, as mentioned above, increasingly many will turn out to be wrong about that), for many new immigrants to Canada (as noted above), older Canadians, or Canadians with disabilities, the extended family model and the pooling of family resources in multi-generational households is nothing new, unexpected, or alarming (Che-Alford and Hamm 1999; Milan, LaFlamme, and Wong 2015; Sun 2008).

For more on aging families, see Chapter 7; for more on living with disabilities, see Chapter 13.

Table 1.2 Counting Census Families

Census year	Family type, number, and/or per cent	Historical context; changes in census enumeration
1921	1.8 million Census families	First World War; large number of war widows; first Census to distinguish between households and families
1931	86.4% married; 13.6% lone parent	Great Depression; marriage and fertility rates decline; reference to food, shared tables, and housekeeping are dropped from Census, eradicating hints of women's domestic labour (Bradbury 2000); single-parent heads of households counted for the first time
1941	87.8% married; 12.2% lone parent	Second World War; women at work in factories; 1942 Dominion-Provincial Wartime Day Nurseries Agreement, funding daycare services in Ontario, Quebec, and Alberta
1951	90.1% married; 9.9% lone parent	Baby Boom (1946–65); fertility rates increase; first Census to clearly allow for single parents with children living with other families to be separately counted
1956	91.4% married; 8.6% lone parent	High marriage rates; high fertility rates; low death rates; rates of single parenthood at their lowest
1961	91.6% married; 8.4% lone parent	High marriage rates; high fertility rates; low death rates; rates of single parenthood remain low
1966	91.8% married; 8.2% lone parent	Mass marketing of birth control pill; contraception is legalized in 1969; changes in Divorce Act, 1968
1971	90.6% married; 9.4% lone parent	Last Census year in which fertility was at "replacement level" of 2:1; lone parents due to divorce now outnumber those due to widowhood
1976	90.2% married; 9.8% lone parent	Mass (re)entry of women into labour force
1981	83.1% married; 5.6% common-law; 11.3% lone parent	Common-law unions first enumerated
1986	80.2% married; 7.2% common-law; 12.7% lone parent	Changes to Divorce Act; divorce rates peak in 1987
1991	77.3% married; 9.8% common-law; 13% lone parent	Married-couple families make up an increasingly smaller proportion of all families in Canada
1996	73.7% married; 11.7% common-law; 14.5% lone parent	Number of stepfamilies sharply on the rise; number of hours spent doing unpaid housework asked for the first time
2001	70.5% married; 13.8% common-law; 15.7% lone parent	Same-sex common-law unions enumerated for the first time; parental leave extended
2006	68.6% married; 15.5% common-law; 15.9% lone parent	Same-sex marriages enumerated for the first time
2011	67.0% married; 16.7% common-law; 16.3% lone parent	Stepfamilies and foster children enumerated for the first time

Table 1.2   (Continued)

Census year	Family type, number, and/or per cent	Historical context; changes in census enumeration
2016	28.2% One-person households 25.8% Couples without children 26.5 % Couples with children 8.9% lone-parent families 2.9 % multigenerational households 3.6% other family households	

Outlining the recent historical evolution of the Canadian Census family (which masks more than it reveals) shows that what we know better reflects how, what, and when we counted, as opposed to exactly who and what we were.
Source: Bradbury 2000, 2011; Statistics Canada 2012b; Statistics Canada 2017a.

A considerable amount of pooling of resources and care work happens across generations, households, even continents, especially by women, in a complex web of exchanges
and support (Connidis and Kemp 2008; Dhar 2011; Eichler and Albanese 2007; Langford, Prentice and Albanese 2017). And while *how* some of this care work happens (for
example, over the internet) may be different, *what* is done, *by whom*, and *for whom*, may
not actually be new. In fact, many of Canada's "new" family forms have always existed,
if in the margins, in the shadows, or during specific historical and economic contexts.
For example, lone-parent families and stepfamilies/remarriages are not new on the
Canadian landscape (see Figure 1.2). Nor are same-sex families or transnational families,

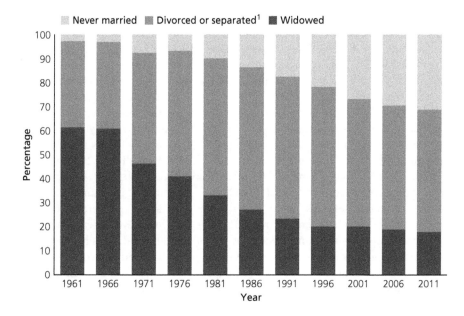

Figure 1.2   Distribution (in percentage) of the Legal Marital Status of Lone Parents, Canada, 1961 to 2011

Note: 1. Divorced or separated category includes "married, spouse absent."
Source: Statistics Canada, 2012b, p. 3

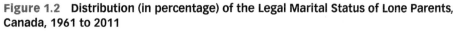

for that matter. Many of these family forms simply went uncounted (Bradbury 2000; see Table 1.2). While diversity seems to best characterize Canadian families today, diversity, adaptability, conflict, and change have always—past and present—been a fact of life for Canadian families.

Contemporary Canadian Family Studies

Studying Canadian families requires students and researchers to stay on top of legal, political, social, and economic changes at the community, sub-national/provincial, national, and international levels. As you will see throughout this book, studying Canadian families often includes understanding and studying aspects of the Canadian economy, policy shifts, changes to health care and longevity, the internet, poverty, immigration, environmental issues, globalization, war/genocide/ethnic conflict, violence, taxation, legal changes, and human rights issues. And much of this has been sparked by what some have called the "big bang" (Cheal 1991) in family theorizing. Before exploring the "big bang" let us first turn to what we mean by *family* and how the changing definition of this concept has had profound implications on access to programs, policies, and privilege in this country.

Changing Definitions of Family

The definition of *family* is in a constant state of flux (Holtzman 2011) (see Box 1.1) and even judicial uses of family definitions—which we would assume to be the most comprehensive—tend to "be inconsistent, unpredictable . . ." and not always "effective" (Holtzman 2011:620). Today we would have a difficult time identifying a single overarching definition of family accepted within and across academic research and disciplines, and formal or informal organizations. This is why we so often use adjectives to qualify *family*, adjectives that allow us to more easily focus in on different incarnations of the family. For example, most agree on the definition of a **nuclear family**, which typically includes a couple and their children, sharing the same household, but may also define one parent and his/her child(ren) (Ambert 2006). Today, with divorce and remarriages, we are also seeing an increase in the number of **bi-nuclear families**—where children of divorced parents move and live across households. For children, the family they "belong to" or originate in is called their "family of origin" or "orientation" (Ambert 2006). There is also the **extended family**, mentioned briefly above, in which several generations or sets of kin—grandparents, aunts, uncles, cousins—share a household. This has also come to be called a multi-generational household. Similarly, terms like **household**, a set of related and unrelated individuals who share a dwelling, are also relatively easily defined.

At the individual level, there are likely as many definitions of *family* as there are families in this country, because the lived reality of "the family" is quite different from the reality privileged through Canadian law and social policy. At the same time, individual level explanations, like some more formal definitions such as the ones in Box 1.1, tend to stress the *structural* or *compositional definition* of the family (Eichler 1983; Gazso 2009). These

Box 1.1

What Is a Family? Evolving Definitions of Family—Is Everyone Accounted For?

Do any of the following definitions exclude your own family? Who else is excluded from the following definitions? Can you spot any other similarities, differences, or problems with these definitions?

Murdock (1949): . . . a social group characterized by common residence, economic co-operation, and reproduction. It includes adults of both sexes, at least two of whom maintain a socially approved sexual relationship, and one or more children, own or adopted, of the sexually cohabiting adults.

Stephens (1963): . . . a social arrangement based on marriage and the marriage contract, including recognition of the rights and duties of parents, common residence for husband, wife, and children and reciprocal economic obligations between husband and wife.

Coser (1974): . . . a group manifesting the following organizational attributes: it finds its origin in marriage; it consists of husband, wife, and children born in their wedlock, though other relatives may find their place close to this nuclear group, and the group is united by moral, legal, economic, religious, and social rights and obligations.

Eichler (1983): A family is a social group which may or may not include adults of both sexes (e.g., lone-parent families), may or may not include one or more children (e.g., childless couples), who may or may not have been born in their wedlock (e.g., adopted children, or children by one adult partner of a previous union). The relationship of the adults may or may not have its origin in marriage (e.g., common-law couples), they may or may not share a common residence (e.g., commuting couples). The adults may or may not cohabit sexually, and the relationship may or may not involve such socially patterned feelings as love, attraction, and awe.

Goode (1995): Doubtless the following list is not comprehensive, but it [family] includes most of those relationships: (1) At least two adult persons of opposite sex reside together. (2) They engage in some kind of division of labor; that is, they do not both perform exactly the same tasks. (3) They engage in many types of economic and social exchanges; that is, they do things for one another. (4) They share many things in common, such as food, sex, residence, and both goods and social activities. (5) The adults have parental relations with their children, as their children have filial relations with them; the parents have some authority over children, and share with one another, while also assuming some obligations for protection, co-operation, and nurturance. (6) There are sibling relations among the children themselves, with, once more, a range of obligations to share, protect, and help one another.

Census Family (1996): Refers to a now-married couple (with or without never-married sons and/or daughters of either or both spouses), a couple living common-law (with or without never-married sons and/or daughters of either or both partners), or a

continued

lone parent of any marital status, with at least one never-married son or daughter living in the same dwelling.

Mandell and Duffy (2000): . . . a social ideal, generally referring to a unit of economic co-operation, typically thought to include only those related by blood, but revised by feminists to include those forming an economically co-operative, residential unit bound by feelings of common ties and strong emotions.

Census Family (2001): Refers to a married couple (with or without children of either or both spouses), a couple living common-law (with or without children of either or both partners), or a lone parent of any marital status with at least one child living in the same dwelling. A couple living common-law may be of opposite or same sex. "Children" in a census family include grandchildren living with their grandparent(s) but with no parents present.

Census Family (2006): Refers to a married couple (with or without children of either or both spouses), a couple living common-law (with or without children of either or both partners) or a lone parent of any marital status, with at least one child living in the same dwelling. A couple may be of opposite or same sex. "Children" in a census family include grandchildren living with their grandparent(s) but with no parents present.

Census Family (2011): . . . is composed of a married or common-law couple, with or without children, or of a lone parent living with at least one child in the same dwelling.

Vanier Institute of the Family (2012): . . . any combination of two or more persons who are bound together over time by ties of mutual consent, birth and/or adoption or placement and who, together, assume responsibilities for variant combinations of some of the following:

- Physical maintenance and care of group members;
- Addition of new members through procreation or adoption;
- Socialization of children;
- Social control of members;
- Production, consumption, distribution of goods and services; and
- Affective nurturance—love.

Census Family (2016). "Census family" is defined as a married couple and the children, if any, of either and/or both spouses; a couple living common law and the children, if any, of either and/or both partners; or a lone parent of any marital status with at least one child living in the same dwelling and that child or those children. All members of a particular census family live in the same dwelling. A couple may be of opposite or same sex. Children may be children by birth, marriage, common-law union, or adoption regardless of their age or marital status as long as they live in the dwelling and do not have their own married spouse, common-law partner, or child living in the dwelling. Grandchildren living with their grandparent(s) but with no parents present also constitute a census family.

Census Family Sources: Statistics Canada, at www.statcan.ca, Census Dictionary 1996, Census Dictionary 2001; Statistics Canada 2010, Census Dictionary 2006; and Statistics Canada 2012c; Statistics Canada, 2017a.

definitions do little more than answer the question: "who makes up a/the/your family"? Family researchers, beginning with key feminists like Margrit Eichler (1983), have long stressed the importance of rethinking our definitions of "the family," to instead focus on questions like "what *makes* a family?" And the Vanier Institute of the Family definition, above, tries to do some of this.

Gazso (2009:157), like Eichler, has highlighted the importance of including "process-based approaches" to "doing family" (much like West and Zimmerman's "doing gender," which assumes gender is "performative"). This type of approach stresses the relations, processes, and activities that individuals share and *do* together—the totality of sets of fluid practices—that make them a family (also see McDaniel and Tepperman 2007; Morgan 1996). This can and likely often does include parenting, intimacy, sharing resources, dividing household work and care work, making important decisions, etc. Similarly, Widmer (2010) treats families as dynamic systems of interdependencies that exist in shifting relational contexts. This allows for the analysis of ever-present tensions and conflicts, and recognizes the fluxes and flows in who is seen to make up a family at any given time.

Gazso (2009) explains that these process-based approaches to defining and understanding families ("doing family") offer the potential to transcend heteronormative, patriarchal, and Eurocentric assumptions about family life, and help capture the diversity and structural constraints embedded in cultural expectations. That said, she recognizes some of the shortcomings of this approach, noting that this approach runs "the risk of embracing individualism and agency to the point of neglecting to consider how agentic choices are shaped by social structure" (Gazso 2009:158). She also reminds us that the structural/compositional definitions of the family, for better and worse, continue to inform eligibility and administration of social policies and programs, and service delivery (Gazso 2009:158).

Eichler, writing on the definition of family, noted that "who is included in the definition of family is an issue of great importance as well as great consequence," because who we include in our definition will determine who is eligible to claim tax benefits, sponsor family members in immigration, claim insurance benefits, claim Indian status, etc. Eichler challenges us to move beyond "who" definitions of family, which focus on group membership and family structure (a mom and a dad and their children, for example), towards a "what" definition of family, which focuses on the services and supports provided by various members. In accepting a "what" definition of family, we would then recognize, reward, and legitimize families for what they do together and for each other, rather than recognize and privilege only those who take the "proper" form, regardless of what happens behind closed doors.

All this said, there remains a disconnect between how individuals themselves, family sociologists, and social policies and policy makers define the idea of family. It also reminds us that *legal/formal definitions*, like the Census family, *social definitions* found within different organizations and social groups, and *personal definitions* of families have been created for different purposes and in different contexts, and so typically remain far apart and distinct.

How we define *family* has profound implications for who is actually counted as a family. Census data, for example, reflect and are constrained by which families are measured and how. As a result, we only know about the types of families we have legally accepted, defined, asked about, and counted. **Quantitative** studies typically mask the actual existence of all other family forms that inevitably exist (see Case in Point box, p. 14).

In sum, when we try to define the idea of family, what is clear and constant is the variability of definitions. This tells us that family is a changing social construct that reflects variations in how states, institutions, and individuals understand, experience, and interact within it. Cheal (2008:14) noted that *family* is "a term whose relevance is defined in social interaction and its referents vary according to the nature of that interaction." Social scientific definitions of family change about as rapidly as other definitions, and often reflect both formal and informal or subjective uses of the term (see Cheal 2008). As you will see, each of the social scientific and theoretical approaches that follow adopts a somewhat different definition and set of assumptions about families, which in turn shape our understanding of it.

CASE IN POINT

Diversity as the Norm? Mixed Unions in Canada

In July 2014, *Maclean's* magazine featured an editorial with the title "Canada is leading the pack in mixed unions—Why we're setting the global standard for multicultural acceptance and integration." The article boastfully noted that "Our country . . . is a Métis nation—and getting more so" (*Maclean's* 2014). The editorial was reporting on the release of data from the 2011 National Household Survey that showed that just over 360,000 couples reported that they were in a mixed union or in a relationship where one partner is "a member of a visible minority" (a term that continues to be used by Statistics Canada) or racialized, while the other is not, or reported being in a relationship where the partners are from different racialized groups.

Maclean's noted that the numbers reveal continued growth in this trend. Statistics Canada (2014) reported a steady trend upwards, with the proportion of mixed unions increasing from 2.6 per cent of all couples in 1991, to 3.1 per cent in 2001, to 4.6 per cent in 2011. The National Household Survey (Statistics Canada 2014) also found that most mixed unions involved partners who were born in different countries. About 20 per cent were unions where both partners were foreign-born, from different countries. Almost half of all mixed couples had one partner who was born in Canada and the other born outside Canada (Statistics Canada 2014).

Interestingly, just over half of mixed unions (52.8 per cent) involved partners from the same religious background—for example, both partners reported being Christian or both were Muslim. Just over 20 per cent of mixed unions reported having no religious affiliation and just over a quarter were of different religious affiliations (compared with only 9.8 per cent of all other couples in Canada; Statistics Canada 2014).

Maclean's (2014) reminded us that mixed unions "are no longer unusual, nor an excuse for cultural conflict or bigotry." They are instead "a commonplace feature of life as it is lived in Canada."

The magazine claimed that we are "setting the global standard for multicultural acceptance and integration." Do you agree?

Questions for Critical Thought

What do you think accounts for the increase in mixed unions? Do you see it as a sign of increased acceptance of diversity in our society? Why? Why not?

Theoretical and Methodological Approaches to Studying Families

Theories are not fixed, complete, or "once and for all" explanations of how things work or are expected to work. They neither emerge as "complete theories," nor remain the same because theory and research are intertwined (Ingoldsby et al. 2004:2). As our understanding or theory changes, so do our research questions. Likewise, as we do research and come up with new observations that run counter to existing theories, our theories change. Even the seemingly unchanging or indisputable theories in the natural sciences are constructed in cultural contexts and so are influenced by social change. For example, Galileo challenged the widely accepted idea that the earth was flat, to the profound disapproval of the Catholic Church, ultimately resulting in his arrest. This shows us that we often accept things to be theoretically sound or "true," frequently despite evidence to the contrary or in the absence of adequate evidence, because of the social climate in which we live.

Paradigm shifts, or radical changes in scientific views, occur after *significant* data have been collected that do not fit the existing theory, to the extent that a new theory is needed to fit the data. This is clearly the case in theorizing on/about families, as family theories have undergone a number of significant shifts and modifications, resulting from challenges and social change.

Theories provide us with a lens through which we look at the social world. With a shift in theory, we take on a different lens with which we try to understand the social world in general and families in particular. Theories then suggest *what* we look at and *how*, because each theory contains underlying assumptions about how the social world works—which in turn guide our research questions and methods. For example, some assume human behaviour is biologically based, and so things like the gender division of labour are not only justified, but deemed natural, inevitable, and unchanging or unalterable. Others assume our behaviour is learned and so can be unlearned, relearned, or learned differently as products of the culture in which we live; and therefore patterns of behaviour can be constructed to support specific groups and interests, at the expense of others. For the first group of theorists, certain kinds of social change are viewed as problematic or dysfunctional, and so they seek to preserve particular existing structures and relations. Others, like those in the second group, recognize power struggles and inequities in existing structures and relations, and so seek change.

Although some approaches seemingly lend themselves to certain methods, as we will see below, it is important to note that sociologists and other family researchers

within each theoretical tradition can and do use multiple types of methods—both qualitative and quantitative—at times, such that theories and methods do not always line up
exactly.

Researchers may use seemingly similar methods but with different theoretical
approaches, and so come to very different results. For example, anthropologists have
been studying families in cross-cultural contexts, and comparative **case studies**, for
a relatively long time. Within the discipline there has also been considerable variation in theorizing. For example, George Murdock (1949), who surveyed 250 human
societies, concluded that the nuclear family was universal and served four basic social
functions: sexual, economic, reproductive, and educational. According to Murdock, a
man and woman constitute an efficient co-operating unit, whereby a man's "superior
physical strength" and ability to "range further afield" to hunt and trade, complements
a woman's "lighter tasks" performed in or near the home. He claimed that all known
societies work this way because of innate and inevitable biological facts and differences
(Murdock 1949:7).

In contrast, Margaret Mead's comparative ethnographic research done in the South
Pacific at approximately the same time is **qualitative** and descriptive in nature. Mead
identified considerable variation across cultures and stressed that the division of labour
in every known society rests firmly on learned behaviour and not simply on biological differences. For example, she noted that if men went away to work in the city, women were
left behind to do the farm labour, which, by Murdock's biological explanation, would be
considered heavy male labour requiring "superior male strength." She did not dismiss or
even minimize biology, but instead argued that "human beings have learned, laboriously,
to be human" (Mead 1949:198).

Clearly, two seemingly similar cross-cultural studies of societies from around the
world came to different conclusions about family life because of differing theoretical
orientations. Let us explore some of these theoretical differences.

Functionalism

In general, structural functionalist theories are based on the idea of organic ontology,
which assumes that society is like a living organism or body, made up of a series of
interrelated parts working together for the good of the whole. Each social institution or
subsystem, like parts of the organism/body, serves specific functions, keeping society in
a state of equilibrium. Individuals within the institutions, like cells in a body, fill specific
and prescribed roles, again, for the proper functioning of the institution and society. From
a functionalist point of view, families are institutions that serve specific functions in
society, and family members are expected to fill prescribed roles within the institution for
the good of society as a whole. Social change, or a challenge to the existing order, is then
undesirable, at best.

Murdock's work exemplifies this approach. He believed we can best understand the
family by examining what it does and how it functions for and within society. Talcott Parsons (1955) also studied the functions of family by looking at the roles men and women
fill within them. According to Parsons, men are biologically better suited to fulfill *instrumental functions*, that is, tasks that needed to be performed to ensure a family's physical

survival, including providing for material needs by earning an income (Parsons and Bales 1955). He believed women are better suited to performing *expressive functions*—the tasks involved in building emotionally supportive relationships among family members—that are needed to foster psychological well-being. In other words, women were expected to fill the nurturing role.

Researchers who begin with a functionalist theoretical orientation are likely to look for cultural universals and aspects of dominant family forms and ask "What purpose do they serve?" They are also likely to look negatively upon rapid social change that could challenge or disrupt the existing social order. Much of this has been criticized, as you will see in the following discussion. More recent neo-functionalist approaches have also tried to address some of the critiques (see Swenson 2008; White and Klein 2008).

Marxism

The functionalist approach to the study of families was particularly popular in North America throughout the 1940s and 1950s. However, competing views also existed and some researchers studying families turned to the earlier work of Friedrich Engels, who provided a very different explanation and approach to the study of families in *Origin of the Family, Private Property and the State* (1972 [1884]). Engels, with Marx, argued that a number of distinct phases in human history shape, alter, and constrain human relations. He explained that the mode of production, or the way we organize economic life— whether hunting and gathering (foraging) in primitive communism, land-based (agrarian) feudalism, or modern industry and profit-driven capitalism—affects the way we organize social life and experience family relations. He claimed that in a period of primitive communism, characterized by a foraging/nomadic existence, the notion of private ownership was absent and there was relative equality between the sexes. Then, with land-based feudalism came a reorganization and privatization of family life and a change in power relations between the sexes. With the advent of the notion of private ownership and male control of land and other property, women lost power and control both within and outside of families. Ideally, for Marxists, the social goal is to abolish private property, re-establish communism, and return to more equitable relations between the sexes. Thus, unlike functionalists, for Marxists, gender differences in power and status, and the domination of men over women, within and outside families, is neither natural nor inevitable but rather is a product of the (re)organization of economic life. This approach, again unlike functionalism, implies that social change is a normal, and at times desirable, part of social life. For family researchers who embrace a Marxist approach, a likely goal would be to identify power relations within the home and connect them to inequities in economic relations outside it.

Symbolic Interactionism

While Marxists looked outside of families to economic forms and relationships in order to understand what was happening within them, others have looked instead within families at social relations and interactions. That is, while Marxists saw economic forces acting on individuals and families, others, like George Herbert Mead, assumed that individuals were active agents or "doers" of social life. In other words, if you want to understand social life in general and family life in particular, you should examine how individuals construct meaning through their daily interactions with others. For example, according to Mead, understanding family involves understanding parent–child relations and "the relationship between the sexes" (Mead 1967 [1934]:238). Exchanges or interactions between them lead to the organization of the family and society. That is, he explained that "all such larger units or forms of human social organization as the clan or the state are ultimately based upon, and whether directly or indirectly are developments from or extensions of, the family" (Mead 1967 [1934]:229). Therefore, in contrast to Marxism, this approach implies that the individuals and interactions within families shape the organization of family life, which in turn helps shape larger organizations like the state. Thus, researchers using this theoretical approach, would likely conduct in-depth, qualitative interviews with family members and/or observe individuals and interactions within families as they happen. At the same time, a researcher would seek to uncover the rich and complex underlying meanings of interactions and relations, often from the point of view of the individuals involved in the exchanges.

Exchange Theory

Social exchange theory is a broad theoretical framework used to examine relational processes within families. It borrows from psychology, sociology, and economics, as it seeks to explain the development, maintenance (including the maintenance of power differences), and decay of "exchange relationships" (Nakonezny and Denton 2008). It focuses on understanding the balance between the costs and rewards that marital partners obtain when choosing to be and remain within a conjugal relationship. In this approach, marital exchange relationships are conceptualized as transactions between partners for valued resources—including love and affection—which culminate in individual or family-level profit or losses. The theory maintains that partners seek positive outcomes based on rewards and costs, but each partner must value the other's activities for relational solidarity to be sustained. It purports that couples who receive favourable reward/cost outcomes from each other—where the distribution of rewards and costs is perceived to be fair (enough)—are more likely to develop solidarity and be more satisfied with their marriage (Homans 1974). These are then the families that are most likely to remain together. Each partner's satisfaction with the relationship is assumed to correlate directly with the perceived rewards of the marital relationship and inversely with the perceived costs (Nakonezny and Denton 2008).

A major risk factor for a relationship's stability is at least one partner's low level of satisfaction with the distribution of costs and benefits. But satisfaction alone is not enough. The theory goes on to explain that the rewards and punishments that individual actors "administer" to each other is a key source of marital power (Nakonezny and Denton 2008). The balance of power generally belongs to that partner who contributes the greater resources to the marriage. Inevitably then "resource differentials" produce "relationship asymmetry," which can then result in exploitation in the marital relationship (Blau 1964). While interesting and seemingly logical, because of its emphasis on micro-level exchanges and their outcomes, this theoretical approach tends to overlook the broader social and cultural contexts that shape, constrain, and alter family life.

Family Systems Theory

Influenced by symbolic interactionism, family systems theory assumes that a family is a relatively closed system of social interactions, or a site of interacting personalities. According to this theory, which happens to be especially popular among family therapists and social workers, an individual's problems and behaviour are best understood in the context of families because it is believed that the locus of pathology is not within the person but in a system dysfunction. In other words, the family is more than a collection of individuals or interactions, it is a natural social system, "with its own rules, roles, communication patterns, and power structure" (Ingoldsby et al. 2004:168).

Urie Bronfenbrenner's ecological theory of human development uses a systems approach to understanding family life by looking at how the home environment, or microsystem, affects child development. Bronfenbrenner's ecological model, however, explains child development as a multi-level interactive process, requiring multi-level analysis of a number of interconnected systems. His bioecological paradigm stresses the importance of reciprocal interactions between individuals and their micro- (family environment), meso- (e.g., school), exo- (institutions beyond a child's immediate environment, like a parent's workplace), and macro systems (customs, values, and laws of the culture in which we live) on developmental and socio-emotional outcomes (Bronfenbrenner 1977). Bronfenbrenner argued that a child's immediate family environment, larger social environment, other systems, and institutions shape development. All of these interacting systems, taken together, provided an understanding of child development.

Doing research from this theoretical perspective would require the researcher to study interactions at multiple levels, modelled like a series of circles, one inside the other. A researcher may first study a child's interactions within the home, the first and smallest circle; then the child's interactions at school, the next and slightly larger circle; then the child's neighbourhood, the next and larger circle, etc. The aim would be to try to understand how the child is affected by and affects relations within each environment or circle.

Developmental Theories

In the 1940s, some family researchers noted that, like individuals, families were influenced by developmental processes, or experienced life cycles, with clearly delineated stages (Ingoldsby et al. 2004). In a report created for the "First National Conference on the Family" established by US president Truman, Duvall and Hill (1948) outlined a relatively new and interdisciplinary approach to the study of families. Evelyn Millis Duvall, a specialist in human development, teamed up with Reuben Hill, a family sociologist, to create the family development theory. Using Freud's work on psychosexual development, Erikson's research on psychosocial development, Piaget's theories on cognitive development, and Kohlberg's ideas on moral development, along with demographic and **longitudinal** research on families, Duvall and Hill argued that families go through a series of eight sequential or developmental stages in the family life cycle (Duvall and Hill 1988). At each life stage—marriage, child-bearing, preschool, school, teen, launching centre, middle-aged, and aging—family members, depending on their physical maturation, are challenged by different developmental tasks and normative events, which can, at times, result in stress, crises, and critical transitions.

Duvall noted that "although the timing and duration of family life cycle stages vary widely, families everywhere try to conform to norms present in all societies in what is expected at each life cycle's stage" (Duvall 1988:130). She explained that the family development theory was unique among theoretical frameworks because:

(a) its family life cycle dimension provides the basis for study of families over time;
(b) of its emphasis on the developmental tasks of individual family members and of families at every stage of their development;
(c) of its built-in recognition of family stress at critical periods in development;
(d) of its recognition ever since 1947 of the need for services, supports, and programs for families throughout their life cycles. (Duvall 1988:133)

More recent research (Cooke and Gazso 2009) using a life-course approach has attempted to capture life-course complexity and gender-specific experiences and trajectories, which were somewhat lacking in the original approach (see Krüger and Levy 2001).

Biases in Traditional Approaches/Theorizing

Within many of the family theories popular throughout the first half of the twentieth century, the family was conceptualized as an important but relatively isolated unit "whose internal structures resulted mainly from negotiated action of adult members" (Krüger and Levy 2001:149). Most of these theories tended to treat all or most families as homogeneous, and questions about gender differences affecting experiences within families, and inequality, generally remained unasked and unanswered. Writing about this, Eichler (1997) noted that, in fact, a great deal of theorizing about families in the past contained a number of hidden assumptions and biases. She identified seven biases in past family literature and theorizing: monolithic, conservative, sexist, ageist, micro-structural, racist, and heterosexist. Thus, theories tended to treat family as a monolithic structure by emphasizing uniformity of experience and universality of functions—*monolithic bias*. In other words, they tended to under-represent the diversity of family forms that actually existed in any given society. She identified a *conservative bias*, where theorists tended to provide only a romanticized view of the nuclear family and regarded recent changes as ephemeral. A *sexist bias* was manifested in a number of ways, including the assumption that there is a "natural" division of functions between the sexes. Theorists also almost exclusively talked about families as involving exchanges between two middle-aged adults, largely excluding children and the elderly in their analysis, producing an *ageist bias*. She identified a *micro-structural bias*, a tendency to treat families as encapsulated units, typically ignoring extraneous/external factors. Theories also often devalued or outright ignored families of culturally or ethnically non-dominant groups—*racist bias*—and treated the heterosexual family as "natural," denying family status to lesbian and gay families—*heterosexist bias*. A large number of these biases have since been addressed by feminist theorizing on families.

The "Big Bang"—Feminist Theories

Feminism is not a new paradigm, and in fact has existed for as long as, if not longer than, sociology itself (for example, see Mary Wollstonecraft, 1759–1797). But what was novel was the force with which feminism was able to challenge existing family theories in the period following the 1960s—a period that David Cheal (1991) called "the big bang." Since then, feminist scholarship and feminist questions have charted a different course for theorizing families. Feminism "is not only an academic school of thought, it is also a broad movement for change" (Cheal 1991:9). Feminism took what, for a long time, had been considered intimate or private matters—sexuality, violence, child-rearing and care, domestic division of labour, etc.—and made them public, social, and political issues. Issues not only worthy of study, but in need of change.

For more on feminist theories, see "Definitions of Domestic Violence" in Chapter 14, pp. 294–6.

Feminist theorizing on families generally challenges the apparently gender-neutral assumptions about family life and roles—often found in other family theories—that mask or ignore inequalities and result in negative outcomes for women. Feminists typically seek to determine who does what, for whom, and with what consequences, often assessing the differential distribution of activities, resources, and power (see Saul 2003). Additionally, feminists believe that gender relations in the home and in other institutions are neither natural nor immutable, but rather historical and socio-cultural products, subject to re-construction (Elliot and Mandel 1998). Typically, feminists subject marriage and family to a series of profound and critical questions, challenge myths about women's roles and abilities, and advocate for change.

Having said this, there is considerable variation within feminism, as feminists them-selves depart from or have developed in response to different intellectual traditions, for example, Marxism, symbolic interactionism, phenomenology, and psychoanalysis. These traditional approaches were "sooner or later all reflected in feminist analysis of family life, and they were in turn transformed by it" (Cheal 1991:2). As a result, within femin-ism there are liberal feminists, Marxist feminists, radical feminists, socialist feminists, psychoanalytic feminists, post-structural feminists, post-colonial feminists, anti-racist feminists, etc. Each focuses on a somewhat different aspect of inequality, often iden-tifying a different source of the problem or problems, and therefore proposing differ-ent solutions. The authors of the chapters that follow reflect some of this diversity. One prominent Canadian example of feminist theorizing on families, discussed in this book, focuses on the notion of **social reproduction** (see Bezanson, Doucet, and Albanese 2015; Luxton 2015). This approach draws on Marxist and socialist feminism to shed light on power and household relations in capitalist economies like ours.

Gazso (2009) points out that for many feminist scholars the theoretical framework of social reproduction offers a sharp focus on both micro-level relations and activities that make up families, and the broader social processes that constrain them. This theoretical approach begins by pointing out that while men's paid work in the public sphere has been historically viewed as productive and socially valuable, the unpaid work so often carried out by women, which meets the care and economic needs to maintain life on a daily basis and contributes to the reproduction of labour in capitalist societies, has for the most part been undervalued and ignored (Bezanson 2006b; Bezanson and Luxton 2006; Fox 2015; Fox and Luxton 2001; Gazso 2009; Luxton 2001).

Researchers embracing this theoretical approach focus their attention on women's care behaviours and relations and work to highlight how women socially reproduce daily life for family members, making it possible to, among other things, allow men to engage in paid work (Fox and Luxton 2001; Luxton 2015). Gazso (2009) notes that social reproduction includes various kinds of work—mental, manual, and emotional—aimed at providing the socially variable care necessary to maintain life and to reproduce the next generation. This theoretical approach, while keenly in tune with the resistance and agency of women from various racialized groups and class backgrounds, has been critiqued for not having done enough to analyze and recognize the experiences of those growing up in LGBTQ families.

Queer theory has provided some additional stimulus in rethinking family theories, because most feminist approaches, as noted above, have been criticized for failing to provide an adequate analysis of lesbian and gay family experiences. For example, while feminists have done important work on family violence and on the subordination of women of different "races," classes, and of other diverse backgrounds, most have failed to note that for lesbian families, "it is not their powerlessness *within* the family that marks their subordination, but rather their *denial of access to* a legitimate and socially instituted sphere of family, marriage, and parenting" (Calhoun 2000:139). This more critical theorizing and activism has resulted in legal and attitudinal changes, yet much remains to be done.

Conclusion

Today, as in the past, Canadian families exist in a number of diverse forms, which, in relation to other social institutions, both aid and constrain individual family members. That is, while a variety of family forms have existed in the past, our changing definitions of family are now making it possible for us to identify, count, and validate a variety of diverse forms. At the same time, our current definitions, theories, and measurement tools are likely to miss or mask a number of family forms that actually exist but remain unrecognized and uncounted, and these family forms may become part of future definitions of family.

Our current and shifting definitions reflect changing social attitudes, economic trends, laws, and policies. At the same time, changing economic trends and social attitudes have changed the age of first marriage; the duration of a marriage; whether marriage occurs at all; family size; the sequence and spacing of life-cycle events; where families live, whether they live together or apart, or across households and/or borders; and how they live.

With changing definitions and trends there have been shifts in how family theorists and researchers study and try to understand family life. Some are critical of change, while others actively seek it. Some look within families to understand them, some look outside them, and still others look at a variety of contexts. Some take a qualitative and descriptive approach, some a quantitative one, and others use both. The chapters that follow will reflect some of this diversity in approaches, as they map out and critically assess some of the trends and changes that are part of the complex collage that makes up Canadian family life.

Study Questions

1. Create a collage of photos of people who you currently see as making up your family. Would all of them be considered part of your family by Statistics Canada's definition of *family*? How is your definition similar? How is it different?

2. If you were asked to develop the official definition of *family* for this country, what would it be?
3. What do you see as the next type of family that the Canadian Census will begin to count in the near future? Why? Has it always existed? Why do you think we have failed to include it thus far?
4. Why do you think Canadians are postponing marriage and childbirth? What do you think is an ideal age (if any) to marry? To have children? Why?
5. If you wanted to study the domestic division of labour within families, how would you study it? Which theoretical orientation would best suit/guide your approach?

Further Readings

Allen, K., and A. Jaramillo-Sierra. 2015. "Feminist Theory and Research on Family Relationships: Pluralism and Complexity." *Sex Roles* 73(3–4): 93–9. This article acts as the introduction for a special series of three consecutive issues of the journal *Sex Roles,* committed to showcasing feminist approaches to the study of families. It launches a collection of theoretical and empirical articles that include critical analyses, case studies, quantitative studies, and qualitative studies that focus on a wide array of substantive topics in the examination of families.

Bezanson, Kate, Andrea Doucet, and Patrizia Albanese. 2015. "Introduction: Critical Feminist Sociologies of Families, Work, and Care." *Canadian Review of Sociology* 52(2): 201–3. This is a brief introduction to a collection of articles in the *Canadian Review of Sociology*, committed to showcasing the strong history of feminist approaches to critical sociologies of families, work, and care. The collection draws together an esteemed set of Canadian voices that have made foundational contributions to feminist and critical family sociologies: Ann Duffy, Margrit Eichler, Bonnie Fox, and Meg Luxton.

Eichler, Margrit. 1997. *Family Shifts: Families, Policies, and Gender Equality.* Toronto: Oxford University Press. This classic text has proven to be a major contribution to the study of Canadian families because it both traces shifts in Canadian family composition and gender roles, and identifies important theoretical and policy implications.

Harrison, Deborah, and Patrizia Albanese. 2016. *Growing Up in Armyville: Canada's Military Families during the Afghanistan Mission.* Waterloo: Wilfrid Laurier University Press. Based on a survey of all youth attending a high school on a Canadian military base and on in-depth interviews with 61 youth from Canadian Armed Forces families, this book assesses the human costs to CAF families resulting from their enforced participation in the volatile overseas missions of the twenty-first century.

Trovato, Frank. 2012. *Population and Society: Essential Readings.* Toronto: Oxford University Press. This text examines, among other things, the relationship between individual action and demographic phenomena including family processes like fertility, marriage, and migration.

Widmer, Eric. 2010. *Family Configurations: A Structural Approach to Family Diversity.* Burlington, VT: Ashgate. This book takes a "configurational approach" to understanding families, which focuses on the complexities and richness of familial relationships and interdependencies within families.

Key Terms

Bi-nuclear family A family consisting of children and their parents who live in two households, usually following a divorce.

Case studies/case study research A qualitative method of inquiry that investigates a contemporary phenomenon within its real-life context; it helps provide in-depth or detailed contextual analysis of a limited number of events or relationships.

Child launch Refers to one of the "early adult transitions," the point at which children leave their parental home. This has been increasingly delayed over the past decade or so, resulting in "cluttered" or "crowded" nests rather than the "empty nests" of the past.

Extended family Takes in both the household and the wider family circle, including kin such as cousins, aunts, uncles, and grandparents. A combination of these family members may share a household, but the extended family does not necessarily reside together.

Household A group of people who occupy the same dwelling or housing unit.

Longitudinal studies/research A study that shows changes over time, usually by tracking a particular group of people or by taking snapshots of different groups at different points in time.

Nuclear family A family that consists of parent(s) and child(ren); also known as the conjugal family unit, this family type includes at most a mother, father, and their dependent children.

Qualitative studies/research A non-numeric analysis of data intended to discover underlying meaning and explore relationships.

Quantitative studies/research A set of statistical analyses intended to discover patterns and trends in data, and causal relationships between variables.

Social reproduction A term taken up by Marxist and socialist feminists to refer to the paid and unpaid processes of reproduction and maintenance of human life that are most often performed by women. This includes activities, emotions, and responsibilities that maintain relationships.

Transgender Individuals who have a gender identity, or gender expression, that differs from their assigned sex.

Transnational, multi-local/satellite family A family that finds itself (temporarily) separated and living across borders, in multiple locations.

Notes

1. The Civil Marriage Act (Bill C-38), adopted on July 20, 2005, made Canada the third country in the world after the Netherlands (2000) and Belgium (2003) to legalize same-sex marriage.

 Interested in finding out more? Visit www.oupcanada.com/Albanese4e for access to a list of recommended websites for this chapter.

2

Canada's Families
Historical and Contemporary Variations

CYNTHIA COMACCHIO

LEARNING OBJECTIVES

- To review the major changes and continuities in the history of Canadian families over the past two centuries

- To discuss how the patriarchal family reinforces hierarchies of class, "race," gender, and age

- To reflect on "the family" as a social construction deriving from the dominant social group's anxieties and objectives at particular historical moments

- To understand that families have always varied in form and composition, despite the force of prevailing ideas about what properly constitutes "the family"

Introduction

Most people throughout history have spent at least some part of their lives in a family or a family setting. Despite common reference to "the family" as though one model and experience are universal across time and place, Canadian families have always been diverse in form and composition. Other chapters in this text will detail how twenty-first century families represent such recent trends as later first marriages and child-bearing; lone-parenting and childlessness by choice; common-law, same-sex, and mixed unions; multiple divorces, remarriages, and family reconstitutions. But some of the characteristics that we associate with contemporary families, such as lone-parent, blended, or multi-generational households, have long existed in both settler and Indigenous communities.

The history of the family was one of the earliest offshoots of the "new social history" that emerged in universities during the turbulent 1960s. Given the historic identification of the family as the basis of an orderly society, it is impossible to consider their histories separately. The shared purpose of historians of either camp was to explore the lives of ordinary people—the majority in any time and place—and to bring to light the experiences of social groups identified, and frequently marginalized, by "race," gender, class, culture, and age. These lived experiences had previously been rarely mentioned, even ignored, because traditional analyses focused on the tiny percentile of those—largely men—who held political and economic power. It is evident, however, that even in histories about monarchs and prime ministers and church leaders, family backgrounds and family networks figured strongly, because families have always played a central role in social formation, political and economic systems, and culture. Family, in short, was an "absent presence" in earlier studies, which family historians, frequently borrowing conceptually and methodologically from social scientists, have attempted to recover. In doing so, they inevitably touch upon the differences that have always existed, and that remain, between what family *means* and what family *is* (Comacchio 2000:177–8).

In keeping with the focus of this collection on Canadian families in their pluralistic contemporary forms, this chapter emphasizes the simple fact that there are many forms and meanings of family in any historical moment. The constant, however, is that no matter what we take to signify "family," families have always been, and remain, important to our individual, social, and national identities. Even as they change over time, as the historical and sociological literature indicates, families persist. They are elemental to self-formation as well as to social formation. Just as family is central to self-identity, class, gender, region, "race," ethnicity, religion, and age are fundamental to experiences of family, past and present.

Families as Historical Actors

Even within the broad range of family experiences that has been documented for the past several centuries, additional variations are found in communities distinguished by "race" and culture: First Nations families, Métis, and Inuit families; francophone Catholic families in Quebec; and immigrant families of diverse religious backgrounds from all parts of the globe. Families adapt to, and also initiate, larger demographic, economic, cultural, and political trends. They are historical actors and not merely passive recipients of changing ideas and practices. Moreover, the emotional elements of family are as important to self and society as are the socio-economic and cultural functions. Families are, and have ever been, at once supportive and restrictive, nurturing and oppressive, protective and abusive, innovative and conservative, liberating and entrapping. Finally, it is important to note that while the form and function of real historical families are adaptive, the symbolic power ascribed to "the family"—a power embedded in culture and memory—has remarkable endurance. The family as an ideal is socially constructed and reconstructed to meet the larger social needs and objectives that are defined by the dominant class, and upheld by the state, in any given time. Until recently, the ideal was the patriarchal, heterosexual male-breadwinner family of white Euro-Canadian middle-class background. This particular social construction of family retains many adherents, even while many contemporary Canadians do not live in families resembling that model. Notwithstanding the public force of the ideal, as well as nostalgia for some "golden age" of the family, many Canadians never have.

Box 2.1

Family Sociology in Canada

The Canadian Conference on the Family, convened by Governor General Georges Vanier in 1964, led to the founding of The Vanier Institute of the Family, which continues to be an important agency for family research and policy. University of Montreal sociologist Frederick Elkin (1918–2011) was charged with preparing the nation's first "state of the art" family survey, published as *The Family in Canada: An Account of Present Knowledge and Gaps in Knowledge about Canadian Families* (1964). Elkin observed that the nation's history, geography, and social structure made it "much too heterogeneous" to have "one or ten or twenty distinctive family types" (Elkin 1964:31–2).

Change is a key concept for any family analyst. The family, with its crucial functions, does not expire, it changes. In varying ways, it adapts and bends and of course, in turn, it influences. (Elkin 1964:8)

The historic centrality of families derives from their vital social functions: reproduction, production, socialization, maintenance, and regulation. Indigenous families in pre-contact times were the basis of all economic, political, and spiritual organization, in varying ways for different peoples and regions, but always functioning collectively to sustain their members and the larger community. The Europeans who arrived in the seventeenth century shared this understanding of family function. The North American colonies were focused on trade with their European mother countries. This economic purpose, as well as the colonists' own need to sustain themselves through agriculture, meant that the familial duties of production and reproduction were also transplanted. The colonization process necessitated certain adaptations to "New World" conditions. Nineteenth-century family theorists contended that the **stem family** or **extended family**, forms that characterized traditional agrarian communities in Europe, were imported intact to the New World. The abundance of cheap land in North America, however, meant that the **nuclear family** form was not the outcome of industrialization as theorized, but actually preceded the growth of the factory system. In the sparsely settled and isolated colonies, the absence of any effective regulatory or policing agency made the family's role as social monitor, alongside the Church and the courts, even more important than in Europe (Dechêne 1992:238–9).

The vital economic role of families as units of production, the importance of land ownership to family fortunes, and the mutual reliance of family members across generations, characterized colonial family life as much as that of the mother countries. All family members were expected to work in some capacity, according to age and gender, from childhood until they "came into their own." Adulthood was signified by early marriage and family formation, usually in separate households, although often on land allotted to sons who had worked for their families without wages since childhood. In this setting, the best possible outcome for the family as a whole required that each member sacrifice self-interest for the good of all. These expectations were embedded in the meanings of family, and reinforced by Church and law. Women were expected to get pregnant shortly after marrying, and could look forward to new babies at regular two- or three-year intervals until at least their mid-forties. Families with a dozen children, ranging from infancy to young adulthood, were not the average experience but were certainly not unusual (Errington 1995:25–6). Childlessness was considered a tragedy and an economic hardship. Adoption, often within family and kin circles, and often without the death of both parents, was commonplace (Strong-Boag 2006, 2011). In a society without social welfare networks, survival depended on family. Few could manage without family ties.

By mid-nineteenth century, the British North American colonies were undergoing a profound structural transformation that would greatly affect their resident families. Stemming from these fundamental economic and demographic changes were political concerns that led to Confederation of the Dominion of Canada in 1867. Production moved out of the artisanal workshop, usually in the home, to ever-larger "manufactories." Work and domestic life were increasingly separated. Within the urban middle class, anglophone and francophone, Protestant and Catholic, family life became less concerned with economic subsistence, and more with maintaining certain living standards in the interests of "respectability." This model of family life was further encouraged by a "cult of domesticity," inspired by Queen Victoria and her growing family, which emphasized separate spheres for men and women. While retaining their traditional patriarchal authority, men belonged to the public sphere of wage labour, business, and politics. Women, newly glorified in their traditional domestic roles, were expected to use their "innate" care-giving skills to make home and family a "haven in a heartless world." More than ever before, mothers were uniquely responsible for children's upbringing in this haven, protected from the external threats posed by the new industrial order (Errington 1995:53).

Because the processes are so entwined, there is no simple way to chart the relationship of structural and familial change through time. What we can identify is the transformative impact of the **modernization** process. Modernization was augmented and accelerated by such transportation and communication advances as canals, railways, and telegraph lines, all of which facilitated the vision of a nation "from sea unto sea" that was realized by the first decade of the twentieth century. In central Canada, the industrialization and urbanization in cities were both further intensified by out-migration from rural areas, where inexpensive land was increasingly scarce, making it difficult to sustain the familial custom of outfitting adult sons with land to settle their own families (Baskerville and Sager 2007).

Unprecedented waves of immigration from Europe also spurred the process. Frequently utilizing the familial practice of **chain migration**, some three million newcomers arrived in Canada between 1896 and 1914. In the decade between the Dominion Census of 1901 and that of 1911, the population grew by 43 per cent, the "foreign-born" then accounting for 22 per cent of all Canadians. Many newcomers were intent on resettling families, kin, and even entire villages, complete with their social institutions, on the prairies. Enticed by the promise of free land, opportunity, and religious tolerance, these families were critical to the vision of a prosperous modern Canada. Others, especially male migrant workers, joined the expanding urban proletariat to make money for their families overseas, perhaps to bring them to Canada after establishing themselves (Knowles 1997:123–4).

Modernization also saw such traditional family functions as educating children and caring for the sick and the elderly gradually transferred out of the household to public institutions, usually funded by churches or charity, and eventually taken over by the state. The first transfer of functions to the state was schooling. Beginning with Ontario in 1871, most provinces enacted compulsory schooling legislation that specified the ages of attendance, generally from age 7 to age 14, as well as the number of days per year that children would be in the classroom. Because needy families could not aspire to a childhood in which school rather than work was the common experience, many children were obliged to keep earning. As a result, during this early stage of public schooling the usual pattern was an erratic school attendance with occasional "time out" to earn wages, help at home, or work on family farms (Sutherland 2000:159–60). The "factory laws" enacted to protect women and children in most provinces at this time reinforced the middle-class male breadwinner family ideal. However well-intentioned, their effect was to take away jobs from women and children for whom personal and family need allowed few options other than wage-earning, whatever the pay and conditions. In the absence of social support networks, the family's material situation, not the law, determined who had to work (Sutherland 2000:24–5; Ursel 1992:97–9).

There is much historical evidence to indicate that working-class families were bearing the brunt of exploitation and deprivation in the midst of these rapid socio-economic changes. In 1900, infant, child, and maternal mortality, orphanhood, and early widowhood disrupted between 35 and 40 per cent of all Canadian families. Rough estimates suggest that as many as one in five babies lost their lives before their first birthdays. The children of the poor were particularly vulnerable to impure water and milk, contagion fostered by crowded living conditions, and the expense of medical care. For women of childbearing age, maternal mortality was the second-ranked threat to life (Comacchio 1993).

As the twentieth century opened, an organized response to the dislocations brought about by modernizing forces was taking form in the urban-based, Protestant, middle-class reform movement known as the **Social Gospel**. Its many campaigns were inspired by the traditional Christian commitment to help the needy, but also by mounting middle-class anxieties about slums, public health threats, alcoholism, infant mortality, prostitution, "racial degeneration," and other horrors, real and imagined, that modernization seemed to have unleashed (Allen 1971; Valverde 1991). Among the movement's members was a growing contingent of women who contended that their "innate" maternal capacity qualified them to conduct the necessary "clean up," material and moral, that the situation demanded. They used such **maternal feminist** arguments to pressure governments to address the problems of poor families, especially those affecting children.

For more on the notion of the male breadwinner and the "male model of employment," see "Paid Work" in Chapter 9, pp. 184–5.

Structural changes, legislation, and new ideas about "the family" effectively reclassified women and children as the non-working dependents of male providers. Work came to be considered exclusively in terms of the wage labour of men functioning as the primary supporters of families. Because this was far from attainable for many families, much work, productive and reproductive, waged and unwaged, remained in the home.

Many women and children continued to contribute to family sustenance, often in ways that were neither paid nor enumerated. On farms, they worked many hours in egg and dairy production; in vegetable, fruit, and small animal cultivation for domestic use and market sale; and as essential seasonal labour for sowing and harvesting. Few working-class families could survive on the wages of a sole breadwinner. Children were kept out of school to earn or to mind younger siblings so that mothers could take paid employment.

Women for whom cultural concepts about respectability prohibited wage labour outside the home, as was the case among many immigrant families, supplemented the breadwinner's wages in less public ways. Many took in boarders, laundry, or "piece work," usually sewing, often assisted by their children and by the elderly family members for whom the dreaded workhouse was the only alternative (Bradbury 1993; Davies 2003; Montigny 1993). The daily domestic labour of caring for children, husbands, and dependent family members—historically "women's work—was undermined by the association of work with waged male labour outside the home. The result was an under-valuation of female labour both in the home and in the marketplace. This assessment of reproductive labour (inside the home) was also applied to women's paid work, which was deemed "feminine" and consequently "menial," justifying their lower wages and reinforcing gender inequality in the home and in the wider society (Frager and Patrias 2005).

To understand the centrality of family on the homesteading frontier in early twentieth century Canada, we need only recall the famous words of Laurier's Minister of the Interior, **Clifford Sifton**, invoking the arrival of the "stalwart peasant in a

---

Box 2.2
Domestic Labour and Social Reproduction

By the 1980s, Canadian feminist sociologists were actively involved in the "domestic labour debates," using historical analysis to emphasize that women's unpaid labour in the home was both productive and reproductive, and that the vital work of social reproduction did, in fact, have substantial economic value in the past as in the present. Meg Luxton's seminal work, *More Than a Labour of Love: Three Generations of Women's Work in the Home* (1980), contended that, in working-class homes, women's unpaid work often made the difference between destitution and family survival. In the present, domestic labour is still mostly "women's work" and remains under-valued.

. . . what women (and men) do, looking after their homes and the people they live with, is work that contributes, not just to the survival of their own households, but to the daily and generational maintenance of the population that sustains the formal economy. Traditionally, the unpaid work women do in their homes, looking after their families, has not been recognized as work, nor valued for its contribution to the economy, and therefore, was not taken into consideration in policy priorities. . . . recent evidence suggests that unpaid domestic labour in Canada continues to be a significant part of the economy, that women do most of it and that without the care work of families, Canadian society would not function. (Luxton 1980:14)

sheepskin coat." The less-cited remainder of this familiar quote refers to the "good quality," in the day's racist terms, represented by the ideal immigrant and his "stout wife and half a dozen children." Immigration was the first priority of the Laurier years (1896–1911), but the "open door" policy that welcomed immigrants of all origins is more mythic than historic. Canadian immigration policy was racially exclusive as well as economically selective (Knowles 2016). For those deemed "undesirable" and "unassimilable"—virtually all prospective immigrants from outside of Great Britain, the US, and Western Europe—federal policy deliberately thwarted the establishment of new families of certain origins, and the reunification of those separated by male migration. Increasingly restrictive regulations achieved this purpose by preventing the settlement of Asian and South Asian families. The 1911 census showed these immigrant communities to be almost exclusively male. In 1923, the **Chinese Immigration Act** closed the doors to Chinese immigrants, including wives and children of those already in Canada, until the new Immigration Act came into being in 1951 (Stanley 2011:43–4, 136).

Indigenous families inarguably suffered the most traumatic effects of a state policy that was designed to further an aggressive, racially exclusive, "nation-building" project. Intent on western "settlement," the federal government ignored the fact that "the Territories" were home to diverse Indigenous peoples long before contact. The influx of white homesteaders threatened their traditional family economies premised on hunting, trapping, and fishing. Their social and political customs, based in extensive networks of family and kin relations, were subjected to the interference of white missionaries, traders, government agents, and settlers alike. The **scientific racism** that fueled Victorian imperialism ensured few challenges to the notion of Indigenous "racial" inferiority. The newcomers were critical of the "mixed" families of white traders and First Nations and Métis women that had long sustained the now-expired fur trade. These families, known as "half-breed" or Métis in reference to their British or French-Canadian paternity, constituted a new society that was not recognized by successive governments as either Canadian or, after the passage of the **Indian Act** (1876), as **Status Indian**. The Act also defined "Indians" as wards of the Crown, officially infantilizing them in their relations with the paternal state and its agents (Coates 2008).

For more Canada's immigration and refugee system and on refugee settlement in Canada, see "Introduction" in Chapter 11, pp. 225–7.

In striving to replicate "the family" of white middle-class ideal, the Indian Act legislated women's subordination by insisting on **patrilineage**, the primacy of reproduction, and the allocation of "Indian" status based on the status of women's husbands. Indigenous men who married white women conferred their status on wives and children. Indigenous women who married white men lost all privileges associated with Indian status, and their children were likewise considered "non-status" (Carter 1999; Dickason 2010).

For more on Indigenous families and the early settlement of Europeans in Canada, see "Contact and the Fur Trade" in Chapter 12, pp. 249–50.

After the land treaties of the 1870s, the establishment of a nation-wide reserve system, and the federal government's plans to transform them into agricultural producers, relegated many families to abject poverty (Dashuk 2013). Indigenous families were threatened with deculturation by means of imposed Euro-Canadian educational,

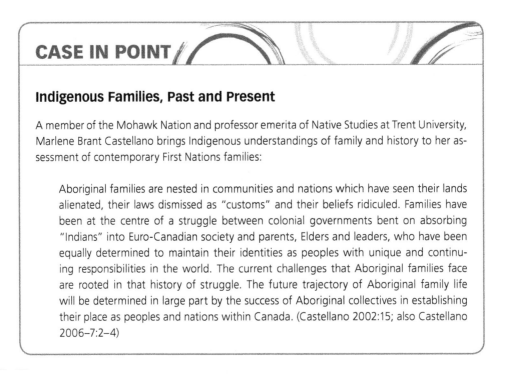

CASE IN POINT

Indigenous Families, Past and Present

A member of the Mohawk Nation and professor emerita of Native Studies at Trent University, Marlene Brant Castellano brings Indigenous understandings of family and history to her assessment of contemporary First Nations families:

> Aboriginal families are nested in communities and nations which have seen their lands alienated, their laws dismissed as "customs" and their beliefs ridiculed. Families have been at the centre of a struggle between colonial governments bent on absorbing "Indians" into Euro-Canadian society and parents, Elders and leaders, who have been equally determined to maintain their identities as peoples with unique and continuing responsibilities in the world. The current challenges that Aboriginal families face are rooted in that history of struggle. The future trajectory of Aboriginal family life will be determined in large part by the success of Aboriginal collectives in establishing their place as peoples and nations within Canada. (Castellano 2002:15; also Castellano 2006–7:2–4)

economic, and domestic institutions, most notably the compulsory **residential schools**. Run by missionaries of both Catholic and Protestant background, their purpose was to disrupt the generational transmission of language and customs by removing children from their families and communities, distancing them from their culture in every sense. It has been estimated that, by the first decade of the twentieth century, as many as 50 per cent of Indigenous children compelled to attend residential schools did not survive to the school-leaving age of 14 years (Miller 1996). The tragic individual, familial, and cultural impact of the residential schools has been manifested generationally into our own day, long after the last school closed in 1996 (National Centre for Truth and Reconciliation 2016).

Despite the evident gap between "the family" of ideal and many real Canadian families, the male breadwinner model was seen to be integral to social stability and national welfare in a time of change and accompanying public anxiety. This construction of the family reflected and reinforced prevailing Euro-Canadian middle-class experiences and objectives. Yet it also appealed to less affluent Canadians, as well as those of different "racial" and religious heritage, including many immigrants whose own cultures were patriarchal. As such, the model dominated public discourses and public policy on families for much of the twentieth century. Those who had historically sustained different notions of family, such as Indigenous peoples, were obliged to abandon them, at times by the force of the state, in favour of a model that held little meaning for them.

Questions for Critical Thought

What explains the widespread embrace of the male breadwinner family ideal, even if it was not attainable for many Canadian families, in a time of intensive socio-economic change that opened up new possibilities for other family models?

The Shape(s) of Modern Families

Inextricably bound with modernizing processes, demographic changes fundamentally affected the size, as well as the life course, of Canadian families over this entire period. Another "family myth" challenged by historical evidence is that late marriage and family limitation are relatively recent developments, occasioned by industrialization and urbanization, and in particular, by increasing opportunities for women. In pre-industrial Canada, large families were economically beneficial because all hands were needed to survive and prosper. As good land became increasingly less available and more expensive, marriages were delayed so that prospective breadwinners could earn wages by "hiring out" as agricultural labourers, or by working in resource industries or urban factories, on canals or railways. By 1900, the average age at marriage for men was 28 years, and for women, 25 years. Later ages at marriage also meant fewer children, evidenced in the corresponding reduction in family size. These demographic trends were not directly caused by the transition to industrial capitalism, for all its significance, but would soon be intensified by it (Sutherland 2000:14).

Also important to the decline in family size were new ideas about the nature of children and the ideal childhood. Proclaimed at home as **Canada's Century** and, internationally, the **Century of the Child**, the new century saw the circulation of ideas about childhood as a special, vulnerable, dependent life-stage associated with play, schooling, and "character formation" rather than work and wages. The middle-class notion of a "new childhood," in calling for more attention to individual children, also called for smaller families. Although these ideas were class- and "race-" defined, urban living, child labour laws, and compulsory schooling actually made smaller families particularly advantageous for the less fortunate. In 1901, women gave birth to an average of 4.6 children; by 1921, this had fallen to 3.5 (Wargon 1997:1) With the notable exception of the early post–Second World War years, the trend toward later marriages and smaller families has continued unabated.

In times when marital dissolution faced tremendous religious disapproval as well as legal obstacles, the social stigma against divorce was intense. The law was very restrictive: divorce was granted only with proof of adultery brought before the courts, and had to be finalized by an Act of Parliament. While no church sanctioned divorce, the Roman Catholic Church, dominant in Quebec, forbade it except by means of its own ecclesiastical annulment process, a lengthy and complex procedure that was only rarely instigated. There were only 11 divorces in all of Canada in 1900 (Snell 1991:9). Desertion was known as "the poor man's divorce." Because women's limited opportunities meant that many were "only a man away from poverty," common-law second marriages were probably far more numerous than statistics can reveal. Many Canadians spent at least some portion of their childhood in single-parent or blended family households, although both single parenthood and remarriage usually resulted from a spouse's death until the divorce laws were eased in 1969 (Milan 2000:3).

Also noteworthy in the history of families is the expanding role of women. Just as the separate spheres ideology was glorifying domesticity, new opportunities were opening up to women—at least the young and unmarried—for paid employment, higher education, and participation in the female organizations that emerged in the late nineteenth century and dominated social reform activity well into the twentieth. The "woman question" that became a dominant theme in the period's public discourses was entirely about the public roles and rights of women; they were simply born into their private roles as dutiful daughters, wives, and mothers. For those men, and women too, who were committed to traditional gender constructions, the woman question quickly became the foremost cause of the crisis in the family, which was women's "proper sphere." Women both unmarried and married joined groups such as the **Women's Christian Temperance Union** (1874), the **National Council of Women of Canada** (1893), and rural **Women's Institutes** (1897). Employing conservative maternal feminist arguments to defend their "unfeminine" public involvement, and to argue for the political rights they needed to effect the reforms they wanted, organized women worked toward an incremental but unprecedented female autonomy. The First World War accelerated both women's public involvement and their entry into paid labour. The federal vote was finally delivered to all women who were British subjects and over the age of majority in 1918, albeit in recognition of their womanly "sacrifice" for the cause of victory rather than that of gender equality (Sangster 2001:201–3).

Questions for Critical Thought

Why would women campaigning for political equality in the early twentieth century opt for a "maternal feminist" argument rather than arguing that they should get the vote simply on the basis of their equality to men?

For anxious observers, such advances implied a "new day" that held great dangers for the family by drawing women away from marriage and motherhood. The First World War cost the under-populated nation some 66,000 men, mostly young fathers and would-be fathers. Added to this was the toll taken by the Spanish influenza epidemic in 1918–19, which hit hardest in the 20- to 40-year-old cohort, the very sector of the population most likely to wed and form families. In the interests of a longed-for return to "normalcy," the 1920s occasioned a renewed public attention on marriage and family formation, and especially to "the crisis in the family."

In 1920, the federal government established the Canadian Council on Child and Family Welfare (later the National Welfare Council), the nation's largest social welfare tribunal, to direct research on families and related policy initiatives. New state agencies and programs called on the rising class of "family experts," drawn from medicine, psychology, sociology, social work, and education, to formulate modern programs and policies. These were largely instructional, centring on parent education, and more specifically education for motherhood (Arnup 1994). Education was considered the most effective, and least expensive, means of promoting healthier, happier families for a productive, "efficient" modern Canada (Comacchio 1993:22–7).

Having expanded their role to conduct the war, the federal and provincial governments continued on their own modernizing path toward the interventionist state, if but slowly and reluctantly. In this manner, the modern state and modern experts developed a new partnership to deliver social welfare programs. In turn, that relationship shaped their modern roles in the historically private family circle. During the interwar years, some of the new "family experts" espoused eugenics, a pseudo-science inspired by Darwinism and premised on the notion of "selective breeding." Eugenicists strove to restrict the immigration that many felt was leading to "racial degeneration." Especially among the newly influential medical profession, many supported anti-contraception campaigns, since "race suicide," as they viewed family limitation, appeared to be largely a practice of educated middle-class "better stock" couples (McLaren 1990:13–17). **Pronatalism** offered the solution to the perceived crisis in the family, by definition a crisis in society. The "better stock" would be encouraged by family experts, governments, voluntary agencies, and the popular media, to marry, have children, and submit to parent education to produce model future citizens. Modern science would replace custom and "superstition," and modern experts, backed by the state, would replace the now outmoded traditional sources of child-rearing wisdom found in family and community (Comacchio 1993:92–3).

If concerns about the "crisis in the family" were intensifying, marriage and family formation remained the choice of most Canadians, although certain "modern" trends were becoming apparent. The 1921 Census revealed a proportionately greater number of married Canadians than at any previous time on record. The 14 per cent decline in the birth rate between 1921 and 1931, however, testified to the continuous spread of birth control despite its illegality. But it also testified to the impact of urban life and the rising costs of living, as well as to the spread of new ideas about childhood, and the growing correlation of small families with a better quality of life. While infant and child mortality remained high, some improvement was being effected through education and improved public health and sanitation measures, especially immunization. Longer life expectancy also increased the average length of marriages. Combined with smaller family size, this development changed the family life course, extending the time between children leaving home and the death of husband or wife. Couples who married in 1920 could expect this post-parental stage to be almost seven years longer than it was for those who married in 1900. This demographic change had important implications for the marital relationship. It also affected the process of "coming into one's own," as postwar adolescents went to high school in higher numbers than ever before, thus postponing leaving home and effectively prolonging that lifestage. The plight of the elderly was intensified as well: as more Canadians lived longer, families were increasingly strained to provide for their dependent young as well as their dependent elders, especially during the Great Depression (Davies 2003:145; Finkel 2006:104–105).

Many of the ambitious plans calling on the state for family welfare purposes were seriously curtailed when the Great Depression began in October 1929. A decade of unrelenting economic hardship, the Depression was effectively a gender crisis, more particularly

Daily Life

During the "Dirty Thirties" Canadians of all ages wrote letters to their provincial premiers, their elected representatives, even Prime Minister Richard B. Bennett, to plead for assistance for their families, usually in the form of work for their male breadwinners. The following is excerpted from a letter written in 1933, the darkest year of the Depression. It was sent to Ontario premier George S. Henry by the eldest girl (no age specified, but probably early teens) in a large family about how her father's unemployment was affecting them all.

February 14, 1933

Dear Mr. Henry:

I take the liberty of writing you to appeal to you to do something for my father.

I am the oldest of the family + am the only one working + we have only $8 coming into the house per week. My Mother + Father are greatly worried and are getting into debt and we can scarcely get the necessities of life and my brothers + sisters need things shoes etc. and we have not the money to get them with. Father has always been good in doing what he could for anyone+ has done much for the Conservative Party . . . He has tried and tried to get a job and met with no success and is just wearing himself out + looking old with worry. He has been a good father to us + if he cannot get anything to do it means the breaking up of our home +we all have been so happy until things became bad with Dad. I appeal to you to do something for him as he has always spoken highly of you. Trusting you will for my sake + for my sisters + brothers.

Yours Faithfully

[Name Omitted]

Source: Letter to the Premier, dated February 14, 1933, Premier George S. Henry correspondence, Reference Code: RG 3-9-0-391, Archives of Ontario.

a crisis of male unemployment. Estimated crudely at between 30 and 50 per cent of the male labour force (ages 14 and older), the extensive joblessness meant that many couples could not take on the financial burdens of marriage and family. Rates of marriage fell notably, from 7.5 marriages per 1,000 of the population in 1928 to 5.9 in 1932. By 1937, the birth rate had fallen to an average of 2.6 children per family, a historic low. The decline is partly explained by delayed marriages, but it was also due to deliberate family limitation by couples who simply could not feed any more children and could not envision better times (Comacchio 1993:158–9; McLaren and McLaren 198:65).

The gap between ideal and reality became painfully evident for more Canadians than ever before as the Depression undermined the material security and quality of life of families usually unaffected by periodic economic contractions. For many, the crisis necessitated returning to the traditional interdependent family economy that middle-class and more prosperous working-class families had been gradually discarding. Anything that any family member could contribute by way of wages took on new importance. While this usually entailed additional employment for women, who were paid much less than men and consequently hired instead of them, it did not strike at the heart of feminine identity in the way that the loss of breadwinner status affected men. In this atmosphere of social collapse, government policy focused on assisting men and "righting" the social order by providing jobs and "relief" for male breadwinners (Baillargeon 1999; Campbell 2009).

The welfare measures of the Depression years were minimal. In September 1939, as Canadians entered into a second world war little more than a generation after the first, the reluctant Liberal government recognized that its citizens, especially the young men in great demand for armed service, could not be asked to fight without assurance of their families' welfare, both "for the duration" and also at war's end (Marshall 2006:73–4). Facing the need to support the war effort and also to address public fears about a possible postwar return to depression, the Mackenzie King government was at last prepared to consider a national social security program. Measures to support the besieged male-breadwinner family were its basis. Unemployment insurance became a reality in 1941, but it left most working women out of its provisions. In 1943, McGill University social scientist Leonard Marsh presented his seminal *Report on Social Security for Canada* to the House of Commons Committee on Reconstruction and Rehabilitation. Its entire purpose was to establish a **social minimum** for all Canadians as a right of citizenship and not on the basis of demonstrated need, as had historically been the case. The Marsh report emphasized that families must have an unequivocal place at the heart of all postwar welfare policy. After much controversy and public debate, the **Family Allowances Act**, the nation's first universal welfare measure, was passed in 1944. The federal government gave mothers five to eight dollars per month for each child 16 years and younger. Popular support for the "baby bonus" was instrumental in assuring another Liberal electoral victory in 1945 (Blake 2009).

Unemployment insurance and family allowances marked the state's definitive entry into the historically sacrosanct patriarchal family. However modern and progressive, they upheld the traditional family and the traditional conceptualization of male and female roles in the home and in the labour force. The federal government would protect male breadwinners and ensure women's role in "home-making," producing children, and nurturing them. Mothers, in effect, were on the public payroll for their work of social reproduction. Once Canadian veterans resettled themselves after the war, many would go home to a family that looked much like the family of middle-class ideal in process since the middle of the previous century.

Families at Mid-century

After so many years of crisis, first with the Depression and then the Second World War, with peace in 1945 most Canadians were only too eager to embrace a version of domesticity that owed more to ideal than reality. The so-called **Reconstruction** interlude saw the return of veterans to civilian life, and, as had happened after the First World War, renewed attention to "the family" (Fahrni 2005; Golz 1993:9–10). Married women who had served the war effort by taking paid employment, often replacing men in skilled or otherwise heavy industrial jobs, now faced open state pressure to return to the home. Family reunion was undoubtedly complicated for both returned soldiers and their wives and children who had become accustomed to life without father. The divorce rate briefly rose to worrying new heights, as some proved unable to resume "normal" family life, perhaps after hasty marriages, infidelity, or simply having grown apart (Fahrni 2005:189). After decades of contraction in marriage and fertility rates, the public desire for a return to normalcy was real, and its effects were profound and long-lasting.

The 1950s mark the golden age of the so-called "normal" family in Canadian history, as always more normative than normal. The "normal" grouping of husband/breadwinner, mother/homemaker, and three or four healthy, well-behaved, intelligent, closely spaced children, became the icon of the day. Much of the "golden" aura of the times has to do with its relatively widespread prosperity. Years of unrealized consumer demand unleashed an economic boom. Production increased and wages rose, doubling for male factory workers between 1945 and 1955. Families headed by unskilled, non-unionized workers, women, and recently arrived immigrants, Indigenous families, African-Canadian and other racialized families, the families of unilingual francophones in Quebec, and those in disadvantaged regions such as Newfoundland (a province from 1949), did not share in the bounty. Postwar psychology emphasized heterosexual marriage and classified homosexuality, still illegal, as deviance (Adams 1997:38; Korinek 2000). Finally, roughly a century after the original "cult of domesticity," more Canadians than in any earlier time were finally able to approximate the Victorian ideal of the male breadwinner family.

At the urging of the newly formed United Nations, the Liberal government revised the Immigration Act in 1951, allowing for a second wave of immigrants, still mostly European, to enter a nation that very much needed skills, labour, and population. Their overall youthfulness guaranteed the increase in population necessary to uphold economic prosperity. Postwar immigration was characterized by family sponsorship: among Italians, one of the largest groups arriving, some 90 per cent were sponsored by relatives (Iacovetta 1992:481). With close to one million newcomers entering Canada by the mid-1950s, social agencies and government policies made concerted efforts to impress upon them the appropriate standards of "Canadian" family life, in keeping with the male breadwinner ideal (Iacovetta 2006).

More than any other historic development of the time, demographic trends reassured family-watchers about commitment to marriage and family formation. Between the late 1940s and the early 1960s, years characterized as the **Baby Boom**, the proportion of children to the rest of the population reached its highest point in the entire twentieth century (Vanier 2004:3). By 1947, young adults were marrying earlier than they had since the late nineteenth century, at an average age of 22 years for women and 24 years for men. The starting point of the Baby Boom, 1947 saw the birth rate increase to 29 per 1,000 of the population (approximately 350,000 babies), higher than since before the Great Depression. It remained between 27 and 28.5 per 1,000 until 1959 (500,000 babies), after which it gradually declined. Over a period of 25 years, the Baby Boom produced about 1.5 million more births than would otherwise have occurred (about 8.6 million), an increase of more than 18 per cent (Vanier 2004:3–4). During this period, a higher number of children than ever before, or since, grew up in the care of both their birth parents. The proportion of lone-parent families declined from about 14 per cent in 1931 to about 10 per cent in 1951, and then to a new low of 8.2 per cent in 1966 (Statistics Canada 1984: Table 1).

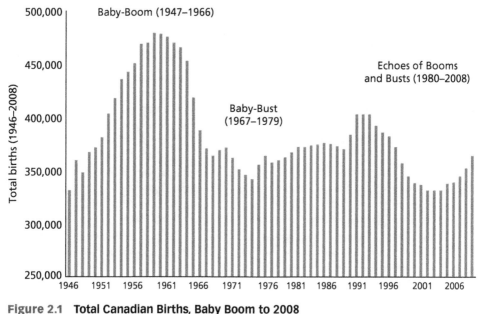

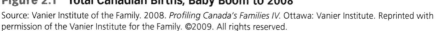

Figure 2.1   Total Canadian Births, Baby Boom to 2008

Source: Vanier Institute of the Family. 2008. *Profiling Canada's Families IV*. Ottawa: Vanier Institute. Reprinted with permission of the Vanier Institute for the Family. ©2009. All rights reserved.

The majority of mothers worked exclusively as full-time homemakers during the 1950s. Despite the popular attachment to this "norm," this was actually an historic departure for many. As we have seen, rural and working-class mothers had always worked, from home or outside the home, or had otherwise supplemented family income, in addition to, and frequently at the same time as, attending to husbands, housekeeping, and children. Although the number of women in the workforce grew slowly during the 1950s, the participation of married women with children remained low. At its peak in 1944, the female labour force participation rate was 27 per cent, a number not reached again for nearly 20 years (Sangster 1995:222).

Also contributing to this family-centric environment was intensified suburbanization. Home ownership has historically been a vital part of family formation for many Canadians, and economic prosperity was making it increasingly accessible. The Depression and the war had virtually halted construction, leaving a serious housing shortage even as marriages increased and families grew. The time was just right for low-density, inexpensive single-family housing to be built on the cheap vacant land encircling urban centres. The federal government established the Central Mortgage and Housing Corporation to oversee and ensure inexpensive mortgages. One million new homes were built between 1945 and 1960, more than two thirds of which were the single detached houses of family-oriented suburban communities (Harris 2004). Suburbia became the site of a modern family life still defined by the traditional hierarchies of gender and age. Many male breadwinners commuted a fair distance from their neighbourhoods to work at reasonably well-paid jobs in stores, offices, sawmills, mines, and factories. During regular

---

Box 2.3

Suburban Family Life and "Home-Making" in the 1950s

In 1956, Canadian family sociologists John R. Seeley, R. Alexander Sim, and Elizabeth W. Loosely published their case study of a middle-class Toronto suburb, identified as Crestwood Heights, a fictitious name. Although they did not emphasize it, they uncovered discontent about the nature and conditions of "full-time homemaker" status among the better-educated women they interviewed:

> Upon marriage, the woman takes charge of the home. When children come, they are her main responsibility. It was exceedingly difficult to find women in Crestwood Heights who had continued their vocations past motherhood. After marriage, the claims of the husband and, late, of the children on the woman's time and energy are so dominant that she must abandon her aspirations towards a career. . . . She was unlikely to think of motherhood itself as a career, even though she felt that she was doing a good job as wife and mother. (Seeley et al. 1956:139–40)

---

daytime working hours, the new, often identical, ranch bungalows and freshly paved streets of suburban enclaves were populated almost exclusively by women and children (Korinek 2000; Strong-Boag 1991).

In the evening, much familial interaction now revolved around the television set. By 1950, there were some 13,600 televisions in Canadian homes; 82.5 per cent of households owned a TV in 1961. Television signified a new epoch as much as did the atomic bomb and the Cold War. With TVs in many Canadian homes, "normalizing" ideas about home and family could be circulated readily, as television watching itself became a family activity. The CBC and Radio-Canada in Quebec specialized in such family programming as the antics of the puppet *Uncle Chichimus*, and, in French, the tragicomic saga of *La famille Plouffe*. Even with limited reception and a restricted channel selection, many Canadians could, and did, watch such American serials as *Leave It to Beaver* and *Father Knows Best*, shows that depicted families at their glowing suburban, nuclear, male-breadwinner best (Sutherland 1997).

The postwar reversal in such long-term trends as higher age at marriage and smaller families was an historic aberration that would be readjusted by the late 1960s. The uniqueness of this moment within the larger context helps to explain why collective memory recalls the 1950s as a brief glorious moment when "family values" permeated society, and family relations were strong and wholesome. Yet many men had only distant relationships with their young children, as long commutes, long workdays, and the emphasis on the mother-centred home kept them vaguely sidelined in the self-enclosed nuclear family circle. For their part, women, with few personal outlets and little personal time thanks to the pressures of modern homemaking, might well find themselves suffering from what American feminist Betty Friedan, drawing upon her own experiences as a 1950s housewife, famously classified "the problem without a name" (Friedan 1963; Rutherdale 2009; Strong-Boag 1991:504).

The children at the centre of this family universe were themselves increasingly subjected to "modern" and "scientific" personality and aptitude tests, in school, at the doctor's office, and even in the family circle, as experts widened the scope of their interventions into the nation's homes. Threats to child health declined, thanks to such wartime medical advances as antibiotics and sulfa drugs, to affordable private medical insurance and state hospital insurance, and, in large part, to prosperity. But the focus on the child's healthy emotional development, and the mother's role in ensuring it, became ever stronger. Intensifying the interwar trend, child psychologists made new inroads into the schools and welfare agencies, and consequently into family life. "The normal child" was stringently defined. The normal mother, in charge of the child's development, had to make herself aware of, and diligent in applying, current child-rearing theories. Such mass-produced paperback manuals as that of the American pediatrician **Dr Benjamin Spock** were ubiquitous in middle-class suburban homes across North America. Despite Dr Spock's reassuring tones, most child-rearing experts of the day blamed mothers for all the physical, emotional, and developmental "problems" that their children might face. These mixed messages about maternal influence and family life once again reflect undercurrents of a larger anxiety about shifting gender roles, age relations, and the relations of family, state, and society (Adams 1997:18–20; Gleason 1999:89–90).

When the first wave of Baby Boomers, born in 1947, entered adolescence in the 1960s, the "youth problem" that had been worrying Canadians since at least the 1920s became a "youthquake." High schools and post-secondary institutions expanded rapidly to accommodate the largest ever influx of young Canadians across class, "racial," regional, and gender boundaries (Owram 1996:159). This historic conjuncture of a specific age group sharing a cohort experience, at a time of social, cultural, and political turbulence, redefined age and generational relations in terms of cultural conflict. The young seemed intent on rejecting the values of their parents and elders, especially regarding sex, marriage, and conventional family life. The political conservatism and social conformity of the 1950s gave way to a resurgence of radicalism in the New Left, in post-colonial liberation movements, in the politicization of groups historically marginalized by class, "race," gender, and sexual orientation, in student protest movements, in Quebec's **Quiet Revolution**, in **second-wave feminism**, and in Indigenous organizations (Palmer 2008:204–5). Although its breadth was exaggerated, the **generation gap** separating youth and their elders was embodied in the "hippie ethic" that challenged sexual taboos and embraced open marriage and communal living. Needless to say, this was interpreted as a generational rejection of all that "the family" represented.

Like youth itself, however, the radical 1960s experiment was transient. Much of it was supported by the prosperity that permitted many young Canadians to finish high school, pursue further education, and find well-paid work. But the economy showed serious signs of flagging by the late 1960s, and a number of international economic shocks gave rise to the low growth, unemployment, and high inflation, characterized as "stagflation," of the 1970s. The early 1980s witnessed the worst recession since the Great Depression. Fewer young people could "come into their own" without considerable parental support and a longer stay in the parental home. These developments dampened youth rebellion and risk-taking, for all that the decade's "sexual revolution" would have lasting effects for individuals—especially women—and for families (Williams 2000:7–8).

The single most important influence on families during the 1960s and 1970s—advances in the status of women—was the outcome of an earlier trend. An effective female contraceptive, popularly known as the Pill, became available in Canada by 1966, finally allowing women control over their fertility and consequently their sexuality. The famous Criminal Code revisions of 1969 decriminalized contraception and consensual adult sexual relations, including homosexual relations, and also opened the way to legal abortion. Long-needed changes to divorce legislation made no fault, uncontested divorce the new basis of marriage dissolution. In the 1970s, the "women's liberation" movement instigated such important political pressure groups as the Committee for the Equality of Women in Canada (1966) and the National Action Committee on the Status of Women (1972). These feminist activists were instrumental in challenging gender inequality in its myriad social, economic, and political forms (Sangster 2001:210).

Although lone-parent families headed by women remained the largest proportion of poor families, higher-paid work opportunities for women, longer lives, and changes to the Divorce Act (1968) made divorce a viable option for unhappy couples. In 1969, 14 per cent of all marriages ended in divorce; by 1975, the rate had doubled, reaching a peak (to date) of 36.2 per cent in 1986. More children than ever would experience at least some part of "growing up" in a lone-parent household, in shared or joint custody arrangements, and in blended families (Beaupré, Dryburgh, and Wendt 2010;). As noted in Chapter 1, the 2011 Census counted the number of stepfamilies for the first time: approximately 12.6 per cent of all Canadian families were step-families, married or common-law parents, with children under the age of 25 years (Vézina 2012:6). Most important, in its impact on both women's social position and on the families that have historically been their "vocation," was the influx of married women and mothers into the labour force. Only one married woman in five worked

Box 2.4
Women's Paid Labour and Contemporary Family Forms

Family sociologists K.A. Duncan and R.N. Pettigrew examined how dual-earner families perceived work–family balance in their own lives by analyzing a nationally representative sample of families from the 1998 and 2005 *General Social Surveys* produced by Statistics Canada. They found that, alongside the increase in the number of dual-worker families, and hours that mothers and fathers each worked, dissatisfaction with work–family balance also grew.

> . . . [T]he greater the time spent in paid work, and the higher the educational status, the less satisfied respondents were with their work–family balance. These findings may point to a value shift, whereby home and family are becoming increasingly important to people compared to career goals. For both men and women the enjoyment of paid work had a strong impact on the experience of work–family balance. . . . even small adjustments that improve the enjoyment of paid work may have substantial positive effects on the perceived balance of earning and caring activities. (Duncan and Pettigrew 2012:420)

for wages in 1961; a decade later, the proportion was one in three; by 1981, one of every two Canadian women was employed outside the home. By the early 1970s, a contracting economy highlighted by the decline of manufacturing where "men's work" was traditionally concentrated, the rising cost of living, and the historically high educational attainments of women, allowed more and better opportunities for women's employment. At the same time, the steadily rising consumerism that also characterized postwar society was demanding two incomes to maintain the standard of living that many Canadian families felt to be their due. For the less affluent and otherwise marginalized, two incomes were, as always, a matter of family need, not personal choice (Williams 2000:8–9).

Families at the Millennium

As the twenty-first century dawned, the average number of children per family declined again, to 1.7, while a new demographic phenomenon, the "childless by choice" union, made significant headway. Due to the steady increase in life expectancy, this meant that a smaller portion of the family life-course, and that of women specifically, was devoted exclusively to the care of infants and preschool children. While the 58.3 per cent of married mothers who worked for wages in 1980 represented a historic peak, by 2000, the proportion was 80 per cent. More than two thirds of working mothers were in the age range of 30–39 years, also the average age range of first marriages and first births. Most women returned to work by the end of the child's first year (Kremarek 2000:165). The introduction of state-supported maternity and parental leave legislation in the 1990s was vital to this "new" configuration of families. Couples could take sequential leave, permitting both parents in turn to be the primary caregiver for the child's first year. Also "new" in historical terms was the growing, though still small, proportion of fathers who interrupted their careers to care for their children while mothers worked as sole breadwinners (Beaupré, Dryburgh, and Wendt 2010:32). Finally, what is probably the single most controversial of all changes affecting families in the entire period under discussion came about with the legal recognition of same-sex marriage in the Civil Marriage Act (2005). Canada became one of only three nations world-wide (at that time) to legalize same-sex unions (Luxton 2011:7). Perhaps most important among the demographic, socio-economic, and cultural changes in the late-twentieth century history for Canadian families, however, were the changing ideas and practices that underlie contemporary understandings of shared parenting, involved fathering, unmarried motherhood and fatherhood, and same-sex parenting as personal choices.

For more on same-sex unions and same-sex parenting, see Chapter 3 and "Deciding to Parent" in Chapter 5, pp. 98–9.

The most recent demographic data confirm the historic relationship of families and societies, and cultural and structural change. The 2011 Census reported a rise in **census families** of 5.5 per cent since the last count in 2006; by 2016, although married couple families no longer predominated (45.0 per cent) in 2016, their decreasing share of the category continued its on-going slide from the late twentieth century. Between 2006 and 2011, for example, the number of common-law couples rose 13.9 per cent, more than four times the 3.1 per cent increase for married couples. In 2016, more than one fifth of all couples were living common law (21.3 per cent). About half of these couples had children.

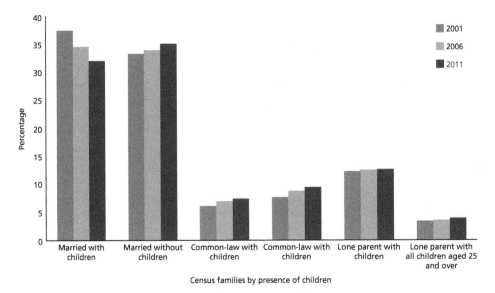

Figure 2.2 Distribution (in percentage) of Census Families by Presence of Children, Canada, 2001 to 2011

Sources: Statistics Canada, censuses of population, 2001 to 2011.

The number of same-sex couples grew 42.4 per cent between 2006 and 2011 (64,575); in 2016, 0.9 per cent of couples were in same-sex partnerships. One third of these were married; about 12 per cent had children. A significant trend first noted in 2006 was a continued widening of the gap between couples with children (39.2 per cent) and those without (44.5 per cent). Between 2011 and 2016, the number of childless couples rose more quickly (+7.2 per cent) than that of couples with children (+2.3 per cent). At 51.1 per cent in 2016, the share of couples with at least one child was the lowest on record (Statistics Canada 2017).

In 2011, Indigenous children aged 14 and under were less likely than non-Indigenous children to live with married parents, twice as likely to live with a lone parent, and twice as likely to live with their grandparents. Although Indigenous children account for only 7 per cent of all children in Canada, almost half of them (48 per cent) were in foster care. The majority of Indigenous children, however, lived with both their parents or with a lone parent (Turner 2016; Castellano 2006–07). The traumatic intergenerational legacy of residential schools and racist child welfare policies continues to haunt Indigenous families (TRC 2012:77–84).

For more on Indigenous families and child welfare, see "Child Welfare: The Millennium Scoop" in Chapter 12, pp. 258–9.

Notwithstanding the endurance of families, the socio-cultural developments affecting them, especially those of the past 25 years, have effectively undermined the tenacious social construction of "the family" in its idealized white middle-class form. This, too, is a historic first. Never as prevalent as its representation, the male breadwinner family is now unequivocally the minority experience among Canadians of all classes, cultural backgrounds, and regions.

Conclusion

This brief overview of the history of Canadian families over the past 200 years was intended to demonstrate one key point: the importance of families to individuals and to society is a constant, both in ideal and in practice, but the form and experience of actual families have always been diverse. Among the major historical influences contributing to changing family forms during these two centuries are

- structural changes, particularly the late-nineteenth century shift from domestic to factory production, and, during the past 40 years, the decline of industry and the rise of digital technology;
- demographic changes sparked by later marriages, the decreases in family size and infant mortality rates, prolonged adolescence and life expectancy, single parenthood, same-sex and childless-by-choice unions;
- changes in the status of women, especially regarding higher education, professional training, wage-earning opportunities, and public acceptance of the employed wife/mother, the childless woman, and the dual-earner family;
- the changing relations between the private sphere of families and the public interest increasingly represented by "experts" and the state, especially by means of family policies that have, until recently, privileged the male-breadwinner family model; and
- the contemporary societal and legal recognition of the rightful family status of so-called non-traditional family groups, including lone-parent, common-law, same-sex, and mixed union families.

The history of Canadian families consists of the varied stories of varying families, functioning in many different ways toward their goal of being families in their own way. Despite the multiple, ongoing changes and challenges of the past two centuries, usually interpreted in the dark language of crisis, the majority of Canadians have always lived, for however much or little of their lives, in families or family settings. This holds true for most Canadians in our own times.

Study Questions

1. Whose family is "the family" of ideal, in terms of "race" and class? Why do notions about "the family" as socially constructed, persist despite the diverse experiences of many Canadian families?
2. Since the ideal reflects, and in turn reinforces, certain social trends, it tends to change over time, in keeping with socio-economic change. Consider how this applies to particular periods, or even to particular decades of intense change.
3. How do we understand ongoing public concern about "the family in crisis" even though contemporary statistics reveal the continued commitment to family formation among Canadians?

4. How has the relationship between the family and the state changed over time? Are there continuities in that evolving relationship?
5. Women's history is not the same as the history of families, but the historic relationship of women and families is a vital element of both. How has that relationship been transformed since the 1960s? What are some of the continuities that still exist, despite the changing status of women over the last half-century?

Further Readings

Baillargeon, Denyse. 1999. *Making Do: Family and Home in Montreal during the Great Depression*. Translated by Yvonne Klein. Waterloo: Wilfrid Laurier University Press. One of the earliest family histories to make use of oral testimony, this focused case study uncovers working-class family strategies in difficult times, highlighting the vital role of women.

Clément, Dominique. 2016. *Human Rights in Canada: A History*. Waterloo: Wilfrid Laurier University Press. Much of the history of families in Canada is concerned with the state's response to evolving ideas about citizenship rights as fundamental human rights; Clement documents these complex developments and their effects.

Comacchio, Cynthia. 1999. *The Infinite Bonds of Family: Domesticity in Canada, 1850 to 1940*. Toronto: University of Toronto Press. Although this book follows family history only to the beginning of the Second World War, it is a comprehensive overview that fills in much of what this chapter sketches.

Campbell, Lara. 2009. *Respectable Citizens: Gender, Family, and Unemployment in Ontario's Great Depression*. Toronto: University of Toronto Press. Campbell examines the ways in which the international crisis of capitalism affected women and men differentially because of gender constructions, and how this affected families.

Dagenais, Daniel. 2008. *The (Un)Making of the Modern Family*. Translated by Jane Brierley. Vancouver: University of British Columbia Press. Sociologist Dagenais explores the deconstruction of "the family" in the past half-century; especially valuable is its discussion of francophone Quebec families.

Macdougall, Brenda. 2012. *One of the Family: Metis Culture in Nineteenth-Century Northwestern Saskatchewan*. Vancouver: UBC Press. Macdougall examines the centrality of family and kin relations in nineteenth-century Métis culture within the context of white "settlement" of the west.

Strong-Boag, Veronica. 2011. *Fostering Nation? Canada Confronts Its History of Childhood Disadvantage*. Waterloo: Wilfrid Laurier University Press. An inaugural historical study of fostering, this book shines much light on social constructions of family and how state and society support them for reasons not necessarily beneficial to children.

Sutherland, Neil. 2000. *Children in English-Canadian Society: Framing the Twentieth Century Consensus*, 2nd ed. Waterloo: Wilfrid Laurier University Press. Originally published in 1976, this seminal study remains critical to understanding how and why childhood was redefined by the 1920s, and how class, gender, and "race" were significant forces in framing modern childhood.

Key Terms

Baby Boom The sharp increase in birth rates in industrialized countries in the 1950s and 1960s; a demographic phenomenon that saw a historic jump in the number of births per 1,000 inhabitants (the usual standard of measurement) between 1946 and 1959. Between 1940 and 1960 the annual number of births rose from 253,000 to 479,000, producing about 8.6 million babies. [see Reconstruction]

Benjamin Spock, Dr The American pediatrician whose *Common Sense Book of Baby and Child Care*, first published in 1941, became the child-rearing bible of the Baby Boom generation. The book sold almost 50 million copies internationally, in 42 languages. Unlike his predecessors, Spock advocated instinctive parenting; his critics contended that he advocated permissive child-rearing, thereby fuelling the "youth revolt" of the 1960s. [see Generation gap]

Canada's Century Meant to convey optimism about the national and international prospects for the young Dominion at the start of the twentieth century; in effect, an unofficial national slogan offered by the Liberal prime minister Sir Wilfrid Laurier (1841–1919; in office 1896–1911) who presided over the boom years at its start. [see Clifford Sifton]

Census family One of the formal and changing definitions of *family* as outlined in the Canadian Census. In the 2006 Census, it refers to a married couple and the children, if any, of either or both spouses; a couple living common-law and the children, if any, of either or both partners; or, a lone parent of any marital status with at least one child living in the same dwelling and that child or those children. All members of a particular census family live in the same dwelling. Grandchildren living with their grandparent(s) but with no parents present also constitute a census family.

Century of the Child An objective put forward by Swedish writer, feminist, social reformer, and child welfare advocate Ellen Key (1849–1926), who wrote a highly influential international bestseller, *Barnets århundrade* (1900), translated into English as *The Century of the Child* (1909). Key argued that child welfare should be the foremost social cause of the new century. Her book became the acknowledged child welfare manifesto of the times. [see Social Gospel; Maternal feminist]

Chain migration A family-based immigration strategy which entails an individual or small group, usually male and often from the same family and community, leaving their country of origin to resettle in another country, and then assisting other family, kin, and community members to join them. Canadian immigration policy has historically favoured chain migration. [see Chinese Immigration Act]

Chinese Immigration Act (1923) The culmination of a series of racist federal government policies intended to restrict Chinese immigration to Canada. The Act effectively prohibited Chinese people from entering the country, except for merchants, diplomats, and students, thereby also barring the entry of Chinese women since these were male occupations. Because many Chinese immigrants were men intending to bring over wives and children, it also prevented the reunification of families in Canada until it was repealed in 1947. [see Chain migration; Scientific racism]

Clifford Sifton (1861–1929) The politician who represented Brandon, Manitoba, as a Liberal Member of Parliament during the reign of Sir Wilfrid Laurier (1896–1911). Sifton was the highly influential Minister of the Interior (1896–1905) in Laurier's Cabinet. He directed an aggressive and successful immigration campaign that resulted in the entry to Canada of roughly one million immigrants during the first decades of the twentieth century.

Extended family Takes in both the household and the wider family circle, including kin such as cousins, aunts, uncles, and grandparents. A combination of these family members may share a household, but the extended family does not necessarily reside together.

Family Allowances Act (1944) Implemented by the Mackenzie King Liberal government in 1944, and also known as the "Baby Bonus," the Act was Canada's first universal social welfare program. Starting in 1945, monthly cheques were mailed to every Canadian mother, the amount dependent on the number of children 16 years and under. [see Reconstruction, Baby Boom]

Generation gap A concept attesting to generational differences—at times clashes—in values, mores, and mindset, especially as evidenced in the relationship between parents and children, or, more widely, between elders and youth. The term gained popularity during the so-called "youthquake" of the 1960s. [See Benjamin Spock, Dr]

Indian Act (1876) Federal legislation to "contain" and assimilate Indigenous peoples by emphasizing their subordinate position as "wards" of the paternalistic state. The Superintendent General of Indian Affairs was given wide powers over their communities and their lands, including the power to decide who could be identified as "status Indian." [see "Status Indian"]

Maternal feminism A sector of the late nineteenth and early twentieth century women's movement that emphasized women's "innate" domesticity as the basis of their public service, and consequently the political power, entailed in the vote, that they needed to perform it effectively. Maternal feminists carried the biologically ordained maternal role out of private homes and into the public sphere. [see Social Gospel; National Council of Women; Women's Christian Temperance Union; Women's Institutes; Second-wave feminism]

Modernization A sociological term describing the historical process in which a pre-industrial agrarian society reaches modernity, generally by means of a series of developments driven by industrialization, urbanization, and mass education. In Canada, modernization developed during the second half of the nineteenth century, and intensified with the immigration wave of the pre-First World War years.

National Council of Women of Canada Established in 1893 by Lady Ishbel Aberdeen, wife of Governor-General Lord Aberdeen. It served as a federation of local and provincial women's voluntary organizations and was the largest and most important of the women's reform associations in Canada until well into the twentieth century. The NCWC emphasized social and political reform to meet the needs of women, children, and families. [see Maternal feminist; Social Gospel; Women's Christian Temperance Union; Women's Institutes]

Nuclear family A family that consists of parent(s) and child(ren); also known as the conjugal family unit, this family type includes at most a mother, father, and their dependent children. [see Census family]

Patrilineage Descent traced through the paternal line to determine family and kin relations; it is the basic determinant of both heritage and inheritance in patriarchal societies that privilege the economic, social, and political power of men.

Pronatalism An ideology promoting human reproduction and glorifying parenthood, especially motherhood as the principal vocation of all women. Pronatalists call upon the state to support policies and to create legislation that limits, or actually criminalizes, access to contraception and abortion, while also advocating state-mandated economic and social incentives to encourage marriage and child-bearing. Closely entwined with the status of women, pronatalism was prominent in Canada in the immediate aftermath of the First World War. [see Maternal feminist; Family Allowances Act]

Quiet Revolution The period of intensive political, economic, and socio-cultural change characterizing the 1960s in the province of Quebec; known in French as the *Révolution tranquille*. It is associated with the election of Liberal Jean Lesage in June 1960. It was characterized by the provincial government's campaign to catch up to the modern world by means of secularization, the creation of a welfare state, government control of natural resources, education and health care, and opting out of certain federal programs in favour of its own. The Quiet Revolution also saw the rise of the Parti Québécois as a viable separatist movement.

Reconstruction Federal government plans for the transition to a peacetime economy after the Second World War. The Department of Reconstruction was established in June 1944 to safeguard production and employment. It was superseded by the Department of Resources and Development in 1950. [see Family Allowances Act]

Residential schools An extensive school system set up by the Canadian government in the 1880s and administered by the Roman Catholic, Anglican, Presbyterian, and United Churches. Intended to provide a nominal "white" education, the schools forcibly removed Indigenous children from their families and communities in order to disrupt the generational transmission of their languages and cultures. Children were indoctrinated into Christianity, forbidden to use their own languages and customs, their contact with parents and kin was severely restricted, and they were subjected to harsh rules, punishment, and physical labour. The mortality rate, and the extent of physical, sexual, and psychological abuse at the hands of school staff, were horrendous. The individual, familial, and socio-economic repercussions persist to the present. On June 11, 2008, Prime Minister Stephen Harper issued a formal apology for the residential schools system on behalf of all Canadians to Indigenous communities. [see Indian Act]

Scientific racism A trend in scientific study that resulted from mid-nineteenth century scientific developments, in particular Charles Darwin's evolutionary theory, which seemingly encouraged the racialization of the world's population. "Races" were defined as groups that shared certain biological characteristics, especially skin colour. Based on these physical traits, it was held that, in evolutionary terms, the white "race" represented the pinnacle of human achievement, while other "races" were progressively lower in the social hierarchy, the darkness of their skin a measure of their mental ability and "civilization." Scientific racism legitimized imperialism and the conquest and colonization of the "lesser races" by those deemed superior, especially the British. It was also the basis of eugenics.

Second-wave feminism The women's movement of the 1960s–1980s, also called the women's liberation movement, it was the second such organized movement to take place in Canada. Its equal rights basis distinguished it from the first wave of feminist organization (1870s–1920s) [see Maternal feminism]. The second wave was fundamentally about social, political, legal, economic, and sexual equality.

Social Gospel An umbrella term used to signify activist, largely urban, middle-class, Protestant Christian reform campaigns focused on remedying the worst abuses of industrial capitalism. Commencing in the last quarter of the nineteenth century, the Canadian movement peaked shortly after the First World War. It was inspired by similar progressive voluntarist movements in Great Britain and the United States. [see Maternal feminist]

Social minimum Refers to the financial resources needed by individuals and families to ensure a minimal standard of living in a given society at a given moment. The modern welfare state is premised on the provision of publicly funded institutions and policies to protect its citizens from falling below a reasonable bottom relative to others in that society. [see Reconstruction, Family Allowances Act]

Status Indian The legal definition of who could be classified "Indian" under the Indian Act (1876). The Act specified that "Indian" referred to any man of Indigenous heritage registered on the federal government's Indian Register as a member of a particular band; any offspring of a such a person; any woman, regardless of "race," currently or once married to such a person. Indigenous women who married non-Indigenous men, as well as any children of the union, lost Indian status. The Act denied Indian status to the Métis, persons of mixed Indigenous and European descent, and the Inuit. [see Indian Act]

Stem family An anthropological term that describes a household in which married adult children, typically the eldest male, reside with their spouse and their own children in the parental home.

Women's Christian Temperance Union The first women's social reform organization that attempted to apply Christian principles to the eradication of "the liquor evil." Founded in Ohio in 1873, the first Canadian branch was established in Owen Sound, Ontario, in 1874. It was the largest non-denominational women's organization of its time, though its membership consisted primarily of anglophone middle-class Protestant women, reflecting that of the larger Social Gospel movement. [see Maternal feminist; Social Gospel; National Council of Women of Canada; Women's Institutes]

Women's Institutes Founded in Stoney Creek, Ontario, by maternal feminist and child welfare advocate Adelaide Hoodless in 1897. By 1913 the primarily rural-based institutes were established in all the provinces. In 1919, the Federated Women's Institutes of Canada was formed. The group's motto, "For Home and Country," indicates its focus on patriotism, rural life, and the concerns of women, children, and families. [see Maternal feminist; Social Gospel]

    Interested in finding out more? Visit www.oupcanada.com/Albanese4e for access to a list of recommended websites for this chapter.

3

Same-sex Marriage in Canada

DOREEN M. FUMIA

LEARNING OBJECTIVES

- To be able to distinguish between marriage as a private lived experience between two people and marriage as a relationship between two people and the state

- To learn about key events and debates that led to the adoption of the Civil Marriage Act (Bill C-38) in Canada

- To understand why same-sex couples feel compelled to be recognized by the state through marriage

- To understand why some supporters of same-sex relationships oppose same-sex marriage

- To consider whether we need the institution of marriage at all in the twenty-first century

---

Introduction

Marriage is both a personal relationship and a public institution. To view marriage as an institution is to step back from viewing it as a relationship *between two people* and, rather, view it as a relationship between *two people and the state*. When we focus on marriage between two people, we focus on the love between them, their suitability, their shared interests, and so on. When we focus on marriage between two people and the state, we are less interested in the specificity of any one couple and more interested in which couples fit into state regulations that define and protect family relations. To engage in a legal marriage is to take one's personal experience of coupledom and seek citizenship legitimacy from the state. The legitimate relationship between citizens and the state is tested in a number of ways throughout our lives. Our citizenship legitimacy is tested when we seek birth certificates, passports, or driver's licences, or when we sign up for access to public education or public health care. If we do not meet the specified criteria, the state can disqualify and deny us as unfit for some or all of the rights offered to its "legitimate" citizens.

Questions for Critical Thought

Can you think of an example when you, or your parents on your behalf, successfully sought the state's approval of your citizenship? What would happen if you had been denied this citizenship right?

Prior to the passing of Bill C-38, the 2005 Civil Marriage Act in Canada, people who declared their same-sex love for each other were denied the citizenship right to a state-approved marriage, not because they were not legal citizens, but rather because their form of love did not fit into the state criteria for what legitimated marriage. These couples were delegitimized as **sexual citizens** (Bell and Binnie 2000). Marriage was for coupledom that was exclusive to one man and one woman. Barbara Findlay, QC, stated (2013) that this not only affects personal relationships, it also may have ripple effects for additional citizenship rights resulting from laws that set the criteria for other activities such as adoption, estate planning, and divorce. As we know, this exclusionary notion of marriage has been successfully challenged, but this did not happen overnight; it took many years to get to this point in Canada.

The first section of this chapter will focus on a brief historical overview of what marriage has been and is now for. This entails the roles that the institution of marriage has played from pre-industrial times to post-industrial times. Drawing on citizenship challenges to traditional, heterosexual definitions of marriage, we will examine reasons why people in same-sex relationships continue to celebrate same-sex marriage as important, progressive social change.

We will then discuss how legalizing same-sex marriage in Canada has generated opposition, not simply from those who oppose same-sex relationships, but also from those who support them. It is this very juncture between personal experience and political civic engagement that highlights the aim of this chapter: to tease out the tensions and contradictions between marriage as a relationship between two people on the one hand and, on the other, marriage as a state institution that imposes value-laden constraints on these relationships. The question—what is marriage for?—turns to another question: Who is marriage for?

The chapter concludes by considering whether marriage is a useful institution at all. While some argue that suggesting people operate outside the logic of state institutions, such as family and marriage, means asking them to surrender rights to full citizenship participation, others argue that marriage constrains, excludes, and disadvantages a wide range of non-normative family forms and people who live in them. Given this, is marriage a useful pursuit? The discussion in this chapter invites you to think about these ideas in order to broaden our limited concepts of families, marriage, and citizenship.

For more on commitment and family formation, see "Family Formation, Social Structures, and Change" in Chapter 4, pp. 74–6.

What Is Marriage For?

One scholar who writes about the historically varied and changing criteria for marriage and family relationships in the West is E.J. Graff (2004). Graff provides a historical overview of marriage and notes its changing status based on changing economic and social needs. She explains that in earlier historical periods, marriage was viewed as a contractual business relationship for the family unit based on finance, factors such as income earning, property acquisition, preservation of income from varied sources including farms and dowries, and the status of wives and servants. According to Graff, in later periods of industrial and post-industrial capitalism, less emphasis was placed on money and property for the basis for marriage and an increased emphasis was placed on psychological relationships and the importance of feelings. She does note, however, that even with the emphasis on matters of the heart there continues to be economic interdependence.

The formalized regulation of "coupledom" concerns local communities and the state. Acceptable norms about how to recognize who is and who is not married have varied from simply declaring a commitment before a chosen religious figure to signing documentation that is legally binding. More recently, there has been a departure from religious and legally formalized marriage and an increase in unmarried couples cohabiting in common-law relationships. Common-law relationships are similar to, but not exactly like, marriage. Marriage is taken more seriously—in ways that have both legal and social ramifications—by banks, insurers, courts, employers, schools, hospitals, cemeteries, rental car companies, frequent-flyer programs, and more. Graff (2004:49) remarks that "marriage is a word that is understood to mean that you share not only your bedroom but the rest of the house as well . . . [it] is the marker that allows the courts to assume that you two wanted your relationship to be respected after death."

Different couple relationships are marked by a citizen's relationship to the state and to each other. While marriage and common-law are similar there are significant advantages to state-recognized marriages. While there are few differences, some say the devil is in the details (Findlay 2013). For example, in common-law relationships, unlike marriage, there is no presumption that assets should be divided equally at the end of such a relationship upon separation or death.

Questions for Critical Thought

If you are or plan to cohabit with someone, would you consider the protection of a legal marriage necessary? Did you know that if you cohabit with someone for not less than three years and share your life in significant ways, you are viewed by the state to be in a common-law relationship?

Many of the "devils" in the details relate to money matters. We can trace the roots of these concerns to the desire to protect family wealth, whether handed down from one generation to the next or accrued within the span of a relationship. The more recent de-emphasis on money as the central factor in the institution of marriage has precipitated the erosion of historical taboos that supported the institution, such as those against premarital sex and child-bearing outside marriage. One of the most significant shifts has been that of the heterosexual presumption that has defined marriage, "one man + one woman = marriage," as a placard against same-sex marriage proclaimed at a March 2005 protest in Ottawa. There have been landmark court cases, referred to below, that have redefined the parameters of marriage and family law to include same-sex partners. What these shifts signal is a redefinition of the moral underpinnings of state-recognized

Box 3.1

Key Events in Sexual Minorities Movements in Canada, 1980s–2012

- 1981   Sexual minorities confront police as they raid bathhouses in Toronto and more than 300 people are arrested. This is sometimes referred to as Canada's Stonewall (referring to the 1969 Stonewall riots in New York City that many mark as the beginning of the modern gay rights movement).
- 1985   The Parliamentary Committee on Equality Rights recommends that the Canadian Human Rights Act be changed to make it illegal to discriminate based on sexual orientation.[1]
- 1988   Svend Robinson becomes the first Member of Parliament to declare he is gay.
- 1991   Delvin Vriend, a lab instructor at King's University College in Edmonton, Alberta, is fired from his job because he is gay.
- 1996   Bill C-33 is passed. It adds protections against discrimination based on sexual orientation to the Canadian Human Rights Act.
- 2000   Bill C-23 (Modernization of Benefits and Obligations Act) is passed. It recognizes same-sex couples as common-law partners and provides equality in over 68 federal statutes. Marriage, however, remains the lawful union of one man and one woman to the exclusion of all others.
- 2001   The Canadian Census includes the category common-law same-sex relationships. There were 34,200 same-sex couples enumerated.
- 2003   The Ontario Court of Appeal rules that, effective immediately, same-sex couples should be entitled to marry; denying them wedding licences, the Court determines, would be unconstitutional. Michael Leshner and Michael Stark become first couple to marry.
- 2004   On 9 December the Supreme Court of Canada decides that the federal government, not the provinces, has the authority to legislate the definition of marriage.
- 2005   Seven provinces (Ontario, Quebec, British Columbia, Manitoba, Saskatchewan, Nova Scotia, and Newfoundland and Labrador) and one territory (Yukon) deliver court decisions that provide equal marriage rights to same-sex couples.
- 2005   Since the legalization of same-sex marriages in seven provinces and one territory, 3,000 same-sex weddings have been registered. It is announced that the 2006 Census will include a category, "same-sex married spouse."
- 2005   1 February: Legislation to make same-sex marriage legal in Canada is introduced (Bill C-38).[2] The Act is cited as the Civil Marriage Act.
- 2005   29 June: Bill C-38 passes final reading in the House of Commons with a vote of 158 to 133.
- 2005   19 July: Bill C-38 passes in the Senate with a vote of 47 to 21 (3 abstentions).
- 2005   20 July: Bill C-38 receives royal assent and becomes the law of the land.
- 2006   The first Census to collect data on same-sex married spouses takes place. There are 45,300 same-sex couples enumerated and of these, about 7,500 (16.5 per cent) are married and 37,900 (83.5 per cent) are common-law.
- 2006   The ruling Conservatives attempt to reopen the same-sex marriage debate; however, it is defeated in the House of Commons by a vote of 175 to 123. Minsters on both sides break rank: 12 Tories voted against the motion and 13 Liberals supported it.[3]

- 2012   An unidentified lesbian couple, neither of whom are Canadian residents, married in Canada in 2005 and sought a divorce in 2009. One woman is living in Florida and one in the UK. Since same-sex marriage is not recognized where they live they appealed to Canada for a divorce. However, they were denied their request on the grounds that they did not meet the residency requirements stated in the Divorce Act (one year). Bill C-32 has been introduced to amend the Civil Marriage Act in order to close this gap and allow non-resident same-sex couples who were married in Canada to divorce in Canada. It receives first reading on February 17, 2012, (Library of Parliament Publication number 41-1-C32E).
- 2012   Prime Minister Stephen Harper reiterates that his government will not reopen debates over whether or not same-sex marriage should be legal in Canada.
- 2012   The 2011 Census information posted September 18, 2012, counts 64,575 same-sex couple families, up 42.4 per cent from 2006. Of these couples, 21,015 are same-sex married couples and 43,560 are same-sex common-law couples. The number of same-sex married couples has nearly tripled between 2006 and 2011, reflecting the first five-year period for which same-sex marriage has been legal across the country. Same-sex common-law couples rises 15.0 per cent, slightly higher than the 13.8 per cent increase for opposite-sex common-law couples.[4] (Statistics Canada 2012a)

The 2016 Census data released August 2, 2017 reports the following:

- According to the 2016 Census, there were 72,880 same-sex couples in Canada in 2016, representing 0.9% of all couples.
- From 2006 to 2016, the number of same-sex couples increased much more rapidly (+60.7%) than the number of opposite-sex couples (+9.6%).
- One third (33.4%) of all same-sex couples in Canada in 2016 were married.
- Although Ontario had the most same-sex couples (26,585), Quebec had a higher number relative to its population. Among provinces, Quebec also had the lowest percentage of married same-sex couples.
- Half of all same-sex couples in Canada were living in four of the country's five largest census metropolitan areas: Toronto, Montréal, Vancouver, and Ottawa–Gatineau.
- About one in eight same-sex couples (12.0%) had children living with them in 2016, compared with about half of opposite-sex couples.

(http://www12.statcan.gc.ca/census-recensement/2016/as-sa/98-200-x/2016007/98-200-x2016007-eng.pdf)

Notes

1. The provinces and territories changed their human rights laws to include sexual orientation protections as follows: Quebec, 1977; Ontario, 1986; Manitoba, Yukon, 1987; Nova Scotia, 1991; British Columbia, New Brunswick, 1992; Saskatchewan, 1993; Newfoundland and Labrador, Alberta, and Prince Edward Island, 1998 (Canadian Lesbian and Gay Rights Organization Archives). More recently these rights were extended to trans-identified persons when all but Quebec, New Brunswick, Newfoundland and Labrador, and Yukon added gender identity and/or gender expression to Section (1)(2) in their Human Rights Acts

continued

(Canadian Lesbian and Gay Rights Organization Archives and individual government websites for each province and territory).

2. This enactment extended the legal capacity for marriage for civil purposes to same-sex couples in order to reflect values of tolerance, respect, and equality consistent with the Canadian Charter of Rights and Freedoms. It also made consequential amendments to other Acts to ensure equal access for same-sex couples to the civil effects of marriage and divorce. All parliamentary publications can be found at www.parl.gc.ca.

3. Since same-sex marriage was made legal in Canada there has been little sustained public debate about this topic since 2006.

4. These numbers have been challenged and are thought to be high. In 2012, Census manager Marc Hamel reported that an automatic algorithm might have overestimated (by up to 4,500 couples) the number of same-sex married unions across the country. The error is thought to have occurred because people who live and marry in one province move to another temporarily for work and often move in with a person of the same sex (as a roommate). Thus, reporting they are married and living with a person of the same sex confused the data (CBC News 2012a).

relationships and families. The question that Graff asks in the title of her book is apt here: What is marriage for?

> [O]nce society got rid of the ideas that sex without babies is bad . . . once our philosophy and laws protect sex for pleasure and love, how can same-sex marriage be barred? (Graff 2004:84)

This quote is a good place to begin to think about the legal and moral shifts that have led us to debating whether or not to legitimate same-sex relationships and marriage. And in Canada, more than a decade after same-sex marriage became legal, we need to think about whether or not those shifts can be considered enough.

Chain of Events in Canada

The fight for legal recognition of same-sex relationships and same-sex marriage in Canada has a long history. There are a number of timelines that highlight the major events that moved sexual orientation from the closet to the mainstream (see Box 3.1). In 1969, then Justice Minister Pierre Trudeau successfully sought to decriminalize homosexuality and he is often quoted when referencing the early history of the fight for LGBTQ rights in Canada:

> I think the view we take here is that there's no place for the state in the bedrooms of the nation. I think that what's done in private between adults doesn't concern the Criminal Code.

Between 1995 and 2007 a number of court challenges to issues of discrimination were launched, predicated on the 1995 ruling that LGBTQ rights are included in Section 15 of the Charter of Rights and Freedoms. These court cases sought, sometimes successfully and other times not, the right to protection based on sexual orientation. They included: a "gay professor" who suffered psychological harm from implicit homophobic messages (*Vriend v. Alberta* [1998]); denial of spousal allowance (*Egan v. Canada* [1995]); denial of spousal support (*M. v. H.* [1999]); denial of recognition of a marriage-like relationship and denial of access to same-sex partner's pension (*Canada [Attorney General] v. Hislop* [2007]); and the barring of gay and lesbian materials at the border because they were classified as "obscene" (*Little Sisters Book and Art Emporium v. Canada* [2000]).

Each of these cases pushed legal arguments and public debate toward a social environment in which it is possible for same-sex relationships to be accepted in the same way that heterosexual relationships are, not only in law, but also in the social imagination. The success or failure of such challenges indicates just who is considered worthy of full citizenship rights and protections. Community activism often acts as a catalyst that pushes courts and politicians to open spaces for citizens who have been previously denied certain rights. Such was the case for those in same-sex relationships.

Because of mounting pressure from LGBTQ activists, and with further impetus once federal protections based on Section 15(1) of the Federal Charter of Rights and Freedoms were confirmed in 1995, between 1977 and 1998 the provinces and territories changed their Human Rights Acts to include sexual orientation as grounds for protection against discrimination. With same-sex relationships sanctioned in many legal and political spaces across Canada, focus shifted to a specific target, one that would bring LGBTQ citizens more in line for a greater range of citizenship rights. The focus to pursue greater equality between same-sex and heterosexual relationships was on marriage, viewed by many as a cornerstone of citizenship participation, social respect, and acceptance.

In 2000, Reverend Brent Hawkes of the Metropolitan Community Church in Toronto read the banns of marriage in three consecutive weeks, that is, announced to the congregation the intention of two couples to marry—Kevin Bourassa and Joe Varnell and Elaine and Anne Vautour (Anne had earlier changed her surname). Hawkes claimed that regardless of Canadian law, if the banns were read on three Sundays before the wedding, he could legally marry the couple based on an old Christian tradition. An opportunity to present legitimate reasons to prevent people from marrying is provided to those gathered at the time of reading the banns. Two people stood up to object on the second Sunday claiming that reading the banns for gay people was "lawless and Godless." Reverend Hawkes dismissed this as an illegitimate claim.

In the face of strong and hostile opposition, Hawkes, equipped with a bullet-proof vest and in front of television cameras, married the two couples. However, Bob Runciman, Solicitor General and Registrar of Ontario at the time, refused to recognize the marriage, stating that no matter what Hawkes' church does, the federal law is clear. "It won't qualify to be registered because of the federal legislation which clearly defines marriage as a union between a man and a woman to the exclusion of all others" (CBC News 2012a). Despite this, the bold approach to the fight for same-sex marriage soon led to several provinces passing laws for legalization. By 2005, seven provinces (Ontario, Quebec, British Columbia, Manitoba, Saskatchewan, Nova Scotia, and Newfoundland and Labrador) and one territory (Yukon) had delivered court decisions that provided equal marriage rights to same-sex couples. The rationale for these decisions was that prohibiting gay couples from marrying is unconstitutional and violates the Charter of Rights and Freedoms.

Passing Bill C-38; The Civil Marriage Act

The confluence of events that created the historical-political moment in Canada allowing for the passing of Bill C-38, the Civil Marriage Act, illustrates as much about how debates facilitate political power as how they respond to changing social norms. The Canadian Charter of Rights and Freedoms is foundational to changes in law that protect citizens from discrimination. The section of the Charter that is most relevant to changes to same-sex relationships and marriage is 15(1), which promises to protect all citizens based on the following:

> Constitution Act 1982, Part I: Canadian Charter of Rights and Freedoms
>   Equality Rights
>   Marginal note: Equality before and under law and equal protection and benefit of law
>   15. (1) Every individual is equal before and under the law and has the right to the equal protection and equal benefit of the law without discrimination and, in particular, without discrimination based on race, national or ethnic origin, colour, religion, sex, age or mental or physical disability.

As events leading up to the passing of Bill C-38 unfolded, it was a reminder of two things. First, while Graff's question—"How can same-sex marriage be barred?"—follows a compelling logic, it ignores the fierce opposition based on traditional family values and conservative religious beliefs, an opposition that continues to be given space in public debates, for example in the 2016 US presidential campaign of Donald Trump (Human Rights Campaign 2016). Second, to make claims from the social margins requires a shift not only in law but also in firmly held social norms.

In the public debate on same-sex marriage, arguments from the conservative viewpoint focused on the need to uphold traditional family values. While this stance has its roots in a particular interpretation of religious doctrine, not all religious leaders took the same narrow view. There were nationwide rallies on April 10, 2005, to support gay marriage. In Toronto, a statement of support was issued by the Religious Coalition for Equal Marriage Rights, a multi-faith coalition that wanted to dispel the myth that people of faith must be opposed to same-sex marriage (United Church of Canada 2005). The multi-faith coalition included representatives from liberal and traditional faith communities across Canada, including the United Church of Canada, the Canadian Unitarian Council, the Muslim Canadian Congress, the Canadian Friends Service Committee of the Religious Society of Friends (Quakers), the World Sikh Organization, Canadian Rabbis for Equal Marriage, Metropolitan Community Church, Ahavat Olam Synagogue (Vancouver), Church of the Holy Trinity (Anglican) in Toronto, Apostolic Society of Franciscan Communities–Canada, Saint Padre Pio Congregational Catholic Community (Toronto), and liberal and progressive members of the Buddhist, Catholic, First Nations, Hindu, Mennonite, and Muslim communities (Canadian Christianity 2017). This was a significant shift in the moral fabric of Canada and while these groups did not represent all religious institutions and faiths, they did interrupt the singular religious view on marriage. Another strong voice in support of Bill C-38 came from Canadian lawyers. Over 100 of them signed an open letter opposing Harper's political views based on legal grounds (Open Letter 2005). Unlike previous debates where traditional and religious views were almost overwhelmingly in opposition to the legalizing of same-sex relationships, religious and traditionally conservative voices were increasingly supportive. This demonstrates that ongoing debates do a number of things. They adhere to traditional moral stances, shift moral grounds, and offer new perspectives.

The stage was set for same-sex marriage to come into effect across Canada. However, political parties have their own battles to fight and sometimes these have less to do with the social good and more to do with maintaining a hold on power. While Bill C-38 was well positioned to become the law of the land, a political storm was brewing.

How the "Perfect Storm" Came Together

In 2005, it looked as though Bill C-38 would easily become law under the federal Liberal party, led by Paul Martin. This changed suddenly as the Liberal party came under attack for their alleged culpability in a scandal around the misappropriation of public funds (known as the Gomery Inquiry and informally as the "sponsorship scandal"). The Conservative party, led by Stephen Harper, threatened to call a vote of no confidence, undermining support for the Liberals and capitalizing on their vulnerability to attack the progressive fight to legalize same-sex marriage. In a vulnerable position the Liberal Party faced two choices. One was to align with the Conservatives and be spared losing a no-confidence vote. This meant that Bill C-38, an Act that troubled the family values of Conservative party members, would surely die. The other was to align with the third and smaller party, the New Democrats (NDP), in which case support for Bill C-38 would be expected. At the eleventh hour, Prime Minister Paul Martin and NDP leader Jack Layton, in a bartering of political power, agreed to support a number of demands including Bill C-38, thus enabling the prime minister to maintain a tenuous hold on Liberal power, and, as some pundits had it, making them "queer bedfellows."

After all the political maneuvering, Bill C-38 passed without delay in the House of Commons by a vote of 158 to 133, and came into force July 20, 2005, making same-sex marriage legal in all of Canada. It reads: "Marriage, for civil purposes, is the lawful union of two persons to the exclusion of all others" (Civil Marriage Act 2005).

Same-sex Marriage around the World

While people in different parts of the globe continue to be persecuted, tortured, or even murdered if caught in a same-sex relationship,[1] in other parts of the world laws have supported such relationships. Canada became the fourth country in the world to legalize same-sex marriage. As of July 2017, 22 countries have legalized same-sex marriage (though this list will continue to grow, notably with Taiwan and Germany seeming poised to enact legislation): Argentina (2010), Belgium (2003), Brazil (2013), Canada (nationwide 2005), Denmark (2012), Finland (2017), France (2013), Greenland (2016), Iceland (2010), Ireland (2015) Luxembourg (2015), Mexico (legal in some states; nationwide proposal upheld in principle by the Supreme Court as of 2017) Netherlands (2001), New Zealand (2013), Norway (2009),

Portugal (2010), South Africa (2006), Spain (2005), Sweden (2009), the UK (England and Wales, 2014), the US and territories (nationwide 2015), Uruguay (2013). Lesbian, gay, bisexual, trans, and queer identified (hereafter LGBTQ) groups in many parts of the world are still fighting to legalize same-sex relationships, along with other fundamental rights.

Same-sex debates have not disappeared with the passing of Bill C-38. Socially conservative voices continue to appeal for a return to traditional heterosexual family values, and since its passing, there have been repeated calls to re-visit the bill; fortunately these attempts have been voted down every time.

Laws may change, yet social stigmas are slow to fade. And as we know, social stigma acts as a powerful counterforce to legal rights. Yet the difference may be made by visibility and sheer numbers. Seven years following the legalizing of same-sex marriage in Canada, a 2012 article in the *National Post* stated that 74 per cent of Canadians say they know someone who is lesbian, gay, bisexual, or transgender, 28 per cent say someone in their family is LGBTQ, and two thirds say they support gay marriage (Carlson 2012). Despite this, it would be a mistake to think Canada is free from discrimination. Scott Brison, the Liberal Party's first out gay MP, said in an interview in 2012 that he encountered a "young guy who was demonstrating bravado by making anti-gay comments to me in front of his friends" (Carlson 2012). There are numerous media and online reports of homophobia in Canada, exemplified during the 2010 "It Gets Better Campaign." There are also well-documented accounts in the 2011 *Every Class in Every School, The Final Report of the First National Climate Survey on Homophobia in Canadian Schools*, which gathered data from 3,700 Canadian high school students between December 2007 and June 2009. It stated that homophobic comments were a common and accepted part of school life, even uttered by some teachers. Further, almost two out of three non-heterosexual students did not feel safe in their schools.

Why Queer Folk Want the Right to Marry

Considering the volumes of testimonies in support of same-sex marriage generated by court challenges across Canada, we should consider how people try to makes their lives more livable. As problematic as marriage may be, as a patriarchal institution, it is also hard to think outside the logic of marriage relationships. Further, as Bell and Binnie (2000) point out, advocates insist that, far from **assimilationist strategies** that seek to make same-sex marriage the same as heterosexual marriage, same-sex marriage is ". . . capable of undermining the most solid of social structure ('the family') by infiltrating it and exposing its contradictory logics from within" (57).

While there are those who disagree with the decision to focus so much energy in securing equal rights for both LGBTQ-identified and heterosexual couples, activists continue to focus on this issue as long as marriage underpins the foundation of family and citizenship. Young and Boyd (2006: 214) explain that "many lesbians and gays from other countries have looked to Canada as a model for their own jurisdictions, while others have come to Canada to marry" (Kitzinger and Wilkinson 2004).

In addition to the personal and expert witness accounts in court cases, there are bodies of literature that both support and oppose same-sex marriage. The literature that supports it stems from an equal rights perspective, that is, the same rights for heterosexuals are due to same-sex couples. This stance focuses on freedoms and inclusion and echoes much of what was said in the affidavits of LGBTQ citizens collected during the various legal cases for marriage equality. For instance, Evan Wolfson (1996) suggests, there is no reason to forego the benefits of same-sex marriage since these help us to counter the real harm done to real-life same-sex couples every day. Wolfson further argues that unless marriage is abolished and replaced by a single system to which everyone has access, an ideological and moral distinction will continue to value one relationship form over another. Nan D. Hunter (1995) believes that same-sex marriage could potentially transform the institution of marriage. Part of Hunter's argument rests with the notion that by its unconventional gender structures, same-sex marriage could destabilize the gendered structure of marriage and its patriarchal notions of dependency and authority. Barbara Findlay, QC, says, "Lesbians and homosexual men in Canada have almost the same rights and responsibilities as heterosexual Canadians in family law. But the devil is in the details: 'Almost' equal can mean big problems for same-sex families in Canada. . . . [I]t means that for lesbians and gay men, rights in Canada under family law depend on where they live" (Barbara Findlay 2016). It also depends on the law being interpreted in favour of same-sex relationships, especially when the "best interest" of the child is invoked.

Biddy Martin (1994:47) points out that many LGBTQ folk are just ordinary people, and this is something we must acknowledge. While we may pursue radical **queer politics** that rightfully strive to deconstruct categories that feed discourses of homophobia, such "queer deconstructions of gender cannot do all the earth-shattering work they seem to promise." There were several court challenges to provincial laws regulating marriage by "ordinary" people who happened to be queer. It is useful to get a glimpse of just why people claimed it was important to fight for same-sex marriage. Below is a selection of affidavits and statements that were generated during Ontario's fight.[2] These statements focus on the everyday lived experiences of very ordinary people. They bring to voice some of the reasons people fight for marriage rights. LGBTQ-identified people who are "just ordinary" want the right to marry without waiting for radical changes in order to be considered legitimate, that is, without waiting for changes that rest outside the logic of family and marriage.

By way of contextualizing how the personal is political, the following are examples found at Equality for Gays and Lesbians Everywhere (EGALE) that represent a wide array of **testimonial affidavits** collected prior to the passage of Bill C-38. These testimonials are from expert witnesses[3] and individuals living in same-sex partnerships. They attest to the strong support, desires, and rationales for legalizing same-sex marriage in Canada (see Equal Marriage Materials www.samesexmarriage.ca/legal/on.html#background). The three general themes expressed can be summarized as follows. One is immigration, that is, to bring a non-Canadian partner to live in Canada. Another is equal access to full citizenship participation, that is, to have same-sex relationships and families legally acknowledged in every way that heterosexual relationships are. The third is for social legitimacy, in the eyes of family members, friends, and colleagues.

Below is part of a testimonial affidavit given by Alison Kemper and Joyce Barrett. At the time these lesbian mothers had two children born and raised within their relationship, which began in 1984.

> AK: The reality is that same-sex couples have kids, love them, and want more than anything the best possible lives for our children. Our lives together have been spent overcoming those who would wish us to be apart or invisible. We

are committed to ensuring that our children have as secure and rich a life as possible. Marriage is one more step.

JB: Instead of being recognized as an equal family, we are considered to have an "alternative lifestyle." We're not very alternative. We're very ordinary. We'd like to be married because it's the ordinary thing to do with the feelings and commitments we share.

A portion of Michelle Bradshaw and Rebekah Rooney's affidavit follows. Michelle was a student; she is Black and is hearing-impaired.[4] Rebekah, who is white, was a student and has a learning disability. Both were in their twenties at the time.

MS: I am not afraid, dismayed, or ashamed of my relationship with Rebekah, as some people feel I should be. I am ecstatic, happy, content, calm all in one. But mostly I am proud. I want the world to know! . . . Because in the end, same-sex couples should have the same rights as heterosexual couples to choose if they want to tell, express, yell it to the world and to have the law congratulate/validate/support through legal means *all* who form that special bond of marriage/family.

RR: If the government refuses to validate our relationship, why should the citizens of this country? Homophobia is rampant in our society, in large measure because it continues to be sanctioned by government.

(Equal Marriage Materials www.samesexmarriage.ca/legal/on.html#background)

At the time of the affidavit, Michael Leshner worked as a Crown attorney for the Government of Ontario. Originally from Halifax, Michael Stark is the eldest of five children. They are known as "the Michaels" and had been together for 20 years at the time.

ML: It should not be necessary for me to justify my application for a marriage licence and requiring me to do so would be discriminatory, humiliating, and upsetting. Being denied a marriage licence suggests that Mike and I do not love each other, and that our hopes, our dreams, our life together do not exist. Mike and I, while supposedly equal citizens of this great country, are deemed non-persons, because we are gay.

MS: My brothers and my sister have all been legally married. We have the same parents and upbringing; we all work and pay taxes; and we have all fallen in love and settled down with our partners. Although my relationship is longer than that of any of my siblings, I find myself deposing my first affidavit, and commencing a court proceeding, to seek a marriage licence—simply because I am gay. It is unfair that I have to justify my marriage licence application to anyone, or that I have to convince anyone of my love of Michael. [. . .] I look forward to the day when I can call each of my siblings and invite them to my wedding as they each have done for me.

(Equal Marriage Materials www.samesexmarriage.ca/legal/on.html#background)

These accounts of three same-sex couples reflect the breadth of reasonings provided by the expert affidavits, while also offering a glimpse at the lived experiences behind the arguments. It is clear that the people who wrote these submissions were educated, some were professionals, and represented themselves as deserving to be included in the citizenship body; in other words they present as respectable, "good" lesbians and gay men. The themes the affidavits elicit are many. Alison and Joyce wanted same-sex marriage to help them valid-ate their family, confront homophobia, stabilize family life for children, and transform the notion of "alternate" family units into a more visible, common, and accepted form. Michelle and Rebekah felt that same-sex marriage would allow them to publicly celebrate their love with pride. Pride is a strong theme that underpins all lesbian and gay rights movements, as demonstrated in Pride celebrations around the globe. They also believed, as did the Mi-chaels, that equal rights with heterosexual counterparts were an important factor. Michelle and Rebekah also, as an acknowledgement of the relationship citizens have with the state, implored their government to take responsibility for the harm they experienced in their lives.

Similar to the personal testimonies, the expert witnesses who participated in court challenges in Ontario (see endnote 3) articulated intellectual rationales for legalizing same-sex marriage. Taken together, the testimonies and affidavits demonstrate how very political the personal is.

A strong case was successfully made for legalizing same-sex marriage. It is important to note that the points made during court challenges were in response to older debates that oppose same-sex relationships as well as in service of opening space for more contem-porary arguments to support them.

Debates: Old and New

Even if the institution of marriage is less popular today, it remains the operative logic that underpins family and citizenship, and it is difficult to think outside of that logic. As Barbara Smith says, "[a]s long as we live under this system, all people should have access to the same benefits regardless of sexual orientation" (1997:201). There are many reasons that lesbians and gay men and their allies oppose or support same-sex marriage. These are powerful debates that, when we challenge how we think about same-sex marriage, must incorporate people's lived experiences. Nobody expects same-sex marriage to undo all the harm inflicted by homophobia. Cheshire Calhoun poses an important question when she asks if it is fair to put the onus on lesbians and gay men to "transform gender relations, to remedy class-related inequities, and to end the privileging of long-term, monogamous relations" (2000:138–9). Same-sex marriage just makes it easier for some families.

Many struggles have been undertaken to ensure the right for same-sex relationships to be legally recognized and protected. There are strong arguments that demand a re-consideration of Graff's question: What is marriage for? Perhaps we might ask: What is same-sex marriage for? Then the more relevant question becomes: *Who* is marriage for?

In this next section, we will turn to arguments from those who support same-sex re-lationships yet oppose same-sex marriage. From this position, fighting for same-sex mar-riage is not viewed as a progressive step. Rather, the institution of marriage itself is viewed as unnecessary, and indeed as harmful.

Who Is Marriage For?

Now that same-sex marriage is legal in Canada, we can pause to consider whether this went far enough. That is, who benefits? A central critique of same-sex marriage from supporters of same-sex relationships is that it serves to simultaneously include some and exclude others. For example, Susan Boyd and Claire Young (2005), Diane Richardson (2005), Mariana Valverde (2006), Suzanne Lenon (2008), Nick Mulé (2010), and others strongly support same-sex relationships but oppose same-sex marriage on the basis that such political gains are limited. They argue that in a neo-liberal climate where individualism overshadows the collective good, making same-sex marriage available actually limits it to a select population while it continues to exclude others who have never had access to the benefits of marriage. That is, rather than destabilizing the patriarchal and oppressive institution of marriage—an institution that has always disadvantaged individuals who are female, poor, racialized, and/ or disabled, as well as families that have been historically disrupted by slavery, forced migration, and racist immigration laws—same-sex marriage equality does nothing to address these inequalities and leaves these unequal relations intact. Further, same-sex marriage depends on state-sanctioned conjugal relations that ostracize relationships that do not conform to such arrangements (Baird 2007; Boyd and Young 2005; Brownworth 1996, Card 1996; Eichler 1997). Brownworth writes about class biases in marriage. She reminds us of the lack of formal marriage rites in populations where the expense of a wedding is prohibitive. She also notes that marriage reflects inherently middle class values since low-income couples often just "shack up" (1996:96). Suzanne Lenon (2008) draws on critical race scholar Darren L. Hutchinson (1997) to explicitly point to the "racial" politics of same-sex marriage. The starting point for such a critique is a review of the effect that colonial histories have played in disrupting Black families. Thus, state-sanctioned relationships, offered through the institution of marriage, have never served Black people or supported their relationships.

Who is marriage for? All signs point to the fact that sexual minorities who can be viewed as being closer to the colonial, white, able-bodied, **heteronormative** centre and those who assimilate to the ideal of heterosexual marriage have a greater chance of being socially accepted through the institution of marriage. More marginal sexual minorities—racialized people, Indigenous peoples, people with disabilities, and trans-identified people—not only remain outside the logic of marriage by being identified as "different," but they are further kept from moving into spaces that might have included them if the system of marriage were to be dismantled.

For more on "remaining outside," being labelled different, and "othering," see "The Social Model of Disability" in Chapter 13, pp. 270–1.

Brenda Cossman (1996) argues that family as a social construct is not the problem; rather, the problem lies in the legal and political system that demands people either fit into a presumed heterosexual unit or be excluded from the benefits of a legal family unit. This argument directly parallels discussions on marriages. Nancy Polikoff's (2008) work insists that we abandon the compulsion to arrange familial units based on conjugal relations and think more broadly of valuing all families as economic units, the units Kath Weston discussed in her 1992 book, *Families We Choose*. Martha Fineman (2000) and Carol Smart (1984) and Heaphy et al. (2013) concur and advocate for legal families to be based on caregiving units between dependents and their caretakers.

Many have argued that marriage is underpinned by class and gender biases. For instance, Claire F.L. Young (2006) points to class and gender in her work on tax implications for married same-sex partners in Canada. She states that income splitting for wealthier married couples is a tax advantage and one that is not available to those couples in lower income brackets. In fact, she points out that class and gender operate to expressly disadvantage those with lower incomes, since married or legal common-law couples' income is aggregated, thus often placing them in a higher tax bracket. Lesbian couples are disadvantaged since women commonly earn less than men. Recent figures from a 2016 report for the *Globe and Mail* by Statistics Canada states that women in full-time work earn 73.5 cents to every dollar earned by men, and Indigenous and minority women earn even less (Grant 2016; Patel 2016). Young's work on the tax implications of same-sex marriage includes an analysis that accuses the government of using the legalization of common-law and same-sex marriage as a cash grab (there were increased tax revenues over a five-year period of $9.85 billion). The financial disadvantage demonstrated by comparing two female wages or a single female breadwinner to the data available for middle-class heterosexual couples shows that lesbian couples are additionally disadvantaged.

CASE IN POINT

Tracking Conjugal Relationships

The Canadian state has been interested enough in its citizens' conjugal relationships to track them in Census polls: marriage data from 1921, divorce data from 1972, marriage stats that included common-law from 1981, and same-sex marriage data from 2006. The term *common-law relationship* is formally sanctioned by the state and now includes the category of two non-related same-sex adults living together.

According to the 2016 census data released by Statistics Canada on August 2, 2017, while common-law unions are becoming more frequent in every province and territory, married couples still represent the majority of couples (total population: 35,151,728; married couples: 13,383,455; common-law: 3,510,265). In 2016, over one fifth of all couples (21.3 per cent) were living common law, more than three times the share in 1981 (6.3 per cent) (Statistics Canada 2016).

The arguments advanced from those who support same-sex relationships and oppose same-sex marriage, focus on the institution of marriage, which assumes the authority to sanction not only what a marriage is but who it is for. It is important to continue to fight against state regulations that construct as many exclusions as they do inclusions. It is also important to question how same-sex couples can be expected to change the institution of marriage without the co-operation of opposite-sex couples. That is, unless we all agree to dismantle the institution of marriage, we are all caught in its grip. Whose relationships will the state legitimate and respect, even after death?

Questions for Critical Thought

Do you think fighting for equal rights in marriage for LGBTQ-identified people is useful or should marriage be dismantled altogether?

How Far Have We Really Come?

Currently, there is no national family policy in Canada. There is a decentralized system with two levels of government: federal and provincial. Marriage comes under the purview of federal family law (definitions of marriage) while the solemnization of marriage comes under provincial legislation (who can apply and age requirements). The different provincial legislations regarding marriage, divorce, and custody lead to the claim that a "patchwork of entitlements" has been created (Hurley 2005:3), leaving some couples within the bounds of privileges that marriage has to offer while others remain outside it. It is true that in Canada, same-sex couples have the legal right to live together, be married, and raise their children created by donor insemination, adoption, or in the context of (former) heterosexual relations. Increased visibility of sexual minorities and changing laws make it impossible to ignore the fact that there have been significant changes in the struggle to re-imagine family units. For example, while in 2004 the Anglican Church affirmed same-sex relationships, in 2016 it passed a resolution to allow same-sex marriages. In 2016, the Conservative Party of Canada voted to strike from its party platform the definition of marriage that limited it to a union between one man and one woman (1,036 to 462 delegate votes) (McGregor 2016). Yet, as noted above, social stigmas hold strong well after laws attempt to change the meanings of those stigmas.

Questions for Critical Thought

When you were in high school, was there someone who was bullied because either they identified as LGBTQ or because people assumed they were? Why do you think homophobia, biphobia, and transphobia still exist?

For more on the lack of unified, cohesive family policies in Canada, see "Introduction" in Chapter 15, pp. 313–15.

So, we have come a long way in law and in changing views about who are considered legitimate citizens based on intimate relationships. There is no question that same-sex marriage has destabilized the traditional institution of heterosexual marriage. However as pointed out above, scholars have demanded we consider whether legalizing same-sex marriage has ensured protection and equality for all or for just some.[5]

Daily Life

I ask students in the university classes I teach if there is any such thing as a nuclear family norm in Canada today. Most often the question is pushed back at me. "No. Just look around." Their answer is that the face of the modern family has changed so drastically that there is no one norm. Support for their beliefs arises from their view of marriage as a personal reflection of their own individual, moral, tolerant, and inclusive perspectives. These views are articulated by students saying "it doesn't matter what people do as long as they don't hurt anybody else," and by their references to the openly LGBTQ characters in media, from *The Ellen DeGeneres Show* to *Glee, Modern Family*, and *The L Word*, to more recently

Orange is the New Black and *Transparent*.[6] They also argue that there is same-sex human rights legislation that additionally proves Canada no longer views the traditional heterosexual nuclear family model as the only acceptable family unit. Before I launch into my argument that social stigmas are hard to shift, I ask students to reflect on their personal experience of heteronormativity. I ask them to test whether their relatives—parents, siblings, aunts, uncles, grandparents—accept same-sex relationships or marriage by asking them if they are confident they would be accepted if they were to go home and announce they were in a non-heteronormative relationship.

As they reflect on personal experiences, their answers become more elaborate, qualified, and less assured. When I then ask them to consider their responses if a child of theirs announced that he, she, or they identified with any of the sexual or gender expressions in the LGBTQQIP2SAA family (lesbian, gay, bisexual, transgender, queer, questioning, intersex, pansexual, two-spirit, asexual, allies). They struggle much more as they examine the difficulties their (imaginary) children might face. The ambivalences created by the disjuncture between same-sex marriage as a public institution and as a personal experience confuse them. What this exercise demonstrates to students is that there are conditions placed on the meaning of a legal document (in this case a marriage licence) that is procured within a heavily coded frame of heteronormative presumptions.

To belong to mainstream communities requires more than the legal right to have access, it requires that people meet the criteria tacitly agreed upon by strictly guarded community standards.

Conclusion

This chapter introduced an earlier time when the foundation for marriage was based on preserving property and economic stability, arguing that the shift from money matters to matters of the heart created an opening for asking: What is marriage for? Once the role of marriage was no longer solely linked to economic and biological reproduction, and sex without marriage entered into acceptable social relations, denying same-sex relationships and marriage lost its broad appeal. Looking at the many events that led to changing laws and social attitudes around same-sex relationships and marriage, we have noted that citizen actions force governments to change while changing laws force society to shift traditional norms.

Canada has its own very specific moment when the long-standing law that upheld marriage as a relationship between a man and a woman was struck down. Yet, even though social acceptance of this change is ongoing, social stigmas remain. We examined one argument that advocates for the inclusion of same-sex couples into the institution of marriage. This is viewed as an equal right to full citizenship participation. We also considered the opposing argument that insists this stance is exclusionary and calls for the total dismantling of the institution of marriage altogether. You must analyze the arguments from both sides and decide for yourself. Who is marriage for? Whatever the answer, the questions posed here will hopefully encourage you to engage in social change that chips away at norms that exclude people in order to broaden who can be included.

Study Questions

1. Do you think "What is marriage for?" is a useful question to ask? Why or why not?
2. Why is the right to marry so important to some people and not others?
3. What is the difference between a personal relationship between two married people and a legal relationship between married people and the state?
4. Can you think of another social issue focused around the inclusion or protection of some citizens to the exclusion of others, which requires a change in law?

Further Readings

Foster, Deborah. 2005. "The Formation and Continuance of Lesbian Families in Canada." *Canadian Bulletin of Medical History* 3, 22 (2): 281–97. Foster begins with the history of lesbian and gay rights in Canada from 1969–2002 and discusses issues such as what a lesbian mother is; how she reproduces; and what rights she, her partner, and her children may or may not have. She refers to studies that conclude the children of lesbian mothers do as well or better than those mothered by heterosexual women.

Foucault, Michel. 1990. *The History of Sexuality*. New York: Vintage Books. This account of sexuality, and the identification of "the homosexual" as a (sub)species of "man," covers long and complex histories. One of the many arguments advanced by Foucault is that censorship of sexuality increases rather than decreases people's desire to discuss and practise it.

Graff, E.J. 2004. *What Is Marriage For? The Strange Social History of Our Most Intimate Institution*. Boston: Beacon Press. Graff argues that marriage in Western societies has changed so much over the years that it challenges us to think about its social purpose. Building on a history of marriage, she asserts that there is no longer a reason to deny same-sex couples the right to marry.

Heaphy, B., C. Smart, A. Einardottir. 2013. *Same Sex Marriages: New Generations, New Relationships*. Chippenham and Eastbourne, UK: Palgrave Macmillan. This book considers the complexity of marriage as both personal experience and state institution. It raises many questions about why we consider marriage to be the most logical form of state-supported interdependency and challenges us to think beyond the heteronormative form of family.

MacDougall, Brian. 2000. *Queer Judgments: Homosexuality, Expression, and the Courts in Canada*. Toronto: University of Toronto Press. This book documents human rights-based court challenges that contribute to the rich and diverse history of the struggle for recognition of same-sex relationships in Canada. Along with this history, MacDougall also provides thought-provoking and critical analysis of seeking sexual minority legal status.

Smith, Miriam. 2008. *Political Institutions and Lesbian and Gay Rights in the United States and Canada*. New York and London: Routledge. This book is written by a scholar who has followed the legal and social struggles in the fight for equal rights for LGBTQ people in Canada and the United States. Her research is thorough, informative, and current.

Key Terms

Assimilationist strategies Refers to a process of making the same, or similar to the original. In the case of queer politics (see below), it refers to a process by which LGBTQ movements aim to gain rights in order to be considered the same as heterosexuals. This differs from the political strategies of some queer activists taking a divergent view and fighting for the right to be different.

Heteronormative Assumes that every person is heterosexual (straight) and that their genitalia defines their gender expression. The term also points to privilege and power as heterosexuality informs the dominant notions that set the standard for what is and is not normal and socially acceptable. Example: it is usual and "normal" for straight, white men to be in powerful roles in the government and would be unusual for black transgender women to take on these roles. It is worth noting that *homonormative*, a related term, does not assume that every person is LGBTQ. Rather, it assumes that queer people want to be just like heterosexual people. This term has entered queer politics because holding onto dominant, heteronormative assumptions and institutions (like marriage) sustains those institutions and continues to exclude those who are not able to benefit from them.

Queer politics By refusing to pigeonhole sexuality and gender, queer politics aim to reject assimilation to heterosexual identities and practices (like same-sex marriage). The term *queer* intends to be indefinable rather than defined by categories. Queer activism within political movements builds links with trans, feminist, anti-racist, and disAbility politics.

Sexual citizens Are those who are not identified, by themselves or others, as heterosexual and who may have documents that prove a legal claim to citizenship. Despite this, they are denied privileges afforded to heterosexual citizens. A sexual citizen may also be someone who demands to be included in the citizenship body based on their non-hetero sexual orientation or gender expression.

Testimonial affidavits In a court case, expert witnesses are called upon to give written declarations made under oath before a notary public or other authorized officer. In the case of same-sex marriage, expert witnesses provided formal statements testifying to the legitimacy of LGBTQ character as worthy citizens owed the right to marriage.

Notes

1. One example is Uganda where a law was proposed (October 2009) that not only outlawed same-sex relationships, it states that it will be a punishable crime for anyone to neglect to report people known to them to be in a same-sex relationship for more than 24 hours (*York* 2009). One website names 76 countries in the world where LGBTQ relationships are illegal as of August 2016 (https://76crimes.com/76-countries-where-homosexuality-is-illegal/).

2. On November 5, 2001, an Ontario Court heard the case of eight same-sex couples seeking the right to marry, together with a companion case brought by the Metropolitan Community Church of Toronto. The national lesbian, gay, bisexual, and transgender rights organization EGALE had intervenor status.

3. Below is a selection of expert witness affidavits from *Halpern v. Canada*, June 2003 found at (www.sgmlaw.com/en/about/Halpernv.CanadaAttorneyGeneral.cfm):

    - Affidavit of Barry Adam, www.sgmlaw.com/media/PDFs/Adam.pdf [on the cross-cultural evidence of same-sex partnerships and marriage and the evolution of cultural conceptions of homosexuality]
    - Affidavit of Bettina Bradbury, www.sgmlaw.com/media/PDFs/Bradbury.pdf [on the history and evolution of the institution of marriage in Canada]
    - Reply Affidavit of Bettina Bradbury, www.sgmlaw.com/media/PDFs/BradburyReply.pdf [responding to a government affidavit, sworn by Edward Shorter, which suggested that the recognition of same-sex marriage would threaten the continued existence of heterosexual marriage]

- Affidavit of Margrit Eichler, www.sgmlaw.com/media/PDFs/Eichler.pdf [on the evolution of the family in Canada]
- Affidavit of Katherine Arnup, www.sgmlaw.com/media/PDFs/Arnup.pdf [on the history and evolution of the family in Canada, and how previous changes, now considered innocuous or progressive, were thought to be a threat to the continued existence of marriage, the family, and civilization]
- Affidavit of Andrew Koppelman, www.sgmlaw.com/media/PDFs/Koppleman.pdf [demonstrates the relevance and applicability of the miscegenation analogy to denying gays and lesbians the right to marry and refuting the claim that a registered domestic partnership regime would be an adequate alternative to marriage]
- Affidavit of Susan Ehrlich, www.sgmlaw.com/media/PDFs/Ehrlich.pdf [on the social construction of meaning and whether the term *marriage* could include same-sex couples]
- Affidavit of Adele Mercier, www.sgmlaw.com/media/PDFs/Mercier.pdf [responding to a government affidavit, sworn by Robert Stainton, that claimed the term *marriage* could refer only to heterosexual unions]
- Affidavit of Jerry Bigner, www.sgmlaw.com/media/PDFs/Bigner.pdf [reviews the social science evidence relating to lesbian and gay parenting, showing that lesbians and gays have equal parenting skills to their heterosexual counterparts and that children raised by lesbians and gays are just as healthy and well-adjusted as children with heterosexual parents]
- Affidavit of Judith Stacey and Timothy Biblarz, www.sgmlaw.com/media/PDFs/Stacy.pdf [responding to a government affidavit, sworn by Steven Nock, which suggested that all of the social science evidence on lesbian and gay parenting was worthless, and to an affidavit filed by an intervener coalition of right wing groups, sworn by Craig Hart, which claimed that social science research shows that "natural"—i.e., heterosexual—family structures provide greater security and stability for raising children]

4. The rare "race-" and disabled-identity markers in one affidavit accentuate the dominance of white able-bodied subjects of same-sex marriage.

5. David Bell and Jon Binnie (2000) cogently assemble the views on all sides of the same-sex marriage debates and challenge readers to think to the future for a politics that moves beyond these debates. They highlight much of the leading work on critical sexuality including Lauren Berlant, Judith Butler, Davina Cooper, Eva Pendleton, Yasemin Soysal, Michael Warner, Jeffery Weeks, Kath Weston, and many others.

6. While television programming is important to LGBTQ history (see Gay and Lesbian Milestones in the Media at http://religioustolerance.org/hom_medi.htm for an overview of lesbians and gays on television and in film), you should keep a critical eye on the fact that often roles are played by people who are straight and the script and plot reflect heterosexual presumptions about what it means to be LGBTQ.

 Interested in finding out more? Visit www.oupcanada.com/Albanese4e for access to a list of recommended websites for this chapter.

PART II

The Life Course

Family life changes over time as people have new experiences, such as the birth of a child, and as they undergo the changes associated with aging. Of course, not everyone experiences the same changes. Some people have children whereas others do not; some people get married and then later get divorced, while other married couples remain together; some people live long into old age while others die young. The chapters in Part II, therefore, do not pretend that everyone follows a predictable life cycle. Rather, the contributors set out some of the common changes that occur in family life and some of the stages of the life course, in order to provide a sense of how family experiences may differ at different times of life.

In Chapter 4, Melanie Heath focuses on how people form relationships, some of which result in marriage. This chapter discusses theories and ideologies of intimacy. It also shows how the legal structure of marriage has historically excluded and marginalized some Canadians based on gender, "race" and ethnicity, immigration status, and sexual orientation. Heath discusses technological innovations that have been affecting dating and sexual relationships among young adults. She considers why people choose to be single and the role of friendship for those who live alone, and for those in "families of choice."

Amber Gazso focuses on becoming and being a parent of young children in Canada today in Chapter 5. The chapter outlines some of the everyday activities of parenting, but at the same time shows that the everyday practices or events of parenting are intimately connected to and textured by ideological discourses, culture, individuals' participation in other social spheres (e.g., the labour market), relationships with others, and social policies (e.g., child care). She highlights how differences in family structure and the sexuality of parents inform the *performance* of parenting.

In Chapter 6, Craig McKie focuses on how families fragment through separation or divorce, but often reformulate within the context of a new union. The chapter begins by reviewing the legal context for divorce and presents statistics on divorce. However, McKie notes that these statistics can be misleading because many cohabiting relationships end without legal or statistical consequences. That said, the economic and social effects of separation and divorce are almost always present and are the subject of great interest, and so they are also discussed here. McKie concludes that accounts of post-separation hardships must be weighed against the real risks of physical and emotional trauma in relationships that are full of conflict, risks that are greatly diminished following separation. The chapter considers how separation and divorce are often followed by the formation of new families, either lone-parent families or families that are reconstituted through new relationships.

Two stages of the life course—middle age and "old age"—are considered in Chapter 7. Karen Kobayashi and Anne Martin-Matthews focus on the transitions that mark middle age (e.g., the "empty nest," caregiving) and are triggered by the occurrence of life events in families (e.g., adult children leaving home, care for aging parents). Home-leaving by adult children, Kobayashi and Martin-Matthews note, has been taking longer in recent years, and in many instances adult children return to their natal home after having left. Support for aging parents is becoming a significant issue in Canada as a result of population aging. Of course, the experience of such life events as taking care of aging parents varies according to individuals' situations, and these can be quite diverse. The chapter therefore examines some of the diversity of mid-life families. The chapter includes a discussion of the relationship between mid- and later-life families and social policy.

Intimacy, Commitment, and Family Formation

MELANIE HEATH

LEARNING OBJECTIVES

- To gain an overview of the ways that family demographics have changed in Canada

- To understand why the number of people who cohabit is increasing, why this family form is becoming more socially acceptable, and why some people choose to "live apart together"

- To learn how sociologists theorize the transformation of intimacy and the scholarly debates on the degree of change that has occurred

- To recognize how the legal structure of marriage has historically excluded and marginalized some Canadians based on gender, "race" and ethnicity, immigration status, and sexual orientation

- To discover the definitions of and technological innovations for dating, and the new forms of sexual relationships among adolescents and young adults

- To consider why people choose to be single, and the role of friendship for those who live alone and for those in "families of choice"

Introduction

The institutions of family and marriage have experienced both continuity and change in the past century. Family remains a central social institution to organize individual life trajectories. Yet, the dominant patterns of family life can no longer be characterized by a routine of marriage, child-bearing, and child-rearing to the eventual death of a spouse. Today there is much greater diversity and transition in living arrangements and family forms involving those who cohabit, marry, separate, divorce, parent on their own, or do a combination of these. Family networks now often include parents, step-parents, same-sex partners, children conceived biologically or by artificial insemination, close friends, ex-partners, and ex-sons- and daughters-in-law.

To explain recent trends in family formation, sociologists have emphasized the increasing importance of intimacy and romantic love (Cheal 1987; Giddens 1992; Swidler 2001). In Western societies, the historic norms for marrying have transformed from a union based on the interests of parents, kin, or community to being rooted more in emotional bonds. Historian Stephanie Coontz (2005) traces this transformation back to the Enlightenment when the rise of the "love match" revolutionized the institution of marriage. Today, marriage holds a more diminished role than it once did in society and in people's lives.

What do sociologists mean when they use the term *intimacy*? In common parlance, it is often used to mean strong emotional bonds such as love. Increasingly, sociological understandings define it more precisely as denoting "closeness" and a state of being "special" to another person that involves self-disclosure (Jamieson 2007). Intimacy thus represents a privileged knowledge of inner selves. Scholars in the field of social psychology study personal relationships to uncover the importance of self-disclosure, partner disclosure, and partner responsiveness to what constitutes a "good" couple. Studies of "self-disclosing intimacy" point to the benefits of mutual self-revelation for quality relationships (Jamieson 2007). Sexual intimacy can be an important component (although not a necessary condition), and scholars point to the ways that sexuality has evolved to become an expression of the self. Thus, it is central to the transformations that are taking place in intimate relationships (Giddens 1992).

Expressions of love and commitment are multifaceted. For example, passionate love tends to be unsteady and can end abruptly. In contrast, commitment to someone involves a very different dimension of positive feelings for a partner and to a relationship over time. Scholars who study the meanings of love and commitment have found that relationship satisfaction is higher for companionate love than for passionate love (Hanson Frieze 2007).

Family scholars disagree on the social consequences of transformations in intimate relationships. Some argue that the increasing importance of private intimacy is dislodging civic and community engagement, whereas others view these transformations as offering heightened equality and democracy in personal life that might spread to other domains. Some view both of these as occurring simultaneously. This chapter will consider how intimacy and family life has changed, looking at the debates over the causes and consequences of these transformations to North American societies.

Family Formation, Social Structures, and Change

During the past century the family system in North America has experienced vast changes in marriage and divorce rates and in the influence of changing trends in cohabitation, sexual behaviour, child-bearing, and women's work outside the home. **Family demography** involves the study of changes in family structure—married-couple families (with or without) children, cohabiting-couple families (with or without children), single-parent families, stepfamilies, and so forth—to understand both individual and societal behaviour. Family demographers seek to answer why individuals behave as they do toward each other, and how societies compare in their family configurations and in their political, economic, and cultural institutions (Goldscheider 1995).

How are families configured in Canada today? Based on the 2016 Census, the majority of all families (83.6 per cent) live as married or common-law couples in either heterosexual or same-sex relationships (Statistics Canada 2017a). While most Canadians choose to live as a couple, we also know that the ways in which families are forming has changed dramatically. Similar to the United States and Europe, Canada has experienced substantial increases in rates of divorce, remarriage, and single parenthood, and today there is more societal acceptance of non-marital unions.

One way in which family life has changed substantially is a decrease in marriage rates. In 1961, married couples accounted for 91.6 per cent of Canadian **census families** (see Figure 4.1). By 2016, this number had dropped to 66 per cent (Statistics Canada 2017a). Decreases in marriage rates are linked to economic trends. Data analysis of the Canadian Labour Force Survey from 1976 to 2011 found a significant reduction in Canadian remarriages during recessionary periods, but only small effects on other aspects of family formation (Ariizumi, Hu, and Schirle 2015). Another marker of growing diversity in Canadian families is a substantial decrease in the number of couples living with children, a trend that has been taking place for some time due to the aging population. From 2011 to 2016, the number of couples living without children rose at 7.2 per cent, in comparison to 2.3 per cent for couples living with children. This means that the percentage of couples living with at least one child fell from 56.7 in 2001 to 51.1 in 2016—the lowest level on record (Statistics Canada 2017b).

Another major change in Canadian family life has been a substantial increase in **multigenerational households**—households that include at least three generations of the same family. Although comprising only 2.9 per cent of Canadian households, multigenerational households were the fasting growing household type in the 2016 Census at 37.5 per cent, well above the increase of 21.7 per cent for all households. Two possible explanations for the increase in multigenerational households are: (1) Canada's changing

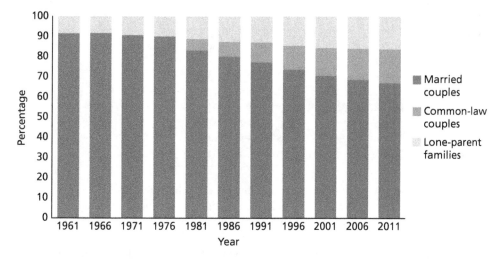

Figure 4.1   Distribution (in percentage) of Census Families by Family Structure, Canada, 1961–2011

Source: Statistics Canada (2012). "Fifty Years of Families in Canada: 1961 to 2011," *Families, Households and Marital Status, 2011 Census of Population.* Catalogue no. 98-312-X2011003; available at http://www12.statcan.gc.ca/census-recensement/2011/as-sa/98-312-x/98-312-x2011003_1-eng.pdf.

ethnocultural composition that includes more multigenerational households among In-digenous and immigrant populations, and (2) the high cost of living in some regions of the country that may compel multiple generations to live together (Statistics Canada 2017b).

While there is an overall decrease in marriage rates, the legalization of same-sex marriage in 2005 offered the possibility for LGBTQ individuals to enter the institution. There has been substantial growth in the numbers of same-sex couples reported by the Census. Between 2001 and 2006, the number grew by one third, from 34,200 to 45,345 (Milan, Vézina, and Wells 2007). By 2016, there were 72,880 same-sex couples in Canada, representing 0.9 per cent of all couples (Statistics Canada 2017c). Strikingly, between 2006 and 2016, the number of same-sex couples increased by 60.7 per cent, compared to just 9.6 per cent for heterosexual couples (Statistic Canada 2017c). One third of all Canadian same-sex couples were married, according to the 2016 Census.

For more on changing divorce law in Canada, see "The Legal Environment for Divorce in Canada" in Chapter 6, pp. 117–19.

Divorce increased substantially in Canada after the passage of the Divorce Act in 1968. This Act expanded the grounds for divorce and made it available across the nation. From 1968 to 1995, there was a five-fold increase (Ambert 2009). Since 1997, the divorce rate has decreased substantially and remained at a lower level with only minor yearly variations. The latest figure from Statistics Canada (2008o) estimates the likelihood of divorce for recently married Canadian couples at 38 per cent. There are currently no rates of divorce available for same-sex couples. Since marriage was so recently legalized for LGBTQ-identifying people, many of these marriages may involve couples who have been in long-term relationships. Thus, the divorce rate may be initially lower for this population than for heterosexual married couples (Ambert 2009).

Another substantial change is an increase in unmarried Canadians. For the first time in 2006, the number of unmarried individuals aged 15 and over surpassed those legally married with just over half unmarried—never legally married, divorced, widowed, or separated (Milan, Vézina, and Wells 2007). Lone-parent homes have also increased for the last four decades. In 2016, lone-parent families represented 16.4 per cent of families, a figure that has almost doubled since 1961. Women head about seven in ten of these (Statistics Canada 2017a).

Questions for Critical Thought

Is the single-parent, two-parent distinction still relevant for understanding family life in Canada? Why or why not?

The increase in marital breakup has meant a parallel increase in the probability of entering into a second or third union. The majority of Canadians repartner after a divorce or separation. Remarriage, however, is now less common because of the increasing propensity to cohabit after divorce (Beaupré 2008). With higher rates of divorce and repartnering, stepfamilies are now more common in Canadian society. The definition of **stepfamilies** includes unions based on marriage and cohabitation, whereas in the US the term refers only to remarried families. Almost half of all stepfamilies are **blended families** that include at least one child from a previous relationship plus one created in the current relationship. In 2011, one in ten children were found to be living in stepfamilies in Canada (Statistics Canada 2017a).

Cohabitation (also known as common-law or consensual unions) has become prevalent in Canada, especially among Canadian youth who commonly cohabit before marrying. While married couples were still the majority of couples in 2016, common-law unions have increased substantially, making up 21.3 per cent of all couples in 2016 (Statistics Canada 2017a). Figure 4.1 maps this growth from 1981, the year data first became available. In that year, common-law unions were only 6.3 per cent of all census families. Between 2006 and 2016, these families grew faster than married and lone-parent families: 27.4 per cent for common law compared to 6 per cent for married couples and 14.1 per cent for lone-parent families (Statistics Canada 2017a). The number of common-law couples was higher in Canada than in the United States: 21.3 per cent compared to 5.9 per cent of couples in non-marital cohabiting unions (in 2010). Canada had a slightly higher proportion than in the United Kingdom at 20.0 per cent in 2015, but a lower proportion than in France at 22.6 per cent in 2011, Norway at 23.9 per cent in 2011, and Sweden at 29.0 per cent in 2010 (Statistics Canada 2017b).

While overall cohabitation rates have grown across Canada, there are some striking regional differences. According to the 2016 Census, Quebec and the three territories had the highest number of common-law unions—39.9 per cent in Quebec, 50.3 per cent in Nunavut, 36.6 per cent in the Northwest Territories, and 31.9 per cent in Yukon. This is in contrast to the rest of Canada, which has an average of 15.7 per cent, excluding Quebec and the three territories (Statistics Canada 2017b). Common-law unions in the rest of Canada more closely align with the US, where individuals with fewer years of education and lower incomes are more likely to cohabit and less likely to marry (Bumpass and Lu 2000; Kerr, Moyser, and Beaujot 2006; Smock and Manning 2004). In terms of Quebec, French-speaking Quebeckers who cohabit are not necessarily economically more vulnerable, and fertility patterns among consensual cohabiting unions result in higher fertility levels overall (Laplante and Fostik 2015). Quebec also differs from the rest of Canada in that cohabitation has become more accepted as a family form in which to become a parent. For the rest of Canada, cohabitation is often seen as a probationary relationship before marriage and not always as an acceptable environment in which to raise a child (Le Bourdais and Lapierre-Adamcyk 2004).

Why the divergence in patterns of cohabitation in Quebec compared with other (Anglo) provinces? Demographers Le Bourdais and Lapierre-Adamcyk (2004) argue that a partial answer can be found in the different religious and cultural backgrounds of the two societies. The Catholic Church played a vigorous role in shaping Quebec society until the 1960s, when the culture shifted towards secularization—known as the Quiet Revolution—that was central to the development of modernity. Most Quebeckers embraced this revolution, abandoning the Church and its doctrines. Paralleling other Catholic societies such as Spain and Italy, women embraced the Pill as a contraceptive method, and the fertility and marriage rate plummeted. In contrast, the Protestant Church exerted less control in other parts of Canada, and non-Catholic Canadians did not feel the same need to separate themselves from religious institutions. Transformations in gender ideologies and practices may also play a role in the difference. The feminist movement has had a stronger history in Quebec than in other parts of Canada, pushing a culture of greater equality between women and men. Studies of the differences between cohabitation and marriage show that the former tends to be more egalitarian. Cohabitation leads to more sharing of domestic work than does marriage, and cohabiting women are more likely to participate in the labour market (Le Bourdais and Sauriol 1998; Shelton and John 1993).

Finally, family change is tied to greater ethnic and "racial" diversity in Canada. On average, 225,000 individuals have immigrated to Canada each year since the early 1990s (Statistics Canada 2007). There has also been substantial growth among Canada's Indigenous population. In 2006, there were 1.2 million self-identified Indigenous individuals—First Nations, Métis, or Inuit (Statistics Canada 2008). Inequality facing racialized families persists, however. For example, a study based on the 2006 Census found that Black families in Canada are culturally heterogeneous, but disparities in family formation and household income have worsened since 1986 when a similar study was conducted. Labour market inequalities, racism, and economic insecurity are factors that contribute to inequality facing Black families in Canada (Livingstone and Weinfeld 2015).

For more on the disparities of experience faced by Indigenous families in Canada, see "Child Welfare: The Millennium Scoop" in Chapter 12, pp. 258–9.

In thinking about these significant demographic changes, family life has emerged as a key focus of discussion. In the next section, we will look at the ways scholars theorize family transformation.

Intimacy: Meanings and Theories

Family demographers tell us about *how* families are configured, but social theorists help us think about the reasons *why* family change occurs. One of the key transformations in family life that theorists have addressed is the increasing separation of sexuality from the constraints of reproduction, a process that has gathered great speed with the rapid innovation in reproductive technologies and contraception.

New reproductive technologies encompass a broad range of technologies that seek to facilitate, mediate, or disrupt the process of reproduction, including conceptive technologies such as in vitro fertilization (a procedure in which eggs from a woman's ovary are removed and fertilized with sperm in a laboratory), antenatal testing (diagnostic procedures performed before the birth of a baby), contraception, and abortion. New reproductive technologies have helped to produce novel family structures and facilitate redefinitions of sexual and intimate relationships (Eichler 1997).

What are the social circumstances enabling contemporary transformations of sexuality, marriage, and child-bearing? Sociologist Anthony Giddens (1992:28) theorizes the emergence of "plastic sexuality" as enabling the transformation of intimacy, especially for women who are experiencing a "revolution in female sexual autonomy." Malleable eroticism offers a form of self-expression at the individual level and within the realm of social norms. Sexuality is not only increasingly detached from reproduction, but it has also been largely freed from the constraints of patriarchy (a social system structured by male headship), religion, and other means of social control. Giddens argues that individuals today shape their erotic needs according to individual identity and on pleasure and performance. Plastic sexuality results not only from the sexual freedom made possible by contraceptive and new reproductive technologies, but by the increasing economic and social independence of women. Emancipatory social movements—such as the women's and LGBTQ rights movements—have called into question traditional gender norms.

This emancipatory potential is also present in the emergence of the **pure relationship**, which Giddens (1992:2) defines in terms of "confluent love," a "relationship of sexual and emotional equality" between partners. In contrast to romantic love, usually thought to require a lifetime commitment, confluent love is more contingent on the emotional satisfaction and pleasure that a relationship offers at any particular moment. Compared to times past when women had few options outside of marriage and family life, women and men are now free to participate in the pure relationship as long as it offers satisfaction. Thus, the domestic norms of getting married, staying together, and raising children no longer constitute a pressing moral obligation.

Similar to Giddens, sociologists Beck and Beck-Gernsheim (2002:22) argue that "the ethic of individual self-fulfillment and achievement is the most powerful current in modern society." For them, membership in family life has become more contingent as a matter of choice. Individualization or the idea that the individual is becoming the central unit of social life has changed the nature of social ties within and between families to create the "post-familial family," which offers a new understanding of family based on its diverse manifestations (Beck-Gernsheim 1998).

Many theorists place LGBTQ relationships at the forefront of these cultural shifts that are transforming intimacy. Giddens (1992) argues that LGBTQ-identified people are forging new pathways for everyone, regardless of sexuality. Research on same-sex relationships has illuminated the ways that LGBTQ people are recouping the values of care and intimacy, against the grain of competitive individualism (Adam 2004). Weeks, Donovan, and Heaphy (1999:85) state that "one of the most remarkable features of domestic change over recent years is . . . the emergence of common patterns in both homosexual and heterosexual ways of life as a result of these long-term shifts in relationship patterns." Thus, social change in the way that intimacy is organized influences the wider organization and structure of sexuality.

Theories on the democratization of intimacy offer a broadly optimistic account of the changing nature of family life, and some empirical research confirms the move towards the pure relationship among certain populations. Demographer David Hall, for example, used data from the 1995 Canadian General Social Survey to examine how Canadian couples living in what he called egalitarian "pure relationships" (married and cohabiting) desired fewer or no children. He concluded that child-bearing and the ideal of the pure relationship often work at cross-purposes. Kate Hughes (2005) conducted a qualitative study of adult children of divorce from Generation X—the generation following the postwar Baby Boomers—who no longer felt pressure to stay married. She found that these Gen Xers connected their sense of personal growth with the formation and termination of intimate relationships. These studies confirmed the importance of the ideal of the pure relationship to family change.

Scholars have criticized the tendency in some of this literature to overstate the degree of family transformation that is occurring in society. Others point to a lack of attention to pervasive gender inequalities and class differences in intimate life (Jamieson 1998). One approach that does consider inequality has come out of an interactionist tradition to examine the links between intimate relationships and gender stratification (Dozier and

Schwartz 2001). This growing literature studies the ongoing interactions that both create and sustain difference and inequality. Sociologist Barbara Risman (1998), for example, has examined the ways that ongoing interactions perpetuate an unequal division of labour in the home and the workplace. She shines light on how gender structures work, family, and community to perpetuate dominant gender norms that support men's economic and social superiority.

Sociologist Neil Gross (2005) critiques the idea that romantic/sexual intimacy is fuelling what social theorists have called "detraditionalization"—the decline or reconfiguration of tradition—in the late modern era. Gross argues that there has been a decline in "regulative traditions," which in the past worked to exclude those who failed to participate in the culturally dominant nuclear, heterosexual, married family. This decline has not necessarily meant, however, the replacement of ultimate fluidity and agency in relationships. Instead, "meaning-constitutive traditions"—commonsense understandings passed down from one generation to the next—still reinforce the regulative tradition of heterosexual marriage as the dominant ideal.

Marriage Debates: Legal Structures and Cultural Privilege

There is general agreement among sociologists and demographers regarding changes to family life in the past five decades. Widespread debate, however, exists over how to interpret these transformations. Much of the debate concerns the relationship between marriage and children's well-being. Is the married, nuclear family consisting of wife/mother, husband/father, and their children the essential form of family—the only configuration for carrying out the vital function of rearing the next generation? Can other family patterns (e.g., single mothers, single fathers, two women, or two men) be as successful?

Questions for Critical Thought

How do we define and measure "the family"? Can a variety of legal sexual and intimate relationships benefit individuals and society?

The current state of the research on these questions has offered mixed conclusions. On the one hand, scholars find evidence that children raised in two-biological-parent married families tend to have better educational, social, cognitive, and behavioural outcomes than children from married step-, cohabiting, and single-parent families. The differences in these family types are modest, however, and there are mediating factors in the relationship between marriage and better outcomes, including economic resources, parents' own socialization, and family conflict/stress (Brown 2010). Moreover, some of the advantages scholars measure are due to selection factors rather than marriage itself. In other words, it is not marriage that causes financial success and happiness; rather, individuals who are happier and financially secure are more likely to marry. In addition, growing evidence finds that children raised by lesbian parents fare as well as those raised by heterosexual married parents; less is known at this stage about children of gay male parents (Biblarz and Stacey 2010; Stacey and Biblarz 2001).

CASE IN POINT

The Changing Legal Path of Marriage and Cohabitation

Laws and attitudes concerning marriage have changed substantially since the 1960s, and the state of marriage and the family is now contested terrain among scholars, policy-makers, and politicians. Many view its fate as in such dire straits as to necessitate greater restrictions on access to divorce, and to call for more narrowly legislating access to marriage's benefits and responsibilities. In the US, the law reserves many rights and privileges to married persons to encourage people to marry. Cohabitation, on the other hand, carries none of these rights and privileges. The 1996 welfare reform law focused on the need for policies to promote and maintain two-parent, married families. Since then, the federal government and individual states have allocated welfare funds to support initiatives and research to promote marriage, especially among low-income couples who have some of the lowest marriage rates. While the goal of these policies is to reduce poverty by encouraging marriage, there is no evidence that these programs have increased marriage rates or strengthened unions between un-married parents (Heath 2012).

The US model of marriage promotion has no equivalent in Canada. For a time, Canada appeared to be moving in a contrary policy direction in recognizing the legal rights of un-married couples. Beginning in the 1970s, unmarried couples and children born outside of marriage began receiving rights and obligations, such as spousal support and property rights. In 2002, however, this legal path changed direction when the Supreme Court of Canada declared it constitutional to exclude unmarried cohabiting individuals from family property laws (Bailey 2004). This decision effectively revived the legal significance of mar-riage in Canada.

What will be the direction of Canadian family law in the future? If the socially conserv-ative Institute of Marriage and Family has its way, Canada would move towards explicit mar-riage promotion policies similar to the United States, offering public awareness campaigns, positive portrayals of marriage in advertising, and tax credits for married families (Cross and Mitchell 2014). Such policy recommendations remain controversial in a country that has a history of seeking to support diverse families.

The marriage debate concerns what role law and public policy should play in sup-porting and regulating the family. Historically, there have been diverse arrangements for societal recognition of marriage in Canada. From the late seventeenth to the early nineteenth century, fur traders of the Hudson's Bay Company contracted marriages "à la façon du pays (or according to the custom of the country)" (Eichler 1997:44). Diverse forms of marriage could also be found among Indigenous populations, including polygamy and same-sex marriage (Carter 2008). As a British colony, colonial politicians in Canada distinguished the "civilized" tradition of marriage as the only legally and socially accepted form of intimate relationship from the "ancient barbarians, 'heathens,' and other peoples they characterized as uncivilized" (Bradbury 2005:105).

The Canadian state promoted marriage rights as a way to build the nation (Carter 2008). It did this by encouraging marriage among desirable white Europeans and by preventing family formation among non-white populations. An early example involves roughly 700 impoverished women, called the *filles du roi* (*daughters of the king*), who were sent from France to Quebec between 1663 and 1673 to marry men they had never met and raise families in New France. In the 1800s, thousands of Chinese men immigrated to work on the Canadian Pacific Railroad. When it was completed in 1885, the Canadian state began instituting policies to obstruct Chinese migration and nuclear family reunification. Federal legislation imposed an expensive head tax on Chinese wage labourers and on the spouses and children of Chinese men already in Canada. In this way, authorities sought to control the migration of Chinese women and thwart procreation among Chinese families that could eventually displace white people's labour power (Satzewich 1993).

For more on The Indian Act, see "Treaties and the Indian Act" in Chapter 12, pp. 250–1.

Regulating families was also a tool used to control Indigenous populations of Canada. The Indian Act of 1876 defined Indian identity and established legal and non-legal categories that had bearing on the rights of Indigenous people (Bourassa, McKay-McNabb, and Hampton 2004). Under the Act, Indian women who married non-Indian men were denied their Indian status, their band membership, education and treaty rights, and the right to pass on status to their children. In comparison, an Indian man who married a non-Indian woman kept his Indian status, and the non-Indian woman and her children received status. The Act imposed a patriarchal model on Indigenous families by making legal status and citizenship rights depend on the husband.

Thus, marriage at the turn of the nineteenth century was considered so central as to be "the bulwark of the social order" (Snell 1991:2). It remained largely patriarchal, with most married women economically dependent on their husbands. Obtaining a divorce was very difficult, and children born outside of marriage were thought of as "illegitimate," subject to social stigma and holding fewer rights than children born in wedlock. Laws and attitudes concerning marriage have changed substantially over time. The Divorce Act made divorce more common and easier to obtain, and further revisions occurred in 1985 to ease the adversarial aspects by introducing "no fault" provisions. The stigma surrounding cohabitation and unwed child-bearing has also declined. Another major change has been the recognition of the constitutional right for same-sex marriage in Canada.

Canada became the fourth country in the world to legalize same-sex marriage with the ratification of the Civil Marriage Act in 2005, and its legalization has been accompanied by significant shifts in attitudes towards the LGBTQ community. In particular, Anderson and Fetner (2008) found a noteworthy degree of change in attitudes among all age groups in Canada and the US. At the same time, the fact that lesbians and gay men were barred from legally marrying for decades now shapes their responses to legal marriage. Qualitative research of lesbian couples who adopted or planned a child found that they often do not marry, and those who did marry tend to be critical of and eschew dominant rituals attached to the "white wedding" (Fetner and Heath 2015; Kelly 2011).

In Canada, there are varying cultural practices of marriage that pose a challenge to Canadian laws and norms involved in regulating family life. Despite the growing dominance of the "love-marriage," arranged marriages—marriages in which parents or extended kin determine the choice of spouse—are still prevalent in many societies, including in South Asia. South Asian women who migrate to Canada through marriage—often through an arranged marriage—represent a vulnerable population due to their tenuous legal status, and immigration policy can intensify this vulnerability by granting the resident spouse control of the process (Walton-Roberts 2004).

Many South Asian women in arranged marriages come to Canada with very little knowledge of their spouses. Before policy changes set forth in the new Immigration and Refugee Protection Act of 2002, there were numerous reports of women who, after experiencing intense emotional and physical abuse from resident husbands and extended kin, were abandoned. New family sponsorship policies seek to reduce the risk of women being mistreated by considering the men's criminal record or history of domestic violence, reducing the number of years of required sponsorship, and adding language to sponsorship contracts outlining women's rights. A qualitative study that examined understandings of sponsorship among South Asian brides who entered Canada after the new immigration policy found that English-proficient women were cognizant of their rights and reported significant support. In contrast, non-English-proficient women did not fully understand the conditions of sponsorship and were subject to more severe abuse and neglect (Merali 2009). This research points to the need for further changes to immigration policy to support non-English-proficient women.

Children of immigrants who grow up in Canada tend to view marriage very differently from their parents. Many studies of South Asian families find evidence of serious intergenerational conflict over marriage customs, with the second generation demanding more say in decisions to marry and desiring more gender egalitarian relationships (Zaidi and Shuraydi 2002). One qualitative study found that youth and their parents were making compromises to reduce such tensions (Netting 2006). Indo-Canadian youth who chose their own mates would pick someone in their own caste or at least religion to make the choice more acceptable to their parents. Parents often begrudgingly accepted these choices, showing the importance of the intergenerational bond to these families. If parents did find something seriously wrong with the partner, the young adults expressed their willingness to reconsider their choice. In the next section, we will continue our consideration of the changing landscape of dating, marriage, and commitment among youth.

CASE IN POINT

Should Canada Criminalize Polygamous Families?

The issue of polygamy has posed a difficult challenge to the role of the state in recognizing relationships in Canada. Polygamy is a global phenomenon, most commonly practised as polygyny in which one man has several wives. The practice is illegal in Canada, raising the question of whether individuals should have the right to participate in this family form without it being criminal. In 2010, the British Columbia Supreme Court addressed this question in a reference case to determine the constitutional validity of polygamy's criminal prohibition in Canada. In his ruling, Justice Bauman found that while the law does infringe on religious freedom, it is warranted by the harm polygamy causes to children, women, and

continued

society. In addition, the Justice ruled that the prohibition does not cover the various forms of "polyamory"—the practice of having two or more consensual intimate relationships at one time—except in cases where polygynous relationships are formalized with a ceremony.

The idea that criminalization of polygynous relationships depends on a formal ceremony—whether legal or not—highlights the tensions in seeking to regulate diverse family forms in multicultural societies. In 2015, Canada's Parliament passed the Zero Tolerance for Barbaric Practices Act, which bans immigrants in polygamous marriages from entry into Canada and allows for deportation if they engage in polygamy while residing here. Political scientist Sarah Song (2007:165) criticizes these kinds of laws that focus attention on immigrant communities, which serve "to reinforce a false dichotomy between oppressive minority cultures and egalitarian Western majority cultures . . . that shield the dominant culture's own patriarchal practices from criticism."

Is it possible to consider polygamy as a workable form of marriage in this new and changing landscape of intimacy and love? This is a legal and theoretical question that will continue to weigh on multicultural and liberal societies.

The Changing Landscape of Young Adult Relationships: Dating and Hooking Up

While marriage rates have dropped in Canada, the median age at first marriage has risen substantially. In 2008, the average age for men to marry was 31.1 years—a six-year increase from its record low in 1970, and the average age for women was 29.1 years—a 6.5-year increase from its record low in the 1960s (Vanier Institute 2010). The rising age of first marriage has meant that most young adults experience a period in their life course called the **independent life stage**, which encompasses a period of relative social independence (Rosenfeld 2007). The rise of the independent life stage has reduced parental control over the dating and mate selection choices of their children. How do youth today form sexual and romantic relationships?

Historically in North America, romantic relationships among heterosexual unmarried youth shifted from courtship—a defined period preceding engagement and marriage—to dating, which took many forms and had less focus on commitment. Dating involves social activities between two people over time to discover the possibility of a committed relationship. It arose in the 1920s after the invention of the automobile, which offered youth more mobility and privacy (Bailey 1988). Until the late 1960s, dating was the dominant model in which young people found a mate, and it was structured in relation to specific codes for dress and behaviour, including defined gender expectations (Coontz 1993). Men asked women to go out, paid for the date, and initiated intimacy and sex.

Social historian Beth Bailey asserts that "it has been more than a quarter of a century since the dating system lost its coherence and dominance" (1988:141). She argues that a "new system of courtship" was established in the mid-1960s in American society. While scholars have acknowledged dramatic changes among youth in their sexual behaviour after 1965, some things have remained the same. In the early twenty-first century, Canadians pursued their first romantic relationships at a similar average age to that of their grandparents (about 16 and 17 years old). On the other hand, there have been numerous changes in attitudes toward premarital sex. In 2004, about 90 per cent of Canadians said they would accept the reality of premarital sex among adults, whereas this figure was quite low before 1965 (Bibby 2004).

The big change in sexual behaviour came with the Baby Boom generation. The National Health and Social Life Survey documents that Americans born after 1942 were more sexually active at younger ages than those born between 1933 and 1942. This trend, however, appears to stop or reverse among the youngest cohort born between 1963 and 1972 (Armstrong, Hamilton, and England 2010). One study found that the number of women who have had premarital sex by age 20 (65–76 per cent) is roughly the same for all cohorts born after 1948 (Finer 2007). The 1990s did witness a brief drop in this number for adolescents between the years 1991 and 2001 (Centers for Disease Control and Prevention 2002). Still, nearly one half of US high school students have had sexual intercourse in their lifetime (Centers for Disease Control and Prevention 2002a). In the past few decades, there has been an increase in the incidence of oral sex: over one half of American adolescents have either received or performed oral sex, a sharp rise from mid-century findings (Leichliter et al. 2007). Laumann et al. (1994:102) described this increase as the most "basic change in the script for sex between women and men" in the twentieth century.

Today, adolescents most often begin dating through involvement with mixed-gender friendship groups (Connolly, Furman, and Konarski 2000). Social and romantic activities are integral to the development of relationships among adolescents, and hanging out with their partner and friends, holding hands, and telling others they are in a relationship generally precedes sexual activity (O'Sullivan et al. 2007). Sexual encounters outside of a relationship are practised by a large number of adolescents for their first and subsequent sexual experiences (Grello, Welsh, and Harper 2006).

In recent years, studies have begun to explore the phenomenon of "hooking up" among heterosexual university students (Bogle 2008). Glenn and Marquardt (2001:4) define a hookup as: "when [partners] get together for a physical encounter and don't necessarily expect anything further." They discovered that hooking up has become quite common in the university environment. One study of undergraduate students in a northeastern university in the United States found that 78.3 per cent of men and women sampled hooked up (Paul et al. 2000). Yet, this high number can be a bit deceiving. Another study found that on average 80 per cent of students hook up less than once per semester over their entire university experience, and many of these hookups involve relatively light sexual activity—one third included sexual intercourse, and the other two thirds involved other activities like oral sex or just kissing and non-genital touching (Armstrong, Hamilton, and England 2010).

Some researchers assess casual sexual encounters as detrimental for heterosexual young women (Bogle 2008); others frame them as offering women sexual agency apart from time-consuming relationships (Hamilton and Armstrong 2009). In the past, studies of adolescent girls found a stronger emphasis on personal relationships and romance in contrast to adolescent boys who can be less emotionally engaged and who focus on sexual competition and scoring (e.g., Gilligan 1982; Martin 1996). One study of high-school adolescent boys found them to be relatively less confident in initiating physical sex and more emotionally engaged in romantic relationships than these previous characterizations

(Giordano, Longmore, and Manning 2006). Yet, research suggests that as boys gain more social maturity, dominant gender dynamics of male confidence in initiating dating and sexual encounters prevail.

Researchers have assessed patterns of dating in terms of dominant scripts—the cognitive schema people use to organize the world around them (Ginsburg 1988). **Sexual scripts** refer to the cognitive models and cultural patterns that inform desire and influence behaviour (Simon and Gagnon 1986). A prevalent sexual script bolsters the "sexual double standard"—the idea that women should limit their sexual activities to committed relationships while men have the liberty to pursue sex within or outside of a relationship. The sexual double standard labels women who have casual sex as "sluts," whereas men who hook up are just doing what guys do (Crawford and Popp 2003). This double standard contributes to broader patterns of gender inequality by privileging men's desires and needs over women's.

The phenomenon of hookups has not necessarily challenged dominant sexual scripts, and heterosexual dating remains highly gender-typed (Eaton and Rose 2011). In their study of 273 undergraduate students in a large public university in the southern United States, Reid, Elliott, and Webber (2011) studied student responses to a vignette that described a heterosexual hookup followed by a first date that did not involve sex. They found that students viewed both women and men as sexual beings with desires that could be

Daily Life
SlutWalk: Dismantling Sexual Scripts

In times past, women who engaged in sex outside of marriage were deemed immoral. Today, the focus has turned to women who have sex with multiple men, often labelled "sluts." Men who have sex with multiple women, however, do not face the same moral opprobrium. The sexual double standard—the fact that one set of sexual rules applies for men and boys, and another, unequal, one applies for women and girls—has led to many false beliefs that shape sexual scripts and justify male sexual aggression against women. To fight this double standard, a group of students reclaimed a word and started an international movement.

In 2011, a Toronto police officer gave a speech to students on preventing rape, remarking: "I've been told I'm not supposed to say this. However, women should avoid dressing like sluts in order not to be victimized" (Mendes 2015:90). His statement articulated a sexual script that blames women for their victimization and perpetuates the myth that women are at fault when they are raped due to the way they dress. In response, Canadian students organized a protest they called SlutWalk, reclaiming the word *slut* to raise awareness about victim-blaming for sexual assaults. The first SlutWalk was organized in Toronto, Ontario, in 2011, and drew 3,000 protesters. Since then, the SlutWalk has gone global, being organized in hundreds of cities across the globe. The continued need for women to fight against sexual scripts that demonize them as sluts points to the durability of a system of sexual stratification based on the idea that women's sexuality should be confined to long-term, committed relationships that ultimately lead to heterosexual marriage (Rubin 1984).

fulfilled through hookups, a "semianonymous, casual, and mutually pleasurable affair that carries few long-term consequences" (Reid et al. 2011:564). This non-stereotypical assessment changed, however, when discussing the first date. Students described the need for the woman, but not the man, to engage in impression management as a way to ensure her potential as "dating material." Thus, the sexual double standard, reduced in the party setting, was reaffirmed in a dating situation where the woman must reframe her behaviour according to the sexual script of the "good" girl who doesn't "put out" on the first date.

Most of the literature on dating and hookups has concentrated on the heterosexual world. Thus, there is limited research on the relationship patterns of LGBTQ youth. Past research found many similarities in dating scripts between white, middle-class heterosexual and LGBTQ youth (Klinkenberg and Rose 1994). Dating among same-sex youth conformed to dominant cultural scripts. For example, lesbians often focused on emotional connections, whereas gay male youth were more likely to participate in sexual activity. On the other hand, there were differences in other cultural scripts between lesbian/gay male and heterosexual youth, including the ways they planned a date and initiated sexual activity.

Same-sex romantic relationships still face the challenge of developing in the face of factors associated with being part of a stigmatized minority. LGBTQ youth often feel isolated and experience verbal and physical abuse in high school (Elze 2003). One small-scale study of LGBTQ youth found that internalized homonegativity—anti-LGBTQ beliefs applied to oneself—brings a decrease in how satisfied youth are with their relationship and in their feelings of mutual attraction (Mohr and Daly 2008). Another small-scale study of gay/bisexual male adolescents in the Castro district of San Francisco found a tension between a desire for love and monogamy and a lack of community support for such relationships (Eyre et al. 2007). With the improving climate for LGBTQ youth, facilitated by the increasing presence of gay–straight alliances—student organizations that provide a safe and supportive environment for LGBTQ students and their straight allies—it will be important to conduct more research on LGBTQ sexual behaviour and romantic relationships to uncover beliefs about sex, love, and compatibility (Fetner et al. 2012).

Techno Transformations: Internet Dating and Cybersex

High rates of union instability and movement mean many people searching for a new mate have been involved in previous marriages and/or cohabitations. With a large pool of individuals in the relationship market, new pathways are available to meet potential partners. Online dating in various forms has flourished over the past decades as a way to facilitate dating or sexual encounters. The internet facilitates online profiles, dating apps, and a variety of technologically mediated ways to meet potential partners. A nascent body of research examines how new technologies, including the internet and matching services based on algorithms, reassert and challenge dominant ideas about what men and women search for in mates.

Research indicates that between 3 and 6 per cent of marriages or long-term partnerships begin over the internet (Sprecher 2009). Studies of targeted segments of internet users offer evidence of its common use to develop personal relationships, but only a small proportion of these actually progress into romantic relationships. Representative surveys further indicate that only a small percentage of existing relationships were initiated following online communications. Instead, it is still more common to meet someone through more traditional networks, such as school or work. However, as the current popularity of online dating continues to increase, it is becoming an important avenue for meeting romantic and/or sexual partners.

Internet users report high levels of personal control over the process of electronically mediated communications to initiate relationships (Ben-Ze'ev 2004). Researchers are finding the effects of online technology to both transform and reproduce dominant cultural practices associated with the initiation and development of intimacy between adults (Barraket and Henry-Waring 2008). **Social exchange theory** understands interpersonal relationships according to the social psychological principle of minimizing costs and maximizing rewards (Myers 1993). For example, relationships that offer more than they take are the ones people tend to sustain. To gain maximum reward, individuals advertise their best traits and seek an exchange for what they view as socially desirable (Phua and Kaufman 2003). This perspective applies to both face-to-face and electronically mediated interactions (Merkle and Richardson 2000). Interactions that take place face to face or in cyberspace involve interpersonal exchanges that seek positive rewards, but differences in online forms of communications do exist, including less need for spatial proximity, greater anonymity, and more emphasis on self-disclosure (Cooper and Sportolari 1997).

Questions for Critical Thought

In your view, how is the internet changing our intimate lives?

Researchers have found that, when choosing a prospective partner, online daters tend to make decisions based on "racial" preferences. Feliciano et al. (2009) sampled profiles from an online dating site to find that white people exclude Black people, Latinos, Asians, those of Middle Eastern descent, East Indians, and Indigenous people as potential dating partners. On average, white men are more willing than white women to date non-whites; however, among those with stated "racial" preferences, white men are more likely to exclude Black people as possible dates. In contrast, white women are more likely to exclude Asian people. The researchers point to the ways that these preferences relate to racialized images of masculinity and femininity that shape who dates, cohabits, and marries. For example, white men who exclude dating Black women may rely on stereotypes that place Black women outside of idealized perceptions of femininity (Collins 2004). Likewise, white women who exclude Asian men draw on stereotypes of Asian men as asexual and lacking masculinity (Espiritu 1997).

Many of the early, more high-profile internet newsgroups, websites, and email discussion lists targeted LGBTQ audiences (Wakeford 2000). Computer-mediated communication has opened new doors for LGBTQ-identified people to find relationships and sexual partners, especially in geographically isolated areas. In his analysis of personal profiles from the now-shuttered LGBTQ web portal PlanetOut, Gudelunas (2005) found that postings differed mainly by gendered identities, and by whether the user came from an urban or rural area. Women in small towns were more likely to identify as butch or femme (masculine or feminine identity), but men and women in large cities mostly failed to answer this question. Overall, Gudelunas found that users maintained their local identities even while they participated in the more global space of PlanetOut.

Cybersex—including more current incarnations such as sexting—has also come of age with the advent of the internet. It involves two or more people engaging in online sexual talk and may include masturbation and orgasm (Daneback, Cooper, and Mansson 2005). There is an emergent body of research on cybersex that moves beyond studying it as a form of addiction (Courtice and Shaughnessy 2017; Daneback et al. 2005; Shaughnessy and Byers 2013, 2014). In their study of cybersex using a sample collected from a Swedish web portal (N = 1828), Daneback et al. (2005) found that almost one third of men and women said they had engaged in cybersex. Shaughnessy and Byers (2014) found that, among heterosexually identified women and women who completed an online survey, significantly more women and men reported participating in cybersex with a primary partner rather than a known non-partner or stranger. In terms of the LGBTQ population, Courtice and Shaughnessy (2017) found that more women engaged in cybersex with a primary partner than men.

Another study explored the mechanics and perceptions of cybersex interactions in MMORPGs, "massively multiplayer online role-playing games." Valkyrie (2011) found that cybersex in the context of online gaming both draws on and expands the original understandings of "cybersex." Players participate in virtual worlds that involve specific tools to augment their practices, including erotic texting accompanied by "emotes" that simulate "virtuophysical touch to heighten the pleasure and intimacy of cybersex" (Valkyrie 2011:91). Players also used eroticized (gendered) avatars as a visual tool to enhance their fantasies and to express themselves erotically. The phenomenon of cybersex blurs the boundaries of the body, sex, and of what counts as being sexual.

Online and electronic communication is shaping the global marketplace of buying sexual services. Sex workers increasingly advertise online and set up appointments with prospective clients via the internet, no longer requiring middlemen (Bernstein 2007). Sociologist Elizabeth Bernstein has studied the ways that electronic communication offers new avenues for intimate encounters; the internet has actually transformed the geographic space and practice of sexual labour, offering greater opportunity to perform sexual labour without the reliance on red light districts and walking the streets.

Living Alone, Families of Choice, and Living Apart Together

The twentieth and twenty-first centuries have witnessed a steady decline in larger household sizes. In recent years, the number of single-person households has increased steadily. According to the 2011 Census, overall household size has decreased in recent decades due to increased shares of one- and two-person households and to decreases in the proportion of large households comprised of five or more people (see Figure 4.2).

For the first time in 2011, the Census counted more one-person households than couple households with children. Between 2001 and 2011, the number of one-person households increased from 25.7 per cent to 27.6 per cent. This trend is not unique to Canada. In fact, about four in ten households in Finland (2010), Norway (2011), and the Netherlands (2011) were one-person. Canada's proportion of single-household families is comparable to the United States and the United Kingdom (Statistics Canada 2011).

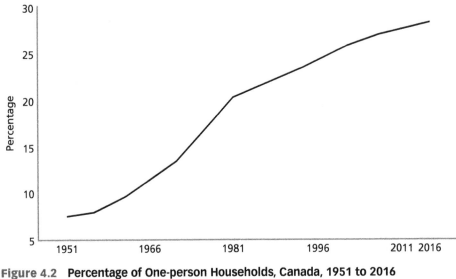

Figure 4.2   Percentage of One-person Households, Canada, 1951 to 2016
Source: Statistics Canada, Census of Population, 1951 to 2016.

Qualitative research indicates that while the number of people who are single has increased, the prevailing meanings regarding singleness are still fairly negative (DePaulo and Morris 2005). Being single is generally thought of as being "selfish, deviant, immature, irresponsible, lonely, unfulfilled, emotionally challenged, lacking interpersonal ties and strong social bonds" (Budgeon 2008:309). The stigma of being single comes from being an outsider to the idealized norm of coupledom in popular culture and in how societal benefits and social policy are distributed.

Shelley Budgeon (2008) conducted in-depth interviews with 51 people aged 24–60 who either were not in a sexual relationship or had a non-cohabiting sexual partnership. She found that participants tended to describe their singleness in a way that distanced them from the couple ideal, bridging a discrepancy between their positive self-identity of being single and their social identity shaped by the negative stereotypes of singleness. Friendships were an important mechanism that participants said they relied on to reduce the stigmatization they faced. By shifting their meaningful relationships towards friendships and away from sexual relationships, the participants embraced the idea of the value of being single as part of social belonging.

Friendships have also been an important component of **families of choice**. Weeks, Donovan, and Heaphy (2001:9) define families of choice as "kin-like networks of relationships, based on friendship and commitment beyond blood." These family configurations can include blood relatives, but the importance of these relationships is based on choice rather than just on blood or legal ties. The concept of families of choice emerged out of the historical exclusion of the LGBTQ community from the heterosexual nuclear family. Acknowledging the importance of particular values of family to everyday life, such as continuity, commitment, and material and emotional support, LGBTQ-identified people created their own families based on these values. Over time, the concept of families of choice has been applied to heterosexual family relationships, as well.

What do sociologists mean by friendship? Pahl and Spencer (2004) note the failure of many sociologists to operationalize the concept in empirical research, instead using an assumed definition. To rectify this, they offer a typology of friendship to clarify the boundaries between relationships that are given (mostly through kinship ties) and the ones that are chosen (both kin and non-kin). They further designate the strength of relationships based on high or low commitment. By elucidating kin and friendship patterns, they find involvement in highly complex sets of relationships within and between generations. Jamieson (1998:88) confirms the importance of strong boundaries in friendship, saying that "actual friendships are often closer to stereotypes of kin and community relationships (for example, based on mutual obligation, kept within careful predefined boundaries) than to the ideal of friendship." People's friendship patterns also change over time (Pahl and Pevalin 2005). Younger people choose their closest friends outside the family, but this tendency changes as people age, and the proportion of individuals who name their relatives as friends increases.

Another emergent family form that has been characterized as placing more importance on friendship is the phenomenon of "living apart together" (LAT), an intimate relationship with a partner who lives somewhere else. LATs are becoming increasingly accepted as a specific way of being in a couple. Studies have found that LATs do not only live apart due to necessity in terms of housing or labour market constraints, but rather that many choose not to live together even when it would be possible for them to do so.

LAT relationships have diverse origins and motivations. Recent research has found that some choose LATs because they are not ready to take the step of living together. Others had external constraints on living together, including affordability or the job and education market. Some intentionally chose to live apart as a more desirable solution to the complexity of modern life (Duncan and Phillips 2010). Many in these relationships expect sexual exclusivity and are highly committed to their partner in terms of love, care, and intimacy (Carter et al. 2016). Another qualitative study of individuals living apart together found that those interviewed offered positive remarks on aspects of not living with their partner, and they portrayed LATs as a valid way of being in a relationship, not as a move in a progression towards a "proper" relationship (Roseneil 2006). In addition, older adults are entering into LAT relationships in large numbers because they afford more freedom from obligation (Benson and Coleman 2016). It is important that individuals are able to make specific choices around the specific configuration of living patterns.

Conclusion

Long-term transformations in marriage, family, and intimacy involve a move away from institutional factors, although these still remain important, towards more relationship fluidity. Women's entry into the labour force in the past 60 years has transformed family structures and marital relationships. Marriage and family, once solidly grounded in familial ties and kinship obligations, now offer a range of options—from relationships embedded in traditional gender roles to those based on individual choice and personal satisfaction. Choice includes the possibility of who to include as part of one's kinship network, whether to marry or remain single, when and how to participate in reproductive relationships, and whether to cohabit or live apart together, among others.

Along with transformations of intimacy have come strains in family life in North America and Europe, marked by high rates of relationship dissolution and concerns over how to balance family and work life. Even though heterosexual relationships have become more gender egalitarian, there are still persistent gendered inequalities, especially within heterosexual marriages where research has found unequal participation between men and women in household and parental tasks. The sources of these persisting differences include institutional barriers for women in entry and earning power in the labour market, the tenacity of deeply held assumptions about the fundamental nature of men and women, and continuing inequalities in power within the household. The growth of income inequality between countries in the global north and south is also generating a hierarchy of families with those at the top retaining economic and social capital to live and work more securely, and those at the bottom experiencing insecure living conditions that force them to uproot to seek the means to survive.

These transformations represent particular challenges to instituting policies and laws to support the numerous manifestations of the family unit in the future. How do we best protect children's interests to secure the support of adults who have formally expressed their commitment to rearing children? How do we strengthen interdependency and personal commitment among adults? The answers will likely depend on finding ways to support the variety of situations with respect to family, to diminish inequality within and among families, and to allow people to form, revise, and pursue the conception of the "good relationship" that is most suitable to their circumstances.

Study Questions

1. In this chapter, you learned about the changes in family formation, the decline in the number of people getting married, and the rise in cohabitation rates. Do you think that marriage is becoming less socially significant in Canada? Why or why not?

2. How has the transformation of intimacy impacted family life in Canada? What is meant by the term *plastic sexuality*, and why is it important to the study of intimacy?

3. What are the social policy implications of the different demographic patterns of cohabitation between French-speaking Quebeckers and the rest of Canada?

4. Studies of youth sexual practices over time show that "hooking up" does not represent a sudden change in youth sexual culture. Apply what you have learned about social exchange theory in this chapter to assess the costs and benefits of the hookup culture for university students.

5. Draw on concepts in this chapter to explain the increased rates of couples who are living apart together (LAT).

6. Friendship is an important intimate and social connection for many people. What role does friendship play in changing family forms, including singleness, "families of choice," and LAT? What is friendship's significance across the life course?

Further Readings

Ansari, Aziz, and Eric Klinenberg. 2015. *Modern Romance*. New York: Penguin Press. Comic Ansari and sociologist Klinenberg conducted surveys and held focus groups to study how people from multiple generations seek romantic partners, how technology has changed the search for a mate, and how instant communication has opened up a bewildering array of options for singles.

Armstrong, Elizabeth A., Laura Hamilton, and Paula England. 2010. "Is Hooking Up Bad for Young Women?" *Contexts* 9: 22–7. The research finds that women's hookup experiences vary from uniformly negative to offering some benefits.

Baker, Maureen, and Vivienne Elizabeth. 2013. *Marriage in an Age of Cohabitation: How and When People Tie the Knot in the Twenty-First Century*. London: Oxford University Press. This book draws on a wide range of international studies—from Canada, Australia, New Zealand, the UK, and the US—on the lives of couples as they negotiate their relationships in the twenty-first century.

Carpenter, Laura, and John DeLamate, eds. 2012. *Sex for Life from Virginity to Viagra, How Sexuality Changes throughout Our Lives*. New York: New York University Press. This collection critically examines sexuality and intimacy across the entire lifespan, including the topics of puberty, sexual initiation, hooking up, coming out, sexual assault, marriage/life partnering, disability onset, immigration, divorce, menopause, and widowhood.

Heath, Melanie. 2012. *One Marriage under God: The Campaign to Promote Marriage in America*. New York: New York University Press. This book is the first ethnography to assess the discriminatory consequences of marriage promotion policies as they are practised on the ground.

Kimport, Katrina. 2014. *Queering Marriage: Challenging Family Formation in the United States*. New Brunswick, NJ: Rutgers University Press. This book draws on in-depth interviews with participants in San Francisco same-sex weddings in 2004 to argue that these new legally sanctioned relationships can both reinforce as well as disrupt the association of marriage and heterosexuality.

Whitty, Monica, Andrea Baker, and James Inman, eds. 2007. *Online Matchmaking*. New York: Palgrave Macmillan. This collection covers various online relationship issues including different internet communication spaces, cybersex and body theories, online subgroups, and cyberstalking.

Key Terms

Blended family The marital union of two people, at least one of whom was previously in a marriage or marriage-like union and is also a parent. A blended family is created when one parent of an established family marries or cohabits with another such partner, and all their children are considered members of the new family.

Census family A heterosexual or same-sex family living in the same dwelling that includes a married couple and the children, if any, of either and/or both spouses; a couple living common law and the children, if any, of either and/or both partners; or a lone parent of any marital status with at least one child living in the same dwelling.

Cohabitation (common-law and consensual unions) An emotional, sexual, and (usually) residential relationship between two people that is not legalized through marriage.

Families of choice Defines family as social networks that include LGBTQ individuals or other people who become members of a self-defined "family."

Family demography A subfield of demography that examines changes in the nature of intergenerational and gender bonds in households and family units.

Independent life stage This is a period in the life stage of young adulthood of social independence that involves living apart from parents before beginning a new family.

Multigenerational household Households that house three or more generations.

New reproductive technologies A broad array of technologies aimed at facilitating or preventing the process of reproduction, such as contraception, abortion, antenatal testing, birth technologies, and conceptive technologies.

Pure relationship Giddens's "pure relationship" describes an ideal relationship based in emotional and sexual intimacy, begun and continued for as long as it satisfies both partners. It relies on sexuality freed from reproduction, intimacy as central to love, and egalitarianism between partners.

Sexual scripts "Sexual scripting theory" was theorized by Simon and Gagnon (1986) to focus on ways that stereotypical scripts enable people to organize the social world and to predict meaningful social interactions.

Social exchange theory Social exchange theory posits that people commodify a range of social characteristics, including physical attractiveness, youth, wealth, education, gender role, and social status and then offer their best traits in trade for traits they desire. This theory is used in studies of dating, cohabitation, and marriage partner choices.

Stepfamilies Families in which at least one of the children in the household is from a previous relationship of one of the parents; a cohabiting or legal union of two adults with at least one member bringing a child or children from previous relationships.

Interested in finding out more? Visit www.oupcanada.com/Albanese4e for access to a list of recommended websites for this chapter.

5

Parenting Young Children
Decisions and Realities

AMBER GAZSO

LEARNING OBJECTIVES

- To introduce the life course perspective and how it can be used to understand the decision to parent and the everyday activities of parenting young children

- To demonstrate how the experience of parenting today is contextualized by changes in Canadian family life over time

- To understand the decision to become a parent as a major life course transition that is connected to gender socialization

- To learn that everyday practices or events of parenting are intimately connected to and textured by discourses, culture, individuals' participation in social spheres other than the family (e.g., the labour market), and relationships with others and social policy (e.g., child care)

- To learn how differences in family structure and the sexuality of parents informs the performance of parenting

---

Introduction

Having and raising children involves parents' constant management and negotiation of their emotions, mental fortitude, and physical energy. At all stages of their growth and development, children can provide parents with feelings of wonderment, accomplishment, and affection, whether it is concerning their first steps or their graduation from high school. Children can also present parents with many, even limitless, challenges that range from sleepless nights and trouble finding child care, to partners who do not equally participate in housework, workplaces that fail to grant days off for caring for sick children, and weak economic support from governments during hard times. Parenting in Canadian society today is, not surprisingly, a fruitful topic of sociological interest.

In this chapter, we will adopt a life course perspective to focus on an important stage in some people's lives—the decision to become a parent—and the subsequent everyday realities of parenting infants and/or young children in their pre-adolescent years, a period when children are especially dependent on others for the meeting of their basic needs. The life course perspective emphasizes transitions, pathways, and trajectories that develop over the course of an individual's life (Elder 1994); becoming a parent is a transition in a person's family trajectory. People are perceived to have agency but the choices they make over their life, such as the choice to raise a child, are understood to be shaped by social structures such as the economy or social policy. Additionally, the choices and opportunities available to any individual are culturally and ideologically mediated and temporally and historically situated; earlier decisions will shape later outcomes (Mitchell 2012). A final principle of this theoretical perspective important in the study of parenting is that of linked lives: the behaviour of one family member shapes and is shaped by the behaviour of other family members, including parents and children (McDaniel and Bernard 2011). The everyday events or practices of parenting are connected to people's relationships in social domains such as paid work and child care, and with others too, including family and friends in networks of support. Through the lens of the life course, we can see the interconnectedness among everyday parenting activities as they are experienced within particular social contexts.

This chapter is organized as follows: the first section begins with a general overview of changes in Canadian families in order to situate the experience of parenting today; the second section considers the factors, including one's gendered sense of self, that underpin the decision to have a child and raise a family,[1] and the third section highlights everyday parenting of young children as linked to other dimensions of social life.

General Overview: Parenting and Social Change

Popular media and rhetoric tends to suggest that parenting occurs most often in **nuclear families**. In fact, people are parenting in arrangements that are more diverse than nuclear families made up of a wife, husband, and children, are doing so at later ages, and are parenting fewer children today than in the past. In fact, according to the 2016 Census, just slightly more Canadians live in single person households than households consisting of couples with children (28.2 per cent versus 26.5 per cent, respectively) (Statistics Canada 2017a). The 2016 Census further revealed that the number of couples living without children has continued to increase and is rising faster than the number of couples living with children. Among those couples who parent children, married couples continue to be the majority, but the numbers of couples living as common-law partners is steadily rising. As well, since 2006, there has been a 60.7 per cent increase in cohabiting same-sex couples, compared to only a 9.6 per cent growth in opposite-sex couples (Statistics Canada 2017b). Parenting young children continues to be more likely among female same-sex couples than male same-sex couples (Milan, Vezina, Wells 2007; Statistics Canada 2017). Parenting young children may also occur in cooperation with younger and older kin relations; the proportion of multigenerational households has grown the fastest among all households between 2001 and 2016 (Statistics Canada 2017a). Finally, the number of children living with grandparents, **skip-generation households**, have been growing in numbers since the early 2000s (Kier and Fung 2014; Statistics Canada 2012).

Parents are older and rearing fewer children than in the past. In 2008 the average age of mothers at childbirth was 29.3, a 2.6-year increase since 1975 (Human Resources and Skills Development Canada 2012). By 2011, mothers gave birth at the average age of 30 years or older (30.2 years of age specifically), and mothers' age at first birth was 28.5; both of these are the oldest average ages on record according to Statistics Canada (Statistics Canada 2016a). In 1959, women had, on average, 3.93 children. By 2007, this number had dropped to 1.7 (Human Resources and Skills Development Canada 2012); it was 1.6 in 2011 (Statistics Canada 2016a). Considering **census families**, there are more couples living with children than without (Statistics Canada 2017). The majority of children aged 0–14 in Canada live with both of their biological or adoptive parents but 3 in 10 children live in one-parent families, a stepfamily, or with a grandparent, other relatives, or as foster children (Statistics Canada 2017c). While lone-mother families continue to be more prevalent in Canadian society, lone-father families are growing in numbers (Statistics Canada 2012). In light of these trends, the popular idea that children are commonly raised by one mother and one father is certainly less than accurate.

Today's parents also raise children in a social climate characterized by fewer or leaner supports for parents. Waves of **welfare state** restructuring have weakened federal income supports designed to assist parents with the daily cost of family life. From 1944 to the mid-1980s, all mothers in Canada were entitled to Family Allowances until their child reached the age of 18. This program provided a monthly benefit amount to assist mothers in their raising of their children regardless of their attachment to the paid labour force or their total household income. In the 1980s, Family Allowances were reformed and targeted at mothers with incomes below a certain threshold. In the early 1990s, the Canada Child Tax Benefit and National Child Benefit replaced Family Allowances but continued to be income-tested programs and so were available to only some parents. While the Harper Conservative government introduced the Universal Child Care Benefit (UCCB) in 2006 to assist with care costs for all families regardless of their income, it was only $100 a month. Families with child care costs over $1,000 a month that yet earned too much money to qualify for child tax benefits often found this benefit to be of little help. Much more recently, in July 2016, Prime Minister Justin Trudeau's Liberal government launched the new Canada Child Benefit to replace the existing system of benefits. This benefit targets support for raising children more narrowly to lower- and middle-income families. It is expected to help reduce poverty experienced by Canadian families to a greater extent than its predecessors because it also offers higher monthly benefit amounts to more families. As to whether this outcome will materialize, especially for very low-income families, is a question for a future chapter on parenting young children.

Besides changes to child benefits, parents have experienced changing support of their paid work participation and lack thereof. Between 1940 and 1996, Unemployment Insurance (UI) provided parents with financial support during times in which they were unemployed. With the replacement of UI with Employment Insurance (EI) in 1996, the federal government introduced new eligibility criteria. Whereas people qualified for UI on the basis of weeks worked for pay, EI eligibility is assessed by hours of work. Parents who work part-time or seasonally are often ineligible for income support from the government if they become unemployed.

Provincial governments have likewise often failed to adequately alleviate financial and care burdens on parents in need. Although social assistance programs provide economic relief in times of need, such as when a person is unemployed but does not qualify for EI, or providing care to young children, restructuring from especially the 1990s onward has resulted in total monthly benefits that are well below Statistics Canada's **low income cut-offs (LICO)**. According to widespread rhetoric, social assistance is a program of "last resort." As a program accessed by parents, however, cuts and restrictions can result in the inability to provide families with enough money for basic needs like adequate housing or nutritious meals (Gazso 2007). Low-income parents also struggle to find suitable child care arrangements should they desire to return to paid work or education. It can be a long wait to receive a subsidy and a space in a licensed child care centre. For two-parent families, even when both parents are engaged in paid work, a good portion of one parent's paycheque goes toward the purchase of outside child care, a topic returned to later in this chapter.

Questions for Critical Thought

How might a person's perception of their capacity to parent be shaped by their awareness that state support for families is often subject to change?

Deciding to Parent

There are many pathways that result in parenthood. Parenthood is no longer the given and natural condition of solely heterosexual and legally married couples (Stacey 2006). Besides a woman conceiving a child with her male partner, straight and LGBTQ individuals can become parents of children through, among other avenues: adoption, artificial insemination, surrogacy, foster care, in-vitro fertilization (IVF), and/or partnering with someone who has children from an earlier union (Foster 2005). For example, IVF technology can enable a woman to conceive and bear a child using a donated ovum and have full legal and social obligations in raising the child; the genetic mother does not share these rights. Or, two gay men may become parents through adoption or surrogacy, where a woman has agreed to conceive a child by being artificially inseminated with one or both of the men's sperm. In her qualitative study, Dempsey (2010:1152–4) explains that lesbian women and gay men can negotiate still more complex reproductive relationships with others through three approaches. In "standard donor" relationships, a male donates sperm to a woman but has no familial relationship with the woman or child. "Social solidarity" relationships involve a donor who could be acknowledged as the child's family member but primary social and legal obligation rest with the woman inseminated. Finally, "co-parenting" relationships can involve two people agreeing to parent a child, conceived by artificial insemination, who do not have to share a residence or be in a sexually intimate couple relationship. As Farrell, VandeVusse, and Ocobock (2012) observe, conventional conceptions of child-bearing and formal, legal definitions of family have been transformed with the advent of such assisted reproductive technologies.

Sociologically, the decision to parent is an interesting one. Stacey (2006) argues that an emotional impetus underlies the decision to parent today, more so than the economic one of the past when children were sources of labour and family financial security. Children promise an emotional intimacy that can be grounding in the midst of a social climate challenged by economic turbulence, violence, crime, and social exclusion. Prior to an adult's perception of the emotional gain associated with children, the development of gender identity and gender socialization over the early life course can underpin the decision of whether to raise a child. From childhood and into later life, women and men interact with multiple discourses that ascribe gender identities and roles such as mother or father according to dominant masculine and feminine stereotypes. The development or achievement of a gendered self, in line or in opposition to this ascription, is a life-long psychological and sociological process.

The family can be a primary site in which boys and girls are taught to view their biological sex as essentially determining their life choices. Boys and girls grow older in a society characterized by institutionalized heterosexuality or **heteronormativity**. The family and other socialization agents such as school and media teach sexuality and reproduction as naturally concomitant (see also Valverde 2009). That is, children tend to be taught that opposites attract and when one partners, one should partner with the opposite sex in order to reach fulfillment of their biological destiny—reproduction. Through these socialization agents, boys learn to view fatherhood as associated with particular masculine characteristics: aggression, leadership authority, power and control, and detached rationality. Girls learn to understand motherhood as assuming characteristics of passivity, submission, and emotional intimacy. Moving along the life course, from adolescence into adulthood, women and men continue to be socialized to understand children as a normal and essential outcome of sexual intimacy. In particular, women are taught to desire children and see the act of mothering as inevitable and natural. To place attention on gender socialization in the decision to parent is not to deny individual agency or psycho-social development of identity. Most people would vehemently argue that they choose to parent at a particular optimal moment in their lives. However, sociologically, we must understand the choice to parent as linked to earlier experiences of gender socialization, particularly the social construction of parenting as a natural event in one's life. Moreover, pressures to parent according to heteronormative configurations of the family are experienced regardless of one's sexuality (Epstein 2009). Individuals who identify as LGBTQ are also exposed to discourses about parenting as a natural outcome of heterosexual coupling. They must navigate gendered constructions of masculinity and femininity in different ways than straight and cis individuals by working against assumptions about their sexuality and prospective child-rearing given their perceived biological bodies, sometimes with the effect of overturning discriminatory law or policy (see Case in Point box below). In some circles within the LGBTQ community, to be queer is to be opposed to constructing families that fit the monolithic nuclear family model, with construction of such families perceived as akin to **homonormativity** (see, for example, Annmaturo 2014). In their study of American gay men who adopted children, Armesto and Shapiro (2011) found that the choice to parent had to be made in opposition to dominant beliefs that fathering and gay identity cannot coexist. Geisler's (2012) qualitative research additionally discovered that American gay men who desire to parent can experience structural barriers in the form of agencies that preclude gay men from adoption and surrogacy arrangements on the basis of discursive constructions of *heterosexual* fatherhood.

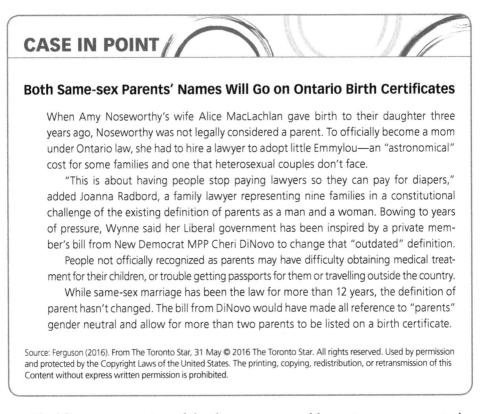

CASE IN POINT

Both Same-sex Parents' Names Will Go on Ontario Birth Certificates

When Amy Noseworthy's wife Alice MacLachlan gave birth to their daughter three years ago, Noseworthy was not legally considered a parent. To officially become a mom under Ontario law, she had to hire a lawyer to adopt little Emmylou—an "astronomical" cost for some families and one that heterosexual couples don't face.

"This is about having people stop paying lawyers so they can pay for diapers," added Joanna Radbord, a family lawyer representing nine families in a constitutional challenge of the existing definition of parents as a man and a woman. Bowing to years of pressure, Wynne said her Liberal government has been inspired by a private member's bill from New Democrat MPP Cheri DiNovo to change that "outdated" definition.

People not officially recognized as parents may have difficulty obtaining medical treatment for their children, or trouble getting passports for them or travelling outside the country.

While same-sex marriage has been the law for more than 12 years, the definition of parent hasn't changed. The bill from DiNovo would have made all reference to "parents" gender neutral and allow for more than two parents to be listed on a birth certificate.

The life course transitions of deciding to parent and becoming a parent must also be connected to societal institutions other than the family. Through qualitative research with parents, Ranson (1998, 2010) has convincingly shown that women's decisions to have a child are connected to their meeting of educational and career goals and available opportunities within the Canadian labour market. Indeed, one of the reasons some women are having children at later ages is because of their spending more time to complete higher education, establish careers, and achieve economic security. In her earlier research with mothers, Ranson (1998) also found that the organization of paid work and whether it was perceived to support child-rearing and care was important to a woman's sense of the "right time" to have children. The Canadian labour market is characterized by occupations that facilitate parenting and those that inhibit it.

For more on fathers taking parental leave see "Child Care" in Chapter 9, pp. 187–9.

Finally, the decision to parent can also be understood as linked to women's and men's relationships with social policy and/or workplace policy. For example, many prospective parents consider whether or not they will be entitled to parental leave, paid by the federal government and/or their employer, should they take time off from their occupations for the birth or adoption of their child. Should they be eligible for Maternity and Parental Benefits under Employment Insurance, monthly benefits from the federal government cover 55 per cent of their average insurable wages for parents to take up to 35 weeks off of paid work; mothers are also entitled up to 15 weeks of maternity leave. Prospective parents may also be entitled to a top-up of their monthly benefits from their employer for a portion or all of their time away from their job. Other available workplace policies can also inform a person's decision to parent, such as provisions for absenteeism if a child is ill.

Several factors underpin a person's decision to rear a child in today's society. Personal choices intersect with whether and how individuals have learned the norms of gender and family life over time and the opportunities within and barriers of other institutions and social structures. The interaction between choice and structure partially underlie some of the wider trends observed earlier, such as having children at later ages and having smaller families. Nonetheless, people are still having children and are parenting. In the next section, we turn to the "hows" and "doings" of parenting and their connection to other everyday activities.

The Performance of Everyday Parenting

The performance of parenting dramatically changes women's and men's lifestyles. Women's and men's independence and autonomy are reconfigured by the presence of an infant or young child who is wholly dependent on them to meet most basic needs including food, shelter, clothing, affection, protection, and socialization. Sleepless nights associated with the parenting of infants are replaced by busy days managing young children's schooling and recreational needs. Parenting practices must be re-imagined again when navigating relationships with young adolescents who become increasingly independent, or when children become adults themselves and need support surrounding life-altering decisions about post-secondary education and/or employment. This section focuses on the everyday practices of parenting infants or young school-aged children (i.e., under the age of 12), and emphasizes how the activities of parenting young children are performed in connection to activities and transitions in other domains of social life, including micro-interactions within the family home and with others and relationships with institutions and structures, such as the workplace and social policy. Parenting young children is influenced by and performed in constant negotiation with one's sense of gender identity, discourses about the practice of parenting, cultural background, attachment to the paid labour market, the division of housework and child care, relationships with social policy, and social support systems, all factors that additionally shape one's overall life course.

Gendered Discourses on Parenting

Just as gender socialization influences the decision to parent, the actual activities of everyday parenting are intimately tied to dominant ideas about masculinity and femininity. Mothers and fathers, regardless of their sexuality, experience powerful Westernized discourses about moral mothering and fathering.

According to Hayes (1996), mothers daily experience pressure for their mothering to conform to the ideology of **intensive mothering**. Gaining traction from the 1900s onward, this ideological discourse prescribes mothering as necessarily involving incredible amounts of time, devotion to the child's well-being first and foremost and regardless of cost, and reliance on expert knowledge. Transforming in tune with mothers' realities over time, the contemporary manifestation of this ideology places great importance on mothers' valuing of paid work as a component of fostering their children's well-being and the subsequent need to find the best expert child care to replace mothers' own care (Hayes 1996). "Good" mothers are ideal role models and creators of an environment for their children that provides for excellent social, physical, and emotional development (Gorman and Fritzsche 2002, as cited in Nelson 2006). Haw's (2015) qualitative research with mothers who engaged in cord blood banking reveals that the creation of a safe environment is even assumed before the child is born. Mothers who bank cord blood in case it is needed at a later date to treat a child's disease can be seen to display the ultimate selflessness assumed of "good" mothering. As Fox (2001) argued over a decade ago, society is also still organized around the assumption that women will want to be fully responsible for an infant's care. Mothers tend to be overwhelmingly represented in both culture and expert discourse as "naturally" suited to caring for infants, compared to fathers (Wall and Arnold 2007). Indeed, Wall's (2013) analysis of cultural representations of motherhood and children in *Today's Parent* magazine in the 1980s and 2000s revealed a shift in magazine content that suggested a growth in intensive mothering discourse; mothers, for example, were assumed to work for pay in articles in the 2000s but were increasingly encouraged (or reminded) to put children first, work second.

"Good" fathering has been long associated with economic provision. Historically, "good" fathers were first and foremost constructed as economic providers to their children, a quality emblematic of the **patriarchy** as associated with a nuclear family model. Today, economic provisioning is still considered central to a father's role in most segments of society (Featherstone 2003). Others' perceptions of fathers' masculinity are tied to their apparent status and power associated with earning. Fathers additionally experience pressure to conform to **hegemonic masculinity** and therefore perform a particular and masculine style of fathering and are largely perceived as rational authority figures or as disciplinarians (Connell 1987; Connell and Messerschmidt 2005). Cultural discourses tend to position fathers as part-time or secondary parents, with their parenting fitting around their paid work attachment (Wall and Arnold 2007).

Some scholars do observe slight changes in the perception and practices of fathering, linked to an increased attention to fathers in the past decade (Este and Tachable 2009; O'Donnell, Johnson, D'Aunno, and Thorton 2005). Compared to mothers, fathers seem to be permitted more choices in terms of their care responsibilities; fathers can be mothers' helpers or children's playmates (Fox 2001). Chuang and Su (2009) find that fathers are active participants within families, not just mere helpers, when they engage in increased levels of caregiving, playing with children, and the doing of household chores.

In a qualitative longitudinal study, Brannen and Nilsen (2006) discovered that there is both change and continuity in the performance of fathering. They studied fathering by different generations of British men born between 1911 and 1931, 1937 and 1953, and 1962 and 1980, and discovered three models. Whereas "work-focused" fathers were fathers from all three generations whose lifestyles were primarily shaped by their paid work attachment, "family men" were fathers from the two older generations who split their time between paid work and child care. "Hands-on" fathers were only those fathers of the youngest generation; few of them had been main earners over the duration of their relationships with their partners. Brannen and Nilsen attribute the hands-on fathering by the younger fathers to weak labour market prospects for these men; fathering could be understood as caregiving, and caregiving was no longer thought as the exclusive domain of women (Brannen and Nilsen 2006).

Sociologist Andrea Doucet has conducted extensive qualitative research on fathering in Canada. Her own study of heterosexual fathers who are primary caregivers revealed these fathers as openly affectionate with their children (Doucet 2006, 2009). Doucet and Merla (2007) additionally discovered that stay-at-home fathers see important differences between their work as fathers and the work of mothers. Fathers did not strive to be a mother or to replace mothers but rather prioritized the promotion of children's physical, emotional, and intellectual independence and risk-taking, involved children in housework, and encouraged independent play. While fathers stressed positive traits of their fathering that matched hegemonic masculinity, they also fathered in ways that successfully integrated feminine psychological traits and skills such as softness and emotional literacy (Doucet 2009; Doucet and Merla 2007). According to Wall and Arnold (2007), there is considerable consensus that "new fathers" are fathers who are nurturing, develop close emotional relationships with children, and share the joy and work of caregiving with mothers. However, there is also considerable academic debate around the extent to which cultural expectations match with conduct of fathers (see also, LaRossa 1988), something that will become quite clear in the below section on paid and unpaid work. Meanwhile, Creighton et al.'s (2015) recent research clearly establishes that there are likely urban and rural differences to the extent that fathers adopt qualities of "new fathering." Their interviews with 32 Canadian heterosexual fathers in urban and rural settings led them to conclude that urban fathers seemed to adopt a more "gender neutral" approach to all aspects of parenting. Men who lived in rural settings seemed to conform more to conventional constructions of fathering, identifying themselves primarily as earners and their partners primarily as carers (Creighton et al. 2015).

Some mothers and fathers would maintain that they are simply parenting in ways that make common sense to them. However, according to psychologist Diana Baumrind's research, there are particular styles of parenting. *Authoritarian* parenting refers to parents who shape, control, and evaluate their children on the basis of a set of criteria or rules or behaviour. Parents know what is "right" and children are to obey them or experience punitive responses. *Authoritative* parenting emphasizes the use of rational, issue-oriented discussion to direct and guide children. Parents performing this style of parenting perceive children as capable of engaging in reasoning and encourage them to participate in discussions about how their behaviour may be changed. Finally, *permissive* parenting refers to parents who permit children to follow their own impulses, desires, and actions and offer little punitive intervention. Children are perceived to be capable of regulating their behaviour and though parents intervene, this is often in an accepting and affirmative manner; they are a child's resource rather than regulator (Baumrind 1966). Horvath and Lee's (2015) survey of North American research leads them to conclude that authoritative parenting is the most common style practised, and within psychological studies it has been found to positively impact children's psychosocial maturity, social relationships with peers and adults, autonomy, and academic achievement (Robinson, Mandleco, Frost Olsen, and Hart 1995).

New(er) styles of parenting have also emerged, concerning all stages from infancy to young adulthood. Coined by pediatrician William Sears, attachment parenting stresses the development of strong emotional intimacy with infants. This style of parenting is achieved through baby-wearing, breastfeeding on demand and for at least one year or more, and co-sleeping (Sears and Sears 2001). Considering university-aged and therefore *adult* children, some parents appear to be very involved in supporting their children's educational and future career outcomes, keeping in constant contact with them through email or smart phones (e.g. text messaging), a style known as "helicopter parenting" (LeMoyne and Buchanan 2011). While sharing some qualities with authoritative parenting, helicopter parenting differs in that parents may intrude in adult children's lives, e.g. making their decisions for them, rather than simply guiding them; this style can actually have the unintended consequence of negatively impacting students' well-being (LeMoyne and Buchanan 2011).

The everyday "hows" and "doings" of parenting are discursively mediated. Women and men who parent do so in the face of prescriptive discourses about "good" mothering and fathering. Whether parenting with someone else or alone, parenting involves consciously acting and behaving with an awareness that activities and behaviours will be perceived as conforming or not conforming to these ideas and the consequences of these perceptions. For example, the social construction of "good" mothering has become so extreme that mothers, especially those that engage in paid work, seem to be destined to be found wanting in some way (see also Wall 2013). This is despite the fact that considerable research does not find paid employment negatively impacts children's development (Nelson 2006:344). Gendered ideas about "good" mothering and "bad" fathering dovetail with actual practices or styles of parenting. In her qualitative study of mothers who breastfed children to "full-term" (approximately three to four years of age), Faircloth (2010) found that mothers' choices to breastfeed in this manner were shaped by expert, scientific discourses that promulgated "good" mothering by equating it with attachment parenting. According to Faircloth, the contemporary ideology of intensive mothering rests on the assumption of mothering performed in the style of attachment parenting. As historically conceptualized, "good" fathering, by contrast, may require parenting as per an authoritarian style. However, there are exceptions to these discursive constructions since newer practices of fathering seem more varied.

Culture and Diversity

Assuming all social groups equally practise parenting according to Westernized gendered discourses can result in overlooking cultural nuances and differences in parenting (Ochocka and Janzen 2008). For example, Ochocka and Janzen (2008) observe that immigrant Chinese and Chinese-American parents practised authoritarian parenting to a greater extent than Euro-American parents. However, while authoritarian parenting was found to predict poor school achievement among Euro-Americans, Chinese children were high achievers under this style. In this section, we focus on a sample of Canadian research that reveals how cultural values and behaviours are tied to "good" parenting in particular racial/ethnic groups.

From a life course perspective, the parenting practices of Indigenous families today are historically contextualized by past cultural genocide, including dispossession of land, mandatory placement of children in residential schools, and the removal of children from their families of origin through foster care or adoption (Fuller-Thomson 2005). Despite, or because of, these enduring troubles, Indigenous communities continue to practise parenting according to deeply engrained traditions and values. Among Indigenous families in Canada, a great deal of importance is placed upon the role of community (Macdougall

For more on Indigenous families, see "Gender Roles and Families" in Chapter 12, pp. 246–9.

2010). While children are recognized as having biological parents, social parents, including extended family members, elders, and neighbours play a prominent role in raising and rearing children (Anderson 2001). According to Anderson (2001), the idea that children are welcome is a persistent and traditional value among Indigenous cultures.

In recent research, Indigenous feminist scholar Angele Alook explored the education, paid work, and family experiences of young adult Indigenous women and men in Alberta who migrate from reserve to city in their decisions about and pursuit of these life course trajectories. The Daily Life box below illustrates Angele's own perspective on family as an Indigenous woman and how her life course transitions intimately connect her to her community.

Other research shows that Indigenous fathers may hold the same traditional values but may face a number of challenges to their involvement in parenting. Compared to other men, Indigenous men are more geographically mobile and nine times more likely to be incarcerated (Ball 2009:30). When adult parents are incapable of parenting because of mental health problems or drug addictions, grandparents can play important instrumental roles. In raising their grandchildren, they are responsible for their mental and physical care and especially to socialize them to cultural traditions and teaching (Fuller-Thomson 2005).

Daily Life
Conceptualizing Family . . .

I remember once hearing in one of my graduate classes, the idea that "your race is your family," meaning your racial identity is influenced by your family relations and your ancestry. So I am going to explain my family background. I am a member of Bigstone Cree Nation and my husband is a Black Canadian with family from Jamaica and Trinidad. We have a mixed race daughter and a mixed race son. In addition, I have a stepson and we are raising my niece who is a very fair-skinned Cree. We have been married for almost a decade, and we have acquired several children in our home, including several other nieces and nephews over on a regular basis. The joining of our two cultural backgrounds has been a challenge at times. My husband claims my culture is too matriarchal and I have felt his culture is too patriarchal. Despite all the gender studies literature I have read, being a member of this family has often tested my feminist values. We've gone through phases where I have been the primary breadwinner while supporting his education, and phases where he has been the primary breadwinner supporting my education, and throughout trying to find as much equal division of labour in our home, trying to value the paid and unpaid labour that we both do.

I have come to realize that being a married couple with children, that our family is an institution in our community. We are parents that try to teach our children about equality, sharing, fairness, and caring for one another. We also strive to have a fairly stable home, we both work in careers we enjoy, and we are in a committed relationship. Unfortunately this means our home has become an institution in our extended families (or maybe we are fortunate for this). Our siblings drop their children off on weekends, our relatives from the reserve treat our home like a hotel when they are in town, and if there is any sensed instability or conflict in our marriage it is cause for concern for our extended family because our home has become this institution. As our family is a valued institution in both our extended families, we also receive help from others when needed. Our home has become an institution of teaching, caring, and providing for others.

Source: Alook (2016:110). Quoted from source.

The experience of immigration is a major life course event and one that is especially revealing of how cultural norms and values impact the everyday performance of parenting young children. Newcomers to Canada experience a social context with cultural norms about child-rearing that may be very different than those in one's country of origin, as well as stereotypes about their culture and family practices (see, for example, Walton-Roberts and Pratt 2005). Settling into life in Canada can be made difficult if economic hardship accompanies the first few years of residence and subsequently creates family troubles like marital instability (Liu and Kerr 2003).[2] Often new immigrant parents must negotiate their children's desires to integrate into broader culture with their own desires to transmit cultural values according to their past styles of parenting (Mitchell 2009). This can lead to family and parent–child conflict (Hassan, Rousseau, Measham, and Lashley 2008). Alternatively, values and practices associated with parenting may change in accordance to new social surroundings of a host country (Chao 1994, as cited in Ochocka and Janzen 2008).

For more on refugee families see "Settlement of Refugees in Canada" in Chapter 11, pp. 228–31.

Este and Tachable (2009) explored the meaning of fatherhood among refugee Sudanese men in Canada. Fathers held strong beliefs that their roles were to instruct their children about the difference between right and wrong and to pass on Sudanese customs and traditions. Because of changes in their family lives as a result of immigration, some fathers assumed a greater role in raising their children in Canada than in their country of origin. Hassan et al. (2008) observed that Caribbean immigrant families are often headed by women who assume both economic and child care responsibilities. For immigrant Caribbean families, the family unit can often be perceived as a source of protection against danger and transmission of filial respect is emphasized (Hassan et al. 2008).

Within South Asian families, familial obligations can be commonly expected to supersede personal desires. Caregiving is also expected to be necessarily multi-generational, involving loyalty to kin beyond one's immediate family of origin, and primarily the purview of women. For example, Spitzer et al.'s (2003:277) study of migrant Chinese and South Asian women revealed that all respondents shared the perception that women, particularly daughters and daughters-in-law, were the "most appropriate caregivers for the elderly and children." Additionally, most respondents rejected the idea of caregiving as a burden despite its association with their exhaustion, ill-health, or anxiety.

Among Chinese families, parenting may be performed in line with generational assumptions about power and responsibility. For Ho (1981, cited in Chuang and Su 2008), Confucianism values of social harmony, clear lines of authority, and the meeting of collective needs are historically embedded in familial relationships including gender expectations, such as the idea that fathers hold power and authority within the family. Some research studies support the notion of "strict father, warm mother" but others reveal higher levels of father involvement in children's lives (Chuang and Su 2008). Chuang and Su (2009) compared the fathering of immigrant Chinese-Canadians and mainland Chinese fathers. They found that mainland Chinese and immigrant Chinese-Canadian fathers were actively involved in making everyday decisions about their children's needs. While fathering practices seem to be shifting, other generational dynamics of support, such as filial responsibility and respect for aging parents, have remained fairly constant. Mainland Chinese and Chinese-Canadian parents both relied on their own adult parents for advice and support (Chuang and Su 2008).

Besides Westernized gendered discourses, rich traditions and values associated with particular cultural groups also inform the performance of parenting. Not surprisingly, clashes can emerge when mothers and fathers have to reconcile competing cultural claims about parenting. Indeed, migration often results in the reconfiguration or renegotiation of familial and gender roles as immigrants encounter different values and new challenges (Spitzer et al. 2003).

Questions for Critical Thought

Consider this hypothetical example: a family of five (mother, father, and three children under the age of eight) have newly immigrated to Canada and only the father can find minimum waged employment to support the family. How might the performance of parenting be especially challenging for these parents?

Paid and Unpaid Work

The parenting of young children involves engagement in paid or unpaid work including household work and child care. Women's and men's workforce and family trajectories have become more similar over time; few couples are able to make ends meet through the earning of one partner alone. Between 1976 and 2015, the proportion of dual earner families with a child under the age of 16 increased from 36 per cent to 69 per cent (Statistics Canada 2016b). The percentage of Canadians aged 16 to 64 who were employed full-time has also increased, from 62 per cent in 1976 to 66 per cent in 2014. As full-time workers, women have begun to fare better in the labour market than men—between this same period, women's engagement in full-time employment increased, from 40 per cent in 1976 to 57 per cent 2014, whereas men's participation decreased, from 84 per cent in 1976 to 74 per cent in 2014 (Hou, Schellenberg, and Morissette 2015).

Paid work provides the main source of income for the majority of family households. Engaging in paid labour permits parents to feed, clothe, and shelter their children as well as facilitate children's engagement in recreational or leisure activities or purchase child care services. Although the median income of economic families with children has increased by between 1999 and 2012, differences emerge in regard to how sufficiently paid work enables parents to achieve these necessities of family life.[3] Dividing families into five income quintiles, Uppal and Larochelle-Côté (2015) find that families at the bottom one fifth of the distribution experienced only a 5.0 per cent increase in their median earnings between 1999 and 2012. In contrast, the one fifth of families at the top of the income distribution experienced a 20.7 per cent increase. Considering family wealth, measured as total assets minus total debt, Uppal and Larochelle-Côté (2015) discovered that families in 2012 in the top quintile had 11.9 times (up from 9.1 times in 1999) the wealth of families in the bottom quintile. Families considered low income and with no wealth, predominantly lone-parent and immigrant families, experienced little change in their situations between 1999 and 2012. Many parents are working for pay full-time and full-year in a societal context increasingly characterized by income security for some and little change in income security for others.

Indeed, having a job is not a guarantee that parents will be able to adequately care for children and other family members. Some parents are already experiencing or risk experiencing worse economic conditions and the challenges associated with these. According to Fleury and Fortin (2006), one in ten adults were among the working poor[4] for at least one year between 1996 and 2001, a finding partially attributed to family characteristics, including number of earners and children. In the city of Toronto, there has been a gradual increase in the working poor between 2000 and 2012 (Stapleton with Kay 2015). Workers who were the sole earner in their family were at greater risk of financial difficulty and this risk increased with the number of children in their care.

Parents' incomes from paid work are connected to child poverty. In 2005, just over 2 per cent of children in couple families with two full-time full-year earners experienced low income. In couple families with one earner, 5.6 per cent of children experienced low income. Female lone-parent families with one full-time full-year earner fared worse than male lone-parent families, with 9.9 per cent of children versus 5.9 per cent of children experiencing low income (Statistics Canada 2008). When parents cannot provide their children with adequate economic resources, children's health and well-being is affected (Fleury and Fortin 2006).

For more on family poverty see "Low Income, Family Change, and Child Poverty" in Chapter 10, pp. 212–13.

Income inequality additionally characterizes the paid work performed by mothers and fathers. Women's increased engagement in paid labour does not change their unequal earnings comparative to men. Although women's tendency to engage in more part-time work, because of caregiving responsibilities, does partially account for their lower earnings,[5] even when both women and men worked full-time full-year in 2008 women's yearly salaries were less than those of men (Statistics Canada 2010). Women employed full-time full-year earned 73.55 cents for each dollar earned by men according to recent data Statistics Canada provided to the *Globe and Mail* (Grant 2016). Mothers may be committed to paid work in the same way as fathers but reap fewer economic rewards associated with this commitment. Moreover, today's mothers are more likely to be balancing the caring of their very young children with paid work. According to Uppal (2015), 36 per cent of mothers with children under the age of five years worked for pay as single earners in 2014, compared to 43 per cent who were part of dual earner families. Focusing on generational cohorts of women aged 25 to 64, Pacaut, Le Bourdais, and Laplante (2011) observe that mothers of two or more children, born between 1967 and 1976, re-engaged with the labour market to a greater extent than mothers born between 1937 and 1946. They speculate that this difference by cohort is linked to the greater availability of parental leave today (Pacaut, Le Bourdais, and Laplante 2011). Compared to fathers, mothers still engage in stay-at-home parenting for longer periods of time and to a greater degree.

Even if they are engaged in paid work, women perform the bulk of caregiving for infants and toddlers within families. Within two-parent families where heterosexual couples are married or cohabiting, women spend more time engaged in domestic labour and child care than men (Beaujot and Ravanera 2009; Gazso 2009). Generationally, the division of paid and unpaid work is slow to change. Considering nuclear families, Marshall (2011) focused on differences in time spent in housework and child care by generation. Women born between 1981 and 1990—Generation Y—spent about 30 minutes less time on housework per day in 2010 compared to women born between 1957–66, late Baby Boomers, in 1986 (two hours and 29 minutes versus three hours, respectively). Late Baby Boomer men spent one hour on housework in 1986 but Generation Y men spent just one and a half hours in 2010 (Marshall 2011).

There have been some changes in fathers' time spent in paid and unpaid work. More fathers are doing more unpaid work within the home (McMullin 2005). Using time-use data from the General Social Surveys conducted in 1992, 1998, and 2005, Beaujot and Ravanera (2009) find increases in the numbers of husbands who perform more unpaid work than their wives (from 1.7 per cent to 3.0 per cent) and in the numbers of couples who equally perform the same amount of time of paid and unpaid work. However, others observe that the experience of providing care is different in kind and quality for fathers. Whereas women spend a greater proportion of their care time in physical care activities (bathing, feeding), research has shown that fathers may engage in play, talking, educational, and recreational activities (Craig 2006).

As well, Ornstein and Stalker's research suggests that the age of children particularly matters to how fathers spend their time. Analyzing data from the 2006 Census, Ornstein and Stalker (2013) discovered that parents with children between age one and five continue to organize paid and unpaid work unequally. The most popular strategy for managing paid work and child care was what they termed "traditional": among 40 per cent of the couples, the mother did not work for pay and engaged in child care and the father worked full-time. Nonetheless, more fathers are choosing to exit paid work and take on full responsibility for their young children's care. In 1976, 1 in 70 fathers were stay-at-home dads. In 2015, 1 in 10 were (Statistics Canada 2016). According to Doucet and Merla (2007:462) fathers choose to stay at home for a number of reasons, including their partner's employment and/ or encouragement from their partner to share caregiving work, preference of home care over daycare, and lack of affordable child care facilities.

For more on the challenges associated with lone parenthood, see "The Lone-parent Family and the Recombined Family" in Chapter 6, pp. 128–9.

Balancing paid and unpaid work is particularly challenging for lone parents. The number of lone mothers engaged in paid work has increased over time (Ferrao 2010) but not all mothers earn wages that sufficiently raise them above low income cut-offs (LICOs). Some lone parents receive social assistance to top up their monthly pay. However, the overall conditions of receiving welfare can further limit their ability to become fully self-sufficient. When lone mothers on social assistance are perceived as employable, they are subject to mandatory education, programming, or job searches in order to remain eligible for monthly benefits (Gazso 2007a). They are also expected to exit social assistance as soon as they find paid work. It is often the case that family care responsibilities hinder their employability efforts and vice versa. For example, Breikreuz, Williamson, and Raine (2010) find that parents cannot always access suitable daycare for their children and so cannot participate in paid work as they may wish. Should they not participate in paid work in the ways dictated by the conditions of their social assistance receipt, they risk being expelled from the caseload. Parenting alone and on social assistance is made more challenging because this parenting is performed in circumstances of poverty, regulated by the government, and without adequate social support, a point discussed further in the next section.

Among gay and lesbian couples who parent young children, researchers find that the conventional gendered division of paid and unpaid work is largely irrelevant. Parents in these families engage in a sharing of paid and unpaid work in different ways. Rather than attempting to conform to traditional gender roles, partners negotiate a fair division of paid and unpaid work by accounting for such things as personal aptitude and desire (Dunne 2000; Sullivan 2004); in female couples, perceptions of work–family conflict can even be reduced by the extent that mothers are "out" in their workplaces (Tuten and August 2006).

The same has been found for male couples. In their study of new gay fathers, Schacher, Auerbach, and Silverstein (2005) discovered that gay couples experienced conflict or role strain when deciding who would relinquish engagement in full-time paid work in order to be the primary caregiver of children. Fathers' shared commitment to "hands-on" fathering was what enabled them to resolve this conflict and "de-gender parenting" or resist seeing roles and duties as ascribed by gender. The gay and lesbian parents who were the focus of these studies seem to more fairly navigate the timing and division of paid labour market attachment and/or full-time responsibility for child care.

Engaging in paid and unpaid work are major responsibilities of parents of young children. The everyday practice of parenting involves a constant act of juggling paid work with other time demands associated with raising young children, such as household labour (e.g., laundry, preparing meals, cleaning) and caregiving (e.g., bathing, feeding). This juggling can prove more difficult when income earned from paid work is insufficient for the meeting of family needs or when parents do not equally participate in housework and child care responsibilities.

For more on child care, see "Child Care" in Chapter 9, pp. 187–9; also see Chapter 15.

Social Policy and Other Supports for Child Care

From a life course perspective, the everyday performance of parenting is interlinked with the caregiving provided by others. Whether a lone parent or partnered with someone else, most parents are supported in their provisions of child care by other people or government programs. Although there is diversity in terms of how families manage caregiving for children and other dependents depending on family members' culture and "race"/ethnicity, conventional kinship ties are still incredibly important to provisions of child care in the early years of parenting (Lashewicz, Manning, Hall, and Keating 2007). Family members across generations provide important sources of physical, financial, and emotional support, ranging from grandparents providing child care relief for a few hours a week to adult children receiving financial aid from their parents (Gazso and McDaniel 2015). Grandparents, particularly grandmothers, are likely to be more involved in raising grandchildren if their child is absent from the household; often, grandparent involvement in parenting a grandchild occurs as an alternative to foster care (Pearson et al. 1997, as cited in Gladstone, Brown, and Fitzgerald 2009). Support structures can include others not part of conventional kinship ties (Beck-Gernsheim 2002; Gazso and McDaniel 2015), as is common with LGBTQ individuals creating "chosen families" (Sullivan 2004).

Currently, there is no national child care program in Canada. Responsibility is often split between federal and provincial or territorial jurisdictions, which produces significant variation in the cost, quality, and source of child care (Albanese 2009). Parents rely on a range of paid services in their communities. Care outside of the home can include licensed care within daycare centres or home care, or unlicensed care within someone else's home. According to Beaujot and Ravanera (2009), children most often received care in the home of a non-relative or from a daycare centre in 2002–3. Fifty-four per cent of children ages six months to five years were in some form of non-parental care compared to 42 per cent in 1994–95 (Bushnik 2006). Compared to two-parent families, lone parents make greater use of licensed, regulated daycare centres, regardless of their employment status (Beaujot and Ravanera 2009). This is partially explained by lone parents' economic situations. Lone parents are more likely to have lower incomes than two-parent families and so are more likely to be eligible to have the cost of their child's licensed daycare subsidized by the government.

Differences emerge when the child care accessed by parents within the province of Quebec is compared to other Canadian provinces. Unlike other provinces, Quebec regulates affordable child care to all parents regardless of their incomes; parents pay $7 a day for child care (Albanese 2006). More Quebec parents who work full-time for pay rely on some form of child care than other parents, 83.7 per cent versus 70.1 per cent, respectively; 42.2 per cent of Quebec children are in daycare versus 21.2 per cent of other Canadian children (Beaujot and Ravanera 2009). Moreover, while other provincial governments are becoming less involved in the provision of child care services, Quebec is the exception as it has been revamping policies to "reflect the increased need and desire to assist families, and women in particular, with the mounting challenges associated with juggling paid and unpaid work" (Albanese 2009:120).

Excluding the unique situation of child care in Quebec, affordable and high quality child care, especially that which is provided by licensed providers such as Early Childhood Educators, is scarce and expensive across Canada. As well, there is a shortage of subsidized child care in Canada, which creates a barrier for those seeking employment and compromises family budgets. Subsidies may not cover the full cost of child care. For example, in Ontario, subsidies are paid by municipal service managers to regulated (both non-profit and for-profit) child care providers on behalf of eligible parents (Canadian Council of Social Development 2009). Municipal service managers are able to set their maximum subsidy below full cost and do so in many communities. According to Albanese (2009), the need for non-parental care has increased along with child care fees but the number of government-regulated and licensed daycare spaces do not meet this demand. In 2014, 24.9 per cent of Canadian children aged 0–12 years could be accommodated by licensed child care centres (Friendly, Grady, Macdonald, and Forer 2015).

Parents may qualify for other tax benefits that support their caregiving of young children. As noted earlier, all parents with children under the age of six were entitled to the Universal Child Care Benefit of $1,200 a year. The UCCB was intended to support families with the costs of their child care choices. Low-income parents may be eligible for the new Canada Child Benefit but even this eligibility may not profoundly change their ability to afford child care, especially if they desired licensed day care and cannot find a subsidized space in their communities.

Even without an immediate, physical connection with children, parents may be caring for young children from afar. This is perhaps best illustrated by the experiences of migrant workers who maintain a constant emotional connection with their children despite the impossibility of physical connection. Canadian immigration policy provides opportunities for persons from developing countries to migrate to Canada for paid work in agriculture and/or as domestic workers. Migrant workers who are mothers or fathers are often separated from their young children for lengthy periods of time. The everyday parenting of young children is then performed most often by other family members. However, migrant workers also engage in **transnational parenting**. Remittances sent home to families provide for children and are of benefit to the wider economy of a migrant worker's country of origin. Mothers and fathers also provide emotional support to children through telephone or internet communication (e.g., Skype). Bernhard, Landolt, and Goldring (2008) find that this performance of transnational parenting by Latin American mothers is often associated with guilt, tension, shame, and isolation. Brigham's (2015) qualitative study reveals that Jamaican mothers' paid work as domestic workers, and their children's care, is supported by others back home but mothers can still feel the pull of intensive mothering ideology and, thus, guilt and anxiety over their not caring for children themselves. Tension surrounding this guilt and anxiety can be further exacerbated by mothers' undocumented migrant status. Transnational parenting can produce short-term benefits for families in economic need but can have long-term consequences of fragmenting family ties.

The caring of young children involves more than parent–child interactions. Other people assist in the raising of Canada's children today. Not all parents can easily find or afford child care, and this suggests that our policy system for child care is woefully inadequate.

Conclusion

Deciding to parent and then raising young children constitute an important period in some people's life courses, one that is shaped by and linked to gender socialization and interactions with others, development of gender identity, educational decisions and pathways, opportunities in the labour market and workforce trajectories, and available supports from the government. The choice to parent must be understood as a choice made in view of other opportunities or constraints. For example, as we have seen, some women and men may desire to parent but place this choice on hold for the time it takes them to gain particular educational credentials and achieve a semblance of income security—other important stages in their life course.

Once a person becomes a mother or father, no matter how this is achieved, their own identities and life courses change, particularly because of the newfound reality of dependent children. Parenting also requires re-imagining one's identity as a parent in the midst of powerful messages about how one should parent. For some parents, dominant Western images of and ideas about parenting must be reconciled with their other specific cultural norms and values. Different cultural groups within Canada have their own historical traditions and practices associated with caring for and raising children. And families migrate to Canada with their own cultural capital on parenting. Ideas about parenting and the actual practice of parenting can be culturally diverse. No matter their "race" or ethnicity, individuals' parenting practices are shaped by past cultural conventions and new ideas about parenting (e.g., attachment parenting) that are popularized in media.

Parenting has also been shown to be interconnected with the meeting of daily needs, for food, shelter, and clothing. The majority of parents engage in paid work in order to care for their children. A mother or father's paid labour informs the child care choices they make. One parent usually stays at home for a period of time in order to provide full-time care, more frequently women, at the risk of gendered power imbalances. In nuclear families, fathers do still spend more time in paid work than mothers. In two-parent families where both parents engage in paid work, most need affordable and adequate child care services during their children's younger years. For many parents, finding good child care is a major source of stress.

To conclude, this chapter has employed a life course perspective to highlight the performance and act(s) of parenting in our current Canadian context. Choosing to parent is a major life course decision, one that has implications for parents' lives—everyday.

Study Questions

1. How does the life course perspective encourage us to understand parenting as but one transition in some individuals' lives?
2. From a life course perspective, how can we see parenting as a series of everyday events or activities?
3. What seems to shape an individual's decision to parent?
4. Consider the concepts of intensive mothering and helicopter parenting. How are these two concepts similar or different? How might they be experienced by parents differently at different stages of their and their children's life courses?
5. What is transnational caregiving? What challenges do parents performing transnational caregiving face that mothers and fathers who live with their children in the same residence do not?
6. How might the child care experiences of lone-parent families be different from those of two-parent families?

Further Readings

Epstein, Rachel, ed. 2009. *Who's Your Daddy? And Other Writings on Queer Parenting*. Toronto: Sumach Press. This edited collection explores what it means to parent from a queer perspective.

Fox, Bonnie. 2009. *When Couples Become Parents: The Creation of Gender in the Transition to Parenthood*. Toronto: University of Toronto Press. This thought-provoking book analyzes the gendered division of labour as it emerges or does not in couples as they move from late pregnancy into early parenthood.

Gazso, Amber, and Susan McDaniel. 2015. "Families by Choice and the Management of Low Income through Social Supports." *Journal of Family Issues* 36(3): 371–95. This article explores the important role that fictive kin—not just biological kin—relationships play in supporting low income parents' experiences providing and caring for their children and families.

Kelly, Fiona. 2013. "One of These Families Is Not Like the Others: The Legal Responses to Non-normative Queer Parenting in Canada." *Alberta Law Review* 51(1): 1–20. This article explores the extent to which the Canadian court system has changed in its accommodation of the parenting rights of queer couples.

Man, Guida, and Rina Cohen, eds. 2015. *Engendering Transnational Voices: Studies in Family, Work, and Identity*. Waterloo: Wilfrid Laurier Press.
This edited collection is devoted to understanding the identities and everyday practices of individuals who participate in transnational caregiving; attention is placed on how families and paid and unpaid work become implicated in this caregiving.

Ranson, Gillian. 2010. *Against the Grain: Couples, Gender, and the Reframing of Parenting*. Toronto: University of Toronto Press.
This exciting book explores how parents work against structural and conventional understandings of mothering and fathering in rearing and caring for their children.

Key Terms

Census families The Statistics Canada definition that equates family with a same- or opposite-sex married or common-law couple, with or without children, or a lone-parent family.

Hegemonic masculinity An image of heterosexual masculinity that is socially constructed to achieve the domination of women and other masculinities.

Heteronormativity The social construction of gender and sexual identities and gender and family relations as distinctly heterosexual and the concomitant normalization of this in discourse.

Homonormativity Refers to the apparent queer assimilation to classist and other privileged definitions and practices of family and gender relations, constructed through the lens of heteronormativity.

Intensive mothering An ideology that prescribes mothering as necessarily involving incredible amounts of time, money, and devotion to a child's well-being, including the reliance on expert knowledge.

Low income cut-off (LICO) A relative measure of low income in which a family is deemed to fall within the low-income category if they spend a greater percentage of their household income on food, clothing, and shelter than the average family.

Nuclear family This is commonly defined as a heterosexual couple with children, i.e. husband, wife, and children.

Patriarchy Refers to the power, authority, and privilege associated with men and ascribed in social interactions and institutions.

Skip-generation household Refers to the phenomenon of grandparents raising grandchildren in households in absence of the adult parents.

Transnational parenting Practices of parenting and caregiving for a child or children, such as providing financial and emotional support, performed by migrant parents who live in countries other than their country of origin, where their child or children still reside.

Welfare state A system of bodies of governance (e.g. federal, provincial) that offer social protection or security to citizens by redistributing, organizing, and ordering social policies and services (e.g. health or child care) according to the agendas of the elected political party.

Notes

1. This chapter focuses on persons who have chosen to deliberately change their life course by having and raising children rather than those who become parents through an unexpected or unplanned pregnancy.

2. Prejudice and discrimination and/or devaluation of foreign education credentials can contribute to immigrants' greater initial earnings deficiency when compared to other Canadians. For example, immigrant women are often concentrated in lower-wage positions in the sales and service industry despite the fact that they are overqualified for these positions (Spitzer et al. 2003). However, as immigrants become familiar with the requirements of their new country's labour markets, this economic hardship can wane (Liu and Kerr 2003).

3. Economic families include all persons related by blood, marriage, or adoption and living in the same dwelling.

4. The working poor are defined as people aged 18 to 64 who engage in paid work for a minimum of 910 hours per year and experience low income according to the market basket measure (MBM).

5. Other structural factors like occupational segregation by gender and/or glass ceilings inhibit women's advancement to higher levels of management and impact their earnings.

 Interested in finding out more? Visit www.oupcanada.com/Albanese4e for access to a list of recommended websites for this chapter.

Separation and Divorce
Fragmentation and Renewal of Families

CRAIG MCKIE

LEARNING OBJECTIVES

- To understand that family breakdown and divorce are separate processes

- To appreciate that many Canadians are choosing not to marry and thus do not require divorce if their relationships dissolve

- To learn that divorce has become increasingly easily available since 1968

- To discover that family breakdown has unfavourable consequences and that these consequences may be made more difficult by a bitter divorce

- To recognize that families that break down often experience a substantial decline in their standard of living

- To understand that members of some religious communities may require additional religious divorce processes in addition to civil divorce in order for a person to remarry within those religious communities

- To show that forming new families brings a new range of adjustments for parents and children

---

Introduction

It is remarkable how rapidly the rights and freedoms of Canadians emerged in family matters and became established in law in the second half of the twentieth century. Canadians are now free to live, love, and cohabit as they wish, and, comparatively easily, to free themselves of previous spousal relationships should they so choose. In about 60 years, we have gone from a rigid and uncongenial divorce regime, which denied divorce with dignity to most Canadians, to the present era in which childless couples can jointly apply for an uncontested divorce by simple written assertion of marriage breakdown and can be certain of receiving one in short order without further complications.

For the first 100 years of its existence, Canadian law in the fields of marriage and of divorce was largely a direct continuation of English law inherited in colonial times prior to Confederation and subject to only minor refinements. English law itself was the product of hundreds of years of judicial decisions and occasional legislation and should be understood in the context of the doctrine of the Church of England. It held to the view that marriage was an indissoluble contract. The core principle was that marital breakdown was a violation of the terms of a legal contract and of a divinely blessed union. Violations, understood as at-fault marital offences, would give rise to claims for money restitution and damages, to community disapproval, and to the impairment of the ability to remarry. Nevertheless, leeway was left such that marriages could, with much difficulty, be legally dissolved in certain circumstances. Church annulments were also used to repair the moral blight of failed marriages in similarly strictly limited circumstances of flawed marriage process. In other words, in the English legal tradition, dissolution of a marriage was infrequent, difficult, and time consuming, but neither the state nor the Church was categorical in its rejection of undoing faulty marriages.[1] And how could it have been otherwise since the Church of England owed its very existence to Henry VIII's requirement for the marital dissolution and remarriage denied him by the Pope in Rome?

For more on historical perspectives on marriage, and on marital dissolution in the past, see "Families as Historical Actors" in Chapter 2, pp. 26–30; "Weddings in the Past" in Chapter 8, pp. 167–8; and "Gender Roles and Families" in Chapter 12, pp. 246–9.

Since the passage of the Divorce Act in 1968, Canada has mostly abandoned both the legal and ideological bases of inherited English law. In addition, provincial family legislation, which covers most separating couples, was completely overhauled when Canadians acquired a Charter of Rights and Freedoms that explicitly guaranteed freedoms of association, religious belief, and other fundamental freedoms that pertain indirectly to the right to live in almost any family context one desires. But divorce, and provincial family law processes, remain potentially litigious and adversarial in nature. In operation, divorce is not often about reaching a civil and peaceful redefinition of future interests. The objective is still a binding, written, and enforceable contract between former marital partners that redefines their obligations to each other in perpetuity.

The fundamental changes in Canadian divorce and provincial family law that occurred in the twentieth century went hand-in-hand with the rapid secularization of Canadian society. The arrival of same-sex marriage (and divorce) in the early twenty-first century is but one more step in the same direction. Few impediments now exist for Canadians to cohabit however and wherever and with whomever they wish, and to subsequently dissolve any such household without fear of legal prosecution. Restrictions are confined to **bigamy** and polygamy where multiple formal marriages are involved, and situations involving the sexual exploitation of minor children and close relatives, provided that they come to the attention of law enforcement authorities.

Questions for Critical Thought

Do you think that we will see a day when polygamy is legalized in Canada? What do you think would need to happen to lead to the change?

The social imperative to clarify and re-label a broken family arrangement remains strong. Clarity is required in sexual access issues, in support obligations, and in the child access rights that inevitably arise when families fragment, through separation or death, to become lone-parent families, then often to reformulate themselves within the context of new marital unions. While the English language lacks complex naming conventions for ex-kin and for step-kin, the law helps to clarify the obligations of complex multiple-family arrangements that have become common in recombined families today. They are more common in part because we typically live longer lives and, as a result, relationships have more time at risk than was the case a few generations ago. The feeling that it is necessary to rectify relationships and renew the nature of obligations seems widespread, though the substance of the rules-making systems differs widely around the world.

The nature of those codes of practice is still in flux. Theological conflict concerning separation and divorce still often derives from the medieval dispute within Christianity over whether marriage is a sacrament (and thus permanent) or not a sacrament and thus dissolvable by the state alone. There is much nuance in this argument as it has developed over the last 500 years, but contemporary Canadian practice clearly is informed by the latter, more liberal and permissive interpretation. The influence of religious views may still be seen in the prohibition of multiple concurrent marriages as bigamy is criminalized in Canada by Section 290 and polygamy by Section 293 of the Criminal Code, and in the requirement for an authoritative legal process to divorce.

While the power of religion over mating behaviour in Canadian society has considerably abated, its residue can still be seen in laws, and in the culture-based behaviour of some Canadians. Customs such as arranged marriages persist in this country though seldom seen or discussed openly. In the end, the personal freedoms conferred by the Charter of Rights and Freedoms and the common law system have allowed Canadians to be innovative in forming and dissolving their social relationships with little fear of ecclesiastical retribution.

No better example of incremental liberalization of family law can be cited than the contemporary extension of marriage rights and obligations, and the inevitable extension of divorce rights and the potential for child custody disputes to same-sex couples. The first Canadian divorce of a former same-sex married couple was awarded in Ontario in September 2004. The unhappy couple, whose marriage lasted only five days, wished to remain anonymous.

For more on same-sex marriage, see "Chain of Events in Canada" in Chapter 3, pp. 56–9.

The Legal Environment for Divorce in Canada

The terms and conditions for granting a divorce or a family law settlement are a reflection of the positive values attributed to an intact marriage (the contract being ended by divorce) or a non-marriage-based family (which is being dissolved and its assets distributed under provincial family law). Dissolution of either cannot seem to be too easy or costless lest offence be given to the ideals of the institution of the **family**. The way in which these values are expressed, however, is very much bound up in the conventional rhetoric of a particular era.

Until the end of the nineteenth century, a marriage was often in essence an economic transaction—one in which many women, if not legally property, passed without real personal autonomy from the protection of fathers, to that of husbands. Making up the transaction were tangible and intangible valuables such as a dowry, mutual enjoyment and protection, and the production of heirs to further the family fortunes. Assent by the actual marrying couple was most often a formal requirement for marriage but coercion was by no means uncommon. Indeed, some aspects of the traditional wedding in Canada still mirror this practice in ritual, as in the giving away of the bride by the father or a stand-in for the father. If we view a marriage in this historical context as a commercial transaction between one man as a seller and another man as purchaser, then it stands to reason that the premature end of a marriage was the occasion for the reassessment of the terms of the initial transaction. If, during a marriage, adultery took place, a male (but not a female) third party could be sued for money damages for what was termed "criminal conversation." Husbands and wives were bound by different standards of behaviour, and the still common expression "a double standard" was often used to signify how morality was applied differently to men and women in society.

For more on how marriages can be contractual building blocks of society, see discussion of Indigenous families and of unions between Indigenous women and European men during the fur trade in "Contact and the Fur Trade" in Chapter 12, pp. 249–50.

A marriage was thus not only a relationship between partners but also a contractual building block of society, somewhat akin to an agreement between clans, in which the state had a vital interest. A married couple had in some sense a capital value, which could be damaged through misbehaviour, and sanctions against (some) offenders were called for.

But in the early twentieth century this view began to change. In this new fashion, the interests of the state and of the parties to a failed marriage came to lie in the peaceful simplification of the contractual tangle. Resolution lay in affixing new and continuing financial obligations, assessing damages, and apportioning the assets of the dissolving union in an orderly and predictable fashion. Once these matters had been resolved, then the marriage contract itself could be dissolved (though the process was costly, tedious, and often involved perjury), in much the same way a business corporation is wound up and its charter surrendered.

Prior to 1968 in Canada, the availability of divorce was a provincial patchwork. Some provinces (for example, Nova Scotia) had their own divorce legislation and others (such as Quebec and Ontario) did not. This situation arose because divorce is a federal power under the Constitution, but successive Canadian governments failed to legislate in this area, leaving pre-Confederation statutes and practices still in place in some provinces. Persons living in provinces without divorce legislation who wished to obtain a divorce had to file a petition with the Senate of Canada providing proof of a marital offence (adultery, desertion, etc.) as grounds. A special committee of the Senate reviewed these petitions and, if it found that the evidence provided was sufficient, the marriage would be ended by an Act of Parliament. This system was unfair since it required the financial means to secure evidence and to file the petition, and also because it led to the falsification of grounds (such as trumped-up adultery with confirming photos). Almost all of this unseemly political theatre, a legacy of centuries of English legal practice, ended in 1968, though adultery remains a ground for divorce to this day.

Modern divorce legislation, which dates from the Divorce Act in 1968, has removed all vestiges of the financial interests of parents as injured parties and changed the conflict to one strictly between the divorcing partners themselves. It lessens the importance of the notion of marital offences (though many, such as bestiality, remained listed as causes for a divorce action from 1968 to 1985) and moved to a predominantly "no fault" basis of settlement that abandons the notion of assessment of damages. But the core of the process remains the same. The parties are obliged to demonstrate marriage breakdown, settle their financial obligations in some fashion, settle custody and residency arrangements for any minor children of the marriage, and divide the assets and future income according to guidelines set out by the state. If the partners are unable to reach a settlement on these issues, a court will do it for them in a judgment. In other words, and in spite of extensive reform, divorce is still treated in many respects as the dissolution of a failed corporation.

The Ebb and Flow of Marital Unions

Most Canadians find themselves in a marriage-like relationship at one time or another in their lives. A small proportion of people remain single for their entire lives. Figure 6.1 shows in rough detail some of the more prominent pathways. A newly formed couple has a number of choices. The partners may choose to cohabit on a short-term trial basis (the dissolution of which does not typically give rise to any legal process at all); they may form a durable common-law union (perhaps out of a preference or perhaps out of necessity if there is an impediment such as a previous undissolved marriage) so as to present themselves to

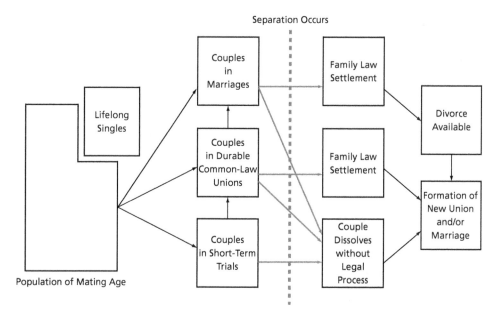

Figure 6.1   The Life Cycle of Marital Union Formation and Dissolution

the world as the equivalent of married. This latter status gives rise to legal consequences under provincial family law if the union dissolves and was of considerable duration. And, of course, the couple can marry, in which case both family law and divorce law apply if the marriage ends in a separation. Finally, members of any of these three types of unions can, if they are agreeable, ignore the law altogether and proceed to the formation of new unions (always provided that, if married, they cannot legally remarry). It goes without saying that many couples remain in one stage or another, perhaps for the life of one of the married couple, then perhaps to enter the cycle again as a widow or widower with a remarriage later in life. The death of a mate is similar in one sense to separation since it demands another kind of family law action, namely the distribution of the assets of the departed spouse, sometimes with probate. When a separated spouse dies, the two types of legal action can become intertwined.

Since the passage of the Divorce Act (1968), the number of divorces granted in Canada increased dramatically as an initial wave of people who could not obtain divorces easily under the previous divorce regime took advantage of the new liberalized legislation. Between 1971 and 1982, the annual total number of final decrees awarded rose from 29,684 to 70,430. A further revision of the Act in 1985 made marriage breakdown the sole grounds for divorce and eased the evidentiary standard to the demonstration of breakdown. Marriage breakdown is now indicated either by (1) separation of one year's duration; (2) adultery that can be proven; or (3) demonstration of intolerable mental or physical cruelty. Once again, after this revision the number of divorces increased, reaching a peak in 1987 at 96,200. Thereafter, total numbers levelled off and then declined (see Figure 6.2).

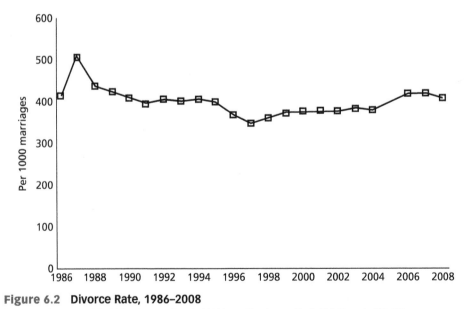

Figure 6.2   Divorce Rate, 1986–2008

Source: Employment and Social Development Canada 2014 (www4.hrsdc.gc.ca/.3ndic.1t.4r@-eng.jsp?iid=76).

From the summary of divorces granted for the years 1998–2008 (Table 6.1) we see that the number has held steady at approximately 70,000 (down from the all-time peak in 1987).[2] This represented a rate of 211 divorces for every 100,000 persons in Canada in 2008. The risk of married couples in Canada divorcing was found to reach a peak after their third anniversary (Kelly 2012: 8) and thereafter declines rapidly.

In about two thirds of cases, child custody decisions were privately settled without judicial intervention. Of the minority of cases that were decided by a court, about 45 per cent of decisions in 2004 were in favour of mothers. A further 46.5 per cent of the decisions involved joint custody, leaving a small minority of cases in which a father was awarded sole custody (about 8 per cent). Paternal sole custody remains unusual. Typically, paternal sole custody is awarded where older children close to the age of majority have expressed a preference (Statistics Canada 2008:73).

The 2011 General Social Survey (GSS) revealed that despite legal changes, the mother's home was still most often (70 per cent) the child's primary residence after a separation or divorce. Some 15 per cent reported that the child lived mainly with their father, while 9 per cent reported that the child had equal living time between the two parents' homes (the remaining 6 per cent indicated other living arrangements; Sinha 2014). The 2011 GSS also revealed that 44 per cent of parents whose child lived with their ex-partner most often saw their child less than three months over the course of the previous year,

Table 6.1 Divorces Granted in Canada, 1998–2008

	1998	1999	2000	2001	2002	2003	2004	2005	2006	2007	2008
Canada	69,088	70,910	71,144	71,110	70,155	70,828	69,644	71,269	74,681	73,167	70,226
NFLD and Labrador	944	892	913	755	842	662	837	789	831	969	907
Prince Edward Island	279	291	272	246	258	281	293	283	287	278	306
Nova Scotia	1,933	1,954	2,054	1,945	1,990	1,907	2,000	1,961	2,161	2,006	1,902
New Brunswick	1,473	1,671	1,717	1,570	1,461	1,450	1,415	1,444	1,527	1,499	1,458
Quebec	16,916	17,144	17,054	17,094	16,499	16,738	15,999	15,423	14,965	14,336	13,899
Ontario	25,149	26,088	26,148	26,516	26,170	27,513	26,374	28,805	31,983	31,242	29,692
Manitoba	2,443	2,572	2,430	2.480	2,396	2,352	2,333	2,429	2,221	2,279	2,241
Saskatchewan	2,246	2,237	2,194	1,955	1,959	1,992	1,875	1,922	1,983	1,850	1,858
Alberta	7,668	7,931	8,176	8,252	8,291	7,960	8,317	8,075	8,329	8,466	8,868
British Columbia	9,827	9,935	10,017	10,115	10,125	9,820	10,049	9,954	10,235	10,071	8,903
NWT including Nunavut	93	85	..	..	..	..	..	..	..	..	..
Northwest Territories	..	..	94	83	68	62	71	65	54	64	58
Nunavut*	..	..	7	8	6	4	15	10	21	12	26

*Nunavut totals are included under NWT for 1998 and 1999. Data for Yukon were not available at time of publication.

Sources: Adapted from Statistics Canada. *Report on the Demographic Situation in Canada 2005 and 2006, 2008*, Table A-6.3, Catalogue no. 91-209-X, p. 75. 2005 data from www.statcan.gc.ca/tables-tableaux/sum-som/l01/cst01/famil02-eng.htm. Unpublished data for the years 2006–2008 provided by Statistics Canada, Health Statistics Division Client Services, April 2012.

and some 18 per cent had no contact at all with their child. Most often, these were fathers (Sinha 2014). As to the probability of the marriages of Canadians ending in divorce, Statistics Canada has reported that the proportion of marriages expected to end in divorce by the thirtieth wedding anniversary was 40.7 per cent in 2008, 41.9 per cent in 2006, and 37.9 per cent in 2004 (Kelly 2012:8). These rates are marginally higher than in the previous decade, being well above a recent low of 34.8 per cent in 1997 (Statistics Canada 2002a), but much below the all-time high of 50.6 per cent established in 1987. The variability of these proportions reflects many factors, such as the extrapolation of the then-current annual divorce totals—but to be clear, the calculation does *not* predict the probability of divorce for any particular married couple.

The average age of those divorcing has gradually increased. By 2004, the average age at divorce was 43.0 years for men and 40.0 years for women (Statistics Canada 2008:72). Preliminary figures for 2008 suggest that the average age for divorcing men continues to rise (44.5 years) and also for women (41.9 years). This gradual increase reflects both the more advanced age at marriage and the increasing number of younger Canadians whose unions are not based on a marriage. For instance, Statistics Canada (2002) reported that by 2001, a clear majority of young Canadians aged 20 to 29 years had chosen *not* to base their first union on a marriage. Later, in the results of the 2006 GSS, Statistics Canada reported that there were approximately equal numbers of persons who terminated a marriage or a common-law union between 2001 and 2006, with approximately one million persons in each category (Statistics Canada 2008:72).

Questions for Critical Thought

Would you rather live in a country with "high" divorce rates or in a country with very low divorce rates? Why is that so?

For more on common-law unions and cohabitation, see "Changing Trends in the Diversity of Family Forms" in Chapter 1, pp. 3–10 and "Family Formation, Social Structures, and Change" in Chapter 4, pp. 74–8.

Within the total of about 70,000 divorces annually, the proportions in each province and territory are roughly the same year after year even though some provincial populations are growing rapidly as a result of immigration (for example, Ontario) and some have lost population as a result of out-migration (such as Newfoundland and Labrador). Since the overall number of Canadians has increased during the period (and more importantly, since the number of Canadians in the marriageable years has increased even more as a result of the general aging of the population), the rate of occurrence might seem to be going down. However, as we have seen, a rapidly increasing number of Canadians do not marry when they form their unions and are thus never in need of a divorce.[3]

Another part of the reason for this apparent decline in the incidence of divorce is to be found in the marked decrease in a type of marriage that was entered into in previous eras as a direct result of extramarital pregnancy. More than a few of our parents and grandparents married at an early age and in a great hurry because of just such a predicament. Today, there is far less stigma attached to having children outside of unions (and it

---

Box 6.1
Rules of Marital Dissolution

The rules pertaining to ending marriages can take two major forms: those embodied in religious assertions and those embedded in law. The two sets of imperatives can exist in conflict. Today, Canadians are free to form and to dissolve whatever alternative mating arrangements they might choose (with the exception that polygamy is forbidden by law).

Rules of marital union dissolution do several things:

- They define the circumstances under which marital pair bonds can be formally dissolved.
- They make adjudication of disputes systematic.
- They define which public figures are entitled to adjudicate marital disputes.
- They attach the obligations for familial support systematically and if necessary unilaterally, and they provide for enforcement of support orders.
- They define the obligations of ex-partners to each other.
- They re-divide social space into realms of those eligible for permissible new pair bonds, define those who are disallowed candidates, and criminalize violations of these boundaries, such as occur, for example, with incest.
- They create permissive space for future intimate behaviour and also define its limits.

---

is actually preferred as a desirable alternative, for some). Abortion is also legal and more readily available than in the past and there is significantly more access to contraceptives that have helped limit the number of panic marriages. Such hasty marriages would have been at great risk of a subsequent separation and divorce because of the youthfulness of the new partners, the tensions of having a young baby in the new household, and the improbability of such partners spending the next 65 years together, as life expectancy figures suggest they might.

Many separations today have no statistical or legal consequences. Further, the current divorce totals for a given year do not reflect the separation reality for that year. This is because of a considerable delay in obtaining a divorce from first filing—and first filing on separation grounds alone can only occur when a year has elapsed following the separation. Part of this delay is the result of satisfying the requirements of the legal process, part is a function of court capacity, and part is the general economic condition that affects the ability of the parties to pay the not inconsiderable costs for the process to proceed to conclusion. And it is certain that many in Canada who will be awarded divorces in Canada this year are already firmly locked into new relationships when the final decree is granted. For instance, for a decade, approximately 35 per cent of new marriages have included at least one previously married spouse. These provisos and qualifications all highlight the importance of considering relationship formation and dissolution (a process in social behaviour) separately from the divorce process (a process in law).

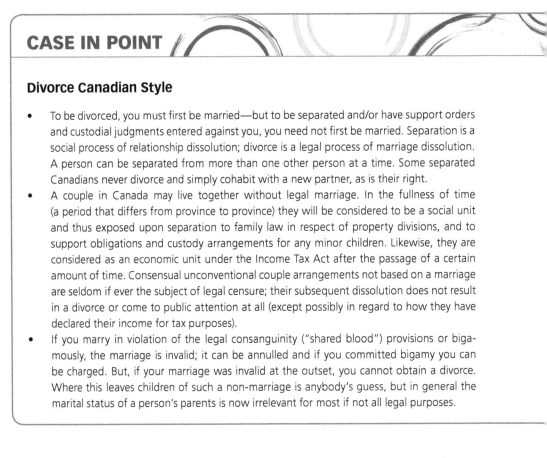

CASE IN POINT

Divorce Canadian Style

- To be divorced, you must first be married—but to be separated and/or have support orders and custodial judgments entered against you, you need not first be married. Separation is a social process of relationship dissolution; divorce is a legal process of marriage dissolution. A person can be separated from more than one other person at a time. Some separated Canadians never divorce and simply cohabit with a new partner, as is their right.
- A couple in Canada may live together without legal marriage. In the fullness of time (a period that differs from province to province) they will be considered to be a social unit and thus exposed upon separation to family law in respect of property divisions, and to support obligations and custody arrangements for any minor children. Likewise, they are considered as an economic unit under the Income Tax Act after the passage of a certain amount of time. Consensual unconventional couple arrangements not based on a marriage are seldom if ever the subject of legal censure; their subsequent dissolution does not result in a divorce or come to public attention at all (except possibly in regard to how they have declared their income for tax purposes).
- If you marry in violation of the legal consanguinity ("shared blood") provisions or biga-mously, the marriage is invalid; it can be annulled and if you committed bigamy you can be charged. But, if your marriage was invalid at the outset, you cannot obtain a divorce. Where this leaves children of such a non-marriage is anybody's guess, but in general the marital status of a person's parents is now irrelevant for most if not all legal purposes.

The Emergence of Shariah Law in Canadian Legal Institutions

Because Canadian society consists of individuals from many places and cultures, it is not possible to generalize about how Canadians actually live out their bonding and dissolution experiences. What we all experience in common is the law. Whether or not religious rules apply is now strictly a matter of individual choice, in striking contrast to earlier periods when the demands of religious edicts were sometimes harsh and imposed with considerable force. Some cultural practices that newcomers to Canada might otherwise be inclined to follow are ruled out by law, as is multiple marriage, or are granted no standing in law, as is religious divorce. Striking departures from this pattern have begun to emerge.

The gradual introduction of Islamic law (shariah) in Canada has raised some difficult questions. Usually, countries have one universal system of civil and criminal codes. Indeed, it is one of the elemental aspects of democracy that all citizens be accorded the same rights and privileges under law. Canada has always been an exception to this rule due to the acceptance of the Civil Code system in Quebec, an integral part of the historic bargain that brought Quebec into Confederation. Other slight departures of a purely

- Children of dissolved marriages or marriage-like unions most often reside with a female parent by well-entrenched habit. This is the result of decades of court decisions and custom both in Canada and elsewhere, which have held custody of and residence with the mother to be preferable. Joint custody now figures prominently in the Canadian picture, though not necessarily joint residence. Access and residential arrangements for dependent children are different from custody. Joint parenting arrangements may exist in the presence of a custody award to one parent.
- Foreign divorces may or may not be recognized in a Canadian province for the purposes of remarrying. As with the status of foreign marriages, out-of-country divorces are honoured out of courtesy most of the time, but an application for recognition in a Canadian province is required. The principle involved is referred to as judicial comity or the accommodation of foreign legal decisions. It might not extend to arranged marriages of minor children or to sham divorces obtained in a foreign country, however. Recent judgments also suggest that same-sex couples who live in another country in which such marriages are not permissible but who marry in Canada may not be able to secure a Canadian divorce. The government has announced the intention to amend the Civil Marriage Act to allow divorces upon mutual application in such cases. This would establish a second channel to divorce designed exclusively for same-sex, non-citizen, Canada-married couples with much narrower grounds than are available to Canadians.
- In Canada, contact with religious authority is not at all necessary for divorce or for the definition of support obligations that arise from dissolved relationships. Nevertheless, some religious communities maintain tradition-based non-legal parallel processes for divorce and for the adjudication of private domestic disputes. Religious divorces and annulments have, in general, no applicability or standing in the civil courts.

optional nature have existed for some time. Among these are the orthodox Jewish requirement for a religious *get*[4] or divorce before remarriage can occur, and a similar Roman Catholic requirement for a religious **annulment**. The *get* has been an especially vexing problem for some divorcing wives because it is granted (or not) exclusively by the husband of the failed marriage. Lawsuits of the common civil variety to compel the delivery of a *get* are not unknown.

The introduction of shariah principles in recent years seems to be qualitatively different. In reflection of the growing diversity of cultural origins present in Canadian society, disputes involving Muslim women's dowries, divorce, inheritance, and property ownership have been arriving in civil court.

In Ontario until 2006, judges might choose to refer such cases to an Islamic tribunal for binding arbitration, provided the parties were willing.[5] However, the matter of parallel justice systems in Ontario came to a head in early 2006 when the government of Ontario ultimately decided against continuing this practice. The Family Statute Law Amendment Act, passed on February 14, 2006, ensures that only Ontario family law can be used in binding arbitrations in Ontario. According to then Attorney General Michael Bryant, "the bill reaffirms the principle that there ought to be one law for all Ontarians" (Gillespie

2006). The previous May, members of the Quebec National Assembly voted unanimously to reject the use of Islamic tribunals in the Quebec legal system.

But in British Columbia, courts have on occasion upheld a Muslim woman's *maher*, a form of prenuptial agreement that defines in advance the amount of payment to be made upon subsequent marriage termination. Acknowledging that a *maher* has force and effect in Canadian courts as a contract (even though it has purely religious legitimacy) is a step in the direction of parallel legal systems, which is completely alien to the Canadian legal context. Although it does have some resonance with sentencing circles and restorative justice initiatives carried out in Indigenous communities across Canada with the blessing of the courts, some separation and divorce proceedings in Canada are taking place in a purely religious context, with judgments only subsequently confirmed (as in "rubber-stamped") in a conventional civil court document. Actions such as that of the province of Ontario in disallowing the use of religion-based tribunals in the settlement of civil disputes may simply drive these activities underground, with judgments officially registered with an Islamic court in another country for instance.

Questions for Critical Thought

What role do you think religion should play in divorce proceedings? Why do you think that?

The Emotional, Social, and Economic Fallout of Marital Discord, Separation, and Divorce

The effects of separation occur independent of any subsequent divorce process. Separation is a social fact, as are the factors that most often give rise to it. Divorce remains an *ex post facto* legal recognition of that social fact; it merely confirms the obvious, though it may have incidental stigmatizing effects on self-identity for those affected.

There is no denying that these effects often arise in the process of ending marital households, and, in particular, economic stress and emotional trauma impinge on the lives of any children of the household. Nevertheless, it would be a mistake to see these as arising from actions in the civil legal system, though that suffering and hardship can undoubtedly become more bitter there. Rather, the operations of provincial family law and the federal Divorce Act seek to bring both accountability and renewal of social futures to the separated couple, together with counsel and advice on reducing disharmony and fostering a positive environment for the fragments of any previously united family. Admittedly, the extent of the success of those efforts is mixed.

Recent literature tends to combine the effects of separation and divorce as if they were a single package—inappropriately. To start, many separations cannot give rise to a divorce because no marriage has been contracted. In conceptually consolidating the consequences of separation and divorce, much literature tends to attribute to divorce effects that might more appropriately be seen as the effects of relationship breakdown, or even results of the prior dysfunctionality of families that ultimately dissolve. In this admittedly complex situation, it cannot be easily established that many observed effects might not have occurred even if the couples in conflict had stayed together.

Keeping in mind this important caveat, what are the observed effects of family sep-arations? Reginald Bibby has addressed this question with published results from a large, classic study of Canadians in 2003 (Bibby 2005:65–70). Bibby finds a large number of impacts, among them (1) social strain with relatives who often disapprove; (2) decreased quality of workplace and school performance of the former spouses and of their children; (3) negative emotional impacts; and (4) financial hardship. But close to nine in ten of Bibby's separated/divorced respondents reported being happier on balance after the sep-aration than before it, though many are hesitant to cohabit again in light of their experi-ences. For the children of separation/divorce, Bibby reports a number of negative effects. For instance, he reports that two thirds of such children later in life report that family dissolution made life "harder for us," more than 50 per cent said they "didn't have enough money," and significant proportions reported feelings of inferiority, embarrassment, and weaker school performance, particularly for male children. Again, it is necessary to re-state that implicit comparisons to intact families rather than to a hypothetical situation had their own conflicted families persisted are shaky.

Anne-Marie Ambert noted the following measurable consequences of divorce: poverty (especially for women); higher incidence of depression, anxiety, and other emo-tional disorders; and increased risk of problems for children of divorced parents including such behaviour problems as fighting and hostility, lower educational attainment, adoles-cent pregnancies, and long-term risk for further marital problems (Ambert 2002:17–19).

Daily Life
How Children Make Friends in Cases of Joint Physical Custody

Prazen, Wolfinger, Cahill and Kowaleski-Jones (2011) assessed how joint physical custody arrangements affect an important component of child well-being, children's neighbourhood friendships. They interviewed 13 parents and 17 children (aged 5–11) in 10 families, selected via convenience and snowball sampling. Their findings suggest that joint custody arrange-ments did not overtly affect how children went about making friends. The children provided accounts of making friends "that did not seem to have anything to do with their custody arrangements. Children started their friendships differently, with initial invitations initiated by both the children themselves and their parents.

- "I just saw them playing and I went over to say, 'Can I play' and then that's how I got in touch with my friends."
- "There were these two kids, Chelsea and Erika, they were walking by and my mom said, 'Hey, do you want to play with them?' and I said, 'Okay' and then we kind of met."

Children's accounts of friendship formation appeared to reflect their immediate circum-stances, not their custody arrangements" (Prazen, Wolfinger, Cahill, and Kowaleski-Jones 2011:253).

More recent research, like that of Jolivet (2011), for example, notes that chronic conflict, in the marriage and in the post-divorce period, is often what leads to children's feelings of chronic stress, insecurity, shame, self-blame, sense of rejection, and guilt. She notes that high-conflict divorces roughly double the rate of behavioural and emotional adjustment problems in children.

Few researchers would deny that divorce negatively affects children, but many researchers also show that a number of mitigating factors, many of which are within the control of parents, can ameliorate the post-separation scenario for children. In fact, some parents have consciously adopted creative solutions and successful parenting arrangements that have made the lives of children experiencing divorce significantly better (Clark 2013; Jamison, Coleman, Ganong and Feistman 2014). When levels of conflict are low, children are best able to continue to go about their daily lives, succeed in school, and build strong peer relationships (see Daily Life box).

What is cause and what is effect? Looking at the precursors of family dissolution, for instance, one obvious dimension of family breakdown involves a tense and potentially violent style of relating between spouses in chronic conflict, a situation that might be one of the more important reasons why one spouse leaves the other. The tension and violence do not arise in isolation. Each might stem from anger at the behaviour of the other, or for oft-cited reasons of financial stress, medical condition, misuse of drugs and alcohol, or infidelity—the list of possible triggering behaviours would be very long indeed. If nothing else, domestic assault figures indicate that the marital household in conflict is one of the primary locations in which Canadian crimes of violence occur. In light of this fact, accounts of post-separation hardships must be weighed against the real risks of physical and emotional trauma, which are greatly diminished by separation.

For more on violence in families, see "Prevalence of Domestic Violence" in Chapter 14, pp. 302–3.

For the balance of family breakdowns, including those unions that never involved a marriage or overt violence, there are as many reasons for discord as there are partners. Unhappiness, frustration, and the "gradual growing apart" prominently mentioned by Bibby as a pre-eminent "cause" are persistent features of the human pair-bonding condition, as is perhaps the resolve to do better the next time. Though there could be no accounting of these causes and effects (and many are both causes and effects), it is certain that all spousal unions of whatever form are subject to such pressures from time to time.

Many children experience at least one episode of living in a lone-parent family at some time during their early years and they tend to experience such interludes as negative. Typically, separation brings with it a decline in standard of living as the expenses of maintaining two households instead of one are absorbed. This must also have effects in constraining what is financially feasible for the children of a dissolved union, and, of course, for the separated partners as well.[6]

The Lone-parent Family and the Recombined Family

The statistical snapshot of Canada's families taken every five years disguises the fact that many of today's families (or fragments therefrom) were once to be found in one of the other categories. For many, family structure is episodic over the long life course typical of today's Canadians: spells of coupledom are interspersed with periods of lone parenthood or being single. For example, in 2006, about half of female lone parents were divorced or separated, 30 per cent had never been married and about 20 per cent were widowed (Milan et al. 2011). Female lone-parent families made up about 18 per cent of all families with children under the age of 24 in both 2001 and 2006 (Milan et al. 2011).

For many years, and continuously since 1991, there have been at least one million lone-parent families in Canada at any given time (and about 1.4 million at the time of the 2006 Census), more than 80 per cent headed by a woman. At the time of each five-year Census, however, this group is not composed of all or even of predominantly the same people as in the previous Census. By any standard single mothers with dependent children are among the poorest of Canadians (by either asset or income measures). For example, in 2013, rates of entry into low income were high among tax filers in lone-parent families—many headed by women (11 per cent), tax filers who had immigrated to Canada less than five years before they filed (9 per cent), and tax filers who were between the ages of 18 and 24 (7.3 per cent) (Statistics Canada 2016).

For more on family poverty among female-headed lone-parent families, see "Has the Problem of Poverty Worsened in Recent Decades?" in Chapter 10, pp. 202–6.

The major difficulties for lone parents relate to child care (expenses, availability, hours of operation, and transport to and from), lack of skills and training (as a result of time spent out of school and/or the labour force), the employment practices of Canadian employers (inflexibility and lack of concern), adequacy and affordability of housing, the continuing effects of elevated stress, and, perhaps most importantly, the unfulfilled need for social and emotional support. Over the long run, low incomes produce low pension entitlements, fewer household and personal assets, and sparse interpersonal networks, all giving rise to the prospect of a potentially troublesome old age.[7]

Many millions of Canadians have experienced episodes of living as children in a lone-parent family. In earlier decades, this was most likely the result of the premature death of a parent, especially during wartime when in addition to mortality there may have been very prolonged absences of a parent without any certainty that he might some-day return. Today, life as a child in a lone-parent family is most likely the result of the separation of parents, whether or not they were ever married. With the passage of time, many lone parents establish new relationships—indeed, that may be the only way out of the lone-parenthood wilderness for many. A relatively small proportion of Canadian two-parent families with children now contain a step-parent, most often a stepfather who occupies the position by virtue of establishing a residential marital relationship with a separated mother and her child or children (Vanier Institute of the Family 2000). Sometimes, newly arrived biological or adoptive children of the current union partners are blended into the family. In addition, one or both partners may have other children who are not living with them. Some may reside with the new couple sporadically and some may live elsewhere but visit the household. These combinations take so many forms, all arising out of the need to satisfy the many conflicting demands on time and money of parents, that neat summation is difficult. In contemporary Canadian family life, innovation is a keyword.

Questions for Critical Thought

What do you think may be some of the unique advantages and challenges associated with living in a stepfamily?

Stepfamilies and Blended Families

When remnants of previously dissolved families combine in a new relationship they tend to become unremarkable in their communities because, for most purposes, they are indistinguishable from their always-intact-family counterparts. Their household income levels are on average much closer to those of "intact families" than they are to those of lone-parent families headed either by a man or by a woman (Juby et al. 2003:6, Figure 1). This parity is attributable almost entirely to having two adult earners in the labour force, a pivotal marker for potential prosperity in Canadian society today.

While immediate friends and family members may know of previous marital dissolutions the newly combining family members may have experienced, for outsiders the cues are subtle. Perhaps there are differing surnames, physical dissimilarities among children of the family, patterns of periodic visits by other adults, or other distinguishing signals. These might give vague clues to outsiders of a non-traditional family history. But even these aspects cannot be taken as decisive for identification purposes. Enough variation exists in the population of Canadian families now that most outsiders have learned not to press questions in the forward manner their grandparents might once have followed. Today's typically high levels of residential mobility—in a society where 80 per cent of the population reside in urban areas—have disrupted the dense web of community knowledge about family genealogy that characterized nineteenth- and early twentieth-century Canadian agrarian society.

Combined families' unremarkable social status is aided by treatment under the law in much the same manner as their more traditional counterparts and significantly also by the fact that until recently the Census of Canada had no questioning directed to family history and did not count **stepfamilies** or **blended families**. This has changed. The 2011 Census was the first to provide information about stepfamilies in Canada. That Census found that 11 per cent of all Canadian children aged 24 and under, or about 1 million children, were in stepfamilies (Bohnert, Milan, and Lathe 2014).

The 2011 Census (and the GSS) counted two distinct kinds of stepfamilies: *simple* and *complex* (Vézina 2012). A simple stepfamily is when only one spouse has children who were born or adopted before the current union and are living in the household. On the other hand, a complex stepfamily is when at least one parent has children from a previous union living in the household and there are also children born into the new union. Complex stepfamilies also include cases where both spouses have children from a previous union living in the household but not necessarily from the current union (Vézina 2012). In 2011, according to the GSS, 49 per cent of stepfamily parents were members of simple stepfamilies and 51 per cent lived in complex stepfamilies (Vézina 2012).

When questioned in the Bibby survey mentioned above, respondents who had entered a new marital relationship that involved step-parenting reported very positively on their experience. About 80 per cent characterized their new relationships as being much happier than their earlier ones. About the same proportion said that they had adjusted very or fairly well to their new partner's children and that the children had adjusted well to them. Men were slightly more positive than women, and those who had been previously married were more positive than those who had never previously married before entering a new combined family with a previously attached spouse and children. However, only about 56 per cent of stepchildren, when asked to look back on their childhoods, reported they got on well with step-parents while 65 per cent reported similarly about relations with stepsiblings. Significant numbers of grown stepchildren were thus indicating strain in the combined family, though it is not clear that this strain is inherently worse than in intact families (Bibby 2005: Tables 6.9–6.11).

A combined family may change the surnames of some members in favour of a single last name, a legal process that is quite easily and inexpensively done. A cost in lost identity may ensue, however, as surnames continue to convey origins and expectations, albeit to a much lesser extent than in the past when the surname often conveyed membership in a mythic kinship collective centred on a particular place on earth.

We might speculate as to the nature of the special strains of the combined family setting, all the more so if the separation and combination cycle happens more than once. There may be non-custodial parental visits, conflicts among parental practices and expectations, awkwardness in formal introductions, and some degree of financial "fallout" from previous relationships. Often there will be new "kin" and kinship relations that make up a larger-than-normal number of extended families, titles for which the language often fails. These exceptional relationships form a more complex kinship puzzle than usual for the children of a combined family, one that can become more complex as time goes by. For adult children of some families this may add extensive obligations to a multiplicity of aging parents along with their other responsibilities as adults. Children of combined families may well find themselves in late middle age with four or more parents to assist in their declining years, parents who may have experienced financial reversals due to previous relationships and who may have remained the poorer for it.

Recent Developments in Divorce and Family Law

A series of court decisions in the early years of the twenty-first century made same-sex marriages legal. These judgments had a set of quite predictable consequences. It was immediately evident that married same-sex couples would require access to divorce and family law financial settlements, access that necessitated the rewriting of much of the existing family legislation. Since some same-sex couples facing divorce will have minor children—whether from a previous relationship, conceived in the same sex union, or adopted—new paradigms of child custody and shared parenting will be required since traditional preference for custody to the mother is still overwhelmingly followed in social practice (it is declining very slowly with time) but is not particularly relevant in the same-sex context.[8]

In addition, there has been some movement in the direction of rehabilitating "fault" or marital misconduct as a factor in financial settlements in divorce. For instance, the British

Columbia Appeals Court held in a judgment in 2004 that a Vancouver woman, Sherry Leskun, whose husband Gary left her for a marriage to another woman, should continue to receive support payments (Schmitz 2004:A2). In the normal course of events this woman might reasonably have expected that her $2,250 monthly support payment would be terminated with the passage of some few years after divorce as the Act intends. There is a general expectation under the legislation that former spouses must begin to support themselves after a transitional period normally limited to a few years (recently specified as eight years in an Alberta decision) and without regard to marital offences committed by the other party. But in this case, the Court ruled that "emotional devastation" caused by adultery had undermined her ability to work. This judgment was upheld by the Supreme Court of Canada on the grounds that while spousal misconduct cannot be considered, its emotional consequences can be. But the British Columbia Appeals Court ruling does raise an important question outside the bounds of law. Why should serious misconduct be subject to sanction in virtually all arenas of social life *except* in marriages?

There is other evidence of a slight hardening of attitude towards former spouses in the throes of a marital dissolution. For instance, in 2007 Ontario increased the maximum debtor prison sentence from 90 to 180 days (served without the normal recourse to early release provisions) for failure to pay child support established under court orders.

Regular payment of child support is important particularly in the case of single-parent families in the post-divorce period, as they tend to be more vulnerable to living on low income. A drop in income from a default on a child support payment in any given month may result in economic hardship for the custodial parent and child(ren). Unacceptably high levels of non-compliance with child support orders (high default rates, particularly on the part of non-custodial fathers) throughout the 1990s led to the creation of Bill C-41, An Act to Amend the Divorce Act (the Family Orders and Agreements Enforcement Assistance Act), and the Garnishment, Attachment and Pension Diversion Act–1997. These amendments of the Divorce Act set out the federal child support guidelines—a simplified series of tables specifying the amount of child support to be paid by the non-custodial parent based on the payer's income (Department of Justice 2006). This federal enforcement legislation was designed to support the efforts of various new provincial enforcement agencies created to help locate spouses in breach of support orders and agreements (so-called "deadbeat" parents). The legislation gave provincial enforcement agencies access to federal sources of information (Revenue Canada data, for example) to allow the agency to garnish funds from income tax refunds, employment insurance benefits, old age security payments, GST credits, etc. to satisfy support orders in default. It included a new licence denial scheme that permits the denial of certain licence applications (such as a passport, pilot and air traffic controller certificates, and other federal licences) in cases of persistent default on child support (Douglas 2001). In 2007, nearly 70,000 children and youth under the age of 19, in 50,000 families, in five reporting provinces and territories, were enrolled in the Maintenance Enforcement Programs—representing 6 per cent of all children in those jurisdictions (Robinson 2009). Despite being enrolled in these enforcement programs, only one third of families received the full amount of the regular payment due every month in 2007/2008. Just over 60 per cent of families received their regular payment in full for at least six months of 2007/2008, while 84 per cent received some support during that year (Robinson 2009). Between 2001 and 2012, the proportion of those fully paying their regular monthly support payments remained stable at about 65 per cent making full payment each month (it was 67 per cent in 2011/2012; Kelly 2013). As of March 31, 2012, there were just over 88,000 cases enrolled in the nine provinces and territories reporting to maintenance enforcement programs (Kelly 2013). Ontario, one of the more aggressive provinces in child support enforcement, created the Family Responsibility Office as part of its Ministry of Community and Social Services. As part of this office, they established a Good Parents Pay initiative, which includes a website containing "most wanted"-style profiles/postings of parents who have defaulted on court-ordered child support payments, aimed at getting the public's help in locating missing defaulters on child support. The individual postings contain the name, alias, age, height, eye and hair colour, photo (where available), occupation, identifying details, and last known whereabouts of the parent, as well as a link for the public to access if they have information to give anonymous tips to help locate the parent (see www.mcss.gov.on.ca/en/goodparentspay/index.aspx).[9] Clearly, defaulting ex-spouses are not uncommon. On a somewhat similar vein, in a Manitoba case (*Schreyer v. Schreyer*) reviewed by the Supreme Court of Canada in 2011, a divorced husband managed to evade a matrimonial property settlement debt by declaring bankruptcy, which protected the husband's principal asset, a farm, from division. In another decision, the Supreme Court of Ontario ruled that a woman who left her common-law husband of more than 20 years some few months before he died is not entitled to the survivor pension she would have received were she to have been married to or still living with the deceased at the time of his death. This ruling has the effect of asserting that *a common-law relationship is over in law at the time of separation.* Continued cohabitation (as signified by the intent of both parties to be together) is required to establish a claim to survivor benefits. Thus, a common-law partner who leaves a relationship immediately acquires the status of divorced spouse no matter the conditions under which he or she left the household. This judgment effectively diminishes the emergent parity between married and common-law couples and holds that married couples have a higher degree of obligation to each other than their unmarried counterparts (Paraskevas 2004:A2).

Finally, in another important decision of the Supreme Court of Canada, in 2008 the Court ruled that divorcing couples should be made to share debts as well as assets, debts such as the unrealized tax liabilities for tax shelter assets not yet liquidated in this case (*Stein v. Stein*). This case arose because current family legislation in the provinces is largely silent on the question of contingent debts such as postponed capital gains taxation (Tibbetts 2008:A5).

In a few cases divorce settlements have been reopened well after the fact to take into account new realities, such as a big lottery win that was hidden and then cashed in only after the family law settlement was signed, or the permanent incapacitation of an ex-spouse occurring after an agreement was reached. These re-openings are very uncommon, as are support awards made against former wives in favour of former husbands. In the future, though, they may become more common. In the *Rick v. Brandsema* case, the Supreme Court of Canada ruled that additional payments over and above the original settlement had to be paid by Mr Brandsema on the basis that he had provided false financial information before the agreement was signed. Additionally, the Ontario Court of Appeal ruled in 2009 that deteriorating economic conditions that have seriously diminished the value of matrimonial assets from that at the date of separation (hereto-fore the standard valuation point) should be reflected in final settlements of equalization payments (*Serra v. Serra*). Should economic conditions become grim at some point in the future, it is likely that some former spouses may seek to have their support payments varied downward for the same underlying reason, involuntary impoverishment.

In practice, support payments and the post-separation splitting of assets seem in-tended to work as parts of a capital redistribution system meant to enhance the economic status of ex-wives and their minor children. In creating such a system, governments hoped that the necessity for large state transfer payments to otherwise bereft ex-spouses would decline. Ex-spouses are additionally instructed (if not already employed) to get a job as soon as possible. Overall, this system, in place for more than 30 years, has been un-successful in addressing the continuing problem of lone-parent poverty, defined either in terms of asset ownership or of income levels. Inadequate enforcement of support payment orders remains a problem, as is the meagre supply of assets and income to attach or divide in very many cases. Poor couples who divide their incomes and assets simply get poorer separately. A study completed for BMO Financial Group in 2011 suggests that potential money woes were well down the list of concerns of Canadians contemplating separation and/or divorce. "Disruption of family life" was listed first by 41 per cent of respondents in contrast to those listing "standard of living" at 14 per cent.[10]

Conclusion

Major changes in social practice and in the legal environment have gone hand-in-hand with demographic changes to greatly enhance the episodic nature of spousal unions in Canada in the last half-century. On the demographic side, the rapid extension of life expectancies and widespread immigration/migration, with consequent dispersal and mixing of previously static populations, have produced a greater awareness of alternatives among people who are experiencing unsatisfactory domestic arrangements. The effect of perceived alternatives has raised the importance accorded to choice in marital matters, or more broadly, to an entitlement to happiness. These and other related factors have in turn contributed to the loosening of once-strict legal regimes for social control in family matters as they applied historically both to cohabitation and to its termination in separation. Likewise, newcomers to Canadian society, who are often adherents to somewhat unfamiliar religious credos and modes of family life, are free to continue in their beliefs and practices when they are not in fundamental conflict with Canadian law.

There are few indications that Canadians are now less likely to cohabit in a marriage or marriage-like union at some point in their lives than they were in the past. Likewise, there is little indication that present unions are now more durable or less conflict-prone than they were in the past. Certainly, the emotional and economic consequences of sep-aration on cohabiting partners and on their children are no easier to endure now than formerly. Often, the result of separation continues to be a descent into a period of intense poverty and personal turmoil.

Looked at in a purely legal context, however, proportionately fewer separating part-ners are in need of a divorce because fewer cohabiting couples are married. Thus, both marriage and divorce have been to some extent pushed towards the margins of social life in the years since the federal Divorce Act was enacted in 1968. On the other hand, provincial family law settlements have become much more central as separating couples unwind their financial entanglements and define the overhang of future support obligations, particularly where minor children are involved. In view of the substantial number of combined families in Canadian society, there seems no slackening in the willingness to try cohabitation again for a second or subsequent time. Each recombinant union contributes in its own unique way to the dense thicket of contemporary kinship charts and support obligations defined with the assistance of the ever-present legal profession.

Study Questions

1. Is lessening the incidence of separation and divorce in Canada a desirable social goal? In your view, what mechanisms might be useful to decrease the incidence of separation and divorce in Canada? Which would be most likely to succeed?
2. Should Canadian law take religious beliefs and practices into account by making the divorce process specific to the various belief communities? Would that expansion include the few small polygamous communities in western Canada such as that at Bountiful, British Columbia?
3. How do Canadian rates of separation and divorce compare to those in other countries? Is there anything Canadians can learn from the experience in other countries?
4. What proportion of Canadian children will experience an episode of living in a lone-parent family in the years to come? Is that proportion likely to rise or fall in the future? Why? Why not?
5. Why has the role of step-parent been portrayed so negatively in the past? This role is a staple of standard storytelling, Cinderella's stepmother being but one example. Can you find any evil stepfathers in this lore?
6. How many same-sex divorces can Canadians expect to see in the years to come? Can you find current data and extrapolate to the future? Do you foresee any unique challenges that might arise in same-sex divorces uniquely?
7. What public policies might be enacted to address and remedy the poverty of post-separation lone-parent families in Canada? Other than enforcement of support orders, what changes could be made to Canadian legislation to make things easier for lone parents?

Further Readings

Brownstone, Harvey. 2009. *Tug of War: A Judge's Verdict on Separation, Custody Battles, and the Bitter Realities of Family Court*. Toronto: ECW Press. This book is an informed insider's view of family court actions in Ontario, including a discussion of reopening and variance of concluded settlements.

Clark, Warren, and Susan Crompton. 2006. "Till death do us part? The risk of first and second marriage dissolution." *Canadian Social Trends*, Summer, Catalogue no. 11–008: 23–33. This article is a short treatment of assessed risk of termination of two main types of marriages.

Debrett's. 2012. *Guide to Civilised Separation: In Association with Mishcon de Reya*. London: Debrett's. This selection provides a fairly detailed guide to conflict reduction in failing British marriages.

Department of Justice. 2013. *Making Plans: A Guide to Parenting Arrangements after Separation or Divorce, How to Put Your Children First*. Ottawa: Department of Justice www.justice.gc.ca /eng/fl-df/parent/mp-fdp/En-Parenting_Guide.pdf and What Happens Next? Information for Kids about Separation and Divorce. Ottawa: Department of Justice. At: www.justice.gc.ca/eng /rp-pr/fl-lf/famil/book-livre/pdf/book-livre.pdf. These booklets, created and distributed by the Department of Justice Canada, can help parents and children learn about family law, and can also help children realize it is normal for them to have an emotional response to their parents' separation.

Department of Justice. 2012. *The Federal Child Support Guidelines: Step-by-Step*. www.justice.gc. ca/eng/rp-pr/fl-lf/child-enfant/guide/index.html. This publication contains general information and aimed at providing convenience and guidance in applying the Federal Child Support Guidelines.

Gillis, John R. 1985. *For Better or Worse: British Marriages 1600 to the Present*. Oxford: Oxford University Press. This scholarly volume documents the various changes and practices in British marriages in the last 400 years.

Grossberg, Michael. 1985. *Governing the Hearth: Law and the Family in Nineteenth-Century America*. Chapel Hill: University of North Carolina Press. This is a detailed scholarly volume on the various changes and practices in America in the nineteenth century.

McKie, Craig, B. Prentice, and P. Reed. 1983. *Divorce: Law and the Family in Canada*. Ottawa: Statistics Canada. This text provides an overall view of marriage, divorce, and family law in Canada from early settlement times to approximately 1982. It contains data from the Central Divorce Registry at the Department of Justice and from the Office of the Official Guardian in Ontario, and a life table indicating the probability of divorce in each year of marriage based on then-available data.

Vézina, Mireille. 2012. 2011 General Social Survey: Overview of Families in Canada—Being a parent in a stepfamily: A profile. Catalogue no. 89-650-X–No. 002. Ottawa: Statistics Canada. (www.statcan.gc.ca/pub/89-650-x/89-650-x2012002-eng.pdf). Using data from the 2011 GSS, this article describes the situation of parents and step-parents aged 20 to 64 living in stepfamilies.

Key Terms

Annulment The retroactive finding that an attempted marriage union violated the requirements for a valid marriage from the outset.

Bigamy The act of entering into a marriage with one person while still legally married to another.

Blended family The marital union of two people, at least one of whom was previously in a marriage or marriage-like union and is also a parent. A blended family is created when one parent of an established family marries or cohabits with another such partner, and all their children are considered members of the new family.

Family A married couple or common-law couple, with or without children of either or both spouses, or a lone parent, regardless of that parent's marital status, having at least one child living under the same roof.

Stepfamilies Families in which at least one of the children in the household is from a previous relationship of one of the parents; a cohabiting or legal union of two adults with at least one member bringing a child or children from previous relationships.

Notes

1. Pre-Christian marriage arrangements persisted in Scottish law until 1939. "Handfasting" provided a one-year trial marriage (August to August) to demonstrate fertility. At the end of the year, this ancient form of trial marriage could be dissolved by either party without consequence (Moffat and Wilson 2011:116–17).

2. Publication of the annual data series on divorces by Statistics Canada ceased with the completion of processing of the 2008 records. The Statistics Canada website reads as follows: "Note: 2008 is the last year for which Statistics Canada will provide information about divorces. The information will remain on the website, and it will not be updated. Data tables for 2006 to 2008 are available by contacting Infostats at 1-800-263-1136 (toll free) or 1-514-283-8300 (international) or via email at STATCAN.infostats-infostats.STATCAN@canada.ca." (www.statcan.gc.ca/eng/help/bb/info/divorce). The data from the final years of 2006 to 2008 were collected from the Central Registry of Divorce Proceedings (CRDP) at the Department of Justice Canada but tabulations have not yet been published. They are available to scholars only on special request. Henceforth, the only source of information on the divorces of Canada will be the Civil Court Survey of administrative files. It covers only seven provinces and territories and the results are somewhat non-comparable, jurisdiction to jurisdiction (see Kelly 2012).

3. According to Statistics Canada, the number of women in Canada getting married has been generally declining since the early 1970s. In 2008, the crude marriage rate in Canada was 444 marriages per 100,000 population, about half the rate recorded in 1972—902 marriages per 100,000 population. (Milan 2013). This is not an isolated Canadian phenomenon. Current marriage totals in 2007 in the United Kingdom were the lowest seen since 1895 when the population was little more than half what it is now. UK divorce rates are also at their lowest level in 26 years.

4. A *get* is a Jewish religious document held to be necessary to separate the combined soul of a married man and woman. Without a proper *get*, even though the man and woman have physically separated, they are still bound together in what believers feel to be mystical fashion—and considered to be still fully married. The great difficulty for contemporary life is that the wife *cannot* initiate the process. Note as well that under Jewish law, divorced women are prohibited from marrying again.

5. The Arbitration Act (1991) in Ontario allowed faith-based arbitration (for Muslims, Jews, and members of other established faiths) in matters of divorce, custody, and property disputes such as inheritance outside the formal court system. Participation was supposed to be voluntary but as sociologists know well, informal social pressure to comply can be intensely coercive. That part of shariah law that pertains to criminal events is clearly contrary to the Charter of Rights and Freedoms, but this does not mean that Canadian Muslims might not someday challenge this aspect as well. The orthodox Jewish arbitration system (*Beth Din*) provides rabbinical decisions, the substance of which are then embodied in a conventional court document of settlement. Rabbinical decisions now deal with separation, division of assets, and other civil matters involving business disputes. This avenue is available in large Canadian cities only where community numbers warrant it.

6. For a graphic view of the economic impacts of being in a lone-parent family, see Chart 4, "Real Median Disposable Income," in Picot and Myles (1995).

7. Michelle Rotermann (2007) discusses findings from the now cancelled National Population Health Survey on associations between marital dissolution and subsequent depression among people aged 20 to 64. She concludes that "Marital dissolution often sets in motion a series of stressful disruptions that create further personal and financial difficulties, which themselves may contribute to depression."

8. In a case in Ontario in 2008 for instance, an Ontario Superior Court judge ordered Connie Springfield to return to northern England with her two adopted daughters to honour the provisions of a shared custody agreement with her former same-sex partner, Sarah Courtney. The judge referred to the deliberate spiriting away of the children in violation of a standing joint custody agreement in the judgment (Wattie 2008:A3). In a more recent case, an Alberta court granted custody of a young girl to a gay man over a claim by his former partner and the biological father of the child (Slade 2011:A7).

9. For a discussion of the various provincial spousal and child support programs, see Steeves (2012).

10. The survey was done for BMO Financial Group by Leger Marketing between August 15–18, 2011, and sampled 1,504 Canadian adults. See Bouzane (2011) for a press account of the results. While the dataset has not been released, an extended discussion of the results is available as "BMO Financial Group Divorce Panel Conference Call, Thursday, October 6, 2011" upon request to BMO.

 Interested in finding out more? Visit www.oupcanada.com/Albanese4e for access to a list of recommended websites for this chapter.

Families in Middle and Later Life
Patterns and Dynamics of Living Longer, Aging Together

KAREN M. KOBAYASHI AND ANNE MARTIN-MATTHEWS

LEARNING OBJECTIVES

- To understand how a life course perspective advances understanding of mid- and later-life family transitions

- To understand how life transitions are changing, and with what implications

- To appreciate the nature of intra- and inter-generational support among family members

- To understand the concept of ambivalence in explaining dynamics in contemporary aging families

- To discover how co-longevity of generations requires the negotiation of new roles and relationships within families

- To consider how social policy impacts families over the life course

---

Introduction

Two key demographic trends are re-shaping family life in fundamental ways: we are having fewer children and we are living longer. Adult children and their older parents today spend more years together over the life course than at any other time in history. A focus on families in mid-life often leads people to think of adults in their forties or fifties, with their own children about to be or already launched (living independently from the parents in a separate household) from home, and with an older parent or parents in their sixties, seventies, or even eighties. But families today are highly variable. Some adult children do not leave home until their parents are about to retire. Some, in their sixties, have a parent or parents aged 90 or older. Others in their late seventies have a living parent, typically a mother, aged 100 years or older.

Family life is often associated with key transitions that reflect a progression into old age. Typical life course transitions are believed to involve home-leaving, marriage, parenthood, grandparenthood, **caregiving**, the death of older relatives, widowhood, and so on. But, as they age, individuals and families become more varied and diverse, not less. Indeed, for many families, this sequence of transitions is no longer the standard. Transitions are delayed, truncated, or altered by societal factors, individual choice, and cultural expectations. For example, unprecedented numbers of people are now living alone—"going solo" (Klinenberg 2012); divorce rates have risen; and widowhood has been delayed until later in life. What are the implications of new, delayed, or **non-transitions** for families?

Some argue that family ties have lost much of their meaning, that bonds and rituals are less salient than they were for previous generations, and that families abandon their older members. What do we know about the dynamics of family life in middle and later life, and what factors seem to explain those dynamics? How are gender, ethnicity, class, and sexual orientation reflected in these dynamics? What role does social policy play in the lives of families as they age? This chapter addresses these issues of demography, transitions, dynamics, diversity, and policy in an effort to understand aging Canadian families in mid- and later life today.

Demography: What Aging Families Look Like

The profile of aging families today is historically unprecedented. Families are smaller, fewer people are marrying, more are childless, first-time parents are older, and we are living longer.

With the increasing demographic complexity of North American families, it is difficult to assign distinct structural markers, such as age, to entrance and exit from life-course stages. In particular, the age range of 45–64 years and 65 and over, previously used to define middle age and later life respectively, are no longer seen as valid or appropriate. Allen et al. (2000:913) note, "there is no agreed upon chronological or processual definition of middle age." The same can be said of old age. Average life expectancy in Canada is 81.3 years (Conference Board of Canada 2016), This means that at age 65, women can expect to live another 20 years; and men, another 16. The general belief is that old age starts at 65, and many policies reinforce that. However, for those who live to age 85, old age can constitute one quarter of their lives; and for those who live to age 95, it may be one third! With such unprecedented longevity, and with multiple generations over the age of 65, the delineation of this number as signaling entry to "old age" is problematic.

For more on changing family trends see "Changing Trends in the Diversity of Family Forms" in Chapter 1, pp. 3–10.

It is the transitions to various stages (e.g., the return to work, the "empty nest," caregiving) triggered by the occurrence of life events in the domains of work and family (e.g., re-entry into the paid labour force, adult children leaving home, care for aging parents), and not age markers per se, that define the parameters of mid- and later-life in the family literature.

"Demographic changes highlight the evolving nature of mid-life" (Antonucci and Akiyama 1997:147). We know that transitions at different points in the life course have implications for family life later on. For example, becoming a father at age 23 and a grandfather at age 51 can be a vastly different experience than becoming a father at age 40 and a grandfather at age 74—for all three generations, the child, parent, and grandparent.

The latter years of mid-life—the years prior to the traditional marker of old age at age 65—have been referred to as the empty nest stage. This pre-retirement stage typically has involved adult children being successfully "launched," leaving aging parents to plan towards their work-free years as a couple (Mitchell 2009, 2016). Over the past few decades, however, with the growing proportion of adult children staying or returning home, the empty nest has increasingly become a cluttered nest.

Questions for Critical Thought

Do you live with your parents? Do you know people your age who live with their parents? When do you/they expect to move out? Is this typical of people you know?

What Families Look Like at Mid-life

Demographic changes in families at mid-life are reflected in the profiles of co-residence, home-leaving, and home returning. Over one third (34.7 per cent) of young adults aged 20–34 years co-reside with their parents (Statistics Canada 2017). It is increasingly typical that parenthood in mid-life comprises extended periods of co-residence with adult children (Arnett 2000; Mitchell 1998a). The Census Metropolitan Areas with the highest proportion of **intergenerational co-residence** (young adults 20–34 years with their parents) are Toronto and Oshawa in Ontario, with 47.4 per cent and 47.2 per cent, respectively, but a number of CMAs across Canada (see Figure 7.1) have high proportions of co-resident young adult children.

For a number of different reasons, the transition to parenthood has been delayed into the thirties for many Canadians.[1] The mean age at first birth for women was 28.5 years in 2011 (Statistics Canada 2016). Canadians are more likely to be well into their forties and fifties—at one time the definition of a middle-age family with launched children—and still have responsibilities for dependent, school-age children. For many, this coincides with having aging parents who themselves are experiencing transitions resulting from less independence and a greater need for support (Allen et al. 2000; Statistics Canada 2013)—something that has been commonly, and at times inaccurately, referred to as the **sandwich generation**.

What Families Look Like in Later Life

Today, more people live *to* old age, and more are living longer *in* old age. Aging families look very different than they did 40 years ago, both in who they include and how members within them relate to one another. Similarly, images of physical and mental decline and loss often associated with later life are changing, as older people are generally healthier than in previous generations. "Seventy is the new fifty" is a contemporary mantra reflecting this change, and it stands in contrast to apocalyptic pronouncements of an epidemic of dementia. However, it is important to recognize that these are two distinct generations in later life.

For more on changing age of first marriage and marriage rates, see "Family Formation, Social Structures, and Change" in Chapter 4, pp. 74–8.

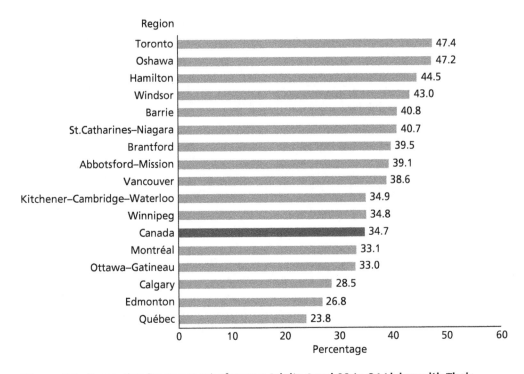

Figure 7.1 Proportion (percentage) of Young Adults Aged 20 to 34 Living with Their Parents, Canada and Selected Census Metropolitan Areas, 2016

Source: Statistics Canada. 2017a. "Census in brief: Young adults living with their parents in Canada in 2016." Ottawa: Statistics Canada. (http://www12.statcan.gc.ca/census-recensement/2016/as-sa/98-200-x/2016008/98-200-x2016008-eng.cfm.)

Advances in medical care and pharmacological interventions mean that many married women no longer lose their partners earlier in life. However, the prevalence of marriage among older women today is changing as more women enter later life unattached as a result of divorce (see Daily Life box) or lifelong singlehood.

A key demographic feature of later life is described by the British sociologist, Phillipson (2013:112), as the "increasing length of our days, and with them, the **co-longevity of different generations**." There are four significant implications of this generational co-longevity.

First, is the increase in the number of years that older adults and at least one of their children are jointly alive. The increases are striking. At age 50, only 16 per cent of children of the 1860 cohort had a surviving parent, compared to 60 per cent of the 1960 cohort. At age 60, the increase is from 2 per cent to a projected 23 per cent. This means that we are spending a longer part of our lives in the role of "child" (Gee 1990).

Second, co-longevity has affected caregiving in later-life families. In the past, most people did not have parents living into advanced age who required care for sustained periods of time. Moss and her colleagues (1997) note that the death of one's last parent is now more common when the adult "child" is him- or herself a "senior citizen." It is not uncommon to know someone aged 77, with a parent who is 104, or a couple in their late 60s, each with mothers of about 100 years of age. As women's lives involve full-time labour force participation, important implications arise. For example, how much care-giving can a 50-year-old woman with a full-time job be expected to provide to four frail parents and parents-in-law? Such challenges are even more pronounced as smaller family sizes result in fewer siblings assisting in the provision of care.

Third, there is a decrease in the proportion of one's adult life spent raising children. The ratio of adult years lived as a child to adult years lived with dependent children is instructive here. In the past, years spent with dependent children exceeded years as an adult child. Now, with fewer children, later age at first birth, much lower median age at birth of last child (a decline of 10 years between the 1860 and 1960 cohorts) and longer life expectancies, the years adults spend with dependent children are shorter than they have ever been. Gee (1990) noted that those born in 1960 will spend 50 per cent more years as an adult child than as a parent of dependent children.

Fourth, co-longevity has resulted in an increase in the number of years spent in the empty nest phase of life—from 6.8 years for those born in 1860 to a projected 30.2 years for those born in 1960 (Gee 1990). This projection is attenuated if there are **boomerang children**.

Questions for Critical Thought

Thinking about your own life, once you leave/have left your parental home, what are some the reasons that might lead you to return?

During this period of co-longevity, members of both generations must negotiate the reframing of their respective roles in the context of a relationship that is no longer based on the adult child as a dependent. There may even be a period when both a mother and a daughter are grandmothers (with, possibly, two generations of grandfathers in the mix as well). This is novel and historically unprecedented. Thus, family members lack "a set of social rules or guidelines to help [us] define, negotiate, and renegotiate [our] intergenerational roles and interactions" (Gee 1990:62).

Co-longevity impacts other family relationships, like sibling ties and marital relations. Sibling ties and relationships, for example, already noted as the longest family ties that most of us will have, are now documented to last well into a person's nineties and beyond (Connidis 2010). Similarly, despite the prevalence of divorce, couples that remain married long enough to celebrate a seventieth wedding anniversary are increasingly common. In both cases, co-longevity results in negotiating what the extension of these family ties mean for everyone involved.

A key message so far is that families change and evolve. For Baby Boomers, and especially the younger members of the Boomer cohort (born in 1960 and turning 65 in 2025), we know that their immediate kin group will be smaller than that of their parents, and that they will have fewer children and grandchildren. Over 25 years ago, Rosenthal (1990:89) predicted that by 2025, ". . . the overall size of both the immediate and wider extended family will have shrunk dramatically."

Transitions throughout Family Life

For much of the twentieth century, transitions have given a particular structure or staging to family life. These stages have included adult children leaving home, often immediately prior to marriage; the arrival of children; marriage-related transitions involving separation, divorce, remarriage, or re-partnering; grandparenthood; episodes of illness for aging parents; death of parents; widowhood; and old age and the onset of frailty. The significance of these transitions is an important area of study in the sociology of the family. Here we focus particularly on a somewhat changing set of mid-life transitions that are becoming increasingly prevalent, those involving children leaving and returning, on childlessness, grandparenthood, and on transitions involving the end of marriage, namely divorce, widowhood, and remarriage. We characterize these as new or non-transitions, and transitions delayed, redefined, and reframed.

For more on separation and divorce, see Chapter 6.

A Transition Delayed: Leaving Home

Earlier, we noted the increase in adult children living in their parents' home. Let us consider what is happening here and its implications for families. Why is it taking longer for cohorts of young adult children to leave the parental home to establish residential independence? Research indicates that children's financial needs are a key factor influencing home-leaving behaviour of young adult children (e.g., Carr 2005; De Marco and Berzin 2008; Iacovou 2010; Mitchell 2006). Mid-life parents, who presumably are in their peak earning years, provide a significant amount of financial and instrumental support to their co-resident children. Assistance takes multiple forms, including the payment of tuition and other fees for post-secondary education and/or vocational training, and, perhaps most importantly, the continued provision of housing, utilities, meals, and transportation. Given increases in un(der)employment rates, declines in affordable housing, and the trend towards extensions in schooling for young adults over the past few decades, parents may continue to be the primary resource for adult children well into later life (Mitchell 2006; Padgett and Remle 2016; Sage and Kirkpatrick Johnson 2012; Settersten Jr 2007).

The delay in home-leaving among young adults can also be attributed to the long-term trend towards the postponement of marriage. Recent statistics indicate that the average age at first marriage was 29.6 years for women and 31.0 years for men in 2008, up from 22.0 and 24.4 years, respectively, in 1975 (Statistics Canada 2013). The increasing age at first marriage results in prolonged periods of intergenerational co-residence in mid-life Canadian families (Mitchell and Gee 1996; Mitchell and Lovegreen 2009).

In addition to this, family structure affects home-leaving behaviour. Young adults living in blended or stepfamilies are more likely to leave home earlier than those in single- or two-parent biological families (Eshleman and Wilson 2001; Mitchell 1994, 2006; Smits et al. 2010; Turcotte 2014). This has been attributed to a weakened sense of mutual obligation that may result from conflict over power relations within these families (Aquilino 2005; Eshleman and Wilson 2001; Smits et al. 2010).

There is also a decreased likelihood that adult children will live at home if parents are divorced or a parent is widowed (Amato 2010). This may be due to the custodial or widowed parent's decreased ability to provide financial support to adult children in co-resident families (Aquilino 2005; DeMarco and Berzin 2008).

While intergenerational co-residence is often said to serve an adult children's needs, Ward and Spitze (1996:537) note that children are not always satisfied with this living arrangement. In fact, they maintain that "co-residence [actually] violates the child's norms and expectations about adulthood and independence, and [that] children may experience greater strain over exchanges in shared households." Research on the quality of intergenerational relationships in mid-life families has identified tension between co-resident parents and adult children (Birditt et al. 2012; Gee and Mitchell 2003; Mitchell 2006). Incongruence over expectations for support has the potential for intergenerational disputes within families (see Case in Point box). And, within more traditional immigrant cultures, parent–child incongruence on adherence to core family and religious values (e.g., filial obligation, family shame) is a primary source of conflict, and may be a precursor to the eventual breakdown of the family unit.

A New Transition: Returning Home

The return of adult children to the parental home in young adulthood is becoming increasingly common. These young adults, commonly referred to as "boomerang kids" (Mitchell 1998b, 2006; Mitchell and Gee 1996; Turcotte 2014) due to their leaving the nest, only to return at some other point(s) over the life course, have been the focus of numerous studies on parent–adult child co-residence (e.g., Dettling and Hsu 2015; Mitchell et al. 2002). Many have examined the antecedents and consequences of a "cluttered" nest for home-returning children and for their parents.

The experience of home-returning is shaped mainly by adult children's economic needs and/or marital status transitions. Indeed, the return of adult children to the parental home is often precipitated by marital disruption (i.e., separation, divorce, or the breakup of a common-law relationship) and/or economic difficulties (i.e., transition from full-time employment to unemployment or underemployment, single parenthood) (Mitchell 1998b, 2006; Turcotte 2014).

The effects of boomerang children on family relationships have ranged from positive to negative. On the positive side, the overall marital satisfaction of mid-life parents has been found to be quite high among those who are living with returning children as parents may receive additional support (emotional, instrumental, financial) from pooled resources (Mitchell and Gee 1996; Ward and Spitze 1996). Thus, returning children may be an antidote to empty nest syndrome for parents. Of negative consequence, however, is the decrease in self-reported relationship satisfaction between parents and adult children in the post-return home period due to conflicts over power relations in the home (Kobayashi 1999). Returning adult children may not adapt well to the reassertion of authority by parents within the household, particularly if the ground rules are not open for negotiation. The negative effects of home-returning are multiplied further in families of children who are "serial home leavers," those who leave and return multiple times (i.e., three or more) over the life course (Mitchell 2006; Mitchell and Gee 1996; Turcotte 2006).

Despite increases in continued and return co-residence of adult children in mid-life families over the past few decades, these experiences are still considered non-normative by Canadian society. The launch of children from the nest is perceived as parents' raison d'être, a key transition point along the family life course trajectory. Given the salience of this event, it is not surprising that incompatibility between parents' expectations and children's behaviour in this regard may often lead to **ambivalence** in intergenerational relationships (Fingerman et al. 2004), as we will discuss shortly.

Transitions Redefined: Grandparenthood

Grandparenthood represents a transition enjoying increased attention among family researchers. We cast this family transition as "redefined" for several reasons. First, as Timonen and Arber have noted, in an aging world, there are "growing numbers of grandparents, who share longer life spans with, on average, smaller numbers of grandchildren" (2012:1). Increasingly, grandparents come to know their grandchildren through adolescence into adulthood. Timonen and Arber cite data indicating that three quarters of 30-year-olds in the US have at least one surviving grandparent. In their seminal book on grandparenthood in global context, Arber and Timonen (2012:247) consider "*doing* grandparenting" as an "active and dynamic family practice"—distinct from other life course transitions of older and younger generations.

Second, it is increasingly recognized that grandparenthood is best understood as mediated in a three-generation context (Arber and Timonen 2012; Hagestad 2006). Research is moving away from an exclusive focus on the grandparent–grandchild dyad, to better understand the ways in which the relationship is mediated by the intermediate or middle generation.

In addition, grandparenthood is experienced differently when there are, simultaneously, two generations of grandparents in a family—as is true as soon as great-grandchildren

Daily Life
After Full Lives Together, More Older Couples Are Divorcing

Hilary Stephens was 57 when she decided she had had enough—enough of her job, of caretaking, of her marriage of 28 years. So she did something many people fantasize about: She walked away from it all.

"Sometimes it's the only solution," said Ms. Stephens, now 58 and the mother of two adult children. She moved from Washington to the Philadelphia area, where she is now vice president for development at Woods Services, a nonprofit.

Late-life divorce (also called "silver" or "gray" divorce) is becoming more common, and more acceptable. In 2014, people age 50 and above were twice as likely to go through a divorce than in 1990, according to the National Center for Family and Marriage Research at Bowling Green State University in Ohio. For those over 65, the increase was even higher. At the same time, divorce rates have plateaued or dropped among other age groups.

One explanation is that many older people are in second marriages; the divorce rate is about two and a half times larger for those who have remarried and are often grappling with blended families or greater financial challenges.

arrive. Similarly, when one or more generations are divorced, or when, not improbably, both the grandparent and parent generations are engaged in full-time employment, the roles, functions, styles, and practices of grandparents may vary.

Transitions Reframed: When Marriage Ends, When New Relationships Begin

Separation and Divorce

Canadian research shows that the proportion of women and men over the age of 50 who are divorced or separated has been increasing. In 2011, about one fifth of Canadians aged 55 to 59 were divorced or separated—three times the proportion found in this age group in 1981 (Milan 2015).

Perhaps the most significant consequences of divorce in mid- and later life are its effects on parent–child relationships and the well-being of children. Indeed, the primary reason for partners remaining in an unhappy marital union and delaying separation is concern over the welfare of their children (McDaniel and Tepperman 2007; Montenegro 2004). With the experience of divorce increasingly becoming a mid-life phenomenon,[2] children who are most likely to be affected by parental divorce are in their late adolescent to young adult years. At this stage in the life course, children are in the process of forming attitudes about marriage and family themselves and may be more vulnerable to the negative impact of parental disagreement or conflict (Kozuch and Cooney 1995). Despite concerns over the long-term effects of divorce on children, there is little evidence to suggest that exposure to the marital disruption of mid-life parents negatively affects the quality of parent–child relationships, children's ability to cope with challenging life events such as moving, or their overall optimism about marriage (Amato 2010; Dunlop and Burns 1995; Landis-Kleine et al. 1995).

Life expectancy also plays a role. In the past, "people died earlier," said Pepper Schwartz, a professor of sociology at the University of Washington in Seattle, and the love, sex and relationship ambassador for AARP. "Now, let's say you're 50 or 60. You could go 30 more years. A lot of marriages are not horrible, but they're no longer satisfying or loving. They may not be ugly, but you say, 'Do I really want 30 more years of this?'"

Besides realizing that "adequate" does not suffice, separation no longer holds the stigma it once did. Just look at Al and Tipper Gore, who split in 2010 after 40 years of marriage and four children (they have yet to make it official). Or the Alabama governor Robert Bentley, and his wife, Dianne, who filed for divorce in August, one month after their fiftieth wedding anniversary.

But perhaps the biggest reason for the increase in late-life divorce is the changing status of women, who initiate about 60 per cent of divorces after age 40, according to AARP. This does not mean that the men aren't disenchanted too. It just means that women actually take the decisive step.

Widowhood

Widowhood is both a status and a process. It is the status of an individual who has not remarried following the death of his or her spouse. Widowhood is also a process of transition, progressing from illness to the death of the spouse and related events involving burial and mourning, grieving, and reconstruction of one's social world (Martin-Matthews 1991). It is both sex-selective and age-related. In many developed countries, one half of all marriages end with the death of the husband, but only one fifth with the death of the wife.

While the incidence (number) of widowed people in the population is increasing due to **population aging**, its prevalence (proportion of the population) is decreasing in many parts of the world. Its duration is also decreasing (Martin-Matthews 2011). Widowhood traditionally was a predictable, "expectable," and a defining characteristic of women's old age; but is less so today (Martin-Matthews 1991, 1999, 2011). Societal trends such as the increased prevalence of divorce and singlehood in later life reduce the prevalence of widowhood. Medical advances also delay its onset. Nevertheless, the predominant trend of a steady increase in average age at widowhood and shorter duration of widowhood have "transformed the intimate landscape for old people" (Allen and Walker 2006:160).

With early studies of widowhood focused on role loss and role exit, the conceptual foundations of widowhood research have shifted away from ". . . the dismal image . . . of the ever-limited, ever-suffering, ever-dependent widow" to one now "more complicated and varied . . . " (Lopata 1996:xiv). Widowhood as a transition in family life intersects in important ways with age, class, gender (including understandings of masculinity), ethnicity, culture, religious affiliation, environment, and to socially structured practices regarding marital status (Connidis 2010).

Generally, there is more economic insecurity for women than for men following widowhood. Widows report significantly more functional extended family relatives (other than children and siblings) than do widowers, and more functional people in their networks in total (including friends). Yet these functional supports may not translate to financial support. Conversely, widowers generally have fewer contacts than do widows, but they do not necessarily report feeling more deprived in terms of support.

Remarriage

Remarriage is a gendered transition: men are more likely than women to remarry, a pattern that holds well into later life (Ambert 2005; Beaupre 2008). One explanation is that divorced or widowed women in middle to older age groups value their new-found independence and thus prefer to remain single (Baker 2001). For men, it may be the case that they find it difficult to make the transition to being "on their own" without the emotional and instrumental support of a partner and subsequently seek out companionship soon after a divorce to fill that void. Research on remarriage indicates that couples are at an increased risk of divorce compared to first marriages (Clark and Compton, 2006). However, remarriages in mid-to-later life seem to have a lower likelihood of marital disruption. This is especially the case when both partners have previously been married (Wu and Penning 1997).

The remarriage of two previously married adults in mid- and later life often involves the "blending" of two families, referred to in the literature as a "complex stepfamily" (Vézina 2015). This reconstitution, or integration of adolescent and/or young adult stepchildren into a new family, brings with it a number of challenges (Sweeney 2010).

In mid- and later-life families the adaptation process for stepchildren is influenced by a number of factors, including children's life course stage at their parent's remarriage, their residential status (co-resident or not), and the quality of the parent–child relationship prior to the remarriage. For example, the difficult period of adjustment that many co-resident children undergo soon after a parent's remarriage may be attributed, in part, to their resentment at the introduction of another authority figure into the home. Depending on the child's age, this may coincide with the development of his/her desire to establish a sense of independence from the family, with the new parent perceived as yet another barrier to the achievement of this goal (Hetherington and Kelly 2002; Smits et al. 2010).

The degree of closeness between parents and their children prior to remarriage also has a significant impact on the adaptation of children to their new family structure. Children who have close relationships with their custodial parent in the pre-remarriage period are likely to adjust better to a stepfamily arrangement than those who have a history of conflicted or strained relations (Ahrons and Tanner 2003).

Dynamics in Aging Families

Here we consider the dynamics of family relationships in aging families in two ways: first, in examining the nature of these dynamics, especially in relation to exchange, support, and care; and then by considering the concept of ambivalence, used by sociologists to help explain these dynamics.

Most studies of later life families have moved away from an almost exclusive focus on family roles, to focus more on family relationships, responsibilities, and connections. Research by Sarah Matthews (2002) explicitly imposes "a vocabulary of relationships" in a study of the dynamics between older parents and their daughters and sons, who are also sisters and brothers. Chambers and colleagues (2009:6) emphasize that family relationships are constructed through interactive processes of negotiation and thus involve more than a simple following of "culturally accepted rules." Throughout the life course, family members construct and negotiate relationships with one another, as circumstances and patterns of dependence, independence, and interdependence shift.

Ultimately, as Streib noted nearly 30 years ago (1988:22), ". . . the principal characteristic that marks the family is not the sheer number or variety of persons to whom one may be related by blood or marriage but the quality of those ties or relationships."

Family dynamics lie at the heart of what family *is*, what it *does*, and what that means to people across generations, and as they age. For many, the dynamics of family life involve knowing that people are kin and that they can be called upon in a crisis, even if that rarely happens. A key feature of family dynamics is the flow of support within and across generations.

There is considerable evidence of "bi-directional flows" between generations, in terms of financial resources, emotional exchanges, and time devoted to caregiving, and for grandchildren, for family members in times of need, and older kin. Overall, however, the dominant direction of financial transfers is down the generations, from the older to the middle and grandchild generations (Attias-Donfut et al. 2005). Flows of financial, instrumental, and emotional support to mid-life children from older parents has become ever more important with major social and economic shifts in society, reflected in an increase in dual-earner families, and a higher incidence of marital breakdown and lone parenthood (Izuhara 2010).

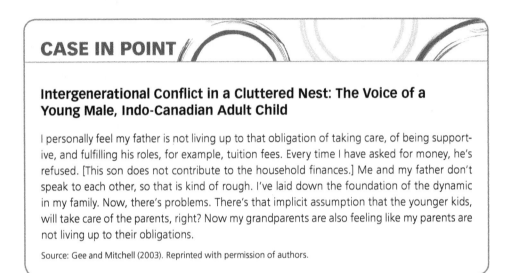

CASE IN POINT

Intergenerational Conflict in a Cluttered Nest: The Voice of a Young Male, Indo-Canadian Adult Child

I personally feel my father is not living up to that obligation of taking care, of being support-ive, and fulfilling his roles, for example, tuition fees. Every time I have asked for money, he's refused. [This son does not contribute to the household finances.] Me and my father don't speak to each other, so that is kind of rough. I've laid down the foundation of the dynamic in my family. Now, there's problems. There's that implicit assumption that the younger kids, will take care of the parents, right? Now my grandparents are also feeling like my parents are not living up to their obligations.

Source: Gee and Mitchell (2003). Reprinted with permission of authors.

This Case in Point nicely illustrates not only conflict in families with a "cluttered" nest but also the expectations of reciprocity and exchange across generations. In all lives, and in all families, there are points when health challenges force a change in patterns of exchange, when, in many cases, family members become "family savers" to one another. Children become ill, accidents happen, individuals age with disabilities, and older relatives become frail. While not characteristic of all families, such experiences can test the mettle of a family. Through a focus on care and support, we gain insight into the dynamics of families in mid- and later life.

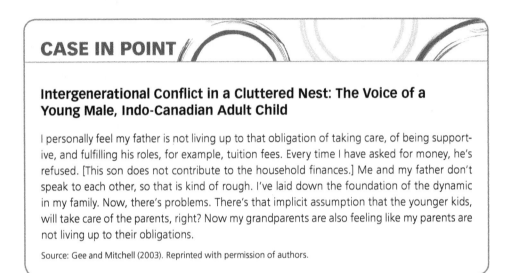
For more on family health, illness, and disabilities, see Chapter 13.

Caring and Support between the Generations

Cutbacks to health care and social services over the past decade in Canada have precipi-tated an increased reliance on the family for care across generations. It is well recognized that most of the care provided to older people near the end of their lives, for example, is provided by family members (McAlister 2013). Such care is unpaid, and erroneously deemed "informal" care. Because today's older adults are often married, for most, the first line of defense is *intra*-generational assistance and support from a spouse (especially from a wife if her husband is ill) (Timonen 2009). Adult children frequently become engaged in assisting parents, especially where one is widowed, or divorced, or experiencing ongoing health challenges due to dementia or stroke.

For the first time in our history, it is estimated that Canadian adults will spend a longer time caring for their aging parents than they spent in raising their children (McDaniel 2005). Given the gendered nature of caregiving in our society, this means that the responsibilities of care continue to fall on women in mid-life and in later life (Dentinger and Clarkberg 2002; Killian et al. 2005; McDaniel 2005; Moen et al. 2009). Although the compression of morbidity to the latter years of old age (80 +) has resulted in a greater number of disability-free years for older people, women—older wives and mid-life daughters—remain the backbone of systems of care within families. Social support (which they may have received and now must provide) consists of three main domains—financial, instrumental, and emotional. The need for assistance in each of these areas is influenced by the timing of later life-course transitions; for example, when the onset of illness and frailty occurs at a time when older parents lack other supportive resources due to widowhood, isolation, or inadequate housing.

In such circumstances, the reliance of older family members on middle-aged adult children increases either temporarily or long term. The extent to which support is provided (the adult child's response) is dictated both by parents' assistance needs and by the quality of the parent–child relationship. For some mid-life adult children, being sandwiched between competing demands—either of caregiving simultaneously for young adult children and older parents, or more commonly, between the demands of work and family—can be extremely stressful, leading to negative financial and/or health outcomes (Gee and Mitchell 2003; Killian et al. 2005; Moen et al. 2009).

Needs for support and care can range from temporary assistance with some activities of daily living, such a bill payments or grocery shopping (instrumental support) to permanent reliance on adult children or other family members for financial help and/or companionship to combat depression (emotional support). Long-term need for assistance may require a complete restructuring of older adult's or adult children's lives as they try to negotiate caregiving with full-time work and spousal and/or parenting roles and responsibilities (Moen et al. 2009).

As people live longer into deep old age, periods of assistance from family members can last for years, or be primarily episodic and intermittent over many years. All in all, the continuity that is achieved by very old people, with the support of their families and friends, requires "real effort and stubborn resilience" (Loe 2011:23), as the very old strive for independent or, in some cases, inter-dependent living. Based on an in-depth three-year ethnographic study of very old people, Loe (2011:45) found that individuals "embrace a wide range of personal and familial resources to achieve self-care, well-being, and comfort in lives characterized by meaning and connection. . . ."

The challenge for many people today is enabling older parents' preferences to **age in place**, that is, to remain living at home, even with complex physical and cognitive challenges (Doyle and Timonen 2008). The (usually) meagre hours of paid **home care** assistance for personal health care needs are supplemented by family members. Canadian research on care workers, older adult clients receiving home care services, and their family members attests to the crucial ways in which paid care workers and unpaid family members "share the care" of older frail family members (Sims-Gould and Martin-Matthews 2010; Sims-Gould et al. 2015).

Understanding Family Dynamics: Ambivalence

Previously considered a primarily psychological construct focused on interpersonal feelings related to needing support but wanting independence, sociological ambivalence considers the ongoing negotiation of contradictions in family relationships and their connections to how social life is organized and structured. Connidis and McMullin (2002) define ambivalence as a more multi-level construct that captures structurally created contradictions that are manifest in interaction. Connidis (2015) notes the particular salience of ambivalence in understanding contradictory cultural expectations due to migration and social change, families, and the welfare state.

The psychological ambivalence created by needing support but wanting independence is also relevant to family ties in mid-life a well as later life. To date, this construct has been used to examine relationships between adult children and their aging parents and in-laws (Lendon et al. 2014; Pillemer and Suitor 2002; Rappoport and Lowenstein 2007; Willson et al. 2003), and to explore the nature of social ties—with both family and friends—in a diverse age sample of adolescents and adults (Fingerman et al. 2004). Findings from Willson et al.'s (2003) study point to the significance of gender in ambivalent social relationships. Mid-life women are more likely to experience ambivalence in their relationships with each other and in their roles as caregivers to older parents and in-laws, suggesting that "structural arrangements give rise to ambivalence and the relationship experience is shaped by gender within the context of socially defined demands and obligations" (Willson et al. 2003:1068). The exception, it seems, is in mid- to later-life sibling relationships, where women (positively) report close ties and the most social contact with their sisters (Connidis 2001; Connidis and Campbell 1995).

Overall, then, there is ample evidence that families matter in the lives of individuals in mid- and later life.

Diversity in Family Forms and Perspectives

In noting the demographic changes, transitions, and dynamics of lives in mid- and late-life families today, we have made reference to some features as "typical," while recognizing the tremendous diversity that characterizes Canadian families today. Here we consider ethnicity and ethno-cultural diversity, the gendered nature of family life, and emerging family forms and dynamics involving sexual orientation.

Ethnicity

Fully 27 per cent of the population aged 65 years and older was born outside Canada, compared with 17 per cent of the population as a whole (Wister and McPherson 2013). These factors impact family relationships, as socio-cultural beliefs and values about families in life course contexts (e.g., filial piety, family shame) intersect with public sector policies and private sector practices.

The intersection of ethnicity and immigrant status has implications for several of the transitions considered here, such as continuing co-residence in mid- and later life families. North American research indicates a stronger sense of obligation to support young adult children in Asian immigrant families (Gee and Mitchell 2003; Kamo 2000; Milan 2016). Gee and Mitchell (2003), in a study of multi-generational households, include an exploration of the co-residential experiences of South Asian and Chinese immigrant families, currently the two largest visible minority populations in Canada (Statistics Canada 2016). Their findings, although limited by a small sample size, highlight the salience of cultural preferences and not economic needs as the key determinants of living arrangements over the family life course. For example, for some mid-life parents it is culturally appropriate to assume all financial responsibility for their young adult children, as a way of expressing parental responsibility for that child. Results from Pacey's (2002) comparative study of Canadian and Chinese Canadian immigrants support these findings in a sample of older adults.

The importance of cultural exigencies is also evident for post-immigrant racialized families. In her study on parent–child relationships in Japanese-Canadian families, Kobayashi (1999) found that third-generation mid-life children recalled that both cultural and socio-economic factors shaped their preferences to co-reside with parents as young adults. Despite the Canadian-born status of the mid-life parents, there was an enduring expectation that the family would stay intact until children, particularly daughters, made the transition to marriage. This cultural "pull factor," combined with economic necessity, in many cases, on the part of adult children to remain at home, formed the basis for intergenerational co-residence in mid-life families.

Similarly, for later-life transitions, ethnicity influences the nature of relationships in families. For example, Canadian research by Martin-Matthews and colleagues (2013) on older Chinese widows indicates that there are differences between Chinese widows and what the literature describes for widows in general. For Chinese people, there tend to be smaller informal support networks, siblings are less prominent as sources of support than was found in other Canadian studies (e.g., Martin-Matthews 1991), and they seem to be less involved with friends. At this juncture, we cannot assess the extent to which these patterns reflect their status as late-life immigrants to Canada (rather than Chinese cultural identity in widowhood *per se*). The study's findings suggest that sharing a household with children is not a bulwark against loneliness, and that even shared households can be lonely places. The preference for independent living is also found in the wider population of older adults and in that sense is not surprising. It does, however, run counter to the popular stereotype of the multigenerational household that is more commonly found in immigrant groups than in the overall population.

Gender

A striking characteristic of Canada's older adult population is the large and increasing imbalance in the proportions of men and women. By age 85, women outnumber men by more than two to one (Statistics Canada, 2016b) as it is well acknowledged that in later life "women get sick, but men die" (Gee and Kimball 1987).

While the gendered nature of family life, and especially of caregiving responsibilities, is widely acknowledged, there is emerging evidence that men are now more engaged as carers over the life course. Expectations of younger fathers have changed in recent decades as they have assumed more nurturing roles in families. With this have come more supports to men, in the form of paternity leaves and the awarding of child custody as they move into mid-life. Further, men in older generations engage more in the care of their wives and their frail parent(s), challenging the feminization of care roles.

These advances are encouraging, although care provision still remains the domain of women in families. Nevertheless, there is evidence that standard methodological approaches in family research, such as relying on women (as sisters) to describe the behaviours of men (their brothers), reinforce men's poor reputation in research regarding the provision and nature of assistance to older parents (Matthews 2002).

Over the past decade, there has been more research on older men's experiences of transitions such as widowerhood (Bennett 2007; van den Hoonaard 2010) and on masculinities more generally. With advances in men's life expectancies, much yet remains to be learned about men's experiences as they navigate the transitions of family life in mid- and later life.

Sexual Orientation

LGBTQ families are becoming increasingly diverse as more and more same-sex partners in middle age are making efforts to "blend" existing families or to have children together either via medical technology or through adoption (Epstein 2003; Miller 2003). Such emergent family forms may be referred to as "new nuclear" or "new blended," with same-sex dyads forming the nucleus of the family unit. Often the result of the end of a heterosexual union(s), the "new blended" family is part of a mid-life phenomenon in Canadian families. As once-married partners come out after years of marriage and child-rearing, they find themselves trying to negotiate both a divorce and a new sexual identity in middle age. For custodial parents, in particular, this may be a difficult period of adjustment for themselves and their adolescent and/or young adult children. Bringing together families who have not yet made their own transitions to a single-parent unit where that parent is LGBTQ may result in conflicted relations early on in the "new blended" family (Epstein 2003).

In addition, recently, the caregiving relationships of LGBTQ-identified people have been recognized as important topics in the literature on social support in families (Fredriksen-Goldsen and Muraco 2010). The experiences of mid-life and older LGBTQ adults caring for chronically ill partners and of same-sex couples caring for parents (Hash 2001) highlight both similarities and differences in caregiving roles. Not surprisingly, homophobic attitudes of informal (family and friends) and formal (health care and human services professionals) resources are major barriers to providing care for chronically ill loved ones. Beyond that, on a structural level, unsupportive policies and practices serve to exacerbate the problem of discrimination and/or non-recognition of same-sex partnerships in the context of caregiving (Fredriksen-Goldsen and Muraco 2010).

While our understandings of widowhood following long-term same-sex unions and marriages is still limited (Whipple 2006), long-partnered but unmarried opposite-sex and same-sex partners often experience what has been termed "disenfranchised grief . . . as official outsiders to family networks, their right to grieve goes unacknowledged even though the bereavement process is similar " (Connidis 2010:117). While the speed of so-cietal change (from criminality to acceptance) of same-sex relationships has been noted (Ibbitson 2016), and with the legalization of same-sex unions in Canada, it remains to be seen how supportive multi-generational families and care workers are of these new forms of family ties.

In ending this section, we acknowledge that there are many more sources and forms of diversity that characterize mid- and later-life families, and their profiles, transitions, and dynamics. Although we leave it to other chapter authors to provide more in-depth dis-cussion on these experiences, we recognize that social and economic markers of inequal-ity, namely class, ethnicity/"race," gender, geographic location, religion, and age, shape the experiences of families and the provision of care throughout the life course. However, so too do the "superstructures" (Timonen 2009) of social and public policies to which we now turn.

Aging Families and Social Policy

Societies vary in how they respond to the changing character of families and the care needs of citizens. Some societies expect individuals and families to absorb the bulk of economic and non-economic costs of care policy, while others develop a range of policies and programs to include maternity and parental leave benefits, child tax cred-its, income transfers to carers, compassionate care leaves, and direct provision of care (Timonen 2009).

Expectations and experiences of families in mid- and later life are significantly im-pacted by social policy in Canada. Three key issues are highlighted here: (1) mid-life parent–young adult co-residence; (2) social support in mid-life child–older parent rela-tionships; and (3) the diversity of aging families.

With young adults finding it increasingly difficult to leave the parental nest (and increasingly necessary to return) for financial reasons, parents have become the social safety net for their children regardless of their own socio-economic position (Beaupre et al. 2008; Mitchell and Gee 1996). Research in this area, for the most part, has focused on middle- to upper-class parents—those with the financial means to assist adult children through co-resident living arrangements—largely ignoring the experi-ences of low-income families. In Canada, the consequences for young adult children are most dire for those whose parents lack the financial means to provide assistance by allowing them to stay at (or return) home. Cuts to social welfare programs over time have weakened the "knots of the safety net" in low-income families, increasing the likelihood of earlier than expected launches and the posting of "no re-entry" signs for children wanting to return home. As a result, young adult children may be forced into a cycle of poverty, living at risk on the streets, suffering from chronic unemployment or underemployment, and subsequently engaging in high-risk behaviours like drug and alcohol abuse.

There is an overall trend to shift responsibility for care in old age from governments onto individuals and families. As a result, older family members are today more fre-quently discharged from hospital and sent home to family care at a point much earlier in their convalescence than in the past, when they are still in need of significant health intervention. The issue of social support to older adults has been of primary interest to governments in light of these reductions to health care spending. At one time, a shared responsibility existed between government and family; now, the provision of social support and caregiving to older adults has been pushed further and further away from the public into the family domain. Responsibility for support has become more "informalized" as hospital and community support service budgets have been cut. Who bears the brunt of this excess burden for care? The onus falls squarely on the shoulders of mid-life women—the sandwich generation—who are the primary caregivers to older parents and parents-in-law, in addition to co-resident adolescent and/or young adult children. As a result of this "caregiving squeeze," middle-aged women have a higher likelihood of transitioning from full-time to part-time employment or of leaving the paid workforce altogether.

Recognition of the diversity in aging Canadian families in the policy domain has been limited for the most part to issues of class, gender, and family structure. For example, governments have focused their efforts on the development of social welfare policy and programs for young to middle-age single mothers (female-headed lone-parent families) living at or below the low income cut-off line (LICO), a group characterized by intersecting identity markers of diversity. With the continuing emergence of diverse family forms, such as LGBTQ families and childless (by choice or not) couples, it is imperative that governments develop and institute policies that address and attempt to break down systemic barriers (e.g., definitions of "parent" in maternity/paternity leave policy, definitions of "family" for caregiving leave) that have, to date, served to marginalize these groups in Canadian society.

As population aging continues to transform Canadian society over the coming decades, we will be confronted with the question: What can we, as a society, reasonably expect of adult children, vis-à-vis adult caregiving? This chapter has suggested what the future portends: increasing life expectancies in many cases combined with lengthening periods of chronic morbidity or disability at end of life, fewer children, who are themselves aging, to provide support, fewer siblings, and many parents and in-laws.

The Vanier Institute of the Family (VIF) has expressed concern about a growing "care gap" in Canada, both for the care of older adults and of children as primary recipients of family care. Increases in dual-earner households, from 36 per cent of couples with children in 1976 to 69 per cent in 2014, drive this care gap; indeed, among three quarters of these couples, both partners are employed full-time. "While this has increased family income, it has also meant there are fewer family members available to help manage work and family responsibilities" (VIF 2016).

Early studies on the intersection of work and family roles focused primarily on a single family member (typically a woman) balancing or "juggling" these two life spheres. However, work–family balance research today examines the complex interplay of multiple roles and multiple players at the intersection of work and home life. Although flexible work arrangements and/or other accommodation for individuals and family members that are "less formal, less bureaucratic, less structured" than in the past have been instituted in some workplaces (VIF 2016), such programs and services still remain elusive for legions of workers.

There are some encouraging signs in focused practices and approaches, if not (yet) in policy. For example, in June 2014 the federal government launched the Canadian Employers for Caregivers Plan (CECP), comprised of industry leaders from small, medium, and large-sized businesses, as well as expert advisors on caregiving. The goal is to identify workplace practices that support those who are balancing their work responsibilities with family caregiving.

Interestingly enough, though much media rhetoric casts conflict between generations, especially pitting "greedy geezers" against millennials, even those who generally agree with this framing tend to add "though not in my family." It is worthwhile to speculate how the connections of family ties may (potentially) moderate intergenerational acrimony—and what this may mean in the long run.

Finally, research and policy must inform one another in the family domain. Given the increasing diversity of the Canadian population in terms of age, class, ethnicity, immigrant status, sexual orientation, and family structure, and so on, it is clear that a broader mandate for family research in this country must be developed. Such an initiative is needed to address some of the critical policy issues for mid- and later-life families and the implications for their aging in the coming decades.

Conclusion

This chapter has provided an overview of key areas in the study of contemporary mid- and later-life families. The focus on changing demographic patterns of families emphasized two key demographic trends re-shaping family life: fewer children and longer lives. The current and projected co-longevity of generations is historically unprecedented, and requires negotiation of family members' roles and responsibilities as individuals remain in the role of "child" for most of their lives.

In aging families, the very nature of life transitions is changing, for example, home-leaving is frequently delayed while home-returning of boomerang children is new and common. In addition, the presumed transition to parenthood is now a non-transition for many, and grandparenthood has been redefined both by its length and its changing nature. Other transitions involving marital roles have also been reframed over the life course.

Bonds of connection across generations continue to imbue family dynamics, with most transfers of resources and support happening from older parents to adult children and grandchildren until frailty and ill health in the older generation alters the focus of support. Typically, intra-generational care precedes care by mid-life children (especially daughters). But most of the care provided to older kin members continues to be provided by family members. The conceptual framework of intergenerational ambivalence advances our understanding of complex relationships that remain fluid, but rooted, over many years.

The bottom line is that families are diverse, with greater heterogeneity in structures and practices in the later stages than in earlier ones. Recognition of gender and ethno-cultural diversity in families alters the picture. New family forms, as with same-sex unions and generational ties, continue to emerge. As population aging continues to transform families and societies, policymakers will be challenged to support families in the face of such changes.

Future cohorts who are aging and older families will be quite different from preceding generations, not only in pronounced co-longevity but also reflecting the historically unprecedented rise in singlehood. Does this trend signal a waning commitment to family life? Thus far the evidence reaffirms that "most people seek the sense of belonging that comes from membership in the family, both immediate and extended" (Rosenthal 1990:90). This discussion on mid- and later-life families confirms a flexibility and adaptability among contemporary Canadian families. Intergenerational relations remain important to both young and old. But time may tell a different story.

Study Questions

1. How are families in Canada today different from how you imagine they will look in the future?
2. Discuss the term *boomerang children*. What factors have contributed to the emergence of this phenomenon in mid-life Canadian families?
3. What does intergenerational ambivalence add to our understanding of older parent–adult child relationships?
4. Discuss why the life course perspective is an appropriate conceptual framework for exploring the nature of intergenerational relationships in mid- and later-life families.
5. Identify some of the key policy issues related to social support in mid- and later-life families.

Further Readings

Arber, Sara, and Virpi Timonen. 2012. *Contemporary Grandparenting: Changing Family Relationships in Global Contexts.* Bristol, UK: Policy Press. This book is unique in taking a sociological approach to the new roles grandparents have, combining theoretical insights with empirical findings in documenting the changing nature of grandparenthood—across the globe. Contributors analyze how grandparenting changes under different welfare states and within different cultural contexts. It examines a range of specific topics, such as challenges facing mid-life families and the gender roles of grandfathers.

Chast, Roz. 2014. *Can't We Talk about Something More Pleasant?: A Memoir.* New York: Bloomsbury Publishing. This book was a *New York Times* Bestseller in 2014 and a National Book Award Finalist. Cartoonist Roz Chast focuses on the topic of aging and the increasing frailty of her parents. The book spans the last years of their lives and relays their story through cartoons, family photos, and Chast's witty (and neurotic) text. It is also about working through the death of parents and dealing with the aftermath of what was ultimately an ambivalent relationship.

Connidis, Ingrid Arnet. 2010. *Family Ties and Aging*. Second edition. Thousand Oaks, CA: Sage. This Canadian book emphasizes diversity in terms of gender, age, class, "race," ethnicity, and sexual orientation as it integrates theory and current research about contemporary mid- to later-life family relationships. It provides valuable insight into how current trends and social arrangements affect family relationships today. Using a life course lens, it considers the implications of current knowledge and circumstances for future research, theory, practice, and policy on family ties and aging.

Donaldson, Christa. 2000. *Midlife Lesbian Parenting*. Binghamton, NY: Haworth Press. This innovative and important book focuses on the experiences of nine mid-life lesbian mothers parenting young children. The findings highlight the structural and individual (personal) challenges that face these middle-aged mothers on a day-to-day basis.

Mitchell, Barbara A. 2006. *The Boomerang Age: Transitions to Adulthood in Families*. Edison, NJ: Aldine. Focusing on families in mid-life, it is the first Canadian book to explore the complex structural and personal dimensions of family relationships and their implications during the transition to adulthood stage of the family life course.

Key Terms

Aging in place Being able to live safely and independently in one's own home or community for as long as one wishes, with necessary levels of health and social supports and services.

Ambivalence Previously considered a primarily psychological construct focused on interpersonal feelings related to needing support but wanting independence, the study of ambivalence by sociologists has focused on the ongoing negotiation of contradictions in family relationships and their connections to how social life is organized and structured.

Boomerang children Refers to young adult/adult children who return home to live with their parents after a period of living independently.

Caregiving The assistance provided to an individual who requires help in completing his or her activities of daily living; a caregiver (or carer) may be either unpaid or paid.

Co-longevity of generations Refers to the increasing period of the life course when members of different generations co-exist; for example, with many adult "children" having at least one living parent when they turn 50 or even 60 years of age.

Home care The provision of health and social services to individuals in their own homes, often combining the services of paid health personnel and the care of family and friends.

Intergenerational co-residence Refers to two or more generations in a family living together.

Non-transitions Not transitioning to culturally expected experiences, e.g., marriage, parenthood, along the family trajectory

Population aging A characteristic of societies where the median age rises due such factors as increasing life expectancy, declining birth rates, and low immigration. Societies are typically considered "old" when 14 per cent or more of the population is aged 65 years and older.

Sandwich generation A generation of adults, usually in mid-life, who provide care to their aging parents while supporting their own children.

Notes

1. A growing number of Canadian adults are opting not to have children, thereby increasing the number of childless couples in mid- and later life.
2. According to Statistics Canada (2008), the age profile of separated and divorced Canadians is changing: from 1986 to 2002, the median age at divorce increased to 44 for men and 41 for women.

 Interested in finding out more? Visit www.oupcanada.com/Albanese4e for access to a list of recommended websites for this chapter.

PART III

Family Issues

Families face many challenges, make many decisions, and develop diverse strategies as they face shifts in social, economic, and political contexts. That said, the challenges that they face and the strategies they adopt inevitably vary between different types of families. One issue that all family members face is that of giving meaning to their lives together. This is done, in part, by family rituals such as wedding ceremonies. Beyond the symbolic meaning of relationships, families also serve as an economic base for most Canadians. In order to meet the material needs of family members, at least one, but increasingly more than one, family member must earn an income so that family can purchase the goods and services that they need to survive. On top of that, there is a great deal of unpaid labour that is essential to a family's well-being.

Families whose members earn low incomes may end up living in poverty and so must cope with the consequences of this. How families cope with the consequences of their situations depends on a number of characteristics. We must therefore pay attention to characteristics such as sexual orientation, minority status, and the presence of disabilities in family members to better understand how Canadian families work.

Chapter 8 takes up the issue of family rituals. Deborah van den Hoonaard focuses special attention on the rituals associated with marriage and death. She begins by looking at pre-marriage rituals and weddings and considers how they have evolved over time. Finally, she discusses rituals of separation, such as funerals, which mark the end of a life together. Important themes in this chapter include the gendered nature of family rituals, and the ways in which family rituals have changed under the influence of conspicuous consumption and individualization. In North America, rituals associated with marriage have come to be defined as women's business, and women tend to be regarded as the proper experts on rituals. At the same time, individuals now exercise greater individuality in their choices about how to conduct rituals. This reflects a long-term trend toward greater individual autonomy in our society.

In Chapter 9, Andrea Doucet describes patterns of paid and unpaid work in families, first by looking at what has been an important topic in sociology: the relationship between gender and paid work. She considers how paid work has been dominated by a male model of employment and then discusses the changes that have occurred to that model in recent years. Historically and even today, unpaid work, like paid work, has been and is gendered. Doucet examines the gender division of labour with respect to the connections between paid and unpaid work, the relationship between paid and unpaid work and state policies, and the differences and inequalities in paid and unpaid work.

Don Kerr and Joseph Michalski demonstrate in Chapter 10 the relevance of family and demographic changes to recent poverty trends, while also considering some of the broader structural shifts in the Canadian economy and in government policies. For example, changes in family structures alone have generated some degree of economic uncertainty, especially for women and children. The authors review poverty trends over time and consider the relationship of low income to family type and number of earners. They also examine the high rates of poverty among female-headed lone-parent families and recent immigrants, and contrast that to family poverty later in life, which has declined substantially in recent years. They show that unlike older Canadians, young families with children have fared less well. The authors discuss the coping strategies that poor families use to survive and consider the evidence on the consequences of poverty for poor people's lives.

In Chapter 11, Amal Madibbo and James Frideres discuss family life among refugee families. They present a socio-demographic overview but also explore socio-economic factors that affect the everyday lives of refugee families. The authors examine the social structure and organization of different types of these newcomer families, with special attention to the unique challenges facing visible minority refugee youth.

A new contribution by Vanessa Watts reviews assimilationist state objectives towards the absorption of Indigenous families in Canada. Chapter 12 focuses on the role that women and families played in Indigenous communities before assimilationist polices were set in place. It includes a detailed overview of how assimilationist policies affected and affect Indigenous family life; and concludes with an important presentation of the new pathways of resistance Indigenous peoples have undertaken in recent years.

Michelle Owen, in Chapter 13, seeks to understand the impact that disability has on families. She begins by discussing the problem of defining disability, with a special focus on the social model of disability. The chapter aims to show that disabled Canadians and their families are marginalized in our society. Owen finds fault with the general lack of support services for caregivers, and describes often onerous caregiving responsibilities within families. Owen explores the economic implications of parental disability in regard to employment and learning, and domestic labour. She also reviews issues pertaining to violence and abuse against disabled women and children. She concludes, among other things, that social perceptions regarding families and disabilities must be radically altered.

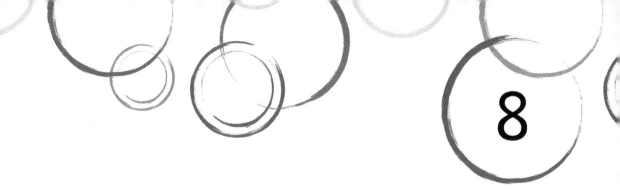

8

Marriage and Death Rituals

DEBORAH K. van den HOONAARD

LEARNING OBJECTIVES

- To understand the role of ritual societal norms in marriage

- To learn about the historical development of rituals associated with marriage

- To understand how rituals reinforce the social meaning of marriage

- To discover how rituals associated with marriage reinforce traditional gender stereotypes

- To learn about the role of consumerism in the evolution of marriage and death rituals

Introduction

Ritual plays a significant role in promoting and maintaining the social norms associated with marriage. You might think first of weddings, but there are many other rituals linked with marriage: bridal showers, bachelor parties, honeymoons, anniversary celebrations, vow renewals, and funerals and mourning practices. How have these rituals changed over time and how do those changes reflect changes in society?

While marriage rituals reinforce gender norms and stereotypes, they also reflect the hyper-individualism that increasingly characterizes society. When we think of rituals, many of us conjure up images of practices related to religious worship. We may also think of the pageantry of weddings or the somber dress and music of traditional funerals. Rituals often identify the sacred in society and always involve symbolism and predictable practices. Rituals bind people to the society in which they live by mediating between their individual experiences and the social structure (Cheal 1988).

The rituals that we associate with marriage, particularly weddings and funerals for spouses, are often religious observances. These milestones demonstrate the religious *ethos* associated with marriage in particular religions, that is, the "codes of behavior [which are] to be lived out in everyday life" (Swenson et al. 2005:535). As fewer people attend religious services on a regular basis—21 per cent in 2005, a decrease from 30 per cent in the 1980s (Lindsay 2008)—marriage ceremonies and funerals may be the only connection that many Canadians have with a religious community.

Rites of passage mark a person's movement from one status to another. For example, a graduation celebrates an individual's transition from being a student to being a non-student. These rites almost always accompany status elevation (Turner in Cheal 1988a). Van Gennep (1960, cited in Cheal 1988) provides the most well-known description of rites of passage. He explains that these rituals have three parts. The first consists of separation from one's previous status. The second and most interesting step involves liminality, or transitional rites. Finally, the third involves rites of incorporation into the new status. The liminal phase associated with marriage—beginning with the engagement through the wedding ceremony—includes a number of rituals. Van Gennep believed that the number of rites of transition reflects the importance of marriage as well as its impact on the community. The rituals we associate with marriage are rites, rituals that are accorded public legitimation (Cheal 1988). Rites of passage that we associate with marriage include bridal showers, weddings, and honeymoons.

Rites of progression, in contrast, celebrate continuity. Erving Goffman referred them as "maintenance rites" which we use to "guarantee the well-being of a relationship . . . as if the strength of a bond deteriorates if nothing is done to celebrate it" (Goffman 1971:73). Rites of progression include anniversary celebrations as well as renewal of marriage vow ceremonies.

Rituals associated with marriage occur before, during, and after marriage. Pre-wedding rituals, such as bridal showers, bachelor parties, and bachelorette parties, take place while a couple is engaged. During the marriage itself, the honeymoon is a rite of passage. Anniversary rituals and the renewal of vows are rites of progression. Rituals associated with the end of marriage traditionally include funerals but also, more recently, divorce rituals. These rituals reflect the norms and moral sentiments current in society (Montemurro 2002: 68).

Pre-wedding Rituals

During pre-wedding rituals, engaged individuals are in the liminal state—they are not quite single but not yet married. The most widespread of these, at least in North America, is the bridal shower, which Beth Montemurro refers to as an "early ritual" that precedes the final stop in the bride's status passage. Through participation in this ritual, the engaged woman demonstrates a commitment to her new status while the women in the community establish their solidarity with her (Montemurro 2002).

Montemurro (2002:13) traces the origins of bridal showers to sixteenth-century Holland, where wealthy, urban women who had access to shops that provided items "suitable to setting up a household" organized events with a ritualized format that bear a very strong resemblance to today's bridal showers. Like today's bridal showers, gathering, eating, socializing, and watching the bride open gifts characterized these early events.

Traditional bridal showers, planned and attended exclusively by women, provide the bride with items she will need in her new status as a wife (Cheal 1988). The appropriate gifts—pots and pans, dishes, linens, small appliances, and others—reflect traditional gender roles and underscore the wife's primary responsibility for cooking and cleaning.

These occasions include a ritual order and expectations of events (Montemurro 2002). The participants know what will happen and in what order. Each woman, from the bride-to-be to the hostess to the guest, knows her obligations. The bride takes centre stage during the entire event. She may feel awkward as the object of intense scrutiny but knows that, particularly during the gift-opening stage, she must act "delighted and grateful" (Montemurro 2002:76).

The hostess is often the maid of honour. Her job is to plan, host, and orchestrate the shower (Goffman 1963, cited in Montemurro 2002:79). For the hostess, this means inviting the right people and organizing the shower as the bride expects and/or approves of.

Women feel an obligation to participate in bridal showers although Montemurro reports that many find them boring. Nonetheless, their attendance demonstrates social solidarity and symbolizes support for the coming marriage and acknowledgment of the bride's new status. Women's attendance fulfills their obligation as members of their gender community (Montemurro 2005:87).

There is no male equivalent of bridal showers. Rather, bachelor or stag parties mark men's departure from their single life. In contrast to the domestic tone of bridal showers, men's parties involve drinking, carousing, and lamenting the end of the groom's sexual freedom (Montemurro 2005).

There have been some adaptations within the last 30 years that suggest a diminution in the conventionally gendered nature of bridal showers. These include the groomal shower and the co-ed shower. Superficially, these invented rituals appear to be evidence of **gender convergence**, but in practice they serve to reinforce conventional gender roles.

Co-ed showers have become quite common. They resemble cocktail parties rather than traditional bridal showers and do not manifest the ritualized format that characterizes bridal showers. Although co-ed showers involve gift giving, the presents are not usually domestic gifts. The gifts appear to be peripheral to the event and gift themes are masculine, for example, "stock-the-bar" motifs directly focused on alcohol (Montemurro 2005:25).

The gift-opening stage of the co-ed shower is a time for joking more than gratitude and emphasizes the masculine. Co-ed showers often include ritualized embarrassment of the groom (Braithwaite 1995; Montemurro 2005), which reinforces men's role of incompetence in shower rituals. They might not know that they are supposed to pass the gifts around after looking at them, and the women tease them about their incompetence. Moreover, men are not supposed to be knowledgeable about wedding tasks (Montemurro 2005). Co-ed showers, rather than leading to gender convergence, reinforce conventional gender expectations of brides and grooms.

Felix Berrardo and Hernan Vera (1981) report on a groomal shower. Berrardo, the groom, was the only man in attendance; his bride-to-be was not present. Berrardo and Vera interpret this shower as an indicator of possible societal and matrimonial changes. The shower symbolized solidarity among friends and a promise that their friendship would not be interrupted—regardless of gender or marital status. Significantly, unlike for brides, there were no domestic gifts. Rather, there were sexual gag gifts that imitated a stag party. Berrardo and Vera (1981:398) describe an atmosphere of "sexual innuendos cast within a friendly atmosphere." Berrardo's women friends understood that cross-gender friendship is unusual and difficult to maintain once the groom-to-be marries. The groomal shower is not common, and it has not presaged fundamental social change.

The other adaptation of pre-wedding rituals that seems to challenge traditional gender scripts is bachelorette parties. These parties arose in direct response to bachelor parties and include elements appropriated from the male model. The symbolic meanings are, however, quite different as they challenge the patriarchal definition of the place of women (Montemurro 2003; Tye and Powers 1998). Bachelorette parties have a ritualized format that includes starting at home where the bride-to-be is dressed up in sexualized gear. The party then moves to a bar, where the bride engages in hyper-sexualized behaviour with men who are strangers to her (sometimes male strippers), and often returns home in a cab. The components of the bachelor party are present but reflect parody and trivialization. The rituals of the bachelorette allow the woman to be sexualized as the subject rather than the object. She is dressed up, sometimes as a bride, and decorated with sexual items. Tye and Powers (1998) describe bachelorettes in Atlantic Canada where the brides wear tee shirts with hard candy attached to the outside; when the women are at a bar, they invite men to suck the candies. The gifts of the bachelorette are highly sexualized gag gifts, and the conversation is light-hearted sexual talk.

Montemurro (2003) explains that the symbols of the bachelorette party suggest that the participants use elements from bachelor parties in order to "get even" with the men. The novelty of male strippers is greeted with humour rather than arousal. The bachelorette mimics and mocks the bachelor party by interpreting the sexual elements as comical rather than sensual.

The sexual character of the bachelorette recognizes that contemporary women are not necessarily virgins but does not supplant the bridal shower, which treats the bride as if she is inexperienced. Bachelorette parties suggest increasing equality but are not wholly a sign of social change. Women are still ambivalent about their sexuality and recognize that even though they are not expected to be naive, sexual innocents, a "good woman" likes sex, but not too much. She conforms to long-term monogamy rather than having many superficial relationships. Nonetheless, the bachelorette symbolically celebrates and ritually laments the bride's "last days of freedom" (Montemurro 2006:33) as the bachelor party does for men. It implies that marriage for women has become a choice, as it has always been for men. Montemurro (2006:147) notes that bachelorette parties' popularity has increased along with the emphasis on lavish weddings.

The bachelorette has a subversive quality that men recognize. In Atlantic Canada their feeling of threat has resulted in the development of "Jack and Jill" or "stag and stagette" parties. This new form reflects the resilience of traditional gender dynamics (Tye and Powers 1998). It may also reflect the women's success at challenging the hegemony of the gendered constructions of "early" marriage rituals.

Questions for Critical Thought

Compare and contrast a wedding shower, bachelorette, and/or bachelor party, you have attended with those described above. How do they reinforce or undermine traditional gender norms about marriage?

The centrepiece of the rituals associated with marriage is the wedding. Traditionally, weddings were religious ceremonies that "enhance[d] the sense of family cohesion and identity and connection to the religious collective" (Chatters and Taylor 2005:520). Clergy members performed weddings that included guidelines that reinforced religious beliefs about marital roles, particularly in the wording of wedding vows. Some traditional Christian wedding vows include the husband's promise to "guide" the wife and the woman's promise to "obey" her husband. As society has moved towards a more equal ideal of marriage, the vows have evolved to become equivalent. The husband and wife make identical promises to one another.

In traditional weddings, one is struck by the symbolic nature of the standard wedding props. Weddings, however, have changed in the twentieth and early twenty-first centuries, pointing to rising individualism in society.

Weddings in the Past

Marriage has always entailed public recognition. In Jewish and Christian traditions, this public recognition originated with biblical stories. As far back as *Genesis*, we witness the marriage of Isaac and Rebekah, during which Isaac led his bride from her family to reside with his. Significantly, although the marriage was arranged by the two families, Rebekah was asked to give her consent before the marriage took place. Biblical accounts of marriage include matchmaking and the union of two families rather than of two individuals. This model of marriage still exists in some parts of the world and continued until the twentieth century in the West (Marcus 2004).

Weddings are necessary for marriage because a social institution "requires public affirmation [and] knowledge." The public nature of weddings and the community's recognition and support of the couple's reciprocal bond explain the need for witnesses to the vows (Cott 2002:1–2). Even when couples elope, a witness is part of the ceremony, as seen in many humorous portrayals in Hollywood films.

Historically, in North America, weddings were "communal celebrations embedded in a system of reciprocity." They were informal events at which "sociability" strengthened both family and community ties. Early weddings were the "loving product of family labor" (Howard 2006:1–2, 11, 14). This type of wedding still exists in small communities. For example, in the Atlantic provinces, I attended wedding receptions held in public halls for which friends and family of the bride and groom provided large, pot-luck feasts. In large part, however, this type of wedding has disappeared, particularly in urban areas.

For more on marriage and family formation in the past, see "Families as Historical Actors" in Chapter 2, pp. 26–30.

Although contemporary weddings use the props of earlier times, their meaning has changed. In nineteenth-century North America, the bride dressed in a white gown that symbolized virginity and "True Womanhood" (Howard 2006:13). Flowers worn as garlands were also symbols of the bride's virtue (Chesser 1980). Giving away the bride originated in the idea that the father "owned" his daughter. Once a woman married, her husband took over ownership. Carrying the bride over the threshold, which has romantic connotations today, also symbolized the husband's ownership of his wife (Sanders, cited in Chesser 1980:206).

One wedding ritual that has almost disappeared is **charivari**, which entailed forcible separation of the bride from the groom after the marriage and tying old shoes or cans to the rear of their car. Charivari was meant to frighten away the devil (Chesser 1980:208). Some small communities still retain forms of this tradition although it is likely that the participants do not know its original meaning. In some parts of the Maritimes, male relatives and friends may "kidnap" the bride from her husband for a few hours, ostensibly to prepare the couple for the unexpected. Today, we are more likely to see a car with a "just married" sign on the back.

Contemporary wedding rituals still use heavily gendered symbols that the wedding industry has co-opted as it has commercialized the wedding ceremonies. In a recent study, Emily Fairchild (2014) found that her interview participants' expectations for their ceremonies took for granted the gendered aspect of rituals, for example, the "gender segregation and heterosexual pairing . . . evident in understanding of bridesmaids and groomsmen" (373). Her participants had also adopted the understanding of the wedding as the bride's event. They used phrases like, "the bride's occasion," and grooms commented that the bride was more invested in the wedding and should get more attention.

Evolution of Weddings through the Twentieth Century

Weddings before the twentieth century were public events with predictable symbols. Everyone knew exactly what to expect as one generation passed down traditions to the next. As the twentieth century got underway weddings became more individualized and increasingly included **consumer rites**, which involve "invented traditions or elaborations of older customs" (Howard 2006:2). As the century went on, the "symbiosis between consumer culture and romantic love" developed (Shissler 2006:118). Wedding vows became more flexible, moving to vows that the couple writes rather than those a religious or civil authority provides. The epitome of the association of romantic love with consumer culture was the 2011 wedding of Kate Middleton and Prince William. People all over the world watched their wedding, which provided the fantasy of a woman's dream of romance and a storybook wedding come true.

Let us look at two components of contemporary weddings and examine how their use and meaning has evolved: wedding rings and wedding dresses.

The wedding ring is the "oldest and most universal marriage symbol." It originally represented trust and power. Men originally wore the ring until it became associated with obedience. From then on, women began wearing it (Chesser 1980:205). In the 1920s, the jewelry industry began to portray marriage as a consumer rite. Stores introduced bridal sets that included matching engagement and wedding rings and constructed them as tokens of romantic love (Howard 2006). At about the same time, jewellers introduced a "male engagement ring campaign" using very masculine images of knights going into jousting tournaments. These images attempted to establish the male engagement ring as a heterosexual tradition and to overcome the link of jewellery with femininity. The time, however, was not right; the woman's engagement ring was a sign of a man's ability to pay for it and a symbol of his love. An engagement ring for men did not fit this story because it was inconsistent with the concept of masculinity of the day (Howard 2003:840–3).

Conversely, the mid-century attempt to introduce a wedding ring for men was successful because the social context had changed, and jewellers were able to provide a symbolic understanding of wedding rings for men that fit with the times. After the Second

World War, middle-class men's identity became more associated with marriage and with personal concerns. A man's wedding ring became a symbol of his maturity. By the 1950s, it had become desirable for a man to "look married." The postwar era and the growth of suburbs put women and men on a more equal plane and encouraged marriages characterized by togetherness (Howard 2006:67). As a result, men adopted the groomal wedding band. Jewellers promoted a double-ring ceremony that "naturalized this conservative version of masculinity, making it seem 'traditional'" (Howard 2003:850). By 1956, the Catholic Church had introduced official double-ring ceremonies.

The white wedding dress that we think of as standard originated with Queen Victoria in 1840. However, it was not until the 1940s that one could simply expect a bride to be dressed in white. As the century progressed, the gown—to be worn only once—began to achieve a special ritual significance as it preserved the individuality of the bride (Howard 2006:175). At this time, the belief that the wedding should reflect the personality of the bride began to supplant the standardized wedding ritual.

The irony, of course, is that women spend hundreds—sometimes thousands—of dollars on a dress that they will wear once while men usually rent a tuxedo, to avoid spending money on something that they might never use again. The wedding gown has achieved a romantic aura while men's wedding clothes have not. The clothing of Kate Middleton and Prince William at their "romantic and regal nuptials" reflects this contrast:

> Kate . . . emerged from a Rolls-Royce wearing a classic fitted white V-neck gown, with a long-sleeved lace overlay and nearly three-metre train. . . . The elegant number was designed by Sarah Burton. . . . Kate also wore a 1936 Cartier "halo" tiara. . . . William, 28, wore the red uniform of the Colonel of the Irish Guards. (CBC 2011)

In 1997, Susanne Friese identified shopping for a wedding dress as the first step in women's realizing they would have a new social status. She concluded that simply walking into a bridal shop and trying on the first wedding dress made women feel that they were entering the liminal state, that their identity was changing. More recently, Carrie Hertz (2013) brought attention to how bridal expos and reality shows like *Say Yes to the Dress* have painted the bridal shop consultant as a ritual specialist and the wedding dress as having ritual power to make a woman feel the reality of her changing status even if she has been living with her partner for years, and her day-to-day life will not change.

"Trashing the dress" is a fad that underlines both the romantic nature of the wedding dress and the increasingly extreme gestures of **conspicuous consumption** (Veblen 1994). To commemorate this practice, wedding photographers take pictures of brides' ruining their dresses by, for example, standing in the ocean while wearing them. This provides a "fairy-tale appeal" that includes the notion that the woman has found the right person, and will not need a wedding dress again. Ironically, couples see trashing the dress as taking a stand against tradition (King 2008).

During the twentieth century, department stores began to take over the role of female relatives in the wedding-planning process. In 1938, Eaton's established its Wedding Bureau. It promoted a service that included all aspects of the wedding ceremony, and its staff ensured that the wedding would go smoothly. As Vicki Howard (2006:132) explains, the Wedding Bureau "standardized the physical outlines of nuptial rites [including] a wider array of ritual props . . . lamps, white ropes, [etc.]." This development presaged the establishment of new professionals—bridal consultants, now called wedding planners—whose presence implied that female members of the family were no longer qualified to plan a wedding (Howard 2006:154).

The evolution of the department-store wedding bureau to the wedding consultant to today's wedding planner has moved weddings even farther away from being communal rites to becoming consumer rites and has reinforced the notion that weddings really belong to the bride. Weddings have become more lavish and have incorporated the symbol of the perfect wedding that fulfills the bride's notion of a dream wedding.

Weddings in the Twenty-first Century

In the twenty-first century, the wedding industry has explicitly adopted the "language of commodity and commerce" (Howard 2006:221). It has eschewed the traditional and become a consumer "spectacle" that focuses on the creation of a perfect day that fulfills each bride's fantasy. The emergence of professionals who do most of the work of planning the wedding echoes the outsourcing of tasks that used to be part of the wife's role in marriage (e.g., cooking and child care). These "wifely chores" have been transformed into consumer services in the process of the commercialization of intimate life (Hochschild 2003, cited in Blakely 2008:639–40; Hochschild 2012).

Outsourcing the task of wedding planning does little to change gendered responsibility. It is the bride who works with the wedding planner; the groom remains inconsequential. Wedding planners reinforce the ideology of the wedding as the achievement of the bride's dream, allowing her to "'have it all': the job, the husband, and the perfect wedding" (Blakely 2008:657–9). For today's couples, who often come from complex families that include divorce and blending, there may be new resonance in how traditional functions of weddings can bring the extended family together. Medora W. Barnes (2014) interviewed white, middle-class women who had had traditional weddings about their experiences. The importance of having all of their family members together in one room was particularly important for those whose parents were divorced, especially if they had half-siblings. Barnes also noted many brides had been walked down the aisle by both parents as a "visible symbol" that both were important, especially because mothers did not have as visible a role in the wedding (71). On reading this article, we might wonder if part of the importance in having the mother of the bride more visible during the wedding ceremony is related to the fact that brides' mothers had a larger role in planning weddings in the past.

Barnes also identified new, made-up rituals that have become common in contemporary weddings. The Unity Candle introduced by the Catholic Church in the 1980s provides a symbol of two halves becoming whole, feels romantic, and may reflect the impact of intense marketing. Another new ritual, the "family medallion" (71) was invented by a Christian minister in 1987. It provides a role in the ceremony for children of the marrying couple, particularly in second marriages (Barnes 2014).

Media coverage of celebrity weddings also contributes to the consumer culture of weddings. In this coverage, the bride is the main character who is both project manager and "emotional childish fantasizer." Sharon Boden (2003) interviewed 15 couples about the planning of their wedding. The couples reported strict gender segregation that constructed the brides as the main character "in the creation of her perfect day" and the groom as incompetent. This segregation intensified on the wedding day, which symbolically started with the bride's donning the wedding dress that turned her into a "fantasy object" and the centre of attention (Boden 2003). Humble, Zvonkovic, and Walker (2008) and Humble (2009) report that couples approach wedding planning in one of three ways: traditional, transitional, or egalitarian. Brides in traditional couples plan the wedding and agree with the ideology that weddings are for the bride rather than the couple. Traditional grooms describe their brides as "natural planners" (2009:11). In contrast, egalitarian couples shared the planning and responsibility, resisted others' gendered expectations, and rejected the ideology that weddings are for brides. Transitional couples expressed a desire to share the planning work, but in actuality, the bride did most of it. Both members of the couple describe the men's work as if they did more than they actually did.

Weddings are big business in North America with estimates of an average cost of $30,717 in Canada in 2015 (O'Brien 2015). Websites such as tietheknot.com showcase weddings in which couples establish their individuality as they throw elegant receptions for over 100 of their "family and closest friends." The site includes slide shows of weddings with descriptors that emphasize the uniqueness of each wedding as well as its success and reviews of their service

> Tie the Knot Wedding Ceremonies is truly fantastic. . . . From the beginning, it was important to us to find an officiant who could understand how we envisioned our ceremony, because we are a non-religious/non-traditional couple with no interest in the standard, cookie-cutter traditions. We were looking for a ceremony that was about who we are together, and our uniqueness that shapes our bond. A ceremony made for our expectations, not the guests'. [The planner] helped us craft and customize our ceremony to reflect our fun personalities, our nerdy tendencies, and the love we share. (www.tietheknot.com)

Very lavish weddings often contribute to a couple's indebtedness, a characteristic of modern marriage. *Money* magazine provides an illustrative example (Chatzky and Gengler 2005) of a couple whose wedding cost $41,000. It included a dress that was "deeply discounted" at $1,100 and a bachelorette party that involved flying the bridesmaids to Las Vegas. Examples of extravagance are fodder for the media, particularly for critics of contemporary weddings. A commentary in *U.S. Catholic* magazine (Conway 2006:26) describes over-the-top weddings that verge on the ridiculous. One marriage ceremony took place in a kick-boxing ring. This extreme illustration is an example of extravagant weddings that emphasize the personalities and affluence of couples rather than solidarity with the community. One growing phenomenon is the "destination wedding." This type of wedding made up about 7 per cent of all Canadian weddings in 2010 (Nelson 2010; Palmer 2008) and 25 per cent of weddings between April and November of 2015 (O'Brien 2015). They are so popular that the Martha Stewart Living brand partnered with a resort chain in the Caribbean to sell destination wedding packages (Nelson 2010). Couples who embrace destination weddings are attracted to exotic places where they will experience "100% romance" (Johnston 2006:192). Some destination weddings involve the movement of whole wedding parties to locales far from home and require significant financial investments for all who attend. In others, the bride and groom go off by themselves, emphasizing the isolation of the couple and the elevation of marriage bonds above all others. The privatization of marriage is complete. Lynda Johnston explored "wedding tourism" in New Zealand. She concludes:

> Wedding tourism separates the couple from their previous social networks, glorifies their relationship . . . over their ties to parents, extended family, friends. . . . In their place, nature steps in . . . a tourist wedding in New Zealand romanticizes both nature and heterosexuality. The couples, like the landscapes, are deemed to be pure, natural, exciting, and romantically "meant to be." (Johnston 2006:203)

Another development of the twenty-first century is the wedding website, often referred to as "wedsites." Couples create these wedsites to communicate details of their wedding ceremony. In a study of wedsites, Laura Beth Daws (2009) discovered that, although they look like joint efforts, brides usually construct wedsites using the term "we" to suggest both members of the couple were involved. Wedsites emphasize a romantic proposal story and manage the change in the couple's identity from single to married. Daws concluded that media messages about fantasy and celebrity weddings were prominent in brides' minds as they developed their wedsites.

Considering these twenty-first century changes, we are prompted to consider the work of sociologist Émile Durkheim, who introduced the concept of the **cult of the individual** (1964, cited in Cheal 1988a:102) to emphasize features of modern culture that make a person feel special and unique. Individualism is rampant in twenty-first century society, and individuals think that they are rebelling against the wider culture by buying into practices like destination weddings and wedsites that celebrate the uniqueness of a couple rather than their integration into social life. Ironically, rather than their plans being original, these couples are part of a common trend. Many of us likely know someone caught up in the same trend—perhaps a friend in New Brunswick whose daughter is heading to South America for her wedding. She had decided on an exotic location as opposed to a church wedding at home because she does not like to conform. Your friend would likely be very surprised to find out that destination weddings, rather than being unique, are the latest thing.

Alternative Approaches

Sometimes we can learn a great deal about mainstream rituals by looking at whom they exclude and by examining different models. To look at whom wedding rituals exclude, we look at the experience of LGBTQ individuals as participants in wedding rituals. The relatively recent legal recognition of same-sex marriage allows us to examine weddings of LGBTQ couples. We will then discuss what wedding ceremonies look like in the Bahá'í Faith, a religion founded by Bahá'u'lláh in nineteenth-century Iran. Finally, we will see how Inuit weddings attempt to incorporate some aspects of Western weddings without focusing on the origins of these aspects.

For more on same-sex marriage in Canada, see Chapter 3.

Ramona Faith Oswald (2000, 2001; Oswald and Suter 2004) has demonstrated the force of heterosexuality as a component of marriage by exploring the experience of LGBTQ research participants as family members or guests at weddings. She argues that wedding rituals implicate LGBTQ family members as "others" or outsiders (2000:350). The exclusion of LGBTQ partners, the need to appear heterosexual in one's dress, the omission of an LGBTQ partner in family portraits, the pressure to participate in the rituals of catching the bouquet and garter, the pressure to dance in heterosexual pairings, and being treated as single women and men who desire heterosexual marriage communicate the sense of not belonging. The marginalizing of LGBTQ participants in wedding ceremonies and receptions reinforces the heterosexual nature of marriage.

One of the outstanding debates of the last 20 years concerns the recognition and legitimation of same-sex marriage. Although the debate still rages on in some quarters, same-sex marriage has been legal in Canada since June 2005. Prior to that point, many LGBTQ couples publicly announced their relationships through commitment ceremonies. This invented ceremony incorporates some aspects of marriage, such as a lifelong commitment, at the same time as it intends to escape the gendered messages of traditional wedding ceremonies. Civil Ceremonies Ltd., for example, defines a commitment ceremony as:

> A meaningful and dignified ceremony for adult couples . . . to make a public declaration of life-long commitment, love, and dedication between two people.

The wording of this definition avoids any mention of gender or sexual orientation. The ceremony upholds the cult of the individual and promotes this invented ritual as a consumer rite. Many LGBTQ websites advertise services and products, including white gowns and flowers that approximate traditional wedding dress.

As soon as same-sex marriage became legal in Canada, LGBTQ couples started marrying and a wedding industry burst into existence. This industry came complete with wedding planners, photographers, and wedding ceremonies that use many traditional wedding symbols (for example, the company IDoinToronto.com, now called prideweddings.ca). Similar to wedding planners who market to heterosexual couples, Pride Weddings Toronto promises that:

> Our wedding services are personalized just for you. We work with our couples to transform wedding dreams into reality. No wedding is too small and no dreams are too big for us to handle. . . . We will be there with you every step of the way, ensuring the perfection of your dream.

Canadian scholars who study how LGBTQ couples plan their weddings found that these rituals, led to their being "'more out' . . . as a result of their public declaration of marriage" (MacIntosh, Reissing, and Andruff 2010:79). Shari R. Lash (2007) and Áine M. Humble (2013) have carried out research into how LGBTQ couples approach their weddings. Lash (2007) interviewed lesbian couples in Toronto who planned their weddings in a liberal Jewish context. She found that, for these women, legal entitlement diminished the need for ritual innovation. Their weddings resembled egalitarian ceremonies for opposite-sex couples. Lash concluded that these couples' Jewish weddings were "meant to assert same-ness [with other weddings] rather than difference." By using traditional Jewish wedding symbols, such as a **chuppah**, the canopy under which couples stand during the ceremony, the women stressed the "equivalency of same-sex love" (Lash 2007:88).

In contrast, Humble (2013) interviewed couples who were over 40 years old when they married and who lived in Nova Scotia. "Intentionality permeated" the planning for these weddings. Couples made carefully thought-out decisions about whom to invite, where they would get married, the incorporation of LGBTQ symbols and avoidance of features associated with heterosexuality, and about the importance of making a good impression on their heterosexual guests that would "represent same-sex marriages well" (2013). Couples' life course experiences of heterosexism and homophobia influenced their decisions.

We can also see a different approach by looking at weddings in the Bahá'í Faith, a religion that emphasizes lack of ritual in everyday life. The Bahá'í Faith has no clergy. No one officiates a Bahá'í wedding; however, two witnesses must be present.

The Bahá'í wedding can be as simple or as elaborate as the couple wishes it to be. In terms of what to wear, what readings or prayers are to be read or sung, what guests

CASE IN POINT

The Marriage of Inuit and Southern Marriage Practices

The following is an account of Jeff and Lisa-Jo van den Scott, who lived in Nunavut for five years. It illustrates how contemporary, commercial props have been added to traditional Inuit weddings without the participants' distinguishing between what we would consider necessary or extra. This mirrors the wholesale continuation of traditional props, like carrying the bride over the threshold, that we include today without much thought.

Tingmihuqaviq (a pseudonym, as are the names below) is a small, remote, Inuit community with a population of roughly 2,200 located in the Kivalliq region of Nunavut, Canada, along the west coast of Hudson Bay. Extremely isolated, Tingmihuqaviq was settled in the late 1950s although there has been a Hudson's Bay Company settlement of *qablunaaq* (people from the south, usually white) since the mid-1920s, when contact with "the South" began in earnest. Prior to the 1920s, contact with white people was nearly non-existent.

> Preparations for the marriage often consist of sewing the bridal clothing. This is becoming more difficult as fewer people know how to sew traditional clothing. When someone from a traditional family gets married, this is not a problem. When Patricia got married, she really wanted to do it right by *qablunaaq* standards so she did not even consider traditional clothing. Katherine wanted to wear the traditional *amoutik*, but she could not get anyone to help her or make a wedding *amoutik* for her. I don't know if the contemporary wedding *amoutik* would be beaded. I think generally not, now, although it was in the past. It used to be a big thing for a bride (with her family) to make her wedding *amoutik*, a very traditional, fancy *amoutik*. Now women get married in an *amoutik* that is half-way between traditional, ceremonial, and everyday use *amoutik*.
>
> Many brides now order items for their weddings from catalogues with the help of their *qablunaaq* friends who have credit cards. Some are connected enough to the South to do it themselves. I have done this twice for friends.

to invite, where it will be held, what food is to be served, or what music is to be played (if any), there are only a few requirements for a Bahá'í wedding to take place. First, the bride and groom must consent to their own marriage (to forestall the practice of arranged marriage). Second, the couple must acquire consent from each of their parents for marriage (such consent does not imply membership in the Bahá'í community).

During the wedding ceremony itself, the only requirement is that the bride and groom each recite the phrase "We will all, verily, abide by the Will of God" as an expression to obey God rather than each other. The Bahá'í local governing body appoints two people to witness the wedding. Bahá'í weddings are legally recognized throughout Canada. Interestingly, New Brunswick requires the local Bahá'í governing body to register a "marriage officer." This person represents the province but does not perform the wedding as a clergy person would.

For more on Indigenous marriage, see "Gender Roles and Families" in Chapter 12 pp. 246–9.

Both times, my friends ordered things I would consider frills at weddings, unimportant items or things associated with the kind of revelry at weddings that is mostly on television. For example, they ordered champagne flutes for the entire bridal party, themselves, and each set of parents. Each one had to be engraved. (Try spelling twelve Inuit names, first and last, over the phone and yes, I was on the phone while my friend sat by since my English was better).

Champagne flutes seemed to be treated as vital to the wedding. Pens were also ordered for the book that people sign. Dresses, a roll-out red carpet, invitations, matchbooks (embossed) . . . this sort of thing. My Inuit friends seem unable to figure out which rituals in the South are "necessary" for the wedding to be defined as a wedding, and which are variations or less integral to the weddingness of a wedding. The dress can be swapped out for a traditional *amoutik*, but the flutes were an absolute necessity for Patricia and Katherine.

When it comes to the wedding itself, the bridal party is dressed up, as are the parents (sometimes traditionally, but often in *qablunaaq* finery). This finery is particularly notable because you can't wear it outside. It is too cold. I have only ever seen women in dresses at their graduation and at weddings. The audience for the wedding is all over the board. A few are dressed up, several are in clean jeans, that are sort of dressed up, and some are still in their ripped sweats and sweatshirts. I have even seen an audience member wearing pajama bottoms. The whole gamut is represented. The average, I would say is to dress normally. People often keep their parkas on, unzipped, but not always. The real show is with the wedding party.

I have a theory that weddings in movies and on TV are so focused on the bride and groom and immediate party that this carries over into what residents think they "should" be focusing on here for a wedding to fulfill all the requirements according to *qablunaaq* standards. The odd part is that often times no *qablunaaq* are even present. Jeff and I were the only ones at one wedding! The preacher immediately came over to us afterwards and apologized for its not having been in English for us. We told him we were very happy that we had the honour of hearing it all in Inuktitut, as indeed we were.

Source: Lisa-Jo van den Scott, personal communication, 2008.

Honeymoons

The final rite of passage to take place during the establishment of a newly married couple—a "late" rite—is the honeymoon. Just like weddings, honeymoons have become both more individualized and more routinized during the twentieth and twenty-first centuries. Women have taken over responsibility for planning the honeymoon, thus emphasizing a more feminized script and further entrenching women's place in the emotional sphere of marriage and family life. Like weddings, honeymoons of the nineteenth-century were community events during which family and friends might accompany the couple, and later became privatized as individuals began to seek fulfillment within the marital relationship rather than in the larger social group.

The honeymoon, as the last rite of passage into marriage, provides the first opportunity for each member of the couple to "discover" the "self" as a marital partner. Even though a couple may have lived together for years, the honeymoon provides their first set of memories as a married couple. Today's honeymoon has a cultural script that includes:

> images of secluded beaches, tropical nights, and sexual passion. If one cannot afford to go to exotic, tropical places, one can always rent the Tropical Room at the Edmonton Mall. (Bulcroft et al. 1997:471)

We, therefore, have seen the development of destinations where one can purchase an escape as well as the romance that contemporary couples crave. Like weddings, honeymoons have come to symbolize the "bride's 'dream' experience" and the couple as "passionate consumers" (ibid:483).

For the most part, rites of passage associated with marriage reinforce conventional gender norms and reflect increasing individualism and consumerism as they have become entrenched in late twentieth- and early twenty-first century cultures. As Nancy Cott (2002:225) has commented:

> Love is exalted in our society—it is the food and drink of our imaginations. Sexual love [has] even more of a halo. . . . But where does marriage stand, when there is widespread awareness that half of all marriages end in divorce? . . . Splendid, elaborately detailed weddings have swelled in popularity, as though money spent on a wedding is ballast designed to keep the marriage afloat.

If spending a lot of money on engagement rituals, weddings, and honeymoons seems like the way to get the right start on a marriage, then rites of progression may help maintain marriage by celebrating the accomplishment of remaining married.

Renewing Vows: A Rite of Progression

Couples have always had private anniversary traditions or routines. In addition, there are socially defined, traditional gifts for each anniversary that symbolize the strength of marriage as it endures. Thus, according to tradition, the ephemeral quality of paper makes it appropriate for a first anniversary while the seventy-fifth anniversary calls for diamonds.

Recently, jewellers and others have developed a more contemporary list that reflects the increased consumerism of contemporary society. Today, clocks have replaced paper for the first anniversary and diamond jewellery replaces tin or aluminum for the tenth (Rose Floral and Greenhouse 2008). Today's jewellers equate a husband's expression of love for his wife on their anniversary with a very expensive diamond ring (*Sun Sentinel* 2008).

The practice of renewing marriage vows gained popularity during the 1990s and received wide media coverage. In addition to individual couples having renewal ceremonies, churches put on mass events. For example, a Catholic Church held a renewal ceremony for 720 couples while a Baptist minister had a special service on Valentine's Day for 75 couples. The rite has become so established that "Dear Abby" had a column in 1992 that included a "protocol of formal vow renewal ceremonies" (Braithwaite and Baxter 1995:117–18).

The vow renewal event, like other marriage rites, has both public and private meanings. The public aspect recognizes the social embeddedness of the marriage relationship as well as the uniqueness of each private relationship. Vow renewals often take place in association with a special, landmark anniversary such as the twenty-fifth or fiftieth anniversary. Other reasons for renewing wedding vows include an opportunity to give thanks after a hardship, an opportunity to have a lavish event when one was not possible at the time of one's wedding, and emerging from a rocky period in one's marriage (Braithwaite and Baxter 1995; Guth 1999).

Marital rites of progression may have become more important in response to high rates of divorce. As maintenance rites, they "pay homage" to the institution of marriage as well as to their "unique marital bond" (Braithwaite and Baxter 1995:179).

As with other rites associated with marriage, anniversary rituals and vows of renewal belong more to the bride or wife than to the husband or man. This is evident in the many jokes revolving around husbands' forgetting their anniversaries. An article in *Esquire* provides humorous advice about how a husband can avoid the vow-renewal event that his wife wants:

> she wants to do it. That's okay, that's good. . . . But trust me, You do not want to do this to your [male] friends. . . . It's a spectacle, it's invariably tacky, and it tends to breed resentment. Still, you love her; you want to make her happy. . . . You might propose . . . a second honeymoon if you wish. . . . And your friends will be cheering you on—from a safe and appropriate distance. (Hamilton 2007)

Daily Life

Marriage rituals comprise not only special occasions, such as weddings, they also include everyday activities, patterned family interactions (Wolin and Bennett 1984), that have symbolic meaning for the couple (Costa 2013). These rituals help to construct a strong sense of identity and reinforce the rhythm of married life. They might include lighting candles for dinner every night, attending a religious service together, or drinking a cup of tea in the evening while sharing the events of the couple's day. The meaning of these rituals can become evident in their loss. Widowed persons I interviewed often avoided activities they had done regularly with their spouse, such as going to church, because they reinforced the absence of their life partner.

Even when marriages are successful and last a very long time, they eventually come to an end through the death of one of the spouses or through divorce. Rituals of separation mark the status passage from being a spouse to being single.

Rites of Separation

The rites of separation associated with death include a funeral or memorial service and the activities and props of mourning, which serve both "integrative and regulatory goals." For the widow or widower, they provide a transformation of the sense of self, the transition to a new social status, and a connection to that which is lost (i.e., the status of wife or husband and the person who has died) (Neimeyer et al. 2002:237).

The social context dictates the degree to which the widowed person must retain or give up the connection to their deceased spouse. In traditional Indian culture, the widow was expected to participate in **suttee**, a practice that required her to jump onto the funeral pyre and be cremated with her husband. This practice, which has been illegal for many years, constructed the wife so that she would have no legitimate status after the death of her husband.

When funerals are celebrated in a recognizable fashion by the community, they communicate its support for the bereaved individual. With the advent of secularization and individualism, these practices have become more fluid and private. Funerals have also become more commercialized as professional funeral directors have taken over from family and clergy.

Before the 1970s, funerals were "fixed events" that offered the widowed person a strong sense of **symbolic communitas** (Turner 1995 [1967], cited in Wouters 2002:2), or connectedness to the whole community. They offered the mourner a sense of "we-feeling" and gave friends and family a concrete way to support the bereaved spouse (Wouters 2002).

Late in the twentieth century, as a culture of individualism increased, people complained that traditional funerals were "stiff" and impersonal. New funeral rituals began to focus on "personalization," that is, funerals focusing on the "unique qualities of the deceased emerged" (Emke 2002; Wouters 2002). In the twenty-first century, options for funerals are broad, and widows and widowers can decide what kind of commemoration they want to arrange. Often the bereaved tries to follow the wishes of the spouse. Thus, the widowed person continues the marital relationship even after death.

With the freedom to make choices about death rituals, some people request that there be no funeral. Some spouses, widowers, in particular, go against the wishes of the deceased spouse (van den Hoonaard 2010) because they, like many people, believe that funerals are really for the living (Emke 2002).

Also associated with secularization is the move to defining the funeral or memorial meeting as a mechanism to "celebrate the life" rather than "mourn the death" (Emke 2002:272). Funeral homes have become "corporatized" resulting in the disappearance of funeral directors who are embedded in the community. They now behave more like salesmen than counsellors and work within a consumer model that involves personalized items that symbolically represent the person who will be remembered (Sanders 2010). These personalized items may include items that "cater to the passions of sports fans" (Huberman 2012:470) or brand-name products, thus remembering the person who died in terms of their "passions" rather than what they have accomplished or momentous events of their lives. Huberman argues that this branding is "yet another example of the way capitalism appropriates human love, labor, and life in its restless pursuit of profit" (472).

Individuals are now memorialized on internet sites like Instagram. Gibbs et al. (2015) have studied photographs tagged with #funeral. They conclude that photographs shared this way provide an "informal, personal, idiosyncratic and highly social practice that is readily appropriated as funerals shift from institutionalized and formal rituals to vernacular events, with individuals and their families . . . engaging in forms of informal and personalized memorialization" (265–6).

Mourning rituals accompany funerals in giving meaning to the end of marriage. Queen Victoria had a great impact on appropriate mourning dress in England and Canada. She was in "full mourning" for three years, and established mourning fashion during the Victorian era (Hell 2001). Mourning fashion reflected both the gendered understanding of widowhood and social class. There were rigid guidelines for widows' dress, but widowers had more latitude and mourned for a shorter period of time (*Harper's Bazaar* 2005 [1886]). Widows' clothes were not only black, but also made from expensive material. One could identify a widow of lower economic standing because she would dye a dress black rather than buy a new one. Thus, Victorian widowhood was "another sphere in which women figured as the pillar of home and society" (Pike 1980:656).

Today there are no rules about how widowed people should dress or how family and community members should support them as they move out of marriage into a new status, an anomic situation. The stigma of widowhood is still there, but there are no norms to tell the members of the community how to act. In some ways, the liminal period, in which the mourner is between being married and single, has almost disappeared. With no concrete norms, bereaved family members may find themselves ostracized by others who have no ritual way to handle an encounter.

There are some vestiges of liminality left. In Jewish culture, for example, many people still sit **shiva**. During this week of confinement from routine duties, the widow or widower allows her- or himself to be cared for by family and close friends (Marcus 2004:216). At the end of the mourning period, the person rejoins society with the new status. Similarly, in Newfoundland, there are several traditional external signs of mourning, for example, keeping one's window blinds lowered (Emke 2002:271). These props of liminality allow the community to acknowledge the loss.

Questions for Critical Thought

How do you think the disappearance of community and religious rituals surrounding death influence the experience of widowhood? To what extent do social media such as Instagram facilitate support for the widowed person?

Becoming widowed is not the only way to leave marriage. As divorce has become more common and socially acceptable, rituals to mark this status passage have appeared. Phil and Barbara Pennington (2001) created a "parting ceremony" during which "the past relationship is carefully honored, difficult feelings are truthfully shared, and the future is gracefully accepted." The Penningtons suggest that friends be present to witness the ceremony, which includes vows and commitments made by the members of the parting couple. If parting ceremonies were to become widely recognized, they would establish the status of a divorced person as legitimate and potentially reduce the stigma.

Conclusion

Our examination of rituals associated with marriage and death shows that secularization, individualization, and commercialization of rituals in society have increased. Nonetheless, these rites, whether of passage, progression, or separation, continue to promote a gendered view of marriage that puts much of the responsibility for their planning in the hands of women. The symbolism and the implicit meanings maintain the belief that issues about the family are really women's issues. If you are a student in a class on Sociology of the Family, there are likely far more women in the class than men, significantly exceeding the proportion one might expect based on the female-to-male ratio at your university.

At the same time, Andrew Cherlin (2004) suggests that we are experiencing a "deinstitutionalization of marriage." This trend is partly the result of the huge growth and acceptability of cohabitation and having children outside of marriage. In Canada, one half of all stepfamilies are formed by cohabitation rather than by marriage. This trend is even more pronounced in Quebec where 84 per cent of unmarried women who had children were cohabiting (Statistics Canada 2002, cited in Cherlin 2004:849–50). Overall, common-law couples made up 19.9 per cent of all couples in Canada (Milan 2013:5) up from 17.9 per cent in 2006 (Institute of Marriage and Family Canada 2009). In Nunavut almost half of couples were common-law (45.6 per cent) while in Quebec the percentage was 38.8 compared to 14.4 in other provinces (Milan 2013).

There has also been a very large increase in never married young adults aged 25–29 in Canada. In 1981, about one quarter of this age group had never married. In 2011, it was 73.1 per cent (Milan 2013:1). Given these changes, it is not surprising that about a quarter of millennials in Canada see marriage as an outdated institution (Mitchell 2016:7).

For more on the future of families, see Chapter 16.

Cherlin suggests that the place of marriage has changed from a social institution with which one associated oneself early in adult life, to an accomplishment, a "capstone" (2004:855). At the same time, the rites of passage, particularly the wedding, which once provided the legal and social approval for having children, has become an event "centred on and controlled by the couple, themselves, having less to do with family approval or having children" (ibid:856). Contemporary lavish weddings, rather than demonstrating the affluence of families of those getting married, "display the attainment of a prestigious, comfortable, stable style of life" of the couple (ibid:857). In addition, Barnes (2014:74) suggests that having a "real" formal wedding that includes all the traditional symbols may serve as "divorce insurance" in times of marital uncertainty. We might say that weddings now straddle the boundary between rites of passage and rites of progression. Although the couple moves into the new status of married people, many have already lived together for some time and plan weddings that underline the success of their lives together so far.

In sum, it appears that couples are depending more on their own resources for marriage and family formation. This move towards privatization means that people cannot or do not depend on their community in times of joy or sorrow. Only the future will tell whether the pendulum may, at some time, swing the other way.

Study Questions

1. What expectations do you have of rites of passage regarding marriage and family for your own life (or what experiences have you had, if you have already married)? To what extent do they fit with the ideas of commercialization and individualization of family rituals that this chapter presents?
2. How do rites of passage, progression, and separation associated with marriage reinforce traditional gendered conceptions of married life?
3. Why does Andrew Cherlin think that marriage has become deinstitutionalized? To what extent do you agree?
4. How has secularization affected rituals associated with marriage and death?
5. How have the internet and social media affected the rituals of family life?
6. If you have shopped for a wedding dress or have accompanied someone who was shopping for a wedding dress, think about what aspects of the shopping trip have become ritualized.

Further Readings

Barnes, Medora W. 2014. "Our Family Functions: Functions of traditional weddings for modern brides and post-modern families." *Qualitative Sociology Review* X (2): 60–78. Medora Barnes interviewed 24 women to discover how women explain how they have reinterpreted features of traditional weddings to be more meaningful for them in the post-modern context.

Emke, Ivan. 2002. "Why the Sad Face?: Secularization and the Changing Function of Funerals in Newfoundland." *Mortality* 7, 3: 269–84. Emke charts changes in funeral practices in Newfoundland and demonstrates the impact of secularization on how funerals are planned and on the disappearance of socially defined mourning rituals.

Goffman, Erving. 1967. *Interaction Ritual*. New York: Pantheon Books.

Goffman, Erving. 1971. *Relations in Public*. New York: Harper Colophon Books. A brilliant observer of social interaction, Goffman's descriptions shed light on small, face-to-face situations that characterize marriage and family rituals.

Hochschild, Arlie R. 2012. *The Outsourced Self: What Happens When We Pay Others to Live Our Lives for Us*. New York: Metropolitan Books. Arlie Hochschild has written some of the most insightful books of the last 30 years. This fascinating read looks not only at how we have outsourced wedding planning, but also many of the tasks that women used to do in their families.

Humble, Áine M. 2009. "The Second Time 'Round: Gender Construction in Remarried Couples' Wedding Planning." *Journal of Divorce and Remarriage* 50: 260–81. This article describes how couples plan their weddings. The author interviewed couples in Nova Scotia who were getting married for the second time to demonstrate how the three categories of traditional, transitional, and egalitarian approaches to gender influence wedding planning.

Tye, Diane, and Ann Marie Powers. 1998. "Gender, Resistance and Play: Bachelorette Parties in Atlantic Canada." *Women's Studies International Forum* 21, 5: 551–61. This article discusses the
subversive nature of bachelorette parties in response to bachelor parties and the success of the
challenge to gendered, pre-wedding ritual scripts.

Key Terms

Charivari The set of practices, traditional in some social contexts, that protect a newly married
couple from the "evil eye" or the devil by separating the bride and groom or attaching loud
items to the back of their departure vehicle.

Chuppah The canopy under which the couple stands in a Jewish wedding.

Conspicuous consumption The lavish and obvious spending on goods and services in order to
display one's wealth and accomplishment.

Consumer rites Consumer activities associated with family rituals, such as weddings, that have
developed the characteristics of rituals, such as shopping for a wedding dress.

Cult of the Individual This concept refers to Emile Durkheim's suggestion that the individual becomes "the object of a sort of religion in advanced societies" (Durkheim 1964:172).

Gender convergence The process through which traditional gender norms and expectations give
way to more equal and less distinct expectations based on gender. The degree to which gender
convergence has taken place is uncertain.

Rite of passage A ritual the marks the movement of an individual from one status to another.
A rite of passage usually has three segments. The first symbolizes the departure of the individual from the previous status. The second, liminality, includes the period when the individual
is between statuses, and the third, incorporation, marks the entrance of the individual to the
new status.

Rite of progression A ritual that recognizes the successful maintenance of a social status. For example, a birthday party marks the progression of an individual as she or he ages.

Shiva The traditional Jewish mourning period, usually a week, during which the family refrains from
its usual activities. During this period friends bring food and visit with the family.

Suttee The Indian custom of a widow's burning herself on her husband's funeral pyre. This practice
is against the law in India today.

Symbolic communitas Anthropologist Victor Turner developed this concept, which refers to the
sense of solidarity and belonging that emerges from the experience of public rites of passage
in which the community expresses its support for the celebrants by its presence.

 **Interested in finding out more? Visit www.oupcanada.com/Albanese4e for
access to a list of recommended websites for this chapter.**

Paid and Unpaid Work
Connecting Households, Workplaces, State Policies, and Communities

ANDREA DOUCET

LEARNING OBJECTIVES

- To examine key issues in the study of paid work and to contest the simplicity of one single model of paid work (i.e., the standard employment model)

- To unpack the diversity and complexity of unpaid work in Canadian households

- To learn about key issues in the study of paid and unpaid work, including connections between paid and unpaid work, links between paid and unpaid work and the state, complexities involved in measuring unpaid work and detailing the costs of care, and why gender differences in paid and unpaid work do matter

- To appreciate the strong gender divisions of labour in both paid and unpaid work, as well as the intricate links between gender, class, and ethnicity

---

Introduction

When I was growing up in a small town in northern New Brunswick in the 1960s and 1970s, my days usually began with the shrill call of the 8 AM whistle at the local paper mill calling the men to their work shifts. My father was one of those men. Along with hundreds of others, he would enter the mill through a front gate that was usually staffed by the mill's only female employee, have his work card punched, and then work 8–12 hours in the papermaking plant. My father worked at the paper mill for nearly 40 years. He received about five weeks of holidays each year, and we were well treated with a generous dental plan and university scholarships, as well as with lobsters in the summer and a large fir tree each Christmas.

Meanwhile, my mother cared for six children. Piecing together a life out of a labourer's salary, she sewed most of our clothes, pickled summer vegetables from my grandmother's garden for the winter, and served beef and fish in an infinite variety of ways from cows reared by my grandfather and fish caught by friends of my father who were seasonal fishermen. My mother's days were filled with the regular family chores of cooking all meals from scratch, housecleaning, washing clothes in an old-fashioned wringer washer in our basement, hanging out loads and loads of laundry, and driving us to various activities when required. She also volunteered at church and school events, diligently brought our old clothes to what were called the "low-rental houses" just down the street from the paper mill, and worked tirelessly to accommodate the countless relatives who drove down from Ontario to visit their New Brunswick homestead each summer.

Through all my growing up years until I took my first course in feminism at York University in the late 1970s, my belief was this: *My father worked. My mother did not work.* The simplicity of that belief and the way in which I did not challenge it still astound me now. Yet, I was not alone. For decades, sociology was concerned only with paid work and with men's work. In Canada in the mid-1970s, a major survey of sociological research on Canadian women pointed out that women's unpaid domestic work in the home had been almost completely ignored (Eichler 1975). Eight years later, the same author concluded again that "by and large housework is excluded from consideration in the social sciences" (Eichler 1983). Thus, housework, as a key form of unpaid work, was neither seen as "work" nor viewed as worthy of study. Since the 1980s, however, all of that has changed and there has been tremendous interest in the study of paid and unpaid work, women's work and men's work, and an ever-expanding area of research and study that falls under the umbrella term of **gender divisions of labour** in paid and unpaid work.

Paid Work

The above description of my father's working life is what researchers have identified as the **standard employment relationship** wherein a worker has continuous full-time employment with the same on-site employer for all or most of his/her working life (Fudge and Vosko 2001; Vosko 2010). This model of work has also been described as one of "48 hours for 48 weeks for 48 years" (Coote et al. 1990) or a "male model of employment" (Brannen and Moss 1991). The word *male* is inserted here for several reasons. First, this model of work has been described as "male" because the continuous unbroken commitment to the labour market has been available mainly to men. Second, the financial remuneration given to women for their paid work has consistently been less than that accorded to men. Third, women's employment has been marked by a dominant pattern of part-time employment while men have consistently worked full-time. Finally, the standard employment relationship has gradually given way to what researchers refer to as non-standard employment.

Gender and Paid Work

The past several decades have witnessed dramatic international growth in the share of women who are part of the paid workforce. In 2015, 82 per cent of all Canadian women aged 25–54 had jobs, up from 52.3 per cent in 1976 (Statistics Canada 2017a). There have been particularly sharp increases in the employment rate of women with children. In 2015, 69.5 per cent of all women with children under age six were part of the employed work force, up from 32.1 per cent in 1976. Women with younger children are still less likely to be employed than women without children under the age of 25; that is, 79.3 per cent of women without children under the age of 25 had jobs compared with the previously mentioned 69.5 per cent of women with children under age six (Statistics Canada 2017a). Table 9.1 shows the employment rates of women aged 25–54 by the age of the youngest child at home for the years 1976–2015.

Gender and Wages for Paid Work

A second reason for the argument that employment is characterized by a male model of work is that women's participation in the labour market, while increasing, has never been on an equal footing to that of men. This is best indicated in the fact that women's earnings continue to be less than those of men. According to a recent report from the Canadian Women's Foundation (2017), a gender wage gap exists in Canada. In 2014, Canada had the seventh highest gender wage gap out of 34 countries in the OECD. The gender wage gap for women workers in Canada varies from women earning 66.7 cents for every dollar earned by men to 87 cents for every dollar earned by men, depending upon how it is calculated. By comparing annual earnings for both full-time and part-time workers, women earn 66.7 cents for every dollar earned by men; by comparing annual earnings of only full-time workers, women earn 74 cents for every dollar earned by men; and finally, by comparing hourly wages, including those for part-time workers, women earn 87 cents for every dollar earned by men. This gender wage gap results from several factors: traditional "women's work" pays less than "men's work," more women work part-time than men (see below), discrimination of racialized people, Indigenous people, and people with disabilities (see below), and most women workers are employed in lower-wage occupations, such as teaching, nursing, health care, and office and administrative work (Canadian Women's Foundation 2017).

For more on the history of changes to paid work, see "Families as Historical Actors" in Chapter 2, pp. 26–30.

Gender and Part-time Work

The labour market has male connotations because it is mainly men who work in full-time continuous work. Women of all ages are more heavily concentrated in part-time work. Many women, between the ages of 25–54, are attracted to part-time service-sector jobs because of their responsibility for children as well as care of the elderly. For women ages 25–54, about one in five worked part-time in 2015 while only a small minority of adult men (less than 6 per cent) did so. Women in the **sandwich generation** who are caring for young children as well as the elderly are also likely to work part-time in comparison to men. Table 9.2 shows the percentages of part-time workers in the labour force in 2015, by sex.

The Rise of Non-standard Employment

A fourth and final point about standard employment, or a male model of work, is how a contrasting model has grown up rapidly alongside it. That is, while my father's

Table 9.1 Employment Rate for Women, by Age of Youngest Child (per cent), 1976 to 2015

Year	Child under 6 years	Child 6–11 years	Child 12–17 years	No child under 25
1976	32.1	45.0	50.4	67.3
1986	53.6	61.0	64.3	73.3
1996	61.7	68.7	72.2	73.2
2006	67.9	76.8	81.5	78.9
2015	69.5	78.1	81.4	79.3

Source: Adapted from Statistics Canada, Labour Force Survey, custom tabulations (Chart 7). www.statcan.gc.ca/pub/89-503-x/2015001/article/14694/c-g/c-g07-eng.htm

work pattern was consistent with the dominant norm of (white) male employment in Canada after the Second World War, this model of paid work began to wane in the late 1970s when other forms of employment, largely filled by women as well as particular groups of men (i.e., men under 25, recent immigrants, and racialized people), became common (Fudge and Vosko 2001; Vosko 2010). Such employment has been variably termed as **non-standard employment** (Krahn 1991, 1995), contingent employment (Polivka and Nardone 1989), precarious employment (Vosko 2000, 2010; Vosko et al. 2003), or temporary employment (Galarneau 2005). Whatever its name, this employment is heavily characterized as part-time, temporary (e.g., short contracts, casual or seasonal work), or self-employment. Such jobs increased almost twice as rapidly as permanent employment in recent years and accounted for almost one fifth of overall growth in paid employment between 1997 and 2003. What all of these jobs share are low wages, insecure working conditions, and limited access to social benefits and statutory entitlements (i.e., Employment Insurance, maternity leave, and parental leave).

Overall, while women experience systemic disadvantages in paid employment, the situation is aggravated for women who are both part of a racialized group and recently arrived immigrants (those women who have lived in Canada for less than seven years) (Chui 2011; Chui and Maheux 2011; Hou and Coulombe 2010; Maitra 2014). An intersectional lens is crucial when analyzing differences in women's and men's experiences of paid work as it recognizes how inequalities are experienced by, and affect, different groups of Canadians, particularly immigrant women and Indigenous women (Pendakur and Pendakur 2011; White, Maxim, and Gyimah 2003)

Table 9.1 shows the percentages of women in the labour force (1976–2015) while Table 9.2 shows male and female part-time participation in the labour force in 2015.

Table 9.2 Percentage of Men and Women Working Part-time, 2015

Age	Women	Men
25–54	18.9%	5.5%

Source: Adapted from Statistics Canada, Labour Force Survey, CANSIM tables. www.statcan.gc.ca/pub/89-503-x/2015001/article/14694/tbl/tbl03-eng.htm

Unpaid Work

Unlike paid work, the definitions and meanings of unpaid work are difficult to pin down. Unpaid work is largely invisible or unnoticed, difficult to measure, and has many subjective meanings that vary according to context. While there are many ways of categorizing unpaid work, most sociologists agree on several dominant types. These include housework, child care, community and inter-household work, subsistence work, informal caregiving, and volunteer work. The first three categories are explored below.

Housework

Several general points can be made about the first category of unpaid work. For one thing, housework is not a universal and homogeneous category. Its detailed composition varies between countries, regions, and classes, and according to such factors as available technologies, number of children, and income level. Second, housework has changed greatly during this century (Cowan 1983; Luxton 1980): while labour-saving devices have made some aspects of housework less onerous (i.e., laundering and dishwashing), growing consumption patterns within households and greater activity levels of children have led to new kinds of housework that entail household management, organization, and planning (Doucet 2006; Taylor et al. 2004). Third, as Olivia Harris pointed out over three decades ago, the degree to which housework is oppressive or burdensome differs greatly and will be influenced by income level as well as by the various forms of co-operation and collectivity between households (Harris 1981).

Child Care

In households with children, the care and upbringing of these children constitute a large part of parents' daily lives. While in this chapter we discuss housework and child care as two separate categories of unpaid work (see also Fox 1998, 2001), they are obviously closely linked. Both kinds of work are usually performed for other household members and thus may be viewed as "familial" work (Delphy 1984). Moreover, some tasks (e.g., cooking for children) may constitute *both* housework and child care activities. Finally, it is important to recognize that both housework and caring activities may have monotonous and routine aspects as well as rewarding and creative dimensions.

Several noteworthy distinctions can, however, be drawn between housework and child care. First, improved technology may have had an impact on household tasks (e.g., cooking and clothes washing) but it has had little impact on caring activities, which are heavily reliant on human input. That is, while the majority of Canadian women do not, in comparison to women in the 1960s and 1970s, wash clothes by hand or with a time-consuming wringer washer, and while most households often buy pre-packaged or takeout food to relieve the demands of cooking every night, the care of children cannot be replaced by technology. While parents may joke or complain that the television and computer have become technological babysitters, the fact is that adults must still supervise their children regardless of what activities they are doing. Infants still require the same amount of time and attention as they have for all of human history, while many school-aged children have high levels of homework and varied levels of participation in extracurricular activities that require time, planning, and organization.

A second distinction between housework and child care is that child care allows for far less flexibility than housework; this is particularly the case with infants and young children where continuous care must be undertaken by household members or must be arranged and organized to be undertaken by others. When children are ill or emotionally troubled, parents often find that they are the ones who need to be with their children. Similarly, while certain aspects of housework can be put on hold, child care cannot. This was beautifully expressed by one particular woman, "Laura," whom I interviewed in Britain in the early 1990s as part of a study on couples attempting to share housework and child care (Doucet 1995, 2000, 2001). Laura made the point that every five years she went on strike over issues of housework. Quite simply, she stopped vacuuming, dusting, doing her husband's laundry, and cooking meals on the weekend. As she put it:

> Every five years I went on strike. I stopped doing certain things so that Richard would start doing more. And sure enough, he started doing more. But I never went on strike around the children. That would have been very unwise. I just would never take those risks with my children. But with housework? Absolutely!

Like Laura, historically and cross-culturally, women overwhelmingly have taken on the work and responsibility of caring for children. Indeed, many researchers have argued that, more than any other single life event, the arrival of children most profoundly marks long-term systemic inequalities between women and men (Brannen and Moss 1991; Dowd 2000; Fox 1998, 2001). This is not to say that fathering and mothering have been static over time. Yet, while women have become secondary workers and wage earners for the household, and sometimes the principal breadwinners, they still remain as primary carers, or shared primary caregivers. Men, on the other hand, have moved from being primary breadwinners but have retained a secondary role in caregiving (Chesley 2011; Doucet 2006; Haas and O'Brien 2010).

While the overwhelming majority of men have not come to share equally in the responsibilities for raising children, there has nevertheless been somewhat of a revolutionary change in father involvement, in Canada as well as in other Western countries. A good indication of Canadian men's increasing involvement in child care is perhaps best revealed in two sets of statistics. The first has to do with fathers at home on a long-term basis while the second has to do with fathers taking parental leave. With regard to the former, recent data from Statistics Canada suggest that stay-at-home fathers (about 54,000 of them in 2010) have increased 25 per cent since 1976 while stay-at-home mothers have decreased by approximately the same figure (Statistics Canada 2010). The second indication of fathers increasing participation in the care of children relates to the extension of parental leave in Canada (from six months to one year) and the increased use of parental leave by fathers to care for infants. A recent study by Statistics Canada reported that in 2010 Canadian fathers took an average of nine weeks of paid parental leave, compared to 28 weeks for women, and the numbers of fathers taking leave increased from 12 per cent of eligible fathers in 2004 to 29 per cent in 2012 (Statistics Canada 2013).

Community and Inter-household Work

An extension of both housework and child care is found in a category of work that has only recently come to be considered in sociological studies on unpaid work. In my own work (Doucet 2000, 2001, 2004, 2006, 2011), I have used the term *community responsibility* to refer to the extra-domestic, community-based responsibility for children. This work of parents *and others* appears in varied guises in a wide body of feminist and sociological research. Terms such as *kin work* (Di Leonardo 1987; Stack 1974), *servicing work* (Balbo 1987), *motherwork* (Collins 1994, 2000), and *household service work* (Sharma 1986) describe domestic work as much wider—spatially, theoretically, and practically—than simply housework and child care. This idea of community responsibility is also explored in the work of scholars working in developing countries, who point to complex webs of social relations within which domestic labour and parenting occur (Goetz 1995, 1997; Moser 1993; Scheper-Hughes 1992). Moreover, Black feminist scholars highlight how community networks and inter-household relations are integral elements of Black motherhood (see Collins 1994, 2000). Canadian author and filmmaker Sylvia Hamilton has illuminated community responsibility and inter-household work in the lives of African-Canadian women living in Nova Scotia (Hamilton 1989).

In summary, both Canadian women and men engage in a considerable amount of unpaid work. But what is the gender divide in unpaid work? It is now a well-recognized cross-cultural and historical fact that women take on the lion's share of unpaid work—whether housework, child care, inter-household work, subsistence work, informal caring, or volunteer work (Bianchi et al. 2000; Coltrane and Adams 2001; Miranda 2011).

Studying Paid and Unpaid Work

As noted earlier, it was not until the 1970s that unpaid work was accorded mention within academic studies, and more specifically within sociology. Three of the "classic" empirical studies of housework (including child care) documented women's "occupation" as domestic labourers within their own homes (Lopata 1974; Luxton 1980; Oakley 1974) and emphasized the isolating and monotonous nature of most housework tasks as well as the fact that housework is overwhelmingly women's work. While these early studies, and the many more that followed, concluded that men did little unpaid domestic work, one criticism of early studies on housework and child care was that they did not fully investigate men's roles in domestic work. In contrast to Ann Oakley's early definition of housework as "an activity performed by housewives within their own homes" (Oakley 1974), many studies have sought to challenge the idea that only housewives do housework. Indeed, the past three decades have produced an astonishing number of case studies on gender

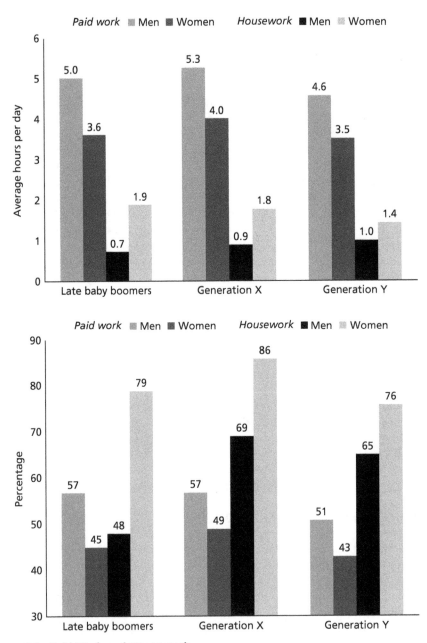

Figure 9.1 Paid Work and Housework

NOTE: Numbers may not add due to rounding. "Other unpaid housework" includes primary child care and shopping for goods and services.

Source: Adapted from Marshall, K. 2011. "Generational change in paid and unpaid work." *Canadian Social Trends*. No. 73. Statistics Canada Catalogue no. 11-008-X. p. 13–24. http://www.statcan.gc.ca/pub/11-008-x/2011002/article/11520-eng.pdf (accessed 1 November 2012).

divisions of labour, that is, on *who* does *what* in relation to unpaid and paid work. These studies generally fall under the rubric of "gender divisions of labour," "work–life balance" (Duxbury et al. 2004) or "work–life integration" (Johnson et al. 2001).

Beginning in the 1970s, Canadian academic studies of gender divisions of labour within the household have collected basically three major types of data on the division of domestic work: *time* (Meissner et al. 1975; Zuzanek 2001), *tasks* (Blain 1994; Marshall 1993), and *responsibility* (Doucet 2001, 2006; Luxton 1980). All three of these areas of study have revealed constant movement and change. For example, Statistics Canada data from 2010 show that gender differences in the time spent in paid and unpaid work had narrowed over three generations. In young "Generation Y" couples (aged 20–29), the gender differences in the time spent in paid and unpaid work were smaller than they were for couples the same age in 1986 (Marshall 2011). Still, the data consistently show women putting in more time, taking on more tasks, and, most importantly, having the greatest responsibility for housework and child care. In focusing on work–life balance issues, Canadian researchers have employed a combination of large-scale surveys as well as in-depth interviews (Duxbury et al. 2004; Fast and Keating 2001). These studies have pointed to how, although men have increasingly come to appreciate the importance of work–family balance, most of the balancing or juggling of home and work continues to fall on women.

In pointing out the persistent connection between women and the time, tasks, and responsibilities associated with caring for children and with domestic life more widely, and their holding the weight of balancing work and family life, many researchers have also considered *why* gender differences persist in paid and unpaid work and why the progress towards gender equality or symmetry has been slow. Several explanations have repeatedly been put forth, including differing gendered expectations of women and men in relation to earning and caring (Deutsch 1999; Dowd 2000; Pleck 1985; Williams 2010); **gender ideologies** (Deutsch 1999; Gaunt 2012; Hochschild 1989; Williams 2010); discourses of motherhood and fatherhood (Dienhart 1998; Lupton and Barclay 1997; Mandell 2002; Miller 2011); and the role of class and social networks in influencing women's and men's choices and decisions, particularly with regard to earning and caring (Barker 1994; Bott 1957; Doucet 2000, 2001; Morris 1985; Shows and Gerstel 2009).

In addition to these findings on gender equality and gender differences, four key areas of study have been emphasized: the connections between paid and unpaid work; the relationship between paid and unpaid work and state policies; the differences and inequalities in paid and unpaid work; and, finally, the overarching question, "What difference does difference make?"

Connections between Paid and Unpaid Work

Talcott Parsons most famously promoted within sociology the notion of complementary spheres of home and work and corresponding gender divisions of labour, with women taking on unpaid work in the "private" sphere and men taking on paid work in the "public" sphere (Parsons 1967; Parsons and Bales 1955). This dichotomy between home and work, paid and unpaid work, and a household model with men as breadwinners and women as homemakers, characterized to some extent the early stages of industrial capitalism where the reorganization of production physically separated the home from the workplace. As described earlier, it was a time when men left the home each morning to go to work while women stayed at home. Spatially, practically, and ideologically, the spheres seemed to be separate.

There are, however, several problems with this dichotomy between home and work and between paid and unpaid work. First, many women, especially women in low-income households as well as African-Canadian women, have always worked outside the home (Carty 1994). Cross-cultural research has clearly demonstrated that many working-class households have always required more than the male wage; thus, women have contributed to the maintenance of the household either by intensifying domestic and self-provisioning work inside the home, by earning money through the informal economy, or by earning a wage themselves (Bradbury 1984, 1993; Tilly and Scott 1987).

A second problem specific to the home/work distinction is the debatable extent to which a clear line of demarcation existed between home and work. This thesis is challenged by the fact that a considerable number of women, as well as men, have always been employed as outworkers or homeworkers. This false distinction between home and work is well captured in the concept of the "household work strategy," which, as defined by Ray Pahl, is "how households allocate their collective effort to getting all the work that they define has, or feel needs, to be done" (Pahl 1984:113). The household work strategy of each household blurs the distinction between home and work because it combines basically three kinds of work that can be done at various sites, including the household, the workplace, and within other households: (1) domestic work; (2) various forms of work in the informal or voluntary economy; and (3) paid employment in the formal economy. While Pahl developed his concept of the household work strategy within a British context, similar ideas have been developed in Canada by Meg Luxton and Bonnie Fox, through the articulation of family households as sites of "social reproduction" (Fox and Luxton 2001), which refers to "the activities required to ensure day-to-day and generational survival" (Luxton 1998).

Since the 1980s, numerous books have appeared with titles including the words "women, work, and family" wherein scholars have investigated the impact of women's labour force participation on gender roles within the household, as well as the inter-relationship between the spheres of home and work (Lamphere 1987; Lewis et al. 1988; Zavella 1987). All of these studies have argued in varied ways that women's experiences of paid and unpaid work cannot be treated as entirely separate things. By the late 1980s and early 1990s it became clear that the issue was not simply a woman's issue and that leaving men out was further solidifying the binary distinction between paid and unpaid work that these analyses were seeking to dissolve. While a few scholars picked up on the importance of examining men, work, and family in the early 1980s (Lewis 1986; O'Brien 1987), this crucial focus came to be part of mainstream sociological research on work and family in the 1990s and in the new millennium. Indeed, research on men as fathers, as domestic partners, and as carers has created a burgeoning literature (Hoffmann 2011; Marsiglio and Roy 2012; Unger 2010; Williams 2010).

The issue of fatherhood as a burgeoning area of research and public attention is addressed in the Case in Point box below. This material is a reduced version of an op ed that I wrote for Father's Day in June 2012. Drawing on my two decades of research on stay-at-home fathers, I reflect on what the category "stay-at-home" father means, the evolution of the concept and the lives of men who inhabit the concept, and the need to re-think how we understand paid and unpaid work.

CASE IN POINT

The Evolution of the Stay-at-home Dad

Twenty years ago, the stay-at-home father was a curiosity, a spectacle, viewed with a mixture of suspicion and praise. I know this because I began to conduct research on these men two decades ago. They were hard to find and reluctant to speak about being the odd man out in a sea of mothers or what one father called "estrogen-filled worlds."

Today, stay-at-home dads seem to be everywhere. They walk proudly with their babies in slings; they're daddy bloggers creating online and community dad groups; and they're injecting a male presence at library story time and infant play groups. The term "stay-at-home dad" (SAHD) is part of our twenty-first century discourse and is used in a taken-for-granted manner by academics, journalists, and bloggers. The term is important. It signals a radical shift in traditional gendered forms of breadwinning and caregiving. Yet I think it's time to re-think the stay-at-home dad label.

First, it is difficult to know to whom it refers. According to Statistics Canada, a stay-at-home dad is part of a husband–wife couple who have dependent children at home (at least one under 16) and where the wife is employed and the dad is not employed; they also note that this means dad is "not going to school and not looking for work, but able to work—meaning not disabled." Using this definition, in 2011, there were 60,875 Canadian stay-at-home dads (13 per cent of all stay-at-home parents).

While these numbers indicate a three-fold increase since 1986, they also seriously underestimate the numbers of fathers who provide much of the daily care of children.

Excluded from these numbers are secondary, irregular, flexible, or part-time earners; part-time students; work-at-home dads (WAHDs); unemployed job-seekers, the underemployed, and discouraged workers. Moreover, statistics that follow only husband–wife families exclude a growing number of single, divorced, and gay fathers.

A second problem with the SAHD label is the now outdated distinction between work and home. This distinction, rooted in the early stages of industrialization when there was a physical separation between factory and home, led to a mythologized view of home as a separate world—a refuge behind a white picket fence, or as historian Christopher Lasch called it, a "haven in a heartless world."

This separation still pervades our understandings of work and care. We assume that the worker goes off to work while the caregiver stays at home. In today's world, however, these lines are blurred. Employed parents may work via their smartphones while they are at school events and take on some parenting duties while at work. Stay-at-home parents, on the other hand, may take on paid work while infants are napping, while kids are at school, or when another parent or caregiver is available. As I argued in my book *Do Men Mother?*, while most stay-at-home dads are the home-based, flexible, or secondary earner, they nevertheless maintain some connection to the labour market.

continued

Instead of stay-at-home dads, should we think instead of work-at-home dads (as well as work-at-home moms)? This would connect to a large body of research on how women have long created lives composed of a patchwork of paid work and unpaid work.

More and more men are now living such lives. Perhaps the most compelling story of fatherhood in 2012 is not about the rise of stay-at-home dads (SAHDS) but about the richly nuanced lives of work-at home dads (WAHDS).

Adapted from an op ed in the *Ottawa Citizen*.

Source: Doucet (2012).

Questions for Critical Thought

What do you think of the stay-at-home parent as a term or label to describe someone? With work lives changing due to technology and with high costs of child-rearing, do you think there will be more or less stay-at-home parents in the future? And what about men? Do you think that mothering and fathering will become more or less similar as men take on more caregiving and as women continue to be breadwinners?

Connections between Paid and Unpaid Work and State Policies

While connections need to be emphasized between home and work, they also need to be drawn between home, work, and state policy. That is, in examining the "choices" and actions of women and men as they negotiate paid and unpaid work—who stays home and who works, how housework is divided, and who takes responsibility for varied aspects of domestic life, caring, and earning—we are reminded, as sociologists, that such actions, decisions, and "strategies" must be situated in a wide set of social relations where women's and men's lives are structured differently. In this vein, state policies in relation to paid and unpaid work do matter.

For more on child care policy see, "Social Policy and Other Supports for Child Care" in Chapter 5, pp. 110–12.

One positive aspect of state support for parenting is Canada's generous parental leave policy. Nevertheless, Canada's parental leave program has weaknesses in that its connection with Employment Insurance (EI) means that many workers—including those who work part-time and those who are not working the required hours in the year before the birth of their child—are largely excluded from both maternity benefits and parental leave (McKay, Mathieu, and Doucet 2016). Moreover, there are marked differences between the province of Quebec and the other provinces and territories with regard to support for fathers' take-up of leave as well as the financial remuneration of leave time. We also know very little about Indigenous parents and their access to parental leave. For example, a recent Canadian Centre for Policy Alternatives (CCPA) report recommended that poverty statistics—including data on key policies and programs, including parental leave programs—should be published to give a clear picture of how Indigenous children are affected (Macdonald and Wilson 2016). In their report, Macdonald and Wilson argued for an extension of annual government surveys to reserves and the territories to provide critical poverty and income data—including access to maternity and parental leave benefits—for Indigenous mothers and fathers.

For more on Indigenous families, see Chapter 12.

As indicated below in the Daily Life box, my research conducted with my colleagues Lindsey McKay and Sophie Mathieu highlights some of the inequities in parental leave policy. In this article published about our research in the online publication *Rabble*, a spotlight was especially put on Lindsey McKay who had paid into EI all of her working life but as she was not working full-time (i.e. she was a student) in the year that she gave birth to twins, she did not have access to those benefits.

Daily Life
A Benefit System Disadvantaging Canada's Poorest Children

By Teuila Fuatai
June 14, 2016
Published on *rabble.ca* (http://rabble.ca)
Lindsey McKay, postdoctoral fellow at Brock University's Sociology Department, is among the thousands of Canadian mothers ineligible for maternity benefits.

McKay, who gave birth to twins in 2011, missed out because she was studying at the time.

According to requirements under the Employment Insurance (EI) system, McKay was ineligible for payments because she had not accumulated at least 600 hours' work in the 12 months prior to her twins' births.

"I worked for about a decade [and was contributing to EI], and then I returned to school, so my children were born in a period in which I wasn't working full time," says McKay, who is also a research associate at Brock University's Social Justice Research Institute.

"Three years after the birth, I'm working full time again, and contributing again."

"I think I should be included in the people who are covered by this program, as should be all kinds of mothers."

McKay teamed up with her colleagues Andrea Doucet, Brock University professor of Sociology and Women's and Gender Studies, and Sophie Mathieu, Université de Montréal Sociology Department lecturer, to investigate how income levels impact on access to maternity and parental leave benefits under EI and the Quebec Parental Insurance Plan (QPIP).

Based on 2013 data from Statistics Canada, the trio's analysis found mothers living in lower income households were not accessing maternity benefits as much as their counterparts in higher income brackets. The disparity between income groups was particularly severe under EI, with Quebec's system achieving more regular benefit coverage between income groups. Mothers living in the three territories were not accounted for in the Statistics Canada figures.

Find out more about this research in the *Journal of Industrial Relations*: http://jir.sagepub.com/content/58/4.toc

Gender Differences in Paid and Unpaid Work: What Difference Does Difference Make?

In examining gender differences in paid and unpaid work as well as how ethnicity and class intersect with gender, the question "Why does this matter?" can often arise. Indeed, this question is invariably asked by at least one student each year when I teach the sociology of gender: *What difference does it make that women do most of the unpaid work in society?* Another way to frame this question is to ask a question that I have often raised in my work: *What difference does difference make?* Drawing particularly on the work of feminist legal scholar Deborah Rhode, we can see that the issue of concern is not that of difference per se, but rather "the disadvantages that follow from it" (Rhode 1990). As phrased by Rhode: "The critical issue should not be difference, *but the difference difference makes*" (Rhode 1989).

Thus, what difference does difference make? It matters in several ways. First, ample scholarship has highlighted the economic, social, political, and personal costs to women of the gender imbalance in the "costs of caring" (Folbre 1994, 2001; Ruddick 1995) for the very young, the very old, the sick, and the disabled in all societies. American journalist Ann Crittenden describes the gender disparity in care and the costs to women particularly well in her best-selling book, *The Price of Motherhood: Why the Most Important Job in the World Is Still the Least Valued*. She writes:

> The entire society benefits from well-raised children, without sharing more than a fraction of the costs of producing them. And that free ride on female labor is enforced by every major institution, starting with the workplace. (2010)

In addition to this "free ride" of unpaid labour that society reaps from women, this weighting of the balance of unpaid labour on the side of women has been very costly to the paid work opportunities for many women. That is, the fact that women undertake the bulk of unpaid labour has had a negative impact on many women's work opportunities including: loss of earnings, pensions, and benefits; economic vulnerability in cases of divorce; and long-term poverty for women (Gough and Noonan 2013; Heitmueller and Inglis 2007; Himmelweit 2007).

A third point about the difference is that we must ask *which* women and *which* men are most affected. Indigenous men, and men of racialized groups, particularly recent immigrants, are disadvantaged in paid work in comparison to men and women who are white and middle-class. Yet Indigenous women and racialized women are doubly disadvantaged because they are faced with inequalities in the labour market while still taking on extra shifts of unpaid work.

A further, conceptual problem entails teasing apart the intersecting inequalities between women and men of different ethnic, citizenship, and socio-economic backgrounds. Specifically, there is an increasing pattern whereby middle-class families with ample economic resources rely on other lesser-paid women (e.g., nannies and housekeepers) for domestic work and child care (Bakan and Stasiulis 1997; Boris and Parrenas 2010; Macdonald 2011; Stasiulis and Bakan 2005). Paying others to perform domestic services such as child care and housework ultimately passes on women's traditional domain from one group of women to another, thus complicating and hardening the boundaries that exist around gender and caring. A good example of this trend has been Canada's Live-In Caregiver program, whereby thousands of women have come to Canada, mainly from the Philippines. Working as nannies with low pay and high levels of stress, these women highlight the tremendous inequalities between women based on ethnicity and citizenship rights (Spitzer et al. 2003). The end result is that work and homemaking remain as devalued "women's work" wherein an ever-broadening lower tier of women are paid meager wages to perform a "modified housewife" role while other women do work that is more socially "valuable." As phrased eloquently by one author, this model seems to trap us into "endlessly remaking the world in the same image: some people in the public sphere, the world of power, of importance, and some people in the private sphere, rocking the cradle but never really ruling the world" (Rothman 1989).

Finally, it is important to point out that gender differences in unpaid work can also make a difference to men. While feminists have been calling for men's involvement in housework, child care, and informal caring partly to ease the gendered costs of caring and as one of the routes towards greater gender equality, men have also been busy documenting the personal and relational losses that they incur from not being fully involved in caring. Most of these claims are found in the burgeoning literature on fatherhood, which has drawn attention to the costs of stress and work–family conflict, the burden of being breadwinners, and the lack of opportunities to develop close emotional and relational attachments for men who are distant or absent fathers (Haas and O'Brien 2010; Kvande 2009; Smith 2009). Alternatively, scholars have pointed to the important generative effects for fathers who are highly involved with their children (Allen and Daly 2007; Ashbourne, Daly, and Brown 2011; Devault, Forget, and Dubeau 2015; Lamb 2004;). As summarized in a Canadian overview of fathering research a decade ago, "[i]t is clear from the research that father involvement has enormous implications for men on their own path of adult development, for their wives and partners in the co-parenting relationship and, most importantly, for their children in terms of social, emotional and cognitive development" (Allen and Daly 2002).

Conclusion

My household today has dramatically different configurations of paid and unpaid work to those undertaken by my parents in the 1960s and 1970s. Much of my unpaid work is invested in child care and the community responsibility that I took on for my three children as well as in housework and small bits of informal caregiving. My paid work consists of being a professor at a Canadian university. My paid and unpaid work occurs in relation to that of my partner, who, as a self-employed naturopathic doctor, varies his hours between full-time and part-time paid work. In addition to the housework, child care, and some parts of community responsibility that he has taken on over the years, he has also taken on a fair bit of subsistence work in our household (painting, household repair, gardening, landscaping, and baking). Moreover, our paid and unpaid work have to be considered in relation to the larger structural and ideological changes that have occurred in Canadian society with regard to norms and practices for women and men at work and at home over the past four decades. Unlike my mother, I have used varied private services over the years to assist me with both child care and housework. Unlike my father, I have not been with only one employer but have worked in several different jobs and two different careers over the past three decades. The sites where my paid work is done are multiple: university classrooms, my university office, my home office, and coffee shops where I read and write. My division of unpaid labour with my partner has been symmetrical, intertwining both equality and differences, with varying contributions from each of us at differing times depending on the ages of our children, the pressures from our respective jobs, our backgrounds, and personal inclinations. Our paid and unpaid work opportunities are also structured by class and ethnicity.

As detailed throughout this chapter, the dramatic changes in the paid and unpaid work patterns in my household are directly related to the tremendous changes in ideologies and family forms, as well as the varied types of paid and unpaid work that have proliferated in the past few decades. Families continue to change and evolve and it could well be argued that the traditional family model, which characterized the household where I grew up (with a breadwinner father and child-rearing mother), has been replaced by multiple new family forms (Gerson 2009).

While heterosexual married couples still account for the dominant family form in Canada, these families are gradually on the wane, while other household types are on the rise. According to Statistics Canada data from the 2011 and 2016 Census (Statistics Canada 2012, 2017) the mother-father-two-kids-under-one-roof model that typified Canadian households half a century ago is being gradually replaced by a complex and diverse portrait of Canadian families, characterized by rising numbers of one member households, blended families created through re-marriage and stepchildren, single parent households (both single mother and single father families), LGBTQ households, multiple generational families sharing a home, and rising numbers of senior citizens. Canadian statistics also reveal a long-term decline in family size and in married couples, with a corresponding rise in common-law couples. This evolving diversity, complexity, and plurality in both paid and unpaid work continue to pose exciting theoretical and methodological challenges to sociologists engaged in the study of work and family life.

Study Questions

1. Why is the standard employment model often considered to be a "male" work model?
2. What types of unpaid work do you engage in? Do you consider these to be "work"? Why or why not?
3. Why do scholars consider it important that men take on a fair share of society's unpaid work?

4. Look back to the generations of your parents and grandparents and reflect on how they structured their paid and unpaid work. What challenges and opportunities did women and men face? How was paid and unpaid work structured by gender, ethnicity, and class?
5. What do you think the families of the future will look like? If you plan to become a parent, what policies would you like to see in place for parents? Will you face a situation of aging parents? If so, what policies or programs would you like to see in place? And whether or not these situations (e.g. having children or aging parents) do or do not apply to you, what workplace policies would you like to see in place to support good work-life balance?

Further Readings

Braedley, Susan, and Meg Luxton. Eds. 2010. *Neoliberalism and Everyday Life*. Montreal and Kingston: McGill-Queen's University Press. This book explores and analyzes neo-liberal policies on a global scale, highlighting how neo-liberal ideology has become entrenched in our daily social and political lives. It reveals the ways in which neo-liberal policies, in particular, are designed to support and exacerbate a system of social inequality across lines of gender, "race," class, and ability.

Doucet, Andrea. 2006. *Do Men Mother?* Toronto: University of Toronto Press. This book builds on international literature on fathering and mothering and the narratives of over 100 Canadian fathers who are primary caregivers of children, exploring the interplay between fathering and public policy, gender ideologies, community norms, social networks, and work–family policies. (The second updated edition of this book will be released in early 2018).

Fox, Bonnie. 2009. *When Couples Become Parents: The Creation of Gender in the Transition to Parenthood*. Toronto: University of Toronto Press. Following 40 heterosexual couples during their first year of parenthood, Fox documents and analyzes the challenges they confront, and the support and personal resources they have to do so. She focuses on the way social and material resources combine in the partners' negotiations around work and care, the resulting divisions of paid and unpaid work in their families, and relationship dynamics.

Macdonald, Cameron Lynne. 2011. *Shadow Mothers: Nannies, Au Pairs, and the Micropolitics of Mothering*. Berkeley, CA: University of California Press. This book explores both the strength and warmth of the bonds between mothers and their child care providers, and the "skirmishes" that erupt between the two groups, situating the latter within broader, classed, cultural, and social tensions.

Williams, Joan, 2010. *Reshaping the Work-Family Debate: Why Men and Class Matter*. Cambridge, MA: Harvard University Press. Williams challenges the conventional wisdom that women "decide" to leave work because they would prefer to be stay-at-home mothers—a view that implicitly guides most workplace policy in the US and creates challenges for both women and men.

Key Terms

Gender divisions of labour The study of how labour is divided by gender in paid and unpaid work.

Gender ideologies A set of social beliefs about men and women's roles and relationships in varied social institutions.

Non-standard employment (relationship) Several types of work that are very different from the norm of a full-time, full-year, permanent paid job, including part-time employment, temporary employment, self-employment, or multiple job holding; also referred to as precarious employment or contingent employment.

Sandwich generation Middle-generation cohorts sandwiched between older and younger cohorts in a population; more specifically, adults in mid-life (40–64 years) who have at least one child in the household and at least one living parent for whom they are the primary caregivers and who often resides in the household.

Standard employment relationship A situation where the employee works full-time for one employer on the same premises and receives statutory benefits from that same employer; also called the male model of employment.

 Interested in finding out more? Visit www.oupcanada.com/Albanese4e for access to a list of recommended websites for this chapter.

Family Poverty in Canada
Correlates, Coping Strategies, and Consequences

DON KERR AND JOSEPH H. MICHALSKI

LEARNING OBJECTIVES

- To understand the nature and extent of family poverty in Canada

- To recognize the demographic characteristics of low-income families and how the face of family poverty has changed in Canada over time

- To be able to identify the main factors contributing to the dynamics of family poverty, including socio-demographic, economic, and political factors

- To develop an appreciation for the coping strategies that low-income families use to deal with their relative lack of disposable income

- To understand and be able to identify the most important consequences of family poverty

---

Introduction

Although a rich country by international standards, within Canada there are families who clearly experience economic hardship. Social inequality and poverty have long character-ized Canadian social life, as families confront the daily struggle of making ends meet. In drawing international comparisons across countries with similar levels of socio-economic development, the research consistently finds that Canada falls somewhere between the United States—where levels of poverty and inequality are relatively high—and much of continental Europe—where the incidence of poverty is moderated somewhat by more comprehensive welfare states (Congleton and Bose 2010; OECD 2015; Picot and Myles 2005; Rainwater et al. 2001). Thus despite Canada's considerable wealth, many families face the challenges, and even the stigma, associated with poverty in a context of relative affluence and economic prosperity (Family Service Toronto 2011).

The last two decades of the twentieth century were turbulent years for many Can-adians, coinciding with some notable ups and downs in the North American economy. In examining trends in family income security, Torjman (1999) describes the period as involving both good news and bad news, or "both crests and crashes." For example, Canadians experienced two severe recessions, in the early 1980s and then the early 1990s. After roughly 15 years of sustained economic growth, Canada again witnessed an economic recession in 2008, but without the same sorts of job losses and double-digit unemployment observed earlier. While the Canadian economy grew relatively rapidly through the latter 1990s and early 2000s, the brief Canadian recession in 2008–9 produced an upturn in the unemployment rate from just under 6 per cent in early 2008 to about 8.5 per cent by 2009. The most recent information available from Statistics Canada on family income provides some indication as to the consequences of the economic downturn for Canadian families, in terms of both average income and the incidence of low income.

In this chapter, we focus on data available on the economic circumstances facing low-income families, from the early 1980s through to 2014. Although average family income has increased modestly in *real* terms for several decades (i.e., after adjusting for inflation), many families continue to experience major financial setbacks. Picot et al. (1998) highlight three distinctive types of events as potential explanations: (1) "demographic" events that influence the types of families and living arrangements in which Canadians share and pool income; (2) "economic" events that influence the availability of jobs and the sorts of wages available in the labour market; and (3) "political" events that influence the types of transfer payments that Canadians receive from government. We develop these themes further by demonstrating the relevance of family and **demographic changes** to recent poverty trends, while also considering some of the broader structural shifts in the Canadian economy and in government policies. For example, changes in family structures alone have generated some degree of economic uncertainty, especially for women and children.

We argue that family poverty tends to be linked to key events—not all of which can necessarily be predicted or controlled. Many low-income families thus struggle to survive and, in some cases, successfully escape poverty. The many potential negative consequences, however, should remind us that poverty has potential costs not only to the families immediately affected, but for society at large.

Has the Problem of Poverty Worsened in Recent Decades?

In addressing the issue as to whether poverty has worsened in Canada over time, we must choose some form of statistical indicator with which to work. Yet in reviewing the literature, we encounter a multitude of different working definitions of poverty (Canadian Council on Social Development 2002; Niemietz 2010; Whelan and Maitre 2007). For instance, some researchers have set poverty thresholds at relatively low levels by considering only the most basic of physical needs necessary for short-term survival in their definitions (Fraser Institute 2001; Montreal Diet Dispensary 1998; Sarlo 2008). Others have set the bar much higher in pointing out that the long-term well-being of families implies much more than merely meeting their barest necessities (Canadian Council on Social Development 2006; Federal–Provincial Working Group on Social Development Research and Information 1998).

Here we work with the most commonly cited poverty line in the Canadian literature: Statistics Canada's **low income cut-offs (LICO)** after tax. Owing in part to the credibility of Statistics Canada, many policy analysts, editorialists, and social scientists consider the LICOs to be the preferred indicators. The LICOs are a reasonable compromise insofar as they fall somewhere near the mid-range of the many working definitions currently available. In addition, the LICOs vary by family size and by five different sizes of urban and rural communities. For example, in 2014 the after-tax low-income threshold ranged from $24,934 for a family of four living in a rural locale to $38,117 for such families living in one of Canada's largest cities. In developing the LICOs, Statistics Canada has systematically examined spending patterns and disposable income, since families that spend an inordinate percentage of their income on necessities (food, shelter, and clothing) are likely to be experiencing economic difficulties.

Table 10.1 provides information on recent trends in income poverty in Canada (1980–2014). In addition, Table 10.2 presents comparable information on median family income, or the midpoint in the income distribution where one half of all families falls above and one half falls below. Thus we can move beyond a narrow focus solely on families at the bottom of the income distribution. The low-income rates and **median incomes** are further broken down by family type. This provides some indication as to how people are adapting to some rather fundamental changes in family life over the last couple of decades, especially in terms of changing family structure and the manner in which households pool their resources. The information in Tables 10.1 and 10.2 has been adjusted for inflation, with all figures presented in constant 2014 dollars.

In reading Tables 10.1 and 10.2, we can see how both income poverty and median income have fluctuated over time, while also varying in a rather pronounced manner by family type. As mentioned previously, the last two decades of the twentieth century have been characterized by periodic ups and downs in the North American economy, with two particularly difficult periods during the early 1980s and early 1990s. For example, in considering all **economic families**, income poverty rose during the recession of the 1980s (from 8.7 per cent in 1980 to 10.2 per cent in 1985), whereas median income fell (dropping from $72,900 to $69,000, expressed in constant dollars). Both of these statistical indicators are influenced by the availability of jobs and wages in the Canadian economy, i.e., by labour market events and macroeconomic conditions (see Kenworthy and Pontusson 2005). The increased incidence of low income is not surprising in light of the double-digit unemployment and inflation of the early to mid-1980s, which exacted a heavy toll on many families and, in particular, on families of low or modest means.

The economic upturn of the late 1980s translated into income gains and reduced poverty, both of which are reflected in Tables 10.1 and 10.2. Unfortunately, these gains were once again washed out during a second recession in the early 1990s. Suggestive of the difficulties that many families encountered during this latter period, median income was lower in 1995 ($67,300) than at the beginning of the decade in 1990 ($72,000) and even lower than 15 years earlier in 1980 ($72,900). In working with these income data, many social scientists in the mid-1990s highlighted this lack of progress (Kazemipur and Halli 2000; McFate 1995; Richardson 1996). In terms of low income, the incidence was once again somewhat higher in 1995 (11.4 per cent) than it was at the beginning of the 1980s (8.7 per cent in 1980).

Table 10.1 Incidence of Low Income (after tax) for Selected Family Unit Types, 1980–2014[a]

	1980	1985	1990	1995	2000	2005	2010	2014
All persons	11.6	13.0	11.8	14.5	12.5	10.8	9.6	8.8
Persons in economic families	8.7	10.2	9.0	11.4	9.3	7.5	6.3	5.6
Persons not in an economic family	37.2	34.9	31.3	35.0	32.9	30.5	27.7	25.9
Non-elderly[b]								
Persons in non-elderly families	8.8	10.8	9.7	12.5	9.9	8.1	6.6	6.1
Persons in couples	4.4	5.9	6.7	7.5	6.9	6.3	5.2	4.5
Persons in couple families with children[c]	7.2	9.2	7.5	10.9	8.7	6.9	5.6	5.1
Persons in lone-parent families								
Female lone-parent families	45.2	52.5	48.2	47.5	36.2	29.7	22.2	26.0
Male lone-parent families	17.9	18.5	18.4	21.9	12.3	11.6	14.0	12.8
Unattached								
Males	24.4	30.2	29.4	37.3	32.1	32.5	29.7	29.9
Females	37.3	37.4	36.8	41.7	44.3	37.0	35.0	33.0
Elderly[d]								
Persons in elderly families	7.6	5.2	2.8	2.6	3.5	2.0	3.7	1.8
Elderly persons not in an economic family								
Males	47.0	28.7	20.7	14.4	17.6	13.6	12.6	12.5
Females	57.1	42.1	30.5	27.3	21.7	20.3	17.1	10.6

a. After-tax low income cut-offs (1992 base) were determined from an analysis of the 1992 Family Expenditure Survey data. These income limits were selected on the basis that families with incomes below these limits usually spent 63.6 per cent or more of their income on food, shelter and clothing. Low income cut-offs were differentiated by community size of residence and family size.

b. Families in which the major income earner is less than 65 years old.

c. Families with single children less than 18 years of age. Children 18+ years and/or other relatives may be present. Low income cut-offs were differentiated by community size of residence and family size.

d. Persons 65 years or older.

Sources: Statistics Canada, CANSIM Table 206-0042. Low income statistics by economic family type, annual (accessed March 22, 2017); Income Statistics Division.

In the early 1990s, as with the earlier recession, persistently high rates of unemployment and a decline in real earnings characterized the North American economy. In addition, the political context shifted with the election of more fiscally conservative governments, both federally and across many provinces. Unemployment insurance and income assistance programs became more restrictive, which had a direct impact on the economic well-being of lower-income Canadians (Meyer and Cancian 1996). Federal and provincial budgetary constraints compounded difficulties in the economy because governments that had hitherto run large fiscal deficits reduced their direct transfers to families (Picot et al. 1998).

Table 10.2   Median Income, by Selected Family Types, Constant 2014 Dollars, Annual 1980–2014

	1980	1985	1990	1995	2000	2005	2010	2014
All economic families[a] & persons not in economic families[b]	$59,900	$55,200	$56,000	$51,800	$54,700	$57,100	$59,000	$63,100
Economic families[a]	$72,900	$69,000	$72,000	$67,300	$73,200	$76,000	$80,900	$87,000
Persons not in an economic family[b]	$26,200	$24,900	$26,200	$24,300	$25,800	$27,300	$30,500	$31,900
Non-elderly[c]								
Non-elderly families	$76,000	$72,900	$76,300	$71,600	$78,400	$81,600	$88,300	$94,900
Couple families	$75,000	$69,000	$70,100	$66,900	$73,300	$77,700	$82,400	$87,700
Couple families with children[d]	$78,500	$77,900	$82,800	$79,100	$87,000	$90,900	$98,600	$105,600
Persons in lone-parent families	$31,100	$28,300	$29,100	$30,500	$38,000	$40,900	$43,600	$45,500
Unattached	$33,700	$31,000	$32,200	$27,600	$28,900	$30,500	$32,700	$33,500
Elderly[d]								
Persons in elderly families	$39,900	$40,900	$48,500	$46,800	$47,300	$51,200	$52,200	$58,500
Elderly persons not in an economic family	$15,900	$18,900	$20,500	$21,400	$22,500	$23,500	$25,200	$28,200

a. An economic family refers to a group of two or more persons who live in the same dwelling and are related to each other by blood, marriage, common-law, adoption, or a foster relationship.

b. A person not in an economic family is a person living either alone or with others to whom he or she is unrelated, such as roommates or a lodger. Income is reported for the individual and not household in which he/she lives.

c. Families in which the major income earner is less than 65 years old.

d. Child or children (by birth, adopted, step, or foster) of the major income earner are under age 18. Other relatives may also be in the family.

e. Families in which the major income earner is 65 years or older.

Source: Statistics Canada. Table 206-0021–Income statistics by economic family type and income source, Canada and provinces, annual (accessed March 22, 2017).

As the decade came to a close, Canada's economic situation improved with declining unemployment and poverty rates. By 2000, the unemployment rate fell below 7 per cent for the first time since 1976—and a stark contrast to the 12 per cent peak only seven years earlier. The unemployment rate declined even further into the first decade of the current century, dipping below 6 per cent by early 2008. Macroeconomic conditions improved, including Canada's record high **labour force participation rate** of just over 67 per cent. Hence by 2008 roughly two thirds of all Canadians aged 15 and older were involved in the labour force, working either on a full-time or part-time basis, or actively searching out employment (Statistics Canada 2008). Furthermore, data on income and unemployment show that a smaller proportion of Canadians relied on government transfers as their primary means of support.

Following a period of sustained economic growth and job creation, Canadians made up the ground they lost during the two previous recessions. By 2005, median family income had risen to $76,000 relative to only $67,300 ten years earlier. The most recent economic downturn that began in 2008 did not fully offset these gains, with median income up to $87,000 by 2014. While not reported in Table 10.2, median family income declined slightly from 2008 before rebounding in 2010 onward. In terms of poverty, Statistics Canada reports that 5.6 per cent of all families had an income below the after-tax LICOs as of 2014, which is lower than observed during the early 2000s.

With respect to household earnings, the norm these days consists of two wage earners per family rather than one. The evidence indicates that many Canadians have enjoyed gains, although upper-income families have witnessed greater improvements in their economic circumstances than lower-income families. Overall the first decade and a half of the twenty-first century has been characterized by higher family incomes and a slightly reduced incidence of low income. It is far from certain as to whether this trend will continue as we move into the third decade of the current century.

Low Income, Family Type, and Number of Earners

Despite the most recent gains suggested in Statistics Canada's income statistics, certain types of families continue to be at a much higher risk of experiencing economic hardship. For example, evidence from the Canadian Survey of Labour and Income Dynamics (SLID) indicates that in the year following divorce or separation, women are far more likely to end up in a low-income household as compared with their male counterparts. In addition, these women (especially those under the age of 40) are much more likely to remain in low-income situations for longer periods than men (Gadalla 2008).

For more on poverty in lone-parent families, see "Recent Developments in Divorce and Family Law" in Chapter 6, pp. 131–4.

Table 10.1 documents how the likelihood of low income has long been much higher for female-headed, **lone-parent families**. In 2014, the likelihood of a female-headed, lone-parent family being classified as poor was more than four and a half times that of all families (26.0 per cent compared to 5.6 per cent) and more than five times that for two-parent families with children (5.1 per cent). Similarly, median income varied substantially across family types as well. For instance, the median income of lone-parent families ($45,500) was only 43.1 per cent of the median income of two-parent families with children ($105,600).

Many lone-parent families, the overwhelming majority of which involve mothers rather than fathers, continue to experience great economic hardship and are seriously over-represented among the poor. This observation is especially consequential in light of some of the remarkable changes in patterns of family formation that have characterized Canada (and most other Western countries) over the last few decades. Sociologists these days appreciate the importance of residential living arrangements for the well-being of adults and children alike, and, in particular, with respect to how individuals earn and pool resources (Cheal 1999; Kenney 2004; Kerr and Beaujot 2016). High rates of divorce, union instability, and non-marital fertility have contributed to a rapid increase in the proportion of families headed by a lone parent—which often implies little or no economic contribution coming from a non-resident parent. Although lone-parent families now comprise more than one in four families with children (or 27.1 per cent according to the 2011 census), among families with children classified as income poor, about half (52 per cent) are single-parent families (Statistics Canada 2013; authors' calculations).

Thus recent trends in family structure have important implications for the economic vitality of families. By their very nature, single-parent families are at a disadvantage in a society where the dual-earner family has now become the norm. The traditional breadwinner family, with a clear gender division of labour, no longer exists in majority form. For example, in considering dual-parent families with children, about nine out of ten men and eight out of ten women are in the labour force. Most dual-parent families currently have two earners, which confers upon them a clear economic advantage. The median income of two-earner families with a child was $98,400 in 2011, as compared to a median income of $61,100 among such families with only one earner (Statistics Canada 2013a).

Even among families with young children, there has been a major shift in the labour force participation of their parents. The majority of new mothers return to paid employment after a short respite to care for their newborns. Survey data have revealed that upon giving birth to a child, an overwhelming majority of Canadian women (well over 80 per cent) plan to return to the labour force within two years (Marshall 2003). While many women (and, increasingly, some men) take advantage of parental leave, in most instances the absence from the labour force is temporary. On the other hand, lone-parent families obviously face disadvantages that dual-parent families do not regarding their ability to re-establish themselves in the labour market. For example, single parents often cannot easily share child care responsibilities with a partner (see Wooley 2004). The age of the children has a particularly important impact on labour force participation of lone parents due to the difficulties of simultaneously raising very young children and maintaining a full-time job. The employment rates for female lone parents, therefore, tend to rise sharply as their children age and depending on the availability of other caregivers or social supports (Uppal 2015; Woolley 1998). These difficulties are often compounded by the shortage of suitable and affordable child care spaces for preschool children as parents seek to re-enter the labour force (Friendly et al. 2007; MacDonald and Klinger 2015).

Recent statistics indicate that about three in ten female lone parents with a child under 16 are not employed, which almost guarantees economic hardship (Uppal 2015). Regardless of individual or family circumstances, welfare payments across Canadian provinces fall well below what most Canadians consider adequate for a reasonable standard of living. These programs have complex rules relating to eligibility for assistance. Yet in reviewing these different programs, we find that one generalization certainly applies across jurisdictions: Canadian welfare programs are not particularly generous. The reality is that families that rely on social assistance to make ends meet usually experience severe economic hardship. For instance, in 2015, the total welfare income for a lone-parent family with one child across provinces ranged from an average of only $17,103 in Manitoba to a high of $22,236 in Newfoundland and Labrador (The Caledon Institute of Social Policy 2016).

For more on the shortage of suitable child care, see "General Overview: Parenting and Social Change" in Chapter 5, pp. 96–8.

Box 10.1

Economic Mobility and Family Background: How Does Canada Compare with Other Wealthy Countries?

Being raised in a poor family does not necessarily imply a lifetime of poverty, just as being raised in a wealthy family does not always guarantee prosperity. **Economic mobility** refers to the extent to which individuals or families experience either improved or declining economic circumstances over time. For example, a child raised in a working-class family could obtain a professional degree and high-paying job in adulthood. This mobility can be thought of as either "intra-generational" (within a person's lifetime) or "inter-generational" (across generations).

The extent of economic mobility varies considerably across different societies, as influenced by local labour market conditions, government policy, and the direct day-to-day experiences and decisions of families and individuals. Corak's (2013) comparative study of intergenerational economic mobility across countries indicates that Canada's mobility compares favourably with other wealthy countries, including two countries with which it shares much in common, both culturally and economically: the United States and the United Kingdom. After examining earnings across generations, the data suggest that a poor child in the US or the UK is far more likely to remain poor as an adult than is true of the typical Canadian child. In fact, the degree of economic mobility documented for Canada even compares relatively well with some of the more social democratic countries of Western Europe, including the Scandinavian countries Finland, Norway, Sweden, and Denmark.

Figure 10.1 summarizes this research using a statistic called the index of intergenerational elasticity (Corak 2004). Without getting into technical detail, the index works with data on individual earnings for persons in young adulthood (latter twenties) relative to the earnings of their parents at a similar stage of the life cycle (i.e. across two generations). The index provides evidence on the extent to which disadvantage is passed on from one generation to the next. A score of 1.0 on this index would theoretically imply absolutely no economic mobility, whereas a score of 0 implies that neither advantage nor disadvantage is passed on from one generation to the next (a completely level playing field for all young adults in establishing themselves in the labour market). In reading Figure 10.1, the degree of intergenerational mobility appears to be more than twice as high in Canada than in the United States, Italy, and the United Kingdom.

In recent studies, Corak et al. (2010) and Corak (2013) have highlighted several factors that are relevant in explaining Canada's advantage, while making systematic comparisons with the US. One important factor is the reality that the poor in the US are on average far poorer than those with low incomes in Canada, as public income transfers have long played a more important role in Canada. For example, many Canadian families receive some form of public support, including a federal child tax benefit, which is a progressive system of income transfers as delivered through the income tax system. The generosity of this benefit varies according to the family's market income, along with its number of children under the age of 18. While this benefit has played a rather limited role in reducing the incidence of low income, it has significantly reduced the severity of poverty among those households that are in fact classified in this manner.

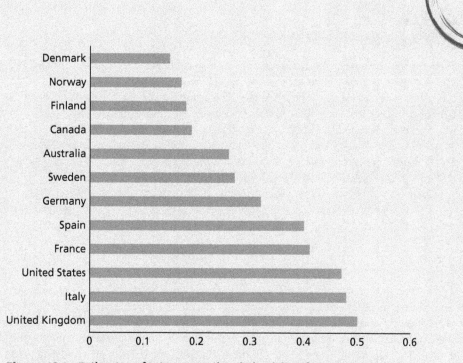

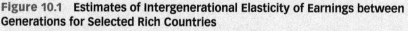

Figure 10.1   Estimates of Intergenerational Elasticity of Earnings between Generations for Selected Rich Countries

Source: Corak et al. (2010), Corak (2009).

Similarly, the wealthiest American households (top 1 per cent) are affluent to a greater extent than their northern neighbours. The overall level of economic inequality in the US is greater in the first place relative to Canada. Taxation and public policies have been described as less "progressive" in the US, failing to compensate to the same degree for family background and labour market inequalities. In essence, because of the difference in the extremes of their earnings distributions, there appears to be notably less mobility at the very top and very bottom of the United States' income distribution.

Finally, children in the US are more likely to be raised in a challenging family context, including being born to young or teenage mothers and/or being raised in a lone-parent family. American parents work longer hours than their Canadian counterparts, while at the same time having fewer benefits, child care opportunities, and job security. In addition, the quality of public education varies more dramatically in the US too, with a smaller proportion achieving at least some post-secondary education. Since quality education is among the most important predictors of economic success in establishing oneself in the workplace, this directly translates into less upward mobility for the most disadvantaged of American families and communities.

Daily Life
Poverty, Stigma, and Social Exclusion

The sociologist Erving Goffman (1963) long ago pointed out how *stigmas* can be associated with specific group affiliations. For example, in the North American context, low income is often associated with social stigma, as the poor are frequently ostracized and discriminated against on the basis of social class. The general public often holds the belief that the poor are somehow responsible for their own economic hardship due to some sort of personal failure or shortcoming such as laziness, irresponsibility, drug or alcohol addiction, family breakdown, or deviant behaviour. This relates to the layperson's understandings of poverty that are often more "individualistic" rather than "structural" in terms of emphasis.

An important contribution of sociology to the study of poverty has been the emphasis on "structural" rather than "individualistic" explanations. For example, instead of focusing narrowly

Lone parents frequently have fewer alternative sources of income to compensate for their lower incomes, as many receive either no child support from former partners or often highly limited support (Marcil-Gratton and Le Bourdais 1999; Stewart 2010). While Canadian law has attempted to enforce the idea that absent parents should maintain financial responsibility for their children, the rates of default on child payments remain high. Among children whose parents have separated or divorced, about one in three of all custodial parents has absolutely no agreement on child support. For those separated parents who have such an agreement, a significant proportion (approaching one half) regularly faces default (Marcil-Gratton et al. 2000). In addition, most non-marital births (i.e., children born to women not in a marital relationship) involve little or no contact with the biological father after the birth, which obviously translates into an absence of child support payments. And those who are poorer, unemployed, with less education, and from racialized backgrounds are overrepresented among those prosecuted for child support debt (Millar 2010).

Moreover, women as lone parents share the same disadvantages that other women face in the Canadian labour market in general (Caragata 2003; Vincent 2013). Women continue to face obstacles in obtaining equal pay for work of equal value, although younger cohorts appear to have been making some significant gains as of late (Schirle 2015). If one further considers the intersection of visible minority status and Indigenous status with gender, the labour market access and earnings differentials become especially pronounced (Gerber 2014; Lee 2000; Smith and Jackson 2002). Beyond issues of "race" and ethnicity, part of the gender-based disadvantage reflects the incidence of low-income families headed by men and women: 12.8 per cent among male lone parents and 26.0 per cent among female lone parents in 2014. On average, male lone parents tend to be older than their female counterparts, are much more likely to be employed, and, when working, earn a significantly higher wage.

on personal problems such as family breakdown or a lack of work ethic, the sociologist points to the underlying structural factors that contribute to poverty and economic inequality in neo-liberal societies. Rather than "blaming the victim" for his or her failures, sociologists examine the limitations of macro-economic conditions, the education system, and/or government policy in terms of promoting job creation, income support, and economic opportunities.

Furthermore, sociologists have demonstrated the negative impacts of social stigma that often attach to low incomes and/or living in low-income neighbourhoods (Hansen, Bourgois, and Drucker 2014). In particular, enduring problems relating to the stigma of poverty can lead to the depletion of social support, lower self-esteem, and greater social exclusion—which only compound the challenges associated with unemployment and/or economic hardships (Pearlin 2010). The linkages between household income and both psychological and physical health are robust: poor people tend to report and experience poorer health in Canada and internationally, even with state-based or universal health care systems in place (Marcus et al. 2015; Maskileyson 2014).

Questions for Critical Thought

On first arriving in Canada, immigrants often experience "greater income" yet simultaneously "lower social status." In other words, while they may have been middle class by the standards of their home country, on first arrival in Canada, they often begin at the bottom, with the lowest status jobs. What do you think are some of the consequences of this simple reality for the well-being of new Canadians and their families? What consequences do you think that this might have with regard to their eventual economic integration and acculturation to life in Canada?

Poverty among Families in Later Life

Older Canadians can be characterized by their diversity in terms of life history, family characteristics, and economic statuses (Chappell and Hollander 2013). In documenting the life history of the elderly, we observe considerable diversity of their life courses, work histories, and patterns of social interaction over a more extended length of time. As an example, some older people have managed to accumulate considerable wealth and property over their lifetimes, whereas others have relatively little. Although some older Canadians benefit from a high income relating to their past investments and/or private pension plans, others are completely reliant on government transfers as they move into later life—which places them at greater risk for being unable to meet their basic needs (Green et al. 2008).

While acknowledging such diversity, we can also draw a few generalizations as to the living arrangements and relative economic status of older Canadians. Most of those aged 65 and older currently live in small households with their spouse, sometimes by themselves, and occasionally with an adult child. Whereas older men are more likely to be living with a spouse in later life, the majority of older women experience widowhood. The data confirm that women outlive men by about four years on average, as well as tending to marry men slightly their senior (Statistics Canada 2016). Although women live longer than their husbands on average, men are more likely to remarry on the event of their spouse's death. Thus women more commonly spend the last years of their lives living by themselves, which has direct ramifications for their economic well-being.

The expansion of the welfare state in Canada during the second half of the twentieth century had a dramatic impact on the economic well-being of elderly Canadians (Myles 2000). Various programs were introduced and expanded, including Old Age Security, the Guaranteed Income Supplement, the Canada Pension Plan, and the Quebec Pension Plan (among other benefits). These programs significantly reduced the risk of sliding into poverty. When the Dominion Bureau of Statistics first started reporting information on the incidence of low income in Canada in the 1960s, Canadians aged 65 and older were more likely to be classified as income poor than any other age group. In fact, more than 40 per cent of elderly families were classified as having low income at that time (Podoluk 1968). Since then, however, the rates of low income have declined substantially and have fallen to levels *below* that of other age groups (Statistics Canada 2015).

Indeed, the expansion of many of the income support programs during the 1970s and 1980s successfully helped reduce the likelihood of economic hardship among the elderly (Myles 2000). Picot and Myles (2005) report that as recently as the late 1970s, the rate of low income (defined as less than half the median family income) among elderly households was nearly 35 per cent. Two decades later, the elderly low-income rate had declined to less than five per cent—a more dramatic decline than for any other group in Canada. As there has been far less support to subsidize families at earlier stages of the life course, the incidence of poverty among families with at least one person over the age of 65 is lower than for any other family or household types. Although the median income of elderly families ($58,500 in 2014) is lower than across all families, average family sizes and the likelihood of income poverty are similarly lower. According to Statistics Canada, the incidence of low income in 2014 after taxes plummets to only 1.8 per cent among elderly families (Tables 10.1 and 10.2).

While most families in later life can avoid poverty by pooling government transfers even without savings or private pension plans, such an option does not exist for the elderly who live alone. For both men and women, the elderly who live alone are more likely to slip into poverty on the death of their spouse. About 10.6 per cent of unattached women aged 65 years or older who lived alone were classified as being in the low-income bracket in 2014, which is comparable to the 12.5 per cent of unattached older men. Clearly, a great many unattached Canadian seniors remain vulnerable, as some have insufficient assets and pension plans to retire in comfort. Whether or not the elderly live in families has a direct effect upon their financial well-being, which once again hints at the importance of living arrangements and the manner in which individuals share resources in predicting low income and economic hardship (Cheal 1999).

Low Income, Family Change, and Child Poverty

Public policy in Canada has been far less generous towards families at earlier stages of their life course than in subsidizing families at later stages. If anything, as governments expanded income support programs for older Canadians in recent decades, income support programs directed at younger families became less generous. For example, during the 1990s, unemployment insurance and income assistance programs became more restrictive, which obviously had a greater impact on younger families (with or without children) than on elderly families. Moreover, the federal government also abandoned its universal Family Allowance program, further reducing the institutional support available for families with children. The net impacts of more limited social transfers for low-income families can be seen in a variety of ways. The evidence from Canada's National Longitudinal Study of Children and Youth, for example, reveals that the welfare reform programs of the 1990s failed to improve the well-being and school readiness of those youngsters living in poverty (Williamson and Salkie 2005).

In short, there has been a major shift in the age distribution of the poor in Canada. While in the 1960s elderly Canadians were about twice as likely as children to be classified as income poor, the situation these days has more than reversed itself, with children more than three times as likely to be income poor relative to the elderly. The shift in the age distribution of poverty highlights one of the most striking changes to characterize the distribution of family income over the last several decades (Cheal 1999). Furthermore, these developments raise troubling questions relating to public policy and generational equity. Many of the aforementioned changes in the structure of the Canadian family—including the increased incidence of lone parenthood—have had a much greater impact on the economic well-being of children than on older age groups.

For more on child poverty see "Impact of Measures on Child Poverty" in Chapter 15, pp. 321–5.

Poverty among Canadian children deserves special mention for a variety of reasons. First, children are particularly vulnerable because of their dependency on parents or caregivers for their economic well-being. Most research on income poverty, however, completely neglects the manner in which resources are shared within families, such as between spouses and between adults and children. The implicit assumption of an equal sharing of financial resources can potentially obscure important differences in the actual level of economic hardship experienced by individual family members (Phipps and Burton 1995; Woolley 1998). Yet the well-being of children ultimately depends on the judgment and goodwill of their parents, as well as the adults' decisions and options regarding family composition, work opportunities, housing, and community locations. Children have far less influence in these areas, despite the significance of such factors in shaping their economic well-being.

While poverty or low-income rates may appear to be somewhat stable in drawing comparisons over time, the actual distribution of individuals and families classified as poor will vary somewhat in response to different life events and especially in terms of changing family characteristics. In Canada, Finnie (2000) has shown that roughly half of those defined as "poor" early in the 1990s escaped poverty within four years, even though a substantial minority remained poor for four consecutive years. Those at greatest risk for such "persistent poverty" were single mothers with children. In addition, Picot et al. (1999) have concluded from their analysis of the Survey of Labour and Income Dynamics that divorces, separations, and remarriages have as great an impact on children entering or leaving poverty as does the changing labour market situation of their parents.

Questions for Critical Thought

The introduction of the Guaranteed Income Supplement for Canadians 65 or older had a major impact in terms of raising the disposable income of lower-income Canadians and reducing poverty rates. As a result, the low-income rate among seniors is now very low by historical standards. Do you think a comparable program could be introduced for all Canadian families, regardless of age, in the form of a "guaranteed annual income"? If so, how high might this income be? If not, why not?

Economic Well-being among Indigenous and Racialized Communities

In Canada, Indigenous peoples are far more likely to be living in low-income situations as compared with other Canadians. For starters, the median income for Indigenous people was estimated to be 31.4 per cent lower than that of non-Indigenous persons (NAEDB 2015). Although the information remains incomplete, the 2006 Census indicates that roughly one in five persons of Indigenous identity lived in a low-income situation (Collin and Jensen 2009). Indigenous women tend to fare even worse than their male counterparts. By extension, nearly 28 per cent of Indigenous children 15 years and younger experienced low income as compared with about 13 per cent of the non-Indigenous population. More specifically, the Indigenous children experiencing low income included 33.7 per cent of First Nations children, 20.8 per cent of Inuit children, and 20.1 per cent of Métis children.

As with Indigenous peoples, those who identified themselves as racialized minorities were also more likely to be living in poverty or below the after tax, low-income cutoffs (22 per cent) as compared with the white majority (9 per cent). The visible minority, or racialized, members of Canadian society living in poverty tend to be rather different in terms of key demographic information in comparison with the non-racialized majority. In particular, racialized individuals living in poverty tend to be younger, married, more educated, immigrants, and unemployed (National Council of Welfare 2012). For example, 32 per cent of racialized persons between the ages of 25–64 with university degrees lived in poverty. Even more dramatically, approximately 90 per cent of racialized individuals living in poverty are newcomers to Canada, or first-generation Canadians (National Council of Welfare 2012). The historical evidence points to a more general decline in the economic well-being of recent immigrants spanning at least three decades (Haan 2008; Picot 2004). The economic struggles of many newcomer families tend to produce other outcomes, such as an exodus of young immigrants from secondary schools, which may serve to perpetuate poverty across generations (Anisef et al. 2010).

Shortcomings of Income-based Measures of Poverty

Income-based indicators of economic well-being have many well-known limitations, most of which have been discussed in detail elsewhere (Collins 2005; Cotton et al. 1998; Head 2008; Hulchanski and Michalski 1994). These measures tend to systematically

under-report or exclude various types of in-kind public assistance, the sharing of resources and services across households and generations, the impact of exchanges in the informal economy, the bartering of goods and services, and various types of employment
benefits such as extended medical insurance and drug plans. This is particularly problematic in documenting the economic well-being of Canadians because these resources and
entitlements can vary considerably across individuals and households.

For example, merely consider the economic situation of a college or university student
temporarily earning a relatively low income, yet receiving generous non-declared income
support from a parent or relative. This situation differs dramatically from a young adult
working full-time at a minimum wage job without any such aid from family. Similarly, a
young adult living precariously close to the poverty line in a low-wage and insecure job has
a vastly different situation from a young university graduate setting out in a career-type
job with an entry-level salary—but with generous benefits, a pension plan, job security,
and the promise of higher income. The aforementioned income statistics do not directly
provide this sort of detailed information necessary to delineate such differences across
individuals and households. In fact, there is currently a scarcity of comprehensive data
at the national level that would allow us to carefully consider many of these issues, both
cross-sectionally and over time.

Most income-based measures of income poverty also exclude information on wealth,
which again varies in an important manner across households. Economists typically define
wealth to mean the stock of assets held by a household or individual that either yields
or has the potential to yield income. Wealth can assume many forms, though usually
is defined as the difference between total assets and total debts. Total assets include
all deposits, mutual fund investments, bonds, and stock holdings, as well as registered
retirement savings plans, locked-in retirement accounts, homeownership, vehicles, etc.
Total debts include mortgage debts, outstanding balances on credit cards, student loans,
vehicle loans, lines of credit, and other money owed. While there is considerable income
inequality in Canada, wealth inequality has a more dramatic skew that appears to have
worsened somewhat in recent years (Uppal and LaRochelle-Côté 2015). For example, in
1999 the top income quintile of all family households in Canada controlled 45.1 per cent
of wealth, but by 2012 this had risen to 46.9 per cent (see Figure 10.2). At the opposite
end of the spectrum, the bottom quintile of income earners owned 5.0 per cent of wealth
in 1999, which declined to 3.9 per cent in 2012.

While households classified as income poor are considerably more likely to have little
wealth or property, there is not a perfect association between income and wealth. For example, consider the economic situation of someone who has paid off his or her mortgage,
has major investments in terms of securities and the stock market, and yet for whatever
reason chooses to live on a relatively low income. Alternatively, consider a new immigrant
to Toronto or to some other large city in Canada trying to establish herself in the labour
market for the first time, without any property or investments. Rising housing costs also
work against the interests of many, including new labour force entrants, whether they are
newly arrived to Canada or have recently completed their education (Zhang 2003). Once
more, these sorts of disparities are not obvious when restricting ourselves exclusively to
the distribution of income across families.

Just as wealth differs enormously across households and individuals, it tends to
vary systematically by life cycle stage as well. In working with Statistics Canada's 2012

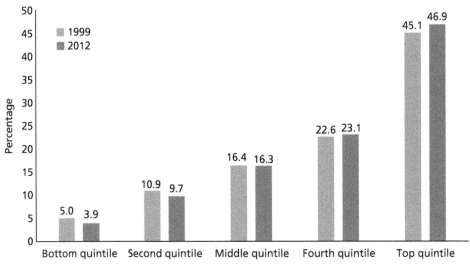

Figure 10.2   Share of Wealth by Income Quintiles, 1999 and 2012, Canada
Source: Statistics Canada, Survey of Financial Security, 1999 and 2012.

Survey on Financial Security, Uppal and LaRochelle-Côté (2015) demonstrate major discrepancies by age group. Among families whose major income recipient was under the age of 35, median assets in 2012 dollars was about $92,700, as compared to a median of over $650,000 for families whose major income recipient was aged 55–64. Everything else being the same, younger people not only tend to have lower incomes, but also typically have far less overall wealth. Similarly, Morissette and Zhang (2006) have documented that median wealth varies significantly by education, immigration status, and number of years residing in Canada. There are also important differences in wealth as documented across family types, in comparing lone-parent families with dual-parent families, elderly with non-elderly families, and households with or without children.

Lone-parent families reported median assets of $89,500 in 2012, which contrasts sharply with dual-parent families with children aged 18 and over, who reported median assets of $578,000. In fact, when we systematically examine differences in wealth across individuals and family types, the inequalities documented in terms of income largely become accentuated. The precariousness of certain types of households and families (e.g., lone-parent families or non-elderly individuals living alone) appears to be even more obvious when we consider differences in terms of assets and wealth. To the extent that those who left income poverty in recent years continue to work in low-wage, insecure jobs with relatively little wealth or property, they are clearly more vulnerable to economic downturns. Many Canadians could easily fall back into poverty with the loss of a low-income job and, in turn, have relatively little wealth to draw from in getting through the worst of economic times.

How Do Low-income Families Cope with and Survive Poverty?

How do low-income families survive, particularly those with limited market incomes and/ or meagre state transfers, such as social assistance? Several commentators have observed that economic factors, globalization, and the subsequent restructuring of the Canadian welfare state have increased the vulnerability of large segments of the population (Caragata 2003; Lightman et al. 2008; McMullin et al. 2002). Social assistance rates declined and eligibility requirements tightened across Canada during the 1990s, as the proportion of unemployed workers eligible for Employment Insurance benefits fell significantly—and the overall size of the Canadian safety net continued to shrink over the next decade (Cooke and Gazso 2009; Krahn et al. 2007; Mendelson et al. 2009). Despite these changes, research reveals that women, in particular, continue to weigh several advantages (e.g., increased income, self-esteem, independence) and disadvantages (e.g., overload, exhaustion, less supervision of children) in evaluating their welfare experiences (Duck 2012; London et al. 2004). The evidence in the North American context further suggests that many of those who move from welfare to employment do not necessarily improve their income situations or family well-being due to the unstable, low-income jobs that they were able to obtain (Lightman et al. 2010; Scott et al. 2004).

As welfare supports tightened up during the 1990s, a variety of community support services developed and in-kind contributions grew. Both Chekki (1999) and Capponi (1999) argued that many agencies—soup kitchens, church and school programs, community centres, Salvation Army centres, and other charitable organizations—expanded their operations in the face of growing demands. In addition, Michalski (2003a) has demonstrated the importance of food banks as a supplemental source of support for low-income families, one that has expanded dramatically over the past two decades, but especially in the 1990s. In the decade from 1999–2009, food bank usage in Canada remained relatively stable as compared with the overall growth in population. The short-term impact of the 2009 recession, however, produced a nearly 10 per cent spike in food bank usage, reaching an all-time high in 2012 as more than 880,000 Canadians accessed food bank programs across the country (Food Banks Canada 2016). Thus food banks continue to be an important coping strategy for about 2.5 per cent of Canadians monthly (see Case in Point box).

Indeed, low-income families typically rely on a broad range of economic survival strategies. The available research demonstrates that these strategies vary in part in response to the degree of urbanization and, more specifically, the resource infrastructures and support networks available in different locales (DeVerteuil 2005; Harvey 2011). The labour market represents one key structural dimension, with the commercial infrastructure providing a variable range of options for low-income households in their efforts to meet their basic needs (Iyenda 2001). In addition, different locales provide distinct opportunities for exchanges, including a variety of non-market and non-governmental economic options such as household production, self-provisioning, and other forms of unpaid work in the informal economy (Felt and Sinclair 1992; Reimer 2006), as well as community-based exchanges (Engler-Stringer and Berenbaum 2007; Raddon 2003), access to social supports and networking (Barnes 2003; Letkemann 2004), and the many non-profit organizations associated with the voluntary sector (Small 2006). Further evidence suggests that women in particular expand their access to resources by engaging in volunteer service and mobilizing to establish greater organizational ties and connections with others (Messias et al. 2005).

CASE IN POINT

What Role Do Food Banks Play in Helping to Sustain Low-income Families?

The first food bank in Canada opened in Edmonton in 1981 as a stopgap measure to assist poor individuals and families on an emergency basis. Throughout the 1980s, the number of food banks continued to grow across Canada, such that by 1989 there were nearly 160 located across the ten provinces (Oderkirk 1992). The number of food banks doubled over the next two years and expanded quite rapidly through the 1990s. In just two decades, the total had grown to roughly 600 food banks working with more than 2,000 agencies dispensing groceries and/or serving meals in every province and territory in Canada (Wilson, with Tsoa 2001). In 2015, Food Banks Canada (2016a) reported working with 550 food banks and more than 3,000 programs across the nation, several of which also provide skills training, community kitchens and gardens, and assistance in the search for employment, affordable housing, and child care.

Figure 10.3 summarizes the trend in food bank usage over the last decade, which fluctuated slightly before a surge on the heels of the 2008–9 economic recession. The relative consistency of these numbers suggest that food banks have become well entrenched as a common response to hunger in Canada (Michalski 2003a). More generally, food banks and emergency food programs are part of the bundle of coping strategies that many low-income individuals and families use to survive (Michalski 2003; Tarasuk 2001; Tarasuk and Dachner 2009). The coping strategies for low-income families include a vast array of budgeting and money-saving schemes, including informal and in-kind work, public transit, maximizing welfare payments, bulk shopping, selling personal possessions, doing without certain basic necessities such as telephones, forgoing recreation and entertainment, simply consuming less food or doing without altogether, and "dumpster diving" (Carolsfeld and Erikson 2013; Edin and Shaefer 2015; Halpern-Meekin et al. 2015). While by no means a comprehensive service or welfare supplement, food banks are an additional source of support among a patchwork of low-income survival strategies (Tarasuk 2001; Tarasuk and Eakin 2003). Indeed, recent evidence indicates that many food-insecure households do not or cannot even access food banks because of the nature of their operations and their target clientele, which usually privilege those in more dire circumstances and/or receiving social assistance (Loopstra and Tarasuk 2015; Tarasuk et al. 2014).

Where job loss occurs and in high unemployment areas, material hardships such as food insufficiency, an inability to meet housing costs, or even the affordability of telephone services routinely crop up (Lovell and Oh 2005). Families with limited resources compensate by reducing their expenses in general, receiving public assistance, retaining a stable residence, and cutting food expenditures (Yeung and Hofferth 1998). Most heads of household, though, prefer to return to the paid labour force. Under Canada's revised Employment Insurance program, the evidence reveals that many individuals accept less than optimal jobs and the prospects of additional training in order to recover lost income more quickly (Martel et al. 2005).

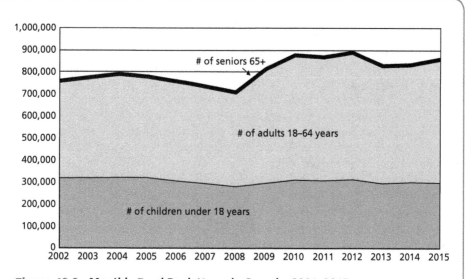

Figure 10.3   Monthly Food Bank Users in Canada, 2001–2015
Source: Food Banks Canada 2016. Reprinted by permission of Food Banks Canada. © 2015. All rights reserved.

The available studies clearly indicate that those who access food banks in urban settings on average tend to have household incomes far below established poverty lines (Michalski 2003a). Their economic statuses are almost always quite precarious, with housing costs consuming the majority of available monthly income (Pegg and Marshall 2011; Vozoris et al. 2002). The depth of their need has been measured more formally over time by comparing their disposable income with household needs (shelter costs, food, clothing, transportation, dental or special health needs, recreation, and so forth). In focusing on Toronto, Michalski (2003) has estimated that the disposable income of food bank users actually declined significantly during the latter 1990s. In this context, it is not surprising that a proportion of Ontario residents became increasingly dependent on public assistance and the voluntary sector to help meet their most basic of needs. Even more remarkably, the most recent evidence indicates that more than one in six households accessing food banks nevertheless live on incomes from employment (Food Bank Canada 2016).

Edin and Lein (1997) studied the importance of three additional strategies above and beyond employment income and welfare supports for sustaining low-income households among women: (1) informal network supports from friends, family, and absentee fathers; (2) side work in the formal, informal, and underground economies; and (3) agency-based strategies from community groups and charitable organizations. Since neither welfare nor low-wage work provided adequate income for living for the families in their study, Edin and Lein (1997:6) reported that "all but one of the 379 mothers spoken to were engaged in other income-generating strategies to supplement their income and ensure their economic survival."

In Ontario, Vozoris et al. (2002) have demonstrated that income from Ontario Works (welfare) alone proved insufficient to cover the core needs for households residing in market rental accommodations on a regular basis. Even if families were fortunate enough to live in rent-geared-to-income housing, a great many expenses beyond the bare necessities (e.g., school expenses, reading materials, gifts) routinely placed them in a deficit-spending position and thus unable to regularly afford a nutritious diet. And Lightman et al. (2008) have shown that the life experiences and even poverty circumstances of food bank users employed in low-income, precarious jobs without benefits do not differ markedly from those households without anyone in paid employment. Herein the importance of relying on informal sources of support or developing a range of alternative coping strategies cannot be overstated.

For example, the majority of food bank users indicated one specific coping mechanism involved simply being hungry once each month or more, while nearly half reported that their children were hungry at least that often, while employing a range of other coping strategies discussed previously (see Michalski 2003). In sum, the research has confirmed that low-income families employ a range of adaptive strategies—informal support networks, unreported and underground work, self-production, and in-kind supports from voluntary and charitable organizations—in their ongoing struggles to secure the basic necessities of life (Bostock 2001; see Jarrett et al. 2010).

Questions for Critical Thought

Critics of food banks have argued that the discourse surrounding them has been hijacked by those who favour the neo-liberal agenda, i.e., that food banks users are subjected to the same kinds of protocols and probing questions that welfare recipients must respond to in order to demonstrate "need" and "deservedness" (Carson 2014). Do food banks actually help *solve* the problem of poverty, or simply continue to perpetuate the problem year after year? What might food banks do to help create systemic change to assist those coping with poverty?

What Are the Consequences of Poverty?

To conclude, we briefly consider an issue that has been examined more extensively than any other aspect of low-income families: What are the consequences of poverty? Many consequences are highly predictable and have been well documented. Others are not entirely obvious or well understood. Health consequences, for instance, have long been associated with a relative lack of family resources and poverty in general. Social scientists have established that a direct relationship exists between socio-economic status (whether measured by income levels or other measures of social class) and health status (Kosteniuk and Dickinson 2003; Phipps 2003). The groundbreaking Whitehall Study of British civil servants determined that those employed at the highest grades had about one third the mortality rate of those in the lowest grades (Marmot and Smith 1997). The study found that death rates were three times higher among junior office support staff as compared with senior administrators, even though these were all white-collar workers in the same offices and living in the same area of the country.

Interestingly, having a sense of control over one's work significantly relates to one's health status—a finding replicated in the second stage of the British research or the Whitehall II Study (Griffin et al. 2002). Higher incomes are linked to improved health not via the ability to purchase adequate housing, food, and other necessities, but also because of the enhanced sense of control and mastery that people have over their lives. Even the level of job insecurity or the threat of losing one's job contributes to greater distress and a decreased sense of control, which have negative effects on self-reported health status.

Tjepkema and Wilkins (2011) have demonstrated that death rates are consistently higher among persons with less than a high school education, who are unemployed or not in the labour force, who work in unskilled jobs, and/or occupy the lowest income brackets. When delineating Canadians by income quintile, for example, the researcher estimated life expectancy at age 25 to be roughly seven years shorter in comparing men in the lowest quintile with those in the highest. Similarly, the evidence confirmed a five-year disadvantage among women in the lowest quintile. Education mattered too: men with less than high school were estimated to have a six-year disadvantage relative to the university educated, with women experiencing roughly a four-year difference.

The chasm between the most educated and wealthiest Canadians and those who were relatively impoverished persists in a context of enduring income inequality, despite an oft-restated commitment on the part of national and provincial governments toward universal health care coverage. Repeated studies have found that Canadians in the highest income bracket reported their health as excellent and lived longer than those in the lower income brackets. Furthermore, statistical evidence revealed that the poor were at greater risk for most types of illnesses and almost all causes of death (Federal, Provincial, and Territorial Advisory Committee on Population Health 1999). Income-related disparities affect the nutritional quality of food selection, which has direct implications for health inequalities (Ricciuto and Tarasuk 2007). In their review of more than a dozen studies using eight data sets across four countries, Benzeval and Judge (2001:1379) concluded the following: "All of the studies that include measures of income level find that it is significantly related to health outcomes."

Even more compelling has been the finding that childhood financial circumstances may be linked to adult health outcomes (Duncan and Brooks-Gunn 1997). Obviously, many other factors may intervene and otherwise affect such long-term outcomes, but the impacts of sustained poverty and the likelihood that children and adolescents may be deprived of various socio-economic advantages cannot be denied (Curtis et al. 2004). In fact, the research verifies that the relative disadvantages for children commence even before they are born, as poor children have significantly greater risks of being born prematurely and with lower birth weights, suffer greater rates of intellectual impairment, and experience higher infant mortality rates (Wilkins and Sherman 1998). By the time poor children have entered formal schooling, the evidence indicates that they have already fallen behind in terms of school readiness, cognitive achievements, and early academic performance (Williamson and Salkie 2005).

Growing up in a poor family has consistently been linked to a variety of negative outcomes, including academic problems, psychosocial morbidity, and, more generally, a range of emotional and behavioural problems (Kornberger et al. 2001; Lipman and Offord 1997). Adolescents who have experienced persistent poverty tend to have lower self-esteem, poorer school performance and attachment, engage in a range of risky or unhealthy practices (e.g., drugs and alcohol abuse), and commit more acts of delinquency and other forms of anti-social behaviour (McLeod and Shanahan 1996; Robinson et al. 2005).

Why should poverty have such negative effects on children, who are often quite resilient? Certainly many children *do* survive and even thrive in the long term *despite* their relatively deprived conditions. The main reason for having potentially negative short-term and long-term effects may be more the result of the problems and stressors that parents face in providing adequate financial, physical, and often emotional resources than anything else. Lone-parent mothers, for instance, often experience a high level of stress in meeting the requirements of both child care and income support. This often leads to poorer health outcomes for both parent *and* child, which in turn introduce additional obstacles to securing gainful employment (Baker 2002). More generally, while the causal connections can be quite complex, research has shown that several home-related or environmental factors such as a difficult physical environment may also mediate the relationship between low income and intellectual development (Brannigan et al. 2002; Guo and Harris 2000). Neighbourhood and community cohesion can serve to lessen the impact of family poverty, as the potential for additional social supports increases (Jarrett et al. 2010; Klebanov et al. 1994). Low-income families tend to live in poorer neighbourhoods and in lower-quality housing, which introduce additional obstacles as they attempt to provide children with the same types of services that most middle- and upper-income Canadians take for granted.

Conclusion

Despite Canada's considerable wealth, many families with low income remain in poverty and continue to face major challenges—especially in light of the most recent recession in 2009. Many statistical indicators highlight various gains, such as the overall growth in the economy, rising family incomes, and reduced low-income rates. In working with Statistics Canada's LICOs, we find that the country experienced several years of declining low-income rates and reliance upon social assistance.

A careful appraisal of the available data, however, leads us to emphasize that some issues of considerable concern should not be downplayed or overlooked. The persistently high incidence of low income among recent immigrants (at about 2.5 times the levels observed for non-immigrants), for example, offers one source of concern in a country increasingly dependent on immigration. The high level of income poverty among female lone-parent families should not be overlooked either, particularly in view of the important consequences for the young. In addition, while many Canadian families witnessed income gains during the late 1990s and early 2000s, the evidence suggests upper-income Canadians experienced the greatest gains. Statistics Canada reports a real upturn in income inequality over this period in terms of family income both "before tax" and, to a lesser extent, "after tax" (Heisz 2007).

As highlighted in this chapter, family change and demographic events have an impact on income poverty, especially to the extent that they influence the types of families and living arrangements in which Canadians share and pool income. Changing family structures in particular have generated some degree of economic uncertainty, especially for women and children. Whereas lone-parent families comprise about one in four families with children, among families classified as income poor, over half are single-parent families (Statistics Canada 2013b). Many of these changes observed in the Canadian family, in terms of non-marital fertility and marital instability, have had a greater impact on the economic well-being of women than they have on men.

The consequences for children have been particularly important, as child poverty persists despite political pronouncements such as the House of Commons' 1989 resolution to end child poverty by the year 2000. Canada has simultaneously witnessed a shift in the age distribution of the poor over past decades. In the 1960s, elderly Canadians were about twice as likely as children to be classified as income poor, but this situation has nearly reversed itself as the likelihood of poverty stands much higher among families with children. Thus the incidence of low income and poverty varies considerably, depending on family type and number of earners, as well as variations linked to age, life course stage, immigration, visible minority status, labour market conditions, and other factors.

Two observations are worth repeating. First, the evidence suggests that for some families and individuals, an exit from welfare over the past decade has actually led to a worsening of an already difficult situation. Second, over this same period, there has been a substantial increase in the number of food banks in Canada, as well as other charities that serve meals and/or provide for other basic necessities. In a sense, food banks have become institutionalized during a period of more restrictive governmental income supports. Thus, while unemployment insurance and welfare payments have been more restrictive since the 1990s, governments have *not* undertaken to reinvest in significant ways that might compensate for these policy changes.

Finally, other problems that low-income families face may be more intractable, especially with respect to dealing with certain unpredictable events and interpersonal decisions that shake families up or leave them vulnerable. Where family poverty cannot be prevented, the research points to the significance of a great many negative outcomes linked to living in poverty over a sustained period of time. From a social transfer standpoint, the costs of dealing with the long-term consequences of family poverty inevitably exceed the costs associated with reducing or preventing such poverty in the first place.

Study Questions

1. The last two decades were turbulent years for many Canadians, with some noticeable ups and downs in the North American economy. Discuss these trends in terms of median income and income poverty, with particular attention to the economic recessions of the early 1980s, the early 1990s, and 2008–9 period.
2. Picot et al. (1998) highlight three distinctive types of events in the explanation of recent trends in terms of income poverty, including "demographic" events, "economic" events, and "political" events. Discuss the relevance of each in reference to recent trends in the economic well-being and poverty of Canadian families.
3. The number of families reliant upon foodbanks remains relatively high in Canada into the second decade of the twenty-first century. What are some of the contributing factors responsible for this? Do you think that this situation will continue over the next several years? Why or why not?
4. What are the most significant effects or consequences of poverty on families? Who, in your view, suffers the most as a result of family poverty?

Further Readings

McKeen, Wendy. 2004. *Money in Their Own Name: The Feminist Voice in Poverty Debate in Canada, 1970–1995*. Toronto: University of Toronto Press. The author presents a feminist perspective on social policy debates regarding poverty over the last three decades of the twentieth century, and also discusses the implications of "women-friendly" social policies.

Sharma, Raghubar. 2012. *Poverty in Canada*. Don Mills: Oxford University Press. This is an overview of poverty and low-income trends in Canada. It provides a concise discussion of specific groups that are most affected by poverty, including child poverty, lone parents, the "working poor," and "ethnic poverty".

Statistics Canada. 2012. *Income in Canada*. Ottawa: Statistics Canada, catalogue no. 75-202-X. The definitive annual publication has been the most reliable source of income statistics in Canada, but has recently been discontinued in its current format. Statistics Canada presents the highlights and summary statistics on income and low income among Canadian families, along with trend data.

Tweddle, Anne, Ken Battle, and Sherri Torjman. Annual. *Welfare in Canada 2015*. Caledon Institute: Ottawa. The report focuses on the income of households and individuals reliant upon social assistance in Canada, commonly known as "welfare." It includes information relating to eligibility by province or territory, as well as the level of income support that can be expected by persons reliant upon this source of income support.

Key Terms

Demographic changes Population shifts related to their size, distribution, and composition (e.g., ethnicities, age structure, family statuses, etc.), changes in them, and the components of such changes, that is, births, deaths, migration, and social mobility (change of status).

Economic family A group of two or more persons who live in the same dwelling and are related to each other by blood, marriage, common-law relationship, or adoption.

Economic mobility refers to the extent to which individuals or families experience either improved or declining economic circumstances over time.

Labour force participation rate The proportion of the population 15 years of age and over that is in the labour force (that is, either employed or looking for work) in a specified reference period.

Lone-parent family One parent with one or more children who have never married, living in the same dwelling.

Low-income cut-offs (LICO) Income levels at which families or unattached individuals are considered to be living in straitened circumstances. Statistics Canada currently produces LICOs before and after tax, which are periodically revised on the basis of changes in the average standard of living of Canadians. These are essentially "relative measures" of low income that vary by family size and degree of urbanization.

Median income That point in the income distribution at which one half of income units (individuals, families, or households) fall above and one half fall below.

 Interested in finding out more? Visit www.oupcanada.com/Albanese4e for access to a list of recommended websites for this chapter.

11

The Settlement of Refugee Families in Canada
Pre-migration and Post-migration Trajectories and Location in Canadian Society

AMAL MADIBBO AND JAMES S. FRIDERES

LEARNING OBJECTIVES

- To understand the socio-economic position of racialized refugee families in Canadian society

- To identify the social structure and organization of different types of families

- To learn about the challenges facing racialized refugee youth

- To understand the role of intersectionality in refugee families

- To discover patterns of conflict in refugee families

Introduction

Today we understand migration to be an international issue. In 2015, there were 215 million migrants around the world compared to 173 million in 2000. In Canada, the growth of the foreign-born population has increased from 10 per cent in 1961 to well over 20 per cent in 2011. As a result, over 25 per cent of families in Canada are immigrant families and immigration is now the main component in population growth; making up nearly 70 per cent of the growth between 2001 and 2011 (Lee and Edmonston 2013). While most (69 per cent) immigrant families have recently entered Canada through the "economic class" category, others have been admitted through the "family class" or "refugee" category (either government assisted or private sponsor). Immigrants coming to Canada through the economic class criteria must obtain a minimum of 67 points (out of 100) over six general criteria: education, ability to speak one of the official languages, experience in approved occupations, age, arranged employment in Canada, and adaptability. Immigrant families share many of the same qualities and characteristics of other Canadian families; at the same time, there is a very rich cultural diversity across immigrant groups. Especially relevant today are refugee families that enter Canada under unique circumstances and different polices than do other immigrant families.

For a brief history of Canadian immigration, see "Families as Historical Actors" in Chapter 2 pp. 26–33.

The combined effects of political instability, armed conflicts, and violations of human rights that unfold around the world have resulted in the displacement of millions within their countries, a group known as **internally displaced persons (IDPs)**, and/or in refugee camps in nearby countries, a group identified as refugees. In 2014, nearly 60 million people were displaced around the world. Moreover, in 2015, there were 19.6 million refugees worldwide compared to 15.9 in 2000. This means that every minute of the day, nearly 100 people are displaced. To help aid the plight of refugees, the United Nations High Commissioner for Refugees (UNHCR) was created in 1950 with the mandate to assist people who had been uprooted from their homes because of the Second World War. The UNHCR endorsed the 1951 Refugee Convention, a key legal document that outlines the rights of the displaced and the legal obligations of states to protect them, and defines a refugee as a person who fears persecution "for reasons of race, religion, nationality, membership of a particular social group or political opinion, is outside the country of his nationality and . . . as a result of such events, is unable or, owing to such fear, is unwilling to return to it." (UN 1951:2).

The UNHCR protects refugees and attempts to help them with assistance, i.e., food, shelter, education, and social services. It also helps to secure for them one of the three durable solutions for refugees: (1) voluntary repatriation to their home countries when these are safe, (2) local integration in the counties they stay in as refugees, and (3) resettlement to a third country that is neither their home country nor the state where they reside as refugees. In this latter case the UNHCR cooperates with countries around the world to relocate refugees within their borders. While the focus of the current refugee crisis has been on the European Union, other areas in the world are equally subject to the refugee process, i.e., North America, South East Asia, Africa. The data show that half of the top ten refugee hosting countries are now located in sub-Saharan Africa (Manozzie 2016).

For its part, Canada generously welcomes families and individuals who are in prolonged and emerging refugee situations. Canada's immigration and refugee system, which is governed by Canada's Immigration and Refugee Protection Act, offers refugees a durable solution by resettling them and providing them permanent residence and citizenship. Canada's refugee system consists of two main parts: (1) the Refugee and Humanitarian Resettlement Program, which is designed for people who seek protection from outside Canada, and (2) the In-Canada Asylum Program, for people who make a refugee claim when they arrive in Canada by land, sea, or air. To facilitate the selection of refugees, the Immigration and Refugee Board of Canada was established in 1989 and is a tribunal that rules on immigration and refugee matters—at the same time being independent of the federal government (El-Assal 2016). Another immigration policy that concerns refugees is the Family Class Sponsorship, which is specifically aimed at family reunification in Canada. It allows permanent residents and citizens to sponsor certain relatives to come to Canada, namely spouses and common-law partners, dependent children, and parents and grandparents. In addition to family members, organizations and groups of citizens can also sponsor refugees and bring them to Canada.

For more on immigrant families in Canada, see "Changing Trends in the Diversity of Family Forms" in Chapter 1 pp. 3–7.

Canada admitted nearly one million refugees from 1979–2014. Around 250,000 immigrants arrive in Canada every year, and approximately 20,000–30,000 of them are refugees. However, the number of refugees admitted to Canada fluctuates in response to world events. For example, in 1956–7 Canada brought in over 30,000 Hungarians; in 1968–9 11,000 Czechoslovakians; in the period 1975–80, nearly 70,000 Vietnamese, Laotian, and Cambodian "boat people" were settled in Canada. The in-take of refugees between 1989 and 1993 averaged nearly 43,000 per year. This large in-take was a result of the Refugee Backlog Clearance Program and the growth of the number of people who had their inland refugee claims accepted by the Refugee Board of Canada. Since then there has been a steady decrease in the number, stabilizing around 20,000 per year for the past decade. Nevertheless, with the acceptance of over 35,000 Syrians in 2015–16, the number of refugees may reach record numbers.

Refugees bring about major positive human and social capital that benefits Canadians. They contribute to economic growth and add to the social cohesion of society (Biles et al. 2009). Despite these benefits and the successes of refugees who have become an integral part of Canada's mosaic, many face structural and social barriers that make their lives in Canada challenging. This outcome hinders the achievement of the goal of the Canadian **policy of multiculturalism**, that seeks to make Canada the most successful pluralist society, where diverse groups live side by side, interact in many ways, and enrich each other and the larger society. The barriers that refugees face need to be numerated because, as Figure 11.1 shows, refugees and their families will continue to arrive in Canada in substantial numbers and they will continue to shape the future of Canada.

This chapter responds to this need by examining the trajectories of refugee families before and after arrival in Canada, along with the challenges that hinder their incorporation into Canadian society. In addition, we will shed light on refugee family structure and

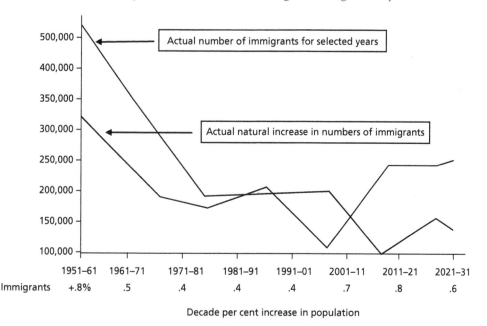

Figure 11.1   Size and Growth of Immigrant Population, Canada, 1951 to 2031

Statistics Canada. 2012. *Population Growth in Canada from 1851 to 2061*. Ottawa; Statistics Canada. 2011. *Immigration and Ethnocultural Diversity in Canada*. Ottawa, National Household Survey; Statistics Canada 2016. *Canadian Demographics at a Glance* (2nd edition), Ottawa. Demography Division.

organization, family conflict, as well as the location of refugee youth in Canadian society. We will focus on two communities—the Afghan and the Sudanese—and pay close attention to refugee family experiences and discuss possibilities to improve the living condition of recent and incoming refugees, such as Syrians, in Canada.

Both Afghanistan and Sudan are war-ravaged countries, ethnically diverse, and associated with Islam. Afghanistan and North Sudan are predominantly Muslim while South Sudan is predominantly Christian, although it also encompasses a Muslim minority. Similarly, the movement of both communities from their respective home countries was triggered by civil wars and armed conflicts; these started in Afghanistan in 1971 and in Sudan in 1955. These wars have displaced large numbers of people. An estimated 2.7 million Afghan refugees—almost 10 per cent of the country's entire population—live outside their country (UNHCR 2011). Meanwhile, an estimated 3.2 million Sudanese are IDP and in IDP-like situations (UNHCR 2016), and the number of the Sudanese refugees worldwide could be as high as one million. Furthermore, most members of both communities are forced into displacement in neighbouring countries prior to arrival in Canada—to Pakistan and Iran in the case of Afghans, and to Egypt, Kenya, Ethiopia, and Chad in the case of Sudanese. The characteristics of the two communities are also similar regarding education and skills. Though some are highly educated and qualified professionals, a common experience of many refugees is having interrupted schooling or education, resulting in a lack of professional skills. A majority in both communities come to Canada under Canada's Refugee and Humanitarian Resettlement Program (Mosaic Institute 2009). Approximately 64,000 Afghans (Statistics Canada 2011) and 35,000 Sudanese reside in Canada (Madibbo 2015). Another similarity between the two groups is associated with the family composition insofar as both communities include people who move to Canada with their families, others who leave their families in refugee camps or other countries, as well as youth.

However, their trajectories differ in that Afghan immigration to Canada is slightly longer established than Sudanese immigration, with the former starting in the 1980s and the latter in the 1990s. Additionally, the number of Afghans in Canada is larger than the Sudanese community. The intersection of "race" and ethnicity, and religion makes South Sudanese a visible minority in Canada while it renders Afghans and North Sudanese both a visible and a religious —Muslim—minority. These convergences and divergences make for a useful case study that allows us to explore how factors such as the time since arrival in Canada, immigration status, family structure, and cultural traditions shape the lives of refugees in Canada. These issues are better understood when we situate them in the context of the initial phase that all refugees and newcomers go through in Canada: the settlement process.

Settlement of Refugees in Canada

During **settlement**, the early years after arrival, refugees have basic needs such as finding housing and schooling for children, language training, and first-time employment. They depend largely on settlement services and friends and community organizations to help orient them to life in Canada. While all newcomers to Canada go through the phase of settlement, the refugee experience is specific insofar as they often face grave difficulties in the pre-migration period, as well as stressful conditions in the post-migration stage, which makes their incorporation into Canadian society strenuous.

Prior to migration to Canada some refugees transition in urban centres in neighbouring countries where their living conditions are relatively comfortable. However, a majority of refugees encounter extreme dangers in the course of displacement, including physical hardships and violent attacks, aerial bombardment, encounters with wild animals or risk of drowning, and threat from military and militia forces. In addition, refugees are targets for sexual violence (Rider 2012), and experience difficult living conditions in refugee camps, such as a lack of proper food and clean water, shelter and security, and medical care. These circumstances are particularly damaging to families since in some cases refugees and their children witness the death or killing of family members, and in others have to abandon dying family members and relatives (Carta et al. 2015). Many Sudanese (Simich et al. 2010) and Afghans (Quirke 2011) are exposed to these losses and disruptions of normal life before moving to Canada.

In the post-migration period, successful settlement requires a good sense of well-being and healthy functioning; for most refugees, the displacement trauma and family losses have both mental (conflict induced trauma) and physical health implications (Brun and Fabos 2015). Many studies have documented the negative effects of trauma on the psychological well-being of adults, children, and youth refugees (Crumlish and O'Rourke 2010). Refugees have been found to have higher rates of post-traumatic stress disorder (PTSD) and depression, and psychological distress after they immigrate (Donnelly et al. 2011; Kirmayer et al. 2011). The two communities under discussion here—the Afghans and the Sudanese in Canada—are no exception since the "Sudanese newcomers [in Canada] as a group are under considerable mental stress," "felt constantly under strain," and have "been upset or disturbed by bad memories" (Culture, Community and Health Studies Program et al. 2004:36); and Afghans are reported to endure similar problems (Guruge et al. 2015; Shakya et al. 2010b). Furthermore, as Hassan et al., (2015) state, a central issue in any war setting is the loss and grief that people have—either for family members or friends. Refugees in the country of resettlement are sometimes unable to communicate with their families, are separated from them for long periods of time, or are uncertain about the fates of family members. This situation is exemplified in the case of the **Lost Boys and Girls of Sudan** who relocated to Canada, some of whom spent up to 20 years without knowing where their families were and whether they were alive. Refugees are also deprived of their extended family and kinship networks, both of which are fundamental social units for social support and psychological well-being. Furthermore, refugees experience financial losses because assets and resources have been diminished to the point of zero. In addition, their assets have been spent and they have no additional funds. These stresses contribute to settlement difficulties and are magnified by additional challenges that refugees encounter in the post-migration period.

Upon resettlement in Canada, refugees are generally unable to document their credentials or work history and do not have Canadian experience in the labour market. Exacerbated by racism in the labour market, this results in low employment rates, high unemployment, and a concentration in low-paying jobs. These trends are in line with research findings that show that the labour force participation rate for recent immigrants (in Canada for less than five years) is about 50 per cent, and that the unemployment rate is about 11 per cent (double the overall Canadian rate), although in some areas it may be as high as 60 per cent (Teelucksingh and Galabuzi 2005; Statistics Canada 2017). In addition, data reveal that the proportion of recent immigrants with family incomes below the poverty line rose to nearly 34 per cent by 2001 (Frenette and Morissette 2003). Over-all, recent immigrants have low-income rates 2.5 times those of Canadian-born residents, resulting in high rates of poverty. In addition, refugees are subjected to other forms of racism in society, such as negative stereotyping and **racial profiling** by the police (Henry and Tator 2006). Furthermore, Muslims encounter **Islamophobia** that dismisses their religious and cultural traditions, and constructs Islam as a religion that promotes violence and Muslims as a threat to national security (Kazemipur 2014). It is worth noting that at-titudes toward Muslims in various Canadian provinces have worsened as they are singled out at airports and public spaces and face increasing hostility (Dua 2007). These chal-lenges trigger feelings of exclusion, and also highlight the settlement needs of refugees as well as the services and program planning that can respond to these needs.

Canada provides settlement services to refugees through settlement agencies that offer services across the country: orientation to life in Canada, language assessment and classes, help finding jobs and housing, support in registering children in school, and offer-ing information about certification of credentials. However, many refugees have been re-luctant to use these services. This is the result of two factors, the first can be solved easily: newcomers are unaware of and experience difficulty accessing these services. The second factor is more complex and requires thorough examination: refugee families and ethnic community organizations perceive the services as not being culturally appropriate. The idea of culturally appropriate services refers to those that are "responsive to . . . beliefs and practices, preferred languages, health-literacy levels, and communication needs" (Howard et al. 2014:198) of "racial," ethnic, and religious groups (Bowes and Wilkinson 2003). From an equity perspective, this perception means that service providers are expected to respond with sensitivity to various values and preferences, and to overcome cultural, language, and communications barriers. It also requires them to enhance effective func-tioning in cross-cultural situations and to increase the representation of the diversity of the population in service agencies. In addition, it necessitates cooperation with community organizations and representatives who are more familiar with the culture of refugees.

When thinking of culture, we should caution ourselves against generalizations, in-cluding the idea that the cultures of visible minorities and religious minorities are dramat-ically different from—or even that they oppose—Canadian cultural norms. Many people from the Global South embrace values similar to Canadian norms, such as tolerance, good work ethics, and respect for human rights. It is these similarities that enable refugees to settle and integrate successfully in society, and help the broader society to enhance settlement and inclusion in society. Although there are cultural differences, some of these differences have positive implications for refugees. For example, Hispanic traditions that promote family co-operation, which is the antithesis of Canadian mainstream norms of individualism, help people to survive in the face of severe circumstances such as displace-ment and exclusion in society. This tendency is depicted through evidence that shows that refugees in Canada rely on family and ethnic community members to help them settle in society. In some cases family relations and relatedness help people to achieve a sense of belonging in Canada (Bragg and Wong 2015; Rytter 2013). Nevertheless, some differences, notably those related to gender, produce negative impacts. Again, we should not fall into the trap of generalization. Previous research pictures immigrant women as passive victims of their culture (men being the oppressors) and their surroundings. While this stereo-type is common for specific ethnocultural groups, it is an oversimplified view that reflects the **ethnocentrism** of the researchers. First, Canadian women are equally oppressed in various ways. Second, it ignores the fact that women and men have their own centres of power and competence and the stereotypes underestimate women as active agents. Third, this stereotype ignores the fact that people from the same country or ethnocultural group do not constitute a homogeneous group and that within some refugee families there are conditions for an equal relationship. Yet it is the case that discriminatory gendered ideas and practices that diverge from the Canadian mainstream approach to gender continue to persist among some refugee cultures. As we will explain in a later section, this difference causes conflict both within refugee families and between these families and society. It is these complex issues that service providers need to comprehend and respond to.

It is important to note that some mainstream settlement agencies are making efforts to be culturally sensitive, and to that end are implementing initiatives, including multi-cultural family counselling and mental health programs, services in different languages, and hiring staff of diverse ethnic and religious backgrounds. Nevertheless, settlement continues to be demanding for many refugees, and many mainstream service agencies are still ineffective in dealing with ethnocultural community issues. For example, values implicit in existing mainstream services often clash with the values of many refugees. Some of the services offered to refugees largely focus on individual rights and empower-ment while refugees may come from a cultural system that believes the values of the community should be of central concern. In this context, the privileging of mainstream Canadian values over others within many service agencies can be explained by a number of factors. Typical service agencies have few connections with immigrant organizations and communities. Moreover, efficient culturally appropriate services in the Canadian context require going beyond culture to address issues of "race": the racism that racialized and Muslim refugees face necessitates anti-oppression and anti-racist policies and train-ing in settlement agencies. Additionally, since discrimination exists in multiple areas of society, it can be argued that, although settlement agencies are responsible for refugees' incorporation into society, successful settlement necessitates more collective efforts that encompass structures such as schools and the child care system.

To rectify this problem, some ethnic community organizations have opted for a par-allel service approach, providing services to their own communities, despite often being underfunded. Others propose a bridging approach (Türegün 2011) that combines resour-ces of mainstream and community organisations to coordinate programs and interven-tions. Although this option could be efficient (Ortega and Frideres 2015), it hasn't become a priority strategy. All these settlement issues require a better understanding of the organ-ization of refugee families and the place they occupy in society.

Family Issues

Family Structure and New Forms of Family

While some refugees and recent immigrants are like many Canadian-born individuals in that many live in nuclear families with no relatives other than parent(s) and children, a sub-stantial number differ in family structure and are more likely to live in extended families that bring together three generations—children, parents, and grandparents, as well as other

Daily Life
From Kabul to Peshawar to Winnipeg: The Dost Family Remains Connected

The Dost family—two parents, five brothers, and four sisters—live in Winnipeg where they arrived in 2004. Their transition from being refugees to becoming Afghan-Canadians has been both successful and complex. After fleeing Kabul in the 1990s due to the persecution that Mr. Dost had faced, they spent more than 10 years as refugees in Peshawar where the children couldn't go to school, and the girls had to wear chadors in public. Mr. Dost's nephew, a Canadian citizen, sponsored them and brought them to Canada.

The family first shared a two-bedroom apartment for a few years, but now has a five-bedroom bungalow. At school, the children felt they were outsiders, but they integrated slowly and have all graduated from high school, except for one sister who is attending high school, and enjoys sports including swimming and boxing. The children have worked in places ranging from

relatives. Nevertheless, people from different countries of origin vary significantly in this regard, i.e., 40 per cent of South Asians live in three-generation households compared to 2 per cent of Canadian-born. One reason may be cultural: in some societies, placing aging parents in senior home care centres runs counter to culturally established norms (Haslam et al. 2014). In these instances, elder care is solely a familial responsibility, with all family members contributing to household activities and support. Adults can stay at their parents' home if they wish, even after marriage and establishing their own families, and grandparents assist with child care. However, the prominence of extended families among refugees and immigrants can also be a result of financial necessity. Recent immigrants are poorer than Canadian-born and many elderly immigrants and relatives are sponsored by their families. Consequently, many of them choose to live with their sponsors. As is the case with many racialized refugees, the Afghan community encompasses substantial numbers of extended families (Guruge et al. 2015; Nourpanah 2014). Although there are fewer Sudanese extended families (Young and Choldin 2012) their number is increasing as Sudanese become more settled in Canada.

For more on aging families, see Chapter 7.

Another difference between Canadian-born and refugees is related to family size. The fertility rate of Canadian women has varied over time but the overall trend has been towards significantly lower birth rates, reaching a low of 1.59 in 2013 (Statistics Canada 2016). However, for new immigrant women, the fertility rate in the past 10 years has been 3.1 children per woman, double the rate of Canadian-born. For immigrant women who arrived in Canada 15 years ago the rate is 1.5. These numbers show that fertility rates among immigrant women decline after they arrive in Canada, eventually reaching a rate equal to women who are native-born Canadians (Ferrer and Adsera 2016). The fastest fertility rate decline is among women from southern Europe. While Asian women have shown a steep decline in the number of children they have, the number of children per woman is still higher than the overall population—1.89 compared to 1.47 for native-born Canadian women. On the other hand, women from other regions, such as South Asia (2.5), Africa (2.4), and Central/West Asia and the Middle East (2.2), far exceed this rate (Bélanger and Gilbert 2005). The fertility rate among Sudanese is higher, in the range of their uncle's restaurant to 7-Eleven. At present, three brothers are car-dealers. One of the sisters is a manager at a Subway restaurant franchise, one of them is a stay-at-home mother. Two sisters travelled to Afghanistan to marry men they knew about through family friends in Winnipeg. They both sponsored their husbands, and one of them waited 16 months before reuniting with her husband in Canada. The husband, who was a physician in Afghanistan, is hoping to work in his field in Canada. The war trauma still haunts their aging father, their mother stays at home, and they all miss the relatives who remained in Afghanistan, and send them remittances. The Dosts have counted on each other throughout, and feel that this connection helped them to survive and thrive.

More information about the Dost family can be found at www.theglobeandmail.com /news/national/eleven-new-canadians-eleven-years-later-one-familys-journey-to-freedom /article25139431/.

4–5 (Milan 2013). Recently arrived communities even exceed this rate, as illustrated by the example of Syrian families who may have up to 10 children.

Other differences are more specific to Muslim communities, including the Afghans and the Sudanese (Al-Krenawl and Graham 2000; Pottie et al. 2015; Rytter 2013). Same-gender parent households are almost non-existent, although they may not self-report if they do exist. In addition, there is a significant number of single people (especially men) within these communities, a trend that is due to the immigration of more single men than single women, and which itself is associated with gendered cultural norms that permit the immigration of single men more than women. Furthermore, arranged marriages are still practised. A new form of family that is becoming increasingly prominent among refugee families is that of "all-youth families," which consist of individuals who have lost their families during the wars and the subsequent displacement. In Canada, they share homes, build support systems, and become each other's family.

Questions for Critical Thought

What do you see as some of the opportunities and challenges that "all-youth families" might encounter?

These patterns highlight differences and similarities in the structure of visible minority refugee families and mainstream Canadian families. The differences could—and do—trigger conflict that has bearing on the refugees' incorporation into society.

Family Conflict

Prior research has identified three conflict patterns in families (Darvishpour 2003). The first pattern emerges when the husband takes on the instrumental role and the wife takes on the emotional role. Over time, if one becomes more isolated, lonely, or

For more on conflict in
immigrant families and
domestic violence, see
"Domestic Violence
among Vulnerable Families"
in Chapter 14
pp. 303–7.

dependent on the other, the one will see the other as ignorant and a burden, and this will lead to spousal conflict. The second pattern occurs when women get new opportunities after marriage, such as a job outside the home, which gives her the self-confidence to challenge the traditional power distribution and role allocation. Alternatively, if the man experiences a status change that decreases his power in the family, he may try to maintain dominance by resorting to old norms and rules that legitimize relations as they were before. Both trends of spousal conflict are found among refugee families in Canada.

After resettlement in Canada, gender roles change as women may become breadwinners and household providers while their husbands may not obtain employment or gain income. This change may make men feel disrespected or that they have lost their status and power. Men also hold perceptions that Canada's justice system guarantees women more rights than men, for example by giving children's custody to the mother over the father, contrary to Muslim societies where fathers have custody over boys after the age of seven and girls over the age of nine (Amar 1984). The change also means that women appreciate the greater freedom they gain in Canada in terms of education, dress code, and employment (keeping in mind that the jobs available to recent immigrant women are mostly low-paying and part-time jobs). They also become aware of their legal rights and therefore are less likely to accept discriminatory traditions. While some families surmount these tensions in a constructive manner, others don't, which results in separation and divorce, domestic violence, and spousal physical abuse—mostly against women, within refugee families.

Questions for Critical Thought

What do you see as some of the similarities between gender relations in Canada and those in countries in the Global South, where racialized and Muslim refugees typically originate?

Raj and Silverman (2002) found a paucity of research on the prevalence of intimate partner violence in refugee and immigrant communities but report that community organizations feel that violence against immigrant women has reached "epidemic proportions." Qualitative studies by Husaini (2001), and Dosanjh et al., (1994) looked at family violence in the South Asian community and found that it was a serious concern. Moreover, they found that battered immigrant women are less likely than non-immigrant women to seek both informal and formal help for intimate partner violence. In cases where spouses have been sponsored, many experience what is called "sponsorship debt" (Côté et al. 2001). Others have found that cultural barriers to receiving help often come from community or religious leaders who compel women to stay in abusive relationships and not to speak publicly about their experiences (Saris and Potvin 2008; Smith 2004). They fear that disclosure to outsiders promotes criticism of their culture or ethnicity. Finally, refugee women are less likely to seek help because of isolation, lack of language skills, fear of deportation, and lack of information with respect to available services. On the other hand, research by Brownridge and Halli (2003) shows that the pattern is not universal. They found that immigrant families from "developed" nations have a lower prevalence of violence than Canadian-born families. Some studies have documented spousal and family conflict in both the Afghan and Sudanese community (Fanjoy 2015). However, there is no mention in the literature of spousal physical abuse within these communities per se, which may be due to the cultural customs that prohibit women from revealing these problems publicly.

The third pattern of conflict that Darvishpour (2003) points out arises between generations within a family. Generational conflicts are endemic to all families, regardless of their ethnicity. The general basis for such conflict is the fact that children are growing up in a different social milieu from that in which their parents and grandparents were raised. In the case of Canadian-born families, the discontinuity is minimal but nevertheless evident. However, racialized refugees may find that they are living in a society that has many different cultural rules from those established during their own childhoods, for example, the shift from an age-graded society in which respect for one's elders was a given to the contemporary twenty-first century Canadian society that stresses individual equality and glorifies youth. As such, cultural gaps between the generations become more pronounced and visible.

Older immigrants have cultural adjustment difficulties to deal with (Liu and Reeves 2016; Moon and Rhee 2010; Park and Kim 2013). In Vietnamese culture, for example, elders are important family members, yet once in Canada they may find themselves marginalized because they don't speak an official language and/or are not consulted on important family decisions. In addition, older immigrants may feel isolated from the community and larger society especially when they spend long hours on their own (Hossen 2012; Treas and Mazumdar 2002). The change of these traditional customs and social interactions fuel tensions within the family. It is important to assert that family conflict involving elders, as well as elder abuse by ethnicity, are rarely mentioned in the literature on family. Similarly, the scarce literature that examines Afghans and Sudanese in Canada does not point out generational conflict involving older immigrants, though this does not mean that such conflict does not exist.

Conflict between parents and their adolescent children often takes its toll on the family. Young refugees tend to assimilate rapidly because young people tend to learn English/French and understand Canadian culture earlier than their parents; they become aware of Canadian expectations much earlier than their parents (Lee and Holm 2011). For their part, parents hold differing perspectives from the mainstream on issues such as disciplining children, the mainstream pop culture of youth, and social norms associated with dating, dress, and alcohol consumption. While refugee parents may not want their children to adopt these norms, youth may have differing ideas. This causes tensions and conflict between parents and youth, which has been observed in both the Afghan (Shakya et al. 2010b) and Sudanese communities. For example, Sudanese parents maintain that "their relationship with their children has changed [in a negative way] since coming to Canada . . . and reported the reason for this as "different Canadian values" and "permissiveness of Canadian society" (Culture, Community and Health Studies Program et al. 2004:36). As it stands, some parents believe they can no longer discipline their

For more on parenting see Chapter 5.

children because of fear of child abuse charges and losing their children to the child care system (Makwarimba et al. 2013).

Family conflicts and relations in general are associated with identity because refugees need to figure out how to positon their culture vis-à-vis the host society. As Berry (2011), and Walters et al. (2006) explain, newcomers and immigrants in multicultural societies such as Canada adopt four strategies of identification: (1) assimilation, when people give up their own cultural heritage and participate fully in the host society; (2) separation, when agents maintain their own cultural identity and distance themselves from the host culture; (3) marginalization, when newcomers simultaneous reject both their ethnic identity and that of the host society; and (4) integration, when individuals maintain their own cultural identity while at the same time embracing the culture of the host society. As it stands, the strategy of integration is the most prominent among newcomer and immigrant racialized people in Canada (Frideres 2002; Kilbride 2014; Mensah 2014). It is popularly known as a **hyphenated identity**, a sense of belonging that links Canadian-ness to an ethnic identity (i.e., an Indo-Canadian or Haitian-Canadian identity). However, the negotiation of the hyphenated identity is still contested, because refugees and other racialized groups feel that while they are keen on embracing Canada and Canadian identity, they are not considered genuine citizens (Frideres 2011). This perception is triggered by the aforementioned barriers, such as negative cultural stereotypes and racism, which make the refugees believe that they receive differential treatment in society (Lee and Yoon 2011). It is also caused by some ethnic communities' perception of the lack of culturally appropriate services and interventions, not only within settlement service agencies, but also other mainstream institutions (Hall 2016). They are critical of the way these institutions respond to family problems that involve children. They believe that the practice of child services, which consists of taking children from their families and placing them elsewhere, is damaging to children and their families because foster families are unlikely to be familiar with the home family's culture and language. This is a major concern that leads ethnic community members and organizations to question their place in Canadian society (Al-Krenawl and Graham 2000; Haslam et al. 2014). These issues demonstrate parental and community concerns about the well-being, identity, and future of their youth in Canadian society.

Refugee Youth

Shakya et al., (2010a) demonstrate that the number of racialized youth in Canada has been steadily increasing. They show that the number of newcomer youth between the ages of 15–24 increased from 28,125 in 1999 to 37,425 in 2008 (a 24.9 per cent increase). About 35,000 immigrants and refugee youth between the ages of 15–24 settle in Canada every year; this represents about 15 per cent of the approximately 250,000 permanent residents that come to Canada per annum. The percentage of youth within the bulk of refugees settling in Canada is higher (20.4 per cent) compared to youth in other groups. The majority (79.8 per cent) of youth who settle in Canada belong to visible minority groups. These trends indicate that racialized refugee and immigrant youth constitute a significant proportion of the youth population in Canada.

Overall, young people from all ethnic groups engage in similar activities—watching television, listening to music, and spending time with their friends. At the same time, racialized refugee youth have different experiences in growing up. The trauma that occurs during displacement causes damaging effects after resettlement (Jakobsen et al. 2014). For example, Mghir et al., (1995) found that Afghan refugee youth who were resettled in the US suffered from "the prevalence of post-traumatic stress disorder (PTSD) and other psychiatric disorders . . . [and] faced major depression" (24). In Canada, many refugee youth bear these effects (Anisef and Kilbride 2000), and encounter additional barriers. For example, linguistic and cultural barriers pose challenges for youth in their ability to understand school routines, and educational rights and responsibilities (Sirin and Rogers-Sirin 2015). Moreover, parents unaware of social support services and their intended role in the education process may hold different expectations than those held by schools. Other factors present difficulties for refugee youth in adjusting to the school system, including the underrepresentation of racialized people in the educational system, the lack of material pertaining to the culture and history of diverse groups in school curricula, high suspension rates, lack of multicultural counselling, and low expectations from teachers (Wilkinson et al. 2012). Added to these factors is the lack of understanding of the specific experience of being a refugee. As a study by Shakya et al., (2010a) on Sudanese and Afghan youth posits, "In Canada, evidence on educational pathways for refugees is particularly thin because the education sector does not collect or consider data about pre-migration experiences or arrival immigration status" (66). As a result, the drop-out rates among refugee and other racialized adolescent and young adults is high and many lack confidence in their ability to pursue postgraduate education (Anisef et al. 2010).

Refugee youth confront other difficulties within society, notably in relation to the criminal justice system. The police profiling of Indigenous and other racialized youth includes Black youth (including those of Sudanese descent) who are often stopped and questioned by the police when no violations have occurred (Commission on Systemic Racism in the Ontario Criminal Justice System 1995; Wortley 2006). In addition, incarceration rates among racialized groups within the Canadian population are disproportionate and are reflective of systemic bias. For example, while Black people comprise 2.5 per cent of the Canadian population, they make up 10 per cent of Canada's prison population. What makes this issue more problematic is that the number of Black people who are incarcerated has increased, there are currently 70 per cent more Black people in Canadian prisons than there were in 2005 (Hunter 2013; Madibbo 2016; Sapers 2015). At the same time, the labour market is not particularly inclusive to refugee youth, which is not surprising considering the results found by Bernard (2015) that reveal that the labour participation rate for immigrant youth is about 15 per cent less than for those who are native born, among the 15–24 age group. Nevertheless many refugee youth are expected to participate in family enterprises, which is why nearly three quarters of immigrant youth occupy low-paying jobs in the labour force. The low-income rate for recent immigrant youth was shown to be three times higher (45 per cent) than that of Canadian-born youth (16 per cent) (Statistics Canada 2017). Employment affects these individuals' ability to spend time on social and extracurricular activities as well as on academic pursuits, and can also create additional challenges: young refugees are subjected to racism and discrimination in the work place because of their skin colour and other identity attributes (Block and Galabuzi 2011).

Muslim refugee youth are more at risk in many social fields insofar as, in addition to barriers due to being part of a racialized population, they face the stereotype of Muslims as "terrorists" and are considered threatening outsiders. The complex needs of Muslim refugee youth with respect to health, education, social services, and the justice system are linked and are played out in the home, at school, and in the community (Berns-McGown 2013). In their cultural adjustment, they often experience cognitive and emotional changes. Issues such as a clash of cultures, changes in family relationships, and the changing roles in the family have been identified as problematic for youth. On one hand, refugee youth must struggle with the changing dynamics within their own families. On the other, they have their own struggles within the mainstream society; they want to be accepted by the mainstream culture but at the same time they want to maintain and affirm their own personal identity. Put together, all these challenges can trigger feelings of exclusion and alienation as well as non-belonging among racialized and Muslim refugee youth. Without many options of inclusion and success, many youth get involved with gangs (Ngo 2009), commit suicide, or develop issues with substance abuse.

Against the backdrop of these challenges, schools have implemented initiatives to pave the way for youth inclusion in society. They have created settlement programs and recreational activities to bridge the gap between schools and refugee youth and their families. Still, perceptions about the educational system failing racialized youth persist, and are based on outcomes such as the youth dropout rate from schools and failure in studies. These outcomes have led some communities to promote alternative schooling options to ensure the success of their youth in Canadian society. Ethno-specific schools such as the Calgary Islamic School or well as the Africentric Alternative School in Toronto, teach what they believe is lacking in the mandated provincial curriculum: the diverse perspectives, experiences, and histories of various peoples. This is done by combining these perspectives—Islamic and African teachings respectively—with the mandated curriculum. In addition, the belief that the school system hinders the self-esteem of minority students pushes these schools to place emphasis on pedagogies aimed at instilling confidence, self-esteem, and a motivation to succeed.

Ethno-specific schools have sparked heated debates in Canada between opponents who perceive them as tools of segregation, and proponents who consider them the best way to help racialized youth succeed in Canada. Like other ethno-specific educational institutions, such as Jewish or German schools, or the schools that eventually became mainstream institutions, such as French-language and Catholic schools, Muslim and Afrocentric schools seek the inclusion of the excluded. This goal overlaps with the Canadian school systems' main intention of creating a sense of inclusion for students from all cultural and religious backgrounds. However, some parents and communities continue to believe that inclusion may never occur in the school system because no efficient initiatives are undertaken to make it a reality. In this context, we observe patterns, on one hand, between the debates surrounding the mainstream settlement service agencies vis-à-vis ethnic community organizations and, on the other, between the perceptions on the school system with regards to ethno-specific schools. Some parents trust only ethno-specific schools to enhance the success and self-esteem of their children in the same way some believe ethnic community organizations to be the most viable option for refugee services. Meanwhile, some parents don't rule out a merger between the two educational systems to enhance inclusion, and some community members are calling for bridging the mainstream and community service providers to facilitate refugee settlement in society (McAndrew et al. 2013; National Anti-Racism Council of Canada 2007; Oakley 1995).

The question of whether ethno-specific schools and ethnic organization services will continue to expand or whether they will be combined with their mainstream counterparts, remains inconclusive. However, this discussion is centred on fundamental issues concerning the kind of institutions and society that best accommodate racialized and Muslim refugees, and diverse ethno-cultural and religious identities (Triki-Yamani et al. 2008). A closer look at the way identity markers (i.e., "race" or gender) influence families and individuals' status and opportunities in society enables us to envision the inclusion of refugee families in society, not in spite of, but because of, their diverse identity characteristics.

Intersectionality of Gender, "Race," Religion, Culture, and Immigration Status

Identity markers such as gender and culture are social constructs that sometimes function independently, but more often in conjunction with each other to influence people's lives. Therefore, they are used as analytical categories to study the ways in which they impact social and institutional dynamics. For example, drawing on gender solely reveals issues such as how women and men confront displacement in similar and different ways. Differences occur in situations where women take on more roles as providers and protectors of families either because husbands die in wars or participate in conflicts. Such circumstances impact not only wives and mothers but the functioning of the family as a unit. However, when two or more identity markers operate together, they produce effects that differ from those that emanate from the impact of one identity marker. This outcome led scholars (Walker 1983; Wane 2004) to develop an **intersectional** approach, which brings to light "variables such as age, sexual orientation, race, social class, and religion . . . [as] distinctive systems of oppression . . . [that are] part of one overarching structure of domination" (Hill-Collins 1990:223). Deborah King (1988) calls this juncture "multiple jeopardy," the situation in which systems of oppression such as patriarchy, homophobia, racism, and ableism work together to limit, control, and exclude some social groups. In this chapter, while using these markers independently enables examining important issues, such as the example of the relation between gender and displacement, perceiving gender, "race," culture, religion, and immigration status (i.e., being a refugee) as being interconnected opens doors for a more thorough understanding of the lives of refugees and their families in a multicultural society like Canada, which is characterized by gender, religious, and ethnic and racial diversity.

Via the lens of intersectionality we are able to identify additional cases where conflicts and displacement impact men and women differently. In some conflicts, the rape of women is used as a weapon of war. In genocidal conflicts women are sometimes purposefully eliminated to prevent the reproduction of a certain "racial" or ethnic group, which happened during the Rwandan Genocide, among other instances. In addition, intersectionality offers us the opportunity to shed light on post-migration processes including those where "religion shapes racially oppressed . . . [people] experiences with race and gender [in Canada]" (Dua 2007:184). In regards to this, Zine (2008) posits "gendered Islamophobia" in relation to the hijab as a depiction of "specific forms of discrimination leveled at Muslim women that proceed from historically contextualized negative stereo-types that inform specific individuals and systemic forms of oppression" (154). In this way, racialized Muslim women who wear hijab are constructed as being submissive, forced into taking off the veil in schools and the workplace, and sometimes denied employment because of wearing hijab. These gendered stereotypes also impact the lived experiences of racialized Muslim men who are constructed as being threatening, in danger of radical-ization, and who face detention without charge as well as deportation to countries where they are at risk of torture (Crocker et al. 2007).

We stated earlier that refugees' separation from their families influences the quality of their life in Canada, and that Canada's family-related immigration policy enables immi-grants to sponsor family members to bring them to Canada. Intersectionality leads us to understand why some refugees find the family reunification process too lengthy and that this is caused by factors associated with their national and geographic background, reli-gion, and immigration status. On one hand, the number of Canadian embassies in some developing countries where refugees await family reunification is very small (Satzewich 2016). On the other hand, Muslim family members are screened and monitored more than non-Muslims. These factors delay the family reunification process further (Culture, Community and Health Studies Program et al. 2004; Makwarimba et al. 2013). Addition-ally, being a refugee often creates financial strains that make it difficult for them to afford living expenses in Canada, sponsorship expenses, and to send remittances to families in other countries, all at the same time.

The intersection of gender and immigration status also reveals that, following family reunification, men and women are treated differently—in this case unfairly—as they settle into Canada. How well each immigrant can integrate depends on a number of factors such as entry status (defined as being "independent" or "dependant"), involvement in the labour market, and involvement in social networks (Boyd and Grieco 2003). As noted earlier, refugees in Canada have access to language-training programs, job-training programs, and a host of other programs that support incorporation into Canadian soci-ety. However, dependants including sponsored spouses have no access to these services.

CASE IN POINT

Family Reunification

Family reunification is important because it reunites refugees and immigrants with their spouses, children, adopted children, and parents in Canada. The Family Class Sponsorship program has been successful in allowing relatives to join their families in Canada, but the re-unification process is sometimes delayed by structural or procedural factors. To speed up this process, the Canadian Council for Refugees has recently requested changes to Canada's refu-gee and immigration policies by implementing an Express entry family reunification to allow refugees to reunite with their families within a few months after arrival in Canada. The sooner families reunite the easier coping with war trauma and adjusting to life in Canada will be.

In Canada, many refugee women enter as dependants and this consequently creates barriers for them to integrate (i.e., they do not have access to language programs). It also impedes their involvement in the labour market, leaves them subject to abuse with no avenue of escape, and limits access to resources.

Questions for Critical Thought

Do you see any advantages or merits of the analysis of family issues through one identity marker, i.e., gender, versus analysis through an intersectional approach?

An intersectional approach also helps us to enhance social justice inasmuch as it enables a better understanding of anti-oppression and can consequently facilitate the development and implementation of inclusive policies and interventions. This is because while these variables intersect to exclude people, they can also be merged to include social actors in society (hooks 1999). For example, when we simultaneously fight oppression based on religion, "race," and gender, we are better situated to eradicate myriad levels of marginalization. Applying this logic to the forms of exclusion that refugees encounter, we can argue that school curricula and programs can be more efficient if attention is given to the ways in which age, immigration status, religion, sexism, racism, and Islamophobia affect refugee youth when they navigate a new educational system and cope with trauma. Similarly, analysis through the intersection of culture, religion, and "race" would be beneficial to the planning of culturally appropriate settlement services. This is because it allows us to reiterate that certain cultural beliefs held by some refugees should not ever justify spousal abuse and, as such, ethnic organizations should fight sexism within their communities while they are fighting racism. It also draws attention to the fact that societal stereotypes about visible and Muslim minorities do not legitimize condemning and marginalizing entire ethnic groups, and that society should question negative stereotypes about refugees and other minority groups with a critical eye. Therefore, intersectionality is beneficial because it raises awareness about the numerous forms of discrimination that impede refugee families, and thus, helps us to identify ways to improve the living conditions for refugees already in Canada, and those recently arrived, including the recent influx of Syrians fleeing the civil war.

Given the socio-cultural, religious, political, and familial features that Syrians (Hassan et al. 2015; Shoup 2008) share with Sudanese and Afghans, it is important to guarantee them better settlement and integration outcomes. Since 2011, nearly half the Syrian population has been displaced: over 8 million within Syria and 4 million outside of the country (Connor and Krogstad 2016; Khalaf and Swing 2015). When Syrian refugees entered Canada in late 2015, some of the families were re-united with relatives that had come before. Adjustment to their new home might be in part aided by these family connections. However, for other families, the volunteer welcoming teams or the sponsoring organizations are the only support initially available to them as they adapt to Canada. In addition to the settlement needs of refugees, the development of trust between refugees and the receiving society becomes a crucial contextual fact (Hall 2016). Canadians in general welcomed Syrian refugee families and the backlash and Islamophobia that surfaced in reaction to their admission and arrival in Canada was minimal, especially when compared to the xenophobia that accompanied their arrival in Europe, and more recently in the US. Nevertheless, these are the very initial phases of the settlement of Syrian families and the rest of the process of their settlement and subsequent integration requires concerted efforts from governments, institutions, and communities to ensure that their life in Canada will be a true depiction of the humanitarian and welcoming tradition that the world ascribes to Canada.

Questions for Critical Thought

What do you think could and should be done to ensure more successful settlement for Syrian refugee families in Canada?

Conclusion

Canada's humanitarian tradition has opened the door to refugees from around the world and created a "racial," ethnic, and religious diversity in our society. This diversity has led to different organizations of family as well as to various processes of socialization. Communities and schools have been overwhelmed by this diversity and are only recently developing strategies for integrating families from diverse backgrounds. In all these cases, families have had to adapt and integrate into Canadian society. Some parents still interpret the world for their children while some children are trying to develop their own strategies to cope with the dynamics of integration and adaptation to Canadian culture. Relatives and kinship relations form networks of social and economic care and interdependence. In some cases these systems span three or four generations. At the same time, the nature and structure of communities can provide more or less support for refugee families. Institutions such as health and social services and the court system are also trying to adapt to incorporate Canada's growing diversity while maintaining equality and justice.

Finally, the backgrounds (human capital) of parent(s) are important in establishing the level of functionality for families. For example, refugee families with high education attainment and secure jobs, and who are not part of a racialized group, find their adjustment less problematic than those without this human capital. Nevertheless, families develop the structure of their children's basic values, and this schema is part of a group's culture. It becomes the basis by which family and individual experiences are processed and evaluated. It is, in short, a world view that serves as a framework for evaluating experiences and gives stability and order to family life. Unfortunately, these structures do not converge across cultural groups and allow all to apply the same schema to each of life's challenges. This endeavour deserves to be addressed in future research to better accommodate refugees and their families. After all, given the current global political climate, punctuated by the election of leaders like Donald Trump whose policies target refugees and Muslims, we are likely to see a growing rather than shrinking need for research in this area.

Study Questions

1. How does the socio-economic status of a refugee family impact its role and function?
2. How does domestic violence impact a family?
3. What are the major characteristics of family life in refugee camps?
4. How could one counter the barriers that refugee youth face?

Further Readings

Adams, L., and A. Kirova, eds. 2006. *Global Migration and Education: Schools, Children, and Families.* Mahwa: Lawrence Erlbaum. This volume illustrates how refugee and immigrant students and their families adapt to schooling in the host society and the challenges that arise in the process. It examines case studies in a few host societies, including in Canada.

Bragg, B., and L. Wong. 2015. "'Cancelled Dreams': Family Reunification and Shifting Canadian Immigration Policy." *Journal of Immigrant and Refugee Studies* 14, 1: 46–65. The authors carry out a series of personal interviews with immigrant families regarding the impact of new restrictive family reunification policies in Canada. The paper explores the impact of this new policy on immigrant families as well as immigrant women and children. The human cost of limiting family reunification is assessed and its impact on integration and belonging is presented.

Dachyshyn. D. 2007. *Refugee Families with Preschool Children: Transition to Life in Canada.* Department of Elementary Education. Edmonton: University of Alberta. This work offers a general explanation of how resettlement impacts the learning of preschool refugee children. It also provides parents and early childhood educators with constructive ways to facilitate the socialization and learning of pre-school refugee children.

Lee, S., and B. Edmonston. 2013. *Canada's Immigrant Families: Growth, Diversity and Challenges.* Discussion Paper Series 1, 1, Article 4. London: Population Change and Life Course Strategies Knowledge Cluster. The authors compare immigrant families with non-immigrant families on various socio-demographic attributes such as family type, size, and language used at home. They then focus on immigrants regarding characteristics such as when they migrated to Canada, place of birth, levels of education, and employment. They identify challenges for immigrant families living in Canada and provide a more detailed analysis of low-income immigrant families.

Key Terms

Ethnocentrism Is the bias or preference for one's own way of life or culture, as reflected in one's thinking or action.

Hyphenated identity Is an adherence that blends social aspects of two cultures, nationalities or heritage.

Internally displaced persons (IDPs) Are people who are forced to leave their homes but remain inside their country.

Intersectional Intersectionality is the theory that takes into consideration the interconnections among various identify markers such as gender, "race," and religion.

Islamophobia Encapsulates discrimination, negative stereotypes, bigotry, and prejudice toward Islam and Muslims.

Lost Boys and Girls of Sudan The name given to over 20,000 Sudanese minors who were displaced during Sudan's Second Civil War (1983–2005), from South Sudan to refugee camps in
Ethiopia and Kenya. They walked for months until they reached these destinations and many
died on the way as a result of starvation, drowning, violence, or animal attack. Hundreds of
them were eventually settled in a few countries, including Canada.

Policy of multiculturalism The policy adopted by Canada in 1971 to support the cultural development of ethno-cultural groups and to help members of these groups overcome barriers to full
participation in Canadian society.

Racial profiling Refers to stereotypical assumptions about "race," ethnicity, colour, religion, or
names that result in action such as arresting, searching, questioning, or beating particular
groups of people.

Settlement Is the adjustment to life in Canada in the early years after arrival, usually the first three
to five years.

**Interested in finding out more? Visit www.oupcanada.com/Albanese4e for
access to a list of recommended websites for this chapter.**

Indigenous Families

VANESSA WATTS

LEARNING OBJECTIVES

- To review assimilationist state objectives towards the absorption of Indigenous peoples

- To understand the role that women and families played in Indigenous communities before assimilationist polices were set in place

- To learn how assimilationist policies affected Indigenous family life

- To explore the trends of Aboriginal policy in Canada

- To discover new pathways of resistance Indigenous peoples have undertaken

---

Introduction

Aboriginal policy in Canada has largely been formed with **assimilationist** objectives towards the absorption of Indigenous peoples into the greater body politic. While the treaty relationship with Indigenous peoples during the late nineteenth century was intended to clear lands of Indigenous communities to make way for incoming settlers through the creation of the **reserve** system, Canada's Aboriginal policies have ultimately been designed to assimilate Indigenous peoples into a Canadian identity. This chapter will trace assimilationist policies as they relate to Indigenous families. In order to situate assimilation, it is necessary to examine how Indigenous understandings of gender and the family were organized prior to forced transitions. We will examine how Aboriginal policy in Canada has attempted to deculturate and re-mean—to cause the loss of cultural characteristics and subsequently impose new values/cultural characteristics—gender roles and family structures within Indigenous societies, as evidenced by discrimination in the Indian Act, residential schools, jurisdictional matters, child welfare, and matrimonial real property. We will also examine how contemporary formations of Indigenous families have been produced by these colonial policies. Finally, this chapter explores how Indigenous advocates and leaders have pushed back against these policies. In order to appreciate the extent of this re-meaning, it is necessary to examine how notions of gender and the family were differentiated in both European and Indigenous societies.

Gender Roles and Families

During the Victorian era, Europeans promoted the safeguarding of men's roles in the public sphere. The public, which included law-making, politics, industry, and ultimately the shaping of national power, was largely occupied by white men in European nations (Smith-Rosenberg 1986). During the nation-building era of Canada, this public space was purposed to increase access to land, wealth, and power in order to encourage European settlement into an emerging nation.

For more on the historical study of families, see "Families as Historical Actors" in Chapter 2, pp. 26–30.

In the private sphere—which includes the home and family life (Siltanen and Stanworth 1984)—wherein European women were expected to fill their roles, purposefulness was defined differently. Smith-Rosenberg (1999) describes the female of the Victorian era as more spiritual, less intellectual, and "closer to the divine." Typically, her only interaction with the political and/or economic was in the tending of her husband and the stresses brought on by political and economic life he would encounter.

The components of the private place included child-rearing, cooking, cleaning, and general maintenance of the home. The public place was and continues to be considered more essential in terms of valuation because not only does it entail more lofty enterprises, but in effect determines the scope of the private place. As such, women were defined by their roles in the private sphere, including the rearing of children, homemaking, and other domestic labour. Yet even when considering the private sphere, in very real terms the home was purchased, shaped, and determined by men—the ability to bestow and inherit was generally accorded to men. Either from father to son, or father to daughter's husband, property moved in the hands of men. The division of labour and its relationship to gender roles during the Victorian era were delineated by the material provisions of men.

Questions for Critical Thought

Can you think of examples in your own life or in the lives of people you know where similar patriarchal values, expectations, and practices continue to shape everyday life?

Inheritance then was not only defined by a gendered intergenerational relationship of property, but was also found in marriage. Victorian women inherited purpose and meaning within a home that was not theirs. What they bestowed in terms of their contributions to society could be found in their mothering. Smith-Rosenberg and Rosenberg (1999) write:

Weaker in body, confined by menstruation and pregnancy, she was both physically and economically dependent upon the stronger, more forceful male. . . .

> A woman who lived "unphysiologically". . . could produce only weak and degen-
> erate offspring. Until the twentieth century, it was almost universally assumed
> that acquired characteristics in the form of damage from disease and improper
> life-styles in parents would be transmitted through heredity . . . (114)

"Unphysiologically" is determined by Smith-Rosenberg and Rosenberg (1999) to
be the engagement with non-feminine activities such as labour outside of the home
(i.e. factory work), reading or studying in "excess," or a sedentary or luxurious lifestyle. For example, women in the Victorian era were believed to be more spiritual
than men, yet were unable to be intellectual enough to engage this spiritual supremacy because of their over-emotional nature—a result of possessing a uterus. And so,
the power of women to be the actors of inheritance was both biologically destined
and biologically stunted.

In contrast, for Indigenous nations, and specifically the **Haudenosaunee**, this literal
reproducing of the nation was not only physiological but also political. Sunseri (2010)
writes: "Oneida women see mothering as a political act, as a way to participate in the
sustainability of the self and the community. They do so by bearing and nurturing their
own children, taking care of others' children and providing for the whole community. . ."
(Sunseri 2010:133). Similar to the Victorian beliefs about reproduction, women were
viewed as bearing the responsibility of ensuring future generations of the nation; the difference lies within the valuation of this act. In Victorian times, childbirth was considered
to be a necessary female biological function that would produce citizens of the nation. Yet
the act itself was indicative of the overly emotional and inward/private place of a woman.
She produced, and the nation would inherit her product. In turn, she would be depleted
from this process, as she was considered weak to begin with. For the Haudenosaunee,
she too produced for the nation, but was empowered by this act. Katsi Cook (2007), a
Mohawk midwife notes:

> Woman is the first environment. In pregnancy, our bodies sustain life. At the
> breast of women, the generations are nourished. From the bodies of women flows
> the relationship of those generations both to society and the natural world. In this
> way the earth is our mother, the old people said. In this way, we the women are
> the earth. (3)

Haudenosaunee women believe that the act of childbirth is connected to the first
human birth on Turtle Island[1] itself. In terms of the valuation of women's role in reproduction, Haudenosaunee women represent Skywoman[2] in their act of birthing. Skywoman's story and impact are intrinsic to the very formation of how relationships are
imbedded into the political, economic, spiritual, and social structure of society. The
belief that land is female in its biology has enormous consequences for the subsequent
belief about Indigenous women as being *of* the earth itself. To believe for instance, that
the land we walk upon is alive and female, and is the result of a woman falling from the
sky, is incredibly powerful when we trace this act to the process of childbirth. It is within
this extension of Skywoman to all of the subsequent births of Haudenosaunee children,
that the value of a woman's role in reproduction is beyond nationalism or biology, but is
a sacred act.

Questions for Critical Thought

How do you think the centrality of the Skywoman story for the Haudenosaunee might affect the status of women in society?

Anderson (2000) comments on a Seneca woman, Betty Laverdure's remarks: "They say that medicine people have certain requirements, near-death experience. Some even have out-of-body experiences. Go into the spirit world and they have constant communication with the spirits. But the woman does this each time she gives birth. It's a near-death experience" (73). Anderson (2000) equates childbirth to a form of spiritual enlightenment. We might also posit that, through a process of place-based inheritance, she is re-affirming the human being's original history of creation. Now it is important to note that this does not therefore imply that women who do not go through the act of childbirth are not fulfilling some sort of biological destiny. There are many women who choose not to have children or are unable to have children. These circumstances are not reflective of more or less value or power. Rather, this understanding of birth as a powerful and authoritative act demonstrates that the female body has the inherent ability to access the spiritual world in a way that is both reflective and contributive in terms of Skywoman's gender role. In addition, it conveys a striking difference between the view of childbirth in Haudenosaunee belief systems as a political and authoritative act that invigorates female authority (Sunseri 2010), and a view of childbirth as a necessary component of maintaining imperial power during the Victorian era, yet ultimately devalued in and of itself (Stoler 2002).

For the Anishinaabe[3] (other Indigenous nations have similar views), family systems held a powerful role in how Anishinaabeg societies function (see Figure 12.1).

Each of the four concentric circles below represents a scope of roles and responsibilities defined within a particular collective. There are many interrelationships that exist within these four levels in different contexts, among various people or groups. The "Individual" is not defined as a position, which exists outside of a larger group, but rather is thought of in terms of how an individual maintains a relationship to a collective. Thus, the term *Individual* does not imply isolation or exclusive capacities, as it is dependent on

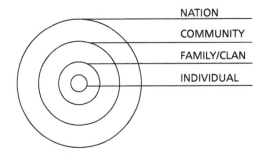

Figure 12.1   Family Systems within Anishinaabeg Societies
Source: Watts 2008.

collective responsibilities and duties for its context. "Family/Clan" is defined as the immediate collective that individuals affect with their own contributions. "Family" consists of both immediate and extended family into the "Clan" system that is also considered a part of the core family collective. Because clans are organized through observance and interaction with the animal world and other aspects of nature, family relationships are also extended beyond a human-to-human structure.

"Community" refers to the governance of the people on a specific territory, comprised of various clans and families. The governance of the people is defined by politics, law-making, ceremonies, health, etc. The roles and responsibilities within the community are reinforced through the ever-present contributions of the individual through their family and clan. This too could be interpreted as possessing attributes of what is considered a Nation, however it is said that *Kaagoogiiwe-Enaakoonige* (Sacred Law) was given to the Anishinaabe nation by *Gzhe-Mnidoo* (the Creator or Great Spirit) through our *Bimaadiziwin* (way of life): our language and concepts, philosophies, ceremonies, and **worldview**. These four levels are not measured in terms of hierarchy, but rather are interdependent on one another in order to function at the most optimal levels, and are anchored in notions of family relationships, roles, and responsibilities (Watts 2006).

In terms of how the family was situated more specifically within a socio-political context, the Royal Commission on Aboriginal Peoples (1996) reported:

> The family in Aboriginal societies stood between the individual and the larger society, playing an interpretive or mediating role. It helped individuals understand and respond to society's expectations, and it helped Aboriginal society engage individuals in constructive ways and discipline them should they venture on a course that conflicted with prevailing social values and expectations of behaviour. . . . If an Aboriginal person has been socialized in a situation where the family is the all-encompassing mediator between the individual and the social, economic and political spheres of the larger society, and that family is subsequently lost or disrupted, then the individual has lost not just one support, but also the principal agency that helps him or her make sense of the world. In effect, the person is set adrift. (Gathering Strength 2, 1.3)

In terms of colonial policy, this disruption impacted all areas of socio-political life. In the following discussion, we will observe how Euro-Canadian policy attempted/attempts to assimilate Indigenous families.

Contact and the Fur Trade

In terms of contact and early settlements of Europeans in Canada, the fur trade is a prime example of how Indigenous notions of gender and family were recognized in Indigenous-European relations before losing their primacy. Van Kirk (1983) describes marriages between Indigenous women and European men as "à la façon du pays," or "according to the custom of the country." That is, most often European traders (mostly Frenchmen) in the provinces now known as Manitoba, Saskatchewan, and Alberta were drawn into the kinship circles of Indigenous communities. Marriage between Indigenous women and European men was recognized as largely social and economic by both

Indigenous peoples and Europeans. For some Indigenous nations, these types of marriages raised the social rank and influence of particular families (Van Kirk 1983). Because Indigenous women held intimate knowledge of the land, and in some communities, authority over distribution of food, wealth, etc., marriage relations and gender roles were organized through Indigenous protocols of gender, family, and community.

The **Métis** people emerged as distinct communities during this time of inter-marriage and economic ties. However, as the fur trade economy began to collapse in the nineteenth century and Métis communities evolved, Indigenous views on gender roles and authority proved a hindrance to the settlement of Canada. Before the collapse of the fur-trade economy, Indigenous women were validated by European traders for their vast knowledge of fur trading territories, yet were simultaneously denied authority over these lands by the Hudson's Bay Company.

While Victorian ideals of gender roles were vastly different from those of Anishinaabe and Cree, European traders adapted to Indigenous ideals for the purposes of profit. This time in history represented a unique circumstance in colonization when Indigenous peoples dominated economic relations in terms of physical presence and knowledge. Yet, while Indigenous gender roles and family relationships were upheld, they were also transforming into a form of commodity. Land that was traditionally non-privatized pre-contact became the corporate property of the Hudson's Bay Company in 1670, and subsequently land title was transferred in the creation of the province of Manitoba in 1870. This transition marked the beginning of Aboriginal policy in Canada.

Treaties and the Indian Act

Westward expansion was one of Canada's top priorities during the latter part of the nineteenth century. The fur trade was coming to a close, and agriculture was thought to be the best option for economic success in the west. In order to do this, Canada required an influx of European settlers, and land for them to begin farming. The treaty process was a means to an end to achieve this goal and the government began an aggressive movement of settling the west through treaty agreements with Indigenous nations (Venne 2007). The idea was to pay Indigenous nations for massive acreages of land in exchange for specific benefits and the creation of reserves to which Indigenous peoples would be restricted.

The Royal Proclamation of 1763 had dictated that no survey or settlement of land could take place without the permission of the Crown or its representatives. The treaty process was meant to achieve three goals for the imperial government: (1) secure military alliances, (2) determine land title, and (3) encourage westward expansion (St. Germain 2004). By 1830 in what is now Canada, jurisdiction over "**Indians**" rested with the British Crown (with the exception of Rupert's Land which was "owned" by the Hudson's Bay Company). During this time, the British began their policy of civilization through assimilation. In 1867, with Confederation, Canada was established as its own self-governing Dominion and this jurisdiction transferred accordingly. The Department of Indian Affairs was transferred from the Secretary of State to the Department of the Interior in 1873, which oversaw Crown lands. After this transfer, treaty-making became the main focus of Government–Indigenous relations (St. Germain 2009). Though a treaty is by definition negotiated between two nation-states, the underlying assumption that Canada made was that this would be the next step in civilizing the "Indian" through an economic transfer of lands. Subsequently, lands set aside in treaty agreements for the use of "Indians," were defined and regulated the Indian Act of 1876.

The Indian Act: Gender and Families

In 1876, nine years after Canada's confederation, the Indian Act was passed. It was the amalgamation of two Acts: (1) the Gradual Civilization Act of 1857, and (2) the Gradual **Enfranchisement** Act of 1869. The Indian Act governs on issues relating to Indian **status**, Indian **bands**, and Indian reserves. It is now administered by Indigenous and Northern Affairs Canada (INAC). The Indian Act dictates almost every aspect of "Indian" life. From 1876 to 1951, there were numerous amendments made to further entrench government control over the lives of "Indians"; here are a few examples:

- In 1844, Indigenous spiritual practices and ceremonies were banned.
- If a reserve was located near a town of 8,000 residents or more, it was made legal in 1905 for the federal government to order the removal and relocation of "Indians" to a more remote area.
- In 1911, municipalities and private companies could expropriate portions of reserves for the purposes of roads, railways, and other public works. (Moss and Gardner-O'Toole 1991)

This interference in the political, economic, and family life by the federal government was further intensified through gender discrimination embedded in the Indian Act. Under section 6(1) of the Indian Act an "Indian" woman lost her Indian status if she married a non-Indigenous person (as well as **non-status Indians**). She was enfranchised as a Canadian citizen, and disenfranchised as an Indian under the Act. She could no longer:

- Live on a reserve
- Hold title on reserve
- Vote in elections on her reserve
- Be buried on her reserve once she passed
- Run in a band election for chief
- Vote in elections on her reserve
- Hold any position on her band council

In 1951, the Indian Act underwent many amendments that lifted bans and limitations. For example, post-1951:

- Ban on Indigenous ceremonies is dropped
- Status women are allowed to vote in band elections
- Ban on raising money for political purposes dropped
- Consumption of liquor in public places is permitted
- Ban on obtaining legal counsel for purposes of a land claim is lifted
  (Royal Commission on Aboriginal Peoples 1996)

However, Indigenous women continued to lose their status as "Indians" under the law if they married a non-Indian. Take the following scenario: a brother and sister are born of two Indigenous parents, both of whom had 6(1) Indian status under the Indian Act. The brother and sister are both **registered** as 6(1) Indians. Both siblings marry non-Indigenous people. The brother's wife becomes a 6(1) **status Indian** and can vote in band elections, hold title on reserve, etc. despite not being Indigenous. The sister's husband however, remains non-Indian, and she in turn loses her status as a 6(1) Indian, making her a non-Indian under the law. She cannot live in her home community, she cannot vote in band elections, and she cannot hold title to property on reserve (Royal Commission on Aboriginal Peoples 1996) (see Figure 12.2).

The children of these two respective unions continue to be recognized differently, despite having the same blood quantum. Let us imagine that the brother had a son with his formerly non-Indian wife—this son would be entitled to 6(1) Indian status, as the law now recognizes the son's mother as an Indian. If the sister had a son, however, he would not be entitled to status under the law, despite his mother formerly being a status Indian before marriage.

During the 1960s and 70s, two cases challenged the discriminatory provisions of the Indian Act that disenfranchised "Indian" women. In 1970, Jeannette Corbiere Lavell married a non-Indian; in 1971, she brought an action contesting that section of the Indian Act as violating the equality clause in the Bill of Rights. She lost her case at trial but won on appeal. Yvonne Bedard lost her status in 1964 when she married a non-Indian. When she separated from her spouse and attempted to return to live in her community in a house she inherited from her mother, she learned that she and her children were no longer entitled to live on the reserve and could not inherit land thereon. The band gave her a year to dispose of the property and Bedard brought legal action. Bedard won her case based on the Lavell precedent but the cases were jointly appealed to the Supreme Court. Bedard and Lavell lost their cases and the "marrying out rule" of the Indian Act was upheld (Holmes 1987).

Questions for Critical Thought

Can you imagine any other circumstances, groups, or cases where similar rules governing women's everyday life would/could exist? Why do you think the Canadian government could get away with policies like these?

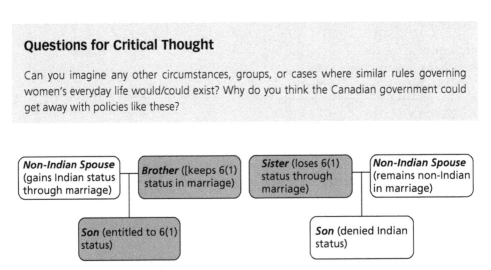

Figure 12.2   Prior to Bill to Amend the Indian Act: How Indian Status was granted and regulated by the Indian Registrar (1876–1984)

Source: Extracted from the Royal Commission on Aboriginal Peoples, 1996, and created by Watts (chapter author), 2016.

In 1974, Sandra Lovelace took this case to the United Nations Human Rights Committee. Sandra Lovelace was a registered Maliseet Indian who lived on the Tobique Reservation until she married a non-Indian man. The marriage ended, and Lovelace returned to the reserve to live with her parents. However, she could not purchase a home on the reserve because the council prioritized housing for members of the group. Ms. Lovelace submitted an application to the Human Rights Committee, claiming that this violated Articles 2(1), 3, 23(1) and (4), 26, and 27 of the International Covenant on Civil and Political Rights (ICCPR) because the Act only strips Indian women who marry non-Indians of their Indian status and not Indian men (Hartley 2007).

In the 1980s, the United Nations Human Rights Committee and the Canadian Human Rights Commission identified Section 12 of the Indian Act as a human rights abuse, as it removed a woman's Indian status if she married a non-Indian man. This is in direct violation the International Covenant on Civil and Political rights that protects a minority's right to belong to their cultural group. The UN ruling in 1982 coincided with the repatriation of the Canadian constitution, which includes the Charter of Rights and Freedoms that guarantees gender equality (Hartley 2007). In 1985, the Indian Act was amended through **Bill C-31** An Act to Amend the Indian Act, and subsequently Indian status was divided as follows:

However, there remain problems of gender discrimination despite the corrective changes of Bill C-31. The granddaughter of the brother in our original scenario still has Indian Status under subsection 6(2), but the granddaughter of the sister still is not entitled to status, despite having the same blood quantum as her cousin. In 2011, the Indian Act was again amended through Bill C-3, Gender Equity in Indian Registration Act, and Indian status was re-defined again (see figure 12.4).

These amendments may seem counterintuitive; that is, why would Indigenous people seek to gain recognition under a discriminatory, "race"-based Act? The answer is that because the treaty relationship between Indigenous peoples and the Crown is largely (and erroneously) prescribed through the Indian Act—access to lands set aside for **First Nations**, rights to members of First Nation bands, etc.—gender discrimination through the Indian Act also means the denial of rights. Additionally, though Indian status is more

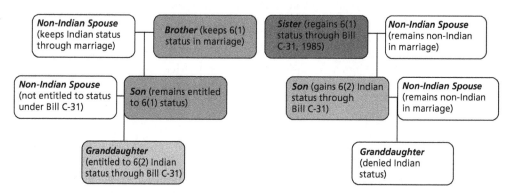

Figure 12.3   Bill C-31, 1985: An Act to Amend the Indian Act, Indian Status

Source: http://blog.oup.com/2013/08/honouring-treaty-gender-equality-canada-stolen-sisters/, with adaptations from Watts (chapter author) to help trace "status" more clearly for readers.

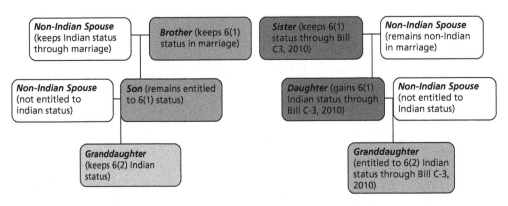

Figure 12.4   Bill C-3, 2010: Gender Equity in Indian Registration Act, Indian Status

Source: Hurley and Simeone (2010) provide the context/analysis from which Watts (chapter author) created this diagram. See: www.lop.parl.gc.ca/About/Parliament/LegislativeSummaries/bills_ls.asp?Language=E&ls=C3&Mode=1&Parl=40&Ses=3&source=library_prb.

reflective of gender equity with the amendments of Bill C-31 and Bill C-3, resources from the federal government for housing or reserve are not adequate to accommodate this increase in membership. This combined with the lack of increase in land bases on-reserves, many newly enrolled status Indians were not able to return home, even if they wanted to.

Residential Schools

In an attempt to "kill the Indian in the child" as infamously phrased by former Deputy Superintendent of Indian Affairs Duncan Campbell Scott, from the mid-nineteenth century the residential schools system became mandated and mandatory for all status-Indian children under the Indian Act, as well as Métis and **Inuit** children. As early as the age of four (three years, in some cases) children were removed from their communities with the aid of Indian Agents (federal employees who monitored reserves), the RCMP, and church officials.

The first federally run residential school was the Mohawk Institute in Brantford, Ontario, in 1831; it was also the longest running school, closing its doors in 1970. The last federally run school to close was in 1996, the Gordon Indian Residential School in Saskatchewan. In 1884, enrollment became mandatory for First Nations children under the age of 16 (Moss and Gardner-O'Toole 1991). Meaning that, for over 150 years, Indigenous families were intruded upon and broken apart.

There were 130 church-operated residential schools during this time and it is estimated that 150,000 First Nations, Métis, and Inuit children attended these schools (Truth and Reconciliation Commission of Canada 2015). The purpose of the residential school system was to Christianize, "civilize," and assimilate First Nations people into the greater body politic of Canada. Notes from the Legislative Assembly of the Province of Canada describe how the "Indian problem" is properly a lack of whiteness:

> The chief obstacles to the advancement of the race are . . . their ignorance or imperfect knowledge of the language, customs, and mode of traffic of the whites;

and that feebleness of the reasoning powers, which are the necessary consequences of the entire absence of mental cultivation. None of these difficulties appear insuperable, and your Commissioners are of opinion, that all the measures of the Government should be directed to their removal, and to the development of those natural capacities which the Indian character exhibits. This may be a difficult task, as regards the majority of the adults, whose habits have been formed, with whom the time for instruction is passed, and who have become familiarized with their condition, but with the youth it will be otherwise. . . ." (Canada 1847: Appendix T)

Many residential schools had high mortality rates due to malnourishment and unsanitary conditions. In 1948, the Department of Indigenous and Northern Development Canada approved a series of five-year experiments recording various interventions and their effects on 1,000 First Nations students in six residential schools. One such experiment tested the effects of riboflavin deficiencies on children. The induced malnourishment of First Nations children in residential schools was thought to be the "ideal scientific laboratory." Rather than improve the health of children during these visits, doctors kept them in a state of ill-health to study the effects of malnourishment in order to learn how to improve the health of non-Indigenous people (Mosby 2013).

Children also experienced atrocious abuses ranging from physical punishment for speaking their language, extreme physical abuse, sexual abuse, and forced abortions (Truth and Reconciliation Commission of Canada 2015).

Daily Life
Chanie Wenjack

In 1967, *Maclean's* magazine released a story about the death of a 12-year old Ojibway boy named Chanie Wenjack in the fall of 1966 (Adams 1967). Chanie was forced to attend the Cecilia Jeffreys Indian Residential School in Kenora, Ontario, at the age of nine. While playing outdoors on the school grounds that day, Chanie and his two friends, Ralph and Jackie Mac-Donald, decided they would run away. Chanie had been spanked by the principal for playing hooky the week before. Many children attending a residential school had tried to escape for many reasons. At Cecilia Jeffreys Indian Residential School, there was a secret path that children would take to avoid the nearby town of Kenora and enter into the bush. Chanie wanted to return home to his father, from whom he had been taken three years before. His home was close to four hundred miles north of the school, in Marten Falls First Nation. After his two friends had met up with their uncle in Redditt, Chanie decided to continue walking through the bush along a railroad track to be with his father. He walked by himself for 36 hours, covering 12 more miles, wearing only a windbreaker. Chanie was found by a railway engineer next to the railroad track, one week after having escaped from Cecilia Jeffreys, having walked over 60 kilometres. He passed away from hunger and exposure.

Today, there are close to 80,000 residential school survivors still living. Many of these survivors are a part of the Indian Residential Schools Settlement Agreement that was negotiated between survivors, the churches, and the federal government. The settlement is believed to be the largest in Canadian history at $5 billion. The implementation process of the settlement began in 2007. All survivors will receive $10,000 for having to attend a residential school and $3,000 in addition for every year attended (Aboriginal Healing Foundation 2007). A separate process was created for those survivors who experienced severe physical and sexual abuse. The federal government hired investigators to look into these claims, adding another level of re-victimization to this process. Payment for abuses was evaluated on a harm scale, in which the level of abuse had a corresponding score, and this score was associated with a dollar amount. The Truth and **Reconciliation** Commission was also funded from this settlement as well as other healing initiatives. Prime Minister Harper made an official apology in 2008; this apology received both acceptance and criticisms from survivors.

Jurisdiction

Jurisdictional matters on-reserve are complex and fraught with human rights implications. When reserves were created systematically through the historic numbered treaties and the Indian Act, they were set aside as federal Crown lands, for the use and occupation of status Indians. This meant/means that status Indians cannot own land outright on-reserve (fee simple), without the advent of a modern day treaty/comprehensive land claim (available as of 1975), or First Nations Land Management Act implementation (available as of 1999). Prior to these dates, neither of these legislative paths were available, and to this day, most reserves are still held as federal Crown lands.

Thus, provincial responsibilities and the standards set within their 27 ministries (some of which include health care, education, labour, and housing) are not a **fiduciary responsibility** of the province on-reserve, nor are they a parliamentary responsibility of the federal government in general. Though the implications are many with regard to chronic underfunding and human rights violation on-reserve (there are no standards for federal health care, as this is a provincial ministry), with regard to the family, three significant jurisdictional issues arise that impact Indigenous communities: child welfare, access to health services on-reserve, and matrimonial real property.

Child Welfare: The Sixties Scoop

As residential schools began to transition into a phase of closure in the 1950s, the complication over jurisdictional disputes is perhaps most severely observed in the child welfare system. In 1951, the Indian Act went through numerous amendments, one of them being in the area of child welfare. In the lead-up to these amendments, the residential school system began transitioning to closure (Milloy 1999). Church groups continued to operate the majority of schools and lobbied the federal government to continue to fund their operations despite reports of physical and sexual abuse, malnourishment, and the disrepair of the schools themselves. The federal government added Section 88 to the Indian Act in 1951, which allowed for some provincial laws to apply to First Nations people living on-reserve; this included child and family services. Social workers of child welfare agencies would now have legal jurisdiction to apprehend children from the reserve.

As of 1951, there were 29 First Nations children in provincial care in British Columbia; this number rose to 1,466 by 1964 (White and Jacobs 1992). Some children were placed in residential schools, which by then operated under the auspices of "child welfare," while some were fostered out to non-Indigenous families. From the 1960s to the 1980s, Indigenous children would come to represent approximately 34 per cent of all children in care nationally (White and Jacobs 1992).

The **Sixties Scoop** refers to the decade when a high number of Indigenous children were "scooped" from their families without proper investigation. The removal of Indigenous children was largely based on assumptions about "race" and character by provincial child welfare agencies. The term was first coined by Patrick Johnston (1983) in a report for the federal department of Social Policy Development entitled, "Native Children and the Child Welfare System." Johnston noted the following when interviewing a former social worker from British Columbia: ". . . with tears in her eyes—that it was common practice in BC in the mid-sixties to 'scoop' from their mothers on reserves almost all newly born children. She was crying because she realized—20 years later—what a mistake that had been" (Sinclair 2007:66). It is estimated that over 20,000 children were fostered out during this time.

Johnston (1983) found that during this time, 70 to 90 per cent of Indigenous children apprehended by provincial child welfare agencies were placed in non-Indigenous foster and adoption homes. The exception to this trend was Quebec, where Cree and Inuit child placements occurred mainly in the home community of the child. (Johnston 1983). The disruptions of specific cultural aspects of family life when an Indigenous child is removed from community are many. Further, the prevalence of stereotypes about Indigenous peoples and their lives as being of less value, can have catastrophic consequences when Indigenous children are "adopted out" in order to protect a child from the familial circumstance:

> When Cameron Kerley was eight years old he witnessed his father being beaten to death. Cameron and three sisters were apprehended by the Children's Aid Society and placed in foster homes. His mother died two years later as a result of heavy drinking.
>
> Cameron was placed for adoption with Dick Kerley, a bachelor who had previously adopted another Aboriginal boy. Cameron soon began to display social problems, skipping school and getting into trouble with the law.
>
> When he was 19 years of age he murdered his adopted father with a baseball bat. Cameron pleaded guilty to second degree murder and was sentenced to life in prison with no eligibility for parole for 15 years. After being sentenced, Cameron alleged that he had been sexually abused by his adoptive father since shortly after he was placed.
>
> Cameron's appeal for a reduced sentence in January 1985 was denied, but his request to be returned to Manitoba to serve his sentence was granted with the

consent of the Canadian government. (Review Committee on Indian and Métis Adoptions and Placements 1985:246)

Cameron Kerley's story is an example of how Indigenous children are vulnerable to the child welfare system. During the Sixties Scoop, Indigenous children were removed from the home in a majority of cases due to neglect—a direct consequence of parents being survivors of the Indian Residential School system (Blackstock 2007). This trend continues today, as Indigenous children continue to be apprehended at disproportionately high rates.

Child Welfare: The Millennium Scoop

In 1991, the federal government established the Royal Commission on Aboriginal Peoples (RCAP). The Commission was designed to address issues pertaining specifically to the status of Aboriginal peoples. The Oka Crisis of 1990 and the Meech Lake Accord in 1987 highlighted historical wrongs and jurisdictional problems that impacted Indigenous peoples and their rights. In 1996, the Commission released its in report, at over 4,000 pages, including 440 recommendations in five volumes. The seven commissioners, after thorough consultation with Aboriginal communities, political leaders, elders, youth, and residential school survivors, made recommendations in areas of **treaty rights**, nation-to-nation relationships, reallocation of lands and resources, governance, and economic development. In terms of the family, RCAP focused on three key policy areas: child welfare reform, family violence, and aspects of family law.

RCAP emphasized how provincial child welfare services were ill-equipped to deal with issues particular to Indigenous communities, namely: **intergenerational impacts** of residential schools, and Indigenous worldviews and cultural practices as they relate to the family. In 1981, INAC authorized for the first time a First Nations agency to have control over child welfare. By the time the RCAP report was released in 1996, 36 Aboriginal child and family services agencies were responsible for child welfare across 212 First Nations communities (Canada 1996). Though this was a progressive step following the release of Johnston's (1983) report, Aboriginal child welfare agencies were underfunded and Aboriginal agencies were not properly equipped to deal with an increasingly urban Aboriginal population. These Aboriginal child welfare agencies increased by 2011 (see Table 12.1).

Despite an increase in Aboriginal child and family services agencies, traditional child-rearing practices and cultural patterns were not recognized as legitimate forms of child care by welfare agencies. The result of this has been children who are alienated from their culture, heritage, and communities. Despite some changes to provincial child welfare practices with respect to Aboriginal peoples, First Nations children are still three times more likely to be in the child welfare system as compared to non-Indigenous children.

Despite comprising just 7 per cent of the child population in Canada, Indigenous children represent 48 per cent of the children in care nationally (Statistics Canada 2011). Blackstock and Trocmé

For more on violence and abuse in Indigenous families, see "Domestic Violence among Vulnerable Families" in Chapter 14 pp. 303–7.

Table 12.1 Number of First Nations, Urban Aboriginal, and Métis Child Welfare Agencies by Province or Territory and Range of Services Offered, 2011

Agencies offering full range of services[b]

Province	Total[a]	All	First Nations	Urban Aboriginal	Métis
Nova Scotia	1	1	1	0	0
New Brunswick	10	10	10	0	0
Quebec	16	8	8	0	0
Ontario	11	6	5[c]	1	0
Manitoba	16	15	13[c]	1	1
Saskatchewan	17	17	17	0	0
Alberta	18	18	18[c]	0	0
British Columbia	31	9	8[c]	1	0
PEI	1	0	0	0	0
Northwest Territories	0	0	0	0	0
Newfoundland and Labrador	0	0	0	0	0
Yukon	0	0	0	0	0
Nunavut		Because Inuit represent the majority ethno-racial group, the distinction between territorial and Aboriginally governed child welfare agencies is unclear			
Total	121	84	80	3	1

a. Includes British Columbia agencies in planning or pre-planning stages.
b. Includes initial investigations and intake, but not adoption services.
c. Includes First Nations agencies serving off-reserve populations.

Source: Sinha, Vandna and Anna Kozlowski (2013). "The Structure of Aboriginal Child Welfare in Canada." Originally published in *The International Indigenous Policy Journal*, 4(2), p. 5. Reprinted by permission.

(2005) argue that Indigenous children and youth are being removed from their homes at a rate three-times higher than during the height of the residential schools system. This phenomenon is known as the **Millennium Scoop**. Indigenous children in the child welfare system are, in the majority of cases, apprehended due to issues of neglect (Sinha et al. 2011). Apprehensions related to sexual and physical abuse are higher among non-Indigenous families (Blackstock and Trocmé 2005). Neglect is accelerated by the intergenerational impacts of residential schools that have not been adequately addressed (Blackstock and Trocmé 2005). That is, the breakdown of the family caused by generations of children being removed from their homes for over 150 years has produced a severe disconnect in family relations. Issues of poverty and discrimination of funding in terms of prevention servi-ces on-reserve (a jurisdictional matter), has only added to how issues of neglect unfold.

For more on poverty in Canadian families, see Chapter 10.

CASE IN POINT

Child Welfare: Jordan's Principle

A key example of how jurisdictional issues on-reserve continue to produce human rights violations against Indigenous families, was brought to the fore in Jordan's Principle. Jordan's Principle is a child-first principle that is intended to ensure that First Nations children do not encounter discrimination in services (either through delay, denial, or disruption) that are normally available to all other children in Canada (The Jordan's Principle Working Group 2015). Jordan's Principle was named in memory of Jordan River Anderson. Jordan River Anderson was from Norway House Cree Nation in Manitoba. He was born with complex medical issues that required at-home care. The Province of Manitoba and the federal government could not agree which government should be responsible for Jordan's at-home care, because his home was on-reserve. Jordan spent two years in hospital, unnecessarily. He died in 2005 while in hospital at the age of five, without ever having spent a day at his family home.

In 2007, Jordan's Principle was adopted in the House of Commons. It provides that First Nations children with Indian status should not experience delay, denial, or disruption of services, regardless of if there is a jurisdictional dispute at play. The federal government has interpreted Jordan's Principle in a more narrow way, wanting to restrict the principle to First Nations children with short-term medical issues and disabilities. This interpretation was criticized in a 2016 ruling by the Canadian Human Rights Tribunal, which ordered the federal government to implement the full scope of Jordan's Principle. The discriminatory measures the federal government took in its narrow interpretation of Jordan's Principle contribute to a larger and exhaustive pattern: the violation of human rights against Indigenous peoples and their families by the federal government in an effort to expend less money and avoid equitable standards in policy (The Jordan's Principle Working Group 2015).

Child Welfare: Canadian Human Rights Tribunal

In 2007, the First Nations Child and Family Caring Society (FNCFC) and the Assembly of First Nations (AFN) filed a complaint against the federal government to the Canadian Human Rights Tribunal (CHRT), citing discrimination in child welfare practices against First Nations children and youth. The subsequent January 2016 ruling by the CHRT was a landmark decision on the issue of First Nations children and child welfare Canada. While ruling that the full scope of Jordan's Principle be implemented, it also found discrimination in other aspects of child welfare and First Nations children.

The CHRT found that the on-reserve child welfare system is chronically under-funded. It receives 38 per cent *less* funding than other child welfare systems elsewhere, despite having higher funding needs in some cases (Native Women's Association of Canada 2015). It also found there was a lack of prevention services to mitigate child apprehension in the case of family crisis affecting First Nations children on-reserve. Additionally, culturally meaningful and relevant child welfare practices and the funding to implement them was cited as an objective of this ruling. These practices are both unique to the multiplicities of cultures among First Nations, as well as unique in terms of the fact that many First Nations families are particularly impacted by the legacy of residential schools. This ruling compels the federal government to fully implement the scope of the CHRT's findings.

Matrimonial Real Property

In the event of the breakdown of a marriage or common-law relationship, or in the event of death of a common-law partner or spouse, families are entitled to the equitable division of property as protected through provincial legislation. Because provinces are not responsible for lands or peoples on-reserve, and the Indian Act had not been legislated with real property implications (it is federal Crown land), Indigenous families and their interests are not protected.

Up until 2013, there were no mechanisms in place for the division of property and assets. Not only does this produce all sorts of inequities, it can impact the custody of children. Take this example:

> A mother and her children are homeless in the city after living for 15 years in their First Nation community. Before leaving for the city they had endured on-going abuse by the father and husband. Because he is the only one who holds the right to the family home, they are now living in a shelter miles away from their friends, family, and support system, leaving behind a comfortable home, prosperous business, clothing, and toys. Without access to applications for emergency protection orders or orders for temporary exclusive occupation of the family home, this woman was not able to protect herself or her children while remaining in the community. (Indigenous and Northern Affairs Canada 2013)

Due to a myriad of reasons, some of which include lack of access to the justice system or women's shelters, etc., the mother in this scenario would have less of a chance of retaining custody because she is not in possession of a home. Further to this, most homes on-reserve are occupied by families through Certificates of Possession. Certificates of possession are predominantly held by men on-reserve. Thus, in the event of the breakdown of a relationship, the mother/wife/common-law partner would not be legally entitled to an equitable division of assets. This threatens her ability to gain custody of her children, remain within her community, and survive (financially or otherwise).

There are many other scenarios that are commonplace on-reserve, resulting in generations of women being denied access to the home to which she contributed either through wages, labour within the home, or both. In 2013, the federal government amended the Indian Act once again with the Family Homes on Reserves and Matrimonial Interests or Rights Act. This Act establishes provisional federal rules to come into effect immediately, while First Nations develop their own matrimonial real property laws under law-making authority within the Act (Native Women's Association of Canada 2014).

The federal rules are similar to provincial rules on matrimonial real property. First Nations law-making authority allows for First Nations to develop mechanisms that are culturally relevant and appropriate to handle such disputes (forms of Aboriginal alternative dispute resolution processes, for example). While this Act and the First Nations authority that comes with it will be an improvement to gendered notions of property on-reserve, there continue to be many families and descendants of families who encountered these types of disputes who will not have equitable access to the assets to which they contributed.

Conclusion

Idle No More, a national social movement of Indigenous peoples across Canada that came together in 2012 and 2013, was a point of momentum in the recognition of Indigenous rights on many issues. While the movement's efforts were widely regarded by media outlets as "protests," it is important to note that efforts in protecting lands for environmental degradation encompasses the protection of "family members." As discussed earlier in the chapter, from an Anishinaabe perspective (and many other Indigenous nations), humans exist in a kinship relationship with other members of a territory (land, animals, the waters, etc.).

This is exemplified powerfully in the Haudenosaunee community of Six Nations of the Grand River in southwestern Ontario, where the Six Nations Birthing Centre was established, and where Haudenosaunee midwives are working with Indigenous women to restore Haudenosaunee midwifery practices (Six Nations Health Services 2006). Based on traditional principles of birthing and mothering, these midwives are renewing cultural aspects of the family within the community.

The residential schools system in Canada, in removing children from their families, not only denied Indigenous children their family structures, but also disavowed Indigenous traditional parenting practices—in effect, preventing the transmission of Indigenous ways of knowing, as well as loving relationships. The intergenerational impacts of residential schools on the family continue to be widely felt by survivors and their families. Whether these effects are observed in the disproportionately high numbers of Indigenous peoples in the justice system and the child welfare system, or in the chronic underfunding of education on-reserve, Indigenous peoples continue to fight against discrimination embedded in Aboriginal policy and access to services.

As noted throughout this chapter, all of the successes Indigenous peoples have achieved in reuniting families and culture and in promoting equitable treatment have been accomplished through hard-fought battles, usually in the Supreme Court. That is, federal and provincial governments have continuously resisted (and continue to resist), righting the wrongs of colonialism. The burden of taking up these disparities continues to be on Indigenous peoples. The Truth and Reconciliation Commission's report released in 2015 included survivor accounts of residential schools and the impacts of residential schools on Indigenous peoples and societies, and presented 94 Calls to Action to address current injustices. In essence, the disparities within Indigenous communities have been produced out of the colonial desire to assimilate Indigenous peoples and appropriate Indigenous lands. This was (and is) predicated on transforming Indigenous notions of gender and family structures, and is further intensified by the state's protection of a racist status quo.

As Cindy Blackstock stated in her response to the Canadian Human Rights Tribunal decision: "Why did we have to bring the government of Canada to court to get them to treat First Nation children fairly? Little kids. . . . Why would it ever be OK to give a child less than other children?" (CBC 2016). Given the era of reconciliation in Canada, why does this remain a question?

Study Questions

1. In what ways do jurisdictional matters impact Indigenous families on-reserve, and how are these impacts discriminatory?
2. How are Indigenous notions of gender and the family different from Victorian-era Western ones?
3. What is Jordan's Principle? How was Jordan's Principle resolved?
4. Describe the different ways in which child welfare systems have evolved as they pertain to Indigenous children in Canada?

Further Readings

Anderson, Kim. 2000. *A Recognition of Being: Reconstructing Native Womanhood*. Toronto: Second Story Press. Anderson offers an excellent resource to understand how Indigenous notions of womanhood and the role of the family were organized during pre-contact times. It also contextualizes these roles in the presence of colonial policy. Anderson includes interviews with midwives, Indigenous knowledge holders, and Elders throughout her book.

Blackstock, Cindy, and Nico Trocmé. 2005. "Community-based Child Welfare for Aboriginal Children: Supporting Resilience through Structural Change." *Social Policy Journal of New Zealand* 24(12): 12–33. This article provides a historical context for how disproportionately high numbers of Indigenous children are involved in the child welfare system. Blackstock and Trocmé document the rates of Indigenous versus non-Indigenous child apprehensions, and focus their discussion on issues of neglect and poverty, as they relate to the residential schools system.

Milloy, J. 1999. *A National Crime: The Canadian Government and the Residential Schools System*. Winnipeg, MB: University of Manitoba Press. Examining the residential schools policy in Canada from the nineteenth to twentieth centuries, this book gives detailed accounts of students' experiences, school curricula, and how church and government policy attempted to break Indigenous culture and families.

Mosby, Ian. 2013. "Administering Colonial Science: Nutrition Research and Human Biomedical Experimentation in Aboriginal Communities and Residential Schools, 1942–1952." *Histoire*

sociale/Social History 46(91): 145–72. This article undertakes an examination of two experiments that took place in two different residential schools during the 1940s. Mosby's research
uncovers data that had not previously been publicly reported.

Sinclair, Raven. 2007. "Identity Lost and Found: Lessons from the Sixties Scoop." *First Peoples Child
and Family Review* (3)1: 65–82. Sinclair examines how adoptees from the Sixties Scoop are
faced with issues surrounding cultural identity after being adopted into non-Indigenous families. Sinclair utilizes social-psychology frames of analysis to draw out this tension, and provides
recommendations for how Aboriginal policy pertaining to Indigenous adoptees can be more
reflective of Indigenous approaches to identity and the family.

Key Terms

Aboriginal The term *Aboriginal* gained currency during the negotiations for the Canadian Constitution, 1982. *Aboriginal* is used to refer to Indian (both status and non-status), Inuit, and Métis.
All three groups have unique heritages, cultural practices, and spiritual beliefs.

Assimilation The process in which one cultural group is absorbed into another, typically dominant,
culture.

Band A group of First Nations peoples for whom lands have been set aside (a reserve) and monies
are held by the Crown. Each has its own governing band council, usually consisting of a chief
and councillors who are elected by band members.

Bill C-31 Indian A person who regains status under the Indian Act (originally of 1869), pursuant to
Bill C-31, 1985. There are many types of non-status Indians in Canada.

Enfranchisement Enfranchisement can be a means of gaining the vote and is viewed by some as
a right of citizenship. Under the Indian Act, enfranchisement meant the loss of Indian status.
Indians were compelled to give up their Indian status and, accordingly, lose their treaty rights,
to become enfranchised as Canadian citizens.

Fiduciary responsibility The trust responsibility toward the Indian People that is vested in the
Minister of Indian and Northern Affairs Canada by the Indian Act, 1876

First Nation(s) This term replaces *band* and *Indian*, which are considered by some to be outdated,
and signifies the earliest cultures in Canada.

Haudenosaunee Also known as Iroquois, *Haudenosaunee* refers to the people of the Six Nations:
the Seneca, Cayuga, Mohawk, Oneida, Onondaga, and Tuscarora. *Haudenosaunee* means
"People of the Longhouse."

Indian The term *Indian* is still a legally defined term used in the Indian Act with the restrictions and
regulations that pertain to it. *Indian* is used to describe the status that is assigned by the Indian
Registrar. However, *Indian* is no longer an acceptable conversational or formal reference for
this specific group of Aboriginal peoples.

Intergenerational impacts The unresolved trauma of Survivors who experienced or witnessed
physical or sexual abuse in the residential schools system that is passed on from generation
to generation through family violence, drug abuse, alcohol abuse, substance abuse, physical
abuse, sexual abuse, loss of parenting skills, and self-destructive behaviours.

Inuit *Inuit* is Inuktitut meaning "the people." The majority of Inuit inhabit the northern regions of
Canada. An Inuit person is known as an Inuk. The Inuit homeland is known as Inuit Nunangat,
which refers to the land, water, and ice contained in the Arctic region.

Métis Métis People are of mixed First Nations and European ancestry who identify themselves as Métis, and are accepted as such by Métis leadership. They are distinct from First Nations and Inuit. Their history and culture draws on diverse ancestral origins such as Scottish, Irish, French, Ojibway, and Cree. Although named as one of the Aboriginal Peoples in Section 35 of the Constitution Act of 1982, there is no national, legal, or formal definition of *Métis*.

Millennium Scoop Refers to the disproportionately high number of Aboriginal children in the child welfare system since 2000.

Non-status Indians Non-status Indians are people who consider themselves Indians or members of a First Nation but who are not recognized by the federal government as Indians under the Indian Act. Non-status Indians are not entitled to the same rights and benefits available to status Indians.

Reconciliation Reconciliation is the process by which individuals or communities attempt to arrive at a place of mutual understanding and acceptance. There is no one approach to achieving reconciliation but building trust by examining painful shared histories, acknowledging each other's truths, and a common vision are essential to the process.

Registered Indian An Indian whose name is recorded in the Indian registrar according to the Indian Act, originally of 1869.

Reserve The Indian Act of 1876 states: "The term 'reserve' means any tract or tracts of land set apart by treaty or otherwise for the use or benefit of or granted to a particular band of Indians, of which the legal title is in the Crown, but which is unsurrendered, and includes all the trees, wood, timber, soil, stone, minerals, metals, or other valuables thereon or therein." Occasionally, the American term *reservation* is used but *reserve* or *Indian Reserve* is the usual terminology in Canada.

Sixties Scoop Refers to the first formal child welfare system for Aboriginal children, where high numbers of Aboriginal children were removed from the home in the 1960s.

Status Those registered (or entitled to be registered) under the Indian Act, originally of 1869.

Status Indian Status Indians are people who are entitled to have their names included on the Indian Register, an official list maintained by the federal government. Only status Indians are recognized as Indians under the Indian Act and are entitled to certain rights and benefits under the law.

Treaty rights The basis of treaty rights are the promises made to First Nations during negotiations, rather than what was specifically written into the texts of the treaties. Neither the federal parliament nor provincial legislatures can alter the existing provisions of Aboriginal or treaty rights under Section 35 of the Constitution Act of 1982.

Worldview The fundamental cognitive orientation of an individual or society encompassing the entirety of the individual or society's knowledge and point of view. A worldview can include natural philosophy; fundamental, existential, and normative postulates; or themes, values, emotions, and ethics.

Notes

1. *Turtle Island* refers to North America; many Indigenous nations in North America refer to their territories as, more broadly, parts of Turtle Island.

2. *Skywoman* refers to the pregnant woman who fell through a hole in the sky to the waters on earth below in the Haudenosaunee origin story. Skywoman is thought to be the bringer of human life to Earth.

3. The Anishinaabe are one of the largest nations in North America. Anishinaabe homelands include territories in the provinces of Ontario, Manitoba, and Saskatchewan, as well as in the American states of Michigan, Wisconsin, and Minnesota. The Anishinaabe include the Ojibway, Algonquin, Odawa, Chippewa, and Saulteaux peoples.

www **Interested in finding out more? Visit www.oupcanada.com/Albanese4e for access to a list of recommended websites for this chapter.**

Lack of Support
Canadian Families and Disability

MICHELLE OWEN

LEARNING OBJECTIVES

- To understand the impact disability has on Canadian families

- To be able to distinguish between the medical and social models of disability

- To recognize the role gender plays in the lives of disabled people

- To describe the relationship(s) between poverty and disability

- To identify the factors that put people with disabilities at increased risk of violence and abuse

---

Introduction

Too many Canadian families experience the poverty, exclusion, and stress that comes from living with disability. As a mother of two disabled children describes it: "I had lost my identity. I had lost control of my life" (CCD 2011). Unfortunately, despite the widespread and growing impact of disability in this country, disabled Canadians and Canadian families continue to experience a lack of support.

In this chapter we will examine disability in Canadian families. As the title suggests, the argument being presented is that disabled Canadians and their families are marginalized in our society. The chapter begins by providing background information regarding definitions, models, and frameworks. It is then divided into three sections: Children and Youth with Disabilities, Parents with Disabilities, and Violence and Abuse.

Disability affects many Canadians and their families. In 2012, 3.8 million people in this country aged 15 or older (almost 14 per cent of the census population, or one in seven) reported that they had a disability (Statistics Canada 2015). While these figures are slightly down from the 2006 data, they most likely do not indicate a decrease in the number of disabled Canadians. Rather the way the federal government measures disability has changed three times over the last thirty years, and unfortunately the surveys are not comparable (Statistics Canada 2014a).

What is important to note is that the 2012 Canadian Survey on Disability (CSD), like the earlier Participation and Activity Limitation Survey (PALS) and the Health and Activity Limitation Survey (HALS), is concerned with what a person can or cannot do at a particular time. This means that some Canadians may not count as having a disability when they fill out the census form. However, the CDS attempts to correct for this by also asking about other long-term health problems or conditions (Statistics Canada 2014a). As in the other surveys people not living in private dwellings were excluded from the CDS (Statistics Canada 2014a). This is significant and means that disabled Indigenous people on-reserve and in institutions, for example, are not part of the data. Finally, the CDS only included adults, so unlike the earlier research, everyone under 15 years of age was left out. The result is that there have been no federal data on children with disabilities since 2006.

For more on the lives of Indigenous families, see Chapter 12.

In addition to the 3.8 million Canadian adults who identify as having a disability or limitation, about 8.1 million Canadians (28 per cent) 15 years and older "provided care to a family member or friend with a long-term health condition, disability or aging needs" (Statistics Canada 2013).

Questions for Critical Thought

Do you have a disability? Are you related to someone who is disabled?

Canada is an aging society, and the prevalence of disability increases with age. In this sense, all people without disabilities can be considered **temporarily able-bodied (TABs)**. While 10.1 per cent of adults (aged 15–64) or 2.3 million working-age Canadians report having a disability, seniors (aged 65 and over) have a rate more than three times higher at 33.2 per cent (Statistics Canada 2015). This increases to 42.5 per cent for Canadians aged 75 and over (Statistics Canada 2015).

For more on aging families in Canada, see Chapter 7.

Canada has one of the highest life expectancies in the world, and women live longer than men although the gap is closing (83.6 years versus 79.4) (Statistics Canada 2016). Women in this country are thus more apt to experience disabilities and concurrent chronic health problems (Statistics Canada and Status of Women Canada 2012:360). In 2012, 14.9 per cent of women in Canada reported having disabilities, compared to 12.5 per cent of men (Statistics Canada 2015). Figure 13.1 shows the rates of disability for women and men in Canada in various age groups. Disabled women are more likely than disabled men to be single, have lower incomes than men with disabilities, and have "less tangible social support" (Des Meules et al. 2004). Furthermore, women and girls with disabilities are oppressed by sexism and **ableism** (and in some cases racism, classism, homophobia, etc.). Demas, for example, argues that Indigenous women with disabilities face "triple jeopardy" (1993a:89).

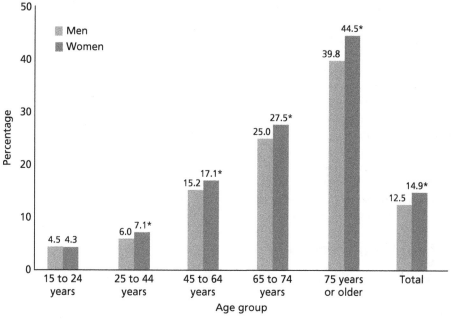

Figure 13.1   Prevalence of Disability, by Age Group and Sex, Aged 15 Years or Older, Canada, 2012

Source: Statistics Canada, Canadian Survey on Disability, (2012).

Defining Disability

There are no easy definitions of *disability*, and the terminology used in disability activism and studies has been hotly debated. Defining words is a political act, as feminist and critical race theorists have struggled to highlight. Some people use a wheelchair or a cane and are conspicuously disabled, while others have chronic illnesses or mental health issues that are not so readily apparent. These are sometimes referred to as **visible** and **invisible disabilities**, a distinction that of course only makes sense if one is sighted. Some disabilities are permanent (paraplegia), while others are temporary (broken limbs), or they come and go (relapsing/remitting multiple sclerosis). Who is disabled and what counts as disability is constantly changing.

Questions for Critical Thought

How do you define *disability*?

The federal government acknowledges that the concept of disability is always shifting and thus "defining disability is not an easy task" (Government of Canada 2002:10). Although national survey data rely on self-identification for a broader range of individuals, much like many community-based organizations and activists, benefits and disability-oriented programs use a far more limiting definition. Neither the Charter of Rights and Freedoms nor the Canadian Human Rights Act unequivocally define disability, although they do prohibit discrimination against persons with physical and/or mental disabilities.

Whenever a definition is not explicitly given by a piece of legislation, it is up to the courts to determine scope and limitations. For example, a 2001 Quebec Supreme Court decision stated that "various ailments such as congenital physical malformations, asthma, speech impediments, obesity, acne and, more recently, being HIV positive, constitute grounds of discrimination" (Office for Disability Issues 2003:14–15). The focus of this ruling is on how society treats (or mistreats) people with non-conformist bodies, which is an example of social model theorizing.

The Social Model of Disability

The **social model of disability** can be understood as "the relationship between a person with impairment and the environment, including attitudes, beliefs, climate, architecture, systems, and services" (Hurst 2005:65). This is in contrast to the earlier **bio-medical or individual models**, which centred disability firmly in bodies (Oliver 1996). These earlier theories served to reinforce disability as a personal tragedy and fuelled feelings of pity in non-disabled people. A good example is the Jerry Lewis telethons, which many people with disabilities find demeaning. It is also useful to distinguish between two types of social model: the materialist or radical, and the idealist or rights interpretation (Sheldon 2005:118–19). According to Alison Sheldon, while a radical social model focuses on capitalism as "the root cause of disablement," rights-based analyses lead to "short-term policy reforms and sticking-plaster solutions" (ibid.:118, 121). From her perspective, the impact of globalization must be taken into account as we theorize disability.

The Union of Physically Impaired Against Segregation (UPIAS) (1976) in the UK was perhaps the first to make an unambiguous distinction between personalized physical **impairments** and the social experience of disability: "In our view it is society which disables physically impaired people. Disability is something imposed on top of our impairments by the way we are unnecessarily isolated and excluded from full participation in society. Disabled people are therefore an oppressed group in society" (cited in Oliver 1996:33).

Hence, since the 1970s, disability activists and theorists have put forth a social model of disability that identifies barriers as being systemically rather than biologically based (Crow, 1996). As Jenny Morris (2001:2) writes, citing a definition used by the British Council of Disabled People:

> Disability is the disadvantage or restriction of activity caused by a society which takes little or no account of people who have impairments and thus excludes them from mainstream activity (therefore, disability, like racism or sexism, is discrimination and social oppression).

Thus, the social model of disability has much in common with analyses that theorize "race" and gender as social constructions and not as biological or "natural." The emphasis in defining "disability," as a result, has shifted from a medical model of (ab)normality (Malec 1993) to a focus on social structures. This has been a significant move in the rethinking of disability and the beginning of political action. Previously, the concept of disability was centred on individual impairments and people with disabilities were "othered" because of their difference from the ableist norm. Within the social model external obstacles, as opposed to individual characteristics, are viewed as disabling (Block and Keys 2002). For example, the lack of a ramp is the problem, not the fact that someone uses a wheelchair.

Despite the progressive thrust of the social model of disability, gender differences have been an ongoing source of tension. However, as Thomas (1999) maintains, experiences of disability are always shaped by gender. A number of academics and activists have struggled for recognition of the double discrimination faced by people who are marked as both "female" and "disabled" (see Wendell 1996). The concept of **gendered disablism** (Thomas 1999:28) is increasingly receiving recognition. Unfortunately, other differences, such as "race" (ibid.) and sexuality (Tremain 1996), have received far less attention. Notably Deborah Stienstra (2012) investigates "race"/ethnicity in the context of Disability Studies, while Eli Clare (2015) and Alison Kafer (2013) write at the intersections of disability, sexuality, and gender.

Theoretical/Methodological Frameworks

Although this chapter is based in the social model of disability, it is important to acknowledge some of the critiques of this mode of theorizing, such as the denial of bodies and pain (Wendell 1996). Not all disabling experiences can be fixed by altering the environment. A cross-disability perspective has been employed, rather than focusing on any one disability or type of disability. This encompasses "visible" and "invisible disabilities," including so-called physical disabilities (mobility, vision, hearing), mental health issues, chronic illnesses, intellectual disabilities, and learning disabilities. Self-identification is critical in this context because it shifts the power of naming away from those in authority and contributes to the cultural identity of people with disabilities. Finally, the terms "persons with disabilities" and "disabled persons" are alternated. The former is derived from "people first" language and is more common in the Canadian context though by no means standard. The intent is to signal that people have many identities in addition to disability. The latter phrase is used more in the UK and fits better with the social model of disability. It is increasingly used by Canadians who want to highlight the disabling features of the social environment.

Children and Youth with Disabilities

Statistics Canada (2007b) reported that in 2006 there were approximately 5.5 million Canadian children aged 14 and under. Of this total, 202,350 (3.7 per cent) had disabilities, representing 2.7 per cent of girls and 4.6 per cent of boys. Boys 14 or younger are more likely than their female counterparts to have disabilities that limit activity, but once they move into the next age category (15–24) this prevalence disappears (Cossette and Duclos 2002). Overall the incidence of disability increases with age of the child—this was found to be true regardless of gender (Statistics Canada 2007a; see Table 13.1).

Table 13.1 Disability Rates for Canadian Children under the Age of 15, by Sex and Age Groups, Percentage, 2006

Age	Child disability rates	Disability rates among boys	Disability rates among girls
0–14	3.7	4.6	2.7
0–4	1.7	2.1	1.2
5–9	4.2	5.3	3.0
10–14	4.9	6.0	3.7

Source: Statistics Canada, *Participation and Activity Limitation Survey, 2008.*

Demographics

Over half (55.1 per cent) of disabled children in Canada are considered to have "mild to moderate disabilities," with Quebec and Ontario having the highest incidences of children with severe to very severe disabilities (48.8 per cent and 39.7 per cent of children with disabilities, respectively) (Statistics Canada 2007b). Of the population of children with disabilities in Canada, 13.6 per cent (27,540) are preschoolers (0–4 years) (Statistics Canada 2007b). The most common type of disability among preschoolers are chronic health conditions such as asthma, severe allergies, heart conditions or disease, kidney conditions or disease, cancer, epilepsy, cerebral palsy, spina bifida, cystic fibrosis, muscular dystrophy, fetal alcohol syndrome, etc. (69.8 per cent) (Statistics Canada 2007b). Developmental delay (62 per cent), including delays in intellectual and/or physical development, and other delays such as speech impairment were the next most prevalent type of disability causing activity limitations for this age group (Statistics Canada 2007b).

The majority (86.4 per cent, or 174,810) of all disabled children are school age (5–14 years) (Statistics Canada 2007b). The most common types of disabilities reported for this age group in 2006 were learning disabilities (69.3 per cent) and chronic health conditions (66.6 per cent) (Statistics Canada 2007a). Boys reported experiencing learning disabilities (4.1 per cent) and chronic disabilities (3.8 per cent) at a higher rate than girls (2.2 per cent for each) (ibid.). That same year a disability related to learning affected 121,080 school-age children, or 3.2 per cent of all children aged 5 to 14 in Canada (ibid.). Learning disabilities are often not diagnosed until children start school, and parents continue to struggle to obtain special education for their children with disabilities (Statistics Canada 2008a). Over 40 per cent of parents with children with disabilities reported in 2006 that they had a difficult time accessing special education, regardless of the type or severity of their child's disability (ibid.). Emotional, behavioural, and psychological conditions such as autism were the most difficult to accommodate (ibid.).

Impact of Children with Disabilities on Families

Many parents of children with disabilities experience considerable frustration, largely stemming from a lack of supports rather than from dealing with their child's disability (Roeher Institute 2000b). While in the past many disabled children were institutionalized, they are increasingly likely to live at home with their families rather than in institutions (Roeher

Institute 2000a). However, in some cases, children are placed in residential or foster care because of inadequate family supports (Howlett 2004). Family breakdown is not uncommon, and children with disabilities are over-represented in female-headed lone-parent families (Fawcett 1996) compared with other children (18.1 and 14.1 per cent, respectively) (NPHS 1996, as cited in Roeher Institute 2000b). Adult Canadian women (15 years of age and over) with disabilities are more likely than similarly aged men with disabilities and women without disabilities to live alone and to be lone parents (Statistics Canada 2009).

Family Income, Employment, and Poverty

The average household income for families with children with disabilities is lower than the household incomes of their peers without disabilities (Table 13.2). In 2006 the average household income for families with disabled children was $69,440, compared to $85,294 for families without children with disabilities (Human Resources and Skills Development Canada 2011a). Further, there is a correlation between the presence of a child with a disability in the household and the likelihood of a family's income falling below the low income cut-off (LICO) (Statistics Canada 2008b). Currently one in five families with children having activity-related disabilities reported falling below the LICO, as compared to one in ten families without children with disabilities (ibid.). Having a disabled child does not only influence income, but it can also impact the employment situation of families. Many families of children with disabilities (nearly 62 per cent of families with preschool children and 54 per cent of those with school-age children) report that their child's condition has impacted the family's employment situation (Government of Canada 2004). The impact was found to be positively correlated to the severity of the child's disability—while 40 per cent of families of children with mild to moderate disabilities reported an impact on their employment, this proportion almost doubled to 73 per cent in families having children with severe to very severe disabilities (Behnia and Duclos 2003).

For information on the negative impact of poverty on health, see "What Are the Consequences of Poverty?" in Chapter 10, pp. 220–2.

Having a child with a disability can thus force families to rethink the way they organize work and family life. In almost half the cases one or more family members make changes to their employment (Human Resources and Skills Development Canada 2011a). Compared to fathers, mothers are most likely to be responsible for providing, arranging, and advocating for care for their disabled children (Roeher Institute 2000a). Hence, women are more likely than men to experience an impact on their employment due to their child's disability. This has been described as "hidden, gender-based oppression" (Home 2002). Mothers' employment is affected almost 90 per cent of the time while fathers' employment is affected about 33 per cent of the time (Human Resources and Skills Development Canada 2011a).

For more on women's employment, see "Gender Differences in Paid and Unpaid Work: What Difference Does Difference Make?" in Chapter 9, pp. 196–7.

Table 13.2 Average Household Income of Canadian Children, 2006

Age	Children with disabilities	Children without disabilities
0–14	$69,440	$85,294

Source: Statistics Canada, *Participation and Activity Limitation Survey,* 2008.

So children with disabilities are more likely to be poor than other children (Human Resources and Skills Development Canada 2011a; Roeher Institute 2000b). "Children with disabilities are twice as likely to live in households relying on social assistance and families of children with disabilities are more likely to live in poverty" (Campaign 2000 2015:8). This trend also goes in the opposite direction: "Children living in poverty are 2.5 times more likely than children in high-income families to have a problem with vision, hearing, speech, or mobility" (Ross and Roberts 1999, as cited in Roeher Institute 2000b:5). According to the Roeher Institute, *poverty can lead to disability* in a number of ways. People living in impoverished conditions have little access to nutritious foods, both during pregnancy and as children grow. Poor people tend to live in areas or circumstances that may increase the risk of injury and also tend to have less access to health services, as well as lower literacy levels, all of which have been linked to increased rates of disability and/or ill health (ibid.). Labelling is a concern for these children, as well: "Poor children, like children who are from visible minorities, are also more likely to be labelled as having a disability than children from more privileged families" (ibid.:6).

The Roeher Institute also suggests that *disability can lead to poverty*. Families with disabled children are more likely to experience "family breakdown" and the corresponding reduced family income. Parents of children with disabilities also experience increased barriers to participation in the paid labour force and must contend with costs that families without disabilities do not face. These expenses include those related to "tutors, special diet, special clothing, transportation, babysitting, medications, supplies and equipment, and home adaptations" (ibid.).

Some parents have no other alternative than to care for their children full-time rather than participating in the paid labour force (Hanvey 2002:11). "For many families of children with disabilities it makes more sense to use social assistance than to take a job with low wages, since they are entitled to receive more disability-related supports when on welfare" (ibid.:6). Because social assistance can provide these disability supports, many parents of children with disabilities simply cannot "afford" to work (see Table 13.3).

Indigenous families with disabled children living on-reserve experience unique problems related to support and social assistance. Because of federal guidelines for support,

Table 13.3 Employment Impact for Parents of Canadian Children with Disabilities by Severity, 2006

Employment impact	Total	Mild to moderate	Severe to very severe
Not taken a job	26.4	16.4	39.8
Quit working	21.6	13.2	32.9
Changed work hours	36.5	26.9	49.4
Turned down promotion	19.7	10.5	31.9
Worked fewer hours	38.4	29.1	50.8
Worked more hours	9.7	6.4	14.2

Source: Statistics Canada, *Participation and Active Living Survey, 2008.*

social assistance on-reserve tends to be lower than elsewhere. And since the mid-2000s money is dispersed to First Nations who in turn distribute funds to individuals (Aboriginal Affairs and Northern Development Canada 2010). Indigenous families caring for a child with disabilities may have to move off-reserve to access the supports they need.

According to Roeher Institute (2000a), 50 to 60 hours of a parent's week is spent providing disability-related supports to their child(ren). Employers are not required to accommodate people caring for children with disabilities, so parents are forced to alter their commitments to their jobs or leave the paid workforce entirely, with very little government assistance (Roeher Institute 2000b). In Canada, a monthly supplement called the Child Disability Benefit (CDB) is available to parents of children with disabilities. It has a maximum amount per child, as well restrictions based on the age of the child, the length of time received, the type of disability, and the severity of the child's disability. The CDB is a tax-free benefit of no more than $2,000 per year, which is only available for "low- and modest-income families, who care for a child under age 18 with a severe and prolonged mental or physical impairment" (Canada Revenue Agency 2005: para. 2).

The Dearth of Supports for Disabled Children

Housework, Family Responsibilities, and Personal Activities

Although having a child with a disability creates additional demands for parents, nearly 60 per cent of parents of preschool children and almost 80 per cent of parents of school-age children with disabilities report not needing additional help with housework and family responsibilities (Government of Canada 2004). Parents of preschool children with disabilities are more likely than parents of school-age children with disabilities to report needing additional help with housework and family responsibilities. Parents of children with severe to very severe disabilities were more likely than parents of children with mild to moderate disabilities to report unmet needs (29.7 per cent versus 10.7 per cent) (Statistics Canada 2008c).

Cost is a major factor preventing parents of disabled school-age children from getting the assistance they require—73.5 per cent cited cost as a reason for not receiving the help they need (Statistics Canada 2008c). Usually, parents (56 per cent of those reporting) resort to "free" help that comes from family members outside the home, though more than a third (36.7 per cent) reported "out-of-pocket" expenses for required assistance (ibid.). As one parent of a child with a disability describes this frustration: "I want them to have a life. They need opportunities to develop. This is not possible for me to do without needed supports and services" (Roeher Institute 2000b:1).

Family access to disability-related supports can be difficult and fraught with problems. According to the Roeher Institute, families report that eligibility screening is too rigid and does not sufficiently take individual family circumstance and disability-related costs into consideration. As a result, families living with disabilities face multiple barriers to gaining access to needed supports. Not just cost, many families report a lack of local resources and a lack of information about local services (Statistics Canada 2008c). In addition, access to services seems to vary between families and regions: "Fewer than four in ten (37.5 per cent) parents reported that special services were not available locally, while 39.5 per cent of parents reported not knowing where to go to find help" (Statistics

Canada 2008c). Families also report being discouraged by long waiting lists and not being able to afford short-term relief care, transportation, and equipment.

Since the late 1990s, the disparity of supports in Canada has left some families caring for disabled children with no option other than to temporarily relinquish guardianship over their children. According to the report of the Ontario ombudsperson, up to 150 families in Ontario signed temporary custody agreements with the Children's Aid Society in order to obtain supports needed by their children with severe disabilities. Douglas Elliott, a lawyer representing many of these families in a class-action lawsuit, argued that "many parents were concerned their children would not continue receiving care once legal custody was restored. Parents had turned to a children's aid society because that was the only way to obtain treatment" (Howlett 2004:A13).

Parental Caregiving Responsibilities

Due to the inadequacy of support services, parents and other familial caregivers are often forced to fill the gap themselves (Statistics Canada 2013). This can result in what a 2003 Canadian study has termed "caregiver strain" (Duxbury and Higgins 2003, cited in Pappone 2005). People in the workforce who are caring for aging parents or children with disabilities are vulnerable to a variety of problems, including depression, fatigue, family conflict, and financial problems. Research illustrates the multiple responsibilities of parents of children with disabilities: nurses, advocates, trainers and educators, and service co-ordinators (Haverstock 1992, cited in Roeher Institute 2000b). One parent interviewed encapsulates this sentiment: "I'm everything—I'm the playmate, storyteller, therapist, disciplinarian, advocate, cook, and parent" (ibid.:10).

For more on parenting see Chapter 5.

Parenting does not end when a child grows up and/or leaves home, particularly for some disabled children. And, as Heather Hewett's story emphasizes (see Box 13.1), a number of people besides parents are included in the "networks of support" for a person with a disability (Hewett 2004). Heather's sister's situation highlights the fact that all of us, people with and without disabilities, are ultimately interdependent. Her family is not unlike other families except that the interdependence is widespread and hence more obvious. While Hewett is writing in the American context, her description of the "intricate web" that allows her sister to live interdependently is relevant for Canadians.

Home and Respite Care

Access to **home care** varies across Canada and even within provinces and territories (Statistics Canada 2014b). In 2012, 792,000 Canadian adults who needed care in the home for disability, long-term illness, or aging reported that their needs were only partly met or not met at all (ibid.).

There is no "consistent or coherent home care coverage, nor standards defining access to basic services" (Roeher Institute 2000b:9). A 2005 report by the Council of Canadians with Disabilities identifies these jurisdictional issues as problematic (Krogh and Ennis 2005).

Families also report needing more **respite care**—those services that give parents/guardians a break from their caregiving responsibilities. The Roeher Institute (2000a), in a study of 50 families of children with disabilities, found that 90 per cent identified

Box 13.1

A Sister's Story

My 31-year-old sister has Down syndrome. She lives in her own house, three miles away from my 70-something parents, and she works part-time busing tables at a local café. An extended network of people help her live on her own: my mother, her full-time advocate and teacher; my father, her biggest fan and supporter; her caseworker, Alicia, who oversees the coordination of her social services; her live-in house companion, Eleanor; her habilitation training specialist, Delores, who helps teach her skills such as balancing her checkbook; her speech pathologist, Judy; her boss, David; her 80-something best friend, Ellen, who gives her rides around town; and finally, her close friends Laurie and Elizabeth, two middle-aged dance therapists who listen to her and provide her with an endless supply of hugs. Then, of course, there's me, but I live thousands of miles away.

From my vantage point, it is particularly evident how much of my sister's daily existence depends on this extended family of friends and professional caregivers. In this respect, her life is not so different from that of other families in our country. Many families rely on similar (though not always as extensive) networks of support; it is just that in my sister's case, the intricate web holding her up cannot be ignored. It is there, in plain view, for all who look.
Source: Hewett 2004.

respite care as one of the most crucial supports needed for them and their children but this need was not being met. Access to respite care is particularly difficult for families in rural areas, as well as for children with exceptional support needs. Demand for in-home respite is high and there are not enough public resources to assist everyone (Dunbrack 2003).

Child Care

Many parents rely on child care services to help meet their family needs. While the majority still rely on a family member in the home, 24.4 per cent (one in five) used after school programs and another 20.7 per cent (one in four) used the child care service of a non-relative outside of the home (Statistics Canada 2008c). Location and transportation to child care services however, makes choosing facilities more complex because the facilities must be able to meet the child's special needs (ibid.). The federal Office for Disability Issues (2003) reported that approximately 20 per cent of parents of disabled preschool children were refused child care or babysitting services due to their child's impairment. This percentage was not found to vary significantly based on severity of disability.

Although the deficiency of child care in Canada is a concern for all Canadians, for parents of children with disabilities accessing child care can be even more difficult. A 2013 Canadian paper frames the inclusion of disabled children in regulated daycare as a human rights issue (Halfon and Friendly 2013). The authors conclude that: "Canada needs a national, publicly funded, publicly managed universal system of high quality early childhood education and child care program that mandates and supports the inclusion of children with disabilities (6). Child care facilities are not required to include children with disabilities, although some do. When child care centres accept children with disabilities, it is usually done on a child-by-child basis, with some disabled children accepted and others not (Roeher Institute 2000b). In 2006, 25 per cent of parents reported that a daycare centre had refused their child with a disability (Statistics Canada 2008c).

According to the Roeher Institute, the problem is inadequate funding—centres would be more inclusive if there were enough money. Getting their children into daycare is not the only problem. Even when they have managed to secure child care, parents may encounter difficulties in getting their child to the centre and back home again, rigid hours of operation, inflexible curricula, or a lack of training among staff about disability (Roeher Institute 2000b:14).

Parents with Disabilities

There is far more information available about disabled children in this country, albeit only up to 2006 on a federal level, than about disabled parents. Neither the CDS nor PALS have collected data pertaining to parents with disabilities. So all we can do is speculate.

Questions for Critical Thought

How might living with disability affect the experience of those who are engaged in parenting?

What we do know is that working age adults with disabilities are not doing as well at forming or maintaining families as their counterparts without disabilities. In 2006, 56.2 per cent of disabled people aged 25–54 were married or in a common-law relationship compared to 71.4 per cent of non-disabled Canadians. People with disabilities are also more likely to be separated or divorced (24.2 per cent) than people without disabilities. Furthermore, the average household income for a single disabled person in this age group is only 67.0 per cent of the average household income for a single non-disabled adult (Human Resources and Skills Development Canada 2011a).

In addition to structural barriers, social stigma and moral regulation surround parenting by disabled people, especially women, who are most affected by medical procedures designed to control fertility and reproduction. In the past, women with disabilities have been denied the right to have children through forced sterilization and chemical birth control (Malacrida 2009: 184; Ridington 1989). Increasingly, women's lives are subject to a process of "geneticization," with common conditions being labelled genetic diseases (Lippman 1993:40). The assumption is that no one would want to raise a disabled child given the choice. A case in point—abortion is currently prohibited for sex selection in Canada but not for the elimination of disability (ibid.:62). Prenatal screening and testing have in fact become routine, opening the doors to a new type of eugenics (Peters and Lawson 2002).

Mothering Challenges

"Mothering or even fathering with a disability is assumed to be potentially 'damaging' for children . . . [and] family 'dysfunction' is presumed to be inevitable" (Blackford 1999:281). It is not uncommon for mothers with disabilities to face disbelief and discrimination regarding pregnancy and parenting, to have their custody challenged, or their children taken away. For example, adaptive measures such as lifting babies by clothing and harnesses on wheelchairs are not always understood or well received by the non-disabled public (Auliff 2001). Kuttai documents many of the challenges women with disabilities face as they become parents including encounters with medical professionals and social judgment (Kuttai 2010).

Blackford (1999:280) argues, however, that "through the intimate experience of caring for and knowing a person with a disability, and through feeling cared-for and understood by a person with a disability, oppression associated with disability prejudice and with **familialism** [restrictive ideas about what constitutes the 'family'] is reduced." In addition, children of disabled parents learn to respect difference and are exposed to a more egalitarian family environment, as well as gain a profound awareness and recognition of the lived experience of space and the body (ibid.).

Daily Life It Could Happen to Anyone

If you haven't experienced disability, you might feel like the information provided in this chapter doesn't apply to you. But disability and chronic illness really can happen to anyone at any time. Consider the story of Nicole Reid, a Canadian mother who experienced postpartum depression and almost lost her children (Tomasi 2015). The Ontario resident had "panic attacks, heart palpitations, worrying thoughts, and insomnia." But Ms. Reid was determined to feel well again, and so she took the medication that her doctor prescribed and spoke to a psychiatrist on a regular basis. However, in 2014 Ms. Reid's physician put her on a new drug and she became sick and very depressed. "I was throwing up, sleeping for hours and I'd start crying at the drop of a hat," she says. "It was scary." When he couldn't help her immediately Ms. Reid was advised to go the local hospital. After a quick assessment, the 27-year-old was sent to the mental health wing and the Children's Aid Society (CAS) was notified. The next day a psychiatrist sent Ms. Reid home, after changing her medication and declaring her "not to be a threat to her children." However, CAS continued to investigate for another month. Ultimately the case was closed but not before damage was done to Ms. Reid and her family. As we've read, it's unfortunately not unusual for parents with disabilities, especially mothers, to undergo scrutiny from authorities and worry about losing custody of their children. Meanwhile mental health issues are widespread and women are more likely to experience depression than men. Canadian society needs to get beyond outmoded stereotypes of disability, and assist rather than punish mothers like Nicole Reid.

Unfortunately disabled women often find themselves isolated. They are almost twice as likely as non-disabled women to live alone (26.2 per cent versus 14.4 per cent), and about half as likely to live with a spouse and children (14.6 per cent versus 27.7 per cent) (Statistics Canada 2009). By comparison disabled men are less likely to live alone (18.1 per cent) and more likely to live with their spouse and children (28.9 per cent) (Statistics Canada 2009) (see Table 13.4).

Despite the challenges, disabled Canadian women are having and raising children. As of 2009 almost 15 per cent of women with disabilities surveyed reported living with their spouse/partner and children, and another 8 per cent indicated that they were lone parents (Statistics Canada 2009). But according to Blackford et al. (1999) the needs of expectant mothers with chronic illnesses and/or disabilities are not being met by current models of prenatal care and education. The authors suggest, "If prenatal education is individualized and culturally respectful, education can be a medium to address the empowerment needs of marginalized expectant mothers" (ibid.:899).

In their research, Blackford and her colleagues interviewed disabled mothers who had given birth to a child within the past two years about their maternity experiences. They found that the women noted six areas of prenatal care that needed improvement: learning resources for self-care, opportunities to voice anxiety, supportive relationships, communication within the family, information pertaining to postnatal care, and special circumstances (ibid.).

Informal Caregiving

In 2012 over 80 per cent of disabled people surveyed indicated that they used at least one aid or assistive device, and 27 per cent reported that they needed an aid or assistive device that they did not have (Statistics Canada 2015). When asked about the kinds of assistance needed, disabled people listed housework, especially help with heavy chores, getting to appointments, and running errands (Statistics Canada 2015). Severity of disability and cost are the main factors influencing whether or not disabled people can get the help they need (Human Resources and Skills Development Canada 2009). Although the most common source of assistance in everyday activities is family, more than one quarter of disabled people say that their friends and families are unable to provide these informal care services (ibid.). In 2012, 80 per cent of disabled people living with family reported receiving assistance from someone in the household, and 56 per cent of people with disabilities who lived alone indicated that they received help from family they did not live with (Statistics Canada 2015). Usually one family member, typically a woman, provides the majority of informal care services: "The role of informal caregiver can be challenging, especially since many caregivers are also employed, are lone parents or have responsibilities besides helping a person with a disability. Caregivers may need support to keep providing quality care to people with disabilities" (Government of Canada 2004:19).

Working-age adults with disabilities are more likely to receive informal care from family members who live with them than from any other resource. According to the Government of Canada, "Informal caregivers often face long-term financial repercussions in the form of, for instance, turning down career opportunities, being unable to update skills, saving less for retirement and experiencing reduced working hours, pay, and pension benefits" (ibid.:20). Re-entering the workforce after a period of full-time caregiving

Table 13.4 Women and Men Aged 15 and over, by Living Arrangement and Activity Limitations Status, Canada, 2009

	Women		Men	
	With activity limitations	Without activity limitations	With activity limitations	Without activity limitations
Living arrangement	Percentage			
Individual living alone	26.2*	14.4	18.1*	13.1
Living with spouse/partner	31.8*	26.4	39.3*	28.4
Living with spouse/partner and children	14.6*	27.7	21.2*	28.9
Lone parent	8.1*	6.5	1.3ᴱ	1.6
Child living with parent(s), siblings	6.5*	12.7	8.3*	16.4
Other arrangements	12.8	12.2	11.8	11.6

ᴱ use with caution
* statistically significant difference from same sex without activity limitations at p < 0.05
Source: Statistics Canada, Canadian Community Health Survey, 2009.
Date modified: 2015-11-30

has also proven to be difficult for these caregivers, and the 2004 government report suggests improved access to respite care, as well as better workplace accommodations for caregivers, to better support these familial caregivers.

For Indigenous Canadians with disabilities, supports to family caregivers are even more limited. Insufficient reimbursement and/or respite care services exist for family caregivers of disabled Indigenous people, even when the caregivers themselves have disabilities. The Aboriginal Reference Group on Disability Issues (1997) cautioned: "In many rural and remote communities there are no respite service providers at all. Lack of respite services is likely to lead to family deterioration and by extension to community deterioration" (ibid.:23).

Employment and Learning

Almost half (47 per cent) of working-age adults with disabilities reported being employed in 2012, compared to 74 per cent of Canadians without disabilities (Statistics Canada 2015). Moreover, disabled workers earn less than non-disabled workers, and women with disabilities in Canada continue to earn less than men without disabilities. In 2010, the median income for working-age disabled people was $20,420, compared with $31,160 for non-disabled people those without disabilities (Statistics Canada 2015, from the 2011 National Household Survey). Although no figures are given, the CSD states that "Regardless of age, men with disabilities reported significantly higher median total incomes than did women with disabilities" (Statistics Canada 2015). Moreover, persons with disabilities "can be doubly disadvantaged by extra costs related to disability" (Government of Canada 2002:44).

Disabled people who are parents of young children experience even more difficulty in finding paid employment opportunities because of their child care responsibilities (Office for Disability Issues 2003). This issue is particularly prevalent among disabled mothers. Fawcett (1996:163) explains, "The greater likelihood of being a lone parent, coupled with lower participation rates among lone parents, contributed to the lower likelihood of labour force participation among women with disabilities." This contributes to "less access to the more generous income support programs, and higher rates of poverty overall" (1996:151). A 2002 discussion paper sums the situation up in this way:

> Canadian research has made it clear that major roadblocks to labour force participation of parents with disabilities exist in the workplace. While there is a need for additional investment in accessible child care, there is also a need for greater awareness on the part of employers about the particular situation of parents with children with disabilities. Flexibility in hours and location of work, recognition of particular needs in benefits packages, and awareness on the part of managers and co-workers are essential. (Hanvey 2002:11)

Post-secondary education narrows the gender gap in labour force participation, as well as the wage gap, for persons with disabilities:

> Among persons with disabilities whose highest level of education was primary school, or less, the participation rate for women was about 53 per cent that of men (25.3 per cent participation rate for women, compared to 48.2 per cent participation rate for men). [However], women's participation rates as a proportion of men's rose to about 92 per cent for those with either a non-university post-secondary diploma (67.6 per cent participation rate for women, compared to 73.4 per cent participation rate for men) or a university degree (69.8 per cent participation rate for women, compared to 76 per cent participation rate for men). (ibid.:153–4)

According to more recent figures, working-age women with disabilities are now surpassing their male counterparts in regard to completing high school (27 per cent versus 23 per cent) and college (24 per cent versus 17 per cent). Disabled men are more likely to attain a trade certificate than disabled women (18 per cent versus 10 per cent). In terms of university degrees, the gap is narrow between women and men with disabilities (13 per cent versus 12 per cent) (Human Resources and Skills Development Canada 2009).

Impact of Dependent Children on Labour Force Participation

Similar to other Canadian women, the labour force participation of disabled women is largely influenced by their (unpaid) domestic labour responsibilities, including the care of dependent children:

> Families of children with disabilities experience an impact on their employment as a result of caring for their children beyond that which is experienced by families of children without disabilities. Caring for children with disabilities can result in a great deal of pressure on families. . . . In almost 50 per cent of cases of

disability in children, one or more family members have altered their employment situation because of the child's condition. . . . In the wide majority of cases, it is the mother's employment situation that is most affected (Employment and Social Development Canada 2011).

In 2006, almost a quarter of families surveyed (24.6 per cent) reported that the presence of a disabled child had an impact on the employment of both parents (Employment and Social Development Canada 2011). However, women's employment was most affected (64.1 per cent) compared with men's (8.3 per cent) (Employment and Social Development Canada 2011). Overall the level of disability had a greater impact on family employment than other factors including age. Parents of severely or very severely disabled children reported having to quit a job because of the child's condition more than twice as often as parents of children with mild or moderate disabilities (26.8 per cent versus 10.2 per cent) (Employment and Social Development Canada 2011).

Domestic Labour

Disabled women are more likely than disabled men to perform most of the basic household chores. This was found to be true, regardless of severity of disability or living arrangements. In this vein, "men with disabilities were much more likely to have assistance with household chores—whether it was required for the disability or not" (Fawcett 1996:165). Men with disabilities were also more likely than women with disabilities to report needing assistance with meal preparation, even if it was not required as the result of their disability.

In Fawcett's words, "While the majority of both women and men with disabilities did not require assistance with basic household chores strictly because of their disability, the majority of men were likely to receive assistance anyway; the majority of women were not" (ibid.:167). The assistance received by men with disabilities may have been from a family member inside or outside of the household, a friend outside the household, or hired help through a service or agency.

Assistance with household chores was very much related to whether or not the individual lived alone or with others. Those who lived with others received much more assistance than those who lived alone (ibid.). Disabled women who live with other people were more likely to perform their own meal preparation.

Blackford (1999:279) found that although oppression in families where a parent has a disability certainly exists, strengths can be gained from the experience: "In organizing the social relations of family life when a parent has a chronic illness like multiple sclerosis, family members often learn to do it differently."

Violence and Abuse

All Canadians with disabilities are at risk of experiencing violence and abuse. The Council of Canadians with Disabilities (CCD) states that the "rates . . . are among the highest for any group in Canada" (Council of Canadians with Disabilities n.d.). Disabled women and children are "particularly vulnerable to threats to their physical safety, and to psychological and verbal abuse and neglect" (Government of Canada 2002:54).

Children

According to the World Health Organization (WHO), "children with disabilities are almost four times more likely to experience violence than non-disabled children" (2017 www .who.int/disabilities/violence/en/). A 2012 international review of two decades of studies pertaining to violence against disabled children concludes that a quarter of young people with disabilities aged 2 to 18 years have experienced violence. Overall the researchers estimate that "disabled children are at nearly four times greater risk of experiencing violence than those without a disability" (Bellis et al. 2012). Moreover, a Manitoba study cites a dramatic increase in the number of disabled children involved with the child welfare system (Fuchs et al. 2007). As the authors state: "Whatever the reasons for the over-representation of children with disabilities among those who are abused and/or neglected, their particular vulnerability is a critical child welfare issue" (127).

According to the Canadian Paediatric Society, "There is clear evidence that young people with a disability or serious chronic condition are at increased risk of being sexual abused." It cites the findings of a large survey that was conducted in a B.C. high school in 2008. Disabled and chronically students were "more than two times as likely as their peers to report having been physically abused (31 per cent versus 15 per cent) or sexually abused (19 per cent versus 7 per cent), and were three times more likely to have experienced both physical and sexual abuse (12 per cent versus 4 per cent)" (Kaufman 2011). These figures are in line with the American and international literature.

Although they are more likely than other children to be victims of abuse, violence against children with disabilities has received little attention. For disabled children, some forms of abuse are so subtle that they are not easily recognized by the law. The Roeher Institute (2000b:18) reports that "abuse may come in the form of restricted movement, invasive 'therapy,' or rough handling while receiving personal care (e.g., for washing, feeding, grooming, using the toilet) . . . abuse could come at the hands of parents, teachers, health professionals, and others."

Where disabled children are most vulnerable is debatable. Ultimately the research is difficult to conduct and there is a dearth of information. DAWN Toronto's (1995:32) research concluded: "The most dangerous place for her [girl with a disability] to be is in her own home. . . . If a girl with a disability is sent to foster homes or institutions, she still faces a high risk of sexual and physical assault." However, other sources maintain that Canadian children who have been institutionalized due to physical and/or intellectual impairments have an increased risk of maltreatment (NCFV 2000). And although protective measures are now in place to prevent this from recurring, children living in institutions continue to be victimized more often than other Canadian children (Doe 1999). The WHO maintains that "Placement of people with disabilities in institutions also increases their vulnerability to violence" (WHO 2017).

Children with disabilities are at an elevated risk for abuse, in part because of the difficult circumstances common to their families (Roeher Institute 2000b). According to the Roeher Institute's 1994 report for the National Clearinghouse on Family Violence (ibid.:18):

Children with disabilities are more likely to be abused within their families when their families experience isolation (which may be increased by demands of caregiving), are overwhelmed by the demands of caregiving, lack opportunity to develop effective coping skills, or engage in difficult caring activities while lacking respite and other supports.

The report goes on to state that additional stresses such as unemployment, as well as a family history of abuse, use of corporal punishment, or substance abuse, can all contribute to the risk of abuse. The authors suggest that this kind of abuse is more prevalent where negative social attitudes towards disability are prominent (Roeher Institute 1994). Over 20 years later the WHO makes a similar point: "Factors which place people with disabilities at higher risk of violence include stigma, discrimination, and ignorance about disability, as well as a lack of social support for those who care for them" (2017).

Child abuse is an issue of power. The risk of disabled children experiencing abuse is often intensified because of their increased levels of dependency and vulnerability (NCFV 2000). Their vulnerability is heightened because of social stereotypes about their impairments. For instance, children with disabilities may experience social isolation within their own families or peer groups due to a family member or friend's negative attitudes towards disability. For example, a child may be left out of a family game, without any accommodations being made to include the child, because of assumptions of the child's inability to participate successfully. Social isolation can lead to an increased vulnerability to abuse (NCFV 2000).

The murder of Tracy Latimer is one of the most high-profile cases involving a child with a disability (see Case in Point box). On October 24, 1993, Robert Latimer, a Saskatchewan farmer, killed his 12-year-old daughter, Tracy, by using a hose to feed carbon monoxide from his truck's exhaust pipe into the cab where he had placed her. She was born with cerebral palsy and was unable to perform many of the so-called activities of daily living without assistance. It is important to read about Tracy's life because so much media attention has been focused on her father and his quality of life. The murder of any child is horrific, but because Tracy was disabled her murder was framed as a type of "mercy-killing."

CASE IN POINT

Tracy Latimer

During his trial, Mr. Latimer's defense to the charge of first degree murder was that he is a loving father who made the heart-breaking decision that Tracy was better off dead. Why did Mr. Latimer say that Tracy was better off dead? Because she had cerebral palsy and he wanted to end her suffering. This is the story that was carried in news media all over the country and which has caused endless painful debate for many Canadians. Let's look at some of the issues surrounding this case.

Tracy did have severe cerebral palsy. She also went to a developmental program at her school every day. She traveled on the same bus as the other children. Tracy liked many different things, including music, watching television, aquatics, animals, being outdoors,

continued

and being hugged. Her mother's own diary captures Tracy's spirit as cheerful, alert, and mischievous up until the day she died. By all accounts she was a happy child. Tracy's disability was not killing her, but her father did. Tracy's disability was part of who she was, but not the sum total of who she was.

However, almost every news report of this story has categorized Tracy as "a twelve year old girl who couldn't walk, talk, or even feed herself." Why was she always described this way? First, it's part of what makes this story newsworthy. Second, Mr. Latimer and his defense lawyer emphasized Tracy's disabilities during the court proceedings and in their press interviews. Unfortunately, what was missing from the public discussion about Tracy's condition is that she could have continued to live a full life, just like other people who have severe disabilities.

Source: MacLeod, Leslie. "Robert Latimer Murdered His Daughter." Council of Canadians with Disabilities Website (www.ccdonline.ca/en/humanrights/endoflife/latimer/2000/06b).

Women

According to the Disabled Women's Network Canada (DAWN), "Violence against women and girls with disabilities is not just a subset of gender-based violence—it is an intersectional category dealing with gender-based and disability-based violence. The confluence of these two factors results in an extremely high risk of violence against women with disabilities" (DAWN-RAFH Canada n.d.). The Canadian Research Institute for the Advancement of Women (CRIAW) states that "Violence is a major cause of injury to women, ranging from cuts and bruises to permanent disability and death" (CRIAW 2002:6). Women who are physically or sexually abused as adults or children are at greater risk of a variety of health problems, including chronic pain, anxiety, and clinical depression (ibid.:7).

As for children with disabilities, violence against women with disabilities often comes in the form of family violence. This can include "physical, psychological, or sexual maltreatment, abuse or neglect of a woman with disabilities by a relative or care-giver. It is a violation of trust and an abuse of power in a relationship where a woman should have the right to absolute safety" (NCFV 1993:1). Disabled women who live in institutions (who are more dependent on a higher number of people) may be at an even greater risk.

Like women without disabilities, violence against women with disabilities is usually perpetrated by someone known to the victim, someone in their inner circle, their "family." Women with disabilities are particularly vulnerable, however, because they often depend on a variety of people to help them in carrying out their everyday lives—"attendants, interpreters, homemakers, drivers, doctors, nurses, teachers, social workers, psychiatrists, therapists, counsellors, and workers in hospitals and other institutions" (ibid.:2). Thus the "family" of a woman with a disability includes "not only parents, husbands, boyfriends, and other relatives, but also friends, neighbours, and caregivers" (ibid.).

Barriers to Obtaining Help

It can be exceedingly difficult for any woman to leave an abusive relationship, but disabled women have additional challenges. DAWN Canada outlines a number of barriers to obtaining help including "difficulty in making contact with shelters or other intervention services, lack of access to information about available services, difficulties in accessing transportation, fear of losing their financial security, their housing, or their welfare benefits and fear of being institutionalized" (DAWN-RAFH Canada n.d.). Moreover, women with disabilities may fear that they won't be believed (ibid.). As a consequence disabled women may remain trapped in a violent situation.

Conclusion

There is a real lack of support for Canadian families living with disabilities. Disability affects many Canadians and their families: 3.8 million adults in this country report having a disability (Statistics Canada 2015), and about 8.1 million Canadians provide care to a disabled or chronically ill family member or friend (Statistics Canada 2013). Moreover, the rate of disability is higher for women and Indigenous people than for other Canadians. And finally, we are an aging society, and rates of disability increase with age.

Disability and poverty are inextricably intertwined: disability leads to poverty and poverty leads to disability. The average household income for families with preschool and school-age children with disabilities is lower than the household incomes of their peers without disabilities. Family breakdown is not uncommon, and children with disabilities are over-represented in lone-parent families. Disabled children, especially those with mental or developmental disabilities, are at increased risk of violence. Cost is a major factor preventing parents from getting the assistance they require. Working-age adults with disabilities are less likely than non-disabled Canadians to be employed, and they have lower average incomes than people without disabilities.

Disabled women are more likely than disabled men to perform most of the basic household chores. Compared with fathers, mothers are most likely to be responsible for providing, arranging, and advocating for care for their children with disabilities. Child care is the primary barrier to participation in the paid workforce for parents (especially mothers) of children with disabilities. Women with disabilities are more likely than women without disabilities to be single, divorced, separated, widowed, and lone parents of dependent children. Parenting, especially mothering, with a disability is surrounded by social barriers and stigma. Violence against disabled women often comes in the form of family violence.

The social model of disability identifies obstacles as being systemically rather than biologically based. From this perspective, the barriers that prevent a full life are the problem, not disabilities themselves. Disabled Canadians clearly need increased support in order to thrive as family members. For example, increased public funds are needed for social assistance, disability supports, health needs, home care, respite care, child care, accessible transportation, adequate housing, education and training, etc. One of the difficulties, as outlined in this chapter, is inconsistency across jurisdictions. This matter needs to be addressed by all levels of government immediately.

In addition, social perceptions regarding families and disabilities must be radically altered. Despite progress in many areas, modern Canadian society is still marked by a strong sense of what is (and is not) "normal." This is most evident when it comes to ideals of the perfect body. Ask yourself, what would you think if you saw a child with cerebral palsy in a classroom full of non-disabled children? Or two young people with intellectual disabilities holding hands and kissing? What about a mother breast-feeding a baby while using her wheelchair? These are images that are not yet common, but hopefully will be one day.

Study Questions

1. Do you consider yourself a disabled person? Do you have family members and/or friends with disabilities? Reflect on the ways in which disability impacts on your life.
2. How is *disability* defined in Canada? What are the implications of the social model of disability?
3. In what sense are many people TABS (temporarily able-bodied)? Have you ever thought about yourself in this way? What about your family or friends?
4. What ableist assumptions underpin the organization of paid and unpaid labour?
5. How does sexism (ageism/racism/heterosexism, etc.) intersect with ableism?
6. What barriers are faced by people with visible disabilities versus so-called invisible disabilities?
7. Why are disabled people so vulnerable to violence? Who is particularly at risk?

Further Readings

Kuttai, Heather. 2010. *Maternity Rolls: Pregnancy, Childbirth and Disability.* Nova Scotia and Winnipeg: Fernwood Publishing. Kuttai employs theory and personal narrative to tell her story about being a woman with a spinal cord injury who becomes a mother. She describes her accident, meeting her current partner, being pregnant, giving birth, and parenting. Significantly, Kuttai maintains that the social stigma around mothering with a disability comes from the belief that disabled women are asexual.

Malacrida, Claudia. 2010. "Discipline and Dehumanization in a Total Institution: Institutional Survivors' Descriptions of Time-out Rooms." Pp. 181–95 in *Rethinking Normalcy: A Disability Studies Reader,* edited by T. Titchkosky and R. Michalko. Toronto: Canadian Scholars' Press Inc. In this chapter Malacrida draws on her interviews with 29 survivors of an institution for "moral defectives" in Alberta. The interviewees, 12 women and 9 men, describe the "Time-out Rooms" used for disciplinary purposes. Although the focus is on one Canadian institution up to the 1980s, the discussion of eugenics and sterilization has broader implications.

Oliver, Michael. 1996. "The Social Model in Context." Pp. 30–42 in *Understanding Disability: From Theory to Practice.* Hampshire and New York: Palgrave. Oliver is one of the first people to write about disability models in general, and the social model in particular. In this piece he traces the development of disability theorizing and calls for the expansion of models. In the 1980s Oliver posited a binary opposition between what he termed the "individual" (which included medicalization and personal tragedy models) and the social models.

Stienstra, Deborah. 2012. "Race/Ethnicity and Disability Studies: Towards an Explicitly Inter-sectional Approach." In *Routledge Handbook of Disability Studies*, edited by N. Watson, A. Roulstone, and C. Thomas. New York: Routledge. In this chapter Stienstra takes up the late Chris Bell's challenge to make Disability Studies more reflective and reflexive about "race" and ethnicity. She is particularly concerned about uncovering and going beyond whiteness.

Wendell, Susan. 1996. *The Rejected Body: Feminist Philosophical Reflections on Disability*. New York: Routledge. Wendell criticizes past feminist theorizing about the body for favouring the able-bodied experience and, for the most part, ignoring the experience of disability. The book sets out to teach feminist scholars why disability is of importance to their work by pointing to disability studies as a significant but often overlooked feminist ally.

Key Terms

Ableism The belief that people without disabilities have more worth than people with disabilities. This view may be explicit or implicit.

Bio-medical model of disability From this perspective disability is centred in a person's body, which is regarded as "flawed." The goal of the medical professionals is to "fix" or "cure" non-conformist bodies in order to make them more "normal."

Familialism According to functionalists the so-called "traditional" nuclear family remains the ideal. This conservative model is based on rigidly gendered roles, and women are expected to provide physical and emotional care to the rest of the family.

Gendered disablism The notion that gender and disability are interlocking and intersecting sites of oppression. Disability is always gendered. There is no generic experience of disability outside of gender (as well as "race," class, sexuality, etc.).

Home care The in-home paid or unpaid assistance provided to a person with a chronic disability or illness, allowing the person with the impairment to remain living at home.

Impairments Characteristics, features, or attributes that may or may not be the result of illness, disease, or injury, for example: mobility impairments, depression, cancer, being hard of hear-ing, psychological impairments, etc.

Respite care Short-term, temporary care, sometimes including overnight, designed to give families that include people with disabilities a break from caregiving.

Social model of disability From this view society is regarded as disabling for persons who have impairments. According to this model, disability refers to the social, environmental, and atti-tudinal oppression faced by persons with non-conformist bodies.

Temporarily able-bodied (TABs) Refers to the inevitable fact that most people will face living with a disability at some point in our lives; when it occurs varies depending upon many life circumstances.

Visible and invisible disabilities Visible disabilities are easily discerned by a second party or, in other words, their barriers are "visible," for example, using a wheelchair, walker, prosthesis, or oxygen. Invisible disabilities—which are not readily apparent—can include debilitating fatigue, pain, heart problems, depression, or neurological damage. A person may have both visible and invisible disabilities.

 Interested in finding out more? Visit www.oupcanada.com/Albanese4e for access to a list of recommended websites for this chapter.

PART IV

Problems, Policies, and Predictions

The final section of this book considers a diverse selection of topics—family violence, family policies in Canada, and the future of the Canadian family.

In Chapter 14, Catherine Holtmann discusses the various definitions of violence and abuse in families and reviews a number of theories that have been used to explain family violence and abuse, including individual pathology models, social learning theories, stress and crisis theories, and feminist explanations of violence. Holtmann examines the available data on violence against women, and discusses problems inherent in the collection of such data. The chapter then examines the consequences of abuse for women and children. She argues that the powerlessness and dependency cycles in families that make women, in particular, vulnerable to maltreatment can be broken. Awareness must be translated into programs for educating and promoting non-violent solutions in social relationships, as well as into social policies that can break the cycle of abuse.

Social policies concerning families have a central importance in Canadian life. They determine how families are defined and formed, which family members are entitled to governmental support, and the amount and type of support that families receive. In Chapter 15, Catherine Krull and Mushira Mohsin Khan examine family policy in Canada with a special focus on those measures that relate to families with children under the age of 18 years. Examples of such policies include arrangements for children in state care, paid maternity and parental leaves, and child and family benefits. Krull and Khan point out that Canada lacks a comprehensive national family policy, unlike some other countries around the world. Rather, family policies in Canada consist of a piecemeal set of programs and policies that either directly or indirectly have an impact on families, often leaving gaps and "cracks" through which some families fall. They demonstrate this through a discussion of the patchwork of child and family benefits aimed at reducing poverty, which yet continue to result in large disparities in poverty rates across family types. Krull and Khan note that Quebec has taken the lead in Canada in terms of implementing policies geared towards supporting families and reducing poverty. They conclude that the rest of Canada has an opportunity to use and build on Quebec's example in the future.

The final chapter in this edition of *Canadian Families Today* offers a view to the future. In the closing chapter, Margrit Eichler discusses issues involved in making predictions about the future of family life, examines past predictions by family sociologists and other experts and how successful they were, and considers the basis on which such predictions are made. Eichler explores which bases for prediction seem to yield more solid results. She concludes that overall there have been a number of spectacular misprognoses—among them that the family is a dying institution and that gender roles within the family are unchanging and unchangeable—as well as some surprisingly accurate predictions on such matters as the nature of sexual relations inside and outside of marriage, cohabitation, fertility, and new reproductive technologies. She draws the conclusion that identifying societal changes and reflecting on their importance for the family are the most useful predictive analyses for family studies, but they are also the most difficult. Eichler concludes her chapter by making some predictions of her own.

14

Violence in Families

CATHERINE HOLTMANN

LEARNING OBJECTIVES

- To define domestic violence and articulate the controversy concerning its definition

- To distinguish between different theories about the root causes of domestic violence

- To recognize the different methods used to determine the prevalence of domestic violence

- To discover the particular vulnerabilities for some sub-groups in the Canadian population

- To identify common intervention strategies for people who experience domestic violence

---

Introduction

Nowadays the media is awash with stories about violence taking place elsewhere in the world—the continuing war on terror in Afghanistan, civil war in Syria, conflict in Iraq, Nigeria, and Israel, and deaths due to tensions between the police and racialized people in the US. It seems as if every time we look online we see images of violence occurring somewhere, maybe even in the city or town where you live. This can give the impression that the world outside our doors is insecure and scary. However, the fact is that violence is most likely to take place inside the doors of the family home. Family violence takes place in every kind of family described in the chapters of this book—but it is like a hidden war. It is taking place all around us but few people have the courage to talk about it in public. Because violence is so much a part of everyday family experiences, some people may not even recognize it when it is happening to them. Violence in families takes place between spouses and common-law partners, it occurs through the abuse of children by parents, it is perpetrated by family members against older persons within the family, and violence is used by siblings against each other. Each of these forms of violence constitute important sub-fields of family violence research with their own theoretical debates, empirical findings, and implications for policy, however one chapter cannot do all of them justice. This chapter will focus on violence between spouses or common-law partners, often referred to as domestic violence. It will highlight different theories about the causes as well as the prevalence of domestic violence. Canada is a world leader in research on domestic violence and this has led to a variety of interventions, some of which will also be explained.

Terminology

There are different terms used in the research and public education literature on domestic violence. These include *intimate partner violence, gender-based violence, spousal abuse*, and *family violence*. The terms *violence* and *abuse* are often used interchangeably. The terms that are used to describe the violence between husbands and wives or between common-law partners are often an indication of the political nature of this social problem. Domestic violence is a topic that provokes strong emotional reactions and conversations about it can quickly become polarized. Gender neutral terms have been used to downplay the fact that **intimate partner violence** is primarily perpetrated by men against women. In recent years, gender neutral terms, such as *gender-based violence*, are used with the intention of being more inclusive of a range of gender identities.

Definitions of Domestic Violence

The contemporary definitions of domestic violence arose from research and activism associated with addressing the social problem of violence against women. Domestic violence is one form of violence against women. Although men are also victims of domestic violence, the majority of victims are women and the majority of perpetrators are men. In this chapter the terminology used will reflect the experiences of the majority, in predominantly heterosexual unions. That said, domestic violence does take place within same sex relationships and a significant body of research exists on abuse in lesbian relationships (Ristock 2002). However, doing justice to this literature would require at least a separate chapter. There are different definitions of domestic violence and these can be categorized as either narrow or broad. A narrow definition of domestic violence consists of any physical or sexual act committed by an intimate partner that causes harm and/or injury to his partner. Violent physical acts include hitting, scratching, punching, slapping, pinching, pulling hair, pushing, grabbing, shoving, choking, biting, cutting, confining, stabbing, and shooting. Sexually violent acts occur when a man forces his partner to perform unwanted sexual acts that violate her sexual integrity. In other words, she does not **consent** to these sexual acts, which can involve a range of behaviours from unwanted touching to penetration. A narrow definition of domestic violence enables researchers to develop measures by which the number and type of acts of physical or sexual violence committed against an individual can be categorized, measured, and analyzed statistically. However, a narrow definition fails to capture the complex dynamics of power and control in violent intimate relationships from the perspective of women survivors.

An example of a broad definition of domestic violence is one that comes from the Women Victims of Abuse Protocols established by the New Brunswick provincial government to be used in the delivery of public services by police, educators, health care, and social workers:

> Women can either be the direct victims of abuse (physical, psychological, verbal, financial, sexual assault/ violence, and/or spiritual abuse) or subjected to threats of abuse to themselves and/or their children, step-children, or other loved ones including pets/farm animals by their boyfriends, girlfriends, partners, or former partners—marital or common-law, heterosexual or same sex (GNB 2014).

This broad definition lists acts of violence beyond those found in the narrow definition including acts of psychological, verbal, financial, and spiritual abuse. Psychological and verbal abuse include name-calling, put-downs, and other attacks on a woman's self-worth such as telling her that she's a bad mother, ugly, stupid, or fat. Psychological abuse may occur using social media like Facebook or Snapchat. Challenging a woman's memories of events or disturbing her sense of reality by "gaslighting" is another form of psychological abuse. (Gaslighting occurs when a perpetrator manipulates a victim into doubting her sanity.) Isolating a woman from her family, friendship, education, and employment social networks is a common psychological control tactic used by abusers. A psychologically abusive partner may monitor a woman's face-to-face and online activities and use a cell phone to constantly call or text her. Sleep deprivation is another form of abuse along with others such as depriving a woman of prescribed medications, a hearing aid, or other necessary health supports. On the other hand, a victim of psychological abuse may be forced to take drugs or drink alcohol with her partner. The many forms of emotional abuse have long-term effects that wear away a woman's self-confidence, sometimes to the extent that she comes to believe in an identity of being worthless imposed on her by her abuser. Financial abuse involves denying a woman knowledge of or access to the family finances. It could also include racking up debts that she must work to pay in order to keep the family finances solvent. Financial abuse creates dependency between an abusive husband and wife or common-law partners that can prevent the woman from taking action to end the relationship, especially if they have children. Notice that the New Brunswick government's broad definition of domestic violence includes both the direct experiences of abuse as well as the threat of violence not only toward the victim but toward the victim's loved ones. Such threats can include one partner threatening to commit suicide if the other seeks help or tries to leave the family home. Often threats of violence are enough to control the victim's actions and are included in the broad definition because of known differences in power between men and women.

Feminists argue that the roots of domestic violence lie in issues of power and control. Historically, and in many ways still today, Canadian society has been almost exclusively structured by patriarchy and many of our social institutions, such as the family, are patriarchal in origin. Patriarchy consists of sets of hierarchies in which some people (men) are given or are believed to have power over others. These beliefs are partly based on observations of differences in biology and physiology between men and women but they are also socially reinforced. Patriarchy is a form of social order in which males have power over females in families, in politics, and in the economy. It contends that husbands naturally have power over their wives and parents naturally have absolute power over their children. Phrases like "the rule of thumb" and "spare the rod and spoil the child" come from what once were considered acceptable violent practices within families. "The rule of thumb" comes from an old English law in which a husband was allowed to hit his wife in order to discipline her but he was limited to using a rod or stick that was no bigger in diameter than his thumb. "Spare the rod and spoil the child" is loosely based on passages from the Bible and refers to physical violence used in the discipline of children by their parents. Historically, the state supported the use of violence within the family to maintain the patriarchal social order. Thus social pressure to conform to particular gender norms, along with husbands' and fathers' threats and perpetration of physical violence were enough to limit and control wives' and children's actions for centuries.

For more on feminist theorizing of families, see "The 'Big Bang'—Feminist Theories" in Chapter 1, pp. 20–2.

The broad definition of domestic violence therefore takes into consideration the history of patriarchy, the social context, and the structural nature of the problem. By doing so, it establishes domestic violence as a public, rather than private, problem that requires systemic change. This is where the political controversy about defining domestic violence arises. Proponents of the narrow definition of domestic violence view it as the specific and limited problem of a particular portion of the population that can be well-defined through the collection of **quantitative data** on crime or through survey research. With the narrow definition, the problem of domestic violence can be addressed by focusing resources on a particular and limited sector of the population. However, proponents of the broad definition of domestic violence point out that the problem of domestic violence is related to the structural inequalities that divide women and men (as well as other groups) in Canadian society. They argue that efforts to address the problem cannot be limited to protecting and healing individuals who are hurt and holding violent individuals to account through the criminal justice system but must include multiple interventions including changes to many of society's foundational institutions such as the family, government, educational systems, and religion.

Questions for Critical Thought

Which definition—the narrow or the broad—do you think is most helpful in understanding domestic violence? Why?

Theoretical Perspectives on Domestic Violence

We have discussed the ways in which the definition of domestic violence is contested. This is largely due to different theories or explanations concerning the source of the problem. This section will outline four theories: feminist, social learning, psychiatric and personality, and social situation/stress and coping. As already mentioned, a feminist theoretical understanding of domestic violence claims that its roots lie in patriarchy and the unequal power relationships between women and men. Patriarchal institutions rely on violence, or the threat of violence, to maintain male power and control over women (Walby 2009). It was during the second wave of the feminist movement in the 1960s that women began to speak publically about their experiences of domestic violence. Women came to realize that their experiences of abuse by husbands, male partners, and boyfriends were not merely isolated incidents but part of a widespread problem of violence against women. The Power and Control wheel in Figure 14.1 below offers a model to explain the tactics used by abusers to assert power and control over victims.

Feminist theories of male dominance over women are very applicable when considering sexual violence, which is almost exclusively perpetrated by men against women (Sev'er 2002). MacKinnon (2006) argues that many women have difficulty distinguishing between "ordinary" sexual acts and sexual violence because the latter is so common between heterosexual couples. Sexual domination of women by men is considered erotic in popular culture and pornography. Many women do not report sexual assaults from intimate partners to the police because they believe that the legal system will not support their statements. Thus the concept of consent has become an important contemporary consideration in theorizing domestic violence and in law (Sheehy 2002).

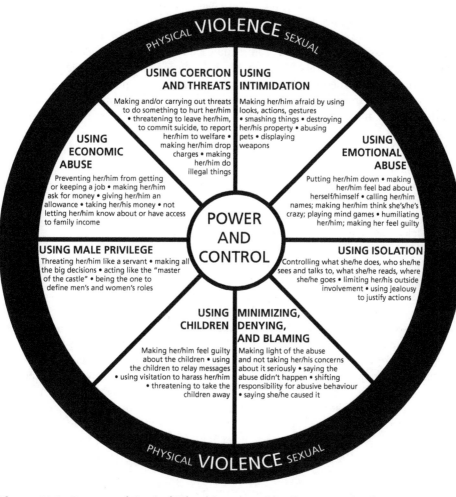

Figure 14.1 Power and Control Wheel Developed by the Domestic Abuse Intervention Programs in Duluth, MN

Source: Developed by the Domestic Abuse Intervention Programs in Duluth, MN. Reprinted by permission of DAIP. All rights reserved.

Feminist theoretical perspectives on domestic violence have expanded to address forms of social inequality beyond gender including "race," class, and sexual orientation (Johnson 2005). Similar to the ways in which patriarchy has socially constructed gender inequality, other forms of inequality based on, for example, "race," class, or sexual orientation, are also constructed and reproduced in society. Different structures of inequality may overlap and either magnify or change particular women's experiences of domestic violence depending on the context under consideration. This is referred to as an intersectional theoretical approach to domestic violence. For example, Indigenous women in Canada today live with the legacy of colonialism that includes repeated waves of trauma from disease, political and economic colonization, the loss of traditional ways of life, the theft of land and resources, the destruction of languages, the state-sponsored residential schools system, and the ongoing removal of children from Indigenous families (Aboriginal Healing Foundation 2003). While this colonial legacy does not excuse contemporary situations of domestic violence in Indigenous families, they must be understood and addressed within a broader historical understanding of structural violence against Indigenous peoples in Canada.

For more For more on Indigenous families and the colonial legacy, see Chapter 12.

Another well-known explanation for the root cause of domestic violence is social learning theory. This theory is based on the assumption that people learn violent and abusive behaviours from their social environment. In traditional forms of families, people of different ages and genders spend a great deal of time together, leading to a range of

Daily Life
A Grandmother's Pain: Scars from the Intergenerational Transmission of Violence

As I look in the mirror, I hardly recognize the person looking back at me, but I am happy with her. I love her, but that wasn't always the case. . . . When I look even deeper and reflect, I can see the emotional scars left behind from when I watched my mother trapped between two beds on the floor with her arm broken in two places after being beaten by my step-father for reasons unknown to me. . . . As I look in the mirror . . . I can see a roadmap of my own broken and tattered past. . . . On the palm of my left hand I see a badly healed scar from where I received five stitches from a wound that I received when my live-in boyfriend of six months pulled a knife on me after badly beating me. . . . At my wrists I see multiple scars where . . . tired of all the hurt and disappointment, I took a piece of broken glass and sliced repeatedly at my wrists trying to end my life. . . . Now I turn to look at you, all grown up with scars of your own . . . I can see the permanent scars on your heart from when you watched me beaten and bloodied and begging for mercy, screaming at you, to go back in your room. . . . I see the scar on your left cheek from when your current husband, the man that you thought was going to take you away from all of the hurt and pain, stomped you in the face. . . . Now I look at your daughter and I see her watching you . . .

Source: © 2017 The Rave Project. https://www.theraveproject.org/faq/ Reprinted with permission.

shared experiences including conflict (Gelles and Straus 1979). Sometimes acts of violence are used to try to solve conflict and sometimes violence and abuse permeate family interactions. Individuals observe and learn from the daily interactions within the family. Children who observe domestic violence between their parents or who experience violence at the hands of a parent or sibling learn from these experiences. They learn that abusive behaviours can take place within the privacy of the family home and they also learn not to talk about their experiences of abuse, especially to people outside of the family. Heterosexual boys who see their fathers abusing their mothers may go on to abuse their girlfriends. Heterosexual girls who witnessed violence between their parents and listen to their mothers make excuses or take the blame for the actions of their fathers are more likely to be victimized in future relationships. This accounts for what is known as the "intergenerational transmission of violence." (See the Daily Life box above for an example.) Violence and abuse can be so common in some family situations that they feel "normal" and individual family members recreate these abusive patterns in other relationships.

In families, abusive behaviours like those described in the Power and Control Wheel in Figure 14.1 co-mingle with non-violent and affectionate behaviours in situations of domestic violence, making it difficult for victims and perpetrators to identify violence and abuse. It is extremely challenging for women to label what they are experiencing in their families as violent because of its implications for their understanding of themselves and of the people who claim to love them. In a woman's process of coming to understand herself as a victim of domestic violence, denial functions as a defense mechanism that allows for the proper pacing of revising her identity and rebuilding her basic assumptions about social and family life (Profitt 2000:66). Disclosure also has implications for action—once violence and abuse are recognized by women there are internal and external expectations of change. Men who act violently also have difficulty accepting responsibility for their actions. They may blame their wives for provoking the abuse or minimize the extent of the harm they cause.

People wonder why women do not leave relationships as soon as the violence becomes apparent. One explanation for this is that domestic violence often occurs in a cyclical or recurring pattern of behaviours. The typical **cycle of violence** has three phases: (1) tension building; (2) violence; (3) honeymoon. In many stories of domestic violence gathered through research, women indicate that they were completely unaware at the beginning of the relationship that their partner had the potential to act violently. However, during the tension building phase there may be signs or factors that indicate that a man does not react appropriately in particular situations. For example, when under stress at work instead of acknowledging and dealing with his feelings, a husband may get angry with his wife over little things such as her being late for a dinner date at a restaurant, or he may be critical of how she is dressed when she joins him at the table. He may try to take charge of the evening and order dinner for the two of them. He might drink too much alcohol in order to try and calm himself down. The wife may voice her concern during dinner at how much her husband has been drinking lately. It is important to note that, in our example, the husband is as likely to be a professor or a foreman, the wife a stay-at-home mom or a dentist—levels of education or socio-economic standing are not barriers to family violence. Taken separately, these kinds of behaviours do not inevitably lead to violence and the pattern only becomes evident after a violent incident occurs. In this case, there are signs that tension is or has been building within the relationship and this can take place during the course of an evening or over an extended period of time such as days, weeks, or months. In a cycle of violence it is practically impossible to predict what will actually trigger a violent outburst. In the case of the husband dealing inappropriately with work stress, the violence could occur in the car on the way home from the restaurant when his wife mentions a conversation she had that day with a male friend. He could fly into a jealous rage, pull her hair and slap her, all while calling her a slut. She could try to ward off his blows with her hands and scream at him as the car swerves dangerously into oncoming traffic. Then, just as suddenly as it began, the violence ends as the husband turns the car onto their street. He parks the car in the driveway and the couple makes their way into the house, both visibly shaken and quickly straightening out their clothes and hair before meeting the babysitter. The days and weeks after the violent evening constitute the honeymoon phase. The husband feels badly and apologizes for what he has done. He cannot believe that the incident actually happened and puts it out of his mind. He promises his wife that it will never happen again. He might bring her gifts of flowers and jewellery suggesting that they plan a vacation together so that they can relax and get away from all of the stress in their lives. His wife may likely agree because she is terrified by her husband's violent outburst. She wonders what she did to provoke his anger. She probably wants to do all that she can to restore the love in her marriage, making sure that she is more understanding of her husband's stress and sensitive to his needs so as not to destroy their children's childhood and her dream of a happy family. It may be that this was an isolated incident of violence, but if this theoretical model holds, then the cycle of violence may continue to unfold in different ways over and over again for many years within this family.

People are exposed to and learn from the violence and abuse that takes place outside of the family home. As stated in the introduction to this chapter, the daily news, whether in print, on the radio or television, or online is usually filled with stories about violence and these stories are often accompanied by graphic visuals. On the one hand it is good that citizens are aware of the current events, even when violent, taking place in the world and closer to home. But on the other hand, constant exposure to violence can dull people's reactions to it—violence becomes so commonplace that it is normalized. This can be a danger when people are regularly inundated with news stories of domestic violence. Likewise through traditional and online forms of media, people can access many movies, music videos, and TV shows that depict explicit scenes of domestic violence and abuse. Many popular video games are very violent. Research has shown that pornography is particularly pernicious in terms of social learning and that men who act abusively towards their intimate partners are more likely than non-violent men to have consumed pornography (DeKeseredy 2011). Exposure to sexually violent pornographic videos increases the likelihood of the viewer committing sexual assault (DeKeseredy and Hall-Sanchez 2016).

An explanation for domestic violence that is quite popular in public discourse is psychiatric or personality theory. Proponents of this theory claim that domestic violence is primarily perpetrated by individuals who have psychological problems, negative personality characteristics, or forms of mental illness that cause them to act violently. The best known researcher associated with this theory is Donald Dutton (Dutton and Bodnarchuk 2005). Dutton argues that psychological trauma experienced by men during their childhood, largely due to dysfunctional relationships with their parents, leads to the development of personality disorders among men who then act violently as adults. These disorders include antisocial, borderline, and over-controlled personalities. Other researchers argue that this psychological theory of the roots of domestic violence only applies to a small proportion of the men who batter women and does not explain the widespread nature of the problem.

Individual personalities have a role to play in explanations concerning the causes of domestic violence but they should be understood in relationship to social and contextual factors that also influence the development and socialization of people. One theoretical framework that incorporates both individual personalities and social structures is referred to as social situational/stress and coping theory (Gelles 1997). Personal problems arise in every individual's life and are influenced by social structures outside of the family. For example, many people associate domestic violence with low-income families. However, poverty is not necessarily a cause of violence and abuse but it certainly is a social source of stress on families and individuals.

For more on poverty among Indigenous and racialized groups, see "Economic Well-being among Indigenous and Racialized Communities" in Chapter 10, p. 214.

Another source of social stress is racism, which, because of its systemic nature, is often associated with low incomes. Economic disadvantage, **visible minority status,** and Indigenous identities are also associated with lower levels of education and higher levels of under- and un-employment in Canada. Subjected to structures of social inequality, **racialized** couples have less resources to help them fulfill the roles of loving parents and caring and supportive wives and husbands. Inadequate access to financial resources means that poor women who are battered are more likely to access public services such as a shelter than are wealthier women who have the option of staying in a hotel. Low-income and racialized men who act violently toward their partners are also more likely to become involved with the criminal justice system because calling the police is another of the limited options available to poor women who seek safety for themselves and their children. The demographic profiles of shelter residents and those charged with violent crimes against their spouses have been made public by researchers and policy-makers but do not necessarily reflect the wide range of victims and perpetrators of domestic violence. Recall that in the example of the cycle of violence the couple was as likely to be well-educated and employed professionals. In that case the husband acted violently toward his wife ostensibly as a way of coping with the stress of his work. Immigrant women in Canada are also likely to lack resources due to structural inequalities, and many do not contact public services in the aftermath of domestic violence because of cultural norms that put pressure on them not to talk about problems outside of the family (Fong 2010).

For more on family stress and refugee families, see "Family Issues" in Chapter 11, pp. 231–3.

Questions for Critical Thought

Which theory do you think best explains the cause of domestic violence? What kind of theorizing is needed to better understand violence in same-sex or trans unions?

Prevalence of Domestic Violence

Canada was the first country to conduct a national survey dedicated to determining the prevalence of different forms of violence against women and their impacts on women's lives. The Canadian Violence Against Women Survey (CVAWS) was developed by Statistics Canada in collaboration with community groups, domestic violence advocates, service providers, women survivors, police, and researchers (Johnson and Dawson 2010). The survey included questions on experiences of sexual harassment, sexual assault, intimate partner violence, and a range of emotionally abusive and controlling behaviours using sensitive and detailed wording. The survey attempted to incorporate the broad definition of domestic violence referred to earlier in the chapter. Interviewers who conducted the survey were specially trained about the impact of violence on women, ready to provide support to those who disclosed experiences of violence (perhaps for the first time), and aware of how women's participation in the survey might increase the risk of violence from their partners. Canadian women 16 years of age and older from all over the country participated in the survey in 1993. The CVAWS results showed that many forms of male violence against women were widespread: 29 per cent of Canadian women reported having experienced some form of violence by a spouse or ex-spouse in their lifetimes and in the year prior to the survey, about 201,000 women had experienced physical or sexual assaults by a spouse or common-law partner (Johnson and Dawson 2010).

The CVAWS was only conducted once and since 1993 **prevalence** rates for domestic violence in Canada have been determined using a combination of data from Statistics Canada's General Social Survey (GSS) on Victimization and crime data collected by police. The 1999 GSS on Victimization incorporated some of the questions used in the CVAWS as part of a modified version of the Conflict Tactics Scale (CTS). The CTS is a set of questions developed by Murray Straus intended to measure three different modes of engagement (reasoning, verbal aggression, violence) used by couples during conflicts (1979). However, it must be kept in mind that the GSS is not a survey dedicated to violence against women. The **sample** included French and English-speaking men and women who were contacted by phone. The GSS on Victimization includes questions about different forms of crime including violent assault, household break and enter, theft, and vandalism. Many people do not think about domestic violence in terms of crime and, as outlined above, disclosing experiences of violence and abuse in intimate relationships is never easy, especially during a telephone interview with a stranger. The questions used to determine the prevalence of domestic violence do not address the context in which the violence takes place, such as the cycle of violence in couples explained above, or the consequences of domestic violence, which tend to be more severe for women than for men. The 1999 GSS data indicate that 8 per cent of women and 7 per cent of men had experienced physical or sexual violence in a current or past relationship in the five years prior to the survey (Jiwani 2002). These statistics prompted critics of the CVAWS and its broad definition of domestic violence to point out that it had overestimated the prevalence of domestic violence in Canada. They were also quick to state that this new data from the GSS indicated that women are as violent as men. However, critics did not take into account the differences in the methodologies of these surveys as well as the differences in time periods under consideration. Remember, the CVAWS predicted lifetime prevalence rates for domestic violence while the GSS considers only the past five years. The GSS data do not show how violence is used differently by women and men. Men often use violence to control women; women tend to use violence in self-defense.

The rates of domestic violence for women and men in Canada have remained relatively steady through subsequent GSSs on Victimization in 2004 (7 per cent) and 2009 (6 per cent). In 2014, analysis of the GSS data indicated a significant decline since 2004 in the rate of physical and sexual violence between spouses and/or common-law partners to 4 per cent for both women and men (Statistics Canada 2016). Although these results must be interpreted in light of the limitations of the survey methodology outlined above, they do provide a snapshot of the types of violence taking place in families across the country. A quarter of those who reported experiencing domestic violence indicated that they had been sexually assaulted, beaten, choked, or threatened with a gun or a knife. Of those who reported spousal sexual assault, 59 per cent reported non-consensual sex as a result of being manipulated, drugged, or coerced (Statistics Canada 2016). Four out of every ten women (40 per cent) reported physical injuries as a result of domestic violence compared to 24 per cent of the men. Twenty-one per cent of victims of domestic violence also reported having witnessed violence between their own parents as a child—evidence of the intergenerational transmission of violence. Many victims of domestic violence (41 per cent) reported incidents that occurred after the relationship had ended and almost half of these victims reported an increase in the severity of the violence compared to when the couple was still in a marriage or common-law relationship (Statistics Canada 2016).

The majority of the men and women who reported experiencing domestic violence in 2013 (70 per cent) did not report it to the police. Even though only a small proportion of domestic violence cases are responded to by the police, crime data provide accurate information about domestic homicides (Statistics Canada 2015). Homicide rates in Canada have declined over the years and are relatively low, but it is a fact that if a woman is murdered, she is more likely than a man to have been killed in the context of an intimate relationship (Johnson and Dawson 2010).

Questions for Critical Thought

Which of the statistics on domestic violence in Canada surprised you the most? Why?

Domestic Violence among Vulnerable Families

Even though research shows that domestic violence occurs in all kinds of families, there remains a perennial question as to whether or not some groups experience higher rates than others. Statistics Canada survey and crime data have consistently revealed higher rates of domestic violence for Indigenous peoples (2016). Indigenous women are two to four times as likely as non-Indigenous women to report experiencing physical or sexual violence at the hands of their spouses or common-law partners (Amnesty International 2009; Brown-ridge 2009). Structural factors contributing to inequality between Indigenous and non-Indigenous people and their contribution to the higher prevalence of domestic violence among Indigenous people in Canada were outlined in the section on intersectional theory above. In some cases, domestic violence pervades entire First Nations communities and has been described as a symptom of intergenerational **post-traumatic stress disorder (PTSD)** (Aboriginal Healing Foundation 2003). In attempting to deal with the multiple forms of trauma that impact their lives, many Indigenous people turn to drugs and alcohol as a coping mechanism, which is a contributing factor in domestic violence (Baskin 2006; Leonard and Quigley 2017). Like the unique experiences of Indigenous people, it is important to understand that domestic violence may be experienced differently in some other groups of people in Canada.

CASE IN POINT

Is Violence More Common among Immigrant Families?

In 2013 the Canadian federal government revised the *Welcome to Canada* guide for new immigrants (CIC). In Chapter 4 on Rights and Freedoms in Canada, there is a section on the equality of men and women in which the guide makes reference to "barbaric cultural practices" such as "spousal abuse, honour killings, female genital mutilation, forced marriage or other gender based violence" (CIC 2013:36). The guide indicates that these are crimes punishable under Canadian law. In 2015 the federal government passed the Zero Tolerance for Barbaric Cultural Practices Act in order to "improve protection for immigrant women and girls" by denying immigration to those who practise polygamy and introducing measures to prevent forced marriages and honour killings (CIC). The revised guide and new laws can give the impression that spousal abuse and honour killings are practices that immigrant families introduce to Canada. Firstly, there is scholarly debate as to whether or not honour killings are a unique form of family violence (Fournier 2012; Korteweg 2012; Korteweg and Yurdakul 2010; Mojab 2012; Papp 2010). But more importantly, there is insufficient evidence that immigrant families are more likely to experience domestic violence than families in the Canadian-born population. The depiction of immigrant families as violent may be part of the social construction of "others," the aim of which is to create boundaries that make the majority feel safer. The immigrant "other" embodies all of those qualities that we judge negatively such as irrationality, inequality, violence, victimization, etc. Korteweg refers to this as "the process of abjection—the psychic casting out of what is other in order to define ourselves as free from that which is abhorrent" (2012:138). In doing so, however, we fail to appreciate the high rates of domestic violence in Canadian society. Instead of participating in the process of abjection, we can critically examine our resistance to multiculturalism and our tolerance for high levels of domestic violence (Beaman 2012).

Brownridge (2009) suggests that researchers look at unique factors associated with certain sub-groups of the population in Canada that make them particularly vulnerable in situations of domestic violence. Using Statistics Canada data, he constructs statistical models to study the factors associated with domestic violence in common-law couples, situations of post-separation, stepfamilies, couples living in public housing, rural and urban contexts, Indigenous peoples, immigrant families, and women with disabilities. The vulnerabilities of two groups will be outlined in greater detail here: that of immigrants and women who belong to conservative religious groups.

As mentioned in the Case in Point Box above, there is a need for more studies of domestic violence among immigrant families in Canada because this is a diverse and rapidly growing sector of the population. It is estimated that by 2031, one in four Canadians will be foreign-born (Statistics Canada 2010). The World Health Organization (2013) compiled data from 79 countries in estimating the global lifetime prevalence rate for intimate partner violence at 30 per cent. Thus we can assume that immigrant women come from contexts in which domestic violence occurs at more or less the same rates as in Canada. Nevertheless it is potentially problematic to address domestic violence among immigrants for fear of fueling existing stereotypes that their families are inherently more violent than non-immigrant families. From what little research there exists on the prevalence of domestic violence among immigrants in Canada, Brownridge's research (2009; Brownridge and Halli 2003) indicates that immigrant women from industrialized countries have lower rates of domestic violence compared to Canadian-born women. He suggests that these results should be interpreted with caution since immigrant women may be more reluctant than Canadian-born women to disclose domestic violence to survey interviewers due to language or cultural barriers. In addition to the barriers to disclosure, there are challenges that immigrant women who experience domestic violence face including cultural differences (Alaggia and Maiter 2013), socio-economic inequality (Fong 2010), racism (Bannerji 2002; Jiwani 2005), unfamiliarity with their legal rights (Wachholz and Miedema 2004) and the public services available to them, the loss of social support networks (Cottrell 2008), and the lack of confidentiality within immigrant groups (Kulwicki, Aswad, Carmona, and Ballout 2010).

For more on immigrant families, see "Changing Trends in the Diversity of Family Forms" in Chapter 1, pp. 3–10; and "Families as Historical Actors" in Chapter 2, pp. 26–32.

When considering the unique vulnerabilities of immigrant women to domestic violence it is important to keep in mind three points: first, that immigrants come to Canada from a wide range of cultural contexts—they are not a homogeneous group in terms of their country of origin, language, ethnicity, or religion. Second, culture does not cause domestic violence but rather shapes and mediates it (Liao 2006). Finally, culture is dynamic and changes over time due to a variety of social and economic factors (Inglehart and Norris 2003). Many immigrant families come from cultural contexts in which patriarchal values are less contested than they are in Canada and social attitudes are more tolerant of domestic violence. While feminist analysis is critical of the ways in which patriarchy subordinates women, not all forms of subordination are necessarily violent (Mahmood 2001). The challenge for Canadian immigrant women is to discern between abusive and non-abusive behaviours in intimate relationships as they become familiar with attitudes towards domestic violence and the resources available to them in their new home.

Qualitative research with immigrant women in the Maritime region of Canada has shown that many immigrant families experience gender role shifts in the years following arrival (Holtmann 2016). Immigrant women report increased autonomy as they become fluent in our official languages, increasingly involved in social networks, and learn to navigate unfamiliar systems of education, employment, and health care. This is in contrast to a decrease in the social status of their husbands who often find it difficult to find employment commensurate with the education and work experience gained in their countries of origin. The shifting status of female and male gender roles can and does lead to conflict in immigrant families not only between husbands and wives but also between parents and children. Conflict due to change is inevitable within families yet this is particularly true for new immigrants. When family conflict is dealt with in abusive and violent ways, immigrant women are very vulnerable. Because Canadian immigration policies create dependency between the primary applicant and dependent family members and due to the precariousness of the pathway to full citizenship (Goldring and Landolt 2011), many immigrant women are unsure of their **immigration status**. This can prevent them from disclosing situations of domestic violence due to fear of deportation.

There is also pressure among immigrants not to publically expose family problems. On the broader social level, immigrant groups do not want to confirm public stereotypes concerning immigrants and family violence. Immigrant women may be concerned that if they disclose domestic violence to others in their social networks, their families will become the subject of gossip. At the level of families, immigrant women tend to understand their individual identities in relationship to their families. In other words, their collective identities are stronger than their individual identities. Immigrant women are embedded in families and are very aware of how their decisions impact others in extended family networks, especially their children. They often put the well-being of their husbands and children before their own. Because intact families are highly valued, attitudes that tolerate violence and abuse are passed down between mothers and daughters from generation to generation. Women are expected to deal with problems on their own or within the family network. Therefore, if word about domestic violence gets out beyond the boundaries of the family, immigrant women may feel that they bring shame and embarrassment upon themselves and their families.

Immigrant women often feel enormous responsibility for the success of their marriages. This sense of responsibility for their families can be reinforced by conservative religious beliefs and practices. Like culture, religion is not a cause of abuse, but particular religious beliefs and practices can make women more vulnerable in situations of domestic violence. For conservative religious traditions of Christianity, Judaism, and Islam the family is considered sacred. Heterosexual family configurations are understood as the foundation of a divinely created social order. Traditional religious teachings on the complementarity of husbands and wives promote the role of a caring mother as the primary identity for women and that of a providing father as the primary identity for men. Thus, when violence occurs within religious families, many women feel that it is somehow their fault. Rhetoric from Christian religious leaders promoting family values, encouraging forgiveness, uncritically preaching self-sacrifice for others, and condemning divorce without the knowledge that rates of domestic violence are the same for religious and non-religious families (Cunradi, Caetano, and Schafer 2002) perpetuates what Nason-Clark refers to as a "holy hush" about the problem of domestic violence among religious groups (2012). As a result, abused religious women suffer in silence filled with guilt and shame while men of faith who abuse their wives are not held accountable for their actions (Nason-Clark and Fisher-Townsend 2015). In some cases, religious texts like the Qur'an are used to justify the physical disciplining of wives by husbands (Ammar 2007) and religious laws are used by controlling Jewish husbands in refusing to grant their wives a divorce (Cares and Cusik 2012). These are examples of religious beliefs and practices that can prevent women who experience domestic violence from taking action in order to ensure their safety and that of their children.

Understanding the particular vulnerabilities to domestic violence for families who belong to sub-groups within the Canadian population is essential in order to intervene in ways that are sensitive to the ethnic, "racial," and religious diversity in our society. We now turn to consider some of the intervention strategies used to bring an end to the problem of domestic violence in Canadian families.

Intervention Strategies

From what we have discussed in this chapter, it should be apparent that domestic violence is a complex problem. Contemporary best practices in responding to domestic violence therefore include a variety of intervention strategies in what is referred to as a **community coordinated response**. Intervention strategies coordinated at the community level can ensure a systematic approach to the problem that incorporates multiple public services as well as participation from diverse community organizations that represent the cultural and religious diversity of its population (Nason-Clark and Holtmann 2013). This section will provide a brief overview of three of these strategies: the shelter movement, the criminal justice response, and **action-oriented research** on family violence.

It was members of the feminist movement that created the first safe houses or shelters for Canadian women fleeing from violent boyfriends, partners, and spouses in the early 1970s (Tutty 2006). In the years since, federal and provincial governments have provided funding for shelters and professionally trained shelter workers have replaced volunteers in supporting survivors. In 2014 there were 627 shelters for abused women and their children in Canada (Beattie and Hutchins 2015). Shelters provide temporary housing as well as other services such as counseling, group programming for residents, safety planning, transportation, advocacy through the criminal justice system and assistance in finding longer-term accommodations. Second-stage housing is an affordable longer-term option for many survivors. However, the strategy of using a publicly funded shelter does not work for all survivors. For example, leaving the home of an abusive spouse can be problematic for rural and farm women (Doherty and Hornesty 2004; Wisniewski et al. 2016) and immigrant women (Agnew 1998; Rupra 2010).

Physical and sexual assault are crimes in Canada and although the majority of victims of domestic violence do not contact the police for help, police do respond to a lot of calls concerning violence in families. For example, in Fredericton, New Brunswick, a city with a population of slightly more than 56,000 people, police respond to between 500 and 600 calls a year related to intimate partner violence—that is almost two per day (Harrop 2016). The adoption of a National Framework for Collaborative Police Action on

Intimate Partner Violence is intended to improve this response across the country (Gill and Fitch 2016). If there is sufficient evidence, police are mandated to arrest and charge perpetrators of spousal assault, a policy originally designed to highlight the criminal nature of domestic violence. This is coupled with a pro-prosecution policy designed to mandate that the Crown prosecute cases where there is sufficient evidence of domestic violence, regardless of the victim's cooperation (Ad Hoc Federal-Provincial-Territorial Working Group Reviewing Spousal Abuse Policies and Legislation 2003). There is evidence that these policies have had the unintended consequence of disempowering women "who may have legitimate reasons for not wanting their abusers arrested and charged" (Tutty et al. 2008:8). Specialized domestic violence courts have been developed in some cities in Canada in recognition of the need for a more coordinated and efficient justice system response (Nason-Clark and Fisher-Townsend 2015). These courts are designed to provide integrated services to victims resulting in an increase in successful prosecutions of perpetrators.

The options of calling the police or seeking safety in a shelter are just two of the most well-known intervention strategies utilized by women in the aftermath of domestic violence. But, as has been pointed out, these options are not necessarily the most effective in many cases of domestic violence given the multiple intersecting inequalities and unique challenges that members of minority groups face. Canada is a world-leader in research on domestic and family violence. There exists a national network of centres of excellence devoted to researching all aspects of family violence including evaluating the effectiveness of intervention strategies used by front-line public service providers and members of subgroups in the population. These centres include:

1. The Freda Centre for Research on Violence against Women and Children at Simon Fraser University (www.fredacentre.com/).
2. The RESOLVE network hosted by the University of Manitoba (http://umanitoba.ca/centres/resolve/index.html) with nodes at the University of Regina (www2.uregina.ca/resolve/) and the University of Calgary (www.ucalgary.ca/resolve/).
3. The Centre for Research and Education on Violence against Women and Children at the University of Western Ontario (www.learningtoendabuse.ca/).
4. Le centre de recherche interdisciplinaire sur la violence familiale et la violence faite aux femmes, Université de Montréal (www.criviff.qc.ca/).
5. The Muriel McQueen Fergusson Centre for Family Violence Research at the University of New Brunswick (www.unb.ca/fredericton/arts/centres/mmfc/).

In most cases, the research is collaborative in nature, bringing together university researchers and community partners to investigate the ever-changing landscape of domestic violence in their regions. The research is often action-oriented, meaning that it is intended to contribute to improvements to local and national intervention strategies as well as to changes in policies and legislation with the aim of reducing and eventually eliminating the problem of family violence from Canadian society. Some of the information presented in this chapter is based on collaborative, action-oriented research conducted through the Muriel McQueen Fergusson Centre for Family Violence Research in Atlantic Canada.

Questions for Critical Thought

Take a look at the website of the family violence research centre closest to you to determine what kinds of research are taking place there. Which research project do you think will have an important impact on the problem of family violence in your region?

Conclusion

Abusive relationships within families are complex and people become accustomed to the interpersonal dynamics with which they grow up and live over the long term. Episodes of violence are interspersed with words of love. Threats mingle with gestures of affection. Identifying oneself as a victim of violence is very difficult because of the implications of this admission for the entire family. Perpetrators and victims often have personal histories in which they saw their fathers abusing their mothers. Many family members suffer in silence, overwhelmed by feelings of shame. In Canada, research over the past thirty years has revealed that almost one in three women has experienced some form of violence or abuse from a spouse or common-law partner. That statistic could be higher for women from racialized groups given their unique vulnerabilities in the face of structural inequalities in Canadian society. Traditional domestic violence interventions have improved over the years, such as the criminal justice system response that holds perpetrators accountable for their actions and the network of women's shelters and programming across the country that help survivors along the road to recovery. New research and new approaches will likely need to be explored as we begin to better understand power dynamics in intimate relationships among same-sex, trans, and other types of partnerships that make up family life in Canada today.

For more on trans people, see "LGBTQ Rights" in Chapter 16, p. 358.

There are many other intervention strategies that are being developed and used in order to help individuals and families bring an end to the violence in their midst. You are invited to learn more about them in the resources listed below.

Study Questions

1. Are there warning signs of abuse in relationships?
2. Why don't women just leave violent marriages?
3. What are some of the differences between patriarchal structures and abuse?
4. How are children impacted by witnessing domestic violence between their parents?
5. If a friend told you that she was the victim of intimate partner violence, how would you respond?
6. What are some of the reasons for the high rates of family violence among Indigenous people in Canada?

Further Readings

Alaggia, R., and C. Vine, eds. 2013. *Cruel But Not Unusual: Violence in Canadian Families*, 2nd edn. Waterloo, ON: Wilfrid Laurier University Press. This edited collection includes contributions from leading scholars and service providers on topics such sexual violence, neglect and the physical punishment of children, violence in Indigenous families, abuse in gender minority communities and among adults with disabilities, domestic violence in immigrant and refugee families, and the abuse and neglect of older adults.

Assay, S.M., J. DeFrain, M. Metzger, and B. Moyer. 2014. *Family Violence from a Global Perspective: A Strengths-Based Approach*. Thousand Oaks, CA: SAGE. The book examines individual, relational, community, and social strengths in approaches to family violence. It provides a global perspective on the issue with authors from 16 countries providing chapters. Information on intimate partner violence, child abuse, and elder abuse is included.

Finkelhor, D. 2008. *Childhood Victimization: Violence, Crime, and Abuse in the Lives of Young People*. New York: Oxford University Press. Child victimization is an under-researched area in the field of family violence. This publication is comprehensive in terms of research on the experiences of juvenile victims of abuse as well as approaches to prevention and treatment. The author also addresses the barriers that victims and their families encounter when seeking help.

Fong, J. 2010. *Out of the Shadows: Woman Abuse in Ethnic, Immigrant and Aboriginal Communities*. Toronto, ON: Women's Press. In addition to promoting an intersectional theoretical framework for the understanding of woman abuse, this edited collection includes chapters on public awareness campaigns, the experiences of activists and service providers, and the experiences of Chinese, South Asian, Ethiopian, and Jewish survivors of domestic violence.

National Clearinghouse on Family Violence. 2008. *Aboriginal Women and Family Violence*. Ottawa, ON: Public Health Agency of Canada. This report was prepared by Ipsos-Reid for Indian and Northern Affairs Canada and is based on Indigenous women's experiences of intimate partner violence as well as those who provide professional support services. The report describes both the resources available to victims and perpetrators in Indigenous families as well as the gaps in resources.

Nason-Clark, N., and B. Fisher-Townsend. 2015. *Men Who Batter*. New York: Oxford University Press. This book is based on data from court-mandated batterer intervention or treatment programs for men who have acted violently towards their intimate partners. The authors interviewed and conducted focus groups with male perpetrators as well as professional staff over a four-year period. It highlights the men's personal histories of abuse and their journeys toward change.

Ploeg, J., L. Lohfeld, and C.A. Walsh. 2013. "What Is 'Elder Abuse'? Voices from the Margin: The Views of Underrepresented Canadian Older Adults." *Journal of Elder Abuse and Neglect* 25, 5: 396–424. Elder abuse is on the rise and this is problematic given Canada's aging population. This article explores the definition of elder abuse as understood by older adults who are members of marginalized groups.

Ursel, J., L. Tutty, and J. LeMaistre. 2008. *What's Law Got to Do with It: The Law, Specialized Courts and Domestic Violence in Canada*. Toronto, ON: Cormorant Press. This book was written by researchers of the RESOLVE network and examines changes in the Canadian justice system's response to domestic violence. Specialized domestic violence courts in Canada are assessed based on the perspective of prosecutors, victims, and researchers.

Key Terms

Action-oriented research A model of research focused on an outcome of social change. It is a collaborative process that brings together university and community partners in the pursuit of practical knowledge and solutions to pressing social problems.

Community coordinated response A strategy that brings together multiple perspectives and areas of expertise to address the problem of family violence, including the criminal justice system, shelters and advocates, therapeutic professionals, public service providers, community groups, researchers, and government. This helps to avoid overlap and prevents members of marginalized groups from falling through the cracks.

Consent Defined in Canadian criminal law as the voluntary agreement to engage in an activity. In regards to sexual activity, men must take "reasonable steps" to ensure that their partners consent to participate. Someone who is unconscious is incapable of consenting to sex.

Cycle of violence A pattern of violent behaviours (emotional, physical, sexual) that recur throughout the course of an intimate relationship.

Immigration status Canada's federal policies include several immigration categories under which people can apply to enter the country: refugee, federal skilled worker, provincial nominee, and family class. A person's immigrant status determines the particular pathway to citizenship. Full, legal citizenship is only granted to permanent residents who have lived and paid taxes in Canada for at least four years and who have passed a citizenship test.

Intimate partner violence (IPV) Includes different forms of violence that occur between people in an intimate relationship. An intimate relationship is defined by regular contact, familiarity, and emotional connectedness and can take the form of a dating, common-law, or marital relationship.

Post-traumatic stress disorder (PTSD) A mental disorder that develops after a person has experienced or witnessed trauma such as sexual or physical assault. Not everyone who experiences or witnesses trauma develops PTSD.

Prevalence Expressed as a fraction, a proportion, a percentage, or as a rate, such as the number of cases per 100,000 people, the prevalence of domestic violence in the population is determined by comparing the number of people who report experiences of domestic violence with the total number of people in the population.

Qualitative research The aim of qualitative research is to understand the complexity of social life. Qualitative methods such as in-depth interviews enable research participants to describe their experiences in rich detail, which is particularly useful to family violence researchers.

Quantitative data Often collected through survey questionnaires administered to a representative sample of the population, these data consist of information about characteristics of a population coded into numerical form.

Racialized Where there has been ethnic or "racial" identities ascribed to a relationship, social practice, or group that did not previously identify itself as such. Ethnic or "racial" identities are usually socially constructed for minority groups by the majority, which in Canada would be people of ethnic Western European origins.

Sample Used in quantitative analysis, it is a representative subset of the population. It is carefully selected to mirror the diversity of population so that results of statistical analysis can be used to predict characteristics or behaviours in the general population.

Visible minority status In Canada, persons who are not Indigenous but who are non-Caucasian or have non-white skin colour are considered to have visible minority status. This definition was established by the federal government for its employment equity policies.

 Interested in finding out more? Visit www.oupcanada.com/Albanese4e for access to a list of recommended websites for this chapter.

15

Investing in Families and Children
Family Policies in Canada

CATHERINE KRULL AND MUSHIRA MOHSIN KHAN

LEARNING OBJECTIVES

- To understand the development of Canada's family policies within a liberal welfare state

- To understand the ideology and implications of a universal approach versus a targeted approach to family policies

- To become aware of Quebec's progressive family policies and how they might serve as a model for the rest of Canada

- To gain a better comprehension as to why Canada's targeted family policies have not yet eradicated child poverty as promised by parliament in 1989

- To become conscious of the reasons why state intervention is necessary if parents, especially mothers, are to successfully integrate employment and family responsibilities, and to recognize how barriers to such integration impact gender equity

- To appreciate the challenges that governments, family policy makers, and advocacy groups face in Canada in developing new child care measures

---

Introduction

Canadian governments have always influenced families: determining who marries, marital age, and how unions end. Generally, governments have a vested interest in reproduction, especially between married adults, in order to perpetuate Canadian culture and supply an adequate number of taxpayers, consumers, and workers—to that end they ask, often bolstered by law and policy, that family members care for and support one another (Baker 1994, 2010). Conversely, Canadians rely on state economic and social support in "balancing" child care with paid work. **Family policy**, therefore, is central for Canadians—it defines families, their forms, which family members are entitled to government support, and the amounts and type of support.

Family policy comprises rules and programs. In this chapter, that policy, narrowly defined, comprises measures affecting families with children under age 18. It includes direct and indirect cash transfers like family allowances and tax relief; benefits for workers with family responsibilities such as maternity–paternity leave; services, including daycare, pre- and after-school care, and early childhood education programs; other benefits affecting housing, education, and health; and legislation affecting abortion and child alimony (Gauthier 2010).

Nonetheless, Canada lacks a comprehensive national policy. State intervention is generally minimal: restricted primarily to child abuse, child neglect, and limited financial support. It varies by gender and different income and cultural groups (Baker 2001, 2008). A governmental "hierarchy of help" exists in assisting families: the labour market first, the family second; if either fails to meet family needs, state involvement occurs in limited, targeted ways (Beauvais and Dufour 2003). However, this system obstructs parents' full participation in family care and paid work, especially women's progress for equality and independence (Krull 2011, 2012, 2014).

Explaining the lack of a cohesive national family policy is complex. Like other countries, an aging population and increasing globalization challenge Canada. Governments must consider the conflicting viewpoints of family-oriented public interest groups—electors of the left and right who put them in office (Evans and Wekerle 1997:13); the debates between these groups encumber cohesive policy. Canada's federal nature also results in constitutional impediments. Ottawa focuses more on income support, emphasizing child protection, while provincial and territorial governments concentrate on welfare assistance and other services (Tézli and Gauthier 2009).

Moreover, families have undergone considerable change over the course of Canadian history (Krull 2011, 2012, 2014). As the 2016 Census indicates, Canadian families are in a state of flux. Census data show that 26 per cent of census families were couples with children, with married couples still accounting for the majority of all census families. However, while married couples account for two thirds of families, this is a marked decline, with the proportion of single-person households and common-law couples increasing, to 28.2 per cent and 21.3 per cent of total census families respectively. The increase in lone-parent families is also important: 19.2 per cent of all children live in households with a single parent, an increase of more than 1 per cent over a decade, with women accounting for 80 per cent of lone parents. The percentage of children living in common-law households has also increased to 16.3 per cent. Stepfamilies—counted for the first time in the 2011 Census—comprise 9.8 per cent of all census families in which children are present. At the same time, 28, 030, or 0.5 per cent of children under age 14 live in foster homes (Statistics Canada 2017a). Clearly, the traditional nuclear family is a social institution facing stiff competition. Indeed, in addition to the increases in single-parent families, blended families, and common-law families, the 2016 Census shows increases in multi-generational families, 6.3 per cent of children living in a household with at least one grandparent; skip-generation families, which account for 0.6 per cent of all households with children; and same-sex households (Statistics Canada 2017b). In whatever form, families constitute the basis of Canadian society and government policy must account for these changes, particularly as they pertain to families raising children. Accordingly, the role of government and the changing requirements of parents, children, grandparents, and other family members in the shape and purpose of family policies are decidedly important.

Canadian family policy falls between western European and American models. Mirroring Western Europe in health and education investments—but at a lower level—and in some federal benefits, they exceed those enjoyed by Americans. In one crucial area, however, Canada joins its southern neighbour: a shameful history of high child poverty rates and low public family expenditures (Brusentsev and Vroman 2007: 28; Chen and Corak 2008: 540).

To understand present Canadian family policy, four questions arise: (1) How have recent policies developed? (2) How have they responded or not responded to changes in Canadian families? (3) What are their strengths and weaknesses? and, responding to criticism, (4) Has the state produced more effective policy? Here, one point needs emphasis. Quebec provides a stellar example of government initiatives that prioritize the family, offering a potential model for developing the rest of Canada's cohesive national policy. Despite constraints on public finance, but confronting increasing family needs, Canada's various levels of government began serious and promising discussions toward a national policy in the late 1990s. But the process remains arduous as Canadian governments oscillate over understanding their role versus that of parents in raising healthy, educated, and well-adjusted children.

Canada's Family and Child-related Policies

Maternity and Parental/Adoption Leave Benefits

Paid maternity and **parental leaves** occupy a central place in Canada's **liberal welfare state**. In specific terms, these policies are meant to assist Canadians in balancing family and employment. However, Canada has not had the best track record in this regard. Although all of Western Europe, Australia, New Zealand, and Japan adopted some form of paid maternity leave legislation by 1939, it took Canada until 1971 to offer women such assistance. The reason was that "the responsibility of protecting pregnant women at work and compensating them for the loss of earnings was not seen as a governmental responsibility" (Gauthier 1998:197).

When the legislation was finally passed, the responsibility for **maternity benefits** (and later parental/adoption leave) was divided between the federal and provincial/territorial governments. The provinces and territories were obligated to determine the length and conditions of maternity leave, while financial replacement fell under the jurisdiction of the federal government's Unemployment Insurance (UI) program. If they had been paying UI premiums, working mothers were initially given 15 weeks of paid leave and received approximately 67 per cent of their regular salary as unemployment benefits. And if they so chose, these women had the option of taking two additional weeks of unpaid leave. Women adopting a child were finally made eligible to receive benefits in 1984. The provinces also offered unpaid maternity leave and, although unpaid, it nevertheless was beneficial because these mothers were guaranteed the right to return to the same or an equivalent job (Jensen and Thompson 1999:13).

Bowing to pressure from women's groups, the federal government introduced 10 weeks of parental leave in 1990, which could be taken by either parent or shared between them; the parent who took leave received unemployment benefits equalling 60 per cent of her/his regular salary. In 1996, two changes were made to maternity benefits: (1) eligibility for maternity benefits was now to be based on the number of hours worked rather than the number of weeks; and (2) the amount women received was reduced from 60 per cent to a maximum of 55 per cent of their regular salary with a ceiling of $413 per week (Baker 2001; OECD 2004). Gauthier (1998) conducted an international comparative study shortly after these changes took place in Canada and found that when both the duration of the leave and maternity pay were taken into consideration, Canada was among the lowest of 22 industrialized countries.

In January 2001, the federal government doubled the amount of time that new parents could receive benefits, from 25 to a maximum of 50 weeks (Government of Canada 2005). While maternity leave remained the same (15 weeks at 55 per cent of insurable earnings), parental leave increased from 10 to 35 weeks at 55 per cent of insurable earnings up to a maximum amount, as of January 1, 2016, of $50,800 per annum, or $537 per week. To be eligible for the maximum, parents had to have worked a minimum of 600 hours of insurable employment in the previous 12 months. Also, for every $100 earned, employers deduct $1.88 until the maximum annual insurable amount is reached. In 2016, the maximum premium to be paid is $955.04 (Government of Canada 2016a).

At present, a mother can add the parental leave to her maternity leave—giving her 50 weeks of paid leave—or she can take maternity leave (15 weeks), return to her employment, and her partner or spouse could then take the 35-week parental leave (ibid.). Although women cannot work while on maternity benefits without having their earnings deducted from their benefits, parents can earn up to $50 per week or 25 per cent of their weekly benefits in part-time work without being penalized (ibid.). Moreover, under the **Working While on Claim** pilot project, until August 11, 2018, once parents have served the waiting period, they will be able to keep $0.50 of the Employment Insurance (EI) benefits for every dollar that they earn, until the 90 per cent threshold of the weekly insurable earnings used to calculate EI benefits has been reached. Any money earned above this threshold is subject to a dollar for dollar deduction from benefits (ibid.).

In its October 2004 report card on Canada's child care system, the Organisation for Economic Co-operation and Development (OECD) praised Canada for its enhanced parental leave, stating that "this has been a tremendous breakthrough for Canadian parents and infants," a finding reaffirmed in the OECD's 2011 Better Life Index (OECD 2004:55; OECD 2011). Canada's birth benefits are also superior to those offered in the US (Brusentsev and Vroman 2007). However, Canada's birth benefits can certainly be criticized for restricting eligibility to employed women who have worked for a minimum of 600 hours—this means that many Canadians are excluded. And despite the changes to parental leave, the majority of Canadian fathers still do not take it, citing as their reasons (1) family choice, (2) difficulty taking time off work, and (3) financial issues (Dube 2008). Despite studies that indicate that greater father involvement positively impacts on a child's cognitive development, educational attainment, and social functioning (ibid.), it seems that cultural expectations of men and insufficient benefits continue to be issues that impede fathers' full involvement in child care. Even so, between 2001 and 2014 there was a nine-fold increase in the percentage of recent fathers taking parental leave, from 3 per cent to 27.1 per cent (Statistics Canada 2015).

Questions for Critical Thought

It is often said that one way to shrink the gender gap in the workplace is to allow both parents to take equal leave upon arrival of the baby. Do you agree with this statement? Why/why not?

From Universal to Targeted Child and Family Benefits

The federal government has been financially supporting Canadian families in some way or another since 1918, when it introduced the Child Tax Exemption, which allowed breadwinners with dependent children an annual fiscal deduction on their income tax (Baker 2001; Lefebvre and Merrigan 2003). In 1945, a monthly Family Allowance was paid to women with children at home. These two contributions were important because they were universal. In other words, they offered financial assistance to all families with dependent children. Family Allowance was also significant because it was paid directly to mothers, which for many women at this time was the only source of income that was theirs alone. These two universal contributions, the Child Tax Exemption and Family Allowance, became known as "child and family benefits" (Baker 2001) and developed as the pillars of Canadian family policy (Lefebvre and Merrigan 2003).

By the late 1980s, Ottawa had become quite concerned about the country's high child poverty rates. Throughout that decade, child poverty rates in Canada ranged from 15.7 to 20.6 per cent—rates that were among the highest in the industrial world and second only to the United States (O'Hara 1998). In 1989, a resolution was unanimously passed in the House of Commons to achieve the goal of eradicating child poverty by the year 2000. The following year, Canada signed the United Nations Convention on the Rights of the Child, a treaty that committed all signatories to protect and ensure children's rights and to hold themselves accountable for this commitment before the international community.

For more on the history of Family Allowance in Canada see "The Shape(s) of Modern Families" in Chapter 2, pp. 33–7.

Between 1988 and 1993, the Conservative government of Brian Mulroney took measures that completely transformed family benefits with the goal of reducing child poverty. "Discussions of poverty focused almost exclusively on 'child poverty,' as children were always seen as the deserving poor, whereas adults drawing social benefits were often suspected of defrauding the welfare system" (Baker 2001:276; also see Stasiulis 2005). The child tax deduction was cancelled in 1988 and replaced with a non-refundable child tax credit, a device that minimized significantly the amount received by wealthier families. In 1993, the Conservative government abolished both Family Allowance and the non-refundable tax credit and introduced the **Child Tax Benefit (CTB)**. The CTB paid low-income families an annual amount for each child, an additional supplement for each subsequent child under seven years of age, and a **Working Income Supplement (WIS)**. These changes marked a monumental change in Canada's approach to family policy—universal benefits (designed to assist all families with dependent children) were substituted with targeted benefits (designed to assist low-income families).

In 1998, the Liberal government of Jean Chrétien developed the **National Child Benefit (NCB)**. The NCB included the **Canada Child Tax Benefit (CCTB)**—just a new name for the previous CTB—and the **National Child Benefit Supplement (NCBS)**, which replaced the WIS. In adhering to the parliamentary commitment to reduce poverty, only low-income families could receive the maximum annual basic amount. Up until 2016 and after several amendments, the CCTB paid an annual maximum of $1,405 per child to families whose net income did not exceed $42,707. An additional supplement of $249 was paid annually for each additional child under the age of seven years but this payment was replaced in July 2007 with the **Universal Child Care Benefit (UCCB)**, a monthly payment of $100 per child under six years of age. This amount was raised to $160 in 2015. In terms of the NCBS benefit, families whose net income did not exceed $24,863 received $2,177 for the first child, $1,926 for the second child, and $1,832 for each additional child (Government of Canada 2012b).

One of the chief criticisms of the NCBS was that it could be fully or partially clawed back by provincial and territorial governments if families were receiving provincial social assistance (welfare). For example, while the provinces of New Brunswick, Newfoundland and Labrador, Nova Scotia, and Manitoba almost always allowed welfare families to collect the full amount allotted by the NCBS, the supplement was fully or partially clawed back in provinces and territories such as British Columbia, Saskatchewan, Ontario, Prince Edward Island, Nunavut, and the Northwest Territories. (National Council of Welfare 2008:142).

The irony is that the federal government increased child benefits but allowed provinces to reduce or deny them altogether for families on social assistance, the families most in need given that welfare rates are well below the poverty line in every province in Canada. Indeed, as of 2007, the last year for which a comprehensive report on NCB was compiled, approximately 320,620 Canadian families continued to have their welfare or child benefits reduced by all or part of the NCBS. While a cursory analysis of NCBS by the Treasury Board of Canada Secretariat noted that provincial and territorial governments were beginning to reduce the clawback so that "the vast majority of children living in low-income families, including those on social assistance, are currently receiving some or all of the [NCBS]," the continued existence of a clawback nevertheless reinforced the idea of the deserving and undeserving poor (Government of Canada 2011b). "Those working for low pay—the deserving poor—get to keep all the NCBS. Those on welfare—the undeserving poor—don't get to keep the NCBS" (National Council of Welfare 2008:86). It also discriminated against single mothers, since they constitute the majority of those who collect welfare and who also had their payments clawed back. Not surprisingly, the **National Council of Welfare**, a federal advisory board with a mandate devoted exclusively to fighting poverty and cutbacks to the welfare system, could find no evidence that the NCBS has assisted welfare families to move to paid employment or obtain employment experience (National Council of Welfare 2008:87–8).

Recognizing these drawbacks in the existing system of family benefits, the Liberal government under Justin Trudeau replaced the CCTB, including the NCBS and the UCCB, with the **Canada Child Benefit (CCB)**. Effective July 1, 2016, the CCB, a tax-free monthly payment made to eligible families, provides a maximum annual benefit of up to $5,400, per child, aged 6 though 17, and $6,400 for children under 6. The CCB is unique in that it is a progressive system of benefits, which targets those families that may need it the most (Government of Canada 2016b). Under the CCB program, families with children with disabilities as well as those in care are expected to see increases in benefits (ibid.). Time alone will judge the overall impact of the CCB on Canada's families but it is certainly a step in the right direction.

Children in State Care

Due to differing ways in which provincial governments classify "out-of-home" care, Canada-wide statistics on state care of children have historically been difficult to calculate (Mulcahy and Trocmé 2010). According to Peter Dudding, executive director of the Child Welfare League of Canada, "the best estimate from two compilation studies is that between 76,000 and 85,000 kids are in foster care. The lack of data means there's no way the provinces, which fund foster care and often stake decisions on statistics and outcomes, can compare themselves against each other for best practices, . . . It's impossible to create good policy without good numbers" (CBC News 2012a). However, according to the 2016 Census, which counted foster children for the first time,[1] 28,030 Canadian children are living in foster care (Statistics Canada 2017b). Despite the variance in definition of foster children and in numbers, there is agreement that the majority of foster children are under the age of 14 years. Moreover, although the Census did not count how many foster children were Indigenous, they did find that the provinces that have the highest proportion of foster children are also the provinces with the highest numbers of Indigenous peoples; namely Manitoba, followed by the Northwest Territories, Nunavut, and Yukon (ibid.). Other surveys report that approximately 40 per cent of foster children are Indigenous; and of these children, the majority are placed in non-Indigenous foster homes (Bokma 2008; Canadian Press 2008, Federation of Aboriginal Foster Parents 2012; Ponti 2008) and as of 2009 more than 8,000 Indigenous children (about 5 per cent of all Indigenous children) have been removed from their homes across Canada (Government of Canada 2010). About one third of foster children have parents whose parental rights have been legally terminated and, as such, are adoptable; yet less than 13 per cent of these children are actually adopted by their foster parents (Bokma 2008). Indigenous groups are challenging the federal government on this overrepresentation of their children in state foster care, arguing that the grossly underfunded child welfare on reserves is a continuation of Canada's colonial history.

For more on other supports for child care, see "Social Policy and Other Supports for Child Care" in Chapter 5, pp. 110–112.

For more on Indigenous families and child welfare, see "Child Welfare: The Sixties Scoop," "Child Welfare: The Millennium Scoop," and "Child Welfare: Canadian Human Rights Tribunal" in Chapter 12, pp. 256–260.

Foster parents receive a monthly basic maintenance fee or per diem from the provincial government to help with the costs of caring for foster children. These costs include food, clothing, personal care items (toiletries and hair care products), general household costs (e.g., wear and tear, cleaning, paper supplies, insurance), spending allowance (minor recreation toys, magazines, and musical recordings), and gifts to and from the foster child. Foster parents can also collect skill fees, which are meant to compensate them for their level of expertise in caring for a child. Specialized rates are also available for children with specialized needs. The amounts that foster parents receive vary considerably depending on the province in which they live. The federal government also pays provincial jurisdictions a Children's Special Allowance (CSA), which is based on the number of children living in that jurisdiction who are under the age of 18 and in state care. This monthly allowance per child in state care is equivalent to the CCB. However, this money does not necessarily get passed on to foster parents. The province determines the allocation of the CSA, and, as such, jurisdictions either pass on the full amount to foster parents, partial amounts, or none at all because they consider it part of their operating revenue (Government of Canada 2008, 2012a).

However, current benefits are often seen as inadequate. Many existing foster parents are struggling and even deciding to quit because of the lack of state support (CBC News 2012a; MacGregor 2006). Canada's foster care system has been fraught with other problems as well. There are not nearly enough foster homes in which to place all children, and foster children often experience an average of seven foster home placements over the course of their childhood (Bokma 2008). Moreover, because of lack of resources and the sheer number of foster children, it is impossible to scrutinize every home on a regular basis. As such, foster children are more vulnerable to neglect and even abuse (CBC News 2012a; Montgomery 2008). It also remains a contested issue as to whether legal responsibility for foster children lies with their foster parents or with the state (Cradock 2007). There exists significant variability in policies, legislation, definitions, and services, largely because foster care operates solely under provincial and territorial jurisdictions—the federal government is responsible only for Indigenous foster children. Foster families are also often excluded from other government benefits that most parents receive. For example, the Ontario government's plan to alleviate poverty excluded foster children living in the province from the new child benefit, denying foster families a total of approximately $5 million (Talaga and Monsebraaten 2008). Most provinces also terminate benefits once a foster child is adopted, which often deters or hampers successful adoptions (Simons 2008). Also troubling is that only 21 per cent of foster children pursue post-secondary education compared to 40 per cent of young people in the general population, while in Ontario children in foster care have a high school graduation rate of 44 per cent compared to a rate among the general populace of 81 per cent (CTV News 2008; OACAS 2011).

Despite these tremendous difficulties, there have also been noteworthy successes. For example, the Alberta provincial government introduced innovative amendments to their Child, Youth, and Family Enhancement Act in 2004. Under **Bill 40**, parents who adopt a child who has been a permanent ward of the provincial government will receive the same benefits given to foster parents until the child turns 18 years of age, a measure still in effect as of mid-2017. This includes a travel allowance for those adopting an Indigenous child so that the child can visit their family reserve and stay connected with their cultural heritage. The rationale for these benefits is that "all children who have been in government care have special needs—not because all foster children have physical or psychological problems but because any child who's been made a permanent ward of the government, for whatever reason, will inevitably have gone through rough times" (Simons 2008). Likewise, the Ontario government has implemented a progressive plan that is meant to increase the enrolment of foster children in post-secondary education. The province has been investing the $100 monthly Universal Childcare Benefit allocated for foster children under the age of six years into a RESP fund. The RESP is being supplemented with other federal funds such as the Canada Learning Bond payments and an annual payment from a Canada educational savings grant. This will translate into $23,000 for a child who is 18 years of age and who entered the foster care system as an infant (CTV News 2008).

Most importantly, it will allow foster children the same possibilities that most Canadian children enjoy. Alongside tuition support, the Ontario government was mulling plans to allow foster children to increase the existing extended care and maintenance age for foster children from 21 to 25, thus providing youth in foster care with the long-term support enjoyed by many of their peers (CBC News 2012b). However, this measure has not been implemented as of 2017. As Reid (2007) argues, "No longer is impersonal and minimal the best approach [to care for foster children]; rather, the most successful programs aim at giving youth the support that any other peer would expect from a parent" (2007:47).

Assessment of Canada's Child and Family Benefits

Impact of Measures on Child Poverty

Canada's child benefits have come under a great deal of criticism. Feminists have long argued that they represent a step backward for women in terms of their full and equal participation in the labour force. McKeen (2001:187) pointed out more than a decade ago that "the move from universal entitlement to means testing on the basis of family income limits women's access to benefits, encourages familial dependency, and turns back progress in the effort to make the recognition of individual autonomy an important policy objective." In essence, Canada's efforts since 1989, when Parliament promised to work towards eliminating child poverty by the year 2000, have failed dismally. In 1989, when the resolution passed, the child poverty rate was 11.9 per cent (after tax). As Figure 15.1 indicates, child poverty rates increased after 1989 until they reached a high of 18.4 per cent in 1996 (based on after tax income). They decreased to 8.2 per cent in 2010, a rate only slightly below the 1989 rate when Canada promised to eradicate child poverty. It also means that 639,000 children, approximately 1 in every 10 children in Canada, continue to live in poverty (calculated by figures reported in Campaign 2000 2011:4). And according to a 2017 United Nations report, wider income inequality, social competition, and stress are making life more difficult for Canada's poorest: Canada ranked 25 out of 41 industrialized countries on the Index of Child and Youth Well-Being and Sustainability (UNICEF 2017). In response to a similar report from 2012, UNICEF Canada's executive director David Morley stated that "The face of poverty in Canada is a child's face—this is unacceptable. It is clearly time for Canada to make children a priority when planning budgets and spending our nation's resources, even in tough economic times" (UNICEF Canada 2012).

Critics of Canada's NCB program have argued for over a decade that focusing on impoverished children rather than on impoverished families relieves governments of the responsibility to alleviate the causes of poverty (see, for example, ibid.; Jensen 2002; Lefebvre and Merrigan 2003; O'Hara 1998). It is important to realize that children are poor because their parents are poor. Moreover, when we focus solely on children, the rights and concerns of adults become marginalized; their voices unheard. Once children have left the nest, poor parents are no longer entitled to benefits and risk falling into deeper poverty. This is not to say that governments should not invest in children but rather that governments also need to focus on alleviating the factors that aggravate adult poverty such as: (1) declining welfare incomes; (2) the low-wage wall (jobs with long hours, no or few benefits, and no opportunities for advancement or wage increases); (3)

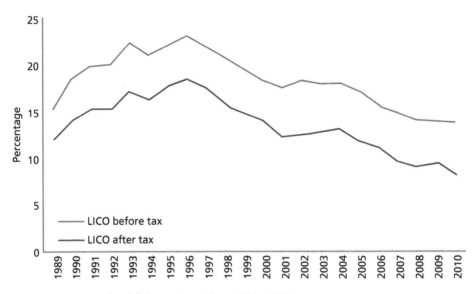

Figure 15.1   Canada Child Poverty Rates, 1989–2010

Source: deBoer, K., Rothwell, D.W. & Lee, C. (2013). "Child and family poverty in Canada: Implications for child welfare research." Canadian Child Welfare Research Portal Information Sheet # 123. Figure developed with data from: Statistics Canada. "CANSIM - 202-0802 - Persons in Low Income Families," 2013. Reprinted by permission of CWRP.

inadequate minimum wages; (4) reduced access to employment insurance; (5) shortages of affordable housing and help for the homeless; and (6) lack of quality, affordable child care spaces (National Council of Welfare 2006:5–7). The Canada Child Benefit recently introduced by the Trudeau Liberals promises to reduce child poverty by 40 per cent, the largest single drop in decades. The program, which is expected to cost approximately $22.4 billion over five years, will pull 300,000 of Canada's children out of poverty (*Toronto Star* 2016). In addition, under the new plan, families are expected to receive nearly $2,300 more annually, benefiting nine out of ten families in Canada (ibid.). But although the CCB is designed to benefit Canada's most vulnerable families, there is a need to develop policies tailored to the specific segments of the population that are most likely to suffer from the hardships that exacerbate poverty. Single mothers are a case in point.

Large disparities in poverty rates exist between family types. According to the 2014 Canadian Income Survey, poverty rates were approximately 11 per cent for two-parent families but 44.9 per cent for families with children under 18 headed by single-parent mothers (Statistics Canada 2016). More recent reports suggest that 20.3 per cent of children under six in Canada live in poverty (Campaign 2000 2015). Moreover, almost half of Indigenous children under the age of six (not living in Indigenous communities) live in a low-income family, while one in four Indigenous youth lives in poverty (Campaign 2000 2011; National Council on Welfare 2011). In addition, in one of the first studies of its kind, a recent report by the Canadian Centre for Policy Alternatives suggests that an alarming 60 per cent of Indigenous children on-reserve live in poverty (CCPA 2016). Further, 32 per cent of immigrant children and 22 per cent of racialized (visible minority) children live in poverty. And not surprisingly, there is also a fair amount of provincial variability in child poverty rates. British Columbia has the highest poverty rate at 20.4 per cent

(First Call BC 2015), whereas Prince Edward Island and Alberta report the lowest (4 per cent and 6.9 per cent, respectively) (Campaign 2000 2011:1).

Quebec has taken the lead in Canada in terms of implementing policies geared towards supporting families and reducing poverty. Since the implementation of its universal child care program and the 2004 **Act to Combat Poverty and Social Exclusion** was put into place, Quebec's child poverty rates have decreased dramatically, from 16.1 per cent in 2004 to 7.7 per cent in 2009 (Campaign 2000 2011:4). The province boasts the highest percentage of mothers who are in the workforce (CCSD 2008; Monsebraaten 2008), and funds have been allocated to promote the development of children living in poverty (Conference Board of Canada 2017). Indeed, according to recent estimates, Quebec had the lowest proportion of stay-at-home families in 2014 (13 per cent) as compared to 59 per cent in 1976 (Uppal 2015). The provincial government's own assessments of where Quebec stands in comparison to other provinces are indeed quite glowing (Ministère de la Famille et des Aînés 2011). Following Quebec's lead, Ontario and Newfoundland and Labrador have also taken poverty reduction initiatives. While it is too early to assess the total impact of these measures, Campaign 2000 has praised the progress shown in Newfoundland and Labrador (Campaign 2000 2011:2). Unfortunately, although the recently introduced CCB is a step in the right direction, Canada has yet to develop a comprehensive poverty reduction plan.

Although being employed offsets poverty to some degree, having only one earner in a family is not adequate for most families. As Campaign 2000's report card (2011:7) highlighted, 63 per cent of low-income children live in two-parent families. Further, one in three of all children in poverty live in families where at least one parent is employed full-time all year (ibid.:2). As a similar report by the Canadian Council on Social Development (2007) noted, even though the number of parents who are working has increased, "working poor parents are stuck behind a 'low wage wall' in poorly paid jobs with few, if any, benefits or opportunities for education, training, and advancement" (ibid.:3). As such, it is unlikely that they will rise above the poverty line without some form of assistance.

Of course, the poverty rate, which measures the risk of poverty within any given group, is important in judging policy. But so, too, is the number or percentage of poor families that exist in Canada. According to the National Council of Welfare (2004:110):

> One of the myths about child poverty is that since single-parent families have high poverty rates, most poor children must live in single-parent families. That has never been the case for any of the years on record. The largest number of poor children has always been the number living in two-parent families.

For example, although two-parent families have a relatively low poverty rate (10 per cent), children living in two-parent families accounted for 54 per cent of all poor children in Canada. In terms of non-two-parent families, 4 per cent of low-income children lived in families headed by single fathers, 40 per cent lived in families headed by single mothers, and 4 per cent were in other living arrangements (Child Care Advocacy Association of Canada 2011:10–11). Also telling is the fact that more than 863,492 Canadians relied on Canadian food banks in 2016, an increase of 1.3 per cent form 2015, and nearly a decade after the end of the 2008–09 recession. Moreover, approximately 36 per cent of food bank users are children (Food Banks Canada 2016). Contrary to the Canadian government's resolution in 1989 to eradicate poverty by the year 2000, the number of Canadians using food banks in 2007—that is, prior to the recession—had increased by 86 per cent (Canadian Council on Social Development 2008:6). The 2008–09 recession only worsened the matter. Furthermore, most food banks in this country continue to operate with little government assistance, with about a third of them operating with no paid staff (ibid.). Of importance too, is that a year before the recession, almost 40 per cent of Canadians believed that they were only one to two paycheques away from living in poverty (CCSD 2008:6).

In May 2002, Canada participated in the United Nations General Assembly Special Session on Children and, along with many other countries, signed the UN Declaration on "A World Fit for Children." In ratifying this document, the federal government promised to develop a national plan of action based on Canada's unique circumstances that took into consideration four priority areas: promoting healthy lives; providing quality education; protecting children against abuse, exploitation, and violence; and combating HIV/AIDS. In 2004, Ottawa released its plan, "**A Canada Fit for Children**," that reaffirmed the federal government's commitment to make children and families a national priority (see full report online at www.sdc.gc.ca).

Despite these efforts, critics have long claimed that the government is still not doing enough. For example, the Canadian Council on Social Development estimated that although the government's social investment has had some impact in that it kept 570,000 children out of poverty, CCTB benefits would need to be increased to $5,100 per child for real progress on child poverty (CCSD 2007:4). The National Council of Welfare (2004) echoed these concerns, charging that despite government promises to give priority to child poverty and work towards eliminating it, it has done little outside of gradually increasing child benefits.

In its latest report on child poverty in Canada, the Conference Board of Canada noted that Canada, at 14.7 per cent, has the second highest child poverty rates among 16 peer countries (Conference Board of Canada 2017). Government policies have obviously been inadequate, and the Canadian poverty rate stood at 12.6 per cent in 2013, up from 9.6 per cent in 2008 (ibid.). Indeed, according to estimates, more than 3.2 million Canadians, including 1 million children, live in poverty; one third of all Canadian children experience poverty for at least one year; one in four workers (2 million adults) are in low-wage employment; low-income two-parent families remain, on average, $7,300 below the poverty line; lone mothers and their children remain the most vulnerable to poverty; the poverty rates for Indigenous people, immigrants, and racialized people are more than double the average for non-racialized groups (National Council on Welfare 2011).

Following the Conservative Party victory in the 2011 federal election, fears among anti-poverty groups of a deepening morass were acute (Maki 2013). The 2012 budget, which included numerous cuts to government services, only deepened fears about increasing poverty (*Toronto Star* 2012). Among these cuts was the closure of the National Council of Welfare. Advocating for families on welfare, the council was a forerunner in fighting against provincial and territorial governments clawing back part of the federal Canada Child Tax Benefit (Kerstetter 2012). These welfare reforms particularly had an adverse impact on single mothers (Maki 2011, 2013). As Campaign 2000 warned at the time:

The federal budget not only ignores the current needs of Canada's children . . . but downloads much of today's costs onto them. The 639,000 children living in poverty will be joined by many more because of a budget that concentrates on business and global markets, while failing to address the critical need for universal childcare and affordable housing, public supports that assist families in realizing their economic potential (2012).

The critics had a point. Canadian families need better policy from their government. The recently introduced Child Care Benefit (CCB) by the Liberal government promises to reduce child poverty in half by benefiting families who need the most help. The extent to which these reforms in Canada's family policy will ameliorate the scourge of child poverty remains to be seen.

Impact of Measures on Child Care

One area where better policy can be helpful concerns child care. Despite all political discourse and efforts to this end over the past four decades, little has been done to provide affordable quality child care. Women have constituted a large part of the workforce for several decades, yet for countless working women the challenge of balancing work and family responsibilities remains daunting (see Case in Point box). Many are *forced out of the labour force* to care for their young children because they cannot afford to pay for child care or they do not have sufficient guarantees of return to employment. Conversely, others are virtually *forced back into employment* because they cannot sustain the income loss, even when receiving the limited unpaid parental leave benefits. Today, fathers have taken on more child care and domestic responsibilities than in the past and, as a consequence, they, too, can find the act of balancing work and family overwhelming. Parents often feel that it is their responsibility to overcome the challenges and problems associated with balancing family life, household work, and market work (Krull and Sempruch 2011b). This message is reinforced by society— one just has to look at the numerous self-help books in any bookstore that offer advice on how to be more creative with time management so to better balance family and work.

Regulated child care has always been a provincial and territorial jurisdiction. It follows that policy, child care services, and funding for child care vary considerably across jurisdictions. And with the exception of Quebec, subsidies are targeted to low-income families, leaving all other families to face exorbitant costs without help. Many parents

CASE IN POINT

Can We (or Should We) Balance Family and Paid Work?

Is it possible to balance family work (caregiving and household work) with paid work (employment)? This issue has challenged feminists, feminist scholars, children's activist organizations, and other family policy advocacy groups, not to mention fathers, mothers, their employers, and all levels of Canadian government. Most of the literature on this subject advocates for better, healthier, and equitable balance between family work and market work. However, others argue that we need to focus on integrating paid work/family work, not balancing the

continued

two as if they are in opposition to one another. Paid work and family have been set against each other, as if they are components in a zero sum game: to not achieve "balance" between the two is equated with failing at our jobs or failing our families (Krull and Sempruch 2011b). Most parents experience the stress of trying to reconcile the demands of their employment with their responsibilities towards—and desire to spend time with—their families. And it's not unusual that parents internalize their difficulties at achieving "balance," often seeing such time crunches as personal failure rather than the failure of our system.

For Maureen Baker, the problem is simple: "Canada and the liberal welfare states offer various programs to assist employed parents, but fathers still earn considerably more than mothers, women still perform more unpaid household work than men, most children remain with their mothers after parental separation, and welfare programs tend to push beneficiaries into low-paid jobs." It follows that existing policy needs to change. Margrit Eichler argues: "In terms of a policy effect, making household workers themselves aware of skills they may possess is only one aspect of a broader issue. Employers, particularly those in positions directly involved in hiring people, need not only to be aware of the skills that may be acquired through unpaid household work, but need to have tools with which to assess them." Margaret Hillyard Little offers a feminist approach: "as feminists, we need to demand increased state support of mothering. While we have been quick to see the limitations of the maternalist discourse of the nineteenth century, we need to make room for a political argument that embraces motherhood and all its demands and duties." Susan McDaniel proposes that "a shared work-valued care model would recognize the value of care as work and redistribute more equitably the costs and benefits of caring for both young and old, both of which, after all, are public 'goods'."

Quebec's family policies, admittedly expensive, offer a model for the rest of the country. Patrizia Albanese explains: "Even with limitations, including long waiting lists, the need to improve quality, and the need for more flexible options, Quebec's model of child care, coupled with its large and generous package of reforms, is unprecedented in North America. . . . at a time when women's work—paid and unpaid—has been central to the international drive for cheap and productive labour, it is high time that the Canadian state contribute, following the Quebec model, to assisting mothers in bearing their disproportionate share of the cost of social reproduction."

The traditional wife–husband/woman–man-based family is only one of a plethora of family forms; government and the private sector employment policies need to be shaped to meet the Canadian reality where more than sole male breadwinners are responsible for their families. As Susan McDaniel argues, it is time "we move beyond the trapeze image of a balancing act between paid work and the rest of our lives."

Source: Krull, Catherine, and Justyna Sempruch, eds. 2011. *A Life in Balance? Reopening the Family-Work Debate.* Vancouver, Toronto: UBC Press. Pp. 62, 95, 143, 204, 218.

cannot afford high-quality care, yet the effect that child care has on children ultimately depends on the quality of that care.

While feminists and advocacy groups have long recognized the urgent need for a government-supported quality child care program based on universality, it has remained elusive. As early as 1970, the Royal Commission on the Status of Women stressed the importance of a subsidized national child care program: "the time is past when society can refuse to provide community child care services in the hope of dissuading mothers from leaving their children and going to work" (in Jensen and Thompson 1999:12). The Royal Commission on Equality in Employment raised the subject again in 1984: "Child care is not a luxury, it is a necessity. Unless government policy responds to this urgency, we put women, children, and the economy of the future at risk. . . . policy should not be permitted to remain so greatly behind the times" (Armitage 2003:119). In 1982, a federally funded National Daycare Conference was held. The Katie Cooke Task Force, an outcome of the Conference, pushed for a universal daycare system over the next few years.

In 1988, the Canada Child Care Act was introduced in Parliament; it proposed an additional 200,000 subsidized child care spaces, doubling the number of existing spaces, which accommodated only 13 per cent of children needing care. The bill was not passed by the House of Commons (Armitage 2003). The issue became politicized, especially given the supposed desire of each federal party in parliament to end child poverty by 2000. Therefore, in 1993, the opposition Liberals provided a detailed proposal for a national child care program in their party manifesto, the so-called "Red Book"; but nothing came of it after they won the general election that year. The reason was simple. Daycare remained expensive—"while child care makes for good electioneering, delivering child care is a somewhat daunting enterprise" due to its enormous expense (Krashinsky 2001:3). Overall, 33 per cent of the cost of raising a child is due to child care costs compared to 23 per cent to provide shelter to a child (Child Care Advocacy Association of Canada 2007).

There also are not enough child care centres in Canada. Despite the fact that mothers comprise 70 per cent of the Canadian labour force, there are only enough regulated spaces for 20 per cent of young children (Child Care Advocacy Association of Canada 2011:3). In its recent Better Life Index, the OECD, which ranked Canada highly in almost all indicators, singled out low child care enrolment as a major issue, citing problems with "affordability and quality" (OECD 2011). As the OECD report went on to emphasize, the problem became especially acute among sole parents, thus necessitating greater governmental investment in child care.

By the late 1990s, talks on this matter resumed between the federal and provincial governments, culminating in a series of agreements that moved forward a national agenda for a universal child care package. In 2003, the Multilateral Framework on Early Learning and Child Care underscored an emerging federal–provincial consensus on the necessity of such a program (CCSD 2004:7). However, costs remained an issue for Paul Martin's Liberal government.

Little progress had been made by the autumn of 2004 when the OECD published its study of Canada's child care system, part of an overall review of such systems in 21 leading industrialized countries. Although the OECD lauded Canada's enhanced parental leave program, it found the country's child care system severely underfunded with no overarching goals, the training of many child care workers to be poor, and the problem of high staff turnover at many centres. Canadian parents were also expected to pay more for child care than in other countries, and despite Canada having one of the highest percentages of employed mothers, the Canadian government contributed half of what many developed countries in Europe did on child care. Less than 20 per cent of Canadian children under the age of seven had a space in a regulated centre, an extremely low figure compared to other industrialized countries such as Belgium (63 per cent), Denmark

(78 per cent), France (69 per cent), Portugal (40 per cent), and the UK (60 per cent) (OECD 2004:7). The OECD report concluded:

> During the 90s, growth in early childhood services slowed significantly in Canada. . . . The result is a patchwork of economic, fragmented services. . . . In the same period, other OECD countries have been progressing toward publicly managed, universal services focused on the development of young children . . . [which are] expected to play a significant role with respect to social cohesion, the alleviation of the effects of child poverty, improved child health and screening, better parenting and family engagement in education. (ibid.:6)

Among its many recommendations, the OECD suggested that Canada double its child care spending to the average of other OECD countries and that the federal and provincial governments each pay 40 per cent of daycare costs, leaving parents responsible for the remaining 20 per cent. It was also strongly recommended that child care workers be given better training and that child care be integrated with kindergarten.

Many Canadians were shocked by these findings. The Child Care Advocacy Association of Canada and the Coalition of Child Care Advocates of British Columbia together recommended that the federal government increase funding for child care from the current level of 0.25 per cent of GDP to 1 per cent (Child Care Advocacy Association of Canada 2011:7). For its part, the Canadian Council on Social Development argued earlier for substantially increased funding from the federal government and a commitment that a developmentally-focused child care system be implemented that achieved the principles of universality, quality, accessibility, and inclusion (CCSD 2004:9), proposals which received scant attention from the Conservative government of Stephen Harper. And despite campaign promises to help struggling families, the Trudeau government deferred urgently needed child care investment to the 2017 Budget. Nonetheless, as of late 2016, the federal and provincial/territorial governments were working to develop a National Child Care Framework, certainly a step in the right direction (Child Care Advocacy Association of Canada 2016). Indeed, many critics of the current system have suggested that the rest of Canada should look at Quebec as a model to build a national cohesive family policy (Albanese 2006, 2007b, 2011; Canadian Policy Research Networks 2003; Krull 2003, 2011; OECD 2004).

Daily Life
Hard Times: Child Care Costs in Canada

How expensive is it raise a child in Canada? Parents across Canada are paying a wide range of fees for child care, from a low of $164 a month in Montreal to a high of $1,649 for infant care in Toronto. And while the federal government has committed to a $500 million investment in child care in the 2017–18 budget, much work still needs to be done in order to offset the dramatically rising costs of child care in Canada (Monsebraaten 2017).

According to David MacDonald and Martha Friendly, researchers at the Canadian Centre for Policy Alternatives (CCPA), child care fees have risen three times faster than inflation, with some parents paying close to $1,000 more per year, per child, than they did two years ago. Toddler fees, in particular, have risen by eight per cent on average between 2014 and 2016, with Quebec City, Longueuil, Laval, and Gatineau witnessing an increase of 18 per cent ($27) during this period, followed closely by Burnaby ($180 per month) and Kitchener ($178 per month) (MacDonald and Friendly 2016).

In addition, MacDonald and Friendly found that cities with set child care fees tend to be more affordable than those that are market-driven; fixing child care fees at the provincial level may, therefore, improve affordability for families with young children. And along with government investment in high quality, affordable child care, there is a need to focus on improving the economic well-being of women so that they are better able to reconcile work and care commitments. As researcher Kate McInturff (2017) suggests in a recently released report, the right policies and choices will go a long way toward fixing Canada's child care problem and bringing much-needed relief to Canada's young families.

Quebec's Family Policies: An Example to Follow

In this context, Quebec's family policies have been distinct from those in the rest of the country in both their evolution and their success. There are several reasons for this. Until 1997, Quebec's family policies had been geared towards promoting population growth: a pro-natal strategy of "strength in numbers" (often referred to as "*la revanche des berceaux*"—"the revenge of the cradle") as a means of overcoming Quebec's subordination to English Canada and safeguarding Québécois culture. Second, there has been more govern-ment intervention and a stronger focus on universal support for families than in the rest of Canada. In this way, Quebec has moved beyond being a "liberal" wel-fare society, like Canada and the United States, and is moving towards a more heavily **state interventionist model**—similar to those in social democratic states such as the Scandinavian countries—but with its own distinctive characteristics. Finally, Quebec is unique in that, since 1997, it has had a comprehensive family policy directed at strength-ening families, assisting parents in balancing paid work and family responsibilities, and promoting parental employability—all of which are still lacking in the rest of Canada (also see Daily Life box).

For more on decision-making processes for parenting young children, see "Deciding to Parent" in Chapter 5, pp. 98–101.

Quebec's Pro-natal Policies

In the past two decades, there have been two major strategies to Quebec's family policy— **pronatalism** (1988–97) and strengthening families (1997–present). Its pro-natal policies were in part a reaction to the many changes that occurred to family life as a result of the province's Quiet Revolution during the premiership of Jean Lesage (1960–6). Quebec's new nationalism, often referred to as the "Quiet Revolution" because it "quietly" but radically transformed and secularized Québécois society, generated liberal values, advanced the French language and education for both sexes, and provided an environment conducive to feminist reform (Behiels 1986; Comeau 1989; Thomson 1984). Consequently, beginning in the 1960s, Quebec society witnessed historic changes to family life and to the status of women, including sharp increases in cohabitation, divorce, and births to unmarried women, as well as substantial declines in religiosity, marriages, and births (Albanese 2006, 2007a, 2007b, 2009, 2011; Baker 1994; Baril, Lefebvre, and Merrigan 2000; Krull 2003, 2007, 2011, 2012; Langlois et al. 1992). The sharp decrease in births—from an average of five children per woman in 1959 to 1.37 in 1987—was particularly alarming to Quebec nationalists, who were concerned that Québécois culture would be in jeopardy if the population continued to decline (Krull 2003; Maroney 1992; Maximova 2004:3).

Advocating direct government intervention, politicians and demographers proposed a monetary incentive program to elevate fertility levels. In a population-engineering effort unprecedented in North America, the Quebec government implemented three programs of direct financial assistance in 1988: allowances for newborns that, after amendments, paid women $500 for a first birth, $1,000 for a second, and $8,000 for third and subsequent births; a family allowance for all children under 18 years; and additional allowances for children under six years. Three rules underscored these programs: universality; monetary increases according to the rank—first, second, and so on—of the child; and more money for young children.

Reactions to the policies varied (Baker 1994; Hamilton 1995; Krull 2003). Non-interventionists argued that fertility decisions were individual, not governmental, responsibilities. Feminists charged that Quebec's pro-natal policies marginalized women, reducing them to objects of demographic policy (Maroney 1992). Social interventionists supported government action, not through pro-natalist intervention but through social policies to improve female equity and assist families. Of particular importance were policies to decrease tensions between employment and family responsibilities. These critiques coincided with a growing awareness that Quebec's incentive policies were not producing expected birth increases—families with three or more children remained atypical. Importantly, policies favouring third and subsequent children were viewed increasingly as contrary to the needs of most families.

From Pronatalism to Pro-family

Quebec radically transformed its family and child support programs in 1997. It created the Ministère de la Famille et de l'Enfance (Ministry of Families and Children) and gave it a budget of $500 million. The new ministry's agenda was threefold (Ministère de la Famille et de l'Enfance 1999). The first objective was to establish a unified child allowance program for low-income families—the amount of allowances would depend on the number of dependent children under 18 years, family type (single-parent, two-parent), and income (a threshold of $15,332 for single-parent families; $21,825 for two-parent families). This allowance was meant to supplement the CCTB, which Quebec found to be insufficient for a family to survive. The second objective was to implement a maternity–parental leave insurance plan whereby parental remuneration increased during and following pregnancy. The third objective was to provide a network of government-regulated, highly subsidized ($5 per day) child care facilities that offered a quality educational program to children from birth to kindergarten age. Parents who qualified for an income supplement program had only to pay $2 per day. By September 1997, all but the parental insurance plan had been implemented.

These three policy initiatives demonstrate the Quebec government's efforts at strengthening families and distinguish Quebec's strategy from those in the rest of Canada, the US, and many European countries. Presently, Quebec is the only province to have universal subsidized daycare. Although the amount that parents pay increased from $5 per day to $7 per day in January 2004, the amount is negligible compared to the amounts paid in other provinces (Albanese 2006, 2007a, 2009; Ministère de l'Emploi, de la Solidarité sociale et de la Famille 2005). The average monthly cost of daycare in Ontario is about $960 compared to $140–$200 in Quebec (Peacock 2012). And in this equation, the portion of cost assumed by the Quebec government is approximately 82 per cent of the overall cost (Hamilton 2004). Parents on social assistance are not charged for the first 23.5 hours per week and, if they enroll in an employability program, they are not charged for additional hours. To facilitate child care, employees can also take an annual maximum of 10 days away from work for family reasons.

In developing universal policy initiatives like low-cost child care services, a range of tax credits, and full-day kindergarten for five-year-olds, Quebec can no longer be classified as a liberal welfare state (Dandurand and Kempeners 2002; Jensen 2002). Policy initiatives in liberal welfare states, such as the rest of Canada and the US, favour targeting specific kinds of families, such as those with low incomes, rather than supporting all of them. Moreover, liberal welfare states are reluctant to involve themselves in the day-to-day activities of family life, including the problems involved with balancing paid work and family life. In this way, based on its child care and family policy initiatives, Quebec is moving towards the more heavily state interventionist model—**social democracy**—of the Scandinavian countries (Beauvais and Dufour 2003).

Quebec's existing family allowance is also innovative. While it targets low-income families with children under 18, the amount paid out is inversely related to the number of adults living in the house: the more adults in the household, the less received in benefits. Thus, single-parent families receive the most in benefits and tax breaks. The design decisions "reflect nothing of the 'moral panic' about lone mothers characterizing some liberal welfare states in the years of welfare reform. Nor do they reproduce the neutrality of programs that do not take into account the particular difficulties faced by lone parents" (Jensen 2002:310). Critics charge that these new initiatives fall short of a universal, non-gender-specific program that assists all types of parenting. The family allowance program provides targeted assistance aimed almost exclusively at working low-income families rather than universal assistance. Moreover, the programs are also expensive and consequently taxes have increased—40 per cent of Quebec's program is now paid for by tax revenues (CUPE Ontario 2008). And in order to offset these costs, Premier Philippe Couillard of the Quebec Liberal Party announced a new "sliding scale" fee structure for Quebec's daycares. Under these new rules, families with a total income of less than

$55,000 will continue to pay the base amount of $7.30, but for those families whose income is more than $150, 000, this could imply having to pay as much as $20 per day per child (CBC News 2014). While critics have soundly criticized these changes, Quebec's daycares continue to be the most affordable in the country.

Further, some critics charge that although Quebec's family policies promote the financial incentive for parents to work, they have inadvertently limited women's choices by offering more assistance to families with employed mothers than to those in which the mother stays at home (Vincent 2000:3). And pro-natal objectives continue to impinge on policy. Quebec's Family Minister in 2005, Michelle Courchesne, said of the proposed parental leave plan: "We feel that this sort of program will encourage . . . families to give birth, and maybe to have more children" (in Wyatt 2005:A5). And according to Stéphane Le Bouyonnec, President of the policy commission for the Action Démocratique du Québec (ADQ), "If we have more babies, it would bring a lot more prosperity to this nation. It's a key factor for investors to invest in Quebec. . . . We have to have a nation that will be strong and survive in 20 years. . . . If we don't change our approach, we will decline as a nation" (Séguin 2008).

Yet, despite these limitations, Quebec continues its efforts to strengthen families and increase the employability of parents. Since March 2004, Quebecers no longer pay provincial sales tax on diapers, baby bottles, and nursing items, and a new child assistance program has replaced family allowances, the non-refundable tax credit for dependent children, and the tax reduction for families (Ministère de l'Emploi, de la Solidarité sociale et de la Famille 2005; Régie des rentes du Québec 2012). While in the 1990s Quebec daycares were frequently overcrowded, had long waiting lists, and were characterized by high teacher to child ratios (Thompson 1999:F7; see also Government of Quebec 1999:Sections 4.4–4.7), the situation in the province is currently quite different. In Quebec, regulated child care spaces provided by the province—all of which are subsidized—increased from 78,388 in 1992 to 368,909 in 2008, the highest such increase in Canada (Childcare Resource and Research Unit, Canada 2007:15; Ministère de la Famille et des Aînés 2011:20). During the September 2012 campaign season, the Parti Québécois rolled out an election platform promising 15,000 additional daycare spots—a place for every child in Quebec—family leave to permit parents to care for children and other family members who are "vulnerable, disabled, or elderly," plus, for families that earn $130,000 or less, a $500 tax credit for children aged 5 to 16 who enroll in sports or arts (Beaudin 2012). Forming a minority government after the election, the Parti Québécois was largely kept from delivering on these expensive promises in an environment of fiscal constraint, a scenario that Quebec's thirty-first premier, Philippe Couillard of the Quebec Liberal Party, is facing today. Nevertheless, Quebec continues to be a pioneer in quality and affordable child care in Canada.

In addition, the new family assistance program, paying out more than the three previous ones together, disburses funds every three months to families with children under the age of 18. The payments are dependent upon the number of children, the family income, and the family situation. The monthly maximum for child assistance is $2,392 for the first child, $1,195 for the second and third children, and $1,793 for each additional child, with an additional $839 for single-parent families. Monthly minimum amounts are $671 for the first child, with $620 for each additional child and $335 awarded to single-parent families (Régie des rentes du Québec 2016). In both cases, the amount paid decreases in a ratio determined by a family's net income exceeding the thresholds. In some circumstances, single-parent families can obtain an additional $700 per year; and in one special case, regardless of parental income, families qualify for a monthly supplement of $189 for each child with a disability (ibid.).

Efforts were also stepped up in 2005 to ensure the employability of parents. A work premium was introduced to encourage low-income parents to remain employed. As with the new child assistance program, the amount of the premium depends on net income and family type to an annual maximum of $3,600 per year for two-parent families and $2,400 for single-parent families (Revenu Québec 2016). In 2006, Quebec withdrew from the federal parental leave program and established its own comprehensive program, which was expected to cost $1.6 billion in 2009, an increase from the 2007 rate of $1.45 billion (Dube 2008; Krull 2007; Ministère des Finances 2009:2). To date, it is the most generous and flexible parental leave program in Canada. The federal program pays new mothers 55 per cent of their insurable earnings for 15 weeks and now covers self-employed women (Government of Canada 2011a). In contrast, the Quebec program offers new mothers, including self-employed mothers, two options: (1) 75 per cent of their insurable earnings for 15 weeks or (2) 70 per cent of insurable earnings for 18 weeks. While both programs offer new parents 35 weeks of shared leave, the Quebec program offers an additional five weeks of paid leave for just fathers. It is not surprising then that 77.6 per cent of Quebec men took paternity leave in 2010 compared to only 11.1 per cent of men in the rest of Canada (Government of Canada 2011a). It is also telling that while child care initiatives dominated Quebec's 2008 provincial election, little attention was given to child care in the federal election campaign that same year, and while the Liberal Party proposed a billion-dollar child care fund in the 2011 federal campaign, the issue was marginal (CTV News 2011).

Quebec's family policies remain the most innovative and ambitious in Canada (Albanese 2011; CPRN/RCPPP 2003; Krull 2011a, 2012; Lefebvre and Merrigan 2003; OECD 2004; Ross 2006). In fact, the Canadian Policy Research Networks (CPRN/RCPPP) claims that "Quebec provides North America's only example of an integrated approach to family policy. It stands as proof that there is room in market-oriented countries for progressive public policies designed specifically for families" (2003:2).

The rest of Canada can take some lessons from Quebec in designing effective national policy directed at strengthening families. Perhaps the strongest lesson that can be learned is the benefit of assisting *all* families to better balance employment and family responsibilities, and that families are strengthened not simply by supplementing incomes with small amounts of money but by increasing employability. For the Quebec government: "Poverty is less present in families with full-time jobs. This is why the government has chosen to fight against it not only through providing financial support to the poorest families but also in the field of employment by offering parents conditions making it easier to balance family and job responsibilities" (quoted in Jensen 2002:311). Quebec's progress is recognized internationally. In its otherwise unfavourable report card on child care in Canada, the OECD praised the "extraordinary advance made by Quebec, which has launched one of the most ambitious and interesting early education and care policies in North America" (OECD 2004:55).

Questions for Critical Thought

Should Canada have a universal daycare system? What might be some advantages and/or disadvantages of such a system?

Looking Back, Looking Ahead

With a policy modelled on Quebec's subsidized daycare program, the Liberal Party led by Paul Martin promised during the 2004 federal election campaign to create 250,000 child care spaces by 2009. On October 5, 2004, just as the OECD findings were being made public, the Martin government used the occasion of the Speech from the Throne to tell Canadians: "For a decade, all governments have understood that the most important investment that can be made is in our children. . . . Parents must have real choices: children must have real opportunities to learn" (Office of the Prime Minister 2004). The next day, Prime Minister Martin laid out his government's commitment to "a strong, Canada-wide program of early learning and care for our children, which is the single best investment we can make in their future and in ours" (ibid.).

By November 2004 the federal and provincial governments had agreed on a series of principles for a national child care program: quality, universal inclusion, accessibility, and a developmental focus (Galloway 2004). Reaching agreement was actually not difficult, as these principles were essentially the same as those proffered consistently for 35 years: from the proposals of the 1970 Royal Commission on the Status of Women, to those of advocacy groups and the Quebec government in the 1980s and after, to the Liberal "Red Book." The problem lay in the details. Even before the principles were agreed, the Quebec government made public its position that it wanted "the right to opt out of any national daycare program with full compensation" since it already had an established child care system and it only needed additional federal funds to make its own improvements (Séguin and Galloway 2004).

In their 2005 budget, the federal Liberal government allocated $5 billion over five years to develop a national system of early learning and child care, adding the proviso that "federal support will need to be ongoing beyond these initial years" (Galloway 2005). But desirous of wanting to get a country-wide system into place, the federal government declared that the "provinces will have access to $700 million [the first year's disbursement] in child care funds to spend virtually as they please."

By the fall of 2005, all 10 provinces finally entered into agreement with the federal government—although the conditions for receiving federal funding varied from province to province. However, the national child care program re-emerged as a divisive yet central political issue during the federal election campaign of December 2005–January 2006. Paul Martin again stressed the importance of a national system of regulated daycare, promising to more than double his government's $5 billion commitment if the Liberals remained in power. Stephen Harper and the Conservative Party, on the other hand, promoted a policy of paying parents $1,200 annually per preschool child, arguing that this would enable parents the freedom of choosing their own child care options. Interestingly, men and women were divided over these competing visions of child care. According to a survey by the Strategic Council, women tended to favour the Liberal policy of a national child care program whereas men typically preferred the Conservative proposal for parents receiving federal funds directly (Laghi 2005:A4).

Having won the 2006, 2008, and 2011 elections, the Conservative Party upheld its family allowance program, the Universal Child Care Benefit, which paid $1,200 annually per preschool child (Canada Revenue Agency 2012), an amount raised to $1,920 in 2015 (Canada Revenue Agency 2015). From its inception, the policy has been heavily criticized. Early critics view it as a step backwards, comparing it to that of Mackenzie King's 1945 Family Allowance (*Globe and Mail* 2005). The Caledon Institute, a think tank that focuses on Canadian child care, also chastised the Conservatives for its child care allowance policy, particularly because it eliminated the young-child supplement of the Canada Child Tax Benefit. In 2006, Ken Battle, the Institute's president, argued that the elimination of the young-child supplement, which is approximately $249 annually, "makes the inequality gap between the child care allowance benefits for low- and modest-income families and high-income families all the wider, because the low-income families are losing that $249 annually whereas higher-income families never got it" (Galloway 2006:A1).

On September 20, 2011, the Harper government tabled the **Helping Families in Need Act** (Press Release 2012). In essence, the Act modified the existing Employment Insurance Act (EI) to give new foster parents speedier parental benefits; allow the self-employed to receive EI maternity, parental, sickness, and compassionate care benefits; improve EI parental benefits for military families; and extend compassionate care benefits for families of the "gravely ill." Additionally, a change to the Canada Labour Code would allow unpaid parental leave in the cases of both "critically ill" children and where children die or disappear as a result of a criminal act. Yet, while certainly an advance, this Act primarily constituted a refinement of fiscal policy—tinkering with EI legislation— rather than formulating any kind of all-inclusive social policy. The Act's purpose was limited, helping important, but select groups: foster parents, the self-employed, military families, and families with children who are either severely ill or have suffered criminal acts. It came into effect on December 14, 2012. Despite its name, however, which might be better expressed as the "Helping Some Families Act," this legislation runs parallel to but is not integrated with family policy. As Philip Toone, former NDP MP for Gaspésie– Îles-de-la-Madeleine (Québec) said just before its passage, "This will make it possible for parents to extend their parental leave by the number of sick days taken during that period. The same goes for time spent serving in the Canadian Forces Reserves. This and many other aspects of the bill are quite worthwhile" (Openparliament.ca 2012a).

On November 4, 2015, the Liberal Party's Justin Trudeau was sworn in as the twenty-third prime minister of Canada. The alleviation of child poverty and support for Canada's middle-income families was a campaign promise that the Liberals are working towards fulfilling. The Trudeau government set the ball rolling with the Canada Child Benefit, which came into effect in July 2016. Nine out of ten Canadian families are expected to benefit from the CCB. Although this is a commendable measure, the momentum needs to be kept going. Stasis in the making of family policy by federal and provincial governments cannot come just as action is needed to address the rapid changes that continue to shape the country's bedrock social institution. As the 2016 and the 2011 Censuses show, Canadian families are now as diverse as they have ever been. In turn, such diversity necessitates active policy-making by government. As one columnist remarked, the Census data suggest "there is room now for new policy specifically designed to address the needs of non-conventional families, and sold as such" (Den Tandt 2012). Canada is a land of immigrants, and multigenerational living is slowly becoming the norm (Khan and Kobayashi forthcoming). Yet the hurdles that must be overcome for those seeking a proactive and progressive approach to family policy in Canada are significant.

Conclusion

Effective family policies must reflect modern Canada, but we have yet to achieve that and policies have not responded to dramatic changes within families: the **individual responsibility family model** needs abandoning (Eichler 1997). It views fathers and mothers as equally responsible for family economic well-being and providing care to family members. State responsibilities arise only when husbands/fathers or wives/mothers are absent or cannot fulfil their responsibilities.

More efficient is the **social responsibility model**: minimizing gender stratification without privileging legal marriage over other relationships. Parents bear responsibility for their children's economic well-being whether residing with them or not. With residency not determining responsibility, caring for children is also society's obligation. Accordingly, the state would not distinguish between same-sex and heterosexual couples/parents entitled to the same state benefits.

Comprehensive child care would integrate family and market employment. Policy-makers often view the home and work place as distinct spheres in "conflict" or in need of "balance" (Krull and Sempruch 2011a). In the male breadwinner model, households and paid work are incompatible. Women labour at home out of love and concern for their families. Market work, conversely, is "real" work, its value determined by wages. Viewing family and work as irreconcilable creates illusions about careful balance: family pressures not interfering with employment and employment pressures not diminishing family life. Policies focused on balancing family and work have the negative side effect of reproducing and reinforcing the normative heterosexual "**gender contract**"—male breadwinner/female caregiver.

Canada needs to emulate the family-centred child care policies of Quebec and of Scandinavian countries that assume parents' right to employment while caring for their families regardless of gender, class, sexuality, or marital status. They integrate family and employment responsibilities. Fathers' involvement in child care is central, breaking hegemonic assumptions about household and child care work as peripheral to market work. Moreover, the heart of these policies assumes a state integral in supporting all family forms and promoting gender equity.

The essential reason for minimal state involvement in overall family policies resides in Canada being a federal liberal welfare state; different governments have different roles in policy-making. Of course, governments have not abdicated responsibility for families.

Paid maternity leave and child and family benefits, plus the plan "A Canada Fit for Children," show state willingness to help. But for every advance, there are failures—the 2005 Liberal national child care program is exemplary.

Instead of a comprehensive national policy, Canada possesses piecemeal family programs and policies; and the state has lagged in meeting the socio-economic changes affecting families. Concerning child care, the rest of Canada has an opportunity to employ Quebec's effective example. Doing so will take more than public money; inter-governmental co-operation and policy require a realistic understanding of contemporary Canadian families. The state and Canadians who give it legitimacy face an immense challenge.

Study Questions

1. What challenges does Canada face in developing a cohesive national family policy?
2. What are the strengths and weaknesses of both targeted and universal family policies?
3. Why have market work and household work been socially construed as distinct spheres? What consequences does this bifurcation have for policy? For gender equity?
4. Discuss why a social responsibility model of the family should improve family policies.
5. Do you think that child poverty can be eradicated by the construction and funding of a comprehensive national child care policy? Explain.
6. In what ways do Canada's current family policies privilege and reinforce the hegemonic nuclear family and traditional gender roles?

Further Readings

Albanese, Patrizia. 2009. *Child Poverty in Canada*. Toronto: Oxford University Press. Focusing on child poverty in Canada, especially since 1989, Albanese discusses why children, especially certain children, are vulnerable. She examines the consequences of child poverty and assesses why Canada has done so poorly in comparison to other countries. She also discusses possible means to obviate child poverty.

Baker, Maureen. 2006. *Restructuring Family Policies: Convergences and Divergences*. Toronto: University of Toronto Press. Adopting a feminist political economy approach and drawing on national and international research, Maureen Baker demonstrates that nation states with the best outcomes for families offer a variety of social supports. She provides a very extensive treatment of the literature on families.

Blake, Raymond. 2008. *From Rights to Needs: A History of Family Allowances in Canada, 1929–92*. Vancouver, BC: UBC Press. Raymond Blake focuses on the historical–political question of how policies are made while examining the history of family allowances in Canada from their debut in the House of Commons in 1929 to their demise under the Mulroney Government in 1992.

Doucet, Andrea. 2006. *Do Men Mother?: Fathering, Care and Domestic Responsibility*. Toronto: University of Toronto Press. Based on extensive interviews with over 100 fathers, Andrea Doucet demonstrates how men are transforming traditional parenting models. The book focuses on the following key questions: What leads fathers to trade earning for caring? How do fathers navigate through the "maternal worlds" of mothers and infants? Are men mothering or are they redefining fatherhood?

Eichler, Margrit. 1997. *Family Shifts: Families, Policies and Gender Equality*. Toronto: Oxford University Press. This is a classic source to see how families and family policy have changed over the past century in Canada. Eichler offers policy-makers a more realistic and improved family model from which to build future family policies.

Gambles, Richenda, Suzan Lewis, and Rhona Rapoport. 2006. *The Myth of Work–Life Balance: The Challenge of Our Time for Men, Women and Societies*. New York: Wiley. These authors challenge the idea that it is the individual's responsibility to "balance" paid work with other parts of life. Drawing research from seven diverse countries—India, Japan, the Netherlands, Norway, South Africa, the UK, and the US—this book demonstrates that "work–life balance" cannot be achieved through quick fixes and suggests ways that work and workplace need to be reorganized so that people can integrate family life with their paid work.

Gilbert, Neil. 2008. *A Mother's Work: How Feminism, the Market, and Policy Shape Family Life*. New Haven, CT: Yale University Press. Neil Gilbert challenges the conventional view on how to balance motherhood and employment, and examines at the national and international levels how the choices women make are influenced by the culture of capitalism, feminist expectations, and the social policies of the welfare state.

Krull, Catherine, and Justyna Sempruch. 2011. *A Life in Balance? Reopening the Family-Work Debate*. Vancouver, BC: UBC Press. This book challenges the notion—often offered in support of neo-liberal agendas—that paid work (employment) and unpaid work (caregiving and housework) are separate and competing spheres, rather than overlapping aspects of a single existence. The premise of the book is that alternative approaches to integrating work and family have to be taken into account if we hope to build truly equitable family and child care policies. Possible means of achieving this are discussed.

Key Terms

A Canada Fit for Children A commitment made by the federal government in 2004 towards making the well-being of children and families a national priority.

Act to Combat Poverty and Social Exclusion (Loi visant à lutter contre la pauvreté et l'exclusion sociale) Introduced in 2002 by the provincial government of Quebec, the Act makes the reduction of poverty and social exclusion an explicit government policy.

Bill 40 Amendments introduced by the Alberta provincial government to their Child, Youth, and Family Enhancement Act in 2004. Under Bill 40, parents who adopt a child who has been a permanent ward of the provincial government will receive the same benefits given to foster parents until the child turns 18 years of age.

Canada Child Benefit (CCB) Under Justin Trudeau, the Liberal government replaced the CCTB, including the NCBS and the UCCB, with the Canada Child Benefit (CCB) in July 2016. The CCB, a tax-free monthly payment made to eligible families, provides a maximum annual benefit of up to $5,400, per child, aged 6 though 17, and $6,400 for children under six.

Canada Child Tax Benefit (CCTB) Introduced by the Liberal government of Jean Chrétien in 1998, this was a new name for the CTB.

Child Tax Benefit (CTB) Introduced by the Conservative government in 1993 by abolishing both Family Allowance and the non-refundable tax credit, the CTB paid low-income families an annual amount for each child, an additional supplement for each subsequent child under seven years of age, and a Working Income Supplement (WIS).

Family policy This term encompasses government sponsored public programs that aim to assist families. Some examples include maternal, paternal, and parental leave benefits; child care subsidies; assistance to low-income families; etc.

Gender contract The idea of an "agreement" between women and men, implying agreed-upon commitments, rights, and responsibilities within the family. It reinforces and reproduces heteronormative values.

Helping Families in Need Act Introduced by the Harper government in 2011, it modified the existing Employment Insurance Act to give new foster parents speedier parental benefits and to allow the self-employed to receive EI maternity, parental, sickness, and compassionate care benefits.

Individual responsibility family model States that husband and wife are equally responsible for the economic well-being of their own selves, each other, their dependent children, and other family members who may require their care.

Liberal welfare state A concept of government based on the principle of market dominance and private enterprise; the state intervenes only to help the very needy; benefits are for the most part means-tested.

Maternity benefits Employment insurance maternity benefits are offered to biological mothers, including surrogate mothers, who cannot work because they are pregnant or have recently given birth.

National Child Benefit (NCB) Introduced in 1998 by the Liberal government of Jean Chrétien, the NCB included the Canada Child Tax Benefit (CCTB)—just a new name for the previous CTB—and the National Child Benefit Supplement (NCBS), which replaced the Working Income Supplement (WIS).

National Child Benefit Supplement (NCBS) Introduced in 1998 by the Liberal government of Jean Chrétien, it replaced the Working Income Supplement (WIS).

National Council of Welfare A federal advisory board with a mandate devoted exclusively to fight poverty and cutbacks to the welfare system and with no private sector equivalent; it was a forerunner in fighting against provincial and territorial governments clawing back part of the federal Canada Child Tax Benefit.

Parental leave An employee benefit, which includes maternity leave, paternity leave, and adoption leave.

Pronatalism The belief that child-bearing and parenthood are socially desirable and beneficial.

Social democracy A democratically elected system of government in which the state aims to provide security and equality for its people.

Social responsibility model States that the public shares responsibility with both parents for the care of dependent children. Parents retain parental responsibilities even if they do not live with children, and society steps in to help when a parent is unable to provide for their dependent children.

State interventionist model A policy perspective that promotes government intervention with an aim to enhance the lives of people.

Universal Child Care Benefit (UCCB) A monthly allowance of $100 (changed to $160 in 2015) for families with children under the age of six, introduced by the Conservative government and in place from July 2007–July 2016.

Working Income Supplement (WIS) An allowance introduced by the Conservative government in 1993 by abolishing both Family Allowance and the non-refundable tax credit. It was paid to low-income families along with the CTB.

Working While on Claim A federal pilot project, which stipulates that, until August 11, 2018, once parents have served the waiting period, they will be able to keep 50 cents of the Employment Insurance benefits for every dollar that they earn, until the 90 per cent threshold of the weekly insurable earnings used to calculate the benefits has been reached. Any money earned above this threshold is subject to a dollar for dollar deduction from benefits.

Note

1. Foster children are defined by Statistics Canada as "'other relatives' in an economic family, that is, a group of two or more persons who live in the same dwelling and are related to each other by blood, marriage, common-law, adoption or foster relationship" (Statistics Canada 2012a:17).

 Interested in finding out more? Visit www.oupcanada.com/Albanese4e for access to a list of recommended websites for this chapter.

The Past of the Future
and the Future of the Family

MARGRIT EICHLER

LEARNING OBJECTIVES

- To learn about the various bases on which predictions can be made

- To appreciate the inherent difficulties in making predictions

- To place the family into a societal context

- To appreciate the extent of environmental changes that will confront families in the future

- To consider the implications of such changes for families

Introduction

Making predictions is a risky business—they may come back to haunt one. My first reaction was dismay when I was invited to contribute a chapter to this book on the future of the family—on what basis could I possibly make any sensible predictions? Then a colleague suggested that I look at past predictions.[1] This has turned what might have been a very difficult and ultimately self-defeating undertaking into an instructive and enjoyable exercise.

I decided to restrict my review of old predictions to those published at the latest in 1975, meaning that enough time has passed to judge whether the predictions have come true or not.

Family sociology within Canada is a relatively young sub-discipline. The first monograph on the family in Canada was written by Frederick Elkin and published in 1964 (Elkin 1964). In her overview of the development of family studies in Canada, Nett identifies the 1970s and 1980s as the "period of Canadianization and policy concerns" (Nett 1988:9), but Canadian publishing about families really only took off in the 1980s. My search for older sources therefore netted primarily American and some British authors. The oldest source I found is from 1930. The search for old predictions turned up some very surprising results. Most prominently, the time at which a prediction was made bore

For more on the history of theorizing in family studies, see "Theoretical and Methodological Approaches to Studying Families" in Chapter 1, pp. 15–22.

no relation to its accuracy. Some older predictions are much more accurate than some that were made significantly later. This being the case, I discarded the notion of ordering the predictions in terms of the time at which they were formulated.

It did not seem advantageous to group predictions in terms of their accuracy or inaccuracy, since I found some of both on virtually every theme. I finally decided to group predictions by topic to avoid repetition and allow for a comparison between successful, unsuccessful, and partially successful predictions under every heading.

This chapter is therefore organized in three parts. First, I examine past predictions about the future of the family, then I consider the basis on which such predictions are made and attempt to determine which bases seem to yield more solid predictions, and third, I engage—with hesitation and much trepidation—in the risky business of making some predictions myself.

Questions for Critical Thought

Before we begin with predictions from scholars of the family, given what you've read in this book, what three predictions would you make about the future of families in Canada?

Past Predictions about the Family

The observations of Baber (1953) on marriage, from over sixty years ago, still seem relevant today:

> There are three types of opinion on marriage: (1) the opinion held by those who consider monogamic, indissoluble [heterosexual] marriage the only divinely sanctioned form and therefore the only one that can ever be tolerated; (2) the opinion held by those few sophisticates at the other extreme that not only is the usefulness of marriage past but also it is now doing a genuine disservice to the family and should be immediately abolished; (3) the opinion held by the vast number of persons in between these extremes that marriage performs valuable service in regularizing sex relations and stabilizing the primary group in which children are reared and that it should be not indissoluble but subject to correction and improvement. The latter are not willing to say that monogamy must always prevail, but only that at present it fits into our total culture pattern better than any other form. It is conceivable that a condition might arise that would call for some other form of marriage (Baber 1953:681–2).

Correspondingly, we have a slew of predictions, from sociologists committed to Baber's second opinion concerning marriage, that the family is dead or dying, and opposing views by those who hold to one of the other opinions.

The Future of the Family/Marriage as an Institution

Predictions that the family is about to disintegrate and disappear seem as old as the family itself. Between 1930 and 1970, there was a lot of concern with the "disintegration of the family." Paul wrote in 1930 in the UK that "the disintegration of the family is going on, and something will have to take its place" (Paul 1930:38). In the US, Sorokin thought in 1941 that the family had "passed from mere instability into the process of actual disintegration" (cited after Baber 1953:678). In 1947, Zimmerman suggested that "the family system will continue headlong its present trend toward nihilism" (Zimmerman 1947:808).

In 1949[2] and again in 1959, Anshen commented that in the US "the present collapse of marriage and the family is a perverted triumph of a profaned passion which in truth now largely consists in a reversion to abduction and rape" (Anshen 1959:512). This is a particularly interesting comment, since the 1950s are often held up as the golden age of the family in North America.

This negative view of the future of the family could easily be carried forward into modern times. To the authors who argued that the family is a dying institution, Nimkoff replied that the same arguments used to demonstrate the collapse of the family can be used to support precisely the opposite. "The issue may be stated thus: Does the individual exist for the family, or does the family exist for the individual?" He suggested that "[t]he totalitarian family organization is as real as the totalitarian state" (Nimkoff 1947:603). In his time, family subservience had given way to individualization—which he saw by and large as a positive development, but which authors who subscribe to marriage as a monolithic, indissoluble institution interpret in wholly negative terms.

By the same token, others have argued that marriage and the family are ongoing concerns that have adapted to very different circumstances for a very long period of time and that they would continue to do so. Linton, an American anthropologist, after reflecting on this issue, concluded simply: "The ancient trinity of father, mother, and child has survived more vicissitudes than any other human relationship. It is the bedrock underlying all other family structures" (Linton 1959:52). He would probably not insist that the father has to be the biological father of the child.

Cavan concluded her book as follows:

> The exact form of family that will emerge cannot be fully predicted, but present research indicates the need for a family that is flexible, with leeway for individual development; adjustable to external social conditions, keyed to mobility and social change; interdependent with other institutions; and ready to accept important though limited functions, such as meeting personal and sexual needs, giving emotional security, and rearing children for life in an industrialized, urban society. (Cavan 1963:533)

Ten years later, Bernard asked rhetorically "does marriage *have* a future?" and answered with an unequivocal "yes," although both its name and form might change. She added, "I do not see the traditional form of marriage retaining its monopolistic sway. I see, rather, a future of marital options" (Bernard 1972:301–2)—which is, of course, what

For more on historical and
contemporary variations of
the family, see Chapter 2.

we find today in Canada: legal and common-law marriages, dual-earner couples, traditional breadwinner couples, and some non-traditional bread-winner couples in which the wife is the breadwinner and the husband the stay-at-home parent and spouse, as well as same-sex couples with and without children.

Communal Family Structures/Group Marriages

The authors cited above who are predicting the disappearance of the monogamous, nuclear family see this as a negative, terrible event, threatening the very existence of civilization. In contrast, by the late 1960s and early 1970s a considerable number of intellectuals and authors believed that this form of the family was basically passé and that alternative structures were needed. This was the time of the hippie movement; significant numbers of communes had sprung up in its wake, and various authors had created attractive fictional accounts of communal families (e.g., Skinner 1948). The women's movement had become a major social force, voicing clear dissatisfaction with the **patriarchal nuclear family**: "our American family model, with its emphasis on 'success' on the one hand and 'domesticity' on the other, appears to be actually a model for marital misery" (Howe 1972:13). The **zero population movement** had been spawned by the environmental movement, and there were conflicting views on fertility (see below, p. 348).

This put the family high on the political agenda. A number of symposia and conferences looked at the future of or alternatives to the family and resulted in publications (e.g., Barbeau 1971; Elliott 1970; Farson et al. 1969; Goode 1972; Otto 1972). In Canada, the report of the **Royal Commission on the Status of Women** was released in 1970. Questioning the role of women inevitably led to a discussion about the future of the family, since until that time women had been largely relegated to and identified with the family.

Monogamous marriage, and the family based on it, was seen as "grim, lifeless, boring, depressing, disillusioning—a potential context for murder, suicide, mental human decay" (Greenwald 1970:63). Contemporary marriage was described as "a wretched institution" that turns beautiful romances into a bitter contract and a relationship that "becomes constricting, corrosive, grinding and destructive" (Marvyn Cadwaller, cited in Otto 1970a:3). In short, the consequences of "continuing family structures as they exist now" were "fearful" (Stoller 1970:145).

Having established that it was dangerous to continue to support the nuclear family of their day, a considerable number of authors proposed and some predicted some form of communal or tribal family, or various forms of group marriage (Downing, 1970; Gerson 1972; Goode 1972; Hochschild 1972; Kanter 1972; Kay 1972; Orleans and Wolfson 1970; Platt 1972; Schulz 1972).

An interesting feature of these discussions is that they focus primarily on the adults and ignore the raising of the children—certainly one of the reasons why this has not become a significant subform of the family. An exception to this is Levett, who developed a model where every boy has a third parent, "a male figure educated, trained, and equipped to serve the socializing needs of male children" (Levett 1970:162). Strangely enough, he did not deal with the socializing needs of female children, who may not have a male figure in their lives at all if they live in female-headed, single-parent families.

Thamm saw the move towards a communal family (people who cohabit, share property, and follow a set of rules/guidelines for daily life) as the outcome of a linear development: stage 1 was characterized by the consanguine family (related through "blood"); stage 2 by the conjugal family (related thought marriage or adoption), which at his time (1975) was in the process of dissolving; thus leading to stage 3, the communal family, which will have wonderful consequences: "The individual and the collectivity will be merged. Conflict and competition will yield to relations of cooperation, and jealous possessiveness will evolve into a loving concern" (Thamm 1975:128–9).

A particular version of some form of communal living was the suggestion of **polygyny** for people over the age of 60. Kassel argued that "the need for polygyny is obvious: there just are not enough men. Therefore, any man over age sixty could marry two, three, four, or five women over sixty" (Kassel 1970:138). He listed the benefits of such an arrangement, which included a better diet, better living conditions, help in illness, help with housework, sex, better grooming: "when there is a choice between uninterested, dowdy, foul smelling hags [i.e., widows who did not find a man to remarry], and alert, interested, smartly dressed ladies [the lucky co-wives], the selection is obvious" (ibid.:141).

Since the women in this scenario continue to do all the cooking and other housework, it is not clear why they need a man to achieve all these benefits—they could simply live together. The only activity reserved for the man is sex, and here again the women might be content with each other.

By contrast, Rosenberg concluded that while polygyny would make sense, given the "ever growing surfeit of old widows" (Rosenberg 1970:181), it is unlikely to actually happen due to the existence of a counter-ideology—the ideology of the nuclear family.

Gender Roles

One of the most important axes of discussion turns around gender roles,[3] specifically, women's roles. Among the more spectacularly wrong predictions we can count those of Parsons and Bales, who argued that the patriarchal family[4] is a *sine qua non* for the welfare of the US. This included very specifically that women not be active in the labour force, which, on the one hand, accomplishes the maintenance of the household and child care and, on the other, "shields spouses from competition with each other in the occupational sphere, which, along with attractiveness to women, is above all the most important single focus of feelings of self-respect on the part of American men" (Parsons and Bales 1955:264–5).

Given that the labour force participation of women today is almost equal to that of men and that the US and Canada have continued to exist and even flourish, clearly the patriarchal breadwinner family is not necessary to the continued survival of these societies. The fact that Parsons and Bales spoke only about the self-respect of men, ignoring what women might desire, lies obviously at the root of some of their misperceptions.

At around the same time, Cavan (1963:515) suggested that the major contribution of the feminist movement, which "has spent its force," has been the transition from the patriarchal family to "the present-day ideal of the partnership family in which husband and wife share equally in rights and responsibilities." It was, of course, precisely the *failure* of the family to live up to this ideal that generated some of the harshest critiques put forth by the second-wave feminist movement—which at that point was readying itself to re-emerge.

Pollak, reflecting on the consequences of **women's lib**, suggested that "partly due to genetic endowment, partly due to shifts in employment policies, women will prove to be frequently more successful in the role of earner than their husbands. The consequence will be power shifts. Women will gain power, men will lose power, and where power is lost, functions will have to be redefined. Unavoidably under such conditions, fathers will be called upon to assume a greater share in child rearing than in the past" (Pollak 1972:71). This has been borne out to a modest degree. While fathers *do* participate more in rearing their children, the lioness' share is still carried by mothers (des Rivières-Pigeon et al. 2002; Haddad 1996; Hossain 2001; John and Shelton 1997; Kitterod 2002; Sanchez and Thomson 1997; Shelton and John 1993; South and Spitze 1994).

Winch predicted that husbands would fail to participate more in housework as their wives become more active in the labour force. However, he then also predicted that we would therefore "presently be returning toward a norm that will give increasing emphasis to the differences between the sexes" (Winch 1970:14) and that we would hence presumably return to the traditional division of labour—something that has not happened.

In spite of the fact that most men are not at this point doing their fair share of housework, the *norms* have changed. Ninety-nine per cent of respondents of a national Canadian sample agreed with the statement that "Parents need to take equal responsibility for raising children" and 94 per cent agreed that "Couples should share household duties equally" (Bibby 2005:6). This suggests that we will continue to move gradually towards a more even balance with respect to housework and care work. In 2000, only 3 per cent of fathers took time off to care for their newborns. In 2014, 27 per cent of all recent fathers reported that they took time off or intended to do so (Vanier Institute of the Family 2016). Nevertheless, the gender imbalance is still stark. In 2012, fathers with youngest child aged zero to four spent an average 9.6 hours per week on domestic work, compared with 19.8 hours for mothers (Vanier Institute of the Family 2016a).

This bears out what Eichler noted in 1975: "there is no equalitarian family in existence in Canada at the present time. . . . It is clear that equality in the family can come neither quickly nor easily, nor in isolation from far-reaching changes in the legal, economic, educational, and political systems" (Eichler 1975:230). While some of the needed changes have occurred, others are still missing (for instance, a high quality, affordable national daycare system).

Sexuality

Many authors—besides those who argue for alternative family forms—have reflected on the nature of sexual relations within and outside of marriage, although this is almost uniformly restricted to heterosexual relations. Except for one side comment (Schulz 1972:420), no one predicted that we would have same-sex marriage in Canada or the US by now. Nonetheless, numerous authors predicted the loosening of restrictions on non-marital sex. Ogburn and Nimkoff predicted that due to technological innovations sexuality would be separated from procreation, and that "the sex act may occur for pleasure rather than for procreation" (Ogburn and Nimkoff 1955:308). This, of course, would require "a disappearance of moral and legal sanctions against extra-marital sex" (Winch 1970:12). This has certainly happened.

Davids predicted that "the law will accept abortion, all forms of birth control will be seen as medical problems, free of any statutory limitation" (Davids 1971:190–1), both of which have happened in Canada.

Divorce and Cohabitation as Alternatives to Permanent Monogamous Marriages

In a 1967 journal article on the future of the family, Edwards argued that:

> Economic overabundance . . . in the long run will have a repressive effect on the rate of marriage. The recognition of alternatives to wedlock, as that concerning alternatives to premarital chastity, will not occasion sudden behavioral consequences. But change is overdue. When women, already imbued with the economic ethos, fully realize their equality in this sphere, much of the *raison d'être* of marriage will no longer be present. . . . Women will no longer find economic dependence a virtue and worthy by-product of marriage, for, given the opportunity, they will succeed for themselves as ably as any male might. (1967:510)

Hobbs noted that "*we are in the process of abandoning the permanence of marriage, while maintaining* (in law and in principle, even if less in reality than ever before) *its sexual exclusiveness*" (Hobbs 1970:37, emphasis in original). He then suggested that we should turn this around.

Winch (1970:15) also predicted a decrease in marriage (which has happened) as well as in birth rates (which has also taken place), as did the Birds: "with fewer mutual responsibilities, these marriages, we can expect, will have less permanence as their goals and interests change, so will their choice of mates" (Bird and Bird 1971:6). However, they assumed that cohabitation would increase because there would be more free time—in fact the amount of time people with jobs in North America spend on their paid work has increased, not decreased.

Cohabitation has increased, as predicted by a number of people, including the Canadian sociologist Whitehurst who dealt with the topic by calling it "Living Together Unmarried" (LTU). He suggested that LTU "will come to be seen as a kind of period like engagement is today, a trial period in which it becomes (legally or informally) possible to try out one or two live-in situations before making a commitment to long-term marriage" (Whitehurst 1975:441). In fact, cohabitation in Canada today exists in three forms: as a premarital arrangement, as Whitehurst suggested, as a permanent alternative to legal marriage, and as a type of post-divorce union. It is particularly prevalent in Quebec and in the northern territories, which have a high proportion of Indigenous people (Wu 2000:53). As can be seen in Table 16.1, in 2011, 20 per cent of all couples lived common-law, including 0.6 per cent of same-sex couples.

For more on the future of marriage, see "Who Is Marriage For?" in Chapter 3, pp. 52–6.

Table 16.1 Distribution (Number and Percentage) of Census Families by Family Structure[1]

	2001	%	2006	%	2011	%
Total census families	8,371,020	100	8,896,840	100	9,389,700	100
Married opposite-sex couples	5,901,425	83.6	6,098,445	81.5	6,272,935	79.8
Married same-sex couples[2]	—	—	45,345	0.6	64,575	0.8
Common-law opposite-sex couples	1,124,200	15.9	1,338,980	17.9	1,524,345	19.4
Common-law same-sex couples	34,200	0.5	37,885	0.5	43,560	0.6
Lone-parent female-led	1,065,360	12.7	1,132,290	12.7	1,200,295	12.8
Lone-parent male-led	245,825	2.9	281,775	3.2	327,545	3.5

1. Statistics Canada, www12.statcan.ca/census-recensement/2011/as-sa/98-312-x/2011001/tbl/tbl1-eng.cfm, collated from tables 1 and 3, accessed May 29, 2016

2. Same-sex marriage became legal across Canada in 2005 only.

Notes: "Couple" households and "lone-parent family" households refer to one-family households.

Sources: Statistics Canada, censuses of population, 2001 to 2011.

Fertility and Fertility Control

The issues around fertility are particularly interesting. Writing at almost the same time, some authors feared that we are moving towards extinction because women do not have enough babies, while others were concerned about overpopulation and fear that women have too many children. Zimmerman wrote about the "sit-down strike on having and rearing children" (Zimmerman 1947:793) due to a drop in the birth rate. This, he argued, was particularly problematic because "the sources of immigration (what the Romans called the 'good barbarians')" are now exhausted. "Between 1820 and 1920, the United States imported forty million immigrants from Europe. These are now no longer available." When the surplus population of the Mexicans and French Canadians are exhausted, "almost the only fertile peoples of the western world now available to us—we too will begin the grand finale of the crisis" (ibid.). He did not apparently see people from non-Western countries as a viable source for immigration. Nimkoff went even further in his projections. He worried about "the problem of the maintenance of the population"—which could, he feared, lead to the extinction of the human race if it declines over a sufficiently long period of time (Nimkoff 1947:604).

For more on pathways to parenthood, see "Deciding to Parent" in Chapter 5, pp. 98–101.

In contrast to those who worried about humanity dying out because of the lack of children, others worried about overpopulation. Goode, for instance, noted that the population in the US was still increasing while they were using proportionately much more of the world's resources than anyone else. Since most of the children were wanted, he saw no easy solution to this problem, except for one he judged destructive but helpful in the population crisis: "to focus our lives away from the family itself. Totally free abortion, late marriage, all women working, no tax benefits for children, and so on" (Goode 1972:123).

Motivated by a similar fear of overpopulation, the Canadian sociologist Davids suggested:

> There will be public control of reproduction—less than 1/3 of marriages will produce children, would-be parents will be strictly screened and rigorously trained in a large number of subject areas, with examinations and a license for parenthood at the end. The age difference between husbands and wives will disappear, childbirth will be delayed into the middle and late thirties. (1971:190–1)

Davids was not alone in proposing/predicting a regulatory approach to population control. Paul E. Ehrlich, Garrett Harding, and Kenneth E. Boulding also put forward this proposition (Blake 1972:59), in line with the zero population movement. He was, however, accurate in predicting the postponement of childbirth into the thirties, though certainly not under the conditions he proposed. By 2011, the average age of women giving birth was 30.2 years, the oldest on record. (Statistics Canada 2016) Canada's fertility rate has been below replacement level (which is calculated as 2.1 children per women) since the early 1970s, (Health Canada 2008) but Canada's population continues to grow because of immigration. However, worldwide, we are now facing a crisis because of the rapidly increasing human population.

The increase in the global human population and the overconsumption in rich countries, such as Canada, along with wars, are the greatest drain on natural resources, and are three of the driving factors in generating environmental problems.

New Reproductive and Genetic Technologies

In the mid-1950s Ogburn and Nimkoff anticipated much of what actually happened with respect to **new reproductive and genetic technologies** in the 1980s and later. On the basis of scrutinizing animal experiments, they predicted the widespread use of birth control pills, increased artificial insemination, in vitro fertilization, use of donor eggs, sex selection of fetuses, Viagra and its female equivalent, hormone replacement therapy, and longer life expectancies.[5] Their view is a rare exception compared to that of others, the vast majority of whom ignored evidence pointing in these directions.

On the basis of these predictions, they suggested "when the procreational function is modified by biological research, the effect will be considered revolutionary" (Ogburn and Nimkoff 1955:307). Among other things, they argued that the status of women within the family would rise, for one, because women would no longer be blamed for "barrenness," and for another since the various factors would likely result in a decrease of the birth rate, which, in turn, would lead to encouraging child-bearing (fostered by nationalistic–militaristic elements) and hence to an appreciation of motherhood. The latter part, of course, did not materialize—most likely due to the fact that immigration levels have continued to be high in the US (and Canada, as well). They also predicted a refocus on eugenics, which has certainly occurred in the guise of prenatal and

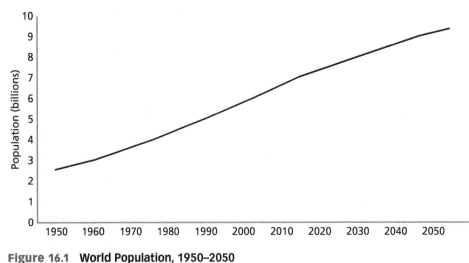

Figure 16.1 World Population, 1950–2050

Source: US Census Bureau, International Data Base, July 2007 version.

pre-implantation diagnoses, although they did not foresee the plotting of the genome and hence assumed that the "hereditary endowment" of an individual would not be easy to establish.

Unanticipated Trends

Overall, then, there have been a number of spectacular misprognoses as well as some surprisingly accurate predictions. In addition, some trends have taken place that no one predicted. Among these is the return of young people to living with their parents for longer periods of time. In 1981, 27.5 per cent of Canadians aged 20–29 lived with their parents (Beaujot 2000:15); by 2016, more than one in three—or almost 35 per cent of young adults aged 20 to 34 lived with at least one parent—a tremendous increase in a rather short time (Statistics Canada, 2017a). Even more dramatically, if same-sex relations were dealt with at all, it was under the heading of sexual deviance. No one anticipated same-sex marriage. As we saw in Table 16.1, in 2011 64,575 of married couples were of the same sex, and in addition there were another 43,560 couples living common-law, by 2016, this number had risen to a total of 72,880 same-sex couples in Canada in 2016, representing 0.9 per cent of all couples and a 12.9 per cent increase since 2011 (Statistics Canada, 2017b). While this is a very small percentage of all Canadian couples, it nevertheless represents a stunning change from the way homosexuality was treated just a few decades ago. Further, with the exception of Ogburn and Nimkoff, sociologists did not foresee the emergence of the new reproductive and genetic technologies and the moral, legal, and social dilemmas they would generate (Basen et al. 1993). No one assumed that people would spend more time working in their paid jobs—if the issue of leisure was considered, the general assumption was that there would be a need to educate people to deal with their ample free time.

The Various Bases for Making Predictions about the Family

In 1964, Reuben Hill identified four methods to predict the future:

1.   extrapolation from trends into the future;
2.   projection from generational changes;
3.   the impact of inventions; and
4.   the family specialists' future family.

To this we can add Goode's criterion:

5.   identifying societal changes and reflecting on their importance for the family (Goode 1972).

All of the authors I examined used one or more of these methods to come up with their predictions.

1. Extrapolation from trends into the future. Looking at each of these methods, Hill, along with other authors, realized that extrapolation can only go so far. He judged this "an exciting but dangerous method" (Hill 1964:21) because some trends are short-term or not linear, and because assumptions about the social and economic circumstances would need to be crystal clear if predictions are based on them.

2. Projection from generational changes. Hill refers to this method as carrying the same hazards but worth attention. It involves studying three generations of the same family, determining consistent differences that persist through the three generations, and projecting on the basis of trends observed in the youngest married-child generation. In another context, Goode (1972:125–6) made a comment that is pertinent to this method of prediction. Parent–youth conflicts, he suggested, have probably always existed, but parents at least used to know what a child is like at that age because they, too, were once that age. He went on to note that "when the whole era changes, that similarity no longer exists" (ibid.:125).

The rate of technological and other change has accelerated enormously over the past few decades. Young children today grow up in a world that is fundamentally very different from the one in which their parents and certainly their grandparents grew up. The internet and social media shape their world view. Children today spend an enormous amount of time in front of various screens, to the detriment of physical activity, the recommended minimum of which is only 60 minutes per day—yet 92 per cent of boys and 96 per cent of girls aged 6 to 17 failed to meet this standard in 2011 (Statistics Canada 2013). This affects their health, and, among other things, contributes to higher rates of obesity.

Canadian high school students are growing used to electronic monitors and uniformed police officers in their schools, and youth and parents fear stabbings and murders as well as drug dealers in high schools. Warfare in Syria, Afghanistan, Iraq, in various parts of Africa, and elsewhere is almost daily fare; millions of people are refugees, many thousands are dying while trying to flee intolerable conditions. Since 9/11, we have grown used to an abrogation of human rights in the name of fighting terrorism. Never in the history of humanity has the gap between the haves and the have-nots been as great as today. In North America, rampant consumerism has to a large degree displaced the values formerly preached by organized religion. Climate change has already resulted in a steep increase in natural disasters, and the rate can be expected to continue to grow.

This fragile world is qualitatively different from that of even three decades ago. On this basis, it would be perilous to assume that children today experience the world as similar to the one their parents experienced when they were their age.

For more on poverty among racialized people, see "Economic Well-being among Indigenous and Racialized Communities" in Chapter 10, p. 214.

Mothers are predominantly in the paid labour force. In Canada, as in the world at large, child poverty is a fact of life. In 2013, almost one out of every five Canadian children lived in poverty. That translates into 1,334,930 Canadian children in need. (Global News 2015) The situation of Indigenous children is particularly dire. In 2016, several reserves declared states of emergency because of a suicide epidemic among their children.

Counter to predictions that we would not know how to use our free time, young parents experience a lack of time to accomplish all that must be done. Most children have no or only one biological sibling, although more have stepsiblings.

Given these rapid and far reaching changes, it does not seem promising to use projections from generational changes as a basis for making predictions. There is another problem with doing so: such data are not presently available for Canadian families. Given that I would expect the pace of change not only to continue, but perhaps even to accelerate (see below) the next generation is likely to face conditions very different from those experienced at present by their parents. Hence the behaviour of their parents may not be the best guide for predicting the future behaviours of the next generation.

3. *The impact of inventions.* A number of authors looked at technological inventions to predict the future of the family. Hill called this method "exciting but hazardous" (Hill 1964:24) and argued that we have overestimated the speed with which certain inventions would be merchandised. He restricted his analysis to household conveniences, though if we extend this approach to look at all technological inventions, this is certainly an important part of the world that impacts on the family. Ogburn and Nimkoff's predictions concerning the new reproductive and genetic technologies provided a startling testimony to the efficacy of this approach.

4. *The family specialists' future family.* This method looks at the type of family advocated by family professionals through their writing and publishing. Hill characterized this method as novel, interesting, but leading to normative statements rather than predictions. This is very evident in the large spate of unsuccessful predictions and prescriptions around 1970 about communal replacements of marriage and the family.

5. *Identifying societal changes and reflecting on their importance for the family.* Goode argued that all family issues are structural and what we really need to know if we wish to predict how the family will change is how society will change. This seems to me the most promising but also the most difficult method.

Some Tentative Predictions about the Future of Canadian Families

Given the assessment of the various methods of how to predict what will happen with respect to future families, I am here concentrating on projected societal changes in my attempt to look into the crystal ball.

Worldwide Changes

Unfortunately, the future promises major challenges. At the global level, **climate change** is undoubtedly the single most important issue confronting humanity. The rate and severity of natural disasters have increased manifold in the early twenty-first century. Further increases can be expected. In 2016, Canada experienced its worst set of wild fires, with the most disastrous ones centred in Alberta around Fort McMurray.

Daily Life
Fort McMurray Family Flees City with Flames at Their Heels

Some things can never be replaced.

Like the tiny house Erica Decker and her husband bought when they found out she was pregnant with their child, a daughter named Piper.

A treasure chest of letters her family and friends wrote on the day of her baby shower, notes meant to be opened on Piper's 16th birthday.

Baby pictures. Intricate portraits she painted on the walls of her daughter's room.

All reduced to ashes. . .

. . .When a massive wildfire ripped through Fort McMurray on Tuesday afternoon, the Beacon Hill neighbourhood was hit hard and Decker's home burned to the ground.

Now safe in an Edmonton hotel room with her husband and her child, she wonders what's left of the neighbourhood she called home for three years.

"We're trying to keep it together for our kids. My daughter, she keeps looking at me and saying, 'Mommy, don't be scared,' because she doesn't understand what's going on. And I'm just trying so hard to keep it together for her."

Decker said her daughter is too young to understand the gravity of the loss. . .

. . .Decker and her family were among the tens of thousands of people forced to flee when the fire raged into the city. . .

. . ."It's absolutely devastating. It's been beyond hard. We're all numb. We're all living with this false sense that there's something to go back to."

Source: Wallis Snowdon, CBC News. "Fort McMurray family flees city with flames at their heels." May 04, 2016. CBC Licensing.

Questions for Critical Thought

The rate of natural disasters has increased greatly in the past decade and will likely increase further. What would be needed to prepare for natural disasters for your family and for society at large?

We can thus expect more severe natural disasters, and more sudden swings in climate, with negative effects on the world's crops. In Canada, we have so far not experienced the worst effects of climate change. However, some small island nations are already in the process of preparing for the time in which their land will be flooded and disappear.[6] Unfortunately, the world has so far not taken much interest in the fact that due to rising sea levels these islands will likely become uninhabitable, and as a result entire countries will be forced from their land.

Climate change is a legacy of the exploitation of natural resources by the world's richest countries (which include Canada), of over-consumption and the reckless burning of fossil fuels that, among other things, power an ever-increasing number of cars; of the exploitation of resources that would have been renewable if they had been used in a sustainable manner (such as fish in Newfoundland); deforestation; the type of meat-rich diet we consume; and other factors that contribute to the emission of greenhouse gases (GHG). Armies and wars are, of course, the greatest contributors to greenhouse gases, yet are rarely considered in this context.

At the same time, more topsoil and forest cover are lost every year, while water tables are falling (Brown 2003). Food prices in Canada are projected to increase by between 2 and 4 per cent, following increases of 4.1 per cent in 2015 (The Food Institute 2016). These increases are due to our high rate of importation of food, crop failures elsewhere, and the low Canadian dollar. Given the current and projected increase in the global human population, and the prevalence of natural disasters, we can expect problems to worsen rather than to improve.

Worldwide, the division of people into haves and have-nots has never been as great as it is today. The personal wealth of a few individuals is almost unimaginable. In 2015, just 62 individuals held the same wealth as all that held by 3.6 billion people—the bottom half of humanity. This figure was down from 388 individuals as recently as 2010. The wealth of the richest 62 people rose by 45 per cent in five years—that's an increase of more than half a trillion dollars ($542 billion), to $1.76 trillion. Meanwhile, the wealth of the bottom half fell by just over a trillion dollars in the same period—a drop of 38 per cent. Since the turn of the century, the poorest half of the world's population has received just 1 per cent of the total increase in global wealth, while half of that increase has gone to the top 1 per cent (OXFAM 2016).

Millions of children in low-income countries grow up malnourished; millions of people die of malnutrition, starvation, and diseases brought on by poverty every year while obesity is recognized as the new epidemic in North America. Canada mirrors the situation worldwide in the sharp distinction between rich and poor and the increasing gap between them. "Five Canadians have the same wealth as the bottom 30 per cent of our population—more than 11 million people. The poorest 10 per cent of Canadians only make about $2.30 more per day than they did 25 years ago. The wealth of the five richest Canadians has risen by $16.9 billion since 2010, a 44 per cent increase" (Global News 2016).

This sharp divide between rich and poor is likely to continue, and possibly increase further, unless governments—in Canada and in the rest of the world—start to regulate and restrict off shore tax havens that allow the superrich to protect their wealth from taxation. In 2015, a massive leak of documents, known as "the Panama papers," revealed the names and details of over 200,000 entities using tax havens. The worldwide attention the leak brought to the issue may potentially push governments to move on this issue.

The world economic system is so interconnected that political, financial, and economic crises in one part of the world have repercussions across the globe.

Climate change has already led to crop failures and food shortages in many parts of the world. The Pentagon is predicting wars due to the consequences of climate change (cf. Dyer 2009). It is the emissions of the rich countries that disproportionately cause climate change, but the consequences are first suffered by countries in Africa, South Asia, and Latin America. Unless rich countries start almost immediately reducing their GHG emissions up to 80 per cent, the situation will get much worse. If left unchecked, the planet may become uninhabitable for humans.

Canada shamefully won the "Fossil of the Year Award" five years in a row, from 2007 to 2011, for its obstreperous role in international climate negotiations (Climate Action Network 2011). The change in the federal government after the 2015 election led to an abrupt turn-around on this issue. To what degree this will result in actual policy changes remains to be seen. World-wide we have passed a "grim milestone" with scientists predicting that we will see continued high accumulations of greenhouse gases, which drive climate change (Mooney 2016).

The cumulative effects of these various trends are likely to result in ever-increasing international turmoil as the countries that have benefited least from the "progress" of the last century pay the highest price.

To this mix we must add the uncertain dangers posed by genetically modified (GM) crops. While resistance to GM crops in Europe has been very strong, Canada sees bio-technologies as an important growth area and is committed to develop this sector further.

It is not clear what the long-term effects of these technologies will be. One of the troubling factors is that the vast majority of genetically modified organisms (GMOs) are oriented towards making plants resistant to the herbicide Roundup, which contains glyphosate, which in turn has been identified as carcinogenic (PAN 2015).

Nuclear weapons continue to pose a serious global threat. The overall effects of these trends are likely to be global economic, social, and political turmoil.

Effects of World and Societal Changes on Families

More Three-generation Families

Unhappily, if these predictions are right, the pressures on Canadian families are likely to increase significantly. Economic uncertainties may result in people moving together in larger units, thus reversing the trend of shrinking household size. We have already seen that young people live longer with their parents than they used to. We may experience a modest trend to more three-generation families. This might happen partially because of economic uncertainties generated by worldwide political, economic, and environmental instability, as well as by increased immigration from countries in which three-generation families are still the norm.

 For more on complex living arrangements see "Demography: What Aging Families Look Like" in Chapter 7, pp. 140–1.

Decrease in Life Expectancy

I expect life expectancy to decrease, rather than increase. The people whose lifespan has been expanding over the past century grew up in a period where pollution levels and other environmental stressors were considerably lower. Today, many people have compromised immune systems. This means that at a time in which environmental stressors are likely to be greater, the physical capacity of people to deal with them will be lower. There is a constant stream of information about newly identified problems. For instance, flame retardants (PBDEs) are now commonplace in the breast milk of Canadian mothers (Picard 2005a). In addition, lifestyles of both children and older people have resulted in a sharp increase in obesity, which will likely result in more health problems. Furthermore, obese mothers are more likely to give birth to babies with health problems than are non-obese mothers (Picard 2005b:A15). The overuse of antibiotics has resulted in the emergence of viruses that are resistant to the medications. This may result in epidemics that may kill many people.

It may be that the life expectancy of people who are quite old will continue to increase for a while, while that of people born later may be curtailed at the same time. If this were the case, a trend towards lower life expectancies might not show up in general statistics for a while. To check the accuracy of this prediction, we would have to examine cohort-specific mortality rates.

Furthermore, social upheaval can quite literally shorten people's life span. The Russian Federation presents a drastic example of this. By 1989, the Soviet Union, although it still existed, had started to disintegrate. It was the year in which the Berlin Wall fell, and many of the satellite states were moving towards independence. In that year, life expectancy for men in what is now the Russian Federation was 64.2 years. Within the next four years it dropped precipitously to 57.6 years—a stunning drop of 6.6 years! By 2015, men were back to a life expectancy of 64.2 years, while women's life expectancy is 75.6, a gap of 11.4 years (Gao 2015).

The Russian example demonstrates that assuming that life expectancy will continue to rise is not a safe assumption. Taking health issues together with the effects of climate change and other environmental factors that are likely to produce serious social changes, it is likely that life expectancy will also decrease in Canada. If this happens, we will face a situation of lower life expectancy for people who are currently parents of young children. They married later and had children later. When their children grow up and have children themselves, fewer of these children would have all their grandparents alive, and fewer of the parents might receive help from their own parents. For the older people it would, of course, mean that fewer of them would be alive to enjoy their grandchildren.

Overall Low Fertility Coupled with High Immigration Rates and Indigenous Population Explosion

I expect the fertility rate to remain below replacement values, as it is at present. Worldwide, fertility decreases as women attain higher levels of education and take on paying jobs. At present, more Canadian women than men attend university. We will therefore have a highly educated group of women of child-bearing age. This picture holds true for non-Indigenous people. In recent decades the Indigenous ancestry population experienced what Statistics Canada calls an explosion. It identifies three distinct periods of population growth (Indigenous and Northern Affairs Canada 2013):

- 1901–1941 Slow Growth
- 1941–1971 Rapid Growth
- 1971–2011 Explosion

Consequently, the Indigenous population is significantly younger than the non-Indigenous population, hence more likely to bear children, and its percentage of the Canadian population is increasing.

At the same time, the pressure for people to come as refugees or to immigrate to Canada for political, economic, and, increasingly, environmental reasons is likely to increase. The Canada of the future is likely to have a population with a higher percentage of racialized people and of Indigenous people.

For more on refugee families in Canada, see Chapter 11.

Sexuality

Same-sex marriage is legal in Canada. This is a major achievement in terms of human rights that should be celebrated. While there is still discrimination on the basis of sexual orientation, and while there is still a significant minority of people who object to same-sex marriage, this is an instance of a rapid evolution of social attitudes and policies.

New Reproductive and Genetic Technologies

The new reproductive and genetic technologies as applied to humans have developed extremely rapidly. They have fundamentally changed, indeed revolutionized, how reproduction is considered within society. Mass media have popularized alternative forms of conception such as in vitro fertilization (IVF). Nevertheless, only a minority of people are directly affected by such techniques, while almost all pregnant women are offered various prenatal diagnostic techniques. Since the intent is usually to abort the fetus if a characteristic perceived as undesirable is detected, this is a form of eugenic gatekeeping. This is being challenged by disability rights activists (Wolbring 2001). It is unclear what will happen. If religious fundamentalism were to rise in Canada, this practice may diminish. On the other hand, strong economic pressures may keep the practice alive.

Gender Roles

Women in the past 30 years have taken on most of the roles that men used to play, but men have not taken up women's roles to the same degree. Nevertheless, men do contribute more to housework and to child care than they did in earlier decades. I would expect that trend, modest as it has been, to continue into the future, on the basis that normatively almost all Canadians—male and female—agree that housework and child care should be shared (Bibby 2005). Even though the behaviour lags behind the norms, there has been a continuous slow move to reconcile the two.

LGBTQ Rights

On May 17, 2016—the International Day Against Homophobia, Transphobia and Biphobia—the federal Liberal government tabled Bill C-16, an Act to amend the Canadian Human Rights Act and the Criminal Code. Now passed into law, it brings broad protections by classifying discrimination on the basis of gender identity and gender expression as a hate crime. This includes hate speech. The changes offer not only legal protection for transgender and gender diverse people in Canada, but also empower law enforcement to track homophobic and transphobic hate crimes. It marks significant progress in recognizing the human rights of transgender people (UNIFOR 2016).

Divorce and Cohabitation as Alternatives to Permanent Monogamous Marriage

At present, the trend towards cohabitation as a precursor and alternative to marriage as well as a post-divorce form of union seems strong. A number of factors are likely to strengthen this trend; however an obvious one is the economic uncertainty experienced by a growing portion of the population because of precarious employment. The proportion of good jobs has significantly decreased, while more and more people hold precarious jobs, including multiple part-time jobs without fringe benefits and job security (EQCOTESST 2011; Lewchuk et al. 2015) Although I expect cohabitation to become even more popular than it is today, I would not expect it to displace legal marriage altogether. In times of political and economic turmoil, more people may turn to more fundamentalist forms of religion. For this part of the population, at least, marriage would retain (or regain) its religious value, and therefore I would expect marriage to continue to keep an important place in Canadian culture.

For more on separation and divorce, see Chapter 6.

It is possible that my predictions about the future of Canadian families may be as wrong as those of so many eminent sociologists before me. Indeed, in some cases I hope so. However, even if the negative events predicted do occur in their broad outlines, there could potentially be some positive outcomes, if people and governments seize the opportunities.

People are protesting against the absurd division of riches, where 62 individual people have as much wealth as the bottom half of humanity. There is mounting concern about climate change, and some moves to contain it—although not yet enough at this writing. As Naomi Klein argued in her book *This Changes Everything*, ". . . the real trick, the only hope, really is to allow the terror of an unlivable future to be balanced and soothed by the prospect of building something much better than many of us have previously dared to hope" (Klein 2014:28). To work towards this goal is clearly what is needed.

CASE IN POINT

Families and the Environment

In 2008 the Vanier Institute of the Family published an issue of their journal, *Transition*, committed to understanding the relationship between families and the environment. In the introduction of that issue they explained that the Institute's editorial board struggled to find individuals with academic expertise in the two areas. When they could not find anyone, they decided to begin the discussion (and the issue) with an interview with an environmentalist and a family studies expert with an interest in the environment. They invited me and David Chernushenko, a sustainability advocate and member of Canada's National Roundtable on the Environment and the Economy, to the Vanier Institute to discuss a series of questions on families and the environment. Here is an excerpt from that interview.

LOWE: Let's explore the relationship between families and the environment a little bit further. It seems clear that the short and long-term health of families depends on a healthy and sustainable environment. Does a healthy and sustainable environment depend on healthy families?

CHERNUSHENKO: I like this question because it comes from both directions. Clearly, a healthy environment contributes to a healthier family in all of the pure senses of health. We may define a healthy environment broadly to be one in which people are safe. This will affect levels of stress and mental health. And on the flip side, a healthy family, both physically and in terms of family dynamic, is more likely to have people discussing things with each other. You may have children coming home and sharing with their parents what they learned at school about recycling.

EICHLER: That's interesting. I have quite a different take on this one. I find this question perplexing, complex, and difficult. We all agree that in order to have healthy families we need a healthy environment because we depend on it. But is it necessary to have healthy families for a healthy planet? I think it depends on the level at which we're putting this discussion. At the global level, I would say yes, because if you look at the environment as a global issue, which of course it is, you cannot try to achieve sustainability without social equity because a lot of environmental problems are generated through poverty and other types of inequity. And you only have families that are healthy when they live in an equitable society, because I would define health as a state of complete wellbeing in physical, mental, social, and spiritual terms. So if you look at it at that level, I would say yes. But if you look at it in terms of Canada, first of all, we do not now have a sustainable society, and the majority of families are probably not healthy; many are poor, many have health problems, many have violence problems, and so on. I do believe these issues need to be addressed jointly. On the other hand, I could imagine a dictator pushing us towards an environmentally more sustainable society. That would then generate unhappy families, as I don't think you have happy families under a dictatorship. The real question, therefore, is how to move

continued

toward becoming more sustainable, and whether we need families for that. If we consider this question, I would say the answer is yes.

Source: Except from an Interview with David Chernushenko and Margrit Eichler in Hanchet, Simone. 2008. "Families and the Environment: A Discussion," *Transition* (Vanier Institute of the Family), Spring 2008: 4–5 (www.vanierinstitute.ca/include/get. php?nodeid=738). Reprinted with permission of the Vanier Institute for the Family. All rights reserved.

Conclusion

In this chapter, we have looked at a number of predictions that were made about families from 1930 to 1975. Some of these predictions were spectacularly wrong; others were surprisingly accurate. The time at which predictions were made was not a predictor of their accuracy. Instead, the important aspect seemed to be the basis on which they were made: those predictions based on societal or technological changes were more likely to be accurate than those based on extrapolation of trends or predictions of family experts. A fifth method, projection from generational changes, was not employed by enough people to gauge its effectiveness.

Given these findings, I have identified some changes that I anticipate for the future, in particular, climate change and a resulting increase in the rate of natural disasters, with on-going social, political, and economic turmoil. If these things occur, I expect the future will see a modest trend towards three-generation families as one response to economic uncertainties and political turmoil, a decrease in life expectancy, continuing overall low fertility with high immigration, less homophobia, a continuing slow erosion of strictly defined gender roles, and a continuing increasing diversity of unions, including common-law and legal marriages and same-sex marriages with and without children. The projected increase in natural disasters would mean that families would have to learn to prepare themselves for a variety of crises.

In other words, families will continue to exist—some will prosper, others less so—and children will continue to be raised within family settings, which will probably be even more diverse than at present.

Study Questions

1. Select a basis on which to make predictions, choose one significant trend (e.g., birth rate, divorce rate, labour force participation of women), and predict how this trend will develop within the next 20 years. Explain why you make this prediction.

2. What are some of the societal factors that affect your own life course and that of one other family member of a different generation?

3. What might be some of the positive ways in which Canada might react to the climate crisis and how would they affect families?

4. Imagine that it became too expensive for most people to drive cars. How would Canadian cities change? How would this affect your own life and that of your family?

5. What could you and your family do to reduce your carbon footprint?
6. Imagine you were living in one of the island nations that can expect to see their entire territory flooded. How would you feel about highly industrialized countries that created this situation? What would you teach your children about this situation?

Further Readings

Alternatives Journal This periodical provides background analyses as well as positive examples of how to deal with environmental problems. The website of the journal is www.alernativesjournal.ca.

CCPA Monitor As the publication of the Canadian Centre for Policy Alternatives, the *CPPA Monitor* provides good up-to-date analyses of current social and environmental issues.

Klein, Naomi. 2015. *This Changes Everything. Capitalism vs. the Climate.* USA: Penguin Random House. In this book, Klein tackles one of the most profound threats that we have ever faced— the war that our current economic model is waging against our planet and our lives.

Simms, Andrew. 2009. *Ecological Debt: The Health of the Planet and the Wealth of Nations*, 2nd edn. London: Pluto Press. A highly readable book, Simms outlines how the rich countries created climate change, and how poor countries carry the consequences.

Todd, Nancy Jack. 2005. *A Safe and Sustainable World: The Promise of Ecological Design*. Washington: Island Press. Written in a personal style, this is a report of various very impressive successful experiments and projects, using ecological design, to lessen humanity's negative impact on the earth.

Vanier Institute of the Family. 2008. "Families and the Environment," *Transition* 38, 1. This entire issue of the journal of the Vanier Institute of the Family is dedicated to a discussion how environmental issues affect Canadian families.

Key Terms

Climate change The long-term change in the climate of a specific region or for the planet as a whole.

New reproductive and genetic technologies A broad array of technologies aimed at facilitating or preventing the process of reproduction, such as contraception, abortion, antenatal testing, birth and contraceptive technologies.

Patriarchal nuclear family A hierarchical family structure in which the husband/father is dominant and the wife and/or children are subordinate to his authority.

Polygyny The practice of one man having more than one wife.

Royal Commission on the Status of Women An extremely important commission that, with the release of its report in 1970, ushered in a new era in gender relations in Canada.

Women's lib (women's liberation) The early name for second-wave feminism, which started in the 1960s.

Zero population movement The social movement that started in the late 1960s advocating that the number of births should be restricted so that the human population would not outstrip the capacity of the Earth to sustain humanity.

Notes

1. I owe the idea to Patrizia Albanese, who also lent me some of her old family sociology textbooks and gave me feedback on this paper. Lingqin Feng found a number of old articles and books for me. I would like to thank Gregor Wolbring and David Cheal for helpful comments on the paper. My sincere thanks go to all of them.
2. In the first edition of the book; I am using the second edition.
3. I have consistently opted to use modern terms when discussing phenomena, but it needs to be noted that the term *gender roles* only started to be used in the mid-to-late 1970s.
4. This is not a term they use, but it is certainly an accurate one.
5. I am using modern terms. For the most part this does not reflect the language employed by the authors, but the phenomena under discussion are the same.
6. For the situation in the Maldives, see Agrell 2008; for the situation in Tuvalu, see Simms 2009, Chapter 3; for Kiribati, the Marshall Islands, Palau, and Micronesia, see UN News Centre 2008.

 Interested in finding out more? Visit www.oupcanada.com/Albanese4e for access to a list of recommended websites for this chapter.

References

Chapter 1

Allen, Katherine, and Ana Jaramillo-Sierra. 2015. "Feminist Theory and Research on Family Relationships: Pluralism and Complexity." *Sex Roles* 73(3–4): 93–9.

Ambert, Anne-Marie. 2006. "One Parent Families: Characteristics, Causes, Consequences, and Issues." Vanier Institute of the Family. Available at (www.vifamily.ca/library/cft/oneparent.pdf).

Beaujot, Roderic. 2004. *Delayed Life Transitions: Trends and Implications*. Ottawa: Vanier Institute of the Family.

Beaupré, Pascale, Pierre Turcotte, and Anne Milan. 2006. "When Is Junior Moving Out? Transitions from the Parental Home to Independence." *Canadian Social Trends* 82: 9–15.

Beiser, Morton, Alasdair Goodwill, Patrizia Albanese, Kelly McShane, Matilda Nowakowski. 2014. "Predictors of Immigrant Children's Mental Health in Canada: Selection, Settlement Contingencies, Culture, or All of the Above?" *Social Psychiatry and Psychiatric Epidemiology* 49(5): 743–56.

Bélanger, Alain. 2006. *Report on the Demographic Situation in Canada, 2002*. Ottawa: Statistics Canada, Demography Division (Catalogue no. 91-209-XIE).

Bernhard, Judith K., Patricia Landolt, and Luin Goldring 2006a. "Transnational, Multi-local Motherhood: Experiences of Separation and Reunification among Latin American Families in Canada." *Policy Matters* 24: 1–7.

———. 2006b. *Gender, The State and Social Reproduction: Household Insecurity in Neo-liberal Times*. Toronto: University of Toronto Press.

Bezanson, Kate, Andrea Doucet, and Patrizia Albanese. 2015. "Introduction: Critical Feminist Sociologies of Families, Work, and Care." *Canadian Review of Sociology* 52(2): 201–03.

———, and Meg Luxton. 2006. "Introduction: Social Reproduction and Feminist Political Economy." Pp. 3–10 in *Social Reproduction: Feminist Political Economy Challenges Neo-liberalism*, edited by K. Bezanson and M. Luxton. Montreal: McGill-Queen's University Press.

Blau, P.M. 1964. *Exchange and Power in Social Life*. New York: John Wiley.

Bradbury, Bettina. 2000. "Single Parenthood in the Past: Canadian Census Categories, 1891–1951 and the 'Normal' Family." *Historical Methods* 33(4): 211–17.

Bronfenbrenner, Urie. 1977. "Towards an Experimental Ecology of Human Development." *American Psychologist* 32: 513–31.

Burholt, Vanessa. 2004. "Transnationalism, Economic Transfers and Families' Ties: Intercontinental Contacts of Older Gujaratis, Punjabis and Sylhetis in Birmingham with Families Abroad." *Ethnic and Racial Studies* 27(5): 800–29.

Calhoun, Cheshire. 2000. *Feminism, the Family and the Politics of the Closet*. New York: Oxford University Press.

Campaign 2000. 2007. *Oh Canada! Too Many Children In Poverty for Too Long: 2006 Report Card on Child and Family Poverty in Canada*. Available at (www.campaign2000.ca/rc/rc06/06_C2000NationalReportCard.pdf).

Castellano, Marlene Brant. 2002. *Aboriginal Family Trends: Extended Families, Nuclear Families, Families of the Heart*. Ottawa: The Vanier Institute of the Family.

CBC News. 2015. "Family of transgender girl, 12, opens up about first year." CBC Online. Retrieved April 14, 2015 (www.cbc.ca/news/canada/ottawa/family-of-transgender-girl-12-opens-up-about-first-year-1.3031418).

———. 2016. "Sixties Scoop survivors recall painful memories in Ontario" CBC Online. Retrieved August 23, 2016 (www.cbc.ca/news/canada/toronto/sixties-scoop-supporters-1.3732037).

Che-Alford, Janet, and Brian Hamm. 1999. "Under One Roof: Three Generations Living Together." *Canadian Social Trends* 53: 6–9. Available at (http://dsp-psd.pwgsc.gc.ca/Collection-R/Statcan/11-008-XIE/0019911-008-XIE.pdf).

Cheal, David. 1991. *Family and the State of Theory*. Toronto: University of Toronto Press.

———. 2008. *Families in Today's World: A Comparative Approach*. London: Routledge.

Citizenship and Immigration Canada. 2007. "Recent Immigrants in Metropolitan Areas: Canada—A Comparative Profile Based on 2001 Census, Part F: Housing." Available at (www.cic.gc.ca/english/resources/research/census2001/canada/partf.asp).

———. 2015. "Facts and Figures 2014—Immigration overview: Permanent Residents Canada—Permanent Residents by Gender and Category, 1989 to 2014." Ottawa: CIC. Available at (www.cic.gc.ca/english/resources/statistics/facts2014/permanent/01.asp).

Connidis, Ingrid A., and Candace Kemp. 2008. "Negotiating Actual and Anticipated Parental Support: Multiple Sibling Voices in Three-generation Families." *Journal of Aging Studies* 22: 229–38.

Cooke, Martin, and Amber Gazso. 2009. "Taking a Life Course Perspective on Social Assistance use in

Canada: A Different Approach." *Canadian Journal of Sociology* 34(2): 349–72.

Coser, Rose Laub. 1974. *The Family: Its Structure and Functions*, 2nd edn. New York: St Martin's Press.

Davies, Megan. 2003. *Into the House of Old: A History of Residential Care in British Columbia*. Montreal: McGill-Queen's University Press.

Dhar, V Erica. 2011. "Transnational Caregiving: Part 1, Caring for Family Relations Across Nations." *Care Management Journals* 12(2): 60–71.

Dobson, Jarod, Hélène Maheux, and Tina Chui. 2013. *Generation Status: Canadian-born Children of Immigrants*. Social and Aboriginal Statistics Division. Ottawa: Statistics Canada. Available at (www12 .statcan.gc.ca/nhs-enm/2011/as-sa/99-010-x/99-010-x2011003_2-eng.pdf).

Duffy, Ann, June Corman, and Norene Pupo. 2015. "Family Finances: Fragility, Class and Gender." *Canadian Review of Sociology/Revue canadienne de sociologie* 52(2): 222–31.

Duvall, Evelyn Millis, and Ruben Hill. 1988. "Family Development's First Forty Years." *Family Relations* 37(2): 127–34.

Eichler, Margrit. 1983. *Families in Canada Today: Recent Changes and Their Policy Consequences*. Toronto: Gage.

———. 1997. *Family Shifts: Families, Policies and Gender Equality*. Toronto: Oxford University Press.

———, and Patrizia Albanese. 2007. "What Is Household Work? A Critique of Assumptions Underlying Empirical Studies of Housework and an Alternative Approach." *Canadian Journal of Sociology* 32(2): 227–58.

Elliot, Patricia, and Nancy Mandell. 1998. "Feminist Theories." Pp. 2–21 in *Feminist Issues: Race, Class and Sexuality*, edited by N. Mandel. Toronto: Prentice-Hall Allyn and Bacon Canada.

Fowler, Erin. 2012. "A Queer Critique on the Polygamy Debate in Canada: Law, Culture, and Diversity." *Dalhousie Journal of Legal Studies* [1188-4258], 21: 93–125.

Fox, Bonnie. 2015. "Feminism on Family Sociology: Interpreting Trends in Family Life." *Canadian Review of Sociology/Revue canadienne de sociologie* 52(2): 204–11.

———, and Meg Luxton. 2001. "Conceptualizing Family." In *Family Patterns and Gender Relations*, edited by B. Fox. Toronto: Oxford University Press.

Gazso, Amber. 2009. "Reinvigorating the Debate: Questioning the Assumptions about and Models of the 'Family' in Social Assistance Policy." *Women's Studies International Forum* 31(2): 150–62.

Goode, William J. 1995. "The Theoretical Importance of the Family." Pp. 1–14 in *Diversity and Change in Families: Patterns, Prospects and Policies*, edited by

M.R. Rank and E.L. Kain. Englewood Cliffs, NJ: Prentice-Hall.

Harrison, Deborah, and Patrizia Albanese. 2016. *Growing Up in Armyville: Canada's Military Families during the Afghanistan Mission*. Waterloo: Wilfrid Laurier University Press.

Holtzman, Mellisa. 2011. "Nonmarital Unions, Family Definitions, and Custody Decision Making." *Family Relations* 60(5): 617–32.

Homans, G.C. 1974. *Social Behavior: Its Elementary Forms*. New York: Harcourt Brace Jovanovich.

Ingoldsby, Bron, Suzanne Smith, and J. Elizabeth Miller. 2004. *Exploring Family Theories*. Los Angeles: Roxbury.

Krüger, Helga, and René Levy. 2001. "Linking Life Courses, Work, and the Family: Theorizing a Not so Visible Nexus between Men and Women." *Canadian Journal of Sociology* 26(2): 145–66.

Langford, Rachel, Susan Prentice, and Patrizia Albanese, eds. 2017. *Caring for Children: Social Movements and Public Policy in Canada*. Vancouver: UBC Press.

Luxton, Meg. 2001. "Family Coping Strategies: Balancing Paid Employment and Domestic Labour." Pp. 318–37 in *Family Patterns, Gender Relations*, 2nd edn. edited by B. Fox. New York: Oxford University Press.

———. 2015. "Feminist Scholarship and Family Sociology: New Ways of Thinking, Outstanding Questions." *Canadian Review of Sociology/Revue canadienne de sociologie* 52(2): 212–21.

Maclean's. 2014. "Editorial: Canada is leading the pack in mixed unions: Why we're setting the global standard for multicultural acceptance and integration." (July 29, 2014). Available at (www.macleans.ca/society/there-is-no-better-index-of-racial-and-cultural-integration-than-mixed-unions-and-canada-is-leading-the-pack/).

Mandell, Nancy, and Ann Duffy. 2000. *Canadian Families: Diversity, Conflicts and Change*, 2nd edn. Toronto: Nelson Thomson.

McDaniel, Susan, and Lorne Tepperman. 2007. *Close Relations: An Introduction to the Sociology of Families*, 3rd edn. Toronto: Pearson Prentice Hall.

Mead, George Herbert. 1967 [1934]. *Mind, Self and Society*. Chicago: University of Chicago Press.

Mead, Margaret. 1949. *Male and Female: A Study of the Sexes in a Changing World*. New York: Dell Publishing, Laurel Editions.

Milan, Anne. 2016. "Insights on Canadian Society Diversity of Young Adults Living with Their Parents." *Insights on Canadian Society*. Catalogue no. 75-006-X. Ottawa: Statistics Canada. Available at (www.statcan.gc.ca/pub/75-006-x/2016001/article/14639-eng.pdf).

———, Nadine Laflamme, and Irene Wong. 2015. "Diversity of Grandparents Living with Their Grandchildren." *Insight on Canadian Society.* Catalogue no. 75-006-X, no. 2015001. Ottawa: Statistics Canada. Available at (www.statcan.gc.ca/pub/75-006-x/2015001/article/14154-eng.pdf).

Mitchell, Barbara A. 1998a. "The Refilled Nest: Debunking the Myth of Family in Crisis." Paper presented at the ninth annual John K. Friesen Conference, "The Overselling of Population Aging." Simon Fraser University, 14–15 May.

———. 1998b. "Too Close for Comfort? Parental Assessments of 'Boomerang Kid' Living Arrangements." *Canadian Journal of Sociology* 23: 21–46.

Morgan, David H.J. 1996. *Family Connections: An Introduction to Family Studies.* Cambridge: Polity Press.

Murdock, George P. 1949. *Social Structure.* New York: Macmillan.

Nakonezny, Paul A., and Wayne H. Denton. 2008. "Marital Relationships: A Social Exchange Theory Perspective." *American Journal of Family Therapy* 36 (5): 402–12.

National Council of Welfare. 2013. *Poverty Profile: Special Edition.* Ottawa: Her Majesty the Queen in Right of Canada.

Newendorp, Nicole DeJong. 2008. *Uneasy Reunions: Immigration, Citizenship, and Family Life in post-1997 Hong Kong.* Stanford: Stanford University Press

Parsons, Talcott. 1955. "The American Family: Its Relations to Personality and to the Social Structure." In *Family Socialization and Interaction Process,* edited by T. Parsons and R.F. Bales. Glencoe, IL: Free Press.

———, and Robert Bales. 1955. *Family, Socialization and Interaction Process.* New York: Free Press of Glencoe.

Saul, Jennifer Mather. 2003. *Feminism: Issues and Arguments.* New York: Oxford University Press.

Statistics Canada. 1996. *1996 Census Dictionary.* Available at (www.statcan.ca/english/freepub/92-351-UIE/04fam.pdf).

———. 2001. *2001 Census Dictionary.* Available at (www12.statcan.ca/english/census01/Products/Reference/dict/index.htm).

———. 2005. "The Socio-Economic Progress of the Children of Immigrants'," *The Daily,* 25 Oct.

———. 2010. *2006 Census Dictionary.* Ottawa: Statistics Canada. Available at (www12.statcan.gc.ca/census-recensement/2006/ref/dict/pdf/92-566-eng.pdf).

———. 2012a. "Portrait of Families and Living Arrangements in Canada." Analytical Document. (Cat no. 98-312-X2011001). Ottawa: Statistics Canada.

———. 2012b. "Fifty Years of Families in Canada: 1961 to 2011." Census in Brief. (Cat no. 98-312-X2011003). Ottawa: Statistics Canada. Available at

(www12.statcan.gc.ca/census-recensement/2011/as-sa/98-312-x/98-312-x2011003_1-eng.pdf).

———. 2012c. 2011 Census of Population Families and Living Arrangements in Canada: Concept Brief (July 12, 2012). Retrieved July 27, 2012 (www42.statcan.gc.ca/smr10/pdf/smr10_2011_002-eng.pdf).

———. 2014. Study: Mixed unions in Canada, 2011. *The Daily* (June, 17, 2015). Ottawa: Statistics Canada. (www.statcan.gc.ca/daily-quotidien/140617/dq140617b-eng.htm).

———. 2017. "Census Family" Dictionary, Census of the Population, 2016. Ottawa: Statistics Canada.

———. 2017a. Infographic 1. Overview of household types, Canada, 2016. Ottawa: Statistics Canada. (www.statcan.gc.ca/daily-quotidien/170802/g-a001-eng.htm).

———. 2017b. "Families, households and marital status: Key results from the 2016 Census." *The Daily.* August 2, 2017. Ottawa: Statistics Canada. (www.statcan.gc.ca/daily-quotidien/170802/dq170802a-eng.htm)

———. 2017c. Census in Brief—Same Sex Couples in Canada, 2016. Ottawaw: Statistics Canada. (www12.statcan.gc.ca/census-recensement/2016/as-sa/98-200-x/2016007/98-200-x2016007-eng.cfm_).

———. 2017d. Portrait of children's family life in Canada in 2016. Census in Brief. Ottawa: Statistics Canada. (www12.statcan.gc.ca/census-recensement/2016/as-sa/98-200-x/2016006/98-200-x2016006-eng.cfm)

Stephens, William. 1963. *The Family in Cross-Cultural Perspective.* New York: Holt, Rinehart and Winston.

Sun, Shirley Hsiao-Li. 2008. "Housework and Gender in Nuclear Versus Extended Family Households: Experiences of Taiwanese Immigrants in Canada." *Journal of Comparative Family Studies* 39(1): 1–17.

Swenson, Don. 2008. *The Religion and Family Link: Neo-Functionalist Reflections.* New York: Springer.

Tsang, A. Ka Tat, Howard Irving, Ramona Alaggia, Shirley B.Y. Chau, and Michael Benjamin. 2003. "Negotiating Ethnic Identity in Canada: The Case of 'Satellite Children'." *Youth & Society* 34(3): 359–84.

Tyyskä, Vappu. 2001. *The Long and Winding Road: Adolescents and Youth in Canada Today.* Toronto: Canadian Scholars' Press.

Vanier Institute of the Family. 2012. "Our Approach to Family—Definition of Family." Retrieved July 31, 2012 (www.vanierinstitute.ca/definition_of_family#.UBfg8bRfF9k).

Waters, Johanna L. 2001. "Migration Strategies and Transnational Families: Vancouver's Satellite Kids." Working Paper Series, No. 01–10. Vancouver: Vancouver Centre of Excellence, Research on Immigration and Integration in the Metropolis. Available at (http://ceris.metropolis.net/frameset_e.html).

White, James, and David Klein. 2008. *Family Theories,* 3rd ed. Los Angeles: Sage.

Widmer, Eric. 2010. *Family Configurations: A Structural Approach to Family Diversity*. Burlington, VT: Ashgate.

Wollstonecraft, Mary. 1988 [1792]. *A Vindication of the Rights of Women*. New York: Norton.

Chapter 2

Adams, Mary Louise. 1997. *The Trouble with Normal: Postwar Youth and the Making of Heterosexuality*. Toronto: University of Toronto Press.

Allen, Richard. 1971. *The Social Passion: Religion and Social Reform in Canada, 1914–1928*. Toronto: University of Toronto Press.

Arnup, Katherine. 1994. *Education for Motherhood: Advice for Mothers in Twentieth-Century Canada*. Toronto: University of Toronto Press.

Baillargeon, Denyse. 1999. *Making Do: Women, Family and Home in Montreal during the Great Depression*. Waterloo: Wilfrid Laurier University Press.

Baskerville, Peter A., and Eric W. Sager. 2007. *Household Counts Canadian Households and Families in 1901*. Toronto: University of Toronto Press.

Beaupré, Pascale, Heather Dryburgh, and Michael Wendt. 2010. "Making Fathers Count." *Canadian Social Trends* (8 June).

Blake, Raymond B. 2009. *From Rights to Needs: A History of Family Allowances in Canada, 1929–1992*. Vancouver: UBC Press.

Bradbury, Bettina. 1993. *Working Families: Age, Gender, and Daily Survival in Industrializing Montreal*. Toronto: McClelland & Stewart.

Campbell, Lara. 2009. *Respectable Citizens: Gender, Family, and Unemployment in Ontario's Great Depression*. Toronto: University of Toronto Press

Carter, Sarah. 1999. *Aboriginal People and Colonizers of Western Canada to 1900*. Toronto: University of Toronto Press.

Castellano, Marlene Brant. 2006–07. "Healing Narratives: Recovery from Residential School Trauma." Vanier Institute of the Family: *Transitions*: 2–4.

Coates, Ken. 2008. *The Indian Act and the Future of Aboriginal Governance in Canada*. West Vancouver: National Centre for First Nations Governance

Comacchio, Cynthia. 1993. *Nations are Built of Babies: Saving Ontario's Mothers and Children, 1900–1940*. Montreal: McGill-Queen's University Press.

———. 2000. "'The History of Us:' Social Science, History, and the Relations of Family in Canada." *Labour/ Le Travail* Special Millennium issue 46: 167–220.

Daschuk, James W. 2013. *Clearing the Plains: Disease, Politics of Starvation, and the Loss of Aboriginal Life*. Regina: University of Regina Press.

Davies, Megan. 2003. *Into the House of Old; A History of Residential Care in British Columbia*. Montreal: McGill Queen's University Press.

Dechêne, Louise. 1992. *Habitants and Merchants in Seventeenth Century Montreal*. Montreal: McGill-Queen's University Press.

Dickason, Olive. 2010. A Concise History of Canada's First Nations, 2nd edn. Don Mills, ON: Oxford University Press.

Duncan, K.A., and R.N. Pettigrew. 2012. "The Effect of Work Arrangements on Perception of Work-Family Balance." *Community, Work & Family* 15(4): 403–23.

Elkin, Frederick. 1964. *The Family in Canada: An Account of Present Knowledge and Gaps in Knowledge about Canadian Families*. Ottawa: Vanier Institute of the Family.

Errington, Elizabeth Jane. 1995. *Wives and Mothers, Schoolmistresses and Scullery Maids: Working Women in Upper Canada, 1790–1840*. Montreal: McGill-Queen's University Press.

Fahrni, Magda. 2005. *Household Politics: Montreal Families and Postwar Reconstruction*. Toronto: University of Toronto Press.

Finkel, Alvin. 2006. *Social Policy and Practice in Canada: A History*. Waterloo: Wilfrid Laurier University Press.

Frager, Ruth A., and Carmela Patrias. 2005. *Discounted Labour: Women Workers in Canada, 1870–1939*. Toronto: University of Toronto Press.

Friedan, Betty. 1963. *The Feminine Mystique*. New York: Norton.

Gleason, Mona. 1999. *Normalizing the Ideal: Psychology, Schooling, and the Family in Postwar Canada*. Toronto: University of Toronto Press.

Golz, Annalee. 1993. "Family Matters: The Canadian Family and the State in the Postwar Period." *Left History* 1(2;Fall): 9–49.

Harris, Richard. 2004. *Creeping Conformity: How Canada Became Suburban, 1900–1960*. Toronto: University of Toronto Press.

Iacovetta, Franca. 1992. *Such Hard-Working People: Italian Immigrants in Postwar Toronto*. Montreal: McGill-Queens University Press.

———. 2006. *Gatekeepers: Reshaping Immigrant Lives in Cold War Canada*. Toronto: Between the Lines.

Knowles, Valerie. 1997. *Strangers at our gates: Canadian immigration and immigration policy, 1540–1997*. Toronto: Dundurn Press.

———. 2007. *Strangers at Our Gates: Canadian Immigration and Immigration Policy, 1540–2015*, 2nd edn. Toronto: Dundurn Press.

———. 2016. *Strangers at Our Gates: Canadian Immigration and Immigration Policy, 1540–2015*, 4th edn. Toronto: Dundurn Press.

Korinek, Valerie. 2000. *Roughing It in the Suburbs: Reading Chatelaine Magazine in the Fifties and Sixties*. Toronto: University of Toronto Press.

Kremarik, Frances. 2000. "Urban Development." Special Issue: 100 Years of Education. *Canadian Social Trends* 59 (Winter): 18–22.

Luxton, Meg. 1980. *More Than a Labour of Love: Three Generations of Women's Work in the Home.* Toronto: Women's Press.

———. 2011. *Changing Families, New Understandings.* Ottawa: Vanier Institute of the Family (June).

Marshall, Katherine. 2006. "Converging Gender Roles." *Perspectives* 7(7): 5–17. Available at (www.statcan .gc.ca/pub/75-001-x/10706/9268-eng.htm).

McLaren, Angus. 1990. *Our Own Master Race: Eugenics in Canada, 1885–1945.* Toronto: McClelland and Stewart Inc.

———, and Arlene Tigar McLaren. 1997. *The Bedroom and the State: The Changing Practices and Politics of Contraception and Abortion in Canada, 1880–1997.* Toronto: Oxford University Press.

Milan, Anne. 2000."100 Years of Families." *Canadian Social* Trends, 56 (Spring).

Miller, J.R. 1996. *Shingwauk's Vision: A History of Native Residential Schools.* Toronto: University of Toronto Press.

Montigny, Edgar-A. 1993. *Foisted Upon the Government? State Responsibilities, Family Obligations, and the Care of the Dependent Aged in Late Nineteenth-Century Ontario.* Montreal: McGill-Queen's University Press.

National Centre for Truth and Reconciliation. 2016. *A Knock on The Door: The Essential History of Residential Schools from the Truth and Reconciliation Commission of Canada.* Edited and abridged. Winnipeg: University of Manitoba Press.

Owram, Doug. 1996. *Born at the Right Time: A History of the Baby Boom Generation.* Toronto: University of Toronto Press.

Palmer, Bryan. 2008. *Canada's 1960s: The Ironies of Identity in a Rebellious Era.* Toronto: University of Toronto Press.

Rutherdale, Robert. 2009. "Just Nostalgic Family Men? Off-the-Job Family Time, Providing, and Oral Histories of Fatherhood in Postwar Canada, 1945–1975." *Oral History Forum* 29: 1–25.

Sangster, Joan. 1995. *Earning Respect: The Lives of Working Women in Small-Town Ontario, 1920–1960.* Toronto: University of Toronto Press.

———. 2001. "Women's Activism and the State." In *Framing Our Past: Canadian Women's History in the Twentieth Century*, edited by S.A. Cook, L. McLean, and K. O'Rourke. Montreal: McGill-Queen's University Press.

Seeley, John, R., Alexander Sim, and Elizabeth W. Loosely. 1956. *Crestwood Heights: A Study of the Culture of Suburban Life.* Toronto: University of Toronto Press.

Snell, James G. 1991. *In the Shadow of the Law: Divorce in Canada, 1900–1939.* Toronto: University of Toronto Press.

Stanley, Timothy J. 2011. *Contesting White Supremacy: School Segregation, Anti-Racism, and the Making of Chinese Canadians.* Vancouver: University of British Columbia Press.

Statistics Canada. 1984. *Canada's Lone Parent Families.* Ottawa: Statistics Canada.

———. 2012. Families, Households and Marital Status, 2011 Census of Population. Available at (www12 .statcan.gc.ca/census-recensement/2011/as-sa/98-312-x/98-312-x2011001-eng.pdf).

———. 2012a. "Fifty years of families in Canada: 1961 to 2011." Census in Brief. (Cat no. 98-312-X2011003). Ottawa: Statistics Canada. Available at (www12 .statcan.gc.ca/census-recensement/2011/as-sa/98-312-x/98-312-x2011003_1-eng.pdf).

———. 2017. "Families, households and marital status: Key results from the 2016 Census." The Daily. August 2, 2017. Ottawa: Statistics Canada. (www.statcan. gc.ca/daily-quotidien/170802/dq170802a-eng.htm)

Strong-Boag, Veronica. 1991. "Home Dreams: Women and the Suburban Experiment in Canada, 1945–60." *Canadian Historical Review* 72.

———. 2006. *Finding Families, Finding Ourselves: English Canada Encounters Adoption, from the Nineteenth Century to the 1990s.* Don Mills: Oxford University Press.

———. 2011. *Fostering Nation? Canada Confronts its History of Childhood Disadvantage.* Waterloo: Wilfrid Laurier University Press.

———. Census Highlights 2016. (www.12.statcan.gc.ca/)

Sutherland, Neil. 1997. Growing Up: Childhood in *English Canada from the Great War to the Age of Television.* Toronto: University of Toronto Press.

———. 2000. *Children in English-Canadian Society: Framing the Twentieth-Century Consensus*, 2nd edn. Waterloo: Wilfrid Laurier University Press.

Truth and Reconciliation Commission of Canada. 2012. *They Came for the Children.* Winnipeg, Manitoba.

Turner, Annie. 2016. "Living Arrangements of Aboriginal Children Aged 14 and Under." Ottawa: Statistics Canada. Available at (www.statcan.gc.ca/pub/75-006-/2016001/article/14547-eng.htm).

Ursel, Jane. 1992. *Private Lives, Public Policy: 100 Years of State Intervention in the Family.* Toronto: Women's Press.

Valverde, Mariana. 1991. *The Age of Light, Soap and Water: Moral Reform in English Canada, 1885–1925.* Toronto: McClelland and Stewart.

Vanier Institute of the Family. 2004. *Profiling Canada's Families III.* Ottawa: Vanier Institute.

Vézina, Mireille. 2012. *The 2011 General Social Survey: Overview of Families in Canada—Being a Parent in a Stepfamily.* Ottawa: Statistics Division.

Wargon, Sylvia. 1997. *Children in Canadian Families*. Ottawa: Statistics Canada.

Williams, Cara. 2000. "Income and expenditures." Special Issue: 100 Years of Education. *Canadian Social Trends*, 59 (Winter).

Chapter 3

Baird, B. 2007. "'Gay Marriage,' Lesbian Wedding." *Gay & Lesbian Issues and Psychology Review* 3(3): 161–70.

Barbara Findlay QC. 2016. www.barbarafindlay.com/

Bell, D., and J. Binnie. 2000. *The Sexual Citizen: Queer Politics and Beyond*. Cambridge: Polity Press.

Boyd, S.B., and C.F.L. Young. 2005. "From Same Sex to No Sex? Trends towards Recognition of (Same-Sex) Relationships in Canada." In *Open Boundaries*, edited by B.A. Crow and L. Gotell. Toronto: Pearson Prentice Hall.

Brownworth, V. 1996. "Tying the Knot or the Hangman's Noose: The Case against Marriage." *Journal of Lesbian, Gay and Bisexual Identity* 1: 91–8.

Calhoun, Cheshire. 2000. *Feminism, the Family and the Politics of the Closet*. New York: Oxford University Press.

Canada (Attorney General) v. Hislop. 2007. 1 S.C.R. 429, 2007 SCC 10.

Canadian Christianity. 2017. Christian Info Society. Available at (https://canadianchristianity.com/).

Canadian Lesbian and Gay Rights Organization Archives. Retrieved June 28, 2017 (www.clga.ca).

Card, C. 1996. "Against marriage and motherhood." *Hypathia* 11: 1–23.

Carlson, Kathryn B. 2012. "The true north LGBT: New poll reveals landscape of gay Canada." *National Post*. Available at (http://news.nationalpost.com/news/canada/the-true-north-lgbt-new-poll-reveals-landscape-of-gay-canada).

CBC News. 2012. "Census may have counted roommates as married couples." Available at (www.cbc.ca/news/canada/census-may-have-counted-roommates-as-married-gay-couples-1.1153344).

———. 2012a. "Timeline—Same-sex rights in Canada." Retrieved June 28, 2017 (www.cbc.ca/news/canada/timeline-same-sex-rights-in-canada-1.1147516).

Civil Marriage Act. 2005. Supreme Court of Canada c. 33.

Constitution Act. 1982. Part I: Canadian Charter of Rights and Freedoms. Available at (http://laws-lois.justice.gc.ca/eng/Const/page-15.html).

Cossman, Brenda. 1996. "Same Sex Couples and the Politics of Family Status." Pp. 223–53 in *Women and Canadian Public Policy*, edited by J. Brodie. Toronto: Harcourt Brace & Company.

Egan v. Canada. 1995. 2 S.C.R. 513. Available at (www.icj.org/sogicasebook/egan-v-canada-supreme-court-of-canada-25-may-1995/).

Eichler, Margrit. 1997. *Family Shifts: Families, Policies and Gender Equality*. Toronto: Oxford University Press.

Equal Marriage Materials from October 2003 Supreme Court of Canada Motion to Appeal Supporting Affidavits. Available at (www.samesexmarriage.ca/legal/on.html#background).

Erasing 76 Crimes. 2016. "77 countries where homosexuality is illegal." Available at (https://76crimes.com/76-countries-where-homosexuality-is-illegal/).

Fineman, M. 2000. "Cracking the Foundational Myths: Independence, Autonomy and Self Sufficiency." *Gender, Social Policy and the Law*, 13.

Graff, E.J. 2004. *What Is Marriage For? The Strange Social History of Our Most Intimate Institution*. Boston: Beacon Press.

Grant, Tavia. 2016. "Women still earning less money than men despite gains in education: study." *Globe and Mail*. Available at (www.theglobeandmail.com/news/national/women-still-earning-less-money-than-men-despite-gains-in-education-study/article29044130/).

Halpern v. Canada (AG). 2003. O.J. No. 2268 Available at (www.sgmlaw.com/en/about/Halpernv.CanadaAttorneyGeneral.cfm).

Heaphy, B., C. Smart, and A. Einardottir. 2013 *Same Sex Marriages: New Generations, New Relationships*. Chippenham and Eastbourne, UK: Palgrave Macmillan.

Human Rights Campaign. 2016. "Donald Trump: Opposes Nationwide Marriage Equality." Retrieved August 20, 2016 (www.hrc.org/2016RepublicanFacts/donald-trump-opposes-nationwide-marriage-equality).

Hunter, N. 1995. "Marriage, Law and Gender: A Feminist Inquiry." Pp. 107–2 in *Sex Wars: Sexual Dissent and Political Culture*, edited by L. Duggan and N. Hunter. New York: Routledge.

Hurley, M.C. 2005. *Bill C-38 The Civil Marriage Act, A Legislative Summary*. Retrieved March 27, 2012 (www.parl.gc.ca/About/Parliament/Legislative Summaries/Bills_ls.asp?ls=c38&Parl=38 &Ses=1).

———. 2007. Charter of Equality Rights: Interpretation of Section 15 in Supreme Court of Canada Decisions. Available at (www.lop.parl.gc.ca/content/lop/research-publications/bp402-e.htm).

Hutchinson, D.L. 1997. "'Out Yet Unseen': A Racial Critique of Gay and Lesbian Legal Theory and Political Discourse." *Connecticut Law Review* 29 (2): 590.

Kitzinger, C., and S. Wilkinson. 2004. "The Re-Branding of Marriage: Why We Got Married Instead of Registering a Civil Partnership." *Feminism and Psychology* 14: 127–50.

Lenon, S. 2008. *A White Wedding? The Racial Politics of Same-Sex Marriage in Canada*. Toronto: University of Toronto Press.

LGBTQ Nation. 2017.Available at (www.lgbtqnation.com/tag/gay-marriage/).

Little Sisters Book and Art Emporium v. Canada (Minister of Justice). 2000. 2 S.C.R. 1120. Available at (https://scc-csc.lexum.com/scc-csc/scc-csc/en/item/1835/index.do).

M. v. H. 1999. 2 S.C.R. 3. Available at (www.leaf.ca/m-v-h/).

Martin, B. 1994. "Extraordinary Homosexuals and the Fear of Being Ordinary." *Differences* 6 (2–3): 100–25.

McGregor, Janyce. 2016. "Freedom and respect: Conservatives strike marriage definition from party policy." *CBC News*. Available at (www.cbc.ca/news/politics/conservative-convention-saturday-votes-1.3604990).

Mulé, N. 2010. "Same-Sex Marriage and Canadian Relationship Recognition—One Step Foward, Two Steps Back: A Critical Liberationist Perspective." *Journal of Gay & Lesbian Social Services* 22(1–2): 74–90.

Ontario Consultants on Religious Tolerance. 2008. "Gay, lesbian, and bisexual milestones in the media." Available at (www.religioustolerance.org/hom_medi.htm).

Open Letter to the Hon. Stephen Harper from Law Professors Regarding Re-Opening Same-Sex Marriage. 2005. Available at (https://egale.ca/open-letter-to-the-hon-stephen-harper-from-law-professors-regarding-re-opening-same-sex-marriage/).

Patel, A. 2016. "Canada's gender pay gap: Why Canadian women still earn less than men." *Huffington Post*. Available at (www.huffingtonpost.ca/2016/03/08/canada-gender-pay-gap_n_9393924.html).

Polikoff, N. 2008. *Beyond (Straight and Gay) Marriage*. Boston: Beacon Press.

Richardson, Diane. 2005. "Desiring Sameness? The Rise of a Neoliberal Politics of Normalisation" *Antipode* 37(3): 515–535.

Smart, C. 1984. "Ties That Bind." *Canadian Journal of Law and Society* 9 (1): 15–38.

Smith, B. 1997. "Where Has Gay Liberation Gone? An Interview with Barbara Smith." In *Homo Economics: Capitalism, Community, and Lesbian and Gay Life*, edited by A. Gluckman and B. Reed. London: Routledge.

Statistics Canada. 2012. "Portrait of families and living arrangements in Canada." *Analytical Document*. (Cat no. 98-312-X2011001). Ottawa: Statistics Canada.

———. 2016. http://www12.statcan.gc.ca/census-recensement/2016/dp-pd/prof/details/page.cfm?Lang=E&Geo1=CSD&Code1=3506008&Geo2=PR&Code2=01&Data=Count&SearchText=ottawa&SearchType=Begins&SearchPR=01&B1=All .

Trudeau, Pierre. 1969. "There's no place for the state in the bedrooms of the nation." Available at (www.cbc.ca/archives/entry/omnibus-bill-theres-no-place-for-the-state-in-the-bedrooms-of-the-nation).

United Church of Canada. 2005. "Religious Faithful Rally in Support of Same-sex Marriage Legislation." Press Release, April 11, 2005. Available at (http://www.marketwired.com/press-release/religious-faithful-rally-in-support-of-same-sex-marriage-legislation-559276.htm).

Valverde, Mariana. 2006. "A New Entity in the History of Sexuality: The Respectable Same-sex Couple." *Feminist Studies* 32 (1): 155–62.

Vriend v. Alberta. 1998. 1 SCR 493. Available at (www.lop.parl.gc.ca/content/lop/researchpublications/bp402-e.htm).

Wolfson, E. 1996. "Why We Should Fight for the Freedom to Marry: The Challenges and Opportunities That Will Follow a Win in Hawaii." *Journal of Gay, Lesbian and Bisexual Identity* 1: 70–89.

York, Geoffrey. 2009. "Uganda's anti-gay bill causes Commonwealth uproar," *Globe and Mail*, 25 November, A1. Available at (www.theglobeandmail.com/news/world/ugandas-anti-gay-bill-causes-commonwealth-uproar/article4196948/).

Young, C. 2006. "What's Sex Got To Do with It? Tax and the 'Family' in Canada." *Journal of the Australasian Tax Teachers Association* 2 (1).

———, and S. Boyd. 2006. "Losing the Feminist Voice? Debates on the Legal Recognition of Same Sex Partnerships in Canada." *Feminist Legal Studies* 14(2): 213–40.

Chapter 4

Adam, Barry D. 2004. "Care, Intimacy and Same-sex Partnership in the 21st Century." *Current Sociology* 52(2): 265–79.

Ambert, Anne-Marie. 2009. *Divorce: Facts, Causes, and Consequences*, 3rd edn. Ottawa: Vanier Institute of the Family.

Andersen, Robert, and Tina Fetner. 2008. "Cohort Differences in Tolerance of Homosexuality: Attitudinal Change in Canada and the United States, 1981–2000." *Public Opinion Quarterly* 72: 311–30.

Ariizumi, Hideki, Yaqin Hu, and Tammy Schirle. 2015. "Stand Together or Alone? Family Structure and the Business Cycle in Canada." *Review of Economics of the Household* 13:135–61.

Armstrong, Elizabeth A., Laura Hamilton, and Paula England. 2010. "Is Hooking up Bad for Young Women?" *Contexts* 9: 22–7.

Bailey, Beth. 1988. *From Front Porch to Back Seat: Courtship in 20th Century America*. Baltimore: The Johns Hopkins University Press.

Bailey, Martha. 2004. "Regulation of Cohabitation and Marriage in Canada." *Law & Policy* 26(1): 153–75.

Barraket, Jo, and Millsom Henry-Waring. 2008. "'Getting it On(line)': Sociological Perspectives on E-dating." *Journal of Sociology*, 44: 149–65.

Beaupré, Pascale. 2008. *I Do. Take Two? Changes in Intentions to Remarry Among Divorced Canadians During the Past 20 Years*. Statistics Canada, Catalogue no. 86-630-X, July. Available at (www.statcan.gc.ca/pub/89-630-x/2008001/article/10659-eng.pdf).

Beck-Gernsheim, Elizabeth. 1998. "On the Way to a Post-familial Family: From a Community of Needs to Elective Affinities." *Theory, Culture and Society* 15(3-4): 53–70.

Ben-Ze'ev, Aharon. 2004. *Love Online: Emotions on the Internet*. Cambridge: Cambridge University Press.

Benson, Jacquelyn J., and Marilyn Coleman. 2016. "Older Adults Developing a Preference for Living Apart Together." *Journal of Marriage and Family* 78: 797–812.

Bernstein, Elizabeth. 2007. *Temporarily Yours: Intimacy, Authenticity, and the Commerce of Sex*. Chicago: University of Chicago Press.

Bibby, Reginald. 2004. *The Future Families Project: A Survey of Canadian Hopes and Dreams*. Ottawa: The Vanier Institute of the Family.

Biblarz, Timothy, and Judith Stacey. 2010. "How Does the Gender of Parents Matter?" *Journal of Marriage and Family* 72: 3–22.

Bogle, Kathleen A. 2008. *Hooking Up: Sex, Dating, and Relationships on Campus*. New York: New York University Press.

Bourassa, Carrie, Kim McKay-McNabb, and Mary Hampton. 2004. "Racism, Sexism and Colonialism: The Impact on the Health of Aboriginal Women in Canada." *Canadian Woman Studies/les cahiers de la femme* 24(1; Fall): 23–9.

Bradbury, Bettina. 2005. "Colonial Comparisons: Rethinking Marriage, Civilization and Nation in the Nineteenth-century White Settler Societies." Pp. 135–58 in *Rediscovering the British World*, edited by P. Buckner and R.D. Frances. Calgary: University of Calgary Press.

Brown, Susan L. 2010. "Marriage and Child Well-being: Research and Policy Perspectives." *Journal of Marriage and Family* 72: 1059–77.

Budgeon, Shelley. 2008. "Couple Culture and the Production of Singleness." *Sexualities* 11(3): 301–25.

Bumpass, Larry, and Hsien-Hen Lu. 2000. "Trends in Cohabitation and Implications for Children's Family Contexts." *Population Studies* 54: 29–41.

Carter, Julia, Simon Duncan, Mariya Stoilova, and Miranda Phillips. 2016. "Sex, Love and Security: Accounts of Distance and Commitment in Living Apart Together Relationships." *Sociology* 50(3): 576–93.

Carter, Sarah. 2008. *The Importance of Being Monogamous: Marriage and Nation Building in Western Canada*. Edmonton: University of Alberta Press.

Centers for Disease Control and Prevention. 2002. "Trends in Sexual Risk Behaviors among High School Students–United States, 1991–2001." *Morbidity and Mortality Weekly Report* 51: 856–9.

———. 2002a. "Youth Risk Behavior Surveillance– United States, 2001." *Morbidity and Mortality Weekly Report* 51: 1–64.

Cheal, David. 1987. "'Showing Them You Love Them': Gift Giving and the Dialectic of Intimacy." *The Sociological Review* 35(1): 150–69.

Collins, Patricia Hill. 2004. *Black Sexual Politics: African-Americans, Gender and the New Racism*. New York: Routledge.

Connolly, Jennifer, Wyndal Furman, and Roman Konarski. 2000. "The Role of Peers in the Emergence of Heterosexual Romantic Relationships in Adolescence." *Child Development* 71: 1395–408.

Coontz, Stephanie. 1993. *The Way We Never Were: American Families and the Nostalgia Trap*. New York: Basic Books.

———. 2005. *Marriage, a History: From Obedience to Intimacy or How Love Conquered Marriage*. New York: Viking Penguin.

Cooper, Alvin, and Leda Sportolari. 1997. "Romance in Cyberspace: Understanding Online Attraction." *Journal of Sex Education and Therapy* 22: 7–14.

Courtice, Erin Leigh, and Krystelle Shaughnessy. 2017. "The Partner Context of Sexual Minority Women's and Men's Cybersex Experiences: Implications for the Traditional Sexual Script." *Sex Roles*. doi:10.1007/s11199-017-0792-5.

Crawford, Mary, and Danielle Popp. 2003. "Sexual Double Standards: A Review and Methodological Critique of Two Decades of Research." *Journal of Sex Research* 40: 13–26.

Cross, Philip, and Peter Mitchell. 2014. "The Marriage Gap between Rich and Poor Canadians: How Canadians Are Split into Haves and Have-nots along Marriage Lines." Institute of Marriage and Family Canada. Available at (www.imfcanada.org/sites/default/files/Canadian_Marriage_Gap_FINAL_0.pdf).

Daneback, Kristian, Al Cooper, and Sven-Axel Mansson. 2005. "An Internet Study of Cybersex Participants." *Archives of Sexual Behavior* 34(3): 321–8.

DePaulo, Bella M., and Wendy L. Morris. 2005. "Singles in Society and Science." *Psychological Inquiry* 16(2-3): 57–83.

Dozier, Raine, and Pepper Schwartz. 2001. "Intimate Relationships." In *The Blackwell Companion to Sociology*, edited by J.R. Blau. Malden, MA: Blackwell Publishing.

Duncan, Simon, and Miranda Phillips. 2010. "People Who Live Apart Together (LATs)—How Different Are They?" *The Sociological Review* 58(1): 112–34.

Eaton, Asia Anna, and Suzanna Rose. 2011. "Has Dating Become More Egalitarian? A 35 Year Review Using Sex Roles." *Sex Roles* 64: 843–62.

Edward O. Laumann, Robert T. Michael and John H. Gagnon. 1994. A Political History of the National Sex Survey of Adults. *Family Planning Perspectives* 26, 1: 34–38.

Eichler, Margrit. 1997. *Family Shifts: Families, Policies and Gender Equality.* Toronto: Oxford University Press.

Elze, Diane. 2003. "Gay, Lesbian and Bisexual Youths' Perceptions of Their High School Environments and Comfort in School." *Children and Schools* 25: 225–39.

Espiritu, Yen Le. 1997. *Asian American Women and Men: Labor, Laws and Love.* Thousand Oaks, CA: Sage Publications.

Eyre, Stephen L., Emily Arnold, Eric Peterson, and Thomas Strong. 2007. "Romantic Relationships and Their Social Context among Gay/bisexual Male Youth in the Castro District of San Francisco." *Journal of Homosexuality* 53(4): 1–29.

Feliciano, Cynthia, Belinda Robnett, and Golnaz Komaie. 2009. "Gendered Racial Exclusion among White Internet Daters." *Social Science Research* 38: 39–54.

Fetner, Tina, Athena Elafros, Sandra Bortolin, and Coralee Drechsler. 2012. "Safe Spaces: Gay–straight Alliances in High Schools." *Canadian Review of Sociology/Revue canadienne de sociologie* 49(2): 188–207.

———, and Melanie Heath. 2015. "Do Same-sex and Straight Weddings Aspire to the Fairytale? Women's Conformity and Resistance to Traditional Weddings." *Sociological Perspectives* 59(4): 721–42.

Finer, Lawrence B. 2007. "Trends in Premarital Sex in the United States, 1954–2003." *Public Health Reports* 122: 73–8.

Giddens, Anthony. 1992. *The Transformation of Intimacy: Sexuality, Love and Eroticism in Modern Societies.* Stanford, CA: Stanford University Press.

Gilligan, Carol. 1982. *In a Different Voice: Psychological Theory and Women's Development.* Cambridge, MA: Harvard University Press.

Ginsburg, Gerlad P. 1988. "Rules, Scripts and Prototypes in Personal Relationships." Pp. 23–39 in *Handbook of Personal Relationships: Theory, Research and Interventions,* edited by S. Duck, D.F. Hay, S.E. Hobfoll, W. Ickes, B.M. Montgomery. Oxford, UK: John Wiley & Sons.

Giordano, Peggy C., Monica A. Longmore, and Wendy D. Manning. 2006. "Gender and the Meanings of Adolescent Romantic Relationships: A Focus on Boys." *American Sociological Review* 71: 260–87.

Glenn, Norval, and Elizabeth Marquardt. 2001. *Hooking Up, Hanging Out and Hoping for Mr. Right: College Women on Dating and Mating Today.* An Institute for American Values Report to the Independent Women's Forum.

Goldscheider, Frances K. 1995. "Interpolating Demography with Families and Households." *Demography* 32(3): 471–80.

Grello, Catherine M., Deborah P. Welsh, and Melinda S. Harper. 2006. "No Strings Attached: The Nature of Casual Sex in College Students." *Journal of Sex Research* 43: 255–67.

Gross, Neil. 2005. "The Detraditionalization of Intimacy Reconsidered." *Sociological Theory* 23: 3.

Gudelunas, David. 2005. "Online Personal Ads: Community and Sex, Virtually." *Journal of Homosexuality* 49(1): 1–33.

Hamilton, Laura, and Elizabeth A. Armstrong. 2009. "Gendered Sexuality in Young Adulthood: Double Binds and Flawed Options." *Gender & Society* 23: 589–616.

Hanson Frieze, Irene. 2007. "Love and Commitment." In *Blackwell Encyclopedia of Sociology,* edited by G.Ritzer. New York: Blackwell Publishing.

Heath, Melanie. 2012. *One Marriage under God: The Campaign to Promote Marriage in America.* New York: New York University Press.

Hughes, Kate. 2005. "The Adult Children of Divorce: Pure Relationships and Family Values?" *Journal of Sociology* 41: 69–86.

Jamieson, Lynn. 1998. *Intimacy: Personal Relationships in Modern Societies.* Cambridge: Polity Press/Blackwell Publishers.

———. 2007. "Intimacy." In *Blackwell Encyclopedia of Sociology,* edited by G. Ritzer. New York: Blackwell Publishing.

Kelly, Fiona. 2011. *Transforming Law's Family: The Legal Recognition of Planned Lesbian Motherhood.* Vancouver: University of British Columbia Press.

Kerr, Don, Melissa Moyser, and Roderic Beaujot. 2006. "Marriage and Cohabitation: Demographic and Socioeconomic Differences in Quebec and Canada." *Canadian Studies in Population* 33: 83–117.

Klinkenberg, Dean, and Suzanna Rose. 1994. "Dating Scripts of Gay Men and Lesbians." *Journal of Homosexuality* 26(4): 23–35.

Laplante, Benoît, and Ana Laura Fostik. 2015. "Disentangling the Quebec Fertility Paradox: The Recent Evolution of Fertility within Marriage and Consensual Union in Quebec and Ontario." *Canadian Studies in Population* 42(1–2): 81–101.

Le Bourdais, Céline, and Annie Sauriol. 1998. "La part des pères dans la division du travail domestique au sein des familles canadiennes [Father's Share in the Division of Domestic Labour among Canadian Families]." *Etudes et Documents* No. 69. Montreal, Quebec: INRS-Urbanisation.

Le Bourdais, Celine and Evelyne Lapierre-Adamcyk. 2004. "Changes in conjugal life in Canada: Is cohabitation progressively replacing marriage?" *Journal of Marriage and Family* 66(4): 929–942.

Leichliter, Jami S., Anjani Chandra, Nicole Liddon, Kevin A. Fenton, and Sevgi O. Aral. 2007. "Prevalence and Correlates of Heterosexual Anal and Oral Sex in Adolescents and Adults in the United States." *Journal of Infectious Diseases* 196: 1852–9.

Liu, L.W., Don Kerr, and Roderic Beaujot. 2006. *Children and Youth in Canada: Recent Demographic Changes* (Discussion Paper No. 06-07). London, ON: University of Western Ontario, Population Studies Centre.

Livingstone, Anne-Marie, and Morton Weinfeld. 2015. "Black Families and Socio-economic Inequality in Canada." *Canadian Ethnic Studies* 47(3):1–23.

Martin, Karin A. 1996. *Puberty, Sexuality, and the Self: Boys and Girls at Adolescence*. New York: Routledge.

Mendes, Kaitlynn, 2015. *SlutWalk: Feminism, Activism and Media*. London: Palgrave Macmillan.

Merali, Noorfarah. 2009. "Experiences of South Asian Brides Entering Canada after Recent Changes to Family Sponsorship Policies." *Violence Against Women* 15(3): 321–39.

Merkle, Erich R., and Rhonda A. Richardson. 2000. "Digital Dating and Virtual Relating: Conceptualizing Computer Mediated Romantic Relationships." *Family Relations* 49: 187–92.

Milan, Anne, M. Vézina, and C. Wells. 2007. *Family Portrait: Continuity and Change in Canadian Families and Households in 2006*. Ottawa: Statistics Canada.

Mohr, Jonathan J., and Christopher A. Daly. 2008. "Sexual Minority Stress and Changes in Relationship Quality in Same-sex Couples." *Journal of Social and Personal Relationships* 25: 989–1007.

Myers, David G. 1993. *Social Psychology*. New York: McGraw-Hill.

Netting, Nancy. 2006. "Two Lives, One Partner: Indo-Canadian Youth between Love and Arranged Marriages." *Journal of Comparative Family Studies*, 37: 129–46.

O'Sullivan, Lucia F., Mariah Mantsun Cheng, Kathleen Mullan Harris, and Jeanne Brooks-Gunn. 2007. "I Wanna Hold Your Hand: The Progression of Social, Romantic and Sexual Events in Adolescent Relationships." *Perspectives on Sexual and Reproductive Health* 39: 100–7.

Pahl, Ray E., and David J. Pevalin. 2005. "Between Family and Friends: A Longitudinal Study of Friendship Choice." *The British Journal of Sociology* 56(3): 433–50.

Paul, Elizabeth L., Brian McManus, and Allison Hayes. 2000. "Hookups: Characteristics and Correlates of College Students' Spontaneous and Anonymous Sexual Experiences." *Journal of Sex Research* 37: 76–88.

Phua, Voon Chin, and Gayle Kaufman. 2003. "The Crossroads of Race and Sexuality: Date Selection among Men in Internet 'Personal' Ads." *Journal of Family Issues* 24(8): 981–94.

Reid, Julie, Sinikka Elliott, and Gretchen Webber. 2011. "Casual Hookups to Formal Dates: Refining the Boundaries of the Sexual Double Standard." *Gender & Society* 25(5): 545–68

Risman, Barbara. 1998. *Gender Vertigo: American Families in Transition*. New Haven, CT: Yale University Press.

Roseneil, Sasha. 2006. "On Not Living with a Partner: Unpicking Coupledom and Cohabitation." *Sociological Research Online* 11: 3.

Rosenfeld, Michael J. 2007. *The Age of Independence: Interracial Unions, Same-Sex Unions, and the Changing American Family*. Cambridge: Harvard University Press.

Rubin, Gayle. 1984. "Thinking Sex." Pp. 267–319 in *Pleasure and Danger: Exploring Female Sexuality*, edited by C.S. Vance. Boston: Routledge.

Satzewich, Vic. 1993. "Migrant and Immigrant Families in Canada: State Coercion and Legal Control in the Formation of Ethnic Families." *Journal of Comparative Family Studies* 24(3): 315–38.

Shaughnessy, Krystelle, and Sandra E. Byers. 2013. "Seeing the Forest with the Trees: Cybersex as a Case Study of Single-item Versus Multi-item Measures of Sexual Behaviour." *Canadian Journal of Behavioural Science*. 45(3): 220–9. doi:10.1037/a0031331.

———, and Sandra E. Byers. 2014. "Contextualizing Cybersex Experience: Heterosexually Identified Men and Women's Desire for and Experiences with Cybersex with Three Types of Partners." *Computers in Human Behavior*. 32: 178–85. doi:10.1016/j.chb.2013.12.005.

Shelton, Beth Anne, and Daphne John. 1993. "Does Marital Status Make a Difference?" *Journal of Family Issues* 14(3): 401–20.

Simon, William, and John H. Gagnon. 1986. "Sexual Scripts: Permanence and Change." *Archives of Sexual Behavior* 15: 97–122.

Smock, Pamela J., and Wendy D. Manning. 2004. "Living Together Unmarried in the United States: Demographic Perspectives and Implications for Family Policy." *Law and Policy* 26: 87–117.

Snell, James G. 1991. *In the Shadow of the Law: Divorce in Canada, 1900–1939*. Toronto: University of Toronto Press.

Song, Sarah. 2007. *Justice, Gender, and the Politics of Multiculturalism*. Cambridge: Cambridge University Press.

Sprecher, Susan. 2009. "Relationship Initiation and Formation on the Internet." *Marriage & Family Review* 45: 761–82.

Stacey, Judith, and Timothy Biblarz. 2001. "(How) Does the Sexual Orientation of Parents Matter?" *American Sociological Review* 66: 159–83.

Statistics Canada. 2007. *Immigrants in Canada: A Portrait of the Foreign-born Population, 2006 Census,* Catalogue no. 97-557-XCB2006006. Available at (www12 .statcan.ca/census-recensement/2006/as-sa/97-557/ pdf/97-557-XIE 2006001.pdf).

———. 2008. *Aboriginal Peoples in Canada in 2006: Inuit, Métis and First Nations, 2006 Census,* Catalogue no. 97-558-XIE. Available at (www12.statcan. ca/english/census06/analysis/aboriginal/pdf/97-558-XIE 2006001.pdf).

———. 2011. "Census in Brief: Living Arrangements of Young Adults Aged 20 to 29." *Families, Households and Marital Status, 2011 Census of Population.* Ottawa: Statistics Canada, p. 7. Available at (www12. statcan.gc.ca/census-recensement/2011/as-sa/98-312-x/98-312-x2011003_3-eng.pdf).

———. 2017a. *Census Profile.* 2016 Census. Catalogue no. 98-316-X2016001. Available at (http://www12. statcan.gc.ca/census-recensement/2016/dp-pd/prof/ index.cfm?Lang=E).

———. 2017b. "Families, households and marital status: Key results from the 2016 Census." *The Daily,* August 2. Available at (http://www.statcan.gc.ca/daily-quotidien/170802/dq170802a-eng.htm).

———. 2017c.*Same-sex Couples in Canada in 2016: Census in Brief.* Catalogue no. 98-200-X2016007. Available at (http://www12.statcan.gc.ca/census-recensement/2016/as-sa/98-200-x/2016007/98-200-x2016007-eng.cfm).

Swidler, Ann. 2001. *Talk of Love: How Culture Matters.* Chicago: University of Chicago.

Valkyrie, Zek Cypress. 2011. "Cybersexuality in MMORPGs: Virtual Sexual Revolution Untapped." *Men and Masculinities* 14(1): 76–96.

Vanier Institute of the Family. 2010. *Families Count: Profiling Canada's Families.* Ottawa: Vanier Institute of the Family. Available at (www.vanierinstitute.ca/ families_count_-_profiling_canadas_families_iv).

Wakeford, Nina. 2000. "Cyberqueer." Pp. 403–15 in *The Cybercultures Reader,* edited by D. Bell and B.M. Kennedy. New York: Routledge.

Walton-Roberts, Margaret. 2004. "Rescaling Citizenship: Gendering Canadian Immigration Policy." *Political Geography* 23: 265–81.

Weeks, Jeffrey, Catherine Donovan, and Brian Heaphy. 1999. "Everyday Experiments: Narratives of Non-heterosexual Relationships." In *The New Family?,* edited by E.B. Silva and C. Smart. London: Sage.

———, Catherine Donovan, and Brian Heaphy. 1999a. "Partners by Choice: Equality, Power and Commitment in Non-heterosexual Relationships." In *The*

Sociology of the Family: A Reader, edited by G. Allen. Oxford: Blackwell.

———, Catherine Donovan, and Brian Heaphy. 2001. *Same Sex Intimacies: Families of Choice and Other Life Experiments.* London: Routledge.

Zaidi, Arshia U., and Muhammad Shuraydi. 2002. "Perceptions of Arranged Marriages by Young Pakistani Muslim Women Living in a Western Society." *Journal of Comparative Family Studies* 33(4): 495–514.

Chapter 5

Albanese, Patrizia. 2006. "Small Town, Big Benefits: The Ripple Effect of $7/day Child Care." *Canadian Review of Sociology* 43(2): 125–40.

———. 2009. *Children in Canada Today.* Don Mills: Oxford University Press.

Alook, Angele. 2016. *Indigenous Life Courses, Racialized Gendered Life Scripts, and Cultural Identities of Resistance and Resilience.* PhD Dissertation. York University.

Anderson, Kim. 2001. *A Recognition of Being: Reconstructing Native Womanhood.* Toronto: Sumach Press.

Annmaturo, Francesca Romana. 2014. "The Right to Privilege? Homonormativity and the Recognition of Same-Sex Couples in Europe." *Social & Legal Studies* 23(2): 175–94.

Armesto, Jorge C., and Ester R. Shapiro. 2011. "Adoptive Gay Fathers: Transformations of the Masculine Homosexual Self." *Journal of GLBT Family Studies* 7(1-2): 72–92.

Ball, J. 2009. "Fathering in the Shadows: Indigenous Fathers and Canada's Colonial Legacies." *The Annals of the American Academy of Political and Social Science* 634(1): 29–48.

Baumrind, Diana. 1966. "Effects of Authoritative Parental Control on Child Behaviour." *Child Development* 37(4): 887–907.

Beaujot, Roderic. 2004. "Delayed Life Transitions: Trends and Implications." Ottawa: Vanier Institute of the Family. Retrieved March 8, 2012 (www.vanierinstitute .ca/include/get.php?nodeid=1143).

———, and Zenaida Ravanera. 2009. "Family Models for Earning and Caring: Implications for Child Care and for Family Policy." *Canadian Studies in Population* 36(1–2): 145–66.

Beck-Gernsheim, Elisabeth. 2002. *Reinventing the Family: In Search of New Lifestyles.* Cambridge: Polity.

Bernhard, Judith K., Patricia Landolt, and Luin Goldring. 2008. "Transnationalizing Families: Canadian Immigration Policy and the Spatial Fragmentation of Care-giving among Latin American Newcomers." *International Migration* 47(2): 3–31.

Brannen, Julia, and Ann Nilsen. 2006. "From Fatherhood to Fathering: Transmission and Change among

British Fathers in Four-Generation Families." *Sociology* 40(2): 335–52.

Breitkreuz, R., D. Williamson, and K. Raine. 2010. "Dis-integrated Policy: Welfare-to-Work Participants' Experiences of Integrating Paid Work and Unpaid Family Work." *Community, Work, & Family* 13(1): 43–69.

Brigham, Susan M. 2015. "Mothering Has No Borders: The Transnational Kinship Networks of Undocumented Jamaican Domestic Workers in Canada." In *Engendering Transnational Voices: Studies in Family, Work, and Identity*, edited by G. Man and R. Cohen. Waterloo: Wilfrid Laurier Press.

Bushnik, Tracey. 2006. "Child Care in Canada." Retrieved May 10, 2010 (www.statcan.gc.ca/pub/89-599-m/89-599-m2006003-eng.pdf).

Canadian Council of Social Development. 2009. "Poverty Reductions Policy and Programs: Poverty in Ontario—Failed Promise and Renewal of Hope." Retrieved April 12, 2012 (www.ccsd.ca/Reports/ON_Report_FINAL.pdf).

———. n.d. "Families: A Canadian Profile." Retrieved May 2, 2012 (www.ccsd.ca/factsheets/family/).

Chuang, S.S., and Y. Su. 2009. "Says Who?: Decision-Making and Conflicts among Chinese-Canadian and Mainland Chinese Parents of Young Children." *Sex Roles* 60(7–8): 527–36.

Cohen, R. 2000. "'Mom Is a Stranger': The Negative Impact of Immigration Policies on the Family Life of Filipina Domestic Workers." *Canadian Ethnic Studies Journal* 32(3): 76–89.

Connell, R.W. 1987. *Gender and Power: Society, the Person and Sexual Politics*. Stanford, CA: Stanford University Press.

———, and J. Messerschmidt. 2005. "Hegemonic Masculinity: Rethinking the Concept." *Gender and Society* 19 (6): 829–59.

Craig, Lyn. 2006. "Does Father Care Mean Fathers Share? A Comparison of How Mothers and Fathers in Intact Families Spend Time with Children." *Gender and Society* 20(2): 259–81.

Creighton, G., M. Brussoni, and J. Oliffe. 2015. "Fathers on Child's Play: Urban and Rural Canadian Perspectives." *Men and Masculinities* 18(15): 559–80.

Dempsey, D. 2010. "Conceiving and Negotiating Reproductive Relationships: Lesbian and Gay Men Forming Families with Children." *Sociology* 44(6): 1145–62.

Doucet, Andrea. 2006. *Do Men Mother? Fathering, Care, and Domestic Responsibility*. Toronto: University of Toronto Press.

———. 2009. "Gender Equality and Gender Differences: Parenting, Habitus, and Embodiment (The 2008 Porter Lecture)." *Canadian Review of Sociology* 46(2):103–21.

———, and L. Merla. 2007. "Stay-at-home Fathering." *Community, Work, & Family* 10(4):455–73.

Dunne, Gillian. 2000. "Lesbians as Authentic Workers? Institutional Heterosexuality and the Reproduction of Gender Inequalities." *Sexualities* 3(2):133–48.

Elder, G.H. Jr. 1994. "Time, Human Agency, and Social Change: Perspectives on the Life Course." *Social Psychology Quarterly* 57(1): 4–15.

Epstein, Rachel, ed. 2009. *Who's Your Daddy? And Other Writings on Queer Parenting*. Toronto: Sumach Press.

Este, D.C., and A. Tachable. 2009. "Fatherhood in the Canadian Context: Perceptions and Experiences of Sudanese Refugee Men." *Sex Roles* 60(7–8): 451–5.

Faircloth, Charlotte. 2010. "What Science Says Is Best: Parenting Practices, Scientific Authority and Maternal Identity." *Sociological Research Online Special Section on 'Changing Parenting Culture'* 15(4).

Farrell, Betty, Alicia VandeVusse, and Abigail Ocobock. 2012. "Family Change and the State of Family Sociology." *Current Sociology* 60(3): 283–301.

Featherstone, B. 2003. "Taking Fathers Seriously." *British Journal of Social Work* 33(1): 239–54.

Ferguson, Rob. 2016. "Both same-sex parents' names will go on Ontario birth certificates." *Toronto Star*, May 31. Retrieved September 28, 2016 (www.thestar.com/news/queenspark/2016/05/31/same-sex-parents-names-to-both-go-on-birth-certificates-under-new-ontario-law.html).

Ferrao, Vincent. 2010. "Women in Canada: A Gender-based Statistical Report, Paid Work." Ottawa: Statistics Canada. Retrieved April 20, 2012 (www.statcan.gc.ca/pub/89-503-x/2010001/article/11387-eng.pdf).

Fleury, Dominique, and Myriam Fortin. 2006. "When Working Is Not Enough to Escape Poverty: An Analysis of Canada's Working Poor." Ottawa: Human Resources and Social Development Canada. Retrieved March 23, 2012 (http://tamarackcommunity.ca/downloads/vc/When_Work_Not_Enough.pdf).

Foster, Deborah. 2005. "The Formation and Continuance of Lesbian Families in Canada." *Canadian Bulletin of Medical History* 22(2): 281–97.

Fox, Bonnie. 2001. "The Formative Years: How Parenthood Creates Gender." *Canadian Review of Sociology and Anthropology* 38(4): 373–90.

Friendly, Martha, Bethany Grady, Lyndsay Macdonald, and Barry Forer. 2015. *Preliminary Data: Early Childhood Education and Care in Canada 2014*. Toronto: Childcare Resource and Research Unit. Retrieved April 16, 2017 (www.cccf-fcsge.ca/2015/10/22/canada2014/).

Fuller-Thomson, Esme. 2005. "Canadian First Nations Grandparents Raising Grandchildren: A Portrait in Resilience." *International Journal of Aging and Human Development* 60(4): 331–42.

Gazso, A. 2007. "Staying Afloat on Social Assistance: Parents' Strategies of Balancing Work and Family." *Socialist Studies* 3(2): 31–63.

———. 2007a. "Balancing Expectations for Employability and Family Responsibilities While on Social Assistance: Low Income Mothers' Experiences in Three Canadian Provinces." *Family Relations* 56: 454–66.

———. 2009. "Mothers' Maintenance of Families through Market and Family Care Relations." Pp. 219–46 in *Feminist Issues: Race, Class, and Sexuality*, edited by N. Mandell. Toronto: Pearson/Prentice Hall.

———. 2009a. "Reinvigorating the Debate: Questioning the Assumptions About and Models of the "Family" in Social Assistance Policy." *Women's Studies International Forum* 31(2): 150–62.

———, and Susan McDaniel. 2015. "Families by Choice and the Management of Low Income through Social Supports." *Journal of Family Issues* 36(3): 371–95.

Geisler, Mark. 2012. "Gay Fathers' Negotiation of Gender Role Strain: A Qualitative Inquiry." *Fathering: A Journal of Theory. Research, and Practice about Men as Fathers* 10(2): 119–39.

Gladstone, James W., Ralph A. Brown, and Kerri-Ann J. Fitzgerald. 2009. "Grandparents Raising Their Grandchildren: Tensions, Service Needs, and Involvement with Child Welfare Agencies." *International Journal of Aging and Human Development* 69(1): 55–78.

Grant, Tavia. 2016. "Women still earning less money than men despite gains in education: study." *Globe and Mail*, March 7.

Hassan, G., C. Rousseau, T. Measham, and M. Lashley. 2008. "Caribbean and Filipino Adolescents' and Parents' Perceptions of Parental Authority, Physical Punishment, and Cultural Values and Their Relation to Migratory Characteristics." *Canadian Ethnic Studies* 40(2): 171–86.

Haw, Jennie. 2015. "Corporeal Commodification and Women's Work: Feminist Analysis of Private Umbilical Cord Blood Banking." *Body & Society* 22(3): 31–53.

Hayes, Sharon. 1996. *The Cultural Contradictions of Motherhood*. New Haven Yale University Press.

Horvath, Catherine A., and Catherine M. Lee. 2015. "Parenting Responses and Parenting Goals of Mothers and Fathers of Adolescents." *Marriage and Family Review* 51: 337–5.

Hou, Feng, Grant Schellenberg, and Rene Morisette. 2015. "Full-Time Employment, 1976 to 2014." *Economic Insights*. Catalogue 11-626-x No. 49. Ottawa: Statistics Canada. Available at (www5.statcan.gc.ca/olc-cel/olc.action?ObjId=11-626-X2015049&ObjType=46&lang=en&limit=0).

Human Resources and Skills Development Canada. 2012. "Canadians in Context: Population Size and Growth." Retrieved April 20, 2012 (www4.hrsdc.gc.ca/.3ndic.1t.4r@-eng.jsp?iid=35).

———. 2012a. "Indicators of Well-Being: Family Life-Age of Mother at Childbirth." Retrieved March 9, 2012 (www4.hrsdc.gc.ca/.3ndic.1t.4r@-eng.jsp?iid=75).

Kier, Cheryl. A., and Tak Fung. 2014. "Adult Outcomes of Being Raised by Grandmothers: Can Social Networks Play a Role?" *Journal of Intergenerational Relationships* 12(2): 141–66.

LaRossa, Ralph. 1988. "Fatherhood and Social Change." *Family Relations* 37: 451–8.

Lashewicz, B., G. Manning, M. Hall, and N. Keating. 2007. "Equity Matters: Doing Fairness in the Context of Family Caregiving." *Canadian Journal on Aging* 26 (Supplement 1): 91–102.

LeMoyne, Terri, and Tom Buchanan. 2011. "Does 'Hovering' Matter? Helicopter Parenting and Its Effect on Well-Being." *Sociological Spectrum* 31: 339–418.

Liu, Jianye, and Don Kerr. 2003. "Family Change and the Economic Well-Being of Recent Immigrants to Canada." *International Migration* 41(4): 113–40.

Macdougall, Brenda. 2010. *One of the Family: Métis Culture in Nineteenth-Century Northwestern Saskatchewan*. Vancouver: UBC Press.

Marshall, K. 2011. "Generational Change in Paid and Unpaid Work." *Canadian Social Trends*. Catalogue 1108-X No. 92. Ottawa: Statistics Canada. Available at (www.statcan.gc.ca/pub/11-008-x/2011002/article/11520-eng.htm).

McDaniel, Susan, and Paul Bernard. 2011. "Life Course as a Policy Lens: Challenges and Opportunities." *Canadian Public Policy* 37(1).

McMullin, Julie Ann. 2005. "Patterns of Paid and Unpaid Work: The Influence of Power, Social Context, and Family Background." *Canadian Journal on Aging* 24(3): 225–36.

Milan, A., M. Vézina, and C. Wells. 2007. "Family Portrait: Continuity and Change in Canadian Families and Households in 2006: Findings." Ottawa: Statistics Canada. Retrieved September 25, 2007 (www12.statcan.ca/english/census06/analysis/famhouse/index.cfm).

———. 2009. *Family Matters: An Introduction to Family Sociology in Canada*. Toronto: Canadian Scholar's Press Inc.

Mitchell, Barbara A. 2012. *Family Matters: An Introduction to Family Sociology in Canada*, 2nd edn. Toronto: Canadian Scholar's Press Inc.

Nelson, Adie. 2006. *Gender in Canada*. Toronto: Pearson Prentice Hall.

Ochocka, J., and R. Janzen. 2008. "Immigrant Parenting: A New Framework of Understanding." *Journal of International Migration and Integration* 6(1): 85–112.

O'Donnell, J.M., W.E. Johnson Jr, L.E. D'Aunno, and H.L. Thorton. 2005. "Fathers in Child Welfare: Caseworkers' Perspectives." *Child Welfare* 84(3): 387–14.

Ornstein, M., and G.J. Stalker. 2013. "Canadian Families' Strategies for Employment and Care for Preschool Children." *Journal of Family Issues* 34(1): 53–84.

Pacaut, Philippe, Celine Le Bourdais, and Benoit Laplante. 2011. "The Changing Impact of Conjugal Status and Motherhood on Employment across Generations of Canadian Women." *Canadian Studies in Population* 38(3–4): 105–32.

Ranson, Gillian. 1998. "Education, Work, and Family Decision Making: Finding the Right Time to Have a Baby." *Canadian Review of Sociology and Anthropology* 35(4): 517–33.

———. 2010. *Against the Grain: Couples, Gender, and the Reframing of Parenting.* Toronto: University of Toronto Press.

Robinson, Clyde C., Barbara Mandleco, Susanne Frost Olsen, and Craig H. Hart. 1995. "Authoritative, Authoritarian, and Permissive Parenting Practices: Development of a New Measure." *Psychological Reports* 77: 819–30.

Schacher, Stephanie Jill, Carl F. Auerbach, and Louise Bordeaux Silverstein. 2005. "Gay Fathers Expanding the Possibilities for Us All." *Journal of GLBT Family Studies* 1(3): 31–51.

Sears, W., and M. Sears. 2001. *The Attachment Parenting Book, A Commonsense Guide to Understanding and Nurturing Your Baby.* London: Little, Brown and Company.

Spitzer, D., A. Neufold, M. Harrison, K. Hughes, and M. Stewart. 2003. "Caregiving in Transnational Context: My Wings Have Been Cut; Where Can I Fly?" *Gender and Society* 17(2):267–86.

Stacey, Judith. 2006. "Gay Parenthood and the Decline of Paternity as We Knew It." *Sexualities* 9(1):27–55.

Stapleton, J., with J. Kay. 2015. "The Working Poor in the Toronto Region: Mapping Working Poverty in Canada's Richest City." Metcalf Foundation. Available at (http://metcalffoundation.com/stories/publications/the-working-poor-in-the-toronto-region-mapping-working-poverty-in-canadas-richest-city/).

Statistics Canada. 2007. "Census Families by Number of Children at Home." Available at (www.statcan.gc.ca/tables-tableaux/sum-som/l01/cst01/famil50a-eng.htm).

———. 2008. *Report on the Demographic Situation in Canada 2005 and 2006.* Ottawa: Statistics Canada.

———. 2010. *Women in Canada: A Gender-Based Statistical Report.* 6th edition. Catalogue no. 89-503-X Ottawa: Statistics Canada. Available at (www.statcan.gc.ca/pub/89-503-x/89-503-x2010001-eng.htm).

———. 2012. "Portrait of Families and Living Arrangements in Canada." Analytical Document. (Cat no. 98-312-X2011001). Ottawa: Statistics Canada.

———. 2016. "Changing Profile of Stay-at-Home Parents." *The Daily*, Canadian Megatrends. Available at (www.statcan.gc.ca/pub/11-630-x/11-630-x2016007-eng.htm).

———. 2016a. "Fertility: Fewer Children, Older Moms." *The Daily*, Canadian Megatrends. Available at (www.statcan.gc.ca/pub/11-630-x/11-630-x2014002-eng.htm).

———. 2016b. "The Rise of the Dual-Earner Family with Children." *The Daily*, Canadian Megatrends. Available at (www.statcan.gc.ca/pub/11-630-x/11-630-x2016005-eng.htm).

———. 2017a. "Families, households, and marital status: Key results from the 2016 Census." *The Daily*. Available at (http://www.statcan.gc.ca/daily-quotidien/170802/dq170802a-eng.htm).

———. 2017b. Same-sex couples in Canada in 2016. Available at (http://www12.statcan.gc.ca/census-recensement/2016/as-sa/98-200-x/2016007/98-200-x2016007-eng.cfm).

———. 2017c. Portrait of children's family life in Canada 2016. Available at (http://www12.statcan.gc.ca/census-recensement/2016/as-sa/98-200-x/2016006/98-200-x2016006-eng.cfm).

Sullivan, Maureen. 2004. *The Family of Woman: Lesbian Mothers, Their Children, and the Undoing of Gender.* Berkeley: University of California Press.

Tuten, Tracy L., and Rachel A. August. 2006. "Work-family Conflict: A Study of Lesbian Mothers." *Women in Management Review* 21: 578–97.

Uppal, Sharanjit. 2015. *Employment Patterns of Parents with Children. Insights on Canadian Society.* Catalogue no. 75-006-X. Ottawa: Statistics Canada. Available at (www.statcan.gc.ca/pub/75-006-x/2015001/article/14202-eng.htm#a6).

Uppal, Sharanjit, and Sébastien Larochelle-Côté. 2015. *Changes in Wealth across the Income Distribution, 1999 to 2012. Insights on Canadian Society.* Catalogue no. 75-006-X. Ottawa. Statistics Canada. Available at: (www.statcan.gc.ca/access_acces/alternative_alternatif.action?l=eng&loc=/pub/75-006-x/2015001/article/14194-eng.pdf).

Valverde, Marianna. 2009. "Heterosexuality: Contested Ground." Pp. 212–18 in *Family Patterns, Gender Relations*, edited by B. Fox. Toronto: Oxford University Press.

Wall, Glenda. 2013. "'Putting Family First': Shifting Discourses of Motherhood and Childhood in Representations of Mothers' Employment and Child Care." *Women's Studies International Forum* 40: 162–71

Wall, G., and S. Arnold. 2007. "How Involved Is Involved Parenting? An Exploration of the Contemporary

Culture of Fatherhood." *Gender and Society* 21(4): 508–27.

Walton-Roberts, M., and G. Pratt. 2005. "Mobile Modernities: A South Asian Family Negotiates Immigration, Gender, and Class in Canada." *Gender, Place, & Culture: A Journal of Feminist Geography* 12(2): 173–95.

Wheeler, Mark, Clarence Lochhead, and Sari Tudiver. 2013. *Policy Implications of Delayed Reproduction and Low Fertility Rates.* Policy Horizons Canada.

Chapter 6

Ambert, Anne-Marie. 2002. *Divorce: Facts, Causes and Consequences*, rev. edn. Ottawa: Vanier Institute of the Family.

Bibby, Reginald. 2005. *Future Families Project: A Survey of Canadian Hopes and Dreams.* Ottawa: Vanier Institute of the Family.

Bohnert, Nora, Anne Milan, and Heather Lathe. 2014. "Living Arrangements of Children in Canada: A Century of Change" *Insights on Canadian Society.* Ottawa Statistics Canada.

Bouzane, Bradley. 2011. "Majority of Canadians underestimate financial burden of divorce: BMO." *Vancouver Sun.*

Clark, Brenda. 2013. "Supporting the Mental Health of Children and Youth of Separating Parents." *Paediatrics and Child Health* 18, 7: 373–7.

Court of Appeal of Ontario. 2009. *Serra v. Serra.* 2009 ONCA 105 (CanLII). Toronto: Court of Appeal of Ontario. Available at (www.canlii.org/en/on/onca/doc/2009/2009onca105/2009onca105.html).

Department of Justice. 2006. *Federal Child Support Guidelines: Step-By-Step.* Ottawa: Minister of Justice and the Attorney General of Canada. Available at (www.justice.gc.ca/en/ps/sup/pub/guide/guide.pdf).

Douglas, Kristen. 2001. *Divorce Law in Canada.* Ottawa: Law and Government Division, Government of Canada.

Employment and Social Development Canada. 2014. "Family Life–Divorce." Ottawa: Employment and Social Development Canada. Available at (www4.hrsdc.gc.ca/.3ndic.1t.4r@-eng.jsp?iid=76).

Gillespie, Kerry. 2006. "Ontario bans binding religious arbitration." *Toronto Star*, 15 February.

Jamison, Tyler, Marilyn Coleman, Lawrence Ganong, Richard Feistman. 2014. "Transitioning to Post-divorce Family Life: A Grounded Theory Investigation of Resilience in Coparentin." *Family Relations* 63, 3: 411–23.

Jolivet, Kendra Randall. 2011. 'The Psychological Impact of Divorce on Children: What Is a Family Lawyer to Do?' *American Journal of Family Law* 25(4): 175–83.

Juby, Heather, Céline Le Bourdais, and Nicole Marcil-Gratton. 2003. *Linking Family Change,*

Parents' Employment and Income and Children's Economic Well-Being: A Longitudinal Perspective. Research Report 2003-FCY-2E. Ottawa: Department of Justice Canada.

Kelly, Mary Bess. 2012. "Divorce Cases in Civil Court, 2010–2011." *Juristat*, March 28.

———. 2013. "Payment Patterns of Child and Spousal Support." *Juristat.* Ottawa: Statistics Canada. Cat. # 85-002-X. Available at (www.statcan.gc.ca/pub/85-002-x/2013001/article/11780-eng.htm).

Milan, Anne. 2013. "Marital Status: Overview, 2011." *Report on the Demographic Situation in Canada.* Statistics Canada Catalogue no. 91-209-X. Ottawa: Statistics Canada. Available at (http://www.statcan.gc.ca/pub/91-209-x/2013001/article/11788-eng.pdf).

———, Leslie-Anne Keown, and Covadonga Robles Urquijo. 2011. *Families, Living Arrangements and Unpaid Work.* Ottawa: Statistics Canada. Available at (www.statcan.gc.ca/pub/89-503-x/2010001/article/11546-eng.pdf).

Moffat, Alistair, and James F. Wilson. 2011. *The Scots, A Genetic Journey.* Edinburgh: Birlinn.

Paraskevas, Joe. 2004. "Survivor pension denial upheld." *Vancouver Sun*, 29 October.

Picot, Garnet, and John Myles. 1995. *Social Transfers, Changing Family Structure and Low Income among Children.* Ottawa: Statistics Canada Research Paper Series, no. 82, Catalogue no. 11F0019MIE, 10.

Prazen, Ariana, Nicholas Wolfinger, Caitlin Cahill, Lori Kowaleski-Jones. 2011. "Joint Physical Custody and Neighborhood Friendships in Middle Childhood." *Sociological Inquiry* 81(2): 247–59.

Robinson, Paul. 2009. "Profile of Child Support Beneficiaries." *Juristat.* Ottawa: Statistics Canada (Cat. # 85-022-X). www.statcan.gc.ca/pub/85-002-x/2009001/article/10784-eng.htm.

Rotermann, Michelle. 2007. "Marital Breakdown and Subsequent Depression." *Health Reports* 18(2): 35. Ottawa: Statistics Canada, Catalogue 82-003

Schmitz, Cristin. 2004. "B.C. ruling puts fault into no-fault divorce." *National Post*, 27 September.

Sinha, Maire. 2014. *Parenting and Child Support after Separation or Divorce.* (Cat. No. 89-652-x). Ottawa: Statistics Canada.

Slade, Daryl. 2011. "Father's gay partner gets custody of girl, 8." *National Post*, 26 October, A7.

Steeves, Chantal. 2012. "Interjurisdictional Cases of Spousal and Child Support." *Jusristat.* Ottawa: Statistics Canada. Catalogue 85-002-X.

Statistics Canada. 2002. "Changing conjugal life in Canada." *The Daily*, 11 July.

———. 2002a. "Divorces." *The Daily*, 2 December.

———. 2005. "Divorces." *The Daily*, 8 March.

———. 2008. *Report on the Demographic Situation in Canada 2005 and 2006.* Ottawa: Statistics Canada.

———. 2016. "Study: Low income dynamics of Canadian taxfilers, 1992 to 2013." *The Daily* (Tuesday, June 21, 2016). Ottawa: Statistics Canada. Available at (www.statcan.gc.ca/daily-quotidien/160621/dq160621c-eng.pdf).

———. 2017b. "Families, households and marital status: Key results from the 2016 Census." *The Daily.* August 2, 2017. Ottawa: Statistics Canada. (www.statcan.gc.ca/daily-quotidien/170802/dq170802a-eng.htm)

Supreme Court of Canada. 2008. *Stein v. Stein.* [2008] 2 S.C.R. 263, 2008 SCC 35. Ottawa: Supreme Court of Canada. Available at (https://scc-csc.lexum.com/scc-csc/scc-csc/en/item/4646/index.do).

———. 2011. *Schreyer v.* Schreyer. 2011 SCC 35, [2011] 2 S.C.R. 605. Ottawa: Supreme Court. Available at (https://scc-csc.lexum.com/scc-csc/scc-csc/en/item/7950/index.do).

Tibbetts, Janice. 2008. "Divorced pair must share future debt." *National Post,* 13 June.

Vanier Institute of the Family. 2000. Profiling Canada's Families II, Section 28, "Mine, Yours and Ours—Canada's 'Blended' Families." Ottawa: Vanier Institute of the Family.

Vézina, Mireille. 2012. 2011 *General Social Survey: Overview of Families in Canada—Being a Parent in a Stepfamily: A Profile.* Catalogue no. 89650X—No. 002. Ottawa: Statistics Canada. Available at (www.statcan.gc.ca/pub/89-650-x/89-650-x2012002-eng.pdf).

Wattie, Chris. 2008. "Lesbian's children to be returned to Britain." *National Post,* 25 July, A3.

Chapter 7

Ahrons, Constance R., and Jennifer L. Tanner. 2003. "Adult Children and Their Fathers: Relationship Changes 20 Years after Parental Divorce." *Family Relations* 52: 340–51.

Allen, Katherine R., Rosemary Blieszner, and Karen A. Roberto. 2000. "Families in the Middle and Later Years: A Review and Critique of Research in the 1990s." *Journal of Marriage and the Family* 62: 911–26.

———, and A.J. Walker. 2006. "Aging and gender in families: A very grand opening." Pp. 155–74 in *Age Matters: Realigning Feminist Thinking,* edited by T.M. Calastani and K.F. Slevin. New York, NY: Routledge, Taylor & Francis Group.

Amato, P.R. 2010. "Research on Divorce: Continuing Trends and New Developments." *Journal of Marriage and Family* 72: 650–66. doi:10.1111/j.1741-3737.2010.00723.x

Ambert, Anne-Marie. 2005. *Divorce: Facts, Causes, and Consequences.* Ottawa: Vanier Institute of the Family.

Antonucci, Toni, and Hiroko Akiyama. 1997. "Concern with OMid-life: Care, Comfort, or Compromise?"

Pp. 147–69 in *Multiple Paths of Mid-life Development,* edited by M.E. Lachman and J.B. James. Chicago: University of Chicago Press.

Aquilino, William S. 2005. "Impact of Family Structure on Parental Attitudes toward the Economic Support of Adult Children over the Transition to Adulthood." *Journal of Family Issues* 26: 143–67.

Arber, S., and V. Timonen. 2012. "Grandparenting in the 21st Century: New Directions." Pp. 247–64 in *Contemporary Grandparenting: Changing Family Relationships in Global Contexts,* edited by S. Arber and V. Timonen. Bristol, UK: The Policy Press.

Arnett, J.J. 2000. "Emerging Adulthood: A Theory of Development from the Late Teens through the Twenties." *American Psychologist* 55: 469–80.

Attias-Donfut, C., J. Ogg, and F.C. Wolff. 2005. "European Patterns of Intergenerational Financial and Time Transfers." *European Journal of Aging* 2(3): 161–73.

Baker, Maureen. 2001. *Families, Labour and Love.* Vancouver: University of British Columbia Press.

Beaupré, Pascale. 2008. *I Do. Take Two? Changes in Intentions to Remarry Among Divorced Canadians During the Past 20 Years.* Statistics Canada, Catalogue no. 86-630-X, July. Available at (www.statcan.gc.ca/pub/89-630-x/2008001/article/10659-eng.pdf).

Bengtson, V.L., and R.E. Roberts. 1991. "Intergenerational Solidarity in Aging Families: An Example of Formal Theory Construction." *Journal of Marriage and the Family*: 856–70.

Bennett, K.M. 2007. "'No Sissy Stuff': Towards a Theory of Masculinity and Emotional Expression in Older Widowed Men." *Journal of Aging Studies* 21(4): 347–56. doi:10.1016/j.jaging.2007.05.002

Birditt, K.S., L.A. Tighe, K.L. Fingerman, and S.H. Zarit. 2012. "Intergenerational Relationship Quality Across Three Generations." *The Journals of Gerontology Series B: Psychological Sciences and Social Sciences* 67(5): 627–38.

Borrie, C. 2015. *The Long Hello: Memory, My Mother, and Me.* Toronto: Simon & Schuster Canada.

Carr, D. 2005. "The Psychological Consequences of Mid-life Men's Social Comparisons with Their Young Adult Sons." *Journal of Marriage and Family* 67: 240–50.

———. 2016. "Grieving for My Abusive Parent? Childhood Maltreatment and Depressive Symptoms among Bereaved Older Adult Children." Paper presentation, American Sociological Association, Seattle, WA. August.

Chambers, P., G. Allan, C. Phillipson, and M. Ray. 2009. *Family Practices in Later Life.* Bristol, UK: The Policy Press.

Clark, W., and S. Crompton. 2006. "Til Death Do Us Part? The Risk of First and Second Marriage

Dissolution." *Canadian Social Trends*, Statistics Canada catalogue no. 11-008 (Summer 2006).

Conference Board of Canada (2016). "Poverty". Retrieved April 24, 2017 (www.conferenceboard.ca/hcp/provincial/society/poverty.aspx).

Connidis, I.A. 1987. "Life in Older Age: The View from the Top." Pp. 451–72 in *Aging in Canada: Social Perspectives*, 2nd edn., edited by V.W. Marshall. Toronto: Fitzhenry and Whiteside.

———. 2001. *Family Ties and Aging*. Thousand Oaks, CA: Sage.

———. 2010. *Family Ties and Aging*, 2nd ed. LA: Pine Forge Press/Sage.

———. 2012. "Interview and Memoir: Complementary Narratives on the Family Ties of Gay Adults." *Journal of Family Theory and Review* 4(2): 105–21. doi:10.1111/j.1756-2589.2012.00127.x.

———. 2015. "Exploring Ambivalence in Family Ties: Progress and Prospects." *Journal of Marriage and Family* 77(1): 77–95. doi:10.1111/jomf.12150.

———, and Lori D. Campbell. 1995. "Closeness, Confiding, and Contact among Siblings in Middle and Late Adulthood." *Journal of Family Issues* 16: 722–45.

———, and C. Kemp. 2008. "Negotiating Actual and Anticipated Parental Support: Multiple Sibling Voices in Three-Generation Families." *Journal of Aging Studies* 22(3): 229–38.

———, and J.A. McMullin. 2002. "Sociological Ambivalence and Family Ties: A Critical Perspective." *Journal of Marriage and Family* 64(3): 558–67.

De Marco, A.C., and S.C. Berzin. 2008. "The Influence of Family Economic Status on Home-Leaving Patterns during Emerging Adulthood." *Families in Society: The Journal of Contemporary Social Services* 89: 208–18.

de Medeiros, K., and R.L. Rubinstein. 2015. "'Shadow Stories' in Oral Interviews: Narrative Care through Careful Listening." *Journal of Aging Studies* 34: 162–8. doi:10.1016/j.jaging.2015.02.009.

Dentinger, Emma and Martin Clarkberg. 2002. "Informal Caregiving and Retirement Timing among Men and Women: Gender and Caregiving Relationships in Late Midlife." *Journal of Family Issues* 23 (7): 857–879.

Dettling, Lisa J., and Joanne W. Hsu. 2015. *Why Boomerang? Debt, Access to Credit, and Parental Co-residence among Young Adults*. FEDS Notes, Board of Governors of the Federal Reserve System (U.S.).

de Vries, B., A.M. Mason, J. Quam, and K. Acquaviva. 2009. "State Recognition of Same-sex Relationships and Preparations for End of Life among Lesbian and Gay Boomers." *Sexuality Research & Social Policy* 6(1): 90–101.

Doyle, M., and V. Timonen. 2008. *Home Care for Ageing Populations: A Comparative Analysis of Domiciliary Care in Denmark, Germany, and the United States*. Northampton, MA: Edward Elgar Publishing.

Dunlop, Rosemary, and Ailsa Burns. 1995. "The Sleeper Effect—Myth or Reality?" *Journal of Marriage and Family* 57: 375–86.

Ellin, Abby. 2015. "After full lives together, more older couples are divorcing." *The New York Times*, 30 October. Available at (https://www.nytimes.com/2015/10/31/your-money/after-full-lives-together-more-older-couples-are-divorcing.html).

Epstein, Rachel. 2003. "Lesbian Families." Pp. 76–102 in *Voices: Essays on Canadian Families*, edited by M. Lynn. Scarborough, ON: Nelson Thomson Learning.

Eshleman, J. Ross, and Susannah J. Wilson. 2001. *The Family*, 3rd Canadian edn. Toronto: Pearson Education.

Fingerman, Karen L., Elizabeth L. Hay, and Kira S. Birdett. 2004. "The Best of Ties, the Worst of Ties: Close, Problematic, and Ambivalent Social Relationships." *Journal of Marriage and Family* 66: 792–808.

Fredriksen-Goldsen, K.I., and A. Muraco. 2010. "Aging and Sexual Orientation: A 25-year Review of the Literature." *Research on Aging* 32: 372–413.

Gee, Ellen M. 1990. "The Changing Demography of Intergenerational Relations in Canada." Pp. 49–69 in *Canadian Gerontological Collection VII: The Aging Family in an Aging Society*, edited by P.A. Conrad and V. White. Ottawa: The Canadian Association on Gerontology.

———, and M.M Kimball. 1987. *Women and Aging*. Toronto: Butterworths Publishers.

———, and Barbara A. Mitchell. 2003. "One Roof: Exploring Multi-generational Households in Canada." Pp. 291–311 in *Voices: Essays on Canadian Families*, edited by M. Lynn. Scarborough, ON: Nelson Thomson Learning.

Gubrium, J.F., and J.A. Holstein. 1998. "Narrative Practice and the Coherence of Personal Stories." *The Sociological Quarterly* 39(1): 163–87. doi:10.1111/j.1533-8525.1998.tb02354.x.

Hagestad, G.O. 2006. "Transfers between Grandparents and Grandchildren: The Importance of Taking a Three-generation Perspective." *Zeitschrift für Familienforschung* 18(3): 315–32.

Hartnett, C.S., K. Fingerman, and K. Birditt. 2016. "Without the Ties that Bind: Young Adults Who Lack Contact with Parents." Paper presentation, American Sociological Association, Seattle, WA. August.

Hash, Kristina. 2001. "Caregiving and Post-Caregiving Experiences of Mid-life and Older Gay Men and Lesbians." PhD thesis, Virginia Commonwealth University.

Hetherington, Mavis, and Joan Kelly. 2002. *For Better or For Worse: Divorce Reconsidered*. New York: Norton.

Iacovou, M. 2010. "Leaving Home: Independence, Togetherness and Income." *Advances in Life Course Research* 15(4): 147–60

Ibbitson, J. 2016. "The speed of change: from criminality to acceptance." *Globe and Mail*, March 2, A4.

Izuhara, M., ed. 2010. *Ageing and Intergenerational Relations: Family Reciprocity from a Global Perspective*. Bristol, UK: The Policy Press.

Kamo, Yoshinori. 2000. "Racial and Ethnic Differences in Extended Family Households." *Sociological Perspectives* 43: 211–29.

Kelly, Christine. 2016. *Disability Politics and Care*. Vancouver: UBC Press.

Kemp, C. 2007. "Grandparent–Grandchild Ties: Reflections on Continuity and Change across Three Generations." *Journal of Family Issues* 28(7): 855–81

Kenyon, G., E. Bohlmeijer, and W.L. Randall, eds. 2010. *Storying Later Life: Issues, Investigations, and Interventions in Narrative Gerontology*. New York: Oxford University Press.

Killian, T., J. Turner, R. Cain. 2005. "Depressive Symptoms of Caregiving Women in Midlife: The Role of Physical Health." *Journal of Women and Aging* 17: 115–27.

Klinenberg, E. 2012. *Going Solo: The Extraordinary Rise and Surprising Appeal of Living Alone*. London: Gerald Duckworth & Co Ltd.

Kobayashi, Karen M. 1999. "*Bunka no tanjyo* (emergent culture): Continuity and Change in Older *nisei* (second generation) Parent–Adult *sansei* (third generation) Child Relationships in Japanese Canadian Families." PhD thesis, Simon Fraser University.

Kozuch, Patricia, and Teresa M. Cooney. 1995. "Young Adults' Marital and Family Attitudes: The Role of Recent Parental Divorce, and Family and Parental Conflict." *Journal of Divorce and Remarriage* 23: 45–62.

Landis-Kleine, C., L. Foley, L. Nall, P. Padgett, and L. Walters-Palmer. 1995. "Attitudes toward Marriage and Family Held by Young Adults." *Journal of Divorce and Remarriage* 23: 63–73.

Lendon, J.P., M. Silverstein, and R. Giarrusso. 2014. "Ambivalence in Older Parent–Adult Child Relationships: Mixed Feelings, Mixed Measures." *Journal of Marriage and the Family* 76(2): 272–84

Loe, M. 2011. *Aging our Way: Lessons for Living from 85 and Beyond*. New York: Oxford University Press.

Lopata, H.Z. 1996. *Current Widowhood: Myths and Realities*. Thousand Oaks, CA: Sage Publications.

McAlister, M. 2013. Valuing Caregivers and Caregiving: Family Caregivers in the Integrated Approach to Palliative Care. Available at (www.hpcintegration.ca/media/37049/TWF-valuing-caregivers-report-final.pdf).

McDaniel, Susan. 2005. "The Family Lives of the Middle-aged and Elderly in Canada." Pp. 181–99 in *Families: Changing Trends in Canada*, edited by M. Baker. Toronto: McGraw-Hill Ryerson.

———, and Lorne Tepperman. 2007. *Close Relations: An Introduction to the Sociology of Families*, 3rd edn. Toronto: Pearson Prentice Hall.

Marshall, V.M., S.H. Matthews, and C.J. Rosenthal. 1993. "Elusiveness of Family Life: A Challenge for the Sociology of Aging." *Annual Review of Gerontology and Geriatrics* 13(1): 39–72.

Martin-Matthews, Anne. 1991. *Widowhood in Later Life*. Toronto: Butterworths/Harcourt Brace.

———. 1999. "Widowhood: Dominant Renditions Changing Demography and Variable Meaning." Pp. 27–44 in *Critical Issues for Future Social Work Practice with Aging Persons*, edited by S.M. Neysmith. New York: Columbia University Press.

———. 2000. "Intergenerational Caregiving: How Apocalyptic and Dominant Demographies Frame the Questions and Shape the Answers." Pp. 64–79 in *The Overselling of Population Aging: Apocalyptic Demography, Intergenerational Challenges and Social Policy*, edited by E.M. Gee and G.M. Gutman. Toronto: Oxford University Press.

———. 2007. "Situating 'Home' at the Nexus of the Public and Private Spheres: Aging, Gender and Home Support Work in Canada." *Current Sociology* 55 (2): 229–49.

———. 2011. "Revisiting Widowhood in Later Life: Changes in Patterns and Profiles, Advances in Research and Understanding." *Canadian Journal on Aging* 30(3): 339–54. doi:10.1017/S0714980811000201.

———. 2016. "Ways of Knowing about Aging, Old Age and Widowhood in Later Life: Insights from Social Media." Presentation in the session "Digital Technologies, Ageing and Everyday Life," Third World Forum of Sociology, International Sociological Association, Vienna, Austria. July 10–16.

———, J. Sims-Gould, and J. Naslund. 2010. "Ethno-cultural Diversity in Home Care Work in Canada: Issues Confronted, Strategies Employed." *International Journal of Ageing and Later Life* 5(2): 77–101.

———, C. Tong, C.J. Rosenthal, and L. McDonald. 2013. "Ethno-cultural Diversity in the Experience of Widowhood in Later Life: Chinese Widows in Canada." *Journal of Aging Studies* 27(4): 507–18.

Matthews, R., and A. Martin-Matthews. 1986. "Infertility and Involuntary Childlessness: The Transition to Nonparenthood." *Journal of Marriage and the Family*: 641–49.

Matthews, S.H. 2002. *Sisters and Brothers/Daughters and Sons: Meeting the Needs of Old Parents*. Bloomington, IN: Unlimited Publishing LLC.

Milan, A. 2015. "Families and Living Arrangements." *Women in Canada: A Gender-Based Statistical Report*. Catalogue no. 89-503-X.

———. 2016. "Insights on Canadian Society: Diversity of Young Adults Living with their Parents." *The Daily*, Statistics Canada, June 15.

Milardo, R.M. 1988. *Families and Social Networks. New Perspectives on Family*. Thousand Oaks, CA: Sage Publications, Inc.

Miller, James. 2003. "Out Family Values." Pp. 103–30 in *Voices: Essays on Canadian Families*, edited by M. Lynn. Scarborough, ON: Nelson Thomson Learning.

Mitchell, Barbara A. 1994. "Family Structure and Leaving the Nest: A Social Resource Perspective." *Sociological Perspectives* 27: 651–71.

———. 1998a. "The Refilled Nest: Debunking the Myth of Family in Crisis." Paper presented at the ninth annual John K. Friesen Conference, The Overselling of Population Aging. Simon Fraser University, 14–15 May.

———. 1998b. "Too Close for Comfort? Parental Assessments of 'Boomerang Kid' Living Arrangements." *Canadian Journal of Sociology* 23: 21–46.

———. 2006. *The Boomerang Age: Transitions to Adulthood in Families.* Edison, NJ: Aldine

———. 2009. *Family Matters: An Introduction to Family Sociology in Canada.* Toronto: Canadian Scholar's Press Inc.

———. 2016. "Empty Nest." In *The Wiley Blackwell Encyclopedia of Family* Studies, edited by C. Sheehan. Hoboken, NJ: Wiley Blackwell.

———, and Ellen M. Gee. 1996. "'Boomerang Kids' and Mid-life Parental Marital Satisfaction." *Family Relations* 45: 442–8.

———, and L. Lovegreen. 2009. "The Empty Nest Syndrome in Midlife Families: A Multi-Method Exploration of Parental Gender Differences and Cultural Dynamics." *Journal of Family Issues* 30(12): 1654–70.

———, Andrew V. Wister, and Ellen M. Gee. 2002. "There's No Place Like Home: An Analysis of Young Adults' Mature Co-residency in Canada." *International Journal of Aging and Human Development* 54: 57–84.

Mitchell, David, and Sharon Snyder. 2003. "The Eugenic Atlantic: Race, Disability, and the Making of an International Eugenic Science, 1800–1945." *Disability & Society* 18: 843–64.

Moen, Phyllis, Kelly Erin, Hill Rachelle. 2009. "Opting to Stay: Does a Work-time Control Intervention Reduce Turnover?" Paper presented at the Population Association of America meetings, Detroit, MI.

Montenegro, Xenia P. 2004. "The Divorce Experience: A Study of Divorce at Mid-life and Beyond." Report published by the AARP, May.

Moss, M.S., and S.Z. Moss. 2014. "Widowhood in Old Age: Viewed in a Family Context." *Journal of Aging Studies* 29: 98–106. doi:10.1016/j.jaging.2014.02.001.

Moss, M.S., N. Resch, and S.Z. Moss. 1997. "The Role of Gender in Middle-age Children's Responses to Parent Death." *OMEGA-Journal of Death and Dying* 35(1): 43–65.

Pacey, Michael. 2002. "Living Alone and Living with Children: The Living Arrangements of Canadian and Chinese-Canadian Seniors." SEDAP Research Paper 74. Hamilton, ON: McMaster University.

Padgett, C., and R.C. Remle. 2016. "Financial Assistance Patterns from Midlife Parents to Adult Children: A Test of the Cumulative Advantage Hypothesis." *Journal of Family and Economic Issues* 36: 1–15.

Pahl, R., and L. Spencer. 2004. "Personal Communities: Not Simply Families of 'Fate' or 'Choice'." *Current Sociology* 52 (2): 199–221.

Phillipson, C. 2013. *Ageing.* London, UK: Polity Press.

Pillemer, Karl, and Jill J. Suitor. 2002. "Explaining Mothers' Ambivalence toward Their Adult Children." *Journal of Marriage and Family* 64: 602–13.

Pyke, K.D., and V.L. Bengtson. 1996. "Caring More or Less: Individualistic and Collectivist Systems of Family Eldercare." *Journal of Marriage and the Family* 58(2): 379–92.

Randall, W.L., and G.M. Kenyon. 2004. "Time, Story, and Wisdom: Emerging Themes in Narrative Gerontology." *Canadian Journal on Aging* 23(4): 333–46. doi:10.1353/cja.2005.0027.

Rappoport, Anat, and Ariela Lowenstein. 2007. "A Possible Innovative Association between the Concept of Intergenerational Ambivalence and the Emotions of Guilt and Shame in Care-giving." *European Journal of Ageing* 4: 13–21.

Rosenthal, C.J. 1990. "Extended Families Today and Tomorrow." Pp. 70–95 in *Canadian Gerontological Collection VII: The Aging Family in an Aging Society*, edited by P.A. Conrad and V. White. Ottawa: The Canadian Association on Gerontology.

———. 1997. "The Changing Contexts of Family Care in Canada". *Ageing International* 24 (1): 13–31.

———, L. Hayward, A. Martin-Matthews, and M.A. Denton. 2004. "Help to Older Parents and Parents-in-law: Does Paid Employment Constrain Women's Helping Behaviour?" *Canadian Journal on Aging* 23 (Supplement 1): S97–S112.

Sage, R.A., and M.K. Johnson. 2012. "Extending and Expanding Parenthood: Parental Support to Young Adult Children." *Sociology Compass* 6: 256–70.

Settersten Jr, Richard A. 2007. "Passages to Adulthood: Linking Demographic Change and Human Development." *European Journal of Population* 23: 251–72.

Sims-Gould, J., and A. Martin-Matthews. 2010. "'We Share the Care': Family Caregivers' Experiences of Their Older Relative Receiving Home Support Services." *Health & Social Care in the Community* 18(4): 415–23.

———, K. Byrne, C. Tong, and A. Martin-Matthews. 2015. "Home Support Workers Perceptions of Family Members of Their Older Clients: A Qualitative Study." *BMC Geriatrics* (Vol 12, 2015), 15: 165. doi: 10.1186/s12877-015-0163-4.

Smits, A., R.I. Van Gaalen, C.H. Mulder. 2010. "Parent-child Coresidence: Who Moves in with Whom and for Whose Needs?" *Journal of Marriage and Family* 72(4): 1022–33.

Statistics Canada. 2011. "Census in Brief: Living Arrangements of Young Adults Aged 20 to 29." *Families, Households and Marital Status, 2011 Census of Population*. Ottawa: Statistics Canada, p. 7. Available at (www12.statcan.gc.ca/census-recensement/2011/as-sa/98-312-x/98-312-x2011003_3-eng.pdf).

———. 2013. "Marital Status: Overview, 2011." *Families, Households and Marital Status, 2011 Census of Population*. Catalogue no. 91-209-X. Ottawa: Statistics Canada.

———. 2016a. "Fertility: Fewer Children, Older Moms." *The Daily, Canadian Megatrends*, Ottawa: Statistics Canada. Available at (www.statcan.gc.ca/pub/11-630-x/11-630-x2014002-eng.htm).

———. 2016b. "Population by Sex and Age Group." *Summary Tables*, Ottawa: Statistics Canada. Available at (http://cansim2.statcan.ca/cgi-win/cnsmcgi.exe?Lan=E&ResultTemplate=CST&CORCMD=GetCRel&CORId=DEMO10A&CORRel=50).

Streib, G.F. 1990. "The Changing Family in an Aging Society." Pp. 1–29 in *Canadian Gerontological Collection VII: The Aging Family in an Aging Society*, edited by P.A. Conrad and V. White. Ottawa: The Canadian Association on Gerontology.

Sweeney, M.M. 2010. "Remarriage and Stepfamilies: Strategic Sites for Family Scholarship in the 21st Century." *Journal of Marriage and Family* 72: 667–84.

Timonen, V. 2009. "Toward an Integrative Theory of Care: Formal and Informal Intersections." Pp. 307–26 in *Pathways of Human Development: Explorations of Change*, edited by J.A. Mancini and K.A. Roberto. Lanham: Lexington Books.

———. and S. Arber. 2012. "A New Look at Grandparenting". Pp. 1–24 in *Contemporary Grandparenting: Changing Family Relationships in Global Contexts*, edited by S. Arber and V. Timonen. Bristol, UK: The Policy Press.

Turcotte, M. 2014. "Staying at Home Longer to Become Home Owners." *Canadian Social Trends*, Statistics Canada catalogue no. 11-008-X.

van den Hoonaard, Deborah K. 2010. *By Himself: The Older Man's Experience of Widowhood*. Toronto: University of Toronto Press

Vanier Institute of the Family (VIF). 2016. Available at (https://vanierinstitute.ca/family-caregiving-in-canada/).

Vézina, M. 2015. "Being a Parent in a Stepfamily: A Profile." *2011 General Social Survey: Overview of Families in Canada*, Statistics Canada. Catalogue no. 89-650-X.

Ward, Russell, and Glenna Spitze. 1996. "Will the Children Ever Leave? Parent–Child Coresidence History and Plans." *Journal of Family Issues* 17: 514–39.

Whipple, V. 2006. *Lesbian Widows: Invisible Grief*. Binghampton, NY: Psychology Press.

Wight, R.G., A.J. LeBlanc, B. De Vries, and R. Detels. 2012. "Stress and Mental Health among Midlife and Older Gay-identified Men." *American Journal of Public Health* 102(3): 503–10.

Willson, Andrea E., Kim M. Shuey, and Glen H. Elder, Jr. 2003. "Ambivalence in the Relationship of Adult Children to Aging Parents and In-laws." *Journal of Marriage and Family* 65: 1055–72.

Wister, A., and B. McPherson. 2013. *Aging as Social Process*, 6th edn. Don Mills, ON: Oxford University Press.

Wu, Zheng, and Margaret Penning. 1997. "Marital Instability after Midlife." *Journal of Family Issues* 18: 459–78.

Chapter 8

Barnes, M.W. 2014. "Our Family Functions: Functions of Traditional Weddings for Modern Brides and Post-modern Families." *Qualitative Sociology Review* X (2): 60–78.

Berrardo, Felix M., and Hernan Vera. 1981. "The Groomal Shower: A Variation of the American Bridal Shower." *Family Relations* 30(3): 395–401.

Blakely, Kristin. 2008. "Busy Brides and the Business Life: The Wedding-planning Industry and the Commodity Frontier." *Journal of Family Issues* 29(5): 639–62.

Boden, S. 2003. *Consumerism, Romance, and the Wedding Experience*. Gordonsville, VA: Palgrave Macmillan.

Braithwaite, Dawn O. 1995. "Ritualized Embarrassment at 'Co-ed' Wedding and Baby Showers." *Communication Reports* 8(2): 145–57.

———, and Leslie A. Baxter. 1995. "'I Do' Again: The Relational Dialectics of Renewing Marriage Vows." *Journal of Social and Personal Relationships* 12(7): 177–98.

Bulcroft, Kris, Richard Bulcroft, Linda Smeins, and Helen Cranage. 1997. "The Social Construction of the North American Honeymoon, 1880–1995." *Journal of Family History* 22: 462–90.

CBC News. 2011. "William, Kate, unite in fairy-tale wedding." 29 April. Available at (www.cbc.ca/news/world/royalwedding/story/2011/04/29/royal-wedding-day.html).

———. 2012a. "Canadian foster care in crisis, experts say." *CBC News*, 19 February. Available at (www.cbc.ca/news/canada/story/2012/02/19/foster-care-cp.html).

Chatters, Linda M., and Robert J. Taylor. 2005 "Religion and Families." In *Sourcebook of Family Theory and Research, edited by* V.L. Bengston, A.C. Acock, K.R. Allen, P. Dilworth-Anderson, and D.M. Klein. Thousand Oaks, CA: Sage.

Chatzky, Jean, and Amanda Gengler. 2005. "The Blowout." *Money* 34(5): 124–9.

Cheal, David. 1988. *The Gift Economy*. New York: Routledge.

———. 1988a. "Relationships in Time: Ritual, Social Structure, and the Life Course." *Studies in Symbolic Interaction* 9: 83–109.

Cherlin, Andrew. 2004. "The Deinstitutionalization of American Marriage." *Journal of Marriage and the Family* 66: 848–61.

Chesser, Barbara Jo. 1980. "Analysis of Wedding Rituals: An Attempt to Make Weddings More Meaningful." *Family Relations* 29: 204–9.

Civil Ceremonies. 2017. Available at (www.civilceremonies.co.uk/).

Conway, Peg. 2006. "A Modest Wedding Proposal." *U.S. Catholic* (November): 24–6.

Costa, R.P. 2013. "Family Rituals: Mapping the Postmodern Family through Time, Space and Emotion." *Journal of Comparative Family Studies* 44 (3): 270–89.

Cott, Nancy F. 2002. *Public Vows: A History of Marriage and the Nation*. Cambridge, MA: Harvard University Press.

Daws, L.B. 2009. *Happily Ever After.com: The Construction of Identity on Wedding Websites*. Lexington, KY: University of Kentucky Press.

Durkheim, E. 1964. *The Division of Labor in Society*, transl. by George Simpson. New York: The Free Press.

Emke, Ivan. 2002. "Why the Sad Face?: Secularization and the Changing Function of Funerals in Newfoundland." *Mortality* 7(3): 269–84.

Fairchild, E. 2014. "Examining Wedding Rituals through a Multidisciplinary Lens: The Analytic Importance of Attending to (In)consistency." *Journal of Contemporary Ethnography* 43(3): 361–89.

Friese, S. 1997. "A Consumer Good in the Ritual Process: The Case of the Wedding Dress." *Journal of Ritual Studies* 11 (2): 51–62.

Gibbs, Martin, James Meese, Michael Arnold, Bjorn Nansen, and Marcus Carter. 2015. "Funeral and Instagram: Death, Social Media, and Platform Vernacular." *Information, Communication and Society* 18(3): 255–68.

Goffman, Erving. 1971. *Relations in Public*. New York: Harper Colophon Books.

Guth, Tracy. 1999. Why not renew your wedding vows? *Good Housekeeping*; New York 228.3: 162.

Hamilton, Kendall. 2007. "Renew your vows (without renewing your vows)." *Esquire* 148, 3: 92.

Harper's Bazaar. 2005 [1886]. "Mourning and funeral usage." *Harper's Bazaar*. Available at (http://harpersbazaar.victorian-ebooks.com).

Hell, Kyshah. 2001. "Victorian Mourning Garb." *Morbid Outlook*. Available at (www.morbidoutlook.com/fashion/historical/2001_03_victorianmourn.html).

Hertz, C. 2013. *White Wedding Dress in the Midwest*. PhD dissertation in Folklore and Ethnomusicology. Bloomington: Indiana University.

Hochschild, A.R. 2012. *The Outsourced Self: What Happens When We Pay Others to Live Our Lives for Us*. New York: Metropolitan Books.

Howard, Vicki. 2003. "A 'Real Man's Ring': Gender and the Invention of Traditions." *Journal of Social History* 36(4): 857–56.

———. 2006. *Brides, Inc.: American Weddings and the Business of Tradition*. Philadelphia: University of Pennsylvania Press.

Huberman, Jenny. 2012. "Forever a Fan: Reflections on the Branding of Death and the Production of Value." *Anthropological Theory* 12 (4): 467–85.

Humble, Áine M. 2009. "The Second Time 'Round: Gender Construction in Remarried Couples' Wedding Planning." *Journal of Divorce and Remarriage* 50: 260–81.

———, 2013. "Moving from 'Meh' to 'Yay': Older Same-sex Couples Get Married in Canada." *Canadian Journal on Aging* 32(2): 131–144.

———, A.M. Svonkovic, and A.J. Walker. 2008. "'The Royal We': Gender Ideology and Assessment in Wedding Work." *Journal of Family Issues* 29(1): 3–25.

Institute of Marriage and Family Canada. 2009. "Cohabitation Statistics." *Quick Stats: Social Policy Statistics at a Glance*. Ottawa.

Johnston, Lynda. 2006. "'I Do Down-under': Naturalizing Landscapes and Love through Wedding Tourism in New Zealand." *ACME: An International E-Journal for Critical Geographies* 5(2): 191–208.

King, Tamara. 2008. "Photographers snap pictures of brides in unexpected places." *Daily Gleaner*, 20 October.

Lash, Shari. R. 2007. "Fitting under the Marriage Canopy: Same-Sex Weddings as Rites of Conformity in a Canadian Liberal Jewish Context." Masters Thesis, Department of Religion and Culture. Waterloo, ON: Wilfrid Laurier University.

Lindsay, Colin. 2008. "Canadians Attend Weekly Religious Services Less Than 20 Years Ago." *Matter of Fact* (June). Ottawa: Statistics Canada.

MacIntosh, H., E.D. Reissing, and H. Andruff. 2010. "Same-sex Marriage in Canada: The Impact of Legal Marriage on the First Cohort of Gay and Lesbian Canadians to Wed." *The Canadian Journal of Human Sexuality* 19(3): 79–90.

Marcus, Ivan G. 2004. *The Jewish Life Cycle: Rites of Passage from Biblical to Modern Times*. Seattle: University of Washington Press.

Milan, A. 2013. *Marital Status Overview, 2011*. Ottawa. Statistics Canada.

Mitchell, P.J. 2016 *Canadian Millennials and the Value of Marriage*. Hamilton, ON: Cardus.

Montemurro, Beth. 2002. "'You Go 'Cause You Have To': The Bridal Shower as a Ritual of Obligation." *Symbolic Interaction* 25(1): 670–92.

———. 2003. 'Sex Symbols: The Bachelorette Party as a Window to Change in Women's Sexual Expression." *Sexuality and Culture* 7(2): 3–29.

———. 2005. "Add Men, Don't Stir: Reproducing Traditional Gender Roles in Modern Wedding Showers." *Journal of Contemporary Ethnography* 34: 6–35.

———. 2006. *Something Old, Something Bold: Bridal Showers and Bachelorette Parties.* Piscataway, NJ: Rutgers University Press.

Neimeyer, Robert A., Holly G. Prigerson, and Betty Davies. 2002. "Mourning and Meaning." *American Behavioral Scientist* 46(2): 235–51.

Nelson, J. 2010. "Your Wedding, by Martha Stewart." *Canadian Business* 83(3): 18.

O'Brien, Jen. 2015. Wedding Trends in Canada. Available at (www.weddingbells.ca/planning/wedding-trends-in-canada-2015/).

Oswald, Ramona Faith. 2000. "A Member of the Wedding?: Heterosexism and Family Ritual." *Journal of Social and Personal Relationships* 17: 349–68.

———. 2001. "Religion, Family, and Ritual: The Production of Gay, Lesbian, Bisexual, and Transgender Outsiders-within." *Review of Religious Research* 43(1): 39–50.

———, and Elizabeth A. Suter. 2004. "Heterosexist Inclusion and Exclusion during Ritual: A 'Straight Versus Gay' Comparison." *Journal of Family Issues* 25(7): 881–99.

Palmer, Bryan. 2008. *Canada's 1960s: The Ironies of Identity in a Rebellious Era.* Toronto: University of Toronto Press.

Palmer, Kimberly. 2008. "For Richer or Poorer?" *U.S. News and World Report,* 15 September, 145(6): 86.

Pennington, Phil and Barbara Pennington 2001. *Healing Divorce: Transforming the End of Your Relationship and Ceremony.* Online publication: Author.

Pike, Martha. 1980. "In Memory of: Artifacts Relating to Mourning in Nineteenth Century America." *Journal of American Culture* 3(4): 642–59.

Pride Weddings Toronto. 2017. Available at (http://pride-weddings.ca/).

Rose Floral and Greenhouse. 2008. *Wedding Anniversary Symbols.* Available at (www.rosefloral.com/wedding.htm).

Sanders, George. 2010. "The Dismal Trade as Culture Industry." *Poetics* 38: 47–68.

Shissler, A. Holly. 2006. "Marriages Made on Madison Avenue?" *Journal of Women's History* 18(4): 118–22.

Sun Sentinel. 2008. *Sun Sentinel,* 2 December, 17a.

Swenson, Don, Jerry G. Pankhurst, and Sharon K. Houseknecht. 2005. "Links between Families and Religion." In *Sourcebook of Family Theory and Research,* edited by V.L. Bengston, A.C. Acock, K.R. Allen, P. Dilworth-Anderson, and D.M. Klein. Thousand Oaks, CA: Sage.

Tye, Diane, and Ann Marie Powers. 1998. "Gender, Resistance and Play: Bachelorette Parties in Atlantic Canada." *Women's Studies International Forum* 21(5): 551–61.

van den Hoonaard, Deborah K. 2010. *By Himself: The Older Man's Experience of Widowhood.* Toronto: University of Toronto Press.

van den Scott, Lisa-Jo. 2008. Personal Communication.

Veblen, Thorstein. 1994. *The Theory of the Leisure Class.* New York: Penguin Classics.

Wolin, Steven J., and Linda A. Bennett. 1984. "Family Rituals." *Family Process* 23(3): 401–420.

Wouters, Cas. 2002. "The Quest for New Rituals in Dying and Mourning: Changes in the We–I Balance." *Body & Society* 8(1): 1–27.

Chapter 9

Allen, Sarah M., and Kerry Daly. 2002. "The Effects of Father Involvement: A Summary of the Research Evidence." Working paper. Carleton Place, ON: Father Involvement Initiative–Ontario Network.

———, and Kerry Daly. 2007. *The Effects of Father Involvement: An Updated Research Summary of the Evidence.* Ottawa: Fatherhood Involvement Research Alliance.

Ashbourne, Lynda, Kerry Daly, and Jamie Brown. 2011. "Responsiveness in Father-Child Relationships: The Experience of Fathers." *Fathering* 9(1): 69–86.

Bakan, Abigail B., and Daiva Stasiulis, eds. 1997. *Not One of the Family: Foreign Domestic Workers in Canada.* Toronto: University of Toronto Press.

Balbo, Laura. 1987. "Crazy Quilts: Rethinking the Welfare State Debate from a Woman's Point of View." In *Women and the State,* edited by A.S. Sassoon. London: Unwin Hyman.

Barker, Richard W. 1994. *Lone Fathers and Masculinities.* Avebury, UK: Aldershot.

Bianchi, Suzanne M., et al. 2000. "Is Anyone Doing the Housework? Trends in the Gender Division of Household Labor." *Social Forces* 79(1): 191–228.

Blain, Jenny. 1994. "Discourses of Agency and Domestic Labor: Family Discourse and Gendered Practice in Dual-earner Families." *Journal of Family Issues* 15(4): 515–49.

Boris, E., and R.S. Parrenas, eds. 2010. *Intimate Labors: Cultures, Technologies, and the Politics of Care.* Redwood City, CA: Stanford University Press.

Bott, Elizabeth. 1957. *Family and Social Networks.* London: Tavistock.

Bradbury, Bettina. 1984. "Pigs, Cows and Boarders: Non-wage Forms of Survival among Montreal Families, 1861–1881." *Labour/Le Travail* 14 (Autumn): 9–46.

———. 1993. *Working Families: Age, Gender, and Daily Survival in Industrializing Montreal.* Toronto: McClelland & Stewart.

Brannen, Julia, and Peter Moss. 1991. *Managing Mothers: Dual Earner Households after Maternity Leave.* London: Unwin Hyman.

Canadian Women's Foundation. 2017. *Fact Sheet: The Gender Wage Gap In Canada.* Available at (www.canadianwomen.org/facts-about-the-gender-wage-gap-in-canada).

Canadianwomen. n.d. The Facts about Violence against Women. Available at (www.canadianwomen.org/facts-about-violence).

Carty, Linda. 1994. "African Canadian Women and the State: 'Labour Only, Please.'" In *We're Rooted Here and They Can't Pull Us Up: Essays in African Canadian History*, edited by P. Bristow. Toronto: University of Toronto Press.

Chesley, N. 2011. "Stay-at-home Fathers and Breadwinning Mothers Gender, Couple Dynamics, and Social Change." *Gender and Society* 25(5): 642–64.

Chui, T. 2011. Immigration and Ethnocultural Diversity Data: 2011 National Household Survey. Statistics Canada.

———, and H. Maheux. 2011. "Visible Minority Women." Component of Statistics Canada.

Collins, Patricia Hill. 1994. "Shifting the Center: Race, Class and Feminist Theorizing about Motherhood." In *Mothering: Ideology, Experience and Agency*, edited by E.N. Glenn, G. Chang, and L.R. Forcey. New York: Routledge.

———. 2000. *Black Feminist Thought: Knowledge, Consciousness, and the Politics of Empowerment*, 2nd edn. London and New York: Routledge.

Coltrane, Scott, and Michele Adams. 2001. "Men's Family Work: Child-centered Fathering and the Sharing of Domestic Labor." In *Working Families: The Man of the American Home*, edited by N.L. Marshall. Berkeley: University of California Press.

Coote, Anne, Harriet Harman, and Patricia Hewitt. 1990. *The Family Way: A New Approach to Policy-Making.* London: Institute for Public Policy Research.

Cowan, Ruth Schwartz. 1983. *More Work for Mothers: The Ironies of Household Technology from the Open Hearth to the Microwave.* New York: Basic Books.

Crittenden, Anne. 2010. *The Price of Motherhood: Why the Most Important Job in the World Is Still the Least Valued.* New York: Picador.

Daly, K., L. Ashbourne, and J.L. Brown. 2009. "Fathers' Perceptions of Children's Influence: Implications for Involvement." *The ANNALS of the American Academy of Political and Social Science* 624(1): 61–77.

Delphy, Christine. 1984. *Close to Home: A Materialist Analysis of Women's Oppression.* London: Hutchinson.

Deutsch, Francine M. 1999. *Halving It All: How Equally Shared Parenting Works.* Cambridge, MA: Harvard University Press.

Devault, A., G. Forget, and D. Dubeau. 2015. *Fathering: Promoting Positive Father Involvement.* Toronto: University of Toronto Press.

Dienhart, Anna. 1998. *Reshaping Fatherhood: The Social Construction of Shared Parenting.* London: Sage.

Di Leonardo, Micaela. 1987. "The Female World of Cards and Holidays: Women, Families and the World of Kinship." *Signs* 12(3): 440–53.

Doucet, Andrea. 1995. "Gender Equality, Gender Differences and Care: Toward Understanding Gendered Labor in British Dual Earner Households." PhD thesis, University of Cambridge.

———. 2000. "'There's a Huge Difference between Me as a Male Carer and Women': Gender, Domestic Responsibility, and the Community as an Institutional Arena." *Community, Work and Family* 3(2): 163–84.

———. 2001. "You See the Need Perhaps More Clearly Than I Have: Exploring Gendered Processes of Domestic Responsibility." *Journal of Family Issues* 22(3): 328–57.

———. 2004. "Fathers and the Responsibility for Children: A Puzzle and a Tension." *Atlantis: A Women's Studies Journal* 28(2): 103–14.

———. 2006. *Do Men Mother?* Toronto: University of Toronto Press.

———. 2011. "'It's not good for a man to be interested in other people's children': Fathers and Public Displays of Care." Pp. 81–101 in *Displaying Families: New Theoretical Directions in Family and Intimate Life*, edited by E. Dermott and J. Seymour. London, UK: Palgrave MacMillan.

———. 2012. "The evolution of the stay-at-home dad" (op ed.), *Ottawa Citizen*, 18 June. Available at (www.ottawacitizen.com/life/evolution+stay+home/6790417/story.html#ixzz1z5gDYTfT).

Dowd, Nancy E. 2000. *Redefining Fatherhood.* New York: New York University Press.

Duxbury, Linda, Chris Higgins, and Karen L. Johnson. 2004. *The 2001 National Work–Life Conflict Study: Report Three—Exploring the Link between Work–Life Conflict and Demands on Canada's Health Care System.* Ottawa: Public Health Agency of Canada.

Eichler, Margrit. 1975. "The Equalitarian Family in Canada?" Pp. 223–35 in *Marriage, Family and Society: Canadian Perspectives*, edited by P.S. Wakil. Toronto: Butterworths.

———. 1983. *Families in Canada Today: Recent Changes and Their Policy Consequences.* Toronto: Gage.

Fast, Janet E., and Norah C. Keating. 2001. *Informal Caregivers in Canada: A Snapshot.* Ottawa: Health Canada.

Folbre, Nancy. 1994. *Who Pays for the Kids? Gender and the Structures of Constraint.* London: Routledge, Chapman and Hall.

———. 2001. *The Invisible Heart: Economics and Family Values.* New York: New Press.

Fox, Bonnie. 1998. "Motherhood, Changing Relationships and the Reproduction of Gender Inequality." In *Redefining Motherhood*, edited by S. Abbey and A. O'Reilly. Toronto: Second Story Press.

———. 2001. "The Formative Years: How Parenthood Creates Gender." *Canadian Review of Sociology and Anthropology* 38: 373–90.

———, and Meg Luxton. 2001. "Conceptualizing Family." In *Family Patterns and Gender Relations*, edited by B. Fox. Toronto: Oxford University Press.

Fudge, Judy, and Leah Vosko. 2001. "Gender, Segmentation and the Standard Employment Relationship in Canadian Labour Law, Legislation and Policy." *Economic and Industrial Democracy* 22(2): 218–310.

Galarneau, Diane. 2005. "Earnings of Temporary Versus Permanent Employees." *Perspectives on Labour and Income*. Ottawa: Statistics Canada.

Gaunt, R. 2012. "Breadwinning Moms, Caregiving Dads: Double Standard in Social Judgments of Gender Norm Violators." *Journal of Family Issues* 4 April. Available at (http://jfi.sagepub.com/content/early/2012/04/01/0192513X12438686).

Gerson, K. 2009. *The Unfinished Revolution: How a New Generation Is Reshaping Family, Work, and Gender in America*. New York: Oxford University Press.

Goetz, Anne Marie. 1995. "Institutionalizing Women's Interests and Accountability to Women in Development." *IDS Bulletin* 26(3): 1–10.

———. 1997. "Getting Institutions Right for Women in Development." In *Getting Institutions Right for Women in Development*, edited by A.M. Goetz. London: Zed Books.

Gough, M., and M. Noonan. 2013. "A Review of the Motherhood Wage Penalty in the United States." *Sociology Compass* 7(4): 328–42.

Haas, L., and M. O'Brien. 2010. "New Observations on How Fathers Work and Care: Introduction to the Special Issue—Men, Work and Parenting—Part I." *Fathering: A Journal of Theory, Research, and Practice About Men as Fathers* 8(3): 271–5.

Hamilton, Sylvia D. 1989. *Black Mother, Black Daughter*. Montreal: National Film Board of Canada.

Harris, Olivia. 1981. "Households as Natural Units." In *Of Damage and the Market: Women's Subordination in International Perspective*, edited by K. Young, C. Walkowitz, and R. McCullagh. London: CSE Books.

Heitmueller, A., and K. Inglis. 2007. "The Earnings of Informal Carers: Wage Differentials and Opportunity Costs." *Journal of Health Economics* 26(4): 821–41.

Himmelweit, S. 2007. "The Prospects for Caring: Economic Theory and Policy Analysis." *Cambridge Journal of Economics*. 31:581–599.

Hochschild, Arlie Russell. 1989. *The Second Shift*. New York: Avon.

Hoffman, J. 2011. *Father Factors: What Social Science Tells us about Fathers and How to Work with Them*. Peterborough, Ontario: Father Involvement Research Alliance.

Hou, F., and S. Coulombe. 2010. Earnings Gap for Canadian-born Visible Minorities in the Public and Private Sectors. *Canadian Public Policy* 36(1): 29–43.

Johnson, Karen L., Donna S. Lero, and Jennifer A. Rooney. 2001. *Work–Life Compendium 2001: 150 Canadian Statistics on Work, Family and Well-Being*. Guelph, ON: Centre for Families, Work and Well-Being, University of Guelph.

Krahn, Harvey. 1991. "Non-standard Work Arrangements." *Perspectives on Labour and Income* (Statistics Canada) 4(4): 35–45.

———. 1995. "Non-standard Work on the Rise." *Perspectives on Labour and Income* (Statistics Canada) 7(4): 35–42.

Kvande, E. 2009. "Work–life Balance for Fathers in Globalized Knowledge Work. Some Insights from the Norwegian Context." *Gender, Work and Organization* 16(1): 58–72.

Lamb, M.E. 2004. *The Role of the Father in Child Development*. New York: John Wiley and Sons.

Lamphere, Louise. 1987. *From Working Daughters to Working Mothers: Immigrant Women in a New England Community*. Ithaca, NY: Cornell University Press.

Lewis, Charlie. 1986. *Becoming a Father*. Milton Keynes, UK: Open University Press.

Lewis, Jane, Marilyn Porter, and Mark Shrimpton, eds. 1988. *Women, Work and the Family in the British, Canadian and Norwegian Offshore Oil Fields*. London: Macmillan.

Lopata, Helena. 1974. *Occupation Housewife*. New York: Oxford University Press.

Lupton, Deborah, and Lesley Barclay. 1997. *Constructing Fatherhood: Discourses and Experiences*. London: Sage.

Luxton, Meg. 1980. *More Than a Labour of Love: Three Generations of Women's Work in the Home*. Toronto: Women's Press.

———. 1998. *Families and the Labour Market: Coping Strategies from a Sociological Perspective*. Ottawa: Canadian Policy Research Networks.

Macdonald, C.L. 2011. *Shadow Mothers: Nannies, Au Pairs, and the Micropolitics of Mothering*. Berkeley, CA: University of California Press.

Macdonald, D., and D. Wilson. 2016, May. *Shameful Neglect: Indigenous Child Poverty in Canada*. Ottawa, ON: Canadian Centre for Policy Alternatives. Available at (www.policyalternatives.ca/publications/reports/shameful-neglect).

Maitra, S. 2014. "The Making of the 'Precarious': Examining Indian Immigrant IT Workers in Canada and Their Transnational Networks with Body-shops in

India." *Globalisation, Societies and Education* 13(2): 194–209.

Mandell, Denna. 2002. *Deadbeat Dads: Subjectivity and Social Construction*. Toronto: University of Toronto Press.

Marshall, Katherine. 1993. "Dual Earners: Who's Responsible for the Housework?" *Canadian Social Trends* 31 (Winter): 11–14.

———. 2011. "Generational Change in Paid and Unpaid Work." *Canadian Social Trends* 92: 13–24.

Marsiglio, W., and K. Roy. 2012. *Nurturing Dads: Social Initiatives for Contemporary Fatherhood*. New York: Russell Sage Foundation.

McKay, L., S. Mathieu, and A. Doucet. 2016. "Parental-leave Rich and Parental-leave Poor? In/Equality in Canadian Labour-Market Based Leave Policies, *Journal of Industrial Relations* 58(4); published online first; May 9, 2016 as doi:10.1177/0022185616643558.

Meissner, Martin, et al. 1975. "No Exit for Wives: Sexual Division of Labour and the Culmination of Household Demands." *Canadian Review of Sociology and Anthropology* 12(4): 424–39.

Miller, T. 2011. "Falling Back into Gender? Men's Narratives and Practices around First-time Fatherhood." *Sociology* 45(6): 1094–109.

Miranda, V. 2011. "Cooking, Caring and Volunteering: Unpaid Work Around the World." OECD Social, Employment and Migration Working Papers, No. 116. Paris: OECD Publishing. doi:10.1787/5kghrjm8s142-en.

Morris, Lydia. 1985. "Local Social Networks and Domestic Organisations: A Study of Redundant Steelworkers and their Wives." *Sociological Review* 33(2): 327–42.

Moser, Caroline. 1993. *Gender Planning and Development: Theory, Practice and Training*. London: Routledge.

Oakley, Ann. 1974. *Housewife*. London: Allen Lane.

———. 2005. *Shared Caring: Bringing Fathers in the Frame*. Manchester, UK: Equal Opportunities Commission.

O'Brien, Margaret. 1987. "Patterns of Kinship and Friendship among Lone Fathers." In *Reassessing Fatherhood: New Observations on Fathers and the Modern Family*, edited by C. Lewis and M. O'Brien. London: Sage.

Pahl, Ray E. 1984. *Divisions of Labour*. Oxford: Blackwell.

Parsons, Talcott. 1967. *Sociological Theory and Modern Society*. New York: Free Press.

———, and Robert Bales. 1955. *Family, Socialization and Interaction Process*. New York: Free Press of Glencoe.

Pendakur, K., and R. Pendakur. 2011. "Aboriginal Incomes in Canada 1995–2005." *Canadian Public Policy* 37(1): 61–83.

Pleck, Joseph H. 1985. *Working Wives, Working Husbands*. London: Sage.

Polivka, Anne E., and Thomas Nardone. 1989. "On the Definition of 'Contingent Work'." *Monthly Labor Review* 112(12): 9–16.

Rhode, Deborah L. 1989. *Justice and Gender: Sex Discrimination and the Law*. Cambridge, MA: Harvard University Press.

———. 1990. *Theoretical Perspectives on Sexual Difference*. New Haven, CT: Yale University Press.

Rothman, Barbara Katz. 1989. "Women as Fathers: Motherhood and Childcare under a Modified Patriarchy." *Gender and Society* 3(1): 89–104.

Ruddick, Sara. 1995. *Maternal Thinking: Towards a Politics of Peace*. Boston: Beacon Press.

Scheper-Hughes, Nancy. 1992. *Death without Weeping: The Violence of Everyday Life in Brazil*. Berkeley: University of California Press.

Sharma, Ursala. 1986. *Women's Work, Class and the Urban Household: A Study of Shimla, North India*. London: Tavistock.

Shows, Carla, and Naomi Gerstel. 2009. "Fathering, Class, and Gender: A Comparison of Physicians and Emergency Medical Technicians." *Gender and Society* 23(2): 161–87.

Smith, J.A. 2009. *The Daddy Shift: How Stay-at-Home Dads, Breadwinning Moms, and Shared Parenting Are Transforming the American Family*. Boston: Beacon Press.

Spitzer, Denise, Anne Neufeld, Margaret Harrison, Karen D. Hughes, and Miriam Stewart. 2003. "Caregiving in Transnational Context: 'My Wings Have Been Cut; Where Can I Fly?'" *Gender and Society* 17: 267–86.

Stack, Carol. 1974. *All Our Kin: Strategies for Survival in a Black Community*. New York: Harper and Row.

Stasiulis, Daiva, and Abigail Bakan. 2005. *Negotiating Citizenship: Migrant Women in Canada and the Global System*. Toronto: University of Toronto Press.

Statistics Canada. 2010. "Paid work." In *Women in Canada: A Gender-Based Statistical Report*. Catalogue no. 89-503-X. Ottawa: Statistics Canada.

———. 2013. Employment Insurance Survey 2012. *The Daily*, November 15, 2013.

———. 2017. Census Profile: 2016 Census. Ottawa: Statistics Canada. Retrieved June 14, 2017 (www12 .statcan.gc.ca/census-recensement/2016/dp-pd/prof/ index.cfm?Lang=E).

———. 2017a. *Women in Canada: A Gender-based Statistical Report*. Available at (www.statcan.gc.ca/ pub/89-503-x/2015001/article/14694-eng.htm).

Taylor, Janelle S., Linda L. Layne, and Danielle F. Wozniak. 2004. *Consuming Motherhood*. New Brunswick, NJ: Rutgers University Press.

Tilly, Louise A., and Joan W. Scott. 1987. *Women, Work and Family*. New York: Holt, Rinehart and Winston.

Unger, D. 2010. *Men Can: The Changing Image and Reality of Fatherhood in America*. Philadelphia: Temple University Press.

Vosko, Leah F. 2000. *Temporary Work: The Gendered Rise of a Precarious Employment Relationship*. Toronto: University of Toronto Press.

———. 2010. *Managing the Margins: Gender, Citizenship, and the International Regulation of Precarious Employment*. Toronto: Oxford University Press.

———, Nancy Zukewich, and Cynthia Cranford. 2003. "Precarious Jobs: A New Typology of Employment." *Perspectives on Labour and Income* 4(10): 16–26.

White, J., P. Maxim, and S.O. Gyimah. 2003. "Labour Force Activity of Women in Canada: A Comparative Analysis of Aboriginal and Non-Aboriginal Women." *Canadian Review of Sociology*, 40(4), 391–415.

Williams, J.C. 2010. *Reshaping the Work-Family Debate: Why Men and Class Matter*. Cambridge, MA: Harvard University Press.

Zavella, Patricia. 1987. *Women's Work and Chicano Families: Cannery Workers of the Santa Clara Valley*. Ithaca, NY: Cornell University Press.

Zuzanek, Juri. 2001. "Parenting Time: Enough or Too Little?" *Canadian Journal of Policy Research* 2(2): 125–33.

Chapter 10

Anisef, Paul, Robert S. Brown, Kelli Phythian, Robert Sweet, and David Walters. 2010. "Early School Leaving among Immigrants in Toronto Secondary Schools." *Canadian Review of Sociology* 47(2): 103–28.

Baker, Maureen. 2002. "Child Poverty, Maternal Health and Social Benefits." *Current Sociology* 50(6): 823–38.

Barnes, Colin. 2003. "What a Difference a Decade Makes: Reflection on Doing 'Emancipatory' Disability Research." *Disability & Society* 18: 3–17.

Barnes, Sandra L. 2003. "Determinants of Individual Neighborhood Ties and Social Resources in Poor Urban Neighborhoods." *Sociological Spectrum* 23(4): 463–97.

Benzeval, Michaela, and Ken Judge. 2001. "Income and Health: The Time Dimension." *Social Science and Medicine* 52(9): 1371–90.

Bostock, Lisa. 2001. "Pathways of Disadvantage? Walking as a Mode of Transport among Low-income Mothers." *Health and Social Care in the Community* 9(1): 11–18.

Brannigan, Augustine, William Gemmell, David J. Pevalin, and Terrance J. Wade. 2002. "Self-control and Social Control in Childhood Misconduct and Aggression: The Role of Family Structure, Hyperactivity, and Hostile Parenting." *Canadian Journal of Criminology and Criminal Justice* 44(2): 119–42.

Caledon Institute of Social Policy. 2016. *Welfare in Canada 2015*. Ottawa: CISP.

Canadian Council on Social Development (CCSD). 2002. *The Canadian Fact Book on Poverty*. Ottawa: CCSD.

———. 2006. "Economic Security: Poverty." CCSD's Stats and Facts. Available at (www.ccsd.ca/factsheets/economic_security/poverty/ccsd_es_poverty.pdf).

Capponi, Pat. 1999. *The War at Home: An Intimate Portrait of Canada's Poor*. Toronto: Viking.

Caragata, Lea. 2003. "Neoconservative Realities: The Social and Economic Marginalization of Canadian Women." *International Sociology* 18(3): 559–80.

Carolsfeld, Anna Lúcia, and Susan L. Erikson. 2013. "Beyond Desperation: Motivations for Dumpster Diving for Food in Vancouver." *Food and Foodways* 21: 245–66.

Carson, Eleanor Anne. 2014. "Canadian Food Banks and the Depoliticization of Food Insecurity at the Individual and Community Levels." *Canadian Review of Social Policy* 70: 7–21.

Chappell, Neena L., and Marcus J. Hollander. 2013. *Aging in Canada*. Don Mills: Oxford University Press.

Cheal, David.1999. *New Poverty: Families in Postmodern Society*. Westport, CT: Greenwood.

Chekki, Dan A. 1999. "Poverty amidst Plenty: How Do Canadian Cities Cope with Rising Poverty?" *Research in Community Sociology* 9: 141–52.

Collin, Chantal, and Hilary Jensen. 2009. *A Statistical Profile of Poverty in Canada*. Ottawa: Parliamentary Information and Research Service, Library of Parliament.

Collins, Stephanie Baker. 2005. "An Understanding of Poverty from Those Who Are Poor." *Action Research* 3(1): 9–31.

Congleton, Roger D., and Feler Bose. 2010. "The Rise of the Modern Welfare State, Ideology, Institutions and Income Security: Analysis and Evidence." *Public Choice* 144: 535–55.

Cooke, Martin, and Amber Gazso. 2009. "Taking a Life Course Perspective on Social Assistance Use in Canada: A Different Approach." *Canadian Journal of Sociology* 34(2): 349–72.

Corak, Miles, ed. 2004. *Generational Income Mobility in North America and Europe*. Cambridge: Cambridge University Press.

———. 2013. *Income Inequality, Equality of Opportunity, and Intergenerational Mobility*. IZA Discussion Paper No. 7520. Bonn, Germany: Institute for the Study of Labour.

———, Lori J. Curtis, and Shelley Phipps. 2010. *Economic Mobility, Family Background, and the Well-Being of Children in the United States and Canada* (Discussion Paper No. 4814). Bonn: Institute for the Study of Labor.

Cotton, C., M. Webber, and Y. Saint-Pierre. 1998. *Should the Low Income Cutoffs Be Updated?* Cat. No. 75F0002MIE-99009. Ottawa: Statistics Canada.

Curtis, Lori J., Martin D. Dooley, and Shelley A. Phipps. 2004. "Child Well-being and Neighbourhood Quality: Evidence from the Canadian National Longitudinal

Study of Children and Youth." *Social Science and Medicine* 58(10): 1917–27.

DeVerteuil, Geoffrey. 2005. "Welfare Neighborhoods: Anatomy of a Concept." *Journal of Poverty* 9(2): 23–41.

Duck, Waverly O. 2012. "An Ethnographic Portrait of a Precarious Life: Getting by on Even Less." *The Annals of the American Academy of Political and Social Science* 642: 124–38.

Duncan, Greg J., and Jeanne Brooks-Gunn, eds. 1997. *Consequences of Growing Up Poor*. New York: Russell Sage Foundation.

Edin, Kathryn, and Laura Lein. 1997. *Making Ends Meet: How Single Mothers Survive Welfare and Low-Wage Work*. New York: Russell Sage Foundation.

———, and Luke Shaefer. 2015. *$2.00 A Day: Living on Almost Nothing in America*. Boston: Houghton Mifflin Harcourt.

Engler-Stringer, Rachel, and Shawna Berenbaum. 2007. "Exploring Food Security with Collective Kitchens Participants in Three Canadian Cities." *Qualitative Health Research* 17(1): 75–84.

Family Service Toronto. 2011. *Revisiting Family Security in Insecure Times: 2011 Report Card on Child and Family Poverty in Canada*. Toronto: Campaign 2000.

Federal, Provincial, and Territorial Advisory Committee on Population Health. 1999. *Statistical Report on the Health of Canadians*. Ottawa: Health Canada and Statistics Canada.

Federal–Provincial Working Group on Social Development Research and Information. 1998. *Construction of a Preliminary Market Basket Measure of Poverty*. Ottawa: Federal Provincial Working Group.

Felt, Lawrence, and Peter Sinclair. 1992. "'Everyone Does It': Unpaid Work in a Rural Peripheral Region." *Work, Employment & Society* 6: 43–64.

Finnie, Ross. 2000. "The Dynamics of Poverty in Canada: What We Know, What We Can Do." C.D. Howe Institute, Commentary No. 145 (Sept.).

Food Banks Canada. 2016. *Hunger Count 2015*. Mississauga: Foodbanks Canada.

———. 2016a. Food Banking in Canada. Retrieved June 30, 2016 (www.foodbankscanada.ca/Hunger-in-Canada/Food-Banking-in-Canada.aspx).

Fraser Institute. 2001. *Measuring Poverty in Canada*. Vancouver: Fraser Institute.

Friendly, Martha, Jane Beach, Carolyn Ferns, and Michelle Turiano. 2007. *Early Childhood Education and Care in Canada 2006*. Toronto: Childcare Resource and Research Unit.

Gadalla, Tahany M. 2008. "Gender Differences in Poverty Rates after Marital Dissolution: A Longitudinal Study." *Journal of Divorce and Remarriage* 49(3–4): 225–38.

Gerber, Linda. 2014. "Education, Employment, and Income Polarization among Aboriginal Men and Women in Canada." *Canadian Ethnic Studies* 46(1): 121–44.

Goffman, Erving. 1963. *Stigma: Notes on the Management of Spoiled Identity*. Englewood Cliffs, NJ: Prentice-Hall.

Green, Rebecca J., Patricia L. Williams, Shanthi C. Johnson, and Ilya Blum. 2008. "Can Canadian Seniors on Public Pensions Afford a Nutritious Diet?" *Canadian Journal on Aging* 27(1): 69–79.

Griffin, Joan M., Rebecca Fuhrer, Stephen A. Stansfeld, and Michael Marmot. 2002. "The Importance of Low Control at Work and Home on Depression and Anxiety: Do These Effects Vary by Gender and Social Class?" *Social Science and Medicine* 54(5): 783–98.

Guo, Guang, and Kathleen Mullan Harris. 2000. "The Mechanisms Mediating the Effects of Poverty on Children's Intellectual Development." *Demography* 37(4): 431–47.

Haan, Michael. 2008. "The Place of Place: Location and Immigrant Economic Well-Being in Canada." *Population Research and Policy Review* 27(6): 751–71.

Halpern-Meekin, Sarah, Kathryn Edin, Laura Tach, and Jennifer Sykes. 2015. *It's Not Like I'm Poor: How Working Families Make Ends Meet in a Post-Welfare World*. Oakland: University of California Press.

Hansen, Helena, Phillipe Bourgois, and Ernest Drucker. 2014. "Pathologizing Poverty: New Forms of Diagnosis, Disability, and Structural Stigma under Welfare Reform." *Social Science and Medicine* 103: 76–83.

Harvey, Mark H. 2011. "Welfare Reform and Household Survival: The Interaction of Structure and Network Strength in the Rio Grande Valley, Texas." *Journal of Poverty* 15, 43–64.

Head, Barbara, 2008. "The Effects of the Partnerships in Comprehensive Literacy Model in Narrowing the Achievement Gap For First Graders in High Poverty School." (Thesis). Little Rock: University of Arkansas of Little Rock.

Heisz, Andrew. 2007. *Income Inequality and Redistribution in Canada, 1976–2004*. Ottawa: Statistics Canada Analytical Studies Branch Research Paper Series.

Hulchanski, David, and Joseph H. Michalski. 1994. *How Households Obtain Resources To Meet Their Needs: The Shifting Mix of Cash and Non-Cash Sources*. Toronto: Ontario Human Rights Commission.

Iyenda, Guillaume. 2001. "Street Food and Income Generation for Poor Households in Kinshasa." *Environment and Urbanization* 13(2): 233–41.

Jarrett, Robin L., Stephanie R. Jefferson, and Jenell N. Kelly. 2010. "Finding Community in Family: Neighborhood Effects and African American Kin

Networks." *Journal of Comparative Family Studies* 41(3): 299–328.

Kazemipur, A., and Shiva Halli. 2000. *The New Poverty in Canada: Ethnic Groups and Ghetto Neighbourhoods*. Toronto: Thompson Educational Publishing.

Kenney, Catherine. 2004. "Cohabiting Couple, Filing Jointly? Resource Pooling and U.S. Poverty Policies." *Family Relations* 53(2): 237–47.

Kenworthy, Lane, and Jonas Pontusson. 2005. "Rising Inequality and the Politics of Redistribution in Affluent Countries." *Perspectives on Politics* 3(3): 449–71.

Kerr, Don, and Roderic Beaujot. 2016. "Families and Households." In *Population Change in Canada*. Don Mills: Oxford University Press.

Klebanov, Pamela Kato, Jeanne Brooks-Gunn, and Greg J. Duncan. 1994. "Does Neighborhood and Family Poverty Affect Mothers' Parenting, Mental Health and Social Support?" *Journal of Marriage and the Family* 56(2): 441–55.

Kornberger, Rhonda, Janet E. Fast, and Deanna L. Williamson. 2001. "Welfare or Work: Which is Better for Canadian Children?" *Canadian Public Policy* 24(4): 407–21.

Kosteniuk, Julie G., and Harley D. Dickinson. 2003. "Tracing the Social Gradient in the Health of Canadians: Primary and Secondary Determinants." *Social Science and Medicine* 57(2): 263–76.

Krahn, Harvey, Karen Hughes, Graham Lowe. 2007. *Work, Industry, and Canadian Society*. Toronto: Thomson Nelson.

Lee, Kevin. 2000. *Urban Poverty in Canada*. Ottawa: Canadian Council on Social Development.

Letkemann, Paul G. 2004. "First Nations Urban Migration and the Importance of 'Urban Nomads' in Canadian Plains Cities: A Perspective from the Streets." *Canadian Journal of Urban Research* 13(2): 241–56.

Lightman, Ernie S., Andrew Mitchell, and Dean Herd. 2008. "Globalization, Precarious Work, and the Food Bank." *Journal of Sociology and Social Welfare* 35(2): 9–28.

———, Andrew Mitchell, and Dean Herd. 2010. "Cycling Off and on Welfare in Canada." *Journal of Social Policy* 39(4): 523–42.

Lipman, Ellen L., and David R. Offord. 1997. "Psychosocial Morbidity among Poor Children in Ontario." Pp. 239–87 in *Consequences of Growing Up Poor*, edited by G.J. Duncan and J. Brooks-Gunn. New York: Russell Sage Foundation.

London, Andrew S., Ellen K. Scott, Kathryn Edin, and Vicki Hunter. 2004. "Welfare Reform, Work-family Trade-offs, and Child Well-being." *Family Relations* 53(2): 148–58.

Loopstra, Rachel, and Valerie Tarasuk. 2015. "Food Bank Usage Is a Poor Indicator of Food Insecurity: Insights from Canada." *Social Policy and Society* 14(3): 443–55.

Lovell, Vicky, and Gi-Taik Oh. 2005. "Women's Job Loss and Material Hardship." *Journal of Women, Politics, and Policy* 27(3–4): 169–83.

Macdonald, David, and Thea Klinger. 2015. *They Go Up So Fast: 2015 Child Care Fees in Canadian Cities*. Ottawa: Canadian Centre for Policy Alternatives.

Marcil-Gratton, Nicole, and Celine Le Bourdais. 1999. *Custody, Access and Child Support: Findings from the National Longitudinal Survey of Children and Youth*. Ottawa: Department of Justice Canada, Child Support Team.

———, Celine Le Bourdais, and Evelyn Lapierre-Adamcyk. 2000. "The Implications of Parents' Conjugal Histories for Children." *Canadian Journal of Policy Research* 1: 32–40.

Marcus, Andrea Fleisch, Sandra E. Echeverria, Bart K. Holland, Ana F. Abraido-Lanza, and Marian R. Passannante. 2015. "How Neighborhood Poverty Structures Types and Levels of Social Integration." *American Journal of Community Psychology* 56: 134–44.

Marcus, Ivan G. 2004. *The Jewish Life Cycle: Rites of Passage from Biblical to Modern Times*. Seattle: University of Washington Press.

Marmot, Michael G., and George Davey Smith. 1997. "Socio-economic Differentials in Health: The Contribution of the Whitehall Studies." *Journal of Health Psychology* 2(3): 283–96.

Marshall, Katherine. 2003. "Benefiting from Extended Parental Leave." *Perspectives on Labour and Income* (Statistics Canada) 4(3): 5–11.

Martel, Edith, Benoit Laplante, and Paul Bernard. 2005. "Unemployment and Family Strategies: The Mitigating Effects of the Transition from Unemployment Insurance to Employment Insurance." *Recherches Sociodemographiques* 46(2): 245–80.

Maskileyson, Dina. 2014. "Healthcare System and Wealth–Health Gradient: A Comparative Study of Older Populations in Six Countries." *Social Science and Medicine* 119: 18–26.

McFate, Katherine. 1995. "Western States in the New World Order." In *Poverty, Inequality, and the Future of Social Policy*, edited by K. McFate. New York: Russell Sage Foundation.

McLeod, Jane D., and Michael J. Shanahan. 1996. "Trajectories of Poverty and Children's Mental Health." *Journal of Health and Social Behavior* 37(3): 207–20.

McMullin, Julie Ann, Lorraine Davies, and Gale Cassidy. 2002. "Welfare Reform in Ontario: Tough Times in Mothers' Lives." *Canadian Public Policy* 28(2): 297–314.

Mendelson, Michael, Ken Battle, and Shari Torjman. 2009. *Canada's Shrunken Safety Net: Employment*

Insurance in the Great Recession. Ottawa: Caledon Institute of Social Policy.

Messias, DeAnne, K. Hilfinger, Margaret K. DeJong, and Kerry McLoughlin. 2005. "Expanding the Concept of Work: Volunteer Work in the Context of Poverty." *Journal of Poverty* 9(3): 25–47.

Meyer, Daniel, and Maria Cancian. 1996. "Life after Welfare." *Public Welfare* 54(4): 25–9.

Michalski, Joseph H. 2003. "The Economic Status and Coping Strategies of Food Bank Users in the Greater Toronto Area." *Canadian Journal of Urban Research* 12(2): 275–98.

———. 2003a. "Housing Affordability, Social Policy and Economic Conditions: Food Bank Users in the Greater Toronto Area, 1990–2000." *Canadian Review of Sociology and Anthropology* 40(1): 65–92.

Millar, Paul. 2010. "Punishing Our Way Out of Poverty: The Prosecution of Child-support Debt in Alberta, Canada." *Canadian Journal of Law and Society* 25(2): 149–65.

Montreal Diet Dispensary. 1998. *Budgeting for Basic Needs and Budgeting for Minimum Adequate Standard of Living.* Montreal.

Morissette, René, and Xuelin Zhang. 2006. "Revisiting Wealth Inequality." *Perspectives on Labour and Income* 7(12): 5–16.

Myles, John. 2000. "The Maturation of Canada's Retirement Income System: Income Levels, Income Inequality and Low Income among Older Persons." *Canadian Journal on Aging* 19(3): 287–316.

NAEDB. 2015. *The Aboriginal Economic Progress Report 2015.* Gatineau: The National Aboriginal Economic Development Board.

National Council of Welfare. 2012. *A Snapshot of Racialized Poverty in Canada.* Ottawa: National Council of Welfare.

Nietmietz, Kristian. 2010. "Measuring Poverty: Context-Specific but not Relative." *Journal of Social Policy* 30(3): 241–62.

Oderkirk, Jill. 1992. "Food Banks." *Canadian Social Trends* 24(6): 6–14.

OECD. 2015. *In it Together: Why Less Inequality Benefits All.* Paris, France: OECD Publishing.

OECD, Directorate for Education. 2004. *Early Childhood Education and Care Policy.* Canada: Country Note. Paris: OECD.

Pearlin, Leonard I. 2010. "The Life Course and the Stress Process: Some Conceptual Comparisons." *Journals of Gerontology* 65B(2): 207–15

Pegg, Sean, and Cherry Marshall. 2011. *Hunger Count 2011: Feed Nova Scotia.* Toronto: Food Banks Canada,

Phipps, Shelley. 2003. *The Impact of Poverty on Health: A Scan of Research Literature.* Ottawa: Canadian Institute for Health Information.

Phipps, S., and P. Burton. 1995. "Sharing within Families: Implications for the Measurement of Poverty among Individuals in Canada." *Canadian Journal of Economics* 28(1): 177–04.

Picot, Garnett. 2004. "The Deteriorating Economic Welfare of Canadian Immigrants." *Canadian Journal of Urban Research* 13(1): 25–45.

———, and John Myles. 2005. *Income Inequality and Low Income in Canada: An International Perspective.* Analytical Studies Research Paper Series 11F0019MIE2005240. Ottawa: Statistics Canada, Analytic Studies Branch.

———, John Myles, and Wendy Pyper. 1998. "Markets, Families and Social Transfers: Trends in Low Income among the Young and Old, 1973–1995." in *Labour Markets, Social Institutions and the Future of Canada's Children,* edited by M. Corak. Ottawa: Statistics Canada, Catalogue no. 890553–XPB, 11–30.

———, M. Zyblock, and Wendy Pyper. 1999. *Why Do Children Move into and out of Low Income: Changing Labour Market Conditions or Marriage and Divorce?* Analytic Studies Research Paper Series 11F0019MIE1999132. Ottawa: Statistics Canada, Analytic Studies Branch.

Podoluk, Jenny. 1968. *Incomes of Canadians.* Ottawa: Dominion Bureau of Statistics.

Raddon, Mary Beth. 2003. *Community and Money: Men and Women Making Change.* Montreal: Black Rose Books.

Rainwater, Lee, Tim Smeeding, and John Coder. 2001. "Child Poverty across States, Nations and Continents." Pp. 33–74 in *Child Well-Being, Child Poverty and Child Poverty in Modern Nations: What Do We Know?,* edited by K. Vleminckx and T. Smeeding. Bristol, UK: Policy Press.

Reimer, Bill. 2006. "The Informal Economy in Non-metropolitan Canada." *Canadian Review of Sociology and Anthropology* 43(1): 23–49.

Ricciuto, Laurie E., and Valerie S. Tarasuk. 2007. "An Examination of Income-related Disparities in the Nutritional Quality of Food Selections among Canadian Households from 1986–2001." *Social Science and Medicine* 64(1): 186–98.

Richardson, Jack. 1996. "Canada and Free Trade: Why Did It Happen?" In *Society in Question,* edited by R. Brym. Toronto: Nelson.

Robinson, Lynne M., Lynn McIntyre, and Suzanne Officer. 2005. "Welfare Babies: Poor Children's Experiences in Forming Healthy Peer Relationships in Canada." *Health Promotion International* 20(4): 342–50.

Sarlo, Christopher. 2008. *What is Poverty? Providing Clarity for Canada.* Vancouver: Fraser Institute.

Schirle, Tammy. 2015. "The Gender Wage Gap in Canadian Provinces, 1997–2014." *Canadian Public Policy* 41(4): 309–19.

Scott, Ellen K., Kathryn Edin, Andrew S. London, and Rebecca Joyce Kissane. 2004. "Unstable Work, Unstable Income: Implications for Family Well-being in the Era of Time-limited Welfare." *Journal of Poverty* 8(1): 61–88.

Small, Mario Luis. 2006. "Neighborhood Institutions as Resource Brokers: Childcare Centers, Inter-organizational Ties, and Resource Access among the Poor." *Social Problems* 53(2): 274–92.

Smith, Ekuwa, and Andrew Jackson. 2002. *Does a Rising Tide Lift All Boats?* Ottawa: Canadian Council on Social Development.

Statistics Canada. 2008. Labour Force Information. Ottawa: Ministry of Industry.

———. 2013. 2011 Census of Population, Cat nos. 98.312-XCB2011020.

———. 2013a. Cansim Table 202-0410. Average total income, by census family type and number of earners, 2011 constant dollars (discontinued).

———. 2015. Statistics Canada. Table 206-0041—Low income statistics by age, sex and economic family type, Canada, provinces and selected census metropolitan areas (CMAs), Annual, CANSIM (database).

———. 2016. Life tables, Canada, provinces and territories, 2010–2012.

Stewart, Susan D. 2010. "Children with Nonresident Parents: Living Arrangements, Visitation, and Child Support." *Journal of Marriage and Family* 72(5): 1078–91.

Tarasuk, Valerie S. 2001. "Household Food Insecurity with Hunger is Associated with Women's Food Intakes, Health and Household Circumstances." *Journal of Nutrition* 131(10): 2670–6.

———, and Naomi Dachner. 2009. "The Proliferation of Charitable Meal Programs in Toronto." *Canadian Public Policy* 35(4): 433–50.

———, Naomi Dachner, and Rachel Loopstra. 2014. "Food Banks, Welfare, and Food Insecurity in Canada." *British Food Journal* 116(9): 1405–17.

———, and Joan M. Eakin. 2003. "Charitable Food Assistance as Symbolic Gesture: An Ethnographic Study of Food Banks in Ontario." *Social Science and Medicine* 56(7): 1505–15.

Tjepkema, Michael, and Russell Wilkins. 2011. "Remaining Life Expectancy at Age 25 and Probability of Survival to Age 75, by Socioeconomic Status and Aboriginal Ancestry." *Health Reports* 22, 4: 31–6.

Torjman, Sherri. 1999. "Crests and Crashes: The Changing Tides of Family Income Security." Pp. 69–88 in *Canada's Changing Families: Challenges to Public Policy*, edited by M. Baker. Ottawa: Vanier Institute of the Family.

Uppal, Sharanjit. 2015. *Employment Patterns of Families with Children*. Insights on Canadian Society. Statistics Canada, Catalogue no. 75-006-X.

———, and Sébastien LaRochelle-Côté. 2015. *Changes in Debt and Assets of Canadian Families, 1999 to 2012*. Insights on Canadian Society: Statistics Canada. Catalogue no. 75-0060X.

Vincent, Carole. 2013. *Why Do Women Earn Less Than Men? A Synthesis of Findings from Canadian Microdata*. CRDCN Synthesis Series, September 2013.

Vozoris, Nicholas, Barbara Davis, and Valerie Tarasuk. 2002. "The Affordability of a Nutritious Diet for Households on Welfare in Toronto." *Canadian Journal of Public Health* 93(1): 36–40.

Whelan, Christopher T., and Bertrand Maitre. 2007. "Income, Deprivation and Economic Stress in the Enlarged European Union." *Social Indicators Research* 83(2): 309–29.

Wilkins, Russell, and Gregory J. Sherman. 1998. "Low Income and Child Health in Canada." Pp. 102–9 in *Health and Canadian Society: Sociological Perspectives*, edited by D. Coburn, C. D'Arcy, and G.M. Torrance. Toronto: University of Toronto Press.

Williamson, Deanna L., and Fiona Salkie. 2005. "Welfare Reforms in Canada: Implications for the Well-being of Pre-school Children in Poverty." *Journal of Children and Poverty* 11(1): 55–76.

Wilson, Beth, with Emily Tsoa. 2001. *HungerCount 2001: Food Bank Lines in Insecure Times*. Toronto: Canadian Association of Food Banks.

Woolley, Frances. 1998. "Work and Household Transactions: An Economist's View." Pp. 27–55 in *How Families Cope and Why Policymakers Need to Know*, edited by D. Cheal, F. Woolley, and M. Luxton. Ottawa: Canadian Policy Research Networks Study No. F12.

———. 2004. "Why Pay Child Benefits to Mothers?" *Canadian Public Policy* 30(1): 47–69.

Yeung, W. Jean, and Sandra L. Hofferth. 1998. "Family Adaptations to Income and Job Loss in the US." *Journal of Family and Economic Issues* 19(3): 255–83.

Zhang, Xuelin. 2003. *The Wealth Position of Immigrant Families in Canada*. Ottawa: Statistics Canada, Business and Labour Market Analysis Division.

Chapter 11

Al-Krenawl, A., and J. Graham. 2000. "Culturally Sensitive Social Work. Practice with Arab Clients in Mental Health Settings." *Health and Social Work* 25: 9–22.

Amar, A. 1984. *Islam and Marriage*. Saudi Arabia: Dar-Al fiker Al-Arabi (in Arabic).

Anisef, P., R. Brown, K. Physthian, R. Sweet, and D. Walters. 2010. "Early School Leaving among Immigrants in Toronto Secondary Schools." *Canadian Review of Sociology* 47(2): 103–28.

———, and K. Kilbride. 2000. *The Needs of Newcomer Youth and Emerging "Best Practices" to Meet Those Needs: Final Report*. Retrieved September 3, 2016 (www.ohchr.org/Documents/ProfessionalInterest/refugees.pdf).

Bélanger, A., and S. Gilbert. 2005. *The Fertility of Immigrant Women and Their Canadian-born Daughters*. Ottawa: Statistics Canada, Division of Demography.

Bernard, A. 2015. *Youth Labour Force Participation: 2008-2014*. Ottawa: Statistics Canada. Retrieved November 9, 2016 (http://homelesshub.ca/sites/default/files/B%20Youth%20Employment%20Backgrounder.pdf).

Berns-McGown, R. 2013. *"I Am Canadian" Challenging Stereotypes about Young Somali Canadians*. Montreal: Institute for Research in Public Policy.

Berry, J. 2011. "Integration and Multiculturalism: Ways towards Social Solidarity." *Papers on Social Representations* 20: 2.1–2.21.

Biles, J., M. Buirstein, and J. Frideres, eds. 2009. *Immigration and Integration in Canada*. Montreal and Kingston, McGill-Queens University Press.

Block. S., and E. Galabuzi. 2011. *Canada's Colour Coded Labour Market: the Gap for Racialized Workers*. Ottawa: Canadian Centre for Policy Alternatives, and Toronto: The Wellesley Institute.

Bowes, A., and H. Wilkinson. 2003. "'We Didn't Know It Would Get This Bad': South Asian Experiences of Dementia and the Service Response." *Health Social Care in the Community* 11: 387–96.

Boyd, M., and E. Grieco. 2003. *Women and Migration: Incorporating Gender into International Migration Theory*. Washington: Migration Policy Institute.

Bragg, B., and L. Wong. 2015. ""Cancelled Dreams": Family Reunification and Shifting Canadian Immigration Policy." *Journal of Immigrant and Refugee Studies* 14(1): 46–65.

Brownridge, D., and S. Halli. 2003. "Double Advantage? Violence against Canadian Migrant Women from 'Developed' Nations." *International Migration* 41(1): 29–46.

Brun, C., and A. Fabos. 2015. "Making Homes in Limbo? A Conceptual Framework." *Refuge* 1(31): 5–17

Carta, M., M. Moro, and J. Bass. 2015. "War Traumas in the Mediterranean Area." *Social Psychiatry* 61(1): 33–8.

Commission on Systemic Racism in the Ontario Criminal Justice System, 1995. *Report of the Commission on Systemic Racism in the Ontario Criminal Justice System*. Toronto: Queens Printer for Ontario.

Connor, P., and J. Krogstad. 2016. "About Six-in-Ten Syrians Are Now Displaced from Their Homes." *Fact Tank*. Washington: PEW Research Center.

Côté, A., M. Kérisit, and M. Côté. 2001. *Sponsorship for Better or for Worse: The Impact of Sponsorship on the Equality Rights of Immigrant Women*. Ottawa: Status of Women Canada.

Crocker, D., A. Dobrowolsky, E. Keeble, C. Moncayo, and E. Tastsoglou. 2007. *Security and Immigration, Changes and Challenges: Immigrant and Ethnic Communities in Atlantic Canada, Presumed Guilty?* Retrieved September 2, 2016 (www.publicsafety.gc.ca/lbrr/archives/cn5191-eng.pdf).

Crumlish N., and K.A. O'Rourke. 2010. "Systematic Review of Treatments for Post-Traumatic Stress Disorder among Refugees and Asylum-Seekers." *The Journal of Nervous and Mental Disease* 198(4): 237–51.

Culture, Community and Health Studies Program, Centre for Addiction and Mental Health, Association of Sudanese Women in Research, and Research Resource Division for Refugees. 2004. *The Study of Sudanese Settlement in Ontario*. Toronto. Retrieved August 20, 2016 (http://atwork.settlement.org/downloads/atwork/Study_of_Sudanese_Settlement_in_Ontario.pdf).

Darvishpour, M. 2003. "Immigrant Women Challenge the Role of Men: How the Changing Power Relationship within Iranian Families in Sweden Intensifies Family Conflicts after Immigration." *Journal of Comparative Family Studies* 33(2): 271–96.

Donnelly, T., J. Hwang, D. Este, C. Ewashen, C. Adair, and M. Clinton. 2011. "If I Was Going to Kill Myself, I Wouldn't Be Calling You. I Am Asking for Help: Challenges Influencing Immigrant and Refugee Women's Mental Health." *Issues in Mental Health Nursing* 32(5): 279–90.

Dosanjh, R., S. Deo, and S. Sidhu. 1994. *Spousal Abuse in the South Asian Community*. Vancouver: Mimeo.

Dua, E. 2007. "Exploring Articulations of 'Race' and Gender: Going Beyond Singular Categories." Pp. 184–8 in *Race and Racism in 21st Century Canada*, edited by S. Hier and S. Bolaria. Peterborough: Broadview Press.

El-Assal, K. 2016. *2016: A Record Setting Year for Refugee Resettlement in Canada?* Ottawa: The Conference Board of Canada. Retrieved August 20, 2016 (www.conferenceboard.ca/commentaries/immigration/default/16-02-02/2016_a_record-setting_year_for_refugee_resettlement_in_canada.aspx).

Fanjoy, M. 2015. "There Is No Place Like Home(s): South Sudanese-Canadian Return Migration." Pp. 76–99 in *Canada in Sudan, Sudan in Canada: Migration, Conflict and Reconstruction*, edited by A. Madibbo. Montreal and Kingston: McGill-Queen's University Press.

Ferrer, A., and A. Adsera. 2016. "The Fertility of Married Immigrant Women to Canada." *International Migration Review* 50: 475–505.

Frenette, M., and R. Morissette, 2003. *Will They Ever Converge? Earnings of Immigrant and Canadian-born Workers over the Last Two Decades.* Statistics Canada Analytical Studies Research Paper Series. Ottawa: Statistics Canada.

Frideres, J.S. 2002. "Immigrants, Integration and the Intersection of identities." Commissioned by Canadian Heritage. Retrieved August 25, 2016 (http://canada.metropolis.net/events/diversity /immigration.pdf).

———. 2011. "Alberta: Four Strong Winds—Immigration without Direction." Pp. 135–59 in *Integration and Inclusion of Newcomers and Minorities Across Canada*, edited by J. Biles, M. Buirstein, J. Frideres, E. Toley, and R. Vineberg. Montreal and Kingston: McGill-Queens University Press.

Guruge, S., M. Hynie, Y. Shakya, A. Akbari, S. Htoo, and S. Abiyo. 2015. "Refugee Youth and Migration: Using Arts-Informed Research to Understand Changes in Their Roles and Responsibilities." *Forum Qualitative Sozialforschung* 16: 3.

Hall, J. 2016. "Welcoming Syrian refugees." *Canadian Family Physician* 26: 269.

Haslam, C., T. Crawys, and S. Haslam. 2014. "The We's Have It: Evidence for the Distinctive Benefits of Group Engagement in Enhancing Cognitive Health in Aging." *Social Science and Medicine* 120: 57–66.

Hassan, G., L. Kirmayer, A. Mekki-Berrada, C. Quosh, R. El-Chammay, J. Deville-Stoetzel, A. Youssef, H. Jefee-Bahloul, A. Barkeel-Oteo, A. Coutts, S. Song, and P. Ventevogel. 2015. *Culture, Context and the Mental Health and Psychosocial Wellbeing of Syrians: A Review for Mental Health and Psychosocial Support Staff Working with Syrians Affected by Armed Conflict.* Geneva: UNHCR.

Henry, F., and C. Tator. 2006. *Racial Profiling in Canada: Challenging the Myth of 'a Few Bad Apples'.* Toronto: University of Toronto Press.

Hill-Collins, P. 1990. *Black Feminist Thought: Knowledge, Consciousness, and the Politics of Empowerment.* Boston: Unwin Hyman.

hooks, b. 1999. *Yearning: Race, Gender, and Cultural Politics.* Brooklyn: South End Press.

Hossen, A. 2012. "Social Isolation and Loneliness among Elderly Immigrants: The Case of South Asians Living in Canada." *Journal of International Social Issues* 1: 1–10.

Howard K., N. Gracia, and M. Alvarez. 2014. "Culturally and Linguistically Appropriate Services—Advancing Health with CLAS." *The New England Journal of Medicine* 371: 198–201.

Hunter, P. 2013. "Number of Blacks in Canadian Prisons Troubling." *Share.* Retrieved November 9, 2016 (http://sharenews.com/number-of-blacks-in-canadian-prisons-troubling/).

Husaini, Z. 2001. *Cultural Dilemma and a Plea for Justice: Voices of Canadian Ethnic Women.* Edmonton: Intercultural Action Committee for the Advancement of Women.

Jakobsen, M., M. Demott, and T. Heir. 2014. "Prevalence of Psychiatric Disorders among Unaccompanied Asylum-Seeking Adolescents in Norway." *Clinical Practice & Epidemiology in Mental Health.* 10: 53–8.

Kazemipur, A. 2014. *The Muslim Question in Canada: A Story of Segmented Integration.* Vancouver: UBC Press.

Khalaf, R., and W. Swing. 2015. *Migration, Displacement and Development in a Changing Arab Region.* Beirut: United Nations and International Organization for Migration.

Kilbride, K. 2014. *Immigrant Integration, Research Implications for Future Policy.* Toronto: Canadian Scholars' Press.

King, D. 1988. "Multiple Jeopardy, Multiple Consciousness: The Context of a Black Feminist Ideology." *Signs* 14(1): 42–72.

Kirmayer, L., J., Narasiah, M. Munoz, M. Rashid, A. Ryder, J. Guzder, G. Hassan, C. Rousseau, and K. Pottie. 2011. "Common Mental Health Problems in Immigrants and Refugees: General Approach in Primary Care." *Canadian Medical Association Journal* 183(12): E959–67.

Lee, K., and D. Yoon. 2011. "Factors Influencing the General Well-being of Low Income Korean Immigrant Elders." *Social Work* 56: 269–79.

Lee, S., and B. Edmonston. 2013. "Canada's Immigrant Families: Growth, Diversity and Challenges." *Population Change and Life Course Strategies Knowledge Cluster Discussion Paper Series* Vol. 1, No.1, Article 4.

Lee, Y-M., and K. Holm. 2011. "Family Relationships and Depression among Elderly Korean Immigrants." *ISRN Nursing*, Article ID 429249.

Liu, S., and L. Reeves. 2016. "Migration and Aging." Pp. 1–8 in *Encyclopedia of Geropsychology*, edited by N. Pachana. New York: Springer.

Madibbo, A., ed. 2015. *Canada in Sudan, Sudan in Canada: Migration, Conflict and Reconstruction.* Montreal and Kingston: McGill-Queen's University Press.

———. 2016. "The Way Forward: African Francophone Immigrants Negotiate Their Multiple Minority Identities." *Journal of International Migration and Integration* 17(3): 853–66.

Makwarimba, E., M. Stewart, L. Simich, K. Makumbe, R. Shizha, E., and S. Anderson. 2013. "Sudanese and Somali Refugees in Canada: Social Support Needs and Preferences." *International Migration* 51(5): 106–19.

Manozzie, C. 2016. *International Migration Report: 2015*. New York: Department of Economic and Social Affairs, Population Division, United Nations.

McAndrew, M., M. Potvin, and C. Borri-Anadon, eds. 2013. *Le développement d'institutions inclusives en contexte de diversité*. Quebec City: Les Presses de l'Université du Québec.

Mensah, J. 2014. "Black Continental African Identities in Canada: Exploring the Intersections of Identity Formation and Immigrant Transnationalism." *Journal of Canadian Studies* 48(3): 5–29.

Mghir, R., W. Freed, A. Raskin, and K. Wayne. 1995. "Depression and Posttraumatic Stress Disorder Among a Community Sample of Adolescent and Young Adult Afghan Refugees." *Journal of Nervous & Mental Disease* 183(1): 24–30.

Milan, A. *Fertility Overview, 2009 to 2011*. 2013. Ottawa: Statistics Canada. Retrieved July 12, 2016 (www.statcan.gc.ca/pub/91-209-x/2013001/article/11784-eng.htm).

Moon, A., and S. Rhee. 2010. "Immigrant and Refugee Elders." Chapter 12 in *Handbook of Social Work in Health and Ageing*, edited by B. Berkman and S. D'Ambruoso. Oxford Scholarship Online.

Mosaic Institute. 2009. *A "Smart Map" of the Sudanese Diaspora in Canada*. Toronto. Retrieved July 12, 2016 (http://mosaicinstitute.ca/research/a-smart-map-of-the-sudanese-diaspora-in-canada-2009__trashed/).

National Anti-Racism Council of Canada. 2007. *Racial Discrimination in Canada*. Toronto.

Ngo, H. 2009. "Patchwork, Sidelining and Marginalization: Services for Immigrant Youth." *Journal of Immigrant & Refugee Studies* 7: 82–100.

Nourpanah. S. 2014. "A Study of the Experiences of Integration and Settlement of Afghan Government-assisted Refugees in Halifax, Canada." *Refuge* 30(1): 57.

Oakley, R. 1995 "Racism and Education: Structures and Strategies." *Ethnic and Racial Studies* 18(3): 662–4.

Ortega, M., and J. Frideres. 2015. "Immigrant Settlement and Integration: Contributions Through Partnerships." *Canadian Diversity* 11: 5–8.

Park, H., and C. Kim. 2013. "Ageing in an Inconvenient Paradise: The Immigrant Experience of Older Korean People in New Zealand." *Australasian Journal on Ageing* 32: 158–62.

Pottie, K., C. Greenaway, G. Hassan, C. Hui, and L. Kirmayer. 2015. "S'occuper d'une famille de réfugiés syriens nouvellement arrivés, " *CMAJ*. Retrieved November 9, 2016 (www.cmaj.ca/site/misc/caring-for-a-newly-arrived-syrian-refugee-family-fr.pdf).

Quirke, L. 2011. "Exploring the Settlement Experiences and Information Practices of Afghan Newcomer Youth in Toronto." *Canadian Journal of Information and Library Science* 35(4): 345–53.

Raj, A., and J. Silverman. 2002. "Violence against Immigrant Women." *Violence Against Women* 8(3): 367–98.

Rider, E. 2012. "Refugees, Sexual Violence, and Armed Conflict: The Nuances between Victims and Agents." *Wagadu* 10: 72–92.

Rytter, M. 2013. *Family Upheaval: Generation, Mobility and Relatedness Among Pakistani Migrants in Denmark*. New York: Berghahn Books.

Sapers, H. 2015. *Annual Report of the Office of the Correctional Investigator 2014–2015*. Ottawa: Office of the Correctional Investigator.

Saris, A., and J. Potvin. 2008. *Sharia in Canada Family Dispute Resolution among Muslim Minorities in the West*. Ottawa: Canadian Council on Social Development.

Satzewich, V. 2016. *Points of Entry: How Canada's Immigration Officers Decide Who Gets In*. Vancouver: UBC Press.

Shakya, Y., S. Guruge, M. Hynie, A. Akbari, M. Malik, S. Htoo, A. Khogali, S. Mona, R. Murtaza, and S. Alley. 2010a. "Aspirations for Higher Education among Newcomer Refugee Youth in Toronto: Expectations, Challenges, and Strategies." *Refuge: Canada's Journal on Refugees* 27(2): 65–78.

———, N. Khanlou, and T. Gonsalves. 2010b. "Determinants of Mental Health Newcomer Youth: Policy and Service Implications." *Canadian Issues* Summer 2010: 98–102.

Shoup, J. 2008. *Culture and Customs of Syria*. Portsmouth: Greenwood Publishing Group.

Simich, L., D. Este, and H. Hamilton. 2010. "Meanings of Home and Mental Well-being among Sudanese Refugees in Canada." *Ethnicity & Health*: 1–14.

Sirin, S., and L. Rogers-Sirin. 2015. *The Educational and Mental Health Needs of Syrian Refugee Children*. Washington: Migration Policy Institute.

Smith, E. 2004. *Nowhere to Turn? Responding to Partner Violence against Immigrant and Visible Minority Women*. Ottawa: Canadian Council on Social Development.

Statistics Canada. 2009. "2006 Census Release Topics." Retrieved November 9, 2016 (www12.statcan.ca/census-recensement/2006/rt-td/index-eng.cfm).

———. 2011. "Ethnic Origin, Single and Multiple Ethnic Origin Responses and Sex for the Population of Canada." Retrieved November 9, 2016 (www12.statcan.gc.ca/nhs-enm/2011/dp-pd/dt-td/Rp-eng.cfm?LANG=E&APATH=3&DETAIL=0&DIM=0&FL=A&FREE=0&GC=0&GID=0&GK=0&GRP=0&PID=105396&PRID=0&PTYPE=105277&S=0&SHOWALL=0&SUB=0&Temporal=2013&THEME=95&VID=0&VNAMEE=&VNAMEF).

———. 2015. *Labour Force Characteristics by Immigrant Status of Population aged 25–54, and by Educational Attainment.* Ottawa.

———. 2016. "Births and total fertility rate, by province and territory." Retrieved November 9, 2016 (www.statcan.gc.ca/tables-tableaux/sum-som/l01/cst01/hlth85b-eng.htm).

———. 2017. Labour Force Characteristics by Immigrant Status of Population aged 25–54, and by Educational Attainment. Ottawa. Retrieved June 17, 2017 (www.statcan.gc.ca/tables-tableaux/sum-som/l01/cst01/labor90a-eng.htm).

Teeluckingh, C., and G. Galabuzi. 2005. *Working Precariously: The Impact of Race and Immigrant Status on Employment Outcomes in Canada.* Toronto. Canadian Race Relations Foundations.

Treas, J., and S. Mazumdar. 2002. "Older People in America's Immigrant Families: Dilemmas of Dependence, Integration and Isolation." *Journal of Ageing Studies* 16(3): 243–58.

Triki-Yamani, A., M. McAndrew, and P. Brodeur. 2008. *Islam and Education in Pluralistic Societies: Integration and Transformations,* Final Report. Montreal: University of Montreal.

Türegün, A. 2011. *Developing Criteria for Best Practices in Settlement Services: A Report.* Centre for International Migration and Settlement Studies. Ottawa: Carleton University.

United Nations (UN). 1951. *Convention Relating to the Status of Refugees.* Retrieved September 5, 2016 (www.ohchr.org/Documents/ProfessionalInterest/refugees.pdf).

United National High Commissioner for Refugees (UNHCR). 2011. *Population Levels and Trends.* Geneva: UNHCR. Retrieved September 3, 2016 (www.unhcr.org/516286589.html).

———. 2016. *Sudan: Refugees, Asylum-seekers, IDPs and Others of Concern to UNHCR by State as of 30 April 2016.* Retrieved September 4, 2016 (www.refworld.org/docid/573ad3274.html).

Walker, A. 1983. *In Search of Our Mothers' Gardens.* Orlando: Harcourt Brace Jovanovich.

Walters, D., K. Phythian, and P. Anisef. 2006. *The Ethnic Identity of Immigrants in Canada.* CERIS Working Papers No. 38. Toronto: The Joint Centre of Excellence for Research on Immigration and Settlement.

Wane, N. 2004. "Black Canadian Feminist Thought: Tensions and possibilities." *Canadian Woman Studies* 23(2): 145–53.

Wilkinson, L., Y. Hébert, and M. Ali. 2012. "Examining Youth's Perceptions of Safety, Fear, Inclusion and Exclusion in a Canadian City in Adolescent Behavior." Pp. 217–34 in *Adolescent Behavior,* edited by C. Bassani. Haupauge: Nova Science Publishers.

Wortley, S. 2006. *Racial Profiling in Canada: Evidence, Impacts and Policy Debates.* Toronto: Faculty of Law, University of Toronto.

Young, P., and E. Choldin, eds. 2012. *Working with South Sudanese Immigrant Students—Teacher Resources.* Edmonton: Alberta Culture and Community Services Community Initiatives Program.

Zine, J. 2008. *Canadian Islamic Schools: Unraveling the Politics of Faith, Gender, Knowledge, and Identity.* Toronto: University of Toronto Press.

Chapter 12

Aboriginal Healing Foundation. 2007. *Annual Report, 2007.* Available at (www.ahf.ca/downloads/annual-report-2007.pdf).

Adams, Ian. 1967, February. "The Lonely Death of Charlie Wenjack." *Maclean's,* 30–49.

Anderson, Kim. 2000. *A Recognition of Being: Reconstructing Native Womanhood.* Toronto: Second Story Press.

Blackstock, C. 2007. "Residential schools: Did they Really Close or Just Morph into Child Welfare." *Indigenous Law Journal* 6, 71.

———, and Nico Trocmé. 2005. "Community-based Child Welfare for Aboriginal Children: Supporting Resilience through Structural Change." *Social Policy Journal of New Zealand* 24(12): 12–33.

Canada. 1847. *Appendix to the sixth volume of the journals of the Legislative Assembly of the Province of Canada.* [Appendix T]. Available at (http://eco.canadiana.ca/view/oocihm.9_00955_6_1/3?r=0&s=1).

———. 1996. Royal Commission on Aboriginal Peoples. *Report of the Royal Commission on Aboriginal Peoples.* Available at (www.collectionscanada.gc.ca/webarchives/20071115053257/www.ainc-inac.gc.ca/ch/rcap/sg/sgmm_e.html).

CBC. 2016, January 26. "Canada discriminates against children on reserves, tribunal rules." Available at (www.cbc.ca/news/indigenous/canada-discriminates-against-children-on-reserves-tribunal-rules-1.3419480).

Cook, Katsi. 2007. Mother Earth. *National Museum of the American Indian.* Transcript. Available at (http://nmai.si.edu/sites/1/files/motherearth/2007/pdfs/cook_transcript.pdf).

Final Report to the Honourable Muriel Smith, Minister of Community Services. 1985. Winnipeg: Manitoba Community Services.

Hartley, Gerard. 2007. "The Search for Consensus: A Legislative History of Bill C-31, 1969–1985." *Aboriginal Policy Research Volume V Setting the Agenda for Change* 5: 5–34

Holmes, Joan. 1987. Bill C-31, equality or disparity? The effects of the new Indian Act on native women. *Background Paper.* Ottawa: Canadian Advisory Council on the Status of Women.

Hurley, Mary C., and Tonina Simeone. 2010, March. Legislative Summary of Bill C-3: Gender Equity in Indian Registration Act. *Social Affairs Division.* Available at (www.lop.parl.gc.ca/About/Parliament/LegislativeSummaries/bills_ls.asp?Language=E&ls=c3&Parl=40&Ses=3& source=library_prb).

Indigenous and Northern Affairs Canada. 2013. *Scenarios: Matrimonial Real Property on Reserves.* Matrimonial Real Property on Reserves. Available at (www.aadnc-aandc.gc.ca/eng/1317216059784/1317216518944?pedisable=true).

Johnston, Patrick. 1983. *Native Children and the Child Welfare System.* Toronto: James Lorimer and the Canadian Council on Social Development.

Milloy, J. 1999. *A National Crime: The Canadian Government and the Residential Schools System.* Winnipeg, MB: University of Manitoba Press.

Mosby, Ian. 2013. "Administering Colonial Science: Nutrition Research and Human Biomedical Experimentation in Aboriginal Communities and Residential Schools, 1942–1952." *Histoire sociale/Social history* 46(91): 145–72.

Moss, Wendy, and Elaine Gardner-O'Toole. 1991. "Aboriginal People: History of Discriminatory Laws." *Law and Government Division.* Available at (http://publications.gc.ca/collections/collection_2008/lop-bdp/bp/bp175-e.pdf).

Native Women's Association of Canada. 2015, January. NWAC Welcomes Canadian Human Rights Tribunal Ruling in Favour of First Nations Child & Family Caring Society of Canada. *Press Release.* Available at (https://nwac.ca/2016/01/2988/).

———. 2014. *Matrimonial Real Property (MRP) Toolkit.* Centre of Excellence for Matrimonial Real Property. Available at (https://nwac.ca/wp-content/uploads/2015/05/2014-Matrimonial-Real-Property-Toolkit-Version-1.3.pdf).

Review Committee on Indian and Metis Adoptions and Placements. 1985. *No Quiet Place.*

Siltanen, Janet and Michelle Stanworth. 1984. "The Politics of Private Woman and Public Man." *Theory and Society* 13(1): 91–118.

Sinclair, Raven. 2007. "Identity Lost and Found: Lessons from the Sixties Scoop." *First Peoples Child and Family Review* (3)1: 65–82.

Sinha, Vandna, and Anna Kozlowski. 2013. "The Structure of Aboriginal Child Welfare in Canada." *The International Indigenous Policy Journal* 4(2): 1–21

———, Nico Trocmé, Barbara Fallon, Bruce MacLaurin, Elizabeth Fast, Shelley Thomas Prokop, et al. 2011. *Kiskisik Awasisak: Remember the Children. Understanding the Overrepresentation of First Nations Children in the Child Welfare System.* Ontario: Assembly of First Nations.

Six Nations Health Services. 2006. Tsi Non:we Ionnakeratstha Ona:grahsta'. Available at (www.snhs.ca/bcBackground.htm).

Smith-Rosenberg, Carroll. 1986. *Disorderly Conduct: Visions of Gender in Victorian America.* Toronto: Oxford University Press.

———, and Charles E. Rosenberg. 1999. "The Female Animal: Medical and Biological Views of Woman and Her Role in Nineteenth-Century America." In *Women and Health in America: Historical Readings,* edited by J. Walzer Leavitt. University of Wisconsin Press.

Statistics Canada. 2011. *Study: Living arrangements of Aboriginal children aged 14 and under, 2011.* Available at (www.statcan.gc.ca/daily-quotidien/160413/dq160413a-eng.htm?HPA).

St. Germain, Jill. 2009. *Indian Treaty-Making Policy in the United States and Canada, 1867-1877: Making Policy in the United States and Canada 1867–1877.* University of Nebraska Press.

Stoler, A. 2002. *Carnal Knowledge and Imperial Power: Race and the Intimate in Colonial Rule.* Berkeley: University of California Press.

Sunseri, Lina. 2010. *Being Again of One Mind: Oneida Women and the Struggle for Decolonization.* Vancouver: UBC Press.

The Jordan's Principle Working Group. 2015. *Without Denial, Delay, or Disruption: Ensuring First Nations Children's Access to Equitable Services through Jordan's Principle.* Ottawa, ON: Assembly of First Nations. Available at (www.afn.ca/uploads/files/jordans_principle-report.pdf).

Truth and Reconciliation Commission of Canada. 2015. *Honouring the Truth, Reconciling for the Future: Summary of the Final Report of the Truth and Reconciliation Commission of Canada.* Ottawa. Available at (www.trc.ca/websites/trcinstitution/index.php?p=890).

Van Kirk, Sylvia. 1983. *Many Tender Ties: Women in Fur-trade Society, 1670–1870.* University of Oklahoma Press.

Venne, Sharon H. 2007. *Treaties Made in Good Faith in Native and Settlers—Now and Then.* Edmonton: University of Alberta Press.

Watts, Vanessa. 2006. "Towards Anishnaabe Governance and Accountability: Reawakening our Relationships and Sacred Bimaadiziwin." Master's thesis. University of Victoria.

White, Lavina, and Eva Jacobs. 1992. *Liberating Our Children, Liberating Our Nations: Report of the Aboriginal Committee.* Community Panel of Family and Children's Services Legislation Review in British Columbia. Victoria: Minister of Social Services.

Chapter 13

Aboriginal Affairs and Northern Development Canada. 2010. "Income Assistance Program." Available at (www.aadnc-aandc.gc.ca/eng/1100100035256).

Aboriginal Reference Group on Disability Issues. (1997) *One Voice: The Perspective of Aboriginal People with Disabilities*. Ottawa, Ontario.

Auliff, Lily. 2001. "Bringing up Baby: Mothering with a Disability." *WeMedia* 5(1; Jan.-Feb.): 66–9.

BC Institute against Family Violence. 1996. *Overview of Family Violence*. Available at (www.bcifv.org/about/overview/3.shtml).

Behnia, Behnaz, and Édith Duclos. 2003. *Participation and Activity Limitation Survey, 2001: Children with Disabilities and Their Families*. Ottawa: Statistics Canada, Housing, Family and Social Statistics Division.

Bellis, Mark A., et al. 2012. "Prevalence and Risk of Violence Against Children with Disabilities: A Systematic Review and Meta-analysis of Observational Studies." *The Lancet* 30(9845): 899–907.

Blackford, Karen A. 1999. "Caring to Overcome Differences, Inequities, and Lifestyle Pressures: When a Parent has a Disability." Pp. 279–87 in *Feminist Success Stories*, edited by K.A. Blackford, M. Garceau, and S. Kirby. Ottawa: University of Ottawa Press.

Block, Pamela, and Christopher Keys. 2002. "Race, Poverty and Disability: Three Strikes and You're Out! Or Are You?" *Social Policy* 33(1): 34–8.

Campaign 2000. 2015. Available at (http://campaign2000.ca/wp-content/uploads/2016/03/C2000-National-Report-Card-Nov2015.pdf).

Canada Revenue Agency. 2005. "About the Child Disability Benefit (CDB)." Ottawa: Government of Canada. Available at (www.cra-arc.gc.ca/benefits/faq_cdb-e.html#q1).

Canadian Research Institute for the Advancement of Women. 2002. *Violence against Women and Girls Fact Sheet*. Ottawa: CRIAW/ICREF.

Clare, Eli. 2015. *Exile and Pride: Disability, Queerness, and Liberation*. Durham, NC: Duke University Press.

Cossette, Lucie, and Édith Duclos. 2002. *Participation and Activity Limitation Survey: A Profile of Disability in Canada, 2001*. Ottawa: Minister of Industry, Statistics Canada.

Council of Canadians with Disabilities. N.D. Building an Inclusive and Accessible Canada: Supporting People with Disabilities. Available at (www.ccdonline.ca/en/socialpolicy/actionplan/accessible-canada)

———. 2011. "Notes from Presentation by Lived Experience of Poverty Panelist Laurie Larson." Available at (www.ccdonline.ca/en/socialpolicy/poverty-citizenship/income-security-reform/3Nov2011-Larson).

Crow, L. 1996. "Including all of our lives: renewing the social model of disability". In *Exploring the Divide: Illness and Disability*, Edited by: Barnes, C. and Mercer, G. Leeds, UK: The Disability Press.

DAWN-RAFH Canada. "Women with Disabilities and Violence." N.D. Available at (www.dawncanada.net/issues/issues/fact-sheets-2/violence/).

Demas, Doreen. 1993. "Triple Jeopardy: Native Women with Disabilities." *Canadian Woman Studies* 13(4): 53–55.

DesMeules, Marie, Linda Turner, and Robert Cho. 2004. "Morbidity Experiences and Disability Among Canadian Women." Pp. 19–32 in *Women's Health Surveillance Report: A Multidimensional Look at Women with Disabilities*. Ottawa: Canadian Institute for Health Information.

DisAbled Women's Network (DAWN) Toronto. 1995. "The Risk of Physical and Sexual Assault." *Abilities: Canada's Lifestyle Magazine for People with Disabilities* 22 (Spring): 32–3.

Doe, Tanis. 1999. "Ecological view of prevention of violence." Retrieved March 17, 2005 (http://members.shaw.ca/dewresearch/others.html).

Dunbrack, Janet. 2003. *Respite for Family Caregivers—An Environmental Scan of Publicly-funded Programs in Canada*. Available at (www.hc-sc.gc.ca/hcs-sss/pubs/home-domicile/2003-respite-releve/index-eng.php#a1).

Employment and Social Development Canada. 2011. *Disability in Canada: A 2006 Profile*. Available at (www.esdc.gc.ca/eng/disability/arc/disability_2006.shtml).

Fawcett, G. 1996. *Living with Disability in Canada: An Economic Portrait*. Hull, QC: Human Resources Development Canada.

Friendly, Martha, and Shani Halfon. 2013. "Inclusion of Young Children with Disabilities in Regulated Child Care in Canada. A snapshot: Research, Policy and Practice." Childcare Resource and Research Unit. Occasional Paper (No. 27 July 2013). Available at (www.childcarecanada.org/sites/default/files/Occasional%20paper%2027%20FINAL.pdf).

Fuchs, Don, Linda Burnside, Shelagh Marchenski, and Andria Mudry. 2007. "Children with Disabilities Involved with the Child Welfare System in Manitoba: Current and Future Challenges." Pp. 127–45 in *Putting a Human Face on Child Welfare: Voices from the Prairies*, edited by I. Brown, F. Chaze, D. Fuchs, J. Lafrance, S. McKay, and S. Thomas Prokop. Prairie Child Welfare Consortium. Available at (http://cwrp.ca/sites/default/files/publications/prairiebook/Chapter6.pdf).

Government of Canada. 2002. *Advancing the Inclusion of Persons with Disabilities: A Government of Canada Report*. Ottawa: Government of Canada, December.

————. 2004. *Office for Disability Issues. Advancing the Inclusion of Persons with Disabilities: A Government of Canada Report.* Ottawa: Social Development Canada.

Halfon, Shani, and Martha Friendly. 2013. "Inclusion of Young children with disabilities in regulated child care in Canada: A snapshot: Research, policy and practice." Occasional Paper No. 27. Toronto: Childcare Resource and Research Unit.

Hanvey, Louise. 2002. *Children with Disabilities and Their Families in Canada: A Discussion Paper.* National Children's Alliance for the First National Roundtable on Children with Disabilities.

Hewett, Heather. 2004. "My Sister's Family." In *The Scholar and Feminist Online: Young Feminists Take on the Family,* guest edited by J. Baumgardner and A. Richards. Retrieved May 7, 2005 (www.barnard .edu/sfonline/family/hewett_01.htm).

Home, Alice. 2002. "Challenging Hidden Oppression: Mothers Caring for Children with Disabilities." *Critical Social Work* (Vol. 3, No. 1). Available at (www1.uwindsor.ca/criticalsocialwork/challenging-hidden-oppression-mothers-caring-for-children-with-disabilities).

Howlett, Karen. 2004. "Families of disabled children to reunite Monday, judge says." *Globe and Mail,* 4 June, A13.

Human Resources and Skills Development Canada (HRSCD). 2009. *Federal Disability Report: Advancing the Inclusion of People with Disabilities.* Quebec: Publications Service. Available at (www.gov.mb.ca/dio/pdf/2009_fdr.pdf).

————. 2011a. *Disability in Canada: A 2006 Profile.* Available at (www.hrsdc.gc.ca/eng/disability_issues/reports/disability_profile/2011/index.shtml).

Hurst, Rachel. 2005. "'Disabled Peoples' International: Europe and the Social Model of Disability." Pp. 65–79 in *The Social Model of Disability: Europe and the Majority World,* edited by C. Barnes and G. Mercer. Leeds: Disability Press.

Kafer, Alison. 2013. *Feminist, Queer, Crip.* Bloomington: Indiana University Press.

Kaufman, M. 2011. "The Sexual Abuse of Young People with a Disability or Chronic Health Condition." *Pediatrics & Child Health* 16 (6): 365.

Krogh, Kari, and Mary Ennis. 2005. *A National Snapshot of Home Support from the Consumer Perspective: Enabling People with Disabilities to Participate in Policy Analysis and Community Development.* Winnipeg: Council of Canadians with Disabilities.

Kuttai, Heather. 2010. *Maternity Rolls: Pregnancy, Childbirth and Disability.* Halifax and Winnipeg: Fernwood Publishing.

Lippman, Abby. 1993. "Worrying—and Worrying About—the Geneticization of Reproduction and Health." Pp. 39–65 in *Misconceptions,* vol. 1, edited by G. Basen, M. Eichler, and A. Lippman. Quebec City: Voyageur Publishing.

MacLeod, Leslie. "Robert Latimer Murdered His Daughter." Council of Canadians with Disabilities website. Available at (www.ccdonline.ca/en/humanrights/endoflife/latimer/2000/06b)

Malacrida, C. 2009. "Discipline and Dehumanization in a Total Institution: Institutional Survivors' Description of Time-out Rooms." In *Rethinking Normalcy: A Disability Studies Reader,* edited by T. Titchkosky and R. Michalko. Toronto: Canadian Scholars' Press Inc.

Malec, Christine. 1993. "The Double Objectification of Disability and Gender." *Canadian Woman Studies* 13(4): 22–3.

Morris, Jenny. 2001. "Impairment and Disability: Constructing an Ethics of Care that Promotes Human Rights." *Hypatia* 16(5): 1–16.

National Clearinghouse on Family Violence (NCFV), Family Violence Prevention Division. 1993a. *Family Violence against Women with Disabilities.* Ottawa: Health and Welfare Canada. Available at (www.phac-aspc.gc.ca/ncfv-cnivf/familyviolence/pdfs/fvawd.pdf).

————. 2000. *Abuse of Children with Disabilities.* Ottawa: Health and Welfare Canada. Available at (www .phac-aspc.gc.ca/ncfv-cnivf/familyviolence/html/nfntsdisabl_e.html).

Office for Disability Issues. 2003. *Defining Disability: A Complex Issue.* Gatineau, QC: Human Resources Development Canada.

Oliver, Michael. 1996. "The Social Model in Context." Pp. 30–42 in *Understanding Disability: From Theory to Practice.* Hampshire and New York: Palgrave.

Pappone, Jeff. 2005. "Tech workers in 'sandwich generation' often most squeezed." *Ottawa Business Journal.* Retrieved May 4, 2004 (www.ottawa businessjournal .com/305596806034971.php).

Peters, Yvonne, and Karen Lawson. 2002. *The Ethical and Human Rights Implications of Prenatal Technologies: The Need for Federal Leadership and Regulation.* Winnipeg: Prairie Women's Centre of Excellence.

Ridington, Jillian. 1989. "Beating the Odds: Violence and Women with Disabilities." Vancouver: DAWN Canada. Retrieved September 28, 2004 (www.dawn-canada.net/odds.htm).

Roeher Institute. 1994. *Violence and People with Disabilities: A Review of the Literature.* North York, ON: Roeher Institute, for the National Clearing House on Family Violence.

————. 2000a. *Beyond the Limits: Mothers Caring for Children with Disabilities.* North York, ON: Roeher Institute.

————. 2000b. *Count Us In: A Demographic Overview of Childhood and Disability.* North York, ON: Roeher Institute.

Sheldon, Alison. 2005. "One World, One People, One Struggle? Towards the Global Implementation of the Social Model of Disability." Pp. 115–40 in *The Social Model of Disability: Europe and the Majority World*, edited by C. Barnes and G. Mercer. Leeds: Disability Press.

Statistics Canada. 2007a. *2006 Participation and Activity Limitation Survey: A Profile of Disability in Canada, 2006—Analytical Report*. Ottawa: Statistics Canada.

———. 2007b. *2006 Participation and Activity Limitation Survey: A Profile of Disability in Canada, 2006—Tables*. Ottawa: Statistics Canada.

———. 2008a. *2006 Census website*. Available at (www12.statcan.ca/english/census06/analysis/famhouse/ind4a.cfm).

———. 2008b. *2006 Participation and Activity Limitation Survey: A Profile of Disability in Canada, 2006—Labour Force Experience of People with Disabilities in Canada*. Ottawa: Statistics Canada.

———. 2008c. *2006 Participation and Activity Limitation Survey: A Profile of Disability in Canada, 2006—Families of Children with Disabilities*. Ottawa: Statistics Canada.

———. 2009. "Earnings and Incomes of Canadians Over the Past Quarter Century." 2006 Census: Earnings. Available at (www12.statcan.ca/census-recensement/2006/as-sa/97-563/p10-eng.cfm).

———. 2013. *The Daily*. Tuesday, September 10, 2013.

———. 2014a. *Canadian Survey on Disability, 2012: Concepts and Methods Guide*. Available at (www.statcan.gc.ca/pub/89-654-x/89-654-x2014001-eng.htm).

———. 2014b. "Canadians with Unmet Homecare Needs." The Daily, Tuesday, September 9, 2014.

———. 2015. *Canadian Survey on Disability, 2012: A Profile of Persons with Disabilities among Canadians Aged 15 Years or Older, 2012*. Available at (www.statcan.gc.ca/pub/89-654-x/89-654-x2015001-eng.htm#r10).

———. 2016. *Life Tables, Canada, Provinces and Territories, 2010 to 2012*. Available at (www.statcan.gc.ca/pub/84-537-x/84-537-x2016006-eng.htm).

Statistics Canada and Status of Women Canada. 2012. *Women in Canada: A Gender-based Statistical Report*, 6th edn. Ottawa: Minister of Industry.

Stienstra, Deborah. 2012. "Race/Ethnicity and Disability Studies: Towards an Explicitly Intersectional Approach." In *Routledge Handbook of Disability Studies*, edited by N. Watson, A. Roulstone, and C. Thomas. New York: Routledge.

Thomas, Carol. 1997. "The Baby and the Bathwater: Disabled Women and Motherhood in Social Context." *Sociology of Health and Illness* 19: 622–43.

———. 1999. *Female Forms: Experiencing and Understanding Disability*. Philadelphia: Open University Press.

Tomasi, Patricia. 2015. Parents with Disabilities: These Moms Live in Fear of Losing Their Kids. *The Huffington Post Canada*.

Tremain, Shelley, ed. 1996. *Pushing the Limits: Disabled Dykes Produce Culture*. Toronto: Women's Press.

Wendell, Susan. 1996. *The Rejected Body: Feminist Philosophical Reflections on Disability*. New York and London: Routledge.

World Health Organization (WHO). 2017. "Violence Against Adults and Children with Disabilities." Disabilities and Rehabilitation. Available at (www.who.int/disabilities/violence/en/).

Chapter 14

Aboriginal Healing Foundation. 2003. *Aboriginal Domestic Violence in Canada*. Retrieved December 12, 2016 (www.ahf.ca/publications/research-series).

Ad Hoc Federal-Provincial-Territorial Working Group Reviewing Spousal Abuse Policies and Legislation. 2003. *Final Report*. Prepared for the Federal-Provincial-Territorial Ministers Responsible for Justice. Ottawa, ON. Retrieved November 2, 2016 (http://justice.gc.ca/eng/rp-pr/cj-jp/fv-vf/pol/spo_e-con_a.pdf).

Agnew, V. 1998. *In Search of a Safe Place: Abused Women and Culturally Sensitive Services*. Toronto: University of Toronto Press.

Alaggia, R., and S. Maiter. 2013. "Domestic Violence and Child Abuse: Issues for Immigrant and Refugee Families."Pp. 235–70 in *Cruel but Not Unusual: Violence in Canadian Families*, edited by R. Alaggia and C. Vine. Waterloo, ON: Wilfrid Laurier University Press.

Ammar, N.H. 2007. "Wife Battery in Islam: A Comprehensive Understanding of Interpretations." *Violence Against Women* 13(5): 516–26.

Amnesty International. 2009. *No More Stolen Sisters: The Need for a Comprehensive Response to Discrimination and Violence against Indigenous Women in Canada*. London, UK. Retrieved April 12, 2017 (www.amnesty.ca/sites/amnesty/files/amr200122009enstolensistersupdate.pdf).

Bannerji, J. 2002. "A Question of Silence: Reflections on Violence against Women in Communities of Colour." Pp. 353–70 in *Violence Against Women: New Canadian Perspectives*, edited by K.M.J. McKenna and J. Larkin. Toronto: Inanna Publications and Education Inc.

Baskin, C. 2006. "Systemic Oppression, Violence, and Healing in Aboriginal Families and Communities." Pp. 15–48 in *Cruel But Not Unusual: Violence in Canadian Families*, edited by R. Alaggia and C. Vine. Toronto: Wilfrid Laurier University Press.

Beaman, L.G. 2012. "The Status of Women: The Report from a Civilized Society." *Canadian Criminal Law Review* 16(2): 223–46.

Beattie, S., and H. Hutchins. 2015. *Shelters for Abused Women in Canada, 2014.* Retrieved December 10, 2016 (www.statcan.gc.ca/pub/85-002-x/2015001/article/14207-eng.htm).

Brownridge, D.A. 2009. *Violence Against Women: Vulnerable Populations.* New York: Routledge.

———, and S.S. Halli. 2003. "Double Advantage? Violence against Canadian Migrant Women from 'Developed' Nations." *International Migration* 41(1): 29–45.

Cares, A.C., and G.R. Cusik. 2012. "Risks and Opportunities of Faith and Culture: The Case of Abused Jewish Women." *Journal of Family Violence* 27: 427–35.

Citizenship and Immigration Canada (CIC). 2013. *Welcome to Canada: What You Should Know.* Catalogue no. Ci4-60/1-2013. Ottawa, ON.

———. 2015. "Legislation Protects Vulnerable Immigrant Women and Girls [Press release]." Retrieved November 15, 2016 (http://news.gc.ca/web/article-en.do?nid=989099).

Cottrell, B. 2008. "Providing Services to Immigrant Women in Atlantic Canada." *Our Diverse Cities,* 6: 133–7.

Cunradi, C.B., R. Caetano, and J. Schafer. 2002. "Religious Affiliation, Denominational Homogamy, and Intimate Partner Violence among US Couples." *Journal for the Scientific Study of Religion* 41(1): 139–51.

DeKeseredy, W.S. 2011. *Violence against Women: Myths, Facts, Controversies.* Toronto: University of Toronto Press.

———, and A. Hall-Sanchez. 2016. "Adult Pornography and Violence against Women in the Heartland: Results from a Rural Southeast Ohio Study." *Violence Against Women* 1–20. doi:1077801216648795.

Doherty, D., and J. Hornesty. 2004. "Abuse in Rural and Farm Context." Pp. 55–81 in *Understanding Abuse Partnering for Change,* edited by M.L. Stirling, C.A. Cameron, N. Nason-Clark, and B. Miedema. Toronto: University of Toronto Press.

Dutton, D.G., and M. Bodnarchuk. 2005. "Through a Psychological Lens: Personality Disorder and Spouse Assault." Pp. 5–18 in *Current Controversies on Family Violence,* edited by D.R. Loseke, R.J. Gelles, and M.M. Cavanaugh. Newbury Park: SAGE Publications.

Fong, J. 2010. *Out of the Shadows: Woman Abuse in Ethnic, Immigrant and Aboriginal Communities.* Toronto: Women's Press.

Fournier, P. 2012. "Introduction: Honour Crimes and the Law—Public Policy in an Age of Globalization." *Canadian Criminal Law Review* 16: 103–14.

Gelles, R.J. 1997. *Intimate Violence in Families,* 3rd edn. Thousand Oaks, CA: SAGE Publications.

———, and M.A. Straus. 1979. "Determinants of violence in the family: Toward a theoretical integration." Pp. 549–81 in *Contemporary Theories about the Family: Researched Based Theories,* edited by W.R. Burr, R. Hill, F.I. Nye, and I.L. Reiss. New York: The Free Press.

Gill, C., and L. Fitch. 2016. "Developing and Delivering a National Framework for Collaborative Police Action to Intimate Partner Violence in Canada." *Journal of Community Safety and Wellbeing* 1(3): 51–5.

Goldring, L., and P. Landolt. 2011. "Caught in the Work-citizenship Matrix: The Lasting Effects of Precarious Legal Status on Work for Toronto Immigrants." *Globalizations* 8(3): 325–41.

Government of New Brunswick (GNB). 2014. *Women Victims of Abuse Protocols.* Fredericton, NB. Retrieved April 2, 2015 (www2.gnb.ca/content/gnb/en/departments/women/Violence_Prevention_and_Community_Partnerships/content/Public_Awareness_and_Education.html).

Harrop, C. 2016. "Police forces get direction on dealing with family violence: Canadian Association of Chiefs of Police releases new framework at University of New Brunswick." Retrieved December 13, 2016 (www.cbc.ca/news/canada/new-brunswick/police-intimate-partner-violence-1.3850213?cmp=rss).

Holtmann, C. 2016. "Christian and Muslim Immigrant Women in the Canadian Maritimes: Considering their Strengths and Vulnerabilities in Responding to Domestic Violence. *Studies in Religion Sciences Religieuses* 45(3): 397–14.

Inglehart, R., and Norris, P. 2003. *Rising Tide: Gender Equality and Cultural Change around the World.* New York: Cambridge University Press.

Jiwani, Y. 2002. "The 1999 General Social Survey on Spousal Violence: An Analysis." Pp. 63–72 in *Violence Against Women: New Canadian Perspectives,* edited by K.M.J. McKenna and J. Larkin. Toronto: Inanna Publications and Education Inc.

———. 2005. "Walking a Tightrope: The Many Faces of Violence in the Lives of Racialized Immigrant Girls and Young Women." *Violence Against Women* 11(7): 846–75.

Johnson, H., and M. Dawson. 2010. *Violence Against Women in Canada: Research and Policy Perspectives.* New York: Oxford University Press.

Johnson, R. 2005. "Gender, Race, Class and Sexual Orientation: Theorizing the Intersections." Pp. 21–37 in *Feminism, Law, Inclusion: Intersectionality in Action,* edited by G. MacDonald, R.L. Osborne, and C.C. Smith. Toronto: Sumach Press.

Korteweg, A.C. 2012. "Understanding Honour Killing and Honour-related Violence in the Immigration Context: Implications for the Legal Profession and

Beyond. *Canadian Criminal Law Review* 16(2): 135–60.

———, and G. Yurdakul. 2010. *Religion, Culture and the Politicization of Honour-related Violence: A Critical Analysis of Media and Policy debates in Western Europe and North America*. United Nations Research Institute for Social Development. Geneva, Switzerland.

Kulwicki, A., B. Aswad, T. Carmona, and S. Ballout. 2010. "Barriers to the Utilization of Domestic Violence Services among Arab Immigrant Women: Perceptions of Professionals, Service Providers and Community Leaders." *Journal of Family Violence* 25: 727–35.

Leonard, K., and B. Quigley. 2017. "Thirty Years of Research Show Alcohol to Be a Cause of Intimate Partner Violence: Future Research Needs to Identify Who to Treat and How to Treat Them." *Drug and Alcohol Review* 36: 7–9.

Liao, M. A. 2006. "Domestic Violence among Asian Indian Immigrant Women: Risk Factors, Acculturation, and Intervention." *Women and Therapy* 29(1): 23–39.

MacKinnon, C. 2006 [1987]. "Sex and Violence: A Perspective." Pp. 266–71 in *Theorizing Feminisms: A Reader*, edited by E. Hackett and S. Haslanger. New York: Oxford University Press.

Mahmood, S. 2001. "Feminist Theory, Embodiment, and the Docile Agent: Some Reflections on the Egyptian Islamic Revival." *Cultural Anthropology* 16(2): 202–36.

Mojab, S. 2012. "The Politics of Culture, Racism and Nationalism in Honour Killing." *Canadian Criminal Law Review* 16: 115–34.

Nason-Clark, N. 2012. "Christianity and the Experience of Domestic Violence: What Does Faith Have to Do With It?" Pp. 277–88 in *Religion and Canadian Society: Contexts, Identities, and Strategies*, 2nd edn., edited by L.G. Beaman. Toronto: Canadian Scholar's Press.

———, and B. Fisher-Townsend. 2015. *Men Who Batter*. New York: Oxford University Press.

———, and C. Holtmann. 2013. "Thinking about Cooperation and Collaboration between Diverse Religious and Secular Community Responses to Domestic Violence." Pp. 187–200 in *Varieties of Religious Establishments*, edited by L.G. Beaman and W. Sullivan. Farnham Surrey, UK: Ashgate Press.

Papp, A. 2010. *Culturally Driven Violence against Women: A Growing Problem in Canada's Immigrant Communities*. Frontier Center for Public Policy, Series No. 92. Winnipeg, MB.

Profitt, N.J. 2000. *Women Survivors, Psychological Trauma, and the Politics of Resistance*. New York: The Haworth Press.

Ristock, J.L. 2002. *No More Secrets: Violence in Lesbian Relationships*. New York: Routledge.

Rupra, A. 2010. "Experiences of Front-line Shelter Workers in Providing Services to Immigrant Women Impacted by Family Violence." Pp. 134–46 in *Out of the Shadows: Woman Abuse in Ethnic, Immigrant and Aboriginal Communities*, edited by J. Fong. Toronto: Women's Press.

Sev'er, A. 2002. "Exploring the Continuum: Sexualized Violence by Men and Male Youth against Women and Girls." Pp. 73–92 in *Violence against Women: New Canadian Perspectives*, edited by K.M.J. McKenna and J. Larkin. Toronto: Inanna Publications and Education Inc.

Sheehy, E. 2002. "Legal Response to Violence against Women in Canada." Pp. 473–92 in *Violence against Women: New Canadian Perspectives*, edited by K.M.J. McKenna and J. Larkin. Toronto: Inanna Publications and Education Inc.

Statistics Canada. 2010. *Projections of the Diversity of the Canadian Population*. Catalogue no 91-551-X. Ottawa, ON.

———. 2015. *Family Violence in Canada: A Statistical Profile, 2013*. Catalogue no 85-002-X. Ottawa, ON.

———. 2016. *Family Violence in Canada: A Statistical Profile, 2014*. Catalogue no 85-002-X. Ottawa, ON.

Straus, M.A. 1979. "Measuring Intrafamily Conflict and Violence: The Conflict Tactics (CT) Scales." *Journal of Marriage and the Family*, 41(1): 75–88.

Tutty, L.M. 2006. *Effective Practices in Sheltering Women: Leaving Violence in Intimate Relationships*. Retrieved May 3, 2014 (www.ywcacanada.ca).

———, K. Wyllie, P. Abbott, J. Mackenzie, J.E. Ursel, and J.M. Koshan. 2008. *The Justice Response to Domestic Violence: A Literature Review*. Retrieved December 11, 2016 (www.ucalgary.ca/resolve-static/reports/2008/2008-01.pdf).

Wachholz, S., and B. Miedema. 2004. "Gendered Silence: Immigrant Women's Access to Legal Information." Pp. 197–218 in *Understanding Abuse Partnering for Change*, edited by M.L. Stirling, C.A. Cameron, N. Nason-Clark, and B. Miedema. Toronto: University of Toronto Press.

Walby, S. 2009. "Violence." Pp. 191–217 in *Globalization and Inequalities: Complexity and Contested Modernities*. London: SAGE Publications.

Wisniewski, A., R. Arseneault, and M. Paquet. 2016. *Rural Realities Faced by Service Providers and Women Survivors of Intimate Partner Violence When Navigating the Justice System*. Muriel McQueen Fergusson Centre for Family Violence Research, Fredericton, NB. Retrieved April 12, 2017 (www.unb.ca/fredericton/arts/centres/mmfc).

World Health Organization (WHO). 2013. *Global and Regional Estimates of Violence against Women: Prevalence and Health Effects of Intimate Partner Violence and Non-partner Sexual Violence*. Retrieved July 7, 2014 (www.who.int/reproductivehealth).

Chapter 15

Albanese, Patrizia. 2006. "Small Town, Big Benefits: The Ripple Effect of $7/day Child Care." *Canadian Review of Sociology* 43(2): 125–40.

———. 2007a. "Quebec's $7 Day Childcare: Some Preliminary Findings." Pp. 102–4 in *Reading Sociology: Canadian Perspectives*, edited by L. Tepperman and H. Dickinson. Toronto: Oxford University Press.

———. 2007b. "(Under)Valuing Care Work: The Case of Child Care Workers in Small-town Quebec." *International Journal of Early Years Education* 15(2): 125–39.

———. 2009. "$7/Day, $7/Hour, 7 Days A Week: Juggling Commutes, Shift Work and Childcare in a Changing ('New') Economy." Pp. 26–40 in *Road Blocks To Equality*, edited by J. Klaehn. Toronto: Black Rose Books.

———. 2011. "Addressing the Interlocking Complexity of Paid Work and Care: Lessons from Changing Family Policy in Quebec." Pp. 130–43 in *Demystifying the Family/Paid Work Contradiction: Challenges and Possibilities*, edited by C. Krull and J. Sempruch. Vancouver: University of British Columbia Press.

Armitage, Andrew. 2003. *Social Welfare in Canada*, 4th edn. Toronto: Oxford University Press.

Baker, Maureen. 1994. "Family and Population Policy in Québec: Implications for Women." *Canadian Journal of Women and the Law/Revue Femmes et Droit* 7: 116–32.

———. 2001. "Definitions, Cultural Variations, and Demographic Trends." Pp. 3–27 in *Families: Changing Trends in Canada*, edited by M. Baker. Toronto: McGraw-Hill Ryerson.

———. 2008. "Improving Child Well-being? Restructuring Child Welfare Programs in the Liberal Welfare States." *Canadian Journal of Family and Youth* 1(1): 3–26

———. 2010. "Gendering 'Child' Poverty: Cross-national Lessons for Canada in a Deepening Recession." *International Journal of Canadian Studies / Revue internationale d'études canadiennes* 42: 25–46.

Baril, Robert, Pierre Lefebvre, and Philip Merrigan. 2000. "Quebec Family Policy: Impact and Options." *Choices: Family Policy* (IRRP) 6(1): 4–52.

Beaudin, Monique. 2012. "What Quebec's parties are offering in the 2012 election." *Montreal Gazette*, 3 September.

Beauvais, Caroline, and Pascale Dufour. 2003. "Articulation travail-famille: Le contre-exemple des pays dits 'libéraux'?" Canadian Policy Research Networks Family Network. Available at (www.cprn.org).

Behiels, Michael D. 1986. *Prelude to Quebec's Quiet Revolution*. Montreal and Kingston: McGill-Queen's University Press.

Bokma, Anne. 2008. "Being a Foster-care Family." Canadian Living. Available at (www.canadianliving.com/relationships/friends_and_family/being_a_foster_care_family.php).

Brusentsev, Vera, and Wayne Vroman. 2007. "Unemployment Compensation Recipiency in English-speaking Countries". Alfred Lerner College of Business and Economics working paper series, 15.

Campaign 2000. 2011. *Revisiting Family Security in Insecure Times: 2011 Report Card on Child and Family Poverty in Canada*. Toronto: Family Service Toronto. Available at (www.campaign2000.ca/reportCards/national/2011EnglishReportCard.pdf).

———. 2015. *Let's Do This: Let's End Child Poverty for Good*. Available at (http://campaign2000.ca/wp-content/uploads/2016/03/2015-Campaign2000-Report-Card-Final-English.pdf).

Canada Revenue Agency. 2012. "Universal Child Care Benefit (UCCB)." 20 September. Available at (www.cra-arc.gc.ca/bnfts/uccb-puge/menu-eng.html).

———. 2015. Universal Child Care Benefit (UCCB) for previous years. Available at (www.cra-arc.gc.ca/bnfts/uccb-puge/menu-eng.html).

Canadian Centre for Policy Alternatives. 2016. Study reveals Canada's shameful Indigenous child poverty rates. Available at (www.policyalternatives.ca/newsroom/news-releases/study-reveals-canada's-shameful-indigenous-child-poverty-rates).

Canadian Council on Social Development (CCSD). 2004. *One Million Too Many—Implementing Solutions to Child Poverty in Canada: 2004 Report Card on Child Poverty in Canada*. Ottawa: CCSD.

———. 2007. *It Takes a Nation to Raise a Generation: Time for a National Poverty Reduction Strategy: 2007 Report Card on Child and Family Poverty in Canada*. Ottawa: CCSD.

———. 2008. *Family Security in Insecure Times: The Case for a Poverty Reduction Strategy for Canada: 2008 Report Card on Child and Family Poverty in Canada*. Ottawa: CCSD.

Canadian Policy Research Networks (CPRN/RCPP), Family Network. 2003. "Unique Quebec Family Policy Model at Risk." 26 November. Available at (www.cprn.org).

Canadian Press. 2008. "Auditor: Foster care failing native children." *Toronto Star*, 6 May. Available at (www.thestar.com/News/Canada/article/422012).

CBC News. 2012a. "Canadian foster care in crisis, experts say." CBC News, 19 February. Available at (www.cbc.ca/news/canada/story/2012/02/19/foster-care-cp.html).

———. 2012b. "Foster care report in Ontario urges cut-off age rise to 25." *CBC News*, 1 March. Available at (www.cbc.ca/news/canada/toronto/story/2012/03/01/toronto-ontario-wards-state.html).

———. 2014. Quebec daycare fees to climb to $20 per day for highest-earning families. Available at (www.cbc.ca/news/canada/montreal/quebec-daycare-fees-to-climb-to-20-per-day-for-highest-earning-families-1.2841994).

———. 2014. Child-care affordability varies across Canada. Retrieved September 11, 2016 (www.cbc.ca/news/business/child-care-affordability-varies-widely-across-canada-1.2829817).

Chen, Wen-Hao, and Miles Corak. 2008. "Child Poverty and Changes in Child Poverty." *Demography* 45(3): 537–53.

Child Care Advocacy Association of Canada. 2007. "Women's employment patterns and the need for child care." Available at (www.fafia-afai.org/files/fafia_ccaac_childcarefinal.doc).

———. 2011. With the Coalition of Child Care Advocates of British Columbia. "A Tale of Two Canadas: Implementing Rights in Early Childhood." February. Available at (www.cccabc.bc.ca/res/rights/ccright_tale2can_brief.pdf?utm_source=+Advocacy+Update+February+6&utm_campaign=child+care+canada&utm_medium=archive).

———. 2016. "Urgently needed funds for child care left out of this federal budget, put off to next year." Available at (https://ccaac.ca/2016/03/22/child-care-put-off-to-next-year/).

Childcare Resource and Research Unit, Canada. 2007. "Child Care Space Statistics 2007." Available at (www.childcarecanada.org/sites/default/files/ccspacestatistics07_0.pdf).

Comeau, R. 1989. *Jean Lesage et l'éveil d'une nation: les débuts de la révolution tranquille.* Sillery, QC: Presses de l'Université du Québec.

Conference Board of Canada 2017. "Poverty". Retrieved April 24, 2017 (www.conferenceboard.ca/hcp/provincial/society/poverty.aspx).

Cradock, Gerald. 2007. "The Responsibility Dance: Creating Neoliberal Children." *Childhood* 14(2): 153–72.

CTV News. 2008. "RESPs to be set up for children in foster care." 24 April. Available at (www.ctv.ca/servlet/ArticleNews/story/CTVNews/20080424/RESP_benefits_080424/20080424?hub=TopStories).

———2011. "Liberals pledge billion-dollar child care fund." CTV News, 31 March. Available at (www.ctv.ca/servlet/ArticleNews/story/CTVNews/20110331/ignatieff-election-110331/20110331?s_name=election2011).

CUPE Ontario. 2008. "Creator of Quebec child care system to be honoured on Child Care Worker Appreciation Day." 20 October. Available at (www.cupe.on.ca/doc.php?document_id=572&lang=en).

Dandurand, Renée B., and Marianne Kempeneers. 2002. "Pour une analyse comparative et contextuelle de la politique familiale au Québec." *Recherches socio-graphiques* 43(1): 9–78.

Den Tandt, Michael. 2012. "PM must look beyond traditional nuclear family." *Calgary Herald*, 20 September.

Dube, Rebecca. 2008. "The daddy shift." *Globe and Mail*, 24 June: L1–L2.

Eichler, Margrit. 1997. *Family Shifts: Families, Policies and Gender Equality.* Toronto: Oxford University Press.

Evans, Patricia M., and Gerda R. Wekerle, eds. 1997. *Women and the Canadian Welfare State: Challenges and Change.* Toronto: University of Toronto Press.

Federation of Aboriginal Foster Parents. 2012. Fact Sheet. Available at: http://docs.openinfo.gov.bc.ca/d54239412a_response_package_cfd-2012-01396.pdf" Minister Briefing with Steve Brown and Doug Hughes. Vancouver. Online. docs.openinfo.gov.bc.ca/d54239412a_response_package_cfd-2012-01396.pdf

First Call BC. 2015. *First Call's 2015 BC Child Poverty Report Card.* Available at (http://still1in5.ca).

Food Banks Canada. 2016. "Hunger Count." Available at (www.foodbankscanada.ca/getmedia/6173994f-8a25-40d9-acdf-660a28e40f37/HungerCount_2016_final_singlepage.pdf).

Galloway, Gloria. 2004. "Ottawa, provinces agree on child-care principles." *Globe and Mail*, 3 November, A11.

———. 2005. "Money comes with no strings attached." *Globe and Mail*, 24 February, F3.

———. 2006. "Child-care proposal gives least to poorest." *Globe and Mail*, 26 April, A1, A7.

Gauthier, Anne Hélène. 1998. *The State and the Family: A Comparative Analysis of Family Policies in Industrialized Countries.* New York: Oxford University Press.

———. 2010. *The Impact of the Economic Crisis on Family Policies in the European Union.* Brussels: European Commission.

Globe and Mail. 2005. "Harper's prescription for choice in child care." 6 December, A22.

Government of Canada. 2005. *Employment Insurance (EI) and Maternity, Parental and Sickness Benefits.* Ottawa: Department of Human Resources and Skills Development. Available at (www.hrsdc.gc.ca/asp/gateway.asp?hr=en/ei/types/special.shtml&hs=tyt#Maternity).

———. 2010. *Better Outcomes for First Nations Children: INAC'S Role as a Funder in First Nations Child and Family Services Updated: July 2010.* Ottawa: Aboriginal Affairs and Northern Development Canada. Available at (www.aadnc-aandc.gc.ca/

DAM/DAM-INTER-HQ/STAGING/texte-text/
cfsd1_1100100035211_eng.pdf).

———. 2011a. *Employment Insurance Coverage Survey—
2010*. Ottawa: Statistics Canada. 27 June. Available
at (www.statcan.gc.ca/daily-quotidien/110627/
dq110627a-eng.htm).

———. 2011b. *Federal–Provincial/Territorial National
Child Benefit Program Initiative*. Ottawa: Treasury
Board of Canada Secretariat. Available at (www.tbs-
sct.gc.ca/hidb-bdih/initiative-eng.aspx?Hi=42).

———. 2012a. *Children's special allowances (CSA) calculation sheet 2006–2013*. Ottawa: Canada Revenue
Agency. Available at (www.cra-arc.gc.ca/bnfts/cs/
clc_2006_2012-eng.html).

———. 2012b. *Canada Child Tax Benefit (CCTB)
payment amounts—Tax years 2007 to 2011*. Ottawa:
Canada Revenue Agency. Available at (www.cra-arc
.gc.ca/bnfts/cctb/cctb_pymnts-eng.html).

———. 2016a. *Maternity and Parental Benefits—While on
EI*. Available at (www.esdc.gc.ca/en/ei/maternity_par-
ental/while_receiving.page).

———. 2016b. Canada Child Benefit. Overview. Available at (www.cra-arc.gc.ca/bnfts/ccb/menu-eng.html).

Government of Quebec. 1999. *Report of the Auditor
General to the National Assembly for 1998–1999, Summary*. Quebec City, ch. 4.

Hamilton, Graeme. 2004. "Quebec's sacred cow has
quality issues." *National Post*, 9 December.

Hamilton, Roberta. 1995. "Pro-natalism, feminism, and
nationalism." Pp. 135–52 in *Gender and Politics
in Contemporary Canada*, edited by F.-P. Gingras.
Toronto: Oxford University Press.

Jensen, Jane. 2002. "Against the Current: Child Care and
Family Policy in Quebec." Pp. 309–30 in *Child Care
Policy at the Crossroads: Gender and Welfare State
Restructuring*, edited by S. Michel and R. Mahon.
New York: Routledge.

———, and Sherry Thompson. 1999. *Comparative Family
Policy: Six Provincial Stories*. Ottawa: Canadian
Policy Research Networks.

Khan, Mushira Mohsin, and Karen Kobayashi. Forthcoming. "Negotiating Sacred Values: Dharma, Karma
and Kin-Work among Migrant Hindu Women." In
Transnational Aging and Kin Work, edited by P. Dossa
and C. Coe. New Brunswick, NJ: Rutgers University
Press.

Kerstetter, Steve. 2012. "Scrapping welfare council is a
cheap shot by a government that doesn't care about
the poor." *Toronto Star*, 8 April. Available at (www
.thestar.com/opinion/editorialopinion/article/1157655–
scrapping-welfare-council-is-a-cheap-shot-by-a-
government-that-doesn-t-care-about-the-poor).

Krashinsky, Michael. 2001. "Are We There Yet? The
Evolving Face of Child Care Policy in Canada." *Transition* 31(4): 2–5.

Krull, Catherine. 2003. "Pronatalism, feminism and
family policy in Quebec." Ch. 11 in *Voices: Essays
on Canadian Families*, 2nd edn., edited by M. Lynn.
Toronto: Nelson Thomson.

———. 2007. "Placing Families First: The State of
Family Policies in la Belle Province." *Canadian
Review of Social Policy* 50: 93–102.

———. 2012. "Does 'the Family' Exist?" Pp. 90–102 in
Questioning Sociology: Canadian Perspectives, 2nd
edn., edited by M.J. Hird and G. Pavlich. Toronto:
Oxford University Press.

———. 2014. "Investing in Families and Children:
Family Policies in Canada." Pp. 292–317 in
Canadian Families Today: New Perspectives, edited
by D. Cheal and P. Albanese. Ontario: Oxford
University Press.

———, and Justyna Sempruch. 2011a. "Diversifying
the Model, Demystifying the Approach: The
Work-Family Debate Reopened." Pp. 1–11 in
*Demystifying the Family/Paid Work Contradiction:
Challenges and Possibilities*, edited by C. Krull
and J. Sempruch. Vancouver: University of British
Columbia Press.

———, and Justyna Sempruch. 2011b. *A Life in Balance?
Reopening the Family-Work Debate*. Vancouver: University of British Columbia Press.

———, and Justyna Sempruch, eds. 2011. *Demystifying
the Family/Work Contradiction: Challenges and Possibilities*. Vancouver: UBC Press.

Laghi, Brian. 2005. "Poll finds gender gap on daycare."
Globe and Mail, 8 December, A4.

Langlois, S., J. Baillargeon, G. Caldwell, G. Fréchet,
M. Gauthier, and J. Simard. 1992. *Recent Social
Trends in Québec, 1960–1990*. Montreal and
Kingston: McGill-Queen's University Press.

Lefebvre, Pierre, and Philip Merrigan. 2003. "Assessing
Family Policy in Canada: A New Deal for Families
and Children." *Choices: Family Policy* 9: 5.

MacDonald, David and Martha Friendly. 2016. "A growing concern: 2016 child care fees in Canada's big
cities." Canadian Centre for Policy Alternatives.
Available at www.policyalternatives.ca/sites/
default/files/uploads/publications/National%20
Office/2016/12/A_Growing_Concern.pdf

MacGregor, Tracy E., Susan Rodger, Anne L. Cummings,
and Alan W. Leschied. 2006. "The Needs of
Foster Parents: A Qualitative Study of Motivation,
Support, and Retention." *Qualitative Social Work*
5(3): 351–68.

McInturff, Kate. 2017. "The best and worst places to be a
woman in Canada 2017." Canadian Centre for Policy
Alternatives. Available at www.policyalternatives.ca/
sites/default/files/uploads/publications/National%20
Office/2017/10/Best%20and%20Worst%20Places%20
to%20Be%20a%20Woman%202017.pdf

McKeen, Wendy. 2001. "Shifting Policy and Politics of Federal Child Benefits in Canada." *Social Politics* 8(2): 186–90.

Maki, Krystle. 2011. "Neoliberal Deviants and Surveillance: Welfare Recipients under the Watchful Eye of Ontario Works." *Journal of Surveillance and Society* 9(1): 47–63.

———. 2013. "Welfare Surveillance, Neoliberal Policy and the Never-Deserving Single Mother." In *Criminalized Mothers, Criminalizing Motherhood*, edited by J. Minaker and B. Hogeveen. Toronto: Demeter Press.

Maroney, Heather J. 1992. "Who Has the Baby? Nationalism, Pronatalism and the Construction of a 'Demographic Crisis' in Quebec, 1960–1988." *Studies in Political Economy* 39: 7–36.

Maximova, Katerina. 2004. *Memorandum for the Minister—Family-Friendly Policies in Quebec*. Ottawa: Government of Canada, Social Policy Research.

Ministère de l'Emploi, de la Solidarité sociale et de la Famille. 2005. "Financial support for childcare." Available at (www.messf.gouv.qc.ca/Index_en.asp).

Ministère de la Famille et de l'Enfance du Québec. 1999. *Family Policy: Another Step towards Developing the Full Potential of Families and Their Children*. Quebec City: Les Publications du Québec.

Ministère de la Famille et des Aînés. 2011. *Analyse comparative des politiques en matière familiale dans les provinces canadiennes*. Available at (www.mfa .gouv.qc.ca/fr/publication/Documents/analyse_ politiques_fam.pdf).

Ministère des Finances. 2009. *Budget 2009–2010: Status Report on Québec's Family Policy*. Available at (www.budget.finances.gouv.qc.ca/Budget/2009-2010/ en/documents/pdf/FamilyPolicy.pdf).

Monsebraaten, Laurie. 2008. "Copy Quebec daycare, PQ leader says." *Toronto Star*, 24 October.

Monsebraaten, Laurie. 2017. "Federal budget money for child care is a good first step but not nearly enough, advocates say." Toronto Star. Available at www. thestar.com/news/canada/2017/03/22/federal-budget-money-for-child-care-is-a-good-first-step-but-not-nearly-enough-advocates-say.html

Montgomery, Sue. 2008. "Foster parents charged: Accused of sexually abusing children." *Montreal Gazette*, 15 April. Available at (www.canada.com/montreal-gazette/news/story.html?k=15566&id=3f601e2f-9c6f-4734-a02a-1e738f5cb113).

Mulcahy, Meghan, and Nico Trocmé. 2010. "Children and Youth in Out-of-Home Care in Canada." Centres of Excellence in Research for Children's Well-being. Available at (www.cecw-cepb.ca/sites/default/files/ publications/en/ChildrenInCare78E.pdf).

National Council of Welfare. 2004. *Welfare Incomes 2003*. Ottawa: Minister of Public Works and Government Services Canada. Available at (www. ncwcnbes .net/htmdocument/reportWelfareIncomes).

———. 2006. *Welfare Incomes*. Summer Edition. Ottawa Minister of Public Works and Government Services Canada.

———. 2008. *Welfare Incomes 2006 and 2007*. Ottawa: Minister of Public Works and Government Services Canada. Available at (www.ncwcnbes.net/ documentsresearchpublications/OtherPublications/2008Report-WelfareIncomes2006-2007/ Report-WelfareIncomes2006-2007E.pdf).

———. 2011. *The Dollars and Sense of Solving Poverty*. Ottawa: National Council of Welfare.

Office of the Prime Minister. 2004. "Speech from the Throne" and "Reply to the Speech from the Throne." 5 October. Available at (http://pm.gc.ca/eng.ftddt.asp).

OACAS. 2011. Children's Well-Being: The Ontarian Perspective, Child Welfare Report 2011. Toronto: Ontario Association of Children's Aid Societies. Available at (www.oacasgroups.org/uploads/ cwr/11childwelfarereporteng.pdf).

OECD, Directorate for Education. 2004. Early Childhood Education and Care Policy. Canada: Country Note. Paris: OECD.

———. 2011. Better Life Index 2011—Canada. Paris: OECD. Available at (http://oecdbetterlifeindex.org/ countries/canada/).

O'Hara, Kathy. 1998. Comparative Family Policy: Eight Countries" Stories. Canadian Policy Research Networks, no. 15734. Ottawa: Renouf Publishing.

Openparliament.ca. 2012. "Nycole Turmel on Helping Families In Need Act." 27 September. Available at (http://openparliament.ca/debates/2012/9/27/ nycole-turmel-1/only).

Peacock, Lindsey. 2012. "Cost of daycare across Canada." 21 August. Available at (www.shawconnect.ca/money/ features/Cost_of_daycare_across_Canada.aspx).

Ponti, Michael. 2008. "Special Considerations for the Health Supervision of Children and Youth in Foster Care." *Paediatrics & Child Health* 13(2): 129–32.

Press Release. 2012. "Harper government welcomes vote on Helping Families in Need Act." 2 October. Available at (www.msnbc.msn.com/id/49265526/ns/ business-press_releases/t/harper-government-welcomes-vote-helping-families-need-act/# .UHWd-VHcwyw).

Régie des rentes du Québec. 2012. *Régime de rentes du Québec Statistiques de l'année* 2012. Gov. of Québec: Quebec.

———. 2016. "The Quebec Pension Plan at a Glance". Available at (www.rrq.gouv.qc.ca/en/programmes/ regime_rentes/regime_chiffres/Pages/regime_ chiffres.aspx).

Reid, Carrie. 2007. "The Transition from State Care to Adulthood: International Examples of Best Practices." *New Directions for Youth Development* 113: 33–49.

Retraite Quebec. 2016. Amount and Payment of Child Assistance. Available at (www.rrq.gouv.qc.ca/en/programmes/soutien_enfants/paiement/Pages/montant.aspx).

Revenu Quebec. 2016. Requirements for Claiming the Work Premium. Available at (www.revenuquebec.ca/en/citoyen/credits/prime_travail/conditions.aspx).

Ross, Jonathan. 2006. "Get real about child care: Why Harper feels he can go to the polls on the issue." *The Tyee*, 20 April. Available at (http://thetyee.ca/Views/2006/04/20/RealChildCare).

Séguin, Rhéal. 2008. "Make babies, ADQ urges Quebec women." *Globe and Mail*, 13 March. Available at (www.amren.com/mtnews/archives/2008/03/make_babies_adq.php).

———, and Gloria Galloway. 2004. "Some provinces skeptical about federal daycare plan." *Globe and Mail*, 2 November, A6.

Simons, Paula. 2008. "Praiseworthy step will help families: Generous package of benefits means successful adoptions for children in care." *Edmonton Journal*, 25 November.

Stasiulis, Daiva. 2005. "The Active Child Citizen: Lessons from Canadian Policy and the Children's Movement." *Polis, Revue Camerounaise de Science Politique* 12.

Statistics Canada. 2012a. "Portrait of Families and Living Arrangements in Canada." Analytical Document. (Cat no. 98-312-X2011001). Ottawa: Statistics Canada.

———. 2012b. "Age groups and sex of foster children, for both sexes, for Canada, provinces and territories." Available at (www12.statcan.gc.ca/census-recensement/2011/dp-pd/hltfst/fam/Pages/highlight.cfm?TabID=1&Lang=E&Asc=1&PR-Code=01&OrderBy=999&Sex=1&tableID=304).

———. 2015. "Employment Insurance Coverage Survey, 2014." Available at (www.statcan.gc.ca/daily-quotidien/151123/dq151123b-eng.pdf).

———. 2016. Canadian Income Survey, 2014. Available at (www.statcan.gc.ca/daily-quotidien/160708/dq160708b-eng.pdf).

Talaga, Tanya, and Laurie Monsebraaten. 2008. "Benefit bypasses foster kids." *Toronto Star*, 18 February. Available at (http://action.web.ca/home/crru/rsrcs_crru_full.shtml?x=113991).

Tézli, Annette, and Anne Gauthier. 2009. "Balancing Work and Family in Canada: An Empirical Examination of Conceptualizations and Measurements." *Canadian Journal of Sociology/Cahiers Canadiens de Sociologie* 34(2): 433–61.

Thompson, Elizabeth. 1999. "Daycare woes ignored: Auditor report blasts lack of supervision." *Montreal Gazette*, 10 December, F7.

Thomson, Dale C. 1984. *Jean Lesage and the Quiet Revolution*. Toronto: Macmillan.

Toronto Star. 2012. "Federal budget 2012: Ottawa axes National Council on Welfare." Available at (www.thestar.com/news/canada/politics/article/1154445–federal-budget-2012-ottawa-axes-national-council-on-welfare).

———. 2016. CCB benefit to pull record number of kids out of poverty, minister says. Available at (www.thestar.com/news/gta/2016/06/15/child-benefit-to-pull-record-number-of-kids-out-of-poverty-minister-says.html).

UNICEF Canada. 2012. "Canada can do more to protect its children from poverty, new UNICEF report." Available at (www.unicef.ca/en/press-release/canada-can-do-more-to-protect-its-children-from-poverty-new-unicef-report).

———. 2017. "UNICEF Report Card 14: Oh Canada! Our Kids Deserve Better!" At www.unicef.ca/sites/default/files/2017-06/RC14%20Canadian%20Companion_0.pdf

Uppal, S. 2015. "Employment Patterns of Families with Children." Retrieved April 21, 2017 (www.statcan.gc.ca/pub/75-006-x/2015001/article/14202-eng.pdf).

Vincent, Carole. 2000. "Editor's Note." *Choices: Family Policy* (IRRP) 6(1): 2–3.

Violence Against Women Survey (VAWS). 1993. *The Daily*, 18 Nov. Ottawa: Statistics Canada, Catalogue no. 11–001.

Wyatt, Nelson. 2005. "Quebec to operate parental leave plan." *Globe and Mail*, 2 March, A5.

Chapter 16

Agrell, Siri. 2008. "Tiny island nation seeks dry land." *Globe and Mail*, November 13. Available at (www.theglobeandmail.com/news/world/tiny-island-nation-seeks-dry-land/article663097/%7b%7burl%7d%7d/?reqid=%257B%257Brequest_id%257D%257D).

Anshen, Ruth Nanda. 1959. *The Family: Its Function and Destiny*. New York: Harper.

Baber, Ray E. 1953. *Marriage and the Family*. New York: McGraw-Hill.

Barbeau, Clayton C. 1971. *Future of the Family*. New York: Bruce Publishing.

Basen, Gwynne, Margrit Eichler, and Abby Lippman. 1993. *Misconceptions: The Social Construction of Choice and the New Reproductive and Genetic Technologies*, vol. 1. Hull, QC: Voyageur.

Beaujot, Roderic. 2000. *Earning and Caring*. Peterborough, ON: Broadview Press.

Bernard, Jessie. 1972. *The Future of Marriage*. New York: Bantam.

Bibby, Reginald. 2005. *Future Families Project: A Survey of Canadian Hopes and Dreams.* Ottawa: Vanier Institute of the Family.

Bird, Joseph, and Lois Bird. 1971. "Marriage: A Doubtful Future." Pp. 1–10 in *Future of the Family*, edited by C.C. Barbeau. New York: Bruce Publishing.

Blake, Judith. 1972. "Here and Beyond—The Population Crisis: The Microfamily and Zero Population Growth." Pp. 55–68 in *College of Home Economics.*

Brown, Lester R. 2003. *Plan B: Rescuing a Planet under Stress and a Civilization in Trouble.* New York: Norton.

Cavan, Ruth Shonle. 1963. *The American Family.* New York: Thomas Y. Crowell.

Charlebois, Sylvain, Francis Tapon, Michael von Massow, Erna van Duren, Paul Uys, Evan Fraser, Leila Kamalabyaneh, Amit Summan. 2016. *Food Price Report 2016.* Guelph: The Food Institute of the University of Guelph. Available at (http://foodinstitute.ca/wp-content/uploads/2016/06/Food-Price-Report-2016-English.pdf).

Climate Action Network. 2011. Canada Wins Fossil of the Year Award in Durban. Retrieved July 20, 2016 (http://climateactionnetwork.ca/2011/12/09/canada-wins-fossil-of-the-year-award-in-durban/).

Davids, Leo. 1971. "North American Marriage: 1990." *The Futurist* 5(2): 190–4.

des Rivières-Pigeon, Catherine, Marie-Josèphe Saurel-Cubizolles, and Patrizia Romito. 2002. "Division of Domestic Work and Psychological Distress One Year after Childbirth: A Comparison between France, Quebec and Italy." *Journal of Community & Applied Social Psychology* 12: 397–409.

Downing, Joseph J. 1970. "The Tribal Family and the Society of Awakening." Pp. 119–36 in *The Family in Search of a Future: Alternate Models for Moderns*, edited by H.A. Otto. New York: AppletonCenturyCrofts.

Dyer, Gwynne. 2009. *Climate Wars: The Fight for Survival as the World Overheats.* Toronto: Vintage Canada.

Edwards, John N. 1967. "The Future of the Family Revisited." *Journal of Marriage and the Family* 29(3): 505–11.

Eichler, Margrit. 1975. "The Equalitarian Family in Canada?" Pp. 223–35 in *Marriage, Family and Society: Canadian Perspectives*, edited by P.S. Wakil. Toronto: Butterworths.

Elkin, Frederick. 1964. *The Family in Canada: An Account of Present Knowledge and Gaps in Knowledge about Canadian Families.* Ottawa: Vanier Institute of the Family.

Elliott, Katherine. 1970. *The Family and Its Future.* A Ciba Foundation Symposium. London: J.&A. Churchill.

EQCOTESST. 2011. Quebec Survey on Working and Employment Conditions and Occupational Health and Safety. Retrieved June 14, 2016 (www.inspq.qc.ca/es/node/3541).

Farson, Richard E., Philip M. Hauser, Herbert Stroup, and Anthony J. Wiener. 1969. *The Future of the Family.* New York: Family Service Association of America.

Gao, George. 2015. "Why the former USSR had far fewer men than women." Pew Research Center. Retrieved July 20, 2016 (www.pewresearch.org/fact-tank/2015/08/14/why-the-former-ussr-has-far-fewer-men-than-women/).

Gerson, Menachem. 1972. "Lesson from the Kibbutz: A Cautionary Tale." Pp. 326–40 in *The Future of the Family*, edited by L.K. Howe. New York: Simon & Schuster.

Global News. 2015. Nearly 1 in 5 Canadian children living in poverty: Report. Retrieved June 14, 2016 (http://globalnews.ca/news/2360311/nearly-1-in-5-canadian-children-living-in-poverty-report/).

———. 2016. Canada not immune to worsening inequality, Oxfam report suggests. Retrieved July 20, 2016 (http://globalnews.ca/news/2460370/canada-not-immune-to-worsening-inequality-oxfam-report-suggests/).

Goode, William J. 1972. "Social Change and Family Renewal." Pp. 116–33 in *College of Home Economics.*

Greenwald, Harold. 1970. "Marriage as a Non-Legal Voluntary association." Pp. 51–66 in *The Family in Search of a Future: Alternate Models for Moderns*, edited by H.A. Otto. New York: AppletonCenturyCrofts.

Haddad, Anton. 1996. "TheSexual Division of House-Hold Labour: Pragmatic Strategies or Patriarchal Dynamics. An Analysis of Two Case Studies." PhD thesis, York University.

Health Canada. 2008. "Changing Fertility Patterns: Trends and Implications." Retrieved November 23, 2008 (www.hc-sc.gc.ca/sr-sr/pubs/hpr-rpms/bull/2005-10-chang-fertilit/intro-eng.php).

Hill, Reuben. 1964. "The American Family of the Future." *Journal of Marriage and the Family* 26(1): 20–8.

Hobbs, Edward C. 1970. "An alternate model from a theological perspective." Pp. 25–42 in *The Family in Search of a Future: Alternate Models for Moderns*, edited by H.A. Otto. New York: AppletonCenturyCrofts.

Hochschild, Arlie Russell. 1972. "Communal Living in Old Age." Pp. 299–310 in *The Future of the Family*, edited by L.K. Howe. New York: Simon & Schuster.

Hossain, Ziarat. 2001. "Division of Household Labor and Family Functioning in Off-reservation Navajo Indian Families." *Family Relations* 50(3): 255–61.

Howe, Louise Kapp, ed. 1972. *The Future of the Family.* New York: Simon & Schuster.

Indigenous and Northern Affairs Canada. 2013. "Aboriginal Demographics from the 2011 Household Survey." Retrieved July 20, 2016 (www.aadnc-aandc.gc.ca/eng/1370438978311/1370439050610#chp2).

John, Daphne, and Beth Anne Shelton. 1997. "The Production of Gender among Black and White Women and Men: The Case of Household Labor." *Sex Roles* 36(3 & 4): 171–93.

Kanter, Rosabeth Moss. 1972. "'Getting It All Together': Communes Past, Present, Future." Pp. 311–25 in *The Future of the Family,* edited by L.K. Howe. New York: Simon & Schuster.

Kassel, Victor. 1970. "Polygyny after Sixty." Pp. 137–44 in *The Family in Search of a Future: Alternate Models for Moderns,* edited by H.A. Otto. New York: AppletonCenturyCrofts.

Kay, F. George. 1972. *The Family in Transition: Its Past, Present and Future Patterns.* Newton Abbot: David and Charles.

Kitterod, Ragni Hege. 2002. "Mothers' Housework and Childcare: Growing Similarities or Stable Inequalities?" *Acta Sociologica* 45(2): 127–49.

Klein, Naomi. 2014. *This Changes Everything: Capitalism vs. The Climate.* USA: Penguin Random House.

Levett, Carl. 1970. "A Parental Presence in Future Family Models." Pp. 161–82 in *The Family in Search of a Future: Alternate Models for Moderns,* edited by H.A. Otto. New York: AppletonCenturyCrofts.

Lewchuk, Wayne, Michelynn Lafleche, Stephanie Procyk, Charlene Cook, Diane Dyson, Diane Goldring, Karen Lior, Alan Meisner, John Shields, Anthony Tambureno, and Peter Viducis. 2015. *The Precarity Penalty: The Impact of Employment Precarity on Individuals, Households and Communities—and What To Do About It.* Toronto: United Way of Greater Toronto and McMaster University.

Linton, Ralph. 1959. "The Natural History of the Family." Pp. 30–52 in *The Family: Its Function and Destiny,* edited by R.N. Anshen. New York: Harper.

Mooney, Chris. 2016. "The Atmosphere Has Hit a Grim Milestone—and Scientists Say We'll Never Go Back 'Within Our Lifetimes'" *Washington Post,* June 13. Available at (www.washingtonpost.com/news/energy-environment/wp/2016/06/13/the-atmosphere-has-crossed-a-grim-milestone-and-scientists-say-well-never-go-back-within-our-lifetimes/).

Nett, Emily M. 1988. *Canadian Families, Past and Present.* Toronto: Butterworths.

Nimkoff, Meyer F. 1947. *Marriage and the Family.* Boston: Houghton Mifflin.

Ogburn, W.F., and M.F. Nimkoff. 1955. *Technology and the Changing Family.* Boston: Houghton Mifflin.

Orleans, Myron, and Florence Wolfson. 1970. "The Future of the Family." *The Futurist:* 48–9.

Otto, Herbert A., ed. 1970a. *The Family in Search of a Future: Alternate Models for Moderns.* New York: AppletonCenturyCrofts.

Otto, Herbert A. 1970b. "Introduction." Pp. 1–9 in *The Family in Search of a Future: Alternate Models for Moderns,* edited by H.A. Otto. New York: AppletonCenturyCrofts.

Otto, Herbert A., ed. 1972. "New Light on Human Potential." Pp. 14–25 in *College of Home Economics.*

OXFAM. 2016. An Economy for the 1%. 210 Oxfam Briefing Paper, 18 January 2016. Retrieved July 20, 2016 (www.oxfam.org/sites/www.oxfam.org/files/file_attachments/bp210-economy-one-percent-tax-havens-180116-en_0.pdf).

PAN. 2015. "Global health experts say glyphosate 'probably carcinogenic' to humans." Retrieved June 14, 2016 (http://www.panna.org/node/3190).

Parsons, Talcott, and Robert Bales. 1955. *Family, Socialization and Interaction Process.* New York: Free Press of Glencoe.

Paul, Eden. 1930. *Chronos or the Future of the Family.* London: Kegan Paul, Trench, Trubner and Co.

Picard, Andre. 2005a. "Flame retardants building up within us." *Globe and Mail,* A19.

———. 2005b. "Obese moms risk having babies with birth defects." *Globe and Mail,* A15.

Platt, John. 1972. "A Fearful and Wonderful World for Living." Pp. 3–13 in *College of Home Economics.*

Pollak, Otto. 1972. "Family Functions in Transition." Pp. 69–78 in *College of Home Economics.*

Rosenberg, George. 1970. "Implications of New Models of the Family for the Aging Population." Pp. 171–86 in *The Family in Search of a Future: Alternate Models for Moderns,* edited by H.A. Otto. New York: AppletonCenturyCrofts.

Sanchez, Laura, and Elizabeth Thomson. 1997. "Becoming Mothers and Fathers: Parenthood, Gender, and the Division of Labor." *Gender and Society* 11(6): 747–72.

Schulz, David A. 1972. *The Changing Family: Its Function and Future.* Englewood Cliffs, NJ: Prentice-Hall.

Shelton, Beth Anne, and Daphne John. 1993. "Does Marital Status Make a Difference?" *Journal of Family Issues* 14(3): 401–20.

Simms, Andrew. 2009. *Ecological Debt: The Health of the Planet and the Wealth of Nations,* 2nd edn. London: Pluto Press.

Skinner, B.F. 1948. *Walden II.* New York: Macmillan.

Snowdon, Wallis. 2016 (May 4). "Fort McMurray family flees city with flames at their heels." CBC News, Online. Available at (www.cbc.ca/news/canada/edmonton/fort-mcmurray-family-flees-city-with-flames-at-their-heels-1.3567196).

South, S.J., and G. Spitze. 1994. "Housework in Marital and Nonmarital Households." *American Sociological Review* 59(3): 327–47.

Statistics Canada. 2013. "Directly Measured Physical Activity of Canadian Children and Youth, 2007 to 2011." Catalogue no. 82-625-X, May 2013. Retrieved April 2, 2014 (www.statcan.gc.ca/pub/82-625-x/2013001/article/11817-eng.pdf).

———. 2015a. Living Arrangements of Young Adults Aged 20 to 29. Retrieved July 20, 2016 (www12.statcan.gc.ca/census-recensement/2011/as-sa/98-312-x/98-312-x2011003_3-eng.cfm).

———. 2015b. Portrait of Families and Living Arrangements in Canada. Tables 1 and 3. Ottawa: Statistics Canada. Retrieved May 29, 2016 (www12.statcan.ca/census-recensement/2011/as-sa/98-312-x/2011001/tbl/tbl1-eng.cfm).

———. 2016. Fewer Children, Older Moms. Retrieved May 29, 2016 (www.statcan.gc.ca/pub/11-630-x/11-630-x2014002-eng.htm).

———. 2017a. Census in Brief: Young Adults Living with Their Parents in Canada in 2016. Ottawa: Statistics Canada. (www12.statcan.gc.ca/census-recensement/2016/as-sa/98-200-x/2016008/98-200-x2016008-eng.cfm).

———. 2017b. Census in Brief—Same Sex Couples in Canada, 2016. Ottawa: Statistics Canada. (www12.statcan.gc.ca/census-recensement/2016/as-sa/98-200-x/2016007/98-200-x2016007-eng.cfm).

Stoller, Frederick H. 1970. "The Intimate Network of Families as a New Structure." Pp. 145–60 in *The Family in Search of a Future: Alternate Models for Moderns,* edited by H.A. Otto. New York: AppletonCenturyCrofts.

Thamm, Robert. 1975. *Beyond Marriage and the Nuclear Family.* San Francisco: Canfield Press.

The Food Institute. 2016. *Food Price Report 2016.* University of Guelph.

UN News Centre. 2008. "Small island nations' survival threatened by climate change, UN hears." Available at (http://www.un.org/apps/news/story.asp?NewsID=28265&Cr=general+assembly&Cr1=debate#.WWOVazOZP2Q).

UNIFOR. 2016. (May 18) "Federal Government Tables Historic Human Rights Protection." Retrieved July 20, 2016 (www.unifor.org/en/whats-new/news/federal-government-tables-historic-human-rights-protections).

Vanier Institute of the Family. 2016. Timeline: Fifty Years of Men, Work and Family in Canada. Ottawa Vanier Institute. Retrieved June 16, 2016 (http://us10.campaign-archive2.com/?u=51bbc09c0804ce9d04df0b562&id=6f25731625&e=c8c38e26ce).

Vanier Institute of the Family. 2016a. Timeline: Fifty Years of Men, Work and Family in Canada. Ottawa Vanier Institute. Available at (http://us10.campaign-archive2.com/?u=51bbc09c0804ce9d04df0b562&id=6f25731625&e=c8c38e26ce).

Whitehurst, R.N. 1975. "Alternate Life Styles and Canadian Pluralism." Pp. 433–45 in *Marriage, Family and Society: Canadian Perspectives,* edited by P.S. Wakil. Toronto: Butterworths.

Winch, Robert F. 1970. "Permanence and Change in the History of the American Family and Some Speculation as to its Future." *Journal of Marriage and the Family* 32(1): 6–15.

Wolbring, Gregor. 2001. *Folgen Der Anwendung Genetischer Diagnostik Fuer Behinderte Menschen. Enquete-Kommission des deutschen Bundestages: Recht und Ethik der modernen Medizin.* Calgary: University of Calgary.

Wu, Zheng. 2000. *Cohabitation: An Alternative Form of Family Living.* Toronto: Oxford University Press.

Zimmerman, Carle C. 1947. *Family and Civilization.* New York: Harper & Brothers.

Index

"abjection": process of, 304
ableism, 268
Aboriginal policy, 245, 250–1; *see also* Indigenous people; Indigenous women; specific groups
Aboriginal Reference Group on Disability Issues, 281
abortion, 42, 123; disabilities and, 278; as eugenics, 357; future of, 347
abuse: arranged marriage and, 83; disabilities and, 283–7; non-Indigenous families and, 259; residential schools and, 255, 256; sexual, 284, 286; spousal, 294; types of, 295; *see also* violence
Act to Combat Poverty and Social Exclusion, 322
Adams, L., and A. Kirova, 243
adolescents: Baby Boomers as, 41; poverty and, 221–2; refugee, 236–9
adoption, 28, 98; foster care and, 319, 320; Indigenous children and, 257; parental leave and, 315–16; same-sex parents and, 100
adult co-resident children, 7, 141, 144, 145–6, 149, 155, 350
adultery, 33, 118, 132
Afghanistan: refugees from, 228–44
Africa: refugees in, 226
Africentric Alternative School, 238
age: childbirth and, 97, 141; children with disabilities and, 272; disability and, 268; divorce and, 122; marriage and, 33, 84, 144; middle, 140, 141; old, 140, 141–3; poverty and, 35, 211–12, 213, 223; as structural marker, 140
"age in place," 151
aging families, 139–60; characteristics of, 140–3; diversity in, 152–5; social policy and, 155–7
Alaggia, R., and C. Vine, 310
Albanese, Patrizia, 2–24, 111, 326, 337
Alberta, 320, 323
Allen, K.: and A. Jaramillo-Sierra, 23; et al., 140
Alook, Angele, 105
Alternatives Journal, 361
Ambert, Anne-Marie, 127
ambivalence, 147, 149, 152
amoutik, 174–5
Anderson, Jordan River, 260
Anderson, Kim, 104, 248, 263
Anderson, R., and T. Fetner, 82
Anglican Church, 66

Anishinaabe, 248–9
anniversaries, 176–7
annulment, 116, 125
Ansari, A., and E. Klinenberg, 93
Anshen, Ruth Nanda, 343
antibiotics, 356
apprehensions: disabled mothers and, 279; Indigenous children and, 257, 258–9, 260–1
Arber, S., and V. Timonen, 158
Armesto, J.C., and E.R. Shapiro, 99
Armstrong, Elizabeth, et al., 93
artificial insemination, 98, 349
Asia: immigrants from, 31
assault: domestic, 128; *see also* abuse; domestic violence; violence
Assay, S.M., et al., 310
Assembly of First Nations, 260
assets, 215, 216
assimilation: immigrants and, 236; Indigenous people and, 245, 250; residential schools and, 254
assimilationist strategies, 60
assistance: disabilities and, 280–1; intergenerational financial, 144, 145, 149–50; *see also* income assistance; social assistance/welfare
autism, 272

Baber, Ray E., 342
"baby bonus," 37
Baby Boom, 38–9, 41, 143; housework and, 108; sexual behaviour and, 85
bachelor parties, 165, 166
bachelorette parties, 166
Bahá'í Faith, 172, 174–5
Bailey, Beth, 84
Baillargeon, Denyse, 46
Baker, M., 326, 337; and V. Elizabeth, 93
bands, Indigenous, 251
"barbaric cultural practices," 83, 304
Barnes, Medora W., 170, 180, 181
Barrett, Joyce, 61–2, 63
bathhouse raids, 54
Battle, Ken, 335
Bauman, Robert J., 82–3
Baumrind, Diana, 103
Beaujot, R., and Z. Ravanera, 109, 110
Beck-Gernsheim, Elizabeth, 79
Bedard, Yvonne, 252
Bell , D., and J. Binnie, 60
Bennett, Richard B., 36
Benzeval, M., and K. Judge, 221
Bernard, A., 237
Bernard, Jessie, 343–4

Bernhard, J.K., et al., 111–12
Bernstein, Elizabeth, 89
Berrardo, F., and H. Vera, 165–6
Berry, J., 236
bestiality, 119
Better Life Index, 316, 327
Bezanson, Kate, et al., 23
biases: theories and, 20
Bibby, Reginald, 127, 129, 130–1
bigamy, 116, 117, 124
"big bang" theory, 10, 20–2
Bill 40, 320
Bill C-16, 358
Bill C-3, 253, 254
Bill C-31, 253, 254
Bill of Rights, 252
bio-medical model of disability, 270, 271
Bird, Joseph, and Lois Bird, 347
birth control: *see* contraception
birth rate, 33, future of, 348–8, 356–7; in Great Depression, 36; post–First World War, 35; postwar, 38; in Quebec, 330; refugees and, 232–3; *see also* childbirth
Blackford, Karen A., 279, 283; et al., 280
Black people: inequality and, 78; motherhood and, 189; profiling of, 237; same-sex marriage and, 64
Blackstock, Cindy, 263; and Nico Trocmé, 258–9, 263
Blake, Raymond, 337
blood quantum, 252, 253
Boden, Sharon, 170–1
boomerang children, 7, 143, 145–6
Boulding, Kenneth E., 349
Bourassa, Kevin, 57
Boyd, S., and C. Young, 60, 64
boys: fatherhood and, 99; sexual confidence of, 85–6; *see also* gender; men
Bradshaw, Michelle, 62, 63
Braedley, S., and M. Luxton, 199
Bragg, B., and L. Wong, 243
Brannen, J. and A. Nilsen, 102
breadwinner model, 26, 32, 37, 38, 44, 344; caregiving and, 188; future of, 345; gender and, 234; state and, 317, 326, 336; women and, 30, 43; home–work balance and, 191, 197
breastfeeding, 104
Breikreuz, R., et al., 109
Brigham, Susan M., 112
Brison, Scott, 60
British Columbia, 82, 131–2; child poverty in, 322–3; Indigenous children in, 257; Shariah in, 126

British Council of Disabled People, 270
Bronfenbrenner, Urie, 19
Brownridge, D., 305; and S. Halli, 235
Brownstone, Harvey, 135
Brownworth, V., 64
Bryant, Michael, 125
Budgeon, Shelley, 90

Caledon Institute, 335
Calgary Islamic School, 238
Calhoun, Cheshire, 63
Cambodia: refugees from, 227
Campaign 2000, 322, 324–5
Campbell, Lara, 46
Canada: family policy in, 313–40;
 foreign-born population of, 225;
 number of refugees in, 226–7;
 refugee settlement in, 228–31
Canada Child Benefit (CCB), 318–19,
 320, 322, 325, 335
Canada Child Care Act, 327
Canada Child Tax Benefit (CCTB), 97,
 111, 318, 324, 335
"Canada Fit for Children, A," 324, 337
Canada Labour Code, 335
Canada Learning Bond, 320
Canada Pension Plan, 212
Canada's Century, 33
Canada v. Hislop, 57
Canadian Centre for Policy Alternatives,
 194–5, 322, 361
Canadian Conference on the
 Family, 27
Canadian Council for Refugees, 240
Canadian Council on Child and Family
 Welfare, 34
Canadian Council on Social
 Development, 322, 324, 328
Canadian Employers for Caregivers
 Plan, 157
Canadian Forces, 335
Canadian Human Rights Act, 54, 358;
 disability and, 270
Canadian Human Rights Commission,
 253, 260–1, 263
Canadian Policy Research Networks, 333
Canadian Research Institute for the
 Advancement of Women, 286
Canadian Survey on Disability (CSD),
 268, 281
Canadian Violence Against Women
 Survey (CVAWS), 302–3
Canadian Women's Foundation, 185
Capponi, Pat, 217
care: respite, 256–7, 281; state, 319–21;
 see also child care; foster care;
 out-of-home care
"care gap," 156

caregiving: co-longevity and, 142–3;
 disabilities and, 268, 276–7, 280–1;
 employment and, 273, 275, 281,
 282–3, 325–6; full-time, 274;
 gender and, 109, 143, 151, 154–6,
 346; "informal," 150, 280–1;
 intergenerational, 150–1; LGBTQ
 people and, 154; policy on, 155;
 programs for, 197; strain of, 276; as
 transition, 139; *see also* child care;
 foster care; out-of-home care
Carpenter, L., and J. DeLamate, 93
case studies, 16
Castellano, Marlene Brant, 32
Catholic Church, 77; divorce and, 125;
 weddings and, 169, 170, 177
Cavan, Ruth Shonle, 343, 345–6
CBC, 40
CCPA Monitor, 361
Cecilia Jeffreys Indian Residential
 School, 255
Census, 3, 4; family change and, 314,
 336; household size and, 89;
 same-sex marriage and, 54, 55–6,
 65; stepfamilies and, 130
Census families, 5–6, 43, 97; definition
 of, 11–12; historical context of,
 8–9; number of, 75
Central Mortgage and Housing
 Corporation, 39
Le centre de recherche interdisciplinaire
 sur la violence familiale et la
 violence faite aux femmes, 308
Centre for Research and Education
 on Violence against Women and
 Children, 308
Century of the Child, 33
Certificates of Possession, 261
Chambers, P., et al., 149
charities, 217, 219, 223
charivari, 167–8
Charter of Rights and Freedoms, 253;
 disability and, 270; divorce and,
 116, 117; LGBTQ rights and,
 57, 58
Chast, Roz, 158–9
Cheal, David, 21
Chekki, Dan A., 217
Cherlin, Andrew, 180
Chernushenko, David, 359
child allowance: in Quebec, 330–1
"child and family benefits," 317
childbirth, 349; age and, 97, 141;
 disabilities and, 280; Indigenous,
 247–8, 262
child care, 107, 108, 187–9; comprehensive, 336–7; costs of, 325–6,
 327, 328–9, 331; disabled children

and, 277–8; employment and, 109;
 funding for, 328; future of, 357–8;
 international comparison of, 327–8;
 national program for, 326–7, 334–5;
 paid, 197; policy and, 325–9;
 poverty and, 207; in Quebec, 111,
 326, 328–9, 331, 332, 333; spaces
 in, 327, 332; subsidized, 98, 111,
 325–6, 331; supports for, 110–12;
 universal, 322, 331; *see also* care;
 caregiving; foster care; out-of-home
 care
Child Care Advocacy Association, 328
Child Disability Benefit (CDB), 275
child-first principle, 260
child launch, 7; *see also* home-leaving
childlessness, 28, 43, 44
child poverty, 212–14, 315, 317; consequences of, 221–2, 223; family
 policy and, 321–5; rate of, 321,
 322, 324; working parents and, 322
children: abuse of disabled, 284–6;
 access to, 117, 121–2; Baby Boom,
 41; boomerang, 7, 143, 145–6;
 colonial families and, 28; cost of,
 196; custody of, 121, 127, 131,
 279; dependent, 143; development
 of, 19; disabled, 268, 271–8,
 282–3, 287; divorce and, 125, 126,
 127–9, 134; economic mobility
 and, 208–9; exposure to violence
 and, 299, 303; families with, 75;
 fathers and, 103, 109, 188–9,
 192–4, 197, 325; foster care and,
 44, 98, 257, 319–20, 321, 335;
 friends and, 127; idealization of,
 33; "illegitimate," 82; immigrant,
 232–3, 235–6; immigrant custody
 of, 234; Indigenous, 2, 31–2, 44,
 214, 254–62; Indigenous custody
 of, 261–2; later-life divorce and,
 147; lone-parent families and, 97,
 128, 129, 273; marriage and, 80;
 millennium families and, 43–4;
 mothering and, 41, 101–2; number
 of, 139; outside of marriage, 82,
 122–3, 180; parenting of, 95–114;
 parents' employment and, 207;
 postwar, 38; poverty consequences
 and, 221–2, 223; primary residence
 of, 121–2; refugee, 231–2, 236–9;
 remarriage and, 148–9; same-sex
 families and, 3, 55, 131; satellite, 6;
 state care and, 319–21; stepfamilies
 and, 5, 76–7, 130–1; unpaid care
 of, 187–9; "velcro," 7; women
 and paid work and, 184–5, 186;
 work and, 29–30; *see also* adult

co-resident children; caregiving; child care; child poverty; fathering; mothering

Children's Aid Society, 276, 279

Children's Special Allowance (CSA), 319–20

child support payments: poverty and, 117, 132–3, 210

Child Tax Benefit (CTB), 208, 317

Child Tax Exemption, 317

child welfare: child abuse and, 284; Indigenous, 256–62, 258

Child, Youth, and Family Enhancement Act, 320

China: immigrants from, 31, 82

Chinese Immigration Act, 31

Chrétien, Jean, 318

Christianity, 116, 117, 306; refugees and, 228; weddings and, 167

Chuang, S.S., and Y. Su, 102

chuppah, 173

Church of England, 116

churches: residential schools and, 32, 254, 256

citizenship guide, 304

citizenship legitimacy, 51–2, 61

Civil Code, 124

Civil Marriage Act, 43, 54, 55, 82; amendment to, 125; citizenship rights and, 52; passage of, 58–9

clan, Indigenous, 249

Clare, Eli, 271

Clark, W., and S. Crompton, 135

class: domestic violence and, 298; gender division of labour and, 196–7; "economic," 225; "family," 38, 83, 225, 226, 240; paid and unpaid work and, 192; "refugee," 225; same-sex marriage and, 64–5; working, 29

clawback: family benefits and, 318

Clément, Dominique, 46

climate change, 353–5, 358

Coalition of Child Care Advocates, 328

cohabitation, 77, 96, 119–20; future of, 347–8, 358; international comparison of, 77; marriage and, 33–4, 78, 180; rights and, 53, 81; same-sex, 54; see also common-law union

"co-longevity of different generations," 142–3

Comacchio, Cynthia, 25–50

commitment, 74; ceremonies of, 173

Committee for the Equality of Women in Canada, 42

common-law union: durable, 119–20: as term, 77; see also cohabitation

communism, 17

community coordinated response, 307

Conference Board of Canada, 324

conflict: immigrant generational, 235; intergenerational, 83, 150; marital, 126–31; refugee families and, 233–6

Conflict Tactics Scale, 302

Connidis, I.A., 152, 159; and J.A. McMullin, 152

consanguinity, 124

consensual unions: as term, 77; see also cohabitation

consent, 294, 297

Conservative Party: child care and, 328, 334–5; family policy and, 324–5; same-sex marriage and, 54, 59, 66

conspicuous consumption, 169

consumerism: weddings and, 168, 170, 176, 177

consumer rites: weddings as, 168

contraception, 35, 42, 123, 347; cohabitation and, 77; intimacy and, 78

Cook, Katsi, 247

Coontz, Stephanie, 74

"co-parenting," 98

Corak, Miles, 208

cord blood, 102

Coser, Lewis, 11

Cossman, Brenda, 64

Cott, Nancy, 176

Couillard, Philippe, 331, 332

Council of Canadians with Disabilities, 276, 283

"coupledom," 53

Courchesne, Michelle, 332

Courtice, E.L., and K. Shaunessy, 89

courts: disability definitions and, 270; divorce and, 119, 133–4; domestic violence, 308; family law and, 131–2; polygamy and, 82; religious law and, 125–6; Supreme, 132, 133

courtship, 84

Creighton, G., et al., 103

Crestwood Heights, 40

crime: domestic violence and, 302, 303–4, 307–8; hate, 358

Criminal Code, 42, 117, 358

"criminal conversation," 118

criminal justice system: domestic violence and, 307–8; refugee youth and, 237

"crisis in the family," 34–5

Crittenden, Ann, 196

cross-cultural studies, 16

Crown lands, 256

"cult of domesticity," 28

"cult of the individual," 172

culture: aging families and, 153; domestic violence and, 305; immigrants and, 239–42; parenting and, 103, 104–7; settlement services and, 230–1

custody: disabled mothers and, 279; immigrants and, 234; joint, 121, 127; paternal, 121; same-sex marriage and, 131

"custom of the country," 81, 249–50

cybersex, 89

Czechoslovakia: refugees from, 227

Dachyshyn, D., 243

Dagenais, Daniel, 46

Daneback, Kristian, et al., 89

Darvishpour, M., 235

dating, 84–9; online, 87–9

Davids, Leo, 347, 349

Daws, Laura Beth, 172

"deadbeat parents," 132

"Dear Abby," 177

death: rituals of, 163, 178–81; spouse's, 120, 148; see also mortality rates

Debrett's, 135

debtor prison, 132

debts, 215; divorce and, 133

Demas, Doreen, 268

demography: family, 74–8; poverty and, 202

Dempsey, D., 98

Department of Indian Affairs, 250

Department of Indigenous and Northern Development, 255

Department of Justice, 136

desertion, 33

"detraditionalization," 80

developmental delay, 272, 284

developmental theories, 19–20

DiNovo, Cheri, 100

"Dirty Thirties," 36

disabilities, 267–90; barriers to help and, 287; costs and, 274, 275; definitions of, 269–71; eligibility screening and, 275; learning, 272; models of, 270–1, 287–8; obstacles and, 271; prevalence of, 267–8; rights and, 357; self-identification and, 270, 271; social experience of, 270; supports for, 274, 275–8; terms for, 271; violence and abuse and, 283–7; visible/invisible, 269, 271

"disabled persons," 271

Disabled Women's Network Canada (DAWN), 284, 286, 287

disablism, gendered, 271

discrimination: in child welfare system, 260; disability and, 270 divorce, 38, 76, 82, 115–38; age at, 122; boomerang children and, 145; "cause" of, 129; decline of, 122–3; effects of, 126–31; emotional disorders and, 127; "fault" and, 131–2; foreign, 125; future of, 347–8, 358; Indigenous, 126, 261–2; "injured parties" and, 118, 119; later-life, 146–7; no fault, 42, 119; number of, 120–1; probability of, 122; recent developments in, 131–4; rituals of, 179; same-sex, 55, 117; separation and, 123, 126; society and, 118; stigma of, 33

Divorce Act, 42, 76, 82, 116, 119; amendments to, 132

"doing family," 13

"domestic labour debates," 30; see also housework

domestic violence, 128, 294–312; broad definition of, 294–6, 302; definitions of, 294–6; honeymoon phase of, 300; immigrants and, 234–5; intervention strategies for, 307–8; leaving and, 299–300; narrow definition of, 296; outburst of, 300; prevalence of, 302–3, 305; reporting of, 303; tension-building phase of, 299–300; see also abuse; violence

Donaldson, Christa, 159

Dosanjh, R., et al., 234

double-ring ceremony, 169

double standard, 86, 87; divorce and, 118

Doucet, A., 103, 183–200, 337–8; and L. Merla, 103, 109

dress: LGBTQ weddings and, 173; mourning, 179; "trashing the," 169; wedding, 168, 169

Dudding, Peter, 319

Duncan, K.A., and R.N. Pettigrew, 42

Durkheim, Émile, 172

Dutton, Donald, 300–1

Duvall, Evelyn Millis, 19–20

Early Childhood Educators, 111

earnings: gender and, 108; women and, 65; see also income

Eaton's, 169–70

ecological model, 19

economic boom, postwar, 38

Edin, Kathryn, and Laura Lein, 219

education: compulsory, 29; disabilities and, 272, 281–2; economic mobility and, 209; foster care and, 320; modernization and, 29, 35; parenting and, 100; poverty and, 221; women and, 356–7

Edwards, John N., 347

Egan v. Canada, 57

Ehrlich, Paul, 349

Eichler, Margrit, 11, 13, 20, 23, 326, 338; future of the family and, 341–62

elderly, 140, 141–3; disability and, 268; poverty and, 35, 211–12, 213, 223

Elkin, Frederick, 27, 341

Elliott, Douglas, 276

emancipatory social movements, 79

Emke, Ivan, 181

employment: caregiving and, 273, 275, 281, 282–3, 325–6; children and, 29–30, 109, 207; contingent, 186; contract, 186; disabilities and, 273–5, 281–2, 287; families and, 315–16, 325–6; immigrant youth and, 237; men and, 29, 184, 185–6; non-standard, 184, 185–6; parenting and, 107; part-time, 184, 185; precarious, 186; refugees and, 229; self-, 186; standard, 184, 185–6; temporary, 186; women and, 29–30, 34, 36–7, 186; see also labour; paid work; work

Employment Insurance, 218; eligibility for, 97, 195, 217; modified, 335; parental leave and, 100, 194, 316

"empty nest stage," 141, 143

Engels, Friedrich, 17

environment: families and, 359–60; see also climate change

Epstein, Rachel, 113

Equality for Gays and Lesbians Everywhere (EGALE), 61

Erikson, Erik, 19

Este, D.C., and A. Tachable, 106

ethnicity: aging families and, 152–3; family change and, 78; gender division of labour and, 196–7; work and, 197; see also "race"; racialized people; specific groups

ethnocentrism, 231

eugenics, 35, 278, 349–50

Europe: economic mobility in, 208; family policy in, 315; poverty in, 201; refugees in, 226

Europeans: gender roles and, 246; Indigenous contact and, 27, 249–50

exchanges, non-market, 217

experts, family, 34–5, 41

expressive functions, 17

extinction, human, 348

extrapolation: predictions and, 351

"factory laws," 29

Fairchild, Emily, 168

Faircloth, Charlotte, 104

familialism, 279

"familial" work, 187

families: as "absent presence," 26; "all-youth," 233; Asian, 153; assets of, 216; bi-nuclear, 10; blended, 4–5, 34, 76–7, 130–1, 144; change and policy and, 314; changes in, 73; children with disabilities and, 267–90; Chinese, 104, 106, 153; "of choice," 90–1, 110; colonial, 27–8; definitions of, 10–15; disintegration of, 343; diversity of, 2–24; dual-earner, 42–3, 107, 206, 207; economic, 203; employment and, 315–16, 325–6; environment and, 359–60; extended, 7, 9, 10, 27, 231–2; formation of, 73–94; functions of, 27; future of, 341–62; as historical actors, 26–33; history of Canadian, 25–50; immigrant, 6–7, 242, 233–6; Indigenous view of, 249; "intact," 130; later life, 141–3; legal/formal definitions of, 13; mid-century, 37–43; millennium, 43–4; "mixed," 31; modern, 33–7; multi-generational, 106, 314; "new blended," 154; new forms of, 231–3; "new nuclear," 154; "normal," 38; number of, 3, 5–6; older, 211–12; personal definitions of, 13; poverty and, 206–11, 212–14, 321; production and, 27–8; recombined, 128–31; refugee, 229, 231–9; satellite, 6; size of, 33, 35, 43, 97, 232–3; as social construction, 26; social definitions of, 13, 14; stem, 27; structural definitions of, 10–12; structure of, 74–8, 129; theories of, 15–22; three-generation, 355; transition and, 144–9; transnational multi-local, 5–6; trends in, 3–10, 350; violence in, 293–312; weddings and, 170; working-class, 29; world and social changes and, 355–60; see also aging families; Census families; nuclear families

La famille Plouffe, 40

Family Allowances, 97, 213, 317; Act, 37; in Quebec, 331–1, 332–3

family breakdown, 115–38; disabilities and, 273, 274, 287; indications of, 120

Family Homes on Reserves and Matrimonial Interests or Rights Act, 261–2

"family medallion," 170

family policy, 313–40; assessment of, 321–9; definition of, 314; future of,

334–6; history of, 317–19; national, 314, 315; parenting and, 100, 110–12; in Quebec, 329–33, 334, 336; workplace, 100–1
Family Responsibility Office, 133
Family Statute Law Amendment Act, 125
family studies, 10, 27, 34; methods of, 15–16
"family values," 40, 306; same-sex marriage and, 58, 60
Farrell, Betty, et al., 98
fathering, 99, 101, 102–3, 192–4; Chinese, 106; good, 104; hands-on, 102; Indigenous, 105; stay-at-home, 109, 188–9; Sudanese, 106; urban/rural, 103; *see also* parenting
Fawcett, G., 282, 283
federal government: child care, 327–8; child poverty, 324; disabled Indigenous children and, 274–5; family policy and, 314, 317, 334; foster care and, 319–20; Indigenous people and, 250–1, 256–7, 260; parental leave and, 315–16, 333; parenting and, 97, 110; same-sex marriage and, 66
Feliciano, Cynthia, et al., 88
femininity, 101
feminism, 20–2; child care and, 325–6; cohabitation and, 77–8; domestic violence and, 295, 296–8, 307; family policy and, 321; future gender roles and, 345–6; inequality and, 21; maternal, 29; postwar, 42; Quebec family policy and, 330; second-wave, 41; types of, 21
filles du roi, 82
Findlay, Barbara, 52, 61
Fineman, Martha, 64
Finkelhor, D., 310
Finnie, Ross, 213
First Nations, 31, 253–4; disability supports and, 275; low income and, 214; *see also* Indigenous people; specific groups
First Nations Child and Family Caring Society, 260
First Nations Land Management Act, 256
First World War, 34
Fleury, D., and M. Fortin, 108
Fong, J., 310
food, 354, 355
food banks, 217, 218–19, 220, 223, 323–4
Food Banks Canada, 218
Fort McMurray fires, 353
"Fossil of the Year" Award, 355
Foster, Deborah, 68

foster care, 44, 98, 319–20, 335; extended, 321; Indigenous children and, 257, 319; legal responsibility and, 320
Foucault, Michel, 68
Fox, Bonnie, 102, 113, 192, 199
Freda Centre for Research on Violence against Women and Children, 308
Fredericton, NB, 307
Freud, Sigmund, 19
Friedan, Betty, 40
friendship, 91; children's, 127
Friese, Susanne, 169
Fuatai, Teuila, 195
Fumia, Doreen M., 51–70
functionalism, 16–17
funerals, 163, 178–9
fur trade, 249–50

Gambles, Richenda, et al., 338
Garnishment, Attachment and Pension Diversion Act, 132
"gaslighting," 295
Gauthier, Anne Hélène, 316
gays: parenting and, 80, 99; *see also* lesbian, gay, bisexual, trans, queer identified people
Gazso, Amber, 13, 21–2, 95–114; and Susan McDaniel, 113
Gee, Ellen M., 143
Geisler, Mark, 99
gender: aging families and, 154–5; caregiving and, 273; children with disabilities and, 271; disabilities and, 268, 271, 280, 281–2, 287; education and, 282, 283; exposure to violence and, 299; immigrants and, 239–42; Indian Act and, 251–4; learning disabilities and, 272; Marxism and, 17; paid work and, 184–6; parenting and, 101–4; part-time work and, 185; prevalence of violence and, 302–3; refugees and, 230–1, 233–4; same-sex marriage and, 64–5; unpaid work and, 108; wages and, 185; weddings and, 170–1; *see also* boys; girls; men; women
gender–based violence: as term, 294
"gender contract," 336
gender convergence, 165
gender division of labour, 184–6, 191–4; importance of, 196–7; income and, 207
Gender Equity in Indian Registration Act, 253
gender identity: parenting and, 99
gender ideologies, 191

gender roles: future of, 345–6, 357–8; immigrants and, 306; Indigenous, 246–9
gender wage gap, 185
General Social Survey (GSS), 121; on Victimization, 302–3
generation: sandwich, 141, 152, 156, 185; "Generation X," 79; "Generation Y," 108, 191
generation gap, 41
genetically modified (GM) crops, 355
"geneticization," 278
genocide, cultural, 104
get, 125
Gibbs, Martin, et al., 179
Giddens, Anthony, 78–9
gifts: anniversary, 176–7; bridal, 164–5
Gilbert, Neil, 338
Gillis, John R., 136
girls: motherhood and, 99; *see also* gender; women
Glenn, N., and E. Marquardt, 85
Goffman, Erving, 164, 181, 210
Goode, William J., 11, 348–9, 351
Good Parents Pay, 133
Gordon Indian Residential School, 254
government: *see* federal government; provinces; state; specific jurisdictions
Gradual Civilization Act, 251
Gradual Enfranchisement Act, 251
Graff, E.J., 52–3, 56, 58, 63, 68
grandparents, 96, 97, 110, 146–7; Indigenous, 105
Great Depression, 35–7
greenhouse gases, 355
Gross, Neil, 80
Grossberg, Michael, 136
Guaranteed Income Supplement, 212
guardianship: disabled children and, 276
Gudelunas, David, 88–9

half-siblings, 5
Hall, David, 79
Harding, Garrett, 349
Harper, Stephen: child care benefit and, 97, 334–5; family policy and, 328; residential schools apology and, 256; same-sex marriage and, 55, 59
Harris, Olivia, 187
Harrison, D., and P. Albanese, 23
Hassan, G., et al., 106, 229
Haudenosaunee, 247–8, 262
haves/have-nots, 354–5
Haw, Jennie, 102
Hawkes, Brent, 57
Hayes, Sharon, 101

health: caregiving and, 150; children's, 221–2; children with disabilities and, 272; climate change and, 356; future, 359; mental, 279, 284, 359; poverty and, 220, 221, 222; pre–First World War, 29; residential schools and, 255
Health and Activity Limitation Survey (HALS), 268
health care: cuts to, 156
Heaphy, B., et al., 64, 68
Heath, Melanie, 73–94
hegemonic masculinity, 102, 103
Helping Families in Need Act, 335
Henry VIII, 116
Henry, George S., 36
herbicide, 355
Hertz, Carrie, 169
heteronormativity, 64, 99
heterosexuality: LGBTQ weddings and, 172–3, 174
Hewett, Heather, 276, 277
hijab, 239–40
Hill, Reuben, 19, 351, 352
Ho, D.Y.F., 106
Hobbs, Edward C., 347
Hochschild, Arlie R., 181
Holtmann, Catherine, 293–312
home care, 151, 276–7
home-leaving, 7, 144–5
homemakers, 39, 40; see also breadwinner model
home-returning, 145–6; see also adult co-resident children
home–work balance, 156–7, 191, 192, 193, 194–6, 325; breadwinner model and, 191, 197
homicide, domestic, 303, 304
homonormativity, 99
homophobia, 63, 154
homosexuality, 38; decriminalization of, 42, 56; see also lesbian, gay, bisexual, trans, queer identified people; same-sex marriage
honeymoon, 164, 176; as phase of violence, 300
honour killings, 304
"hooking up," 85–7
Horvath, C.A., and C.M. Lee, 103
households, 6, 10; multigenerational, 75–6; same-gender, 233; size of, 89; skip-generation, 96; with/without children, 96, 97
"household work strategy," 192
housework, 107, 108, 187–8; definition of, 189; disabilities and, 275, 283; future of, 346, 357–8; paid, 197; as

unrecognized, 184; see also unpaid work
housing, 39
Howard, Vicki, 169–70
Huberman, Jenny, 179
Hudson's Bay Company, 250
Hughes, Kate, 79
Humble, Áine M., 173, 174, 181; et al., 171
Hungary: refugees from, 227
Hunter, Nan D., 61
Husaini, Z., 234
Hutchinson, Darren L., 64

identity: gender, 99; hyphenated, 236; immigrants and, 236, 239
ideologies, gender, 191
Idle No More, 262
immigrants: aging families and, 152–3; child poverty and, 322; domestic violence and, 301, 304; families of, 6–7, 233–6, 242; independent/dependent, 240–1; individuals as, 233; marginalization of, 236; marriage and, 82–3; parenting and, 106; poverty and, 214, 222; racialized, 7; same-sex marriage and, 61, 233; status of, 239–42, 306
immigration, 225–46; family sponsorship and, 38, 83; future of, 356–7; postwar, 38; pre–First World War, 28, 30–1
Immigration Act, 31, 38
Immigration and Refugee Protection Act, 83, 226
impairments, 270
In-Canada Asylum Program, 226
incarceration rates, 237
income: caregiving and, 155; disabilities and, 273–5, 278, 281; fathering and, 102; food banks and, 219; immigrants and, 229–30; lone-parent families and, 108, 109, 110–11, 129, 132; median, 203, 207, 214; number of earners and, 206–11; parenting and, 107–8; poverty and, 212–14; recombined families and, 130; rising, 206; trends in, 201–2; welfare state and, 97
income assistance, 204, 207, 217; elderly and, 212; families and, 213
Income Tax Act, 124
independent life stage, 84
Index of Child and Youth Well-Being and Sustainability, 321
"index of intergenerational elasticity," 208–9

India: death in, 178
Indian: non-status, 251; as term, 250
Indian Act, 31, 82, 251–4; amendments to, 256–7, 261–2, 253
"Indian problem," 254–5
Indian Residential Schools Settlement Agreement, 256
Indigenous people: adoption and, 257; child-neglect and, 259; children and marriage and, 44; community and, 104, 249; disabilities and, 268, 274–5; disability supports and, 281; divorce and, 126, 261–2; domestic violence and, 298, 301, 304; earnings of, 65; enfranchisement and, 251; European contact and, 249–50; families of, 27, 31–2, 245–66; family systems of, 248–9; foster care and, 44, 257, 319, 320; gender roles and, 246–9; jurisdiction and, 256, 260; land and, 250, 256; marriage and, 31, 81, 82, 249–50, 251–4, 261–2; matrimonial property and, 261–2; "nation" and, 249; organizations of, 41; paid work and, 196; parental leave and, 194, 195; parenting and, 104–5; patrilineage and, 31; policy on, 245, 250–1; population of, 78, 356–7; poverty and, 210, 214, 322; pre-contact families of, 27; profiling of, 237; Sixties Scoop and, 2; worldview of, 249; see also Aboriginal; First Nations; Indigenous women; specific groups
Indigenous and Northern Affairs Canada (INAC), 251, 258
Indigenous women: fur trade and, 250; income of, 65, 214; marriage and, 31, 82, 261–2; "triple jeopardy" and, 268; violence and, 298
individualism: funerals and, 178; Indigenous view of, 248–9; weddings and, 172, 176
individualization: family change and, 79
individual model of disability, 270
individuals: disabled living alone, 280; elderly living alone, 212; immigrants as, 233; living alone, 3, 89–91, 140; unmarried, 76
industrialism, 33
inflation, 203
influenza, 34
Institute of Marriage and the Family, 81
institution: marriage as, 51, 52, 53
institutionalization: abuse and, 284, 286; disabled children and, 272–3

instrumental functions, 16–17
integration: immigrants and, 236; refugees and, 226
inter-/intra-generational mobility, 208–9
intergenerational co-residence, 141; *see also* adult co-resident children
internally displaced persons (IDPs), 226
International Covenant on Civil and Political Rights, 253
Internet, 87–9, 351
intersectionality, 239–42, 298
intervention: domestic violence and, 307–8; state, 314, 329, 330
intimacy, 78–80; definition of, 74
intimate partner violence, 294; immigrants and, 234–5; *see also* abuse; domestic violence; violence
Inuit: low income and, 214; residential schools and, 254; weddings and, 172, 174–5; *see also* Indigenous people
in-vitro fertilization (IVF), 98, 357
Islam, 306; family law and, 124–6; *see also* Muslims
Islamophobia, 230; gendered, 239–40
"It Gets Better Campaign," 60
Italy: immigration from, 38

"Jack and Jill parties," 166
Japanese-Canadian families, 153
Johnston, Lynda, 172
Johnston, Patrick, 257, 258
Jolivet, Kendra Randall, 127
Jordan's Principle, 260
Judaism, 306; death and, 179; divorce and, 125; weddings and, 167, 173

Kafer, Alison, 271
Kassel, Victor, 345
Katie Cooke Task Force, 327
Kelly, Fiona, 113
Kemper, Alison, 61–2, 63
Kerley, Cameron, 257–8
Kerr, D., and J.H. Michalski, 201–24
Kimport, Katrina, 93
King, William Lyon Mackenzie, 37
Klein, Naomi, 358, 361
Knox, Alexis, 4
Kobayashi, Karen M., 153; and Anne Martin-Matthews, 139–60
Kohlberg, Lawrence, 19
Korteweg, A.C., 304
Krull, Catherine: and Justyna Sempruch, 338; and Mushira Mohsin Khan, 313–40
Kuttai, Heather, 279, 288

labelling: disabilities and, 274
labour: gender division of, 184–6, 191–4, 196–7, 207; *see also* employment; paid work; unpaid work; work
labour force, 205, 207; disabilities and, 282–3; immigrant youth and, 237; married women in, 42–3; women in, 39, 210
Laos: refugees from, 227
Lasch, Christopher, 193
Lash, Shari R., 173
Latimer, Tracy and Robert, 284–5
Lavell, Jeannette Corbiere, 252
Laverdure, Betty, 248
law: divorce and, 115–16, 117–19, 123; "factory," 29; family, 116, 131–4; marriage and, 81–2; in Quebec, 124
Layton, Jack, 59
Le Bourdais, C., and E. Lapierre-Adamcyk, 77
Le Bouyonnec, Stéphane, 332
Lee, S., and B. Edmonston, 243
Legislative Assembly of the Province of Canada, 254–5
Lenon, Suzanne, 64
lesbian, gay, bisexual, trans, queer identified people (LGBTQ), 22, 82; aging families and, 154–5; dating and, 87, 88–9; future of, 358; families of choice and, 90–1; intimacy and, 79; paid and unpaid work and, 109–10; parenting and, 98, 99–100; rights of, 56–8; world status of, 59–60; weddings and, 172–4; *see also* homosexuality; same-sex marriage
lesbians: earnings of, 65; as parents, 80
Leshner, Michael, 54, 62, 63
Leskun, Sherry, 132
Levett, Carl, 344–5
Liberal Party: child care and, 327, 328, 334, 335, 337; same-sex marriage and, 59
liberal welfare state: family policy in, 329, 331, 336
life course perspective, 20, 71–2; aging families and, 139–60; parenting and, 96–114
life cycles, 19–20; poverty and, 215–16
life expectancy, 35, 139, 140, 268; decreasing, 356; divorce and, 147; gender and, 212; poverty and, 221
liminality, 164, 179
Linton, Ralph, 343
Little, Margaret Hillyard, 326
Little Sisters v. Canada, 57

Live-In Caregiver program, 197
"living apart together" (LAT), 91
"Living Together Unmarried" (LTU), 347
Loe, M., 151
lone-parent families, 34, 117, 128–31; assets of, 216; children in, 97, 128, 129; disabled children and, 273; divorce and, 42; female-led, 129, 206–11, 222–3; income and, 108, 109, 110–11, 129, 132; men in, 97, 210; number of, 3, 76, 129; policy and, 314; postwar, 38; poverty and, 129, 134, 206–11, 322; in Quebec, 331–1; stress and, 222; support and, 132
longitudinal studies, 19
Lost Boys and Girls of Sudan, 229
Lovelace, Sandra, 253
low-income cut-offs (LICO), 98, 203, 206, 273
Luxton, Meg, 30, 192

McDaniel, Susan, 326
Macdonald, Cameron Lynne, 199
Macdonald, D., and D. Wilson, 195
MacDonald, D. and M. Friendly, 329
MacDougall, Brian, 68
McInturff, Kate, 329
McKay, Lindsey, 195
McKeen, Wendy, 224, 321
McKie, Craig, 115–38
MacKinnon, C., 297
Maclean's, 14
Madibbo, Amal, and James S. Frideres, 225–44
maher, 126
Maintenance Enforcement Programs, 132–3
Malacrida, Claudia, 288
male model of employment, 184, 185–6
Man, Guida, and Rina Cohen, 113
Mandell, Nancy, and Ann Duffy, 12
Manitoba, 250; divorce in, 133
marital dissolution: rules of, 123; *see also* divorce
marital offences, 116, 118, 119, 131–2
marriage: as accomplishment, 180; age at, 33, 84; arranged, 82–3, 117, 233; changes in, 73; coercion and, 118; cohabitation and, 78; colonial, 81; debates on, 80–4; "deinstitutionalization" of, 180; disabled people and, 278; divorce and, 123; as economic contract, 118; equivalence to, 120; Great Depression and, 36; group, 344–5;

historical overview of, 52–3; Indigenous people and, 31, 81, 82, 249–50, 251–4, 261–2; Indigenous/non-Indigenous, 249–50, 251–4; money and, 53; monogamous, 344; parenting and, 96; as personal and public, 51; post–First World War, 35; postponement of, 144; predictions on, 342–4; purpose of, 52–6; rates of, 75; rituals of, 163–78, 180–1; *see also* same-sex marriage

Marsh, Leonard, 37

Marshall, K., 108

Martha Stewart Living, 171

Martin, Biddy, 61

Martin, Paul, 59, 327, 334

Martin-Matthews, Anne, et al., 153

Marxism, 17

masculinity: hegemonic, 102, 103; parenting and, 101, 102

Maternity and Parental Benefits, 100

maternity leave, 43, 194, 195, 315–16; *see also* parental leave

Mathieu, Sophie, 195

Matthews, Sarah, 149

Mead, George Herbert, 17–18

Mead, Margaret, 16

media: domestic violence and, 300; LGBTQ and, 66

Meech Lake Accord, 258

memorials, 178, 179

men: aging families and, 154–5; child care and, 103, 109, 188–9, 192–4, 197, 325; earnings of, 108; employment and, 29, 184, 185–6; future role of, 345–6, 357–8; gender divisions of labour and, 197; gender roles of, 246–7; immigrant, 233, 240–1; Indigenous, 261–2; labour force and, 207; lone-parent families and, 97, 210; marriage and, 33, 84; Muslim, 240; older, 211–12; paid and unpaid work and, 109, 189–91, 194–6; parental leave and, 188–9, 194, 316, 333; patriarchy and, 295–6; refugee, 233–4; remarriage and, 148; separate spheres and, 28; as stay-at-home dads, 109, 188–9, 192–4; stepfamilies and, 130; suburban, 40; unemployment of, 36, 37; violence against women and, 294, 302–3; weddings and, 165, 168–9; widowhood and, 148; *see also* boys; fathering; gender

mental disabilities/health: abuse and, 284; child custody and, 279; environment and 359

"mercy-killing," 284

Métis, 31, 250; low income and, 214; residential schools and, 254; *see also* Indigenous people

Mghir, R., et al., 237

Michalski, Joseph H., 217

Middleton, Kate, and Prince William, 168, 169

migration, 225; chain, 28; parenting and, 111; *see also* immigrants; immigration

Millennium Scoop, 258–60

Milloy, J., 263

Ministère de la Famille and de l'Enfance, 330

Mitchell, Barbara, 159

mixed unions, 14

MMORPGs (massively multiplayer online role-playing games), 89

mobility, economic, 208–9

modernization, 28–9

Mohawk Institute, 254

Montemurro, Beth, 164–5, 166

Morissette, R., and X. Zhang, 216

Morley, David, 321

Morris, Jenny, 270

mortality rate: infant, 29; maternal, 29; poverty and, 220, 221; residential schools and, 255

Mosby, Ian, 263–4

Moss, M.S., et al., 142

"most wanted postings," 133

mothering, 99; child-rearing advice and, 41; disabled parent and, 279–80, 282; good, 104; intensive, 101–2; Victorian v. Indigenous views of, 246–8; *see also* parenting

Mulé, Nick, 64

Mulroney, Brian, 317

multiculturalism, 227

Multilateral Framework on Early Learning and Child Care, 327

Murdock, George, 11, 16

Muriel McQueen Ferguson Centre, 308

Muslims, 230, 233, 239–40; child custody and, 234; family law and, 124–6; racialized, 237–8; as refugees, 228; *see also* Islam

M. v. H., 57

nannies, 197

Nason-Clark, N., 306–7; and B. Fisher-Townsend, 310

National Action Committee on the Status of Women, 42

National Child Benefit (NCB), 97, 318, 321

National Child Benefit Supplement (NCBS), 318

National Child Care Framework, 328

National Clearinghouse on Family Violence, 284–5, 310

National Council of Welfare, 322, 324

National Council of Women of Canada, 34

National Daycare Conference, 327

National Framework for Collaborative Police Action, 307–8

National Health and Social Life Survey, 85

National Household Survey, 14

National Longitudinal Study of Children and Youth, 213

National Post, 60

National Welfare Council, 34

Nett, Emily M., 341

New Brunswick: domestic violence in, 294–5, 307

New Democratic Party, 59

Newfoundland and Labrador: child poverty in, 322; mourning in, 179

new reproductive and genetic technologies, 78, 98, 349–50, 352, 357

"new social history," 25–6

Nimkoff, Meyer F., 343, 348

non-status Indian, 251

non-transitions, 140

Norton, Thomas, 2

nuclear families, 10, 27, 96; patriarchal, 344, 345–6; policy and, 314

Nunavut: cohabitation in, 180

nutrition, 221, 255

Oakley, Ann, 189

obesity, 354, 356

Ochocka, J., and R. Janzen, 104

Office for Disability Issues, 277

Ogburn, W.F., and M.F., Nimkoff, 346–7, 349, 350, 352

Oka Crisis, 258

Old Age Security, 212; *see also* elderly

Oliver, Michael, 288–9

Ontario: child poverty in, 322; child support in, 133; children with disabilities in, 272; divorce in, 132; foster care in, 320; religious law in, 125, 126; same-sex marriage in, 54, 55, 57; welfare in, 220

oral sex, 85

Orenstein, M., and G.J. Stalker, 109

Organisation for Economic Co-operation and Development (OECD): 316, 327–8, 333, 334

orphanhood, 29

Oswald, Ramona Faith, 172–3

out-of-home care, 319–21; *see also* foster care; state care

over-consumption, 354
overpopulation, 348–9
Owen, Michelle, 267–90

Pacaut, Phillippe, et al., 108
Pacey, Michael, 153
Pahl, R., 192; and L. Spencer, 91
paid work, 30, 183–200; gender and,
    184–6; married women and, 42–3;
    parenting and, 97, 100, 104,
    107–10; postwar women and, 39;
    poverty and, 218; state and, 194–6;
    unpaid work and, 191–4; women
    and, 34, 36–7; see also employment;
    work
"Panama papers," 354–5
paradigm shift, 15
parental leave, 43, 188–9, 194, 315–16;
    poverty and, 207; in Quebec, 331,
    332, 333; unpaid, 335
parenting, 95–114; age and, 97;
    Caribbean, 106; children with
    disabilities and, 272–8; Chinese,
    104, 106; decision to, 98–101;
    emotions and, 98–9; "helicopter,"
    104; immigrant, 104, 106, 235–6,
    237, 238, 242; performance of,
    101–12; social change and, 96–8;
    styles of, 103; Sudanese, 106;
    transnational, 111–12
parents: "deadbeat," 132; with
    disabilities, 278–83; employability
    of, 333; ethno-specific schools
    and, 238
Parsons, Talcott, 16–17, 191; and
    Robert Bales, 345
Participation and Activity Limitation
    Survey (PALS), 268
Parti Québécois, 332
passage: rites of, 164, 176
patriarchy: domestic violence and,
    295–6, 305; fathering and, 102;
    nuclear family and, 344, 345–6; as
    social order, 295–6; violence and,
    296
Paul, Eden, 343
Pennington, Phil and Barbara, 179–80
pensions, 133
personality disorders, 301
"persons with disabilities," 271
Philippines: caregivers from, 197
Phillipson, C., 142
Piaget, Jean, 19
Picot, Garnett: and John Myles, 212;
    et al., 202, 213
Pill, the, 42
"plastic sexuality," 78–9
Ploeg, J., et al., 310

police: domestic violence and, 303,
    307–8
policy: Aboriginal, 31–2, 245, 250–1;
    pro-prosecution, 308; see also family
    policies
Polikoff, Nancy, 64
politics: poverty and, 204; queer, 61;
    same-sex marriage and, 59
Pollak, Otto, 346
polygamy, 82–3, 116, 117
polygyny, 345
population, 348–9; aging, 148; explosion
    of, 357; foreign-born, 225; future,
    348–9, 356–7; Indigenous, 78,
    356–7; state and, 330
pornography, 300
post-traumatic stress disorder (PTSD),
    229, 237; intergenerational, 304
poverty, 29, 201–24; consequences
    of, 220–2; coping with, 217–20;
    definitions of, 202–3; "deserving/
    undeserving," 318; disabilities and,
    273–5, 282, 287; divorce and,
    127; domestic violence and, 301;
    elderly and, 35, 211–12, 213, 223;
    explanations for, 202, 210–11;
    family policy and, 315; future, 354;
    immigrants and, 230; income-based
    measures of, 214–16; indications
    of, 202–6; Indigenous, 210, 214,
    322; international comparison of,
    208–9; lone-parent families and,
    129, 134, 206–11, 322; parental
    leave and, 194–5; parenting and,
    97, 108; racialized people and,
    7; stigma of, 210–11; trends in,
    203–6; welfare and, 318; see also
    child poverty
Power and Control wheel, 297, 299
Prazen, Ariana, et al., 127
predictions: future of family and,
    341–62
pregnancy, extramarital, 122–3, 180;
    see also childbirth
premarital sex, 85
Prince Edward Island, 323
pro-prosecution policy, 308
progression: rites of, 164, 176
pronatalism, 35, 329–30
property, matrimonial, 261–2
Protestant Church, 77
provinces: child care and, 325, 327–8;
    child poverty and, 322–3; child
    support enforcement and, 132–3;
    divorce and, 118; family law
    and, 116; family policy and, 314,
    334; Human Rights Acts and,
    57; Indigenous people and, 256,

260; parental leave and, 315–16;
    parental support and, 97–8, 110;
    same-sex marriage in, 54, 57–8,
    66; state care and, 319–21; see also
    specific provinces
psychiatric or personality theory, 296,
    300–1
psychologists, 41
public/private spheres, 191–2, 246
"pure relationship," 79

qualitative studies, 16
quantitative studies, 13, 14
Quebec: child care in, 111, 326, 328–9,
    331, 332, 333; child poverty in,
    322; children with disabilities in,
    272; cohabitation in, 77–8, 180;
    family policy in, 329–33, 334, 336;
    Indigenous children in, 257; law
    in, 124; parental leave in, 194, 195;
    same-sex marriage in, 55; Shariah
    in, 126
Quebec Pension Plan, 212
queer politics, 61
queer theory, 22
Quiet Revolution, 41, 77, 330
quintiles, 107

"race": disability and, 271; domestic
    violence and, 298; immigrants and,
    239–42; online dating and, 88;
    refugees and, 228, 231; see also
    ethnicity; visible minorities
racialized people, 7, 14, 237–8; child
    poverty and, 322; domestic violence
    and, 301; family change and, 78;
    paid work and, 186, 196; poverty
    and, 210, 214; youth as, 236–9
racial profiling, 230, 237
racism: domestic violence and, 301
Radford, Joanna, 100
Radio-Canada, 40
Rae, Karen, 2
Raj, A., and J. Silverman, 234
Ranson, Gillian, 100, 113
rape: as weapon of war, 239
recessions, 41, 202, 203, 204, 205–6
Reconstruction, 37
Refugee and Humanitarian
    Resettlement Program, 226, 228
Refugee Backlog Clearance Program,
    227
Refugee Board of Canada, 227
refugees, 225–44; credentials and, 229;
    danger and, 229; durable solutions
    for, 226; number in Canada, 226–7;
    number of, 226, 228; post-migration,
    229; pre-migration, 228–9;

repatriation and, 226; resettlement and, 226; settlement of, 228–31; top hosting countries for, 226
Reid, Julie, et al., 86–7
Reid, Nicole, 279
religion, 358; cohabitation and, 77; divorce and, 116, 117, 123; domestic violence and, 305, 306–7; family law and, 124–6; immigrants and, 239–42; mixed unions and, 14; refugees and, 228; rituals and, 163–4; same-sex marriage and, 58–9; weddings and, 167; *see also* specific religions
Religious Coalition for Equal Marriage Rights, 58–9
remarriage, 33–4, 76, 148–9; number of, 75
reproduction: disabilities and, 278, 280; new technologies for, 78, 98, 349–50, 352, 357; sexuality and, 78, 99; social, 21–2, 30, 192; Victorian v. Indigenous views of, 247
research, 13, 14, 16; action-oriented, 307, 308
reserves, 31–2, 245, 251; child welfare on, 260–1; jurisdiction and, 256
residential schools, 32, 254–6; consequences of, 258, 259, 262–3; human experiments in, 255; intergenerational impacts and, 258; malnourishment and, 255; survivors of, 256
RESOLVE network, 308
responsibility: community, 189; fiduciary, 256; foster care and, 320; gender division of labour and, 191; individual, 336; social, 336
reunification, family, 240
la revanche des berceaux, 329
Rhode, Deborah, 196
Richardson, Diane, 64
Rick v. Brandsema, 133
rights: citizenship, 52; cohabitation, 53, 81; disabilities and, 357; Indigenous people and, 253, 258; LGBTQ, 56–8
rings, engagement/wedding, 168
Risman, Barbara, 80
rites: consumer, 168; maintenance, 177; marriage and death, 163–82; mourning, 179; of passage, 164, 176; progression, 164, 176; separation, 178–80
Robinson, Svend, 54
Roeher Institute, 274, 275, 276, 278; abuse and, 284–5
romantic love, 74

Rooney, Rebekah, 62, 63
Rosenberg, George, 345
Rosenthal, C.J., 143
Royal Commission on Aboriginal Peoples, 249, 258
Royal Commission on Equality in Employment, 327
Royal Commission on the Status of Women, 326–7, 334, 344
Royal Proclamation of 1763, 250
"rule of thumb," 295–6
Runciman, Bob, 57
Russian Federation, 356
Rwandan Genocide, 239

same-sex marriage, 43, 82, 51–70, 116, 233, 357; adoption and, 100; aging and, 154–5; benefits of, 63–7; critique of, 63–4; debates on, 63; divorce and, 117, 125, 131; families and, 3, 55, 131; history of, 54–60; number of, 44, 55, 65, 76; parenting and, 96; prediction of, 346–7, 350; reasons for, 60–3; violence in, 294; weddings and, 172–4; world status of, 59–60
sandwich generation, 141, 151, 156, 185
Scandinavia: economic mobility in, 208
Schacher, Stephanie Jill, et al., 110
schools: ethno-specific, 238–9; intersectionality and, 241; LGBTQ students in, 60; refugee youth and, 237, 238; *see also* residential schools
Schwartz, Pepper, 147
Scott, Duncan Campbell, 254
screening, prenatal, 278
Sears, William, 103
Second World War, 37
secularization, 116, 178
Seeley, John R., et al., 40
self-employment, 186
Senate: divorce and, 118
separate spheres, 28
separation, 115–38; death and, 120; divorce and, 123, 124, 126; effects of, 126–31; immigrants and, 236; later-life, 147; rites of, 178–80
settlements: divorce, 119, 133–4; residential schools, 256
settlement services, 230–1
settlers, 250
sexting, 88
sexual activity: casual, 85; non-marital, 346–7; oral, 85; premarital, 85
sexual citizens, 52
sexuality: bachelorette parties and, 166; disability and, 271; future

of, 346–7, 357; intimacy and, 74; "plastic," 78–9; reproduction and, 78, 99
sexual orientation: aging families and, 154–5; domestic violence and, 298
sexual scripts, 86
sex work, 89
Shakya, Y.S., et al., 236, 237
Shariah law, 124–6
Sharma, Raghubar, 224
Shaughnessy, K., and S.E. Byers, 89
Sheldon, Alison, 270
shelter movement, 307–8
shiva, 179
showers, pre-wedding, 164–6
siblings: co-longevity and, 143; step-/half-, 5
Sifton, Clifford, 30–1
Simms, Andrew, 361
Sinclair, Raven, 264
Six Nations Birthing Centre, 262
Sixties Scoop, 2, 256–8
Skywoman, 247, 248
"sluts," 86
SlutWalk, 86
Smart, Carol, 64
Smith, Barbara, 63
Smith, Miriam, 68
Smith-Rosenberg, Carroll, 246; and Charles E. Rosenberg, 246–7
social assistance/welfare, 35, 220; disabilities and, 274–5; Great Depression and, 37; lone parents and, 109; marriage and, 81; parenting and, 97–8; poverty line and, 318; reform of, 213
social construction: families as, 26
Social Gospel, 29
socialization, gender, 99
social media, 295, 351
social minimum, 37
social model of disability, 270–1, 287–8
social policy: parenting and, 100, 110–12
social security, 37
"social solidarity relationships," 98
sociology, family, 10, 15–16, 27, 341
Song, Sarah, 83
Sorokin, P., 343
South Asians: aging families and, 153; as immigrants, 31; marriage and, 82–3; parenting and, 106
Spanish influenza, 34
"spare the rod and spoil the child," 295–6
Spitzer, D., et al., 106
Spock, Benjamin, 41
sponsorship, family, 226, 232, 240

spousal abuse: as term, 294; *see also* domestic violence; violence

spousal support, 132, 133–4

Stacey, Judith, 98–9

"stag/stagette" parties, 165, 166

"stagflation," 41

"standard donor," 98

Stark, Michael, 54, 62, 63

state: caregiving and, 155–7, 319–21; domestic violence and, 296; family policies and, 29, 313–40; Great Depression and, 37; Indigenous people and, 31–2, 245, 250–1; interventionist, 35, 329; marriage and, 51–2, 53–6, 81–2; paid and unpaid work and, 194–6; poverty and, 204, 212–13; same-sex marriage and, 66; *see also* federal government; provinces; welfare state; specific jurisdictions

Statistics Canada, 14, 224, 357; disability and, 271; divorce and, 122; domestic violence and, 302, 303; family diversity and, 3; gender division of labour and, 191; household types and, 198; poverty and, 203; same-sex marriage and, 65

status: immigrant, 239–42, 306; "Indian," 31, 251–4

stay-at-home dads (SAHDs), 109, 188–9, 192–4

stepfamilies, 4–5, 129, 130–1; Census and, 42; children and, 97; complex, 130, 148–9; definition of, 76–7; home-leaving and, 144; policy and, 314; simple, 130

stepfather, 129

Stephens, William, 11

Stienstra, Deborah, 271, 289

stigma: living alone and, 90; poverty and, 210–11; same-sex marriage and, 60, 67

Stonewall riots, 54

Strategic Council, 335

Straus, Murray, 302

Streib, G.F., 149

Strong-Boag, Veronica, 46

suburbanization, 39–40

Sudan: refugees from, 106, 228–9, 235, 237

Sunseri, Lina, 247

Supreme Court of Canada, 132, 133

surnames: stepfamilies and, 131

Survey of Labour and Income Dynamics (SLID), 206, 213

Survey on Financial Security, 216

sustainability, 359–60

Sutherland, Neil, 46

suttee, 178

symbolic communitas, 178

symbolic interactionism, 17–18

Syria: refugees from, 227, 241–2

targeting: family policy and, 314, 317–19, 321, 331

tax benefits, 97, 208–9, 317–19, 324, 335; disability and, 275; marriage and, 64–5, 124; parenting and, 111; in Quebec, 331, 332

tax havens, 354–5

technologies: new reproductive and genetic, 78, 98, 349–50, 352, 357; predictions and, 352

telethon, 270

television, 40

temporarily able-bodied (TAB), 268

territories: Human Rights Acts and, 57

"terrorists," 238

testimonial affidavits: same-sex marriage and, 61–3

Thamm, Robert, 345

theories: biases in, 20; developmental, 19–20; disabilities and, 271; domestic violence and, 296–301; exchange, 19; family, 15–22; family systems, 19; psychiatric or personality, 296, 300–1; queer, 22; social exchange, 18, 88; social learning, 296, 298–9; social situation/stress and coping, 296, 301

Thomas, Carol, 271

Timonen, V., and S. Arber, 146

Tjejpkema, M., and R. Wilkins, 221

Todd, Nancy Jack, 361

Toone, Philip, 335

Torjman, Sherri, 201–2

"tourism," wedding, 172

transgender people, 3–4; *see also* lesbian, gay, bisexual, transgender and queer people

transitions: family life and, 139–40, 144–9

trauma: domestic violence and, 304, 305–6; refugees and, 229; *see also* post-traumatic stress disorder

Treas, J., and S. Mazumdar, 235

treaties, 250–1, 258

Trovato, Frank, 23

Trudeau, Justin, 97, 318, 328, 335

Trudeau, Pierre, 56

Trump, Donald, 58, 242

Truth and Reconciliation Commission, 256, 262

Turtle Island, 247

Tweddle, Anne, et al., 224

Tye, D., and A.M. Powers, 166, 182

Uncle Chichimus, 40

unemployment, 202, 203, 205, 218; male, 36

unemployment insurance, 37, 204, 217; program, 97, 315

Union of Physically Impaired Against Segregation, 270

United Kingdom: economic mobility in, 208

United Nations, 321; Convention on the Rights of the Child, 317; Declaration on "A World Fit for Children," 324; High Commissioner of Refugees, 226; Human Rights Committee, 253

United States: cohabitation in, 77; economic mobility in, 208–9; family policy in, 315; marriage in, 81; poverty in, 201; premarital sex in, 85; stepfamilies in, 86

Unity Candle, 170

Universal Child Care Benefit, 97, 111, 318, 320, 335

universality: family policy and, 317–19, 321, 326–7

unmarried people, 76

unpaid work, 30, 39, 183–200; definitions of, 187; as "free ride," 196; paid work and, 191–4; parenting and, 107–10; state and, 194–6; women and, 189; *see also* caregiving; housework; work

Uppal, Sharanjit, 108; and Sébastien Larochelle-Côté, 107, 216

Ursel, J., et al., 310

Valkyrie, Zek Cyprus, 89

Valverde, Mariana, 64

van den Hoonaard, Deborah K., 163–82

Van Gennep, Arnold, 164

Vanier, Georges, 27

Vanier Institute of the Family, 27, 361; "care gap" and, 156–7; definition of family and, 12, 13; family and environment and, 359–60

Van Kirk, Sylvia, 249

Varnell, Joe, 57

Vautour, Elaine and Anne, 57

"velcro kids," 7

Vézina, Mireille, 136

"victim-blaming," 211

Victoria (Queen), 169, 179

Vietnam: refugees from, 227

violence, 234–5, 293–312; cycle of, 299–300; disabilities and, 283–7; disclosure of, 299, 306; exposure to, 293, 298–9, 300; family, 83, 128, 284–5, 286, 294; gender-based,

304; intergenerational transmission of, 298, 299, 303; intimate partner, 234–5, 294; learned, 298–9, 300; physical, 303; sexual, 294, 297, 300, 303; structural, 298; terminology for, 294–6; *see also* abuse; domestic violence

visible minorities: domestic violence and, 301; mixed unions and, 14; *see also* "race"; racialized people

vows: renewal of, 176–8; wedding, 167

Vozoris, Nicholas, et al., 220

Vriend, Delvin, 54

Vriend v. Alberta, 57

wages: gender and, 185; *see also* income

Wall, G., 102; and S. Arnold, 103

Walters, D. et al., 236

war: climate change and, 355; rape and, 239; refugees and, 228

Ward, Russell, and Glenna Spitze, 145

wealth: inequality in, 354–5, 358; poverty and, 215, 216

weddings, 163, 167–75; alternative, 172–4; Bahá'í, 172, 174–5; celebrity, 170; cost of, 171, 180; "destination," 171–2; history of, 167–8; Inuit, 172, 174–5; Jewish, 167, 173; LGBTQ, 172–4; pre-wedding rituals and, 164–7; symbols of, 168; types of, 171; websites for, 172

"wedsites," 172

Weeks, Jeffrey, et al., 79, 90

welfare: *see* social assistance/welfare

welfare state, 329, 331; elderly and, 212; parenting and, 97

Wendell,, Susan, 289

Wenjack, Chanie, 255

Weston, Kath, 64

Whitehall Study, 220–1

Whitehurst, R.N., 347

"whiteness": lack of, 254–5

Whitty, Monica, et al., 93

Widmer, Eric, 13, 23

widowhood, 29, 148; same-sex marriage and, 154–5

Williams, Joan, 199

Willson, Andrea E., et al., 152

Winch, Robert F., 346, 347

Wolfson, Evan, 61

"woman question," 34

women: aging families and, 154–5; Asian, 106; care costs to, 196–7; caregiving and, 143, 151, 156; child care and, 325; children and, 188; disabled, 273, 278, 286, 287; earnings of, 65, 108; future of, 356–8345–6; gender roles of, 246–9; immigrant, 230–1, 232, 240–1; Indian Act and, 251–4; labour force and, 207; lone-parent families and, 129, 206–11, 222–3; marriage and, 33, 84; Muslim, 125, 239–40; older, 142, 212; paid and unpaid work and, 29–30, 34, 36–7, 184–5, 186, 189–91, 194–6; part-time work and, 185; patriarchy and, 295–6; poverty and, 217; refugee, 233–5; remarriage and, 148; role of, 34; separate sphere

and, 28; sexual agency of, 85; South Asian, 82–3; status of, 42; stepfamilies and, 130; suburban, 40; vote and, 34; weddings and, 164–6, 170–1; widowhood and, 148; *see also* gender; girls; Indigenous women; mothering

Women's Christian Temperance Union, 34

Women's Institutes, 34

"women's liberation," 42, 346

women's movement, 344

Women Victims of Abuse Protocols, 294–5

work; community, 189; control of, 221; "familial," 187; kin, 189; paid/unpaid, 183–200; sex, 89; studies of, 189–91; *see also* employment; paid work; unpaid work

work-at-home dads (WAHDs), 193–4

Working Income Supplement (WIS), 317

Working While On Claim, 316

workplace policy: parenting and, 100–1

World Health Organization (WHO), 284, 285, 305

Young, Claire, 64–5

youth, refugee, 236–9

"youthquake," 41

Yukon, 58; same-sex marriage in, 54

zero population movement, 344, 349

Zero Tolerance for Barbaric Cultural Practices Act, 83, 304

Zimmerman, Carle C., 343, 348

Zine, J., 239–40